# THE INTERNATIONAL DIRECTORY OF
# MILITARY AIRCRAFT

## 2002/03

### Gerard Frawley

Published by Aerospace Publications Pty Ltd (ACN: 001 570 458) PO Box 1777, Fyshwick, ACT 2609, Australia.
Phone (02) 6280 0111 Fax (02) 6280 0007 – Publishers of monthly *Australian Aviation* magazine.
www.ausaviation.com.au
mail@ausaviation.com.au

ISBN 1-875671-55-2

Printed in Australia by Pirie Printers Pty Ltd, 140 Gladstone St, Fyshwick, ACT 2609.
Distributed throughout Australia by Network Distribution Company, 54 Park St, Sydney, 2000. Fax (02) 9264 3278
Distribution in North America by Motorbooks International, 729 Prospect Ave, Osceola, Wisconsin, 54020, USA.
Fax (715) 294 4448. Distributed throughout Europe and the UK by Airlife Publishing Ltd,
101 Longden Rd, Shrewsbury SY3 9EB, Shropshire, UK. Fax (743) 232944.

# Contents

**Photographers' websites:**
Paul Sadler - www.southernskyphoto.com.au
Paul Merritt - www.aviationexposure.com
Joris van Boven - www.sentry.hangar1.net
Lassi Tolvanen - www.saunalahti.fi/flyhigh1/
Military Aircraft Photographs (MAP) - www.mar.co.uk

# Introduction

Welcome to the fourth edition of the *International Directory of Military Aircraft*.

This book, like its predecessors, aims to provide an up to date reference work on military aircraft at an affordable price. Further, unlike other aircraft reference books, this volume includes aircraft still in service rather than only those currently in production.

Therefore on the following pages you will find entries on such famous and long lived types as the MiG-21, Hawker Hunter, Douglas C-47, Bell Sioux and scores of others, alongside the very latest in military aviation technology such as the F-22 Raptor, Lockheed Martin's F-35 JSF and Mitsubishi's F-2.

*The International Directory of Military Aircraft* is published every two years. It includes the latest aircraft types under development and updated entries on the established types. This *Military Aircraft* directory supersedes the third edition (2000/01), and itself is due be replaced by an updated edition in early 2004, and so on.

This book is a companion to the successful *International Directory of Civil Aircraft*, first released early in 1995. Likewise, the *Civil Aircraft* directory is superseded by a new and updated edition every two years.

The Military and Civil books are published in alternating years. Together, these all colour volumes are a source of data on just about all the aircraft of the world that are not only in production but also still in everyday use.

To be eligible for coverage an aircraft must still be in operational service or currently under development. There are a very small number of aircraft currently in military service that are not covered in this volume – mainly civil based light aircraft, details of which can be found in the *International Directory of Civil Aircraft*. Other aircraft that are only in the initial stages of development are likely to appear in subsequent *Military Directory* editions when the designs of these aircraft firm and more information is released.

Aircraft are listed alphabetically by manufacturer. Where aircraft manufacturers have changed name, through mergers or acquisitions, aircraft currently in production are listed under their current manufacturer (ie Boeing F/A-18, rather than McDonnell Douglas), while aircraft out of production are listed under the manufacturer's name they are most commonly known by.

Where a type has a long and complicated history with numerous variants (the Hercules, Mirage and F-16 come to mind) the more important models have been split up into their own entries to give the type appropriate coverage.

This edition sees the addition of two new sections providing brief coverage on significant Unmanned Aerial Vehicles (UAVs) and aircraft carriers.

The format of the book is largely self explanatory and hopefully user friendly. (An asterisk in the operators column and in the World Air Power Guide indicates aircraft on order or currently being delivered.)

Both metric and imperial measures are used. While much of the world has now adopted metric as its official system of measure, aviation records its figures in knots, nautical miles and feet.

I'd like to thank those individuals and organisations (including manufacturers, embassies and defence department public relations sections) which have helped in the compilation of this book.

The work of many photographers illustrate these pages. I'd particularly like to acknowledge the contributions of Paul Merritt, Paul Sadler, Joris van Boven of Sentry Aviation News, Santiago Rivas, Lassi Tolvanen and Sebastian Zacharias.

Thank you also to Jim Thorn, Gayla Wilson, and Stewart Wilson of Aerospace Publications, for their support with this project.

Last but not least, my thanks to Justin, Bradley and Kerrie.

Gerard Frawley
Canberra, January 2002.

# Military Aviation in Review

2001 will go down in history as an extraordinary year for military aviation.

Hijacked airliners were used in a warped application of airpower to topple New York's World Trade Center towers and crash through the Pentagon. The might of American airpower - long range B-52, B-1 and B-2 bombers and aircraft carrier based F/A-18s and F-14s dropping laser and GPS guided bombs - almost single handedly toppled the Taliban regime in Afghanistan. And potentially the world's largest arms program, the Joint Strike Fighter, was decided, with Lockheed Martin winning the prize.

In other news since this book's last appearance, long running programs such as the F-22, A400M and T-6 JPATS passed major milestones. A number of military aircraft made first flights, while others achieved milestones such as entering production or service.

The unbelievable events of September 11 2001, which saw fuel laden commercial airliners used as crude but devastatingly effective cruise missiles, soon saw military aircraft on the frontline in the 'War Against Terrorism'. At home in the United States, US Air Force and Air National Guard F-16 and F-15 fighters were soon flying combat air patrols over major cities to guard against further hijacked airliner attacks. NATO swung into action, its pledges of support soon backed by the deployment from Europe of NATO E-3 Sentrys to the US, to help command and control USAF fighters flying patrols over major cities.

But airpower's biggest role to play after September 11 was the bombing campaign against the Taliban regime in Afghanistan. Soon after the September 11 attacks the United States determined blame for the terrorism lay with Saudi born dissident Osama bin Laden and his al-Qaeda terrorist network, who were sheltered by the Taliban in Afghanistan. As a result the US set about dismantling the Taliban and al-Qaeda forces with a stunningly effective bombing campaign.

The air war against the Taliban and al-Qaeda was in some ways a coming of age for airpower. In a few short weeks, USAF bombers and US Navy carrier based F/A-18 and F-14 fighters almost single-handedly led to the fall of the Taliban. The rain of GPS JDAM and laser guided bombs systematically destroyed Taliban and al-Qaeda infrastructure and ground forces. This allowed opposing Northern Alliance ground forces to quickly defeat the Taliban on the ground.

The bombing campaign was as quick as it was effective. It also served to highlight the growing maturity and the high technology of US airpower. The Enduring Freedom air campaign demonstrated the long range reach of US airpower through long range strategic bombers and aircraft carriers, the accuracy of US bombs, and the accuracy and speed of delivery of targeting and intelligence information.

Certainly the Taliban had little to fight back with. The Taliban had no air force and only a few air defence guns to defend itself with. (Such one sided conflicts have given rise to the term asymmetric warfare.) But the US had to contend with distance - initially it could not base fighters or bombers in any adjoining country to Afghanistan.

US bombers and carrier based fighters, plus later tanker supported F-15Es and F-16s, were so effective because of the reconnaissance and intelligence support around them, reducing the time between target detection and then bombing to in some cases within minutes.

The US support fleet included RC-135 Rivet Joint electronic intelligence gatherers, E-8 Joint STARS, EA-6B Prowlers, EC-130H Compass Call communications jammers and RQ-1 Predator UAVs. Such impressive assets meant targets were quickly identified and targeting information was quickly passed on to the bombers and fighters, and Taliban communications were either intercepted, providing valuable intelligence, or jammed.

Perhaps the most remarkable aspect of the air campaign was the use of orbiting B-52s called in to bomb targets as they were found by ground or Fast FACS (Forward Air Controllers) in the style of the 'cab rank' P-47 attacks in the dieing days of World War 2.

Not all the bombing involved precision bombs. B-52s were also used for bombing of Taliban positions using 'dumb' bombs, while a handful of 15,000lb BLU-82 'daisy cutter' Ammonal bombs, the biggest conventional bombs in the US inventory, were dropped by US MC-130 Hercules.

Yet another success for airpower (after Yugoslavia/Kosovo in 1999 and the Gulf War in 1991) suggests that the future of the replacement aircraft for most US tactical fighters - the Joint Strike Fighter - is assured.

Lockheed Martin has beaten Boeing to win the lucrative contract to build the Joint Strike Fighter, the Western world's next fighter plane and the most expensive military program in history.

*One of two Lockheed Martin X-35 JSF concept demonstrators. The US Department of Defense announced that Lockheed Martin's JSF design had been selected for full scale development and production as the F-35, ahead of a Boeing design, in October 2001. (Lockheed Martin)*

The US Department of Defense announced on October 26 2001 that Lockheed Martin's design, validated by the X-35 concept demonstrators, had been selected for development and production as the F-35, ahead of Boeing. Lockheed Martin is partnered with Northrop Grumman and BAE Systems on the aircraft.

The size of the prize is hard to underestimate. Under current schedules and requirements, the US Air Force, Navy and Marines and the UK's Royal Navy and Royal Air Force will buy 3000 F-35s worth $US200bn to replace F-16s, A-10s, F-14s, F/A-18s and Harriers. That number could be doubled with exports.

The new fighter will be built in conventional (USAF and export), CV or carrier capable (USN) and STOVL (USMC) variants. The three different variants are about four-fifths common – the naval F-35 variant features an extended span wing and strengthening for carrier operations, the STOVL version a shaft driven lift fan.

The US DoD's selection of Lockheed Martin allows the program to move to the $US25bn System Development and Demonstration phase (formerly known as Engineering and Manufacturing Development – EMD). Under the SDD phase Lockheed Martin will build 22 development F-35s, with the first of these to fly 48 months after the SDD contract is signed. Of the 22 development aircraft to be built, 14 will fly, comprising six CTOL, four STOVL and four CV versions. They will be built as close to production standard as possible. Two static test aircraft of each variant will be built, together with a single example each for stealth radar signature pole tests and carrier drop tests.

Low rate initial production will start in 2006 and deliveries will begin to the US Marines in 2008, with an initial operational capability (IOC) set for 2010. IOC for the USAF is planned for 2011, the USN and RAF and RN in 2012.

The USAF plans to buy 1763 F-35s, the US Marines 609 STOVL F-35s and the US Navy 480. Combined the RAF and Royal Navy plan to buy around 150 to replace Harrier GR.7s and Sea Harriers (the UK will decide in 2002 whether to buy the CV or STOVL variant). In today's dollars the basic F-35 would have a unit cost of $US40m, with the CV and STOVL variants closer to $US50m.

The UK has signed on as a "Level 1" partner in the JSF's SDD phase, contributing $US2bn of its own funds in return for an 8% program stake. Apart from the UK several other countries are participating in JSF on smaller scales. Italy, the Netherlands and Turkey look likely to join as Level 2 partners with an up to 5% SDD share each. Canada, plus Denmark and Norway combined have been in talks to sign on as Level 3 partners taking up to 2% stakes. Participating countries will likely receive any F-35s they buy before other export customers can take deliveries. F-35s for export may be available as soon as 2011 or as late as 2015.

*US Navy carrier based F/A-18s (pictured) and F-14s were an integral part of the air war against the Taliban in Afghanistan. (US Navy)*

*A veteran fights on. A B-52 departs the British territory of Diego Garcia in the Indian Ocean on a bombing mission to Afghanistan. In the foreground are B-1B Lancers and KC-10 Extender tankers. (USAF)*

The involvement of international partners helps reduce the development bill for the F-35 the US has to pay out of its own pocket. It may also have the added benefit of reducing the likelihood of program cancellation – the US would find it much harder to cancel a development program that has foreign investment and partnerships.

Two engines are being developed for the F-35. The initial standard engine will be Pratt & Whitney's F135, an evolution of the F119 that powers the F-22. General Electric has been working on its JSF-F120 evolution of the F120 (which was the losing engine contender in the ATF program won by the F119) since 1996, and has been funded for flight testing in 2004. The JSF-F120 features a Rolls-Royce designed three stage fan.

The two engines are being designed to be completely interchangeable, so that they can be swapped easily in individual aircraft. GE and P&W will compete for production contracts with their engines from 2011.

For production the F-35's airframe is divided into three major assemblies. Lockheed Martin will build the forward fuselage and undertake final assembly at its Fort Worth, Texas facilities, integrating the rear fuselage built by BAE Systems and the centre fuselage and wing box built by Northrop Grumman.

Where does the loss of the Joint Strike Fighter program leave Boeing? It certainly hurts future earnings prospects, although F/A-18E/F, C-17 and USAF 767 tanker transport buys cushion the blow. Lockheed Martin has also said it would find a significant workshare for Boeing if the US DoD asked it to accommodate its rival.

Boeing also had around 400 design and engineering

*Smooth flying ahead for the A400M at last? A production contract for the Airbus airlifter was signed in December 2001. (Airbus Military)*

fighter programs are also maturing. The Rafale entered service with the French navy in 2001 when the first operating squadron was formed. The Typhoon is now in production and will enter service in 2002. The Eurofighter consortium also remains hopeful that Greece will reinstate its order for the European fighter.

But the biggest news for the European military aerospace industry in 2001 was the signing of production contracts for the Airbus Military A400M airlifter, subject to German parliamentary approval due in early 2002.

The A400M will undoubtedly prove a very capable and advanced airlifter, but, like most other European aircraft programs, has suffered from its fair share of delays. The A400M in its various forms dates back to 1982 - the first aircraft is not due to fly until 2006 with deliveries in 2008. On December 19 2001 eight launch customers signed a formal contract for 196 A400Ms, finally giving the program some certainty. Italy has not signed up for the program, but is not needed if Germany signs up.

In the rotary wing world, the Eurocopter Tiger is now in production and has its first export customer in Australia; both components of the US Marine Corps' H-1 upgrade have made their first flights - the AH-1Z and UH-1Y; the NH 90 scored major export orders from Finland, Norway and Sweden; and the EH 101 has new customers in Denmark and Portugal.

The revolutionary tiltrotor V-22 Osprey has been struggling. Two fatal crashes in 2000 led to program reviews that potentially could have seen the whole project scrapped. In May 2001 limited MV-22 production was authorised while software and hydraulics modifications are incorporated into the design. Certainly the V-22 would have been very useful in the Afghanistan campaign, so its stocks may be on the rise.

In Japan, the Mitsubishi F-2 fighter and OH-1 reconnaissance helicopter both entered service in 2000.

Finally, in New Zealand, December 13 2001 was a black day for that small nation's air force. The Royal New Zealand Air Force's Air Combat force of two squadrons of A-4 Skyhawks and a squadron of Aermacchi MB-339 jet trainers were formally withdrawn from service (without replacement) after the NZ Government controversially decided to retire the combat aircraft as an economy measure.

staff who were working on its JSF bid to be reassigned. Keeping their all important design skills and knowledge is one of Boeing's biggest challenges.

The JSF wasn't the only major US combat program to pass a significant milestone in the last two years. The US Air Force's next air superiority fighter, the Lockheed Martin F-22 Raptor, has finally been cleared for series production. The US Department of Defense approved F-22 low rate initial production in August 2001, authorising a buy of 295 of the advanced fighters. The number of F-22s to be acquired has been cut from 331. If the program achieves savings, more F-22s could be bought.

Another US fighter program passed a major milestone recently. In September 2001 the US Navy took delivery of the first full rate production F/A-18E/F Super Hornet.

Across the Atlantic, one European fighter program that has been kicking goals of late is the Saab Gripen, which towards the end of 2001 picked up two customers - recently joined NATO members Hungary and the Czech Republic.

Europe's Dassault Rafale and Eurofighter Typhoon

# MILITARY
# AIRCRAFT

## ADA Light Combat Aircraft

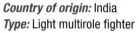

**Country of origin:** India

**Type:** Light multirole fighter

**Powerplant:** Prototypes – One 80.5kN (18,100lb) with afterburning General Electric F404-GE-F2J3 turbofan. Production aircraft – One 52.0kN (11,700lb) dry and 80.1kN (18,000lb) with afterburning GTRE Kaveri turbofan.

**Performance:** Few details released other than an estimated top speed of Mach 1.8 at altitude and a service ceiling of over 50,000ft.

**Weights:** Empty approx 5500kg (12,125lb), clean takeoff approx 8500kg (18,740lb), max takeoff approx 12,500kg (27,530lb).

**Dimensions:** Wing span 8.20m (26ft 11in), length 13.20m (43ft 4in), height 4.40m (14ft 5in). Wing area approx 38.4m² (413sq ft).

**Accommodation:** Pilot only, two seat conversion trainer planned.

**Armament:** One 23mm twin barrel GSh-23 gun. Six underwing and one centreline external stores stations will carry a variety of weaponry, ranging from conventional bombs and rockets to laser guided bombs, air-to-air and air-to-surface missiles.

**Operators:** India*

**History:** India's Light Combat Aircraft, or LCA, program will result in a lightweight multirole fighter in the weight class of Saab's Gripen which will replace the Indian Air Force's MiG-21s.

The LCA is being developed by India's Aeronautical Development Agency (ADA) based in Bangalore. Development work has been underway since 1983 when Indian government approval was given for the new project. The basic design of the LCA was finalised in 1990 and HAL (Hindustan Aeronautics Ltd) began construction of the first prototype in mid 1991.

This first prototype, TD1, rolled out on November 17 1995, about nine months behind schedule. TD1's first flight was planned for June 1996 but was delayed many times (mainly due to flight control system reliability issues) until January 4 2001. A second prototype was also due to fly during 2001. Deliveries of production aircraft are planned for 2005/6. The Indian Air Force requires around 220.

The LCA features a tailless delta configuration. The design includes extensive use of composite materials in its construction, including the wing and vertical tail, and has a fixed external refuelling probe. The cockpit features a HUD, HOTAS controls and two colour LCD multifunction displays, with all avionics linked by dual Mil Std 1553B databuses. The radar will be an Indian developed multimode unit with track while scan and ground mapping features.

Except for the first two prototypes, all LCAs will be powered by the Indian developed Kaveri engine. The Kaveri is in the same size and thrust class as the GE F404 (which powers the first two prototypes) and has been under development with India's Gas Turbine Research Establishment. The engine has been designed specifically to operate in India's hot weather and high altitude conditions.

Three LCA models are planned, the basic single seater, a two seat conversion trainer and a single seat carrier borne variant for the Indian Navy.

An advanced development, the Medium Combat Aircraft, is being studied as a replacement for Indian Jaguars and Mirage 2000s.

**Photo:** The first LCA prototype.

## Aermacchi MB-326

**Country of origin:** Italy

**Type:** Two seat basic and advanced trainer

**Powerplant:** MB-326G – One 15.3kN (3410lb) Rolls-Royce Viper 20 turbojet.

**Performance:** MB-326G – Max speed 867km/h (468kt), max cruising speed 797km/h (430kt). Max initial rate of climb 6050ft/min. Service ceiling 47,000ft. Range with internal fuel and tip tanks 1850km (1000nm), range with underwing tanks 2445km (1320nm). Combat radius (hi-lo-hi) with 770kg (1695lb) payload 650km (350nm).

**Weights:** MB-326G – Basic operating empty 2685kg (6920lb), max takeoff clean 4577kg (10,090lb), max takeoff armed 5215kg (11,500lb).

**Dimensions:** Wing span over tip tanks 10.85m (35ft 7in), length 10.67m (35ft 0in), height 3.72m (12ft 3in). Wing area 19.4m² (208.3sq ft).

**Accommodation:** Seating for two in tandem.

**Armament:** MB-326G – Provision for up to 1815kg (4000lb) of armaments, including bombs, rockets and gun pods on six underwing pylons.

**Operators:** Argentina, Brazil, Congo, Ghana, Paraguay, South Africa, Togo, Tunisia, UAE (Dubai).

**History:** Macchi initiated design of this successful two seat jet trainer in 1954 to meet an Italian air force requirement.

The MB-326 was designed by Dr-Ing Ermano Bazzochi (responsible for the B in the MB prefix) and a prototype first flew on December 10 1957. The prototype was powered by a 7.8kN (1750lb) thrust Bristol-Siddeley (later Rolls-Royce) Viper 8 turbojet and the design featured a low, straight wing and tandem seating.

Prototype flight testing impressed the Italian air force which ordered the type into production. Deliveries began in 1962.

The Italian air force took delivery of 100 basic, 11.1kN (2500lb) Viper 11 powered MB-326s (including 15 preproduction aircraft), and was offered, but did not order, the armed MB-326A with six underwing hardpoints. Similar armed versions were built for other nations, including Ghana (MB-326F) and Tunisia (MB-326B), while the Italian airline Alitalia took delivery of four unarmed MB-326Ds.

South Africa and Australia placed significant orders for the basic Viper 11 powered 326. South Africa took delivery of 191, most of which were assembled locally by Atlas as Impala Mk 1s (two ex SAAF examples are in service with Cameroon). Australia ordered 97 MB-326Hs, the majority of which were built in country by CAC. Australia retired its last 326s in early 2001.

The MB-326G had a more powerful 15.2kN (3140lb) Viper 20 Mk.540 engine, structural strengthening and greater weapons payload. MB-326Gs were delivered to Argentina, Zaire (now Congo) and Zambia. Six similar but Viper 11 powered MB-326Es were delivered to Italy.

Embraer licence built 182 MB-326GCs as the EMB-326 Xavante between 1971-81. These were delivered to Brazil (167), Paraguay (9) and Togo (6). Argentina also took delivery of 11 ex Brazilian AF Xavantes.

The final two seater was the MB-326L, which included features introduced on the single seat MB-326K (described separately). Total MB-326 production was 761.

**Photo:** A Paraguayan EMB-326. (Santiago Rivas)

# Aermacchi MB-326K

*Country of origin:* Italy

*Type:* Single seat light attack aircraft

*Powerplant:* One 17.9kN (4000lb) Rolls-Royce Viper Mk 632-43 turbojet.

*Performance:* Max speed at 5000ft 890km/h (480kt), max speed with armament at 30,000ft 685km/h (370kt). Max initial rate of climb 6500ft/min. Time to 36,000ft 9min 30sec. Service ceiling 47,000ft. Ferry range with external fuel over 2130km (1150nm). Combat radius with 1280kg (2822lb) warload lo-lo-lo 268km (145nm), with a 1815kg (4000lb) payload on a lo-lo-lo mission 130km (70nm), radius on a hi-lo-hi photo reconnaissance mission with two external tanks and recce pod 1040km (560nm).

*Weights:* Empty equipped 2964kg (6534lb), normal takeoff 4210kg (9285lb), max takeoff 5900kg (13,000lb).

*Dimensions:* Wing span with tip tanks 10.85m (35ft 7in), without tip tanks 10.15m (33ft 4in), length 10.67m (35ft 0in), height 3.72m (12ft 2in). Wing area 19.4m² (208.3sq ft).

*Accommodation:* Pilot only.

*Armament:* Max payload of 1815kg (4000lb) on six hardpoints, comprising bombs, wire guided AS.12 ASMs, Matra R550 Magic AAMs, unguided rockets, cannon and reconnaissance pods. Fixed armament comprises two 30mm DEFA 553 cannons with 125 rounds per gun.

*Operators:* Cameroon, Congo, Ghana, South Africa (Impala Mk 2), Tunisia, UAE (Dubai).

*History:* The MB-326K remains the most successful example of a two seat jet trainer being developed into single seat light fighter.

Right from the beginning of the MB-326 jet trainer program, designer Dr-Ing Ermano Bazzochi intended that the aircraft also be capable of light attack duties. The two seater proved to be a stable and effective weapons platform and so a single seater optimised for light attack was a logical development.

The single seat MB-326K was developed well into the 326's career, given that the prototype two seater flew in 1957 and the single seat prototype flew on August 22 1970. The K was based on the MB-326G, which compared to earlier Macchis featured a strengthened airframe and more powerful Viper 20 engine.

The first K prototype featured the 15.2kN (3410lb) Viper 20, while the second had the more powerful 17.9kN (4000lb) Viper Mk 632-43 intended for production aircraft, allowing an increased armament payload compared with two seaters and the fitting of two internal 30mm DEFA cannons. The second seat gave way to avionics and fuel.

Despite a 1970 first flight, the first production machines were not built until 1974 because of a lack of orders. The first customer was Dubai, which eventually took delivery of six MB-326KDs, while others were delivered to Zaire (MB-326KB), Ghana (MB-326KG) and Tunisia (MB-326KT).

South Africa was the MB-326K's largest customer, taking delivery of seven Italian built MB-326KMs and 73 Atlas licence assembled 15.1kN (3360lb) Viper 540 powered Impala 2s. Four ex SAAF Impala 2s are in service with Cameroon.

*Photo:* A Southern African Air Force Central Flying School Impala Mk II. (Keith Gaskell)

# Aermacchi MB-339

*Country of origin:* Italy

*Type:* Advanced trainer, lead-in fighter trainer & light attack aircraft

*Powerplant:* MB-339A – One 17.9kN (4000lb) Rolls-Royce Viper Mk 632-43 turbojet (licence built in Italy). MB-339C – One 19.6kN (4400lb) Viper Mk 680-43.

*Performance:* MB-339A – Max speed at 30,000ft 817km/h (441kt), at sea level 898km/h (485kt). Max initial rate of climb 6595ft/min. Climb to 30,000ft 7min 6sec. Service ceiling 48,000ft. Ferry range with drop tanks 2110km (1140nm), range 1760km (950nm). Combat radius with four Mk 82 bombs and two drop tanks hi-lo-hi 393km (212nm). MB-339C – Max speed 902km/h (487kt). Max initial rate of climb 7085ft/min. Climb to 30,000ft 6min 40sec. Service ceiling 46,700ft. Ferry range with two drop tanks 2035km (1100nm). Combat radius with four Mk 82 bombs hi-lo-hi 500km (270nm).

*Weights:* MB-339A – Empty equipped 3125kg (6889lb), max takeoff 5895kg (13,000lb). MB-339C – Empty equipped 3310kg (7297lb), max takeoff 6350kg (14,000lb).

*Dimensions:* MB-339A – Wing span over tip tanks 10.86m (35ft 8in), length 10.97m (36ft 0in), height 3.99m (13ft 1in). Wing area 19.3m² (207.7sq ft). MB-339C – Same except wing span over tip tanks 11.22m (36ft 10in), length 11.24m (36ft 11in).

*Accommodation:* Seating for two in tandem.

*Armament:* MB-339A – Up to 2040kg (4500lb) of external stores on six hardpoints including bombs, rockets, cannon pods, Matre anti shipping missiles (MB-339AM) and Magic and Sidewinder AAMs. MB-339C – Up to 1815kg (4000lb) of external ordnance, as above, plus Maverick missiles and Vinten reconnaissance pod.

*Operators:* Argentina, Eritrea, Ghana, Italy, Malaysia, Nigeria, Peru, UAE (Dubai).

*History:* The MB-339 is an upgraded successor to the MB-326.

The main change to the 339's airframe compared to the 326 was the reprofiled forward fuselage with stepped tandem cockpits for greatly improved forward vision from the rear seat. Aermacchi also considered new powerplant options, including turbofans and a twin engine configuration, but settled upon the familiar Viper turbojet for its performance, ease of maintenance and lower acquisition cost.

The first of two prototypes flew on August 12 1976, since which time the basic aircraft has been developed into a number of models. The base MB-339A has accounted for most sales and 101 were delivered to the Italian air force.

The improved MB-339C is optimised for lead-in fighter and light attack duties and features advanced nav and attack systems, HUDs, the ability to carry missiles, a more powerful engine, lengthened nose housing a laser rangefinder and larger tip tanks. New Zealand was the only C customer, but its were being offered for sale at the end of 2001.

The Italian air force's Viper 632 powered MB-339CD (and Eritrea's 339CEs) and the export Viper 680 powered MB-339FD feature a digital cockpit, including three colour LCD displays, HUD and HOTAS controls, plus a removable inflight refuelling probe. An Eritrean MB-339CE delivered in 1997 was the 200th 339 built.

The single seat MB-339K Veltro 2 was built in prototype form only.

*Photo:* An Italian air force MB-339CD. (Paul Merritt)

## Aermacchi RediGO & Valmet Vinka

**Countries of origin:** Finland and Italy

**Type:** Two seat basic trainers

**Powerplant:** L-70 – One 150kW (200hp) Lycoming AEIO-360-A1B6 flat four piston engine, two blade prop. LM-290TP – One 335kW (450shp) flat rated Allison 250-B17F turboprop driving a three blade prop.

**Performance:** L-70 – Max speed at sea level 235km/h (127kt), cruising speed at 5000ft 222km/h (120kt). Max initial rate of climb 1120ft/min. Service ceiling 16,405ft. Range 950km (512nm). M-290TP – Max speed at sea level 333km/h (180kt), max cruising speed 354km/h (191kt), economical cruising speed 312km/h (168kt). Service ceiling 25,000ft. Range 1205km (650nm). Endurance 5hr 55min.

**Weights:** L-70 – Operating empty 767kg (1690lb), max takeoff 1250kg (2755lb). M-290TP – Empty equipped 970kg (2138lb), max takeoff with external stores 1900kg (4190lb).

**Dimensions:** L-70 – Wing span 9.63m (31ft 7in), length 7.50m (24ft 8in), height 3.31m (10ft 11in). Wing area 14.0m² (150.7sq ft). M-290TP – Wing span 10.60m (34ft 9in), length 8.53m (28ft 0in), height 3.20m (10ft 6in). Wing area 14.8m² (159.1sq ft).

**Accommodation:** Two side by side. Two extra seats can be installed behind them.

**Armament:** L-70 – Up to 300kg (660lb) on underwing hardpoints, including rockets, gun pods and light bombs. M-290TP – Up to 800kg (1765lb) of armament on six underwing hardpoints. Weapon options similar to L-70.

**Operators:** L-70 – Finland. L-90TP – Eritrea, Finland, Mexico.

**History:** Valmet's L-70 is currently Finland's basic military trainer, and forms the basis for the turboprop powered L-90TP Redigo/M-290TP RediGO development.

The L-70 Miltrainer first flew on July 1 1975. Its conventional configuration includes seating for the student and instructor side by side, fixed tricycle undercarriage and a Lycoming AEIO-360 flat four piston engine driving a two blade prop. Hardpoints under the wings are designed for practice bombs or light armament including gun pods or rockets.

In 1978 the Finnish air force ordered 30 L-70 Miltrainers, which it named Vinka (Blast), to replace its Saab Safir basic trainers. They were delivered between 1980 and 1982. Apart from their basic training role Vinkas serve as liaison aircraft.

The L-90TP Redigo is a turboprop powered development of the Miltrainer with an Allison 250 driving a three blade prop. Other changes to the Redigo include retractable undercarriage, a slight fuselage stretch, lengthened wings and greater external weapons load. First flight was on July 1 1986. Ten were built for the Finnish air force and others went to the Mexican navy (10 serve for COIN missions) and Eritrea.

A second prototype Redigo flew in 1987 powered by a Turbomeca TP 319, but no production aircraft were built with this engine.

The final Valmet built Redigo was delivered in 1995.

In January 1996 Aermacchi purchased the design and production rights to the Redigo and wouold build in Italy any new aircraft ordered as the M-290TP RediGO. None have been ordered.

**Photo:** A Finnish air force L-70. (Lassi Tolvanen)

## Aermacchi SF-260

**Country of origin:** Italy

**Type:** Two seat trainer and light attack aircraft

**Powerplant:** SF-260TP – One 261kW (380hp) Rolls-Royce 250-B17D turboprop driving a three blade propeller.

**Performance:** SF-260TP – Max speed at 10,000ft 426km/h (230kt), max cruising speed 400km/h (216kt), economical cruising speed 315km/h (170kt). Max initial rate of climb 2170ft/min. Service ceiling 24,600ft. Range with max fuel and reserves 950km (512nm).

**Weights:** SF-260TP – Empty equipped 750kg (1654lb), max takeoff 1300kg (2866lb).

**Dimensions:** SF-260TP – Wing span 8.35m (27ft 5in), length 7.10m (23ft 4in), height 2.41m (7ft 11in). Wing area 10.1m² (108.7sq ft).

**Accommodation:** Seating for two side by side, with optional third seat behind.

**Armament:** SF-260TP – Four underwing hardpoints can carry a max ordnance load of 300kg (660lb) including gun pods, bombs, practice bombs and rockets.

**Operators:** Belgium, Brunei, Burundi, Chad, Congo, Indonesia*, Ireland, Italy, Libya, Mauritania, Philippines, Sri Lanka, Tunisia, Turkey, UAE (Dubai), Uganda, Uruguay, Venezuela, Zambia, Zimbabwe.

**History:** The nimble SF-260 is a highly successful piston engine powered military trainer.

The retractable undercarriage SF-260 was designed by respected Italian aircraft designer Stelio Frati in the early 1960s. It was originally flown in 185kW (250hp) Lycoming O-540 powered form by Aviamilano as the F.250. However SIAI-Marchetti undertook production of the new aircraft (initially under licence, it later assumed full responsibility for the program) as the 195kW (260hp) O-540 powered SF.260. The second aircraft to fly was the first built by SIAI-Marchetti and the first powered by the more powerful version of the O-540. This second prototype flew in 1966.

Initial civil production was of the SF.260A and SF.260B. Improvements launched on the military SF.260M included a stronger undercarriage, a redesigned wing leading edge and a taller fin. The M first flew on October 10 1970. The SF.260 has been further developed into E and F models with minor changes, while the definitive SF.260 military piston powered variants are the SF.260E and F Warriors, with a further strengthened airframe and two or four underwing hardpoints for up to 300kg (660lb) of rockets and bombs for light ground attack, weapons training and forward air control. The Warrior's first flight was in May 1972.

The 260kW (350shp) Rolls-Royce (Allison) 250-B17D turboprop powered SF.260TP has been in production since the early 1980s. About 60 have been built for the air forces of Dubai, Ethiopia, the Philippines, Sri Lanka and Zimbabwe.

More than 650 piston powered SF.260s have been built, the vast majority for military customers. Aermacchi acquired SIAI-Marchetti in January 1997 and now builds the SF.260s as the SF-260 (both piston and turbine powered) at its Venegono plant. The Italian air force has been in negotiation with Aermacchi to acquire 40 SF.260Es to replace SF.260AMs.

**Photo:** An SF-260E demonstrator (Aermacchi).

# Aermacchi S.211

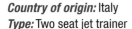

**Country of origin:** Italy

**Type:** Two seat jet trainer

**Powerplant:** S.211 – One 11.1kN (2500lb) Pratt & Whitney Canada JT15D-4C turbofan. S.211A – One 14.2kN (3190lb) JT15D-5C.

**Performance:** S.211 – Max cruising speed at 25,000ft 667km/h (360kt). Max initial rate of climb 4200ft/min. Service ceiling 40,000ft. Combat radius with four rocket launchers hi-lo-hi 555km (300nm), or lo-lo-lo 230km (125nm). Ferry range with external fuel 2485km (1340nm), range with internal fuel 1665km (900nm). Endurance 3hr 50min. S.211A – Max cruising speed at 25,000ft 767km/h (414kt). Max initial rate of climb 5100ft/min. Service ceiling 42,000ft. Ferry range with external fuel 2685km (1450nm). Endurance 4hr 15min.

**Weights:** S.211 – Empty equipped 1850kg (4078lb), max takeoff 3150kg (6955lb). S.211A – Empty equipped 2030kg (4475lb), max takeoff 4000kg (8188lb).

**Dimensions:** Wing span 8.43m (27ft 8in), length 9.50m (31ft 2in), height 3.96m (13ft 0in). Wing area 12.6m² (135.6sq ft).

**Accommodation:** Two in tandem.

**Armament:** Four underwing hardpoints can carry a max external ordnance load of 660kg (1455lb) for bombs, practice bombs, rockets and machine gun pods.

**Operators:** Philippines, Singapore.

**History:** SIAI-Marchetti developed the S.211 as a private venture to fulfil basic/intermediate training and light ground attack roles. The jet is now part of the Aermacchi stable of trainers.

SIAI-Marchetti first displayed models of its new basic jet trainer at the 1977 Paris Airshow. The first of two prototypes made the type's first flight on April 10 1981, while production deliveries began in November 1984.

Major customers/operators are Singapore (30) and the Philippines (24), with both countries assembling most of their S.211s under licence. The former's aircraft are based near Perth in Australia, where they are free to train without Singapore's airspace constraints. The Philippines uses its aircraft for both training and ground attack, but the fleet has suffered from high attrition. Haiti took delivery of four but subsequently sold them in the USA to civilian buyers.

The S.211 features a shoulder mounted wing with four hardpoints for light weaponry. Power is from a single Pratt & Whitney Canada JT15D turbofan, which is used in a number of light business jets (including the Raytheon Beech T-1 Jayhawk), while the crew sit on stepped tandem lightweight Martin-Baker ejection seats. Sixty-one percent of external surfaces are made from composite materials.

The uprated S.211A has yet to find a customer and was unsuccessfully offered by Northrop Grumman (originally Grumman) to meet the USAF/USN's JPATS trainer requirement.

Aermacchi acquired SIAI-Marchetti in January 1997 and any new S.211s ordered would be built at Aermacchi's Venegono plant. However none have been sold since Aermacchi took over the program.

**Photo:** Singapore's S.211s are based in Australia to take advantage of uncongested air space. They share RAAF Base Pearce with RAAF PC-9 turboprops of 2FTS and 79SQN Hawk 127s. (Paul Sadler)

# Aero L-29 Delfin

**Country of origin:** Czech Republic

**Type:** Two seat basic and advanced jet trainer

**Powerplant:** One 8.78kN (1960lb) Motorlet M 701c 500 turbojet.

**Performance:** Max speed at 16,400ft 655km/h (353kt), at sea level 620km/h (335kt), cruising speed at 16,400ft 545km/h (294kt). Max initial rate of climb 2755ft/min. Time to 16,400ft 8min, time to 36,100ft 25min. Service ceiling 36,100ft. Ferry range with drop tanks 895km (482nm), range with internal fuel 640km (345nm).

**Weights:** Empty equipped 2365kg (5212lb), normal takeoff 3280kg (7230lb), max takeoff 3540kg (7805lb).

**Dimensions:** Wing span 10.29m (33ft 9in), length 10.81m (35ft 6in), height 3.13m (10ft 3in). Wing area 19.9m² (213sq ft).

**Accommodation:** Seating for two in tandem.

**Armament:** Max warload of 200kg (441lb) on two underwing hardpoints (one per wing). Armament can include two 7.62mm gun pods, or two 100kg (220lb) bombs, or eight light rockets.

**Operators:** Angola, Azerbaijan, Bulgaria, Czech Republic, Georgia, Ghana, Mali, Romania, Slovakia, Syria.

**History:** The L-29 Delfin saw widespread use in the Soviet Union as its primary advanced jet trainer for more than a decade from the early 1960s, and proved one of the Czech aircraft industry's most successful aircraft designs.

Early design studies for a two seat jet engined trainer were conducted by K Tomas and Z Rubic in 1955. A major feature of the resulting L-29 Delfin (Dolphin) was its design concept of simplicity, including straight forward construction and maintenance and docile handling qualities. Other design features are typical of jet trainers of the era, such as a small turbojet engine, straight wing, tandem seating and lightweight ejection seats. Unlike many of its contemporaries and later jet trainers, the L-29 features a T-tail and can operate from grass, waterlogged or dirt strips.

The first XL-29 prototype was powered by a Bristol Siddeley Viper turbojet and first flew on April 5 1959. A second prototype flew in July 1960, powered by the indigenously developed M 701 turbojet. The following year the Delfin was pitted against the Yak-30 and PZL Mielec TS-11 Iskra in a competitive fly-off. As a result of winning the competition the Delfin equipped the air forces of every Warsaw Pact nation except Poland (which went with the TS-11).

The Soviet Union alone took delivery of more than 2000 Delfins, while significant numbers also served with Czechoslovakia, East Germany and Hungary. In these countries the Delfin was used in all-through training from ab initio to advanced stages. The first Delfins were delivered in 1963, with the last of over 3600 built rolling off the production line in 1974.

Almost all production was of the basic trainer variant (which was given the NATO reporting name 'Maya'), although two other variants did appear. Small numbers of single seat L-29A Delfin Akrobats were built for aerobatics while a prototype L-29R dedicated attack aircraft was also built.

Russia has retired its L-29s, but large numbers serve with ex communist block nations.

**Photo:** A Czech L-29.

## Aero Albatros

**Country of origin:** Czech Republic

**Type:** Two seat advanced trainer and light strike aircraft

**Powerplant:** L-39 ZA – One 16.9kN (3972lb) Progress (nee Ivchenko) AI-25 TL turbofan. L-59 E – One 21.6kN (4850lb) Progress DV-2 turbofan.

**Performance:** L-39 ZA – Max speed at 20,000ft 760km/h (410kt). Max initial rate of climb 4409ft/min. Service ceiling 39,360ft. Range with max internal fuel and reserves 1650km (890nm). Endurance with internal fuel 3hr 19min. L-59 E – Max speed at 16,400ft 876km/h (473kt). Max initial rate of climb 4921ft/min. Service ceiling 38,480ft. Range with reserves 1475km (796nm).

**Weights:** L-39 ZA – Empty equipped 3565kg (7859lb), max takeoff 5600kg (12,345lb). L-59 E – Empty 4030kg (8885lb), max takeoff 7000kg (15,432lb).

**Dimensions:** L-39 C – Wing span incl tip tanks 9.46m (31ft 0in), length 12.13m (39ft 10in), height 4.77m (15ft 8in). Wing area 18.8m$^2$ (202.4sq ft). L-59 – Same except wing span incl tip tanks 9.54m (31ft 4in) and length 12.20m (40ft 0in).

**Accommodation:** Seating for two in tandem.

**Armament:** L-39 C – Unarmed. L-39 ZA & L-59 – Max external warload of 1000kg (2205lb) comprising rockets and pods, plus a 23mm GSh-23 two barrel cannon on centreline station.

**Operators:** L-39 – Algeria, Armenia, Azerbaijan, Bulgaria, Cambodia, Cuba, Czech Republic, Ethiopia, Hungary, Iraq, Libya, Lithuania, Nigeria, North Korea, Russia, Slovakia, Syria, Thailand, Turkmenistan, Uganda, Yemen. L-59 – Egypt, Tunisia.

**History:** Design work on the Albatros, under the leadership of Dipl Ing Jan Vlcek, began in 1966, just three years after the aircraft it was designed to replace, the Delfin, had entered production.

The prototype L-39 first flew on November 4 1968. Two other initial prototypes were built, both for structural testing, while a further four flying prototypes later joined the original aircraft in flight test duties. After a production decision was made in 1972 the L-39 was adopted for widespread use by Warsaw Pact countries (including the Soviet Union) and USSR client states.

A key feature of the L-39 is its modular construction for its ease of manufacture and maintain ability. It is powered by the Russian AI-25 turbofan.

There are numerous variants of the L-39. The L-39 C is the basic two seat, unarmed trainer, and accounts for the majority of L-39 production. The L-39 V is a target tug, the L-39 ZO is an armed weapons trainer with a reinforced wing and four underwing hardpoints, while the L-39 ZA is similar to the ZO, but has reinforced undercarriage and can carry a reconnaissance pod. The L-39 ZA/ART was built for Thailand and features Israeli Elbit avionics.

The L-139 Albatros 2000 was powered by a 18.2kN (4080lb) TFE731 turbofan, featured Bendix/King avionics and Flight Vision HUD and was offered for export. It flew in 1993 but none were ordered.

The L-59 development (and Czech AF L-39 MS) is similar to the L-39 but has a more powerful engine, upgraded avionics and reinforced fuselage.

**Photo:** Lithuania ordered two L 39s in 1998. Almost 3000 L 39s/59s have been built. (Aero)

## Aero L 159 ALCA

**Country of origin:** Czech Republic

**Type:** Light multirole fighter and lead-in fighter trainer

**Powerplant:** One 28.2kN (6330lb) Honeywell/ITEC F124-GA-100 non afterburning turbofan.

**Performance:** L 159A – Max speed at sea level 936km/h (505kt). Max initial rate of climb 12,210ft/min. Service ceiling 43,300ft. Radius with two Mk 82 bombs, two AIM-9s and two external tanks, hi-lo-hi 705km (380nm), with two Mk 82s and two drop tanks hi-lo-hi 780km (421nm). Range with max internal fuel 1570km (848nm), max range with external fuel 2530km (1366nm).

**Weights:** Empty equipped 4320kg (9524lb), max takeoff 8000kg (17,637lb). Internal fuel L 159A 1596kg (3519lb), L 159B 1273kg (2806lb).

**Dimensions:** Wing span incl tip tanks 9.54m (31ft 2in), length 12.72m (41ft 8in), height 4.77m (15ft 8in). Wing area 18.8m$^2$ (202.4sq ft).

**Accommodation:** Pilot only, or two in tandem in L 159T.

**Armament:** Seven external hardpoints can carry a total ordnance/fuel load of 2340kg (5159lb). Weapon options include AIM-9 Sidewinder AAMs, AGM-65 Maverick ASMs, gun pods, rockets and bombs.

**Operators:** Czech Republic*

**History:** The L 159 ALCA (Advanced Light Combat Aircraft) is the latest development of the Aero L 39 family of advanced jet trainers and is being built in single seat light multirole fighter and two seat lead-in fighter trainer forms.

The L 159 combines a slightly longer Albatros airframe with a new engine, modern avionics and a radar. The engine is Honeywell/ITEC's F124 (which in afterburning F125 form powers the Taiwanese AIDC Ching-Kuo fighter) a modern turbofan with FADEC. The Boeing integrated avionics suite is built around a Mil Std 1553B databus linking a head-up display, two colour multifunction liquid crystal displays, Flight Visions dual mission computers, ring laser gyro INS with GPS nav system, and the Italian FIAR Grifo L multimode radar (with look down/shoot down and ground mapping functions).

Other features include HOTAS controls, a BAE Systems Sky Guardian radar warning receiver and Vinten countermeasures (chaff and flares) dispenser, and cockpit armour and a fuel tank inerting system in the single seater, enhancing combat survivability.

Apart from the cockpit armour and fuel inerting system, the single seater differs from the two seater in having an additional fuel tank and avionics in place of the second seat (but with a two seater style canopy). Otherwise the two aircraft are similar.

The L 159 has been under development since late 1992 and is on order with the Czech air force. First flight, of a two seater, took place on August 4 1997, while the first single seater, built to full Czech air force standards, flew on August 18 1998.

The Czech air force ordered 72 L 159s (most are expected to be single seaters) in April 1995. The first production L 159 flew on October 20 1999, the first two were handed over to the Czech air force in April 2000 (about four months late). Rising costs due to the strong US currency may mean deliveries are stretched out.

**Photo:** A production L 159A. Marketing of the L 159 to export customers continues. (Harold van Eupen/Sentry Aviation News)

## Aerospatiale (Fouga) CM 170 Magister

**Country of origin:** France

**Type:** Two seat jet trainer

**Powerplants:** CM 170-1 – Two 3.91kN (880lb) Maborè IIA turbojets. CM 170-2 – Two 4.71kN (1058lb) Maborè VICs.

**Performance:** CM 170-1 – Max speed 715km/h (385kt) at 29,925ft, 650km/h (350kt) at sea level. Max initial rate of climb 3345ft/min. Service ceiling 36,090ft. Ferry range with auxiliary fuel 1200km (650nm), range with standard fuel 925km (500nm). CM 170-2 – Max speed clean at 30,000ft 745km/h (402kt), at sea level 700km/h (378kt). Max initial rate of climb 3540ft/min. Service ceiling 44,300ft. Range 1250km (675nm).

**Weights:** CM 170-1 – Empty equipped 2150kg (4740lb), max takeoff 3200kg (7055lb). CM 170-2 – Empty equipped 2310kg (5093lb), max takeoff 3200kg (7055lb).

**Dimensions:** Wing span over tip tanks 12.15m (39ft 10in), span without tip tanks 11.40m (37ft 5in), length 10.06m (33ft 0in), height 2.80m (9ft 2in). Wing area 17.3m² (186.1sq ft).

**Accommodation:** Standard seating for two in tandem.

**Armament:** Two 7.5mm or 7.62mm fixed machine guns mounted in the nose. Underwing hardpoints can carry bombs, rockets and Nord AS.12 air-to-ground missiles.

**Operators:** Cameroon, El Salvador, Israel, Morocco, Senegal.

**History:** The Fouga/Aerospatiale Magister was the world's first purpose designed jet trainer.

The Magister resulted from a French Armée de l'Air requirement for a jet powered trainer. The basic aircraft was conceived by Fouga designers Castello and Mauboussin (hence the CM prefix in the designation) in 1950. The first of three prototypes first flew on June 27 1951, the type's promising performance leading to an Armée de l'Air order for 10 preproduction aircraft. Prolonged testing and development of the aircraft followed, with the first preproduction aircraft not flying until June 1954 and the first production aircraft (for the French air force) flying on February 29 1956.

The Magister proved well suited for its training role as it was easy to fly with predictable flying characteristics, despite the uncommon two surface butterfly tail arrangement. A total of 387 was eventually built for the French air force while several hundred others were built in France and under licence in Finland, Germany and Israel for a large number of export customers including West Germany, Austria, Belgium, Lebanon and Cambodia. Total French production was 622 (built mainly by Fouga's successors Potez, Sud Aviation and Aerospatiale), while IAI built 36, Finland's Valmet 62 and Germany's Flugzeug Union Sud 188.

The Magister was built in three versions – the initial CM 170-1, the CM 170-2 Super Magister with more powerful engines and ejection seats, and the navalised, carrier capable CM 175 Zéphyr. The French navy took delivery of 30 arrester hook equipped Zéphyrs.

Today the Magister remains in service in dimishing numbers – a number of nations acquired examples second hand. Israel is the largest operator with around 40. Its were upgraded in the 1980s with new avionics and Mabore VI engines.

**Photo:** A Magister in Belgium air force markings. Belgium, like France and Germany, has retired its Magisters. (Belgium SID)

## Aerospatiale TB 30 Epsilon

**Country of origin:** France

**Type:** Two seat basic trainer

**Powerplant:** TB 30B – One 225kW (300hp) Textron Lycoming AEIO-540-L1B5D fuel injected flat six piston engine driving a two blade constant speed Hartzell propeller.

**Performance:** TB 30B – Max speed at sea level 378km/h (204kt), cruising speed at 6000ft 358km/h (193kt). Max initial rate of climb 1850ft/min. Service ceiling 23,000ft. Range 1250km (675nm). Endurance at 60% power 3hr 45min.

**Weights:** TB 30B – Empty equipped 932kg (2055lb), max takeoff 1250kg (2755lb).

**Dimensions:** TB 30B – Wing span 7.92m (26ft 0in), length 7.59m (24ft 1in), height 2.66m (8ft 9in). Wing area 9.0m² (96.0sq ft).

**Accommodation:** Seating for two in tandem.

**Armament:** Togolese aircraft only – Maximum external ordnance of 300kg (660lb) with pilot only, comprising two twin 7.62mm machine gun pods, or four 68mm six rocket tubes, or two 120kg (265lb) bombs, on four underwing hardpoints. Inner pylons stressed for 160kg (350lb), outer pylons 80kg (175lb).

**Operators:** France, Portugal, Togo.

**History:** The Epsilon is the French Armée de l'Air's primary basic trainer.

Aerospatiale's general aviation subsidiary Socata (now both part of EADS) developed the Epsilon in response to an Armée d l'Air requirement for a basic trainer. Initially Socata looked at a jet powered aircraft, then a piston engined aircraft based on its Tobago four seater with two seats side-by-side. When the Armée de l'Air decided it wanted a tandem seating arrangement, Socata redeveloped the basic design and all commonality with the Tobago was lost.

Socata proposed two Epsilon variants differing in the powerplant – the 195kW (260hp) powered TB 30A and the 225kW (300hp) TB 30B, with the latter selected for development and production. The Armée de l'Air awarded a development contract in June 1979 and the TB 30B prototype first flew on December 22 that year.

Testing of the prototype revealed unacceptable pitch/yaw coupling characteristics, so Socata further refined the design to feature extended, rounded, upswept winglets and a redesigned rear fuselage and tail. The first and second prototypes were then modified and flew in this new, definitive configuration from late October 1980.

The first French production order was placed in March 1982 for 30 aircraft. Socata eventually delivered 150 Epsilons to the Armée de l'Air through to 1989, while Togo took delivery of four and Portugal 18, assembled locally by OGMA.

The fully aerobatic Epsilon's fuel system allows it to fly inverted for up to two minutes. Togo's aircraft meanwhile are equipped with four external hardpoints, which can carry gun pods, rockets and light bombs in a counter insurgency role.

The TB 30 also formed the basis for the turboprop Turbomeca Arrius powered TB 31 Omega, which flew in 1985 but never entered production due to a lack of orders.

**Photo:** The Epsilon is France's standard basic trainer. These examples belong to the Armée de l'Air's Cartouche Dore aerobatic team.

## Aerospatiale Alouette II & Lama

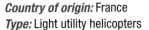

**Country of origin:** France

**Type:** Light utility helicopters

**Powerplant:** SA 313B Alouette II – One 270kW (360shp) Turbomeca Artouste IIC6 turboshaft driving a three blade main rotor and two blade tail rotor. SA 315B Lama – One 650kW (870shp) Turbomeca Artouste IIIB turboshaft, derated to 410kW (550shp).

**Performance:** SA 313B – Max speed 185km/h (100kt), max cruising speed 165km/h (90kt). Max initial rate of climb 825ft/min. Hovering ceiling in ground effect 5400ft. Range with max fuel 300km (162nm), range with max payload 100km (54nm). SA 315B – Max cruising speed 192km/h (103kt). Max initial rate of climb 1080ft/min. Service ceiling 17,715ft. Hovering ceiling in ground effect 16,565ft, out of ground effect 15,090ft. Range with max fuel 515km (278nm).

**Weights:** SA 313B – Empty 895kg (1973lb), max takeoff 1600kg (3527lb). SA 315B – Empty 1020kg (2250lb), max takeoff 1950kg (4300lb), or 2300kg (5070lb) with external sling load.

**Dimensions:** SA 313B – Main rotor diameter 10.20m (33ft 5in), fuselage length 9.70m (31ft 10in), height 2.75m (9ft 0in). SA 315B – Main rotor diameter 11.02m (36ft 2in), length overall 12.92m (42ft 5in), fuselage length 10.26m (33ft 8in), height overall 3.09m (10ft 2in). Main rotor disc area 95.4m² (1026.7sq ft).

**Accommodation:** Typical seating for five. Can carry two stretchers in medevac role. Lama can lift a 1135kg (2500lb) external sling load.

**Armament:** Lancer can carry rockets and guns.

**Operators:** Alouette II – Belgium, Cameroon, Dominican Republic, Guinea-Bissau, Lebanon, Senegal, Tunisia. Lama – Argentina, Chile, Ecuador, India (Cheetah), Togo.

**History:** The Alouette II was based on the original Sud-Est Alouette SE 3120 which first flew on March 12 1955, and for a time was the most successful western European helicopter in terms of numbers built.

Two prototypes were built powered by Salmson 9 piston engines. Production deliveries of the turbine powered SE 313B Alouette II took place from 1957, with the first examples for the French army. Most SA/SE 313B production was for military operators.

The Alouette II was soon followed by a more powerful Turbomeca Astazou powered development. This aircraft was designated the SA 318C Alouette II Astazou, and first flew on January 31 1961. Power was supplied by a 395kW (530shp) Astazou IIA derated to 270kW (360shp), which increased the type's maximum speed and max takeoff weight.

The SA 315B Lama was developed initially as a utility helicopter with excellent hot and high performance for the Indian Army. Called Cheetah in Indian service (where HAL has built it under licence), the Lama mated the Alouette II's airframe with the larger Alouette III's dynamic components including the Artouste IIIB engine. The Lama first flew on March 17 1969. Aerospatiale built 407 through to 1989.

In late 1998 HAL unveiled the armed Lancer development of the Cheetah, capable of carrying anti armour rockets and fitted with two 12.7mm machine guns. The Indian Army has ordered 12 for delivery in 2001. They will be used for counter insurgency work

**Photo:** The HAL Lancer demonstrator. (Sebastian Zacharias)

## Aerospatiale Alouette III

**Country of origin:** France

**Type:** Light utility helicopter

**Powerplant:** SA 316B – One 425kW (570shp) Turbomeca Artouste IIIB turboshaft driving a three blade main rotor and three blade tail rotor. SA 319B – One 450kW (600shp) derated Turbomeca Astazou XIV.

**Performance:** SA 316B – Max speed 210km/h (113kt), max cruising speed 185km/h (100kt). Max initial rate of climb 885ft/min. Hovering ceiling in ground effect 7380ft. Range with max fuel 480km (260nm). SA 319B – Max cruising speed 197km/h (106kt). Max initial rate of climb 885ft/min. Hovering ceiling in ground effect 10,700ft, out of ground effect 5575ft. Range with six passengers 605km (327nm).

**Weights:** SA 316B – Empty 1122kg (2474lb), max takeoff 2200kg (4850lb). SA 319B – Empty 1140kg (2513lb), MTOW 2250kg (4960lb).

**Dimensions:** SA 316B & SA 319B – Main rotor diameter 11.02m (36ft 2in), length overall 12.84m (42ft 2in), fuselage length 10.03m (32ft 11in), height 3.00m, (9ft 10in). Main rotor disc area 95.4m² (1026.7sq ft).

**Accommodation:** Typical seating for seven.

**Armament:** Can carry one 7.62mm machine gun mounted on a tripod firing from right hand doorway, a 20mm cannon fixed to the left hand side of the fuselage, or four or two AS.11 anti tank missiles, or two Mk.44 torpedoes.

**Operators:** Argentina, Austria, Cameroon, Ecuador, France, Ghana, Iraq, Ireland, Malaysia, Mexico, Netherlands, Pakistan, Portugal, Romania, South Africa, Switzerland, Tunisia, Venezuela. Chetak in service with India and Nepal.

**History:** The popular Alouette III is an enlarged development of the Alouette II and remains in widespread service.

Like the Alouette II, the Alouette III traces its development back to the Sud-Est SE 3101 piston powered prototypes, the first of which first flew on July 31 1951. The largest member of the Alouette series, the III flew as the SE 3160 on February 28 1959. Compared with the Alouette II, the Alouette III is larger and seats seven, but in its initial SA 316A form is also powered by a Turbomeca Artouste turboshaft.

The SA 316A Alouette III remained in production for almost a decade until 1969, when it was replaced by the improved SA 316B, with strengthened transmission and a greater max takeoff weight, but the same Artouste III turboshaft.

Further development led to the SA 319 Alouette III Astazou, which, as its name suggests, is powered by a 450kW (600shp) Turbomeca Astazou turboshaft. The more powerful Astazou XIV engine conferred better hot and high performance and improved fuel economy. The SA 319 entered production in 1968.

The SA 319 and SA 316B remained in production side by side through the 1970s and into the 1980s. HAL of India has built more than 300 SA 316B Alouette IIIs under licence as the Chetak, mainly for that country's military, while ICA-Brasov built 230 in Romania through to 1989.

The Romanians also built a two seat anti tank attack helicopter development of the Alouette, the IAR-317 Skyfox, but this flew in prototype form only.

**Photo:** The Argentine navy's Alouette IIIs can deploy aboard its Meko class ships. (Santiago Rivas)

## Aerospatiale Gazelle

**Country of origin:** France

**Type:** Reconnaissance, training, anti tank and utility helicopter

**Powerplant:** SA 342L – One 640kW (858shp) Turbomeca XIVM turboshaft driving a three blade main rotor and Fenestron shrouded tail rotor.

**Performance:** SA 342L – Max cruising speed at sea level 260km/h (140kt). Max initial rate of climb 1535ft/min. Service ceiling 13,450ft. Hovering ceiling in ground effect 9975ft, out of ground effect 7775ft. Range at sea level with standard fuel 710km (383nm).

**Weights:** SA 342L – Empty 999kg (2202lb), max takeoff 2000kg (4410lb).

**Dimensions:** SA 342L – Main rotor diameter 10.50m (34ft 6in), length overall 11.97m (39ft 3in), fuselage length 9.53m (31ft 3in), height overall 3.19m (10ft 6in). Main rotor disc area 86.6m² (932.1sq ft).

**Accommodation:** Seating for five including pilot.

**Armament:** Armament options include rocket pods, four or six HOT wire guided anti armour missiles, two forward firing 7.62mm machine guns, and a single 20mm Giat cannon on starboard side. Yugoslav SA 342Ls equipped with four AT-3 'Sagger' ASMs and two SA-7 AAMs.

**Operators:** Military operators include Angola, Burundi, Cameroon, Cyprus, Ecuador, Egypt, France, Guinea, Iraq, Ireland, Kuwait, Lebanon, Libya, Morocco, Qatar, Senegal, Syria, Tunisia, UAE (Abu Dhabi), UK, Yugoslavia.

**History:** The Gazelle was developed as a replacement to the Alouette II and sold around the world to various military air arms.

The Gazelle pioneered a number of significant technologies namely a rigid main rotor head, composite construction rotor blades and the Fenestron shrouded tail rotor, a feature of a number of Aerospatiale/Eurocopter helicopters since.

The prototype was designated SA 340-01, had conventional rotor blades and first flew on April 7 1967. A second prototype introduced composite blades, while improved preproduction aircraft with a larger cabin were designated the SA 341. The first production Gazelle, with longer cabin, larger tail and uprated Astazou IIIA engine first flew on August 6 1971.

A 1967 Anglo French agreement between Sud Aviation (Aerospatiale from 1970) and Westland covering the Gazelle, Lynx and Puma helicopters saw the Gazelle become a joint production effort between both nations. Initial production Gazelle models were the SA 341B Gazelle AH.1 for the British Army, SA 341C Gazelle HT.2 for the Royal Navy, SA 341D Gazelle HT.3 trainer and SA 341E Gazelle HCC.4 transport for the RAF, the French army SA 341F, civil SA 341G and military export SA 341H.

Over 600 SA 341s of different versions were built before production switched to the more powerful Astazou XIVH powered SA 342. Versions are the civil SA 342J and export optimised SA 342K. Final versions are the export military SA 342L and French army SA 342M, which remained in production through to the mid 1990s with Eurocopter (total civil and military Gazelle production reached 1255).

French SA 342Ms are equipped with HOT anti armour missiles, while earlier SA 341Fs have been converted to fire HOTs. France also equipped 30 Gazelles (the SA 342M ATAM) to fire Mistral AAMs.

**Photo:** A British Army Gazelle AH.1. (Paul Merritt)

## Aerospatiale SA 321 Super Frelon

**Country of origin:** France

**Type:** Utility helicopter

**Powerplants:** SA 321G – Three 1100kW to 1215kW (1475shp to 1630shp) Turbomeca Turmo IIIC turboshafts driving a six blade main rotor and five blade tail rotor.

**Performance:** SA 321G – Max cruising speed at sea level 248km/h (134kt). Max initial rate of climb (inclined) 1214ft/min, 480ft/min on two engines. Hovering ceiling in ground effect 7120ft. Service ceiling 10,170ft. Range 1020km (550nm). Endurance in ASW role 4hr.

**Weights:** SA 321G – Empty 6700kg (14,775lb), max takeoff 13,000kg (28,660lb).

**Dimensions:** Main rotor diameter 18.90m (62ft 0in), length overall 23.03m (75ft 7in), fuselage length 19.40m (63ft 8in), height 6.66m (21ft 10in). Main rotor disc area 280.6m² (3019sq ft).

**Accommodation:** Flightcrew of two. Original SA 321G ASW configuration seats three tactical/sonar operators. Transport configured Super Frelons can seat 30 troops or carry 15 stretcher patients in a medevac configuration.

**Armament:** As originally configured, SA 321Gs could carry four homing torpedoes or two AM 39 Exocet anti shipping missiles. Various export aircraft configured to launch Exocet.

**Operators:** China, France, Iraq, Libya.

**History:** The Super Frelon has the distinction of being the largest helicopter to be built in quantity in western Europe.

The Super Frelon was developed from the smaller, mid size SA 3200 Frelon (Hornet), which first flew on June 10 1959. The Frelon was intended to meet French military requirements but was not ordered into production. Instead the Frelon formed the basis for the much larger Super Frelon which Sud Aviation developed in conjunction with Sikorsky. Sikorsky helped primarily with the development and testing of the main and tail rotor systems, while Fiat of Italy assisted with the gearbox and power transmission (and built those parts for production aircraft).

The first SA 3210-01 prototype Super Frelon first flew on December 7 1962, and was representative of the troop transport configuration. The second prototype, which flew on May 28 1963, was representative of the maritime variant.

Ninety-nine production aircraft were built in three basic models. The SA 321G was initially operated by the French navy as an anti submarine warfare and sanitization aircraft for French nuclear armed submarines, equipped with radar, dunking sonar and torpedoes (now they are used for SAR and transport). Similar SA 321GMs and SA 321Hs were delivered to Syria and Iraq respectively. The SA 321F and SA 321J were civil variants, while the SA 321J is a utility transport. Non amphibious transport versions were sold to South Africa (SA 321L) and Israel (SA 321K), while Libya's SA 321Ms are for SAR and logistics support.

French production ceased in 1983, while Changhe Aircraft Industries Corporation in China licence built the multirole Z-8 development, with 20 in service with the Chinese naval air force. Argentina operated ex Israeli GE T58 re-engined Super Frelons.

**Photo:** A French navy Super Frelon. (Lassi Tolvanen)

# AgustaWestland A 109

**Country of origin:** Italy

**Type:** Multirole light twin helicopter

**Powerplants:** A 109M – Two 477kW (640shp) TO rated Pratt & Whitney Canada PW206C or 500kW (670shp) TO rated Turbomeca Arrius 2K1 turboshafts driving a four blade main rotor and two blade tail rotor. A 109KM – Two 471kW (632shp) max continuous rated Arriel 1K1s.

**Performance:** A 109M – Max cruising speed at sea level clean 263km/h (142kt). Max initial rate of climb 1860ft/min. Service ceiling 19,200ft. Hovering ceiling out of ground effect 11,800ft. Max range 910km (491nm). A 109KM – Max cruising speed 264km/h (143kt). Initial rate of climb 1950ft/min. Service ceiling 20,000ft. Hovering ceiling OGE 13,200ft. Max range 819km (442nm).

**Weights:** A 109M – Empty 1611kg (3548lb), max takeoff 2850kg (6280lb), max takeoff with an external load 3000kg (6608lb). A 109KM – Empty 1657kg (3650lb), max takeoff same.

**Dimensions:** Main rotor diameter 11.00m (36ft 1in), length rotors turning 13.03m (42ft 9in), fuselage length 11.44m (37ft 6in), height 3.50m (11ft 6in). Main rotor disc area 95.0m$^2$ (1023sq ft).

**Accommodation:** Seats up to eight in passenger configuration.

**Armament:** Options on two external hardpoints include eight TOW 2A anti armour missiles, Stinger or Mistral air-to-air missiles, machine gun pods, and rocket launchers, plus doorway pintle mounted guns.

**Operators:** Argentina, Belgium, Ghana, Italy, Peru, South Africa*, Sweden*, UK, Venezuela.

**History:** Although developed primarily for the civil market, the A 109 has been adopted for a range of military and para military roles.

The prototype A 109 first flew on August 4 1971, with the first production machines delivered from 1976. Models since then include the initial A 109A, the A 109A Mk II with improvements to the dynamic systems, the A 109C with a further uprated transmission, composite rotor blades and greater max takeoff weight, the P&WC PW206 powered A 109E Power (the US Coast Guard has ordered four as MH-68As), and the Arrius 2K1 and glass cockpit A 109F.

Argentina was an early operator. Two of its four aircraft were captured by the British during the Falklands War in 1982 and then placed into British Army service in support of SAS operations.

The first major military A 109 customer was Italy, which initially ordered 24 A 109A based A 109EOA armed scout helicopters fitted with sliding main cabin doors, fixed landing gear, roof mounted day sight, laser range finder and the ability to carry weapons.

The A 109C based A 109CM is in Belgium army service. Belgium took delivery of 18 scout and 24 anti armour variants as A 109BAs (designated by Belgium as A 109HO and HA respectively). Similar to the A 109EOA, the scouts feature a Saab roof mounted sight, the attack aircraft Saab/ESCO HeliTOW 2 sights and the capability to carry eight Hughes TOW 2A anti tank missiles.

The A 109K for hot and high operations is fitted with Turbomeca Arriel turboshafts. The A 109KM has sliding doors and a fixed undercarriage and is in service in South America. The A 109M is an offered military variant of the A 109 Power. South Africa has ordered 30 A 109LUHs – Light Utility Helicopters – (plus 10 options).

**Photo:** The A 109CM is in Belgian army service. (AgustaWestland)

# AgustaWestland A 129 Mangusta

**Country of origin:** Italy

**Type:** Two seat multirole attack and scout helicopter

**Powerplants:** A 129 – Two 615kW (825shp) max continuous rated Rolls-Royce Gem 2 Mk 1004D turboshafts (licence built by Piaggio), driving a four blade main rotor and two blade tail rotor. International – Two 1016kW (1362shp) LHTEC T800-LHT-800 turboshafts driving a five blade main rotor and two blade tail rotor.

**Performance:** A 129 – Dash speed 294km/h (160kt), max speed at sea level 250km/h (135kt). Max initial rate of climb 2030ft/min. Hovering ceiling in ground effect 10,300ft, out of ground effect 6200ft. Combat radius with eight TOW missiles, reserves and a 90min loiter time on station 100km (55nm). Max endurance 3hr 5min. International – Cruising speed 269km/h (145kt). Max vertical rate of climb at sea level 2385ft/min. Hovering ceiling in ground effect 13,620ft, out of ground effect 8500ft.

**Weights:** A 129 – Empty equipped 2530kg (5575lb), max takeoff 4100kg (9040lb). International – Max takeoff 5100kg (11,243lb).

**Dimensions:** A 129 – Main rotor diameter 11.90m (39ft 1in), wing span 3.20m (10ft 6in), length overall rotors turning 14.29m (46ft 11in), fuselage length 12.28m (40ft 3in), height overall 3.35m (11ft 0in). Main rotor disc area 111.2m$^2$ (1197.0sq ft). International – Same except fuselage length 12.50m (40ft 11in).

**Accommodation:** Crew of two seated in tandem, pilot in rear seat.

**Armament:** A 129 – Up to 1200kg of stores including rocket and gun pods and TOW 2 and 2A anti tank missiles. International – One 20 mm gun in undernose turret. Options include anti tank missiles, rocket and gun pods and Stinger AAMs.

**Operators:** Italy

**History:** Agusta began firm development of the A 129 Mangusta (Mongoose) in 1978 to meet an Italian army requirement.

The prototype's first flight was on September 11 1983. Features of the aircraft include two Rolls-Royce Gem turboshafts, seating for a gunner/copilot and pilot in separate, stepped cockpits, four blade main rotor with some use of composite construction, a computerised and fully redundant integrated management system designed to reduce crew workload, stub wings with two weapons pylons each, and a Saab/ESCO HeliTOW weapons system with nose mounted sight.

Following funding delays with the HeliTOW system, the A 129 entered service with the Italian army in October 1990.

The A 129 International was developed to attract export sales. Changes include the 20% more powerful LHTEC T800 turboshafts, uprated transmission, a higher max takeoff weight and an optional three barrel 12.7mm gun turret. The A 129 International first flew in 1988, more latterly the prototype flew in 1995 with a five blade main rotor. Armament and equipment options include Stinger AAMs, a Lockheed Martin/GIAT 20mm three barrelled cannon and FLIR.

Italy's last 15 of 60 Mangustas on order are being built to a similar configuration, the A 129 Combat. Italy's existing Mangusta will then be upgraded to Combat standard. The similar A 129 Scorpion was unsuccessfully bidded to Australia in 2001.

**Photo:** A Italian army A 129. All A 129s are due to be upgraded to Combat standard. (AgustaWestland)

# AgustaWestland EH 101 Merlin & Cormorant

**Countries of origin:** Italy and United Kingdom

**Type:** Medium lift utility transport and shipborne ASW helicopter

**Powerplants:** HM.1 – Three 1725kW (2312shp) Rolls-Royce Turbomeca RTM322-01 turboshafts driving a five blade main rotor and four blade tail rotor.

**Performance:** HM.1 – Cruising speed 278km/h (150kt), long range cruising speed 260km/h (140kt), best endurance speed 167km/h (90kt). Endurance with max weapon load, 5hr on station.

**Weights:** HM.1 – Operating empty approx 10,500kg (23,149lb), max takeoff 14,600kg (32,188lb).

**Dimensions:** Main rotor diameter 18.59m (61ft 0in), length overall rotors turning 22.80m (74ft 10in), length main rotor and tail folded (HM.1) 15.75m (51ft 8in), height overall rotors turning 6.62m (21ft 9in), height main rotor and tail folded (HM.1) 5.20m (17ft 1in). Main rotor disc area 271.5m² (2922.5sq ft).

**Accommodation:** Flightcrew of one or two. HM.1 – Two pilots, acoustic sensor operator and observer. Utility version – 30 equipped troops, or 16 stretchers and medical attendants. Max external sling load 5445kg (12,000lb).

**Armament:** Merlin can be fitted with four homing torpedoes in addition to anti ship missiles. Utility version can be fitted with stub wings for rocket pods and a 12.7mm machine gun in a nose turret. HC.3 has provision for pintle mounted machine guns in main doors.

**Operators:** Canada*, Denmark*, Italy*, Portugal*, UK*.

**History:** The three engined EH 101 was initially conceived as an ASW replacement for the Sikorsky/Westland Sea King, but is also on offer in a number of military and civil versions.

EH (or European Helicopter) Industries was formed as a collaborative venture between Westland of the UK and Agusta of Italy (now Agusta-Westland), primarily to develop an anti submarine warfare helicopter for the Royal Navy and Italian navy, plus utility and civil variants. The 50-50 partnership was formed in 1980, full scale program go-ahead was announced in March 1984. First flight of an EH 101 (the Westland built PP1) was on October 9 1987.

The biggest EH 101 is the Royal Navy, which is taking delivery of 44 ASW configured Merlin HM.1s (previously HAS.1) equipped with Blue Kestrel radar, dipping sonar and ESM (the first was rolled out in 1996). The Royal Air Force ordered 22 utility Merlin HC.3s (with defensive aids and provision for FLIR and AAR probe) with delivery from 2000.

The Italian navy has ordered eight ASW EH 101s similar in configuration to the Merlin, four EH 101 utility transports, and four AEW platforms with an Eliradar HEW-784 air and surface radar (with a 3m diameter radome).

The EH 101 is offered with either Rolls-Royce Turbomeca RTM322 or General Electric T700 engines. British Merlins have RTM322s, civil and Italian EH 101s General Electric CT7 engines.

Canada ordered 15 of the AW320 Cormorant development in late 1997 for SAR. Further export orders came from Portugal and Denmark in 2001, the same year that AgustaWestland and Lockheed Martin signed an agreement to market and possibly licence assemble the helicopter in the United States as the US101.

**Photo:** An Italian navy EH 101. (Paul Merritt)

# AIDC AT-3 Tzu-Chiang

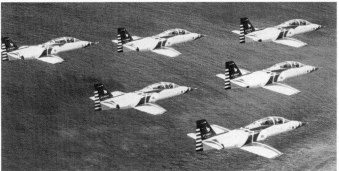

**Country of origin:** Taiwan

**Type:** Two seat advanced trainer and light attack aircraft

**Powerplants:** AT-3 – Two 15.6kN (3500lb) Garrett TFE731-2-2L non afterburning turbofans.

**Performance:** AT-3 – Max speed at 36,000ft 904km/h (488kt), or 900km/h (486kt) at sea level, max cruising speed at 36,000ft 880km/h (475kt). Max initial rate of climb 10,100ft/min. Service ceiling 48,000ft. Range with internal fuel 2280km (1230nm). Endurance with internal fuel 3hr 12min.

**Weights:** AT-3 – Empty equipped 3855kg (8500lb), normal takeoff (trainer, clean) 5215kg (11,500lb), max takeoff 7940kg (17,500lb).

**Dimensions:** AT-3 – Wing span 10.46m (34ft 4in), length including nose probe 12.90m (42ft 4in), height 4.83m (15ft 10in). Wing area 21.9m² (236.1sq ft).

**Accommodation:** Seating for two in tandem. AT-3A seats pilot only.

**Armament:** Can be fitted with gun pods in an internal weapons bay. Armament can be carried on one centreline pylon, four underwing hardpoints and two wingtip launch rails. Can carry bombs, rockets, wingtip mounted AAMs and training bombs.

**Operators:** Taiwan

**History:** The AT-3 Tzu-Chiang was AIDC's second design to enter Taiwanese service, behind the turboprop powered Chung Tsing development of the T-28 Trojan, and serves with the Taiwanese air force as an advanced/weapons trainer and light attack and close support aircraft. Up until the development of the Ching-Kuo fighter, the AT-3 was the most advanced aircraft to be developed by Taiwan's aircraft industry.

Serious design of the AT-3 began in 1975 with the placement of a development contract. The first of two prototypes first flew on September 16 1980, while the first production aircraft flew on February 6 1984. In all, AIDC built 60 AT-3s for the Republic of China Air Force, the last of which was delivered in 1990.

All 60 production aircraft were designated AT-3. The AT-3A Lui Meng meanwhile was a single seat dedicated light ground and maritime attack development. Two prototypes were known to have been built (the first one being converted from a two seat AT-3) and flown in the late 1980s, but development was suspended.

The two seat AT-3B features the nav/attack system initially developed for the Lui-Meng. Twenty AT-3s were converted to AT-3B standard which also features an APG-66 radar and an internal weapons bay that can carry semi recessed machine gun packs. The aircraft can carry a variety of weapons, including wingtip mounted infrared guided AAMs, in addition to bombs and rockets on a centreline and four underwing pylons. The AT-3B's maximum external stores load is 2720kg (6000lb).

Power for the AT-3 is supplied by two Garrett (now Honeywell) TFE731 turbofans, while the airframe design is conventional. Other features include zero/zero ejection seats and the ability to carry and deploy an aerial target towing system.

**Photo:** AT-3s are used by the RoCAF's display team based at Kangshan. In RoCAF service the AT-3 has replaced the turboprop powered T-CH-1 Chung Tsing.

## AIDC Ching-Kuo

*Country of origin:* Taiwan

*Type:* Lightweight multirole fighter

*Powerplants:* Two 26.8kN (6025lb) dry and 41.8kN (9400lb) afterburning ITEC (Honeywell/AIDC) TFE1042-70 (F125) turbofans.

*Performance:* Max level speed at 36,000ft 1295km/h (700kt). Max initial rate of climb 50,000ft/min. Service ceiling 54,000ft. Range figures not published.

*Weights:* Operating empty 6485kg (14,300lb), max takeoff 12,245kg (27,000lb). Internal fuel 2109kg (4650lb).

*Dimensions:* Wing span over wingtip missile rails 8.53m (28ft 0in), length incl nose probe 14.21m (46ft 7in), length exc nose probe 13.26m (43ft 6in), height 4.65m (15ft 3in). Wing area 24.3m² (261.1sq ft).

*Accommodation:* Pilot only, or two in tandem in trainers.

*Armament:* One 20mm M61A1 Vulcan cannon. Six hardpoints for missiles, bombs, guided bombs and cluster munitions including 500lb/225kg GBU-12s, Rockeyes, AGM-65B Mavericks, Hsiung Feng II anti ship missiles, Sky Sword I short range IR guided and Sky Sword II medium range radar homing AAMs.

*Operators:* Taiwan

*History:* The Ching-Kuo has been by far Taiwan's most ambitious aircraft program, and has resulted in a capable multirole fighter.

Development of the Ching-Kuo, initially known as the Indigenous Defensive Fighter (IDF), began in 1982 after the US prevented Taiwan from ordering F-16s or Northrop F-20 Tigersharks. Despite the fighter sales ban, US companies were still able to provide technical support for the IDF program. General Dynamics worked closely with AIDC to develop the airframe, which features a blended fuselage/wing design and leading edge root extensions.

The International Turbofan Engine Company (ITEC) TFE1042 afterburning turbofans were developed in partnership by AlliedSignal (now Honeywell) and AIDC. The Golden Dragon 53 radar (which has a search range of 150km/80nm) is based on the APG-67 originally developed for the F-20, with some elements based on the F-16A's APG-66, and features air and sea search modes and lookdown/shootdown capability. The specifically developed infrared guided Sky Sword I and radar guided Sky Sword II AAMs closely resemble the AIM-9 Sidewinder and AIM-7 Sparrow, respectively. Other features include a side stick controller, two multifunction displays, a HUD and fly-by-wire.

The first prototype Ching-Kuo, a single seater, first flew on May 28 1989, while three other prototypes – one single seater and two two-seaters – and 10 preproduction aircraft followed. The first production Ching-Kuo was delivered in January 1994. Single seaters are designated F-CK-1A, two seaters F-CK-1B.

Taiwan's initial planned buy of 260 Ching-Kuos was halved when the lifting of arms restrictions during the early 1990s allowed it to purchase F-16s and Mirage 2000-5s and cancel a developed version. The final two Ching-Kuos were delivered in January 2000.

In 2001 AIDC was developing an improved Ching-Kuo with greater fuel capacity and improved radar as insurance against future Western bans on fighter sales to Taiwan.

*Photo:* A production two seater Ching-Kuo.

## Airbus Corporate Jetliner

*Country of origin:* Europe (France, Germany, Spain and UK)

*Type:* Long range VIP transport

*Powerplants:* Two 120kN (27,000lb) International Aero Engines IAE V2527M-A5 turbofans (CFM International CFM56s optional).

*Performance:* Max cruising speed Mach 0.82. Max altitude 41,000ft. Range with 12 passengers up to 11,100km (6000nm), range with 40 passengers up to 8300km (4500nm).

*Weights:* Max takeoff 75,500kg (166,400lb).

*Dimensions:* Wing span 33.91m (111ft 3in), length 33.80m (110ft 11in), height 11.80m (38ft 8.5in). Wing area 122.4m² (1317.5sq ft).

*Accommodation:* Flightcrew of two. Six standard layouts offered, seating from 10 to 39 passengers.

*Armament:* None

*Operators:* France*, Italy.

*History:* The Airbus Corporate Jetliner, or ACJ, is a long range corporate jet development of the A319 airliner. It competes directly with the Boeing Business Jet and dedicated long range corporate jets such as the Bombardier Global Express and Gulfstream V and will likely attract a number of military VIP operators.

Airbus launched the ACJ at the 1997 Paris Airshow and the first ACJ rolled out in October 1998. The airframe was then fitted with belly auxiliary fuel tanks and flight test instrumentation prior to making a first flight in May 1999. Certification was awarded in July 1999, with the first delivery to a civil customer that December.

The ACJ was designed as a minimum change development of the A319 124-seat airliner, a member of the highly successful Airbus A320 family. Like the rest of the A320 single aisle family (plus the A330 and A340), the ACJ shares Airbus' common advanced six screen glass flightdeck with sidestick controllers (but with a new flight management system), plus fly-by-wire flight controls. It also features a standard integral airstair and has a higher cruising altitude than the A319 airliner.

The ACJ can be powered by either the IAE V2500 or CFM56, although in October 2000 Airbus signed an agreement with IAE to make the V2500 the 'reference' engine on the aircraft. As a consequence the V2500 powered ACJ is now offered to potential customers as a package arrangement.

The A319's containerised cargo hold means that the ACJ's auxiliary fuel tanks can be easily loaded and unloaded, giving operators flexibility to reconfigure the aircraft for varying payload/range requirements. Another design feature is that the ACJ can be easily converted to an airliner, thus increasing the aircraft's potential resale value.

Airbus supplies green A319CJ airframes to outfitters for interior fitment. Interiors weigh 3.8 tonnes (8500lb) to 4.8 tonnes (10,700lb), and cost from $US8m to $US12m. Outfitting takes from four to eight months.

The first civil ACJ order was announced in December 1997. Italy is the first military customer, ordering two (powered by CFM56s) for use as VIP transports, replacing DC-9-30s. The first of these was delivered in March 2000, the second that August. France ordered two ACJs for VIP transport in October 2000, for delivery in late 2001 and 2004.

*Photo:* An Italian air force A319CJ. (Airbus)

## Airbus A310 & MRTT

**Country of origin:** European consortium

**Type:** A310 – VIP/strategic transport. MRTT – tanker transport

**Powerplants:** A310 – Initially either two 213.5kN (48,000lb) Pratt & Whitney JT9D-7R4D1 or two 222.4kN (50,000lb) General Electric CF6-80A3 turbofans. Current choices of 238kN or 262kN (53,500lb or 59,000lb) GE CF6-80C2A2s or -80C2A8s, or 231kN or 249kN (52,000lb or 56,000lb) P&W PW4152 or PW4156 turbofans.

**Performance:** A310-200 – Max cruising speed 897km/h (484kt), long range cruising speed 850km/h (459kt). Range at typical airliner operating weight with reserves 6800km (3670nm). A310-300 (with CF6-80C2A2s) – Typical airliner range with reserves 7980km (4310nm), or up to 9580km (5170nm) for high gross weight version.

**Weights:** A310-200 with CF6-80C2A2s – Operating empty 80,142kg (176,683lb), max takeoff 142,000kg (313,055lb). A310-300 with CF6-80C2A8s – Operating empty 80,330kg (177,095lb), max takeoff up to 164,000kg (361,560lb).

**Dimensions:** A310 – Wing span 43.89m (144ft 0in), length 46.66m (153ft 1in), height 15.80m (51ft 10in). Wing area 219.0m² (2357.3sq ft).

**Accommodation:** Flightcrew of two. MRTT max palletised passenger seating 270. Max payload 35 tonnes (77,161lb).

**Armament:** None

**Operators:** Belgium, Canada, France, Germany, Spain*, Thailand.

**History:** The A310, a shortened development of Airbus' original A300 widebody airliner, is in limited military service as a transport.

Compared with the A300, the A310 introduced a shortened fuselage, a new higher aspect ratio wing, new and smaller horizontal tail surfaces and a two crew flightdeck.

The A310 first flew on April 3 1982. The basic passenger aircraft is the A310-200, while the A310-300 is a longer range development and has been in production since 1985. The A310-200F freighter and A310-200C convertible are available as new build aircraft or as conversions of existing A310s.

Military A310s operate in a variety of transport functions. Thailand became the first military A310 operator when its sole A310 was delivered in 1991. Germany inherited its A310s from the former East German airline Interflug. France's replaced DC-8s. Canada is the largest A310 operator with five in service, designated the CC-150 Polaris. Two will be converted to tankers from 2003. Belgium acquired two ex airline A310s which replaced 727-100s.

Airbus offers new build and conversion Multi Role Tanker Transport (MRTT) configured A300s and A310s (MRTT 300 and MRTT 310 respectively). Features offered on the MRTT include both boom and probe and drogue refuelling with additional belly fuel tanks, and a quick change main deck layout for freight and/or palletised seating.

Germany contracted DASA and Lufthansa to convert two of its aircraft to MRTT standard in 1997. Initially they were not equipped for air-to-air refuelling. Spain is also converting two ex airliner A310s to tanker configuration to replace 707 tankers.

Raytheon unsuccessfully offered Australia and Turkey the A310 as an AEW&C platform fitted with Elta's phased array radar mounted in a fixed rotodome (in both cases the Boeing 737 AEW&C was chosen instead).

**Photo:** A German A310 MRTT. (Paul Merritt)

## Airbus Military Company A400M

**Countries of origin:** Belgium, France, Germany, Portugal, Spain, Turkey, UK

**Type:** Strategic & tactical transport

**Powerplants:** Four 6900kW (9250shp) class Aero Propulsion Alliance TP400 turboprops driving eight blade propellers.

**Performance:** Cruising speed 555km/h (300kt) or Mach 0.72, normal cruising Mach 0.68. Takeoff run at 116,500kg (256,835lb) 1402m (4600ft), landing run at 93,500kg (206,131lb) 625m (2050ft). Max range with 30 tonnes 4540km (2450nm), max range with 20 tonnes 6578km (3550nm). Ferry range 9075km (4900nm).

**Weights:** Max zero fuel weight 84,250kg (185,740lb), max takeoff 116,500kg (256,840lb). Max tactical payload 25,000kg (55,115lb), max logistics payload 32,000kg (70,547lb).

**Dimensions:** Wing span 42.4m (139 ft 1in), length 42.2m (138 ft 5in), height 14.7m (48ft 3in). Wing area 221.5m² (2384 ft²).

**Accommodation:** Flightcrew of two, with provision for a third flight-deck crew member, plus a loadmaster. Max tactical payload (2.5g) 29,500kg (65,036lb), max logistic payload (2.25g) 37,000 kg (81,571lb). 120 troops or 9 224 x 274cm (88 x 108in) pallets.

**Armament:** None

**Operators:** Belgium*, France*, Germany*, Luxembourg*, Spain*, Turkey*, UK*.

**History:** The A400M transport has its origins in various European requirements to replace C-160s and C-130s.

The A400M began life as the FIMA (Future International Military Aircraft), a high wing, propfan powered design which resulted from a four nation study group formed in December 1982. In 1989 FIMA evolved into EUROFLAG (as in European Future Large Aircraft Group). At the time EUROFLAG envisaged that the FLA would enter service in 2000.

Initial studies of the aircraft carried on into the early 1990s, with turbofans, rather than turboprops, initially preferred. Turbofans were dropped in preference to turboprops in 1994, and a full feasibility study was completed in 1995. Airbus Military Company took over FLA work in 1995, with Airbus to develop and build the aircraft along commercial lines. The FLA was redesignated the A400M, and EADS CASA's Seville facilities will undertake final assembly.

In late 2000 Airbus selected the Aero Propulsion Alliance of Rolls-Royce, SNECMA, MTU, FiatAvio, ITP and Techspace to develop the A400M's TP400 turboprop. The A400M will be built to a common standard which will be capable of being converted into a two point probe and drogue aerial tanker. Features will include fly-by-wire flight controls and an advanced flightdeck with five liquid crystal displays and head-up displays. The A400M could also be developed to fulfil AEW and maritime patrol missions and into a three point aerial tanker.

On December 19 2001 eight launch customers finally signed a formal contract for 196 A400Ms – Belgium (seven), France (50), Germany (73), Luxembourg (1), Portugal (3), Spain (27), Turkey (10) and the UK (25). Italy failed to sign on. The first A400M is due to fly in 2006 with customer deliveries from 2008.

**Photo:** A computer generated image of the A400M. In service the A400M will replace C-160s and C-130s. (Airbus)

# Alenia G222

**Country of origin:** Italy

**Type:** Tactical transport

**Powerplants:** Two 2535kW (3400shp) General Electric T64-GE-P4D turboprops, licence built by Fiat, driving three blade propellers.

**Performance:** Max speed 487km/h (263kt), long range cruising speed 437km/h (236kt). Max initial rate of climb 1250ft/min. Service ceiling 25,700ft. Takeoff run 686m (2250ft). Ferry range 4685km (2530nm), range with max payload 1260km (680nm), range with 36 litters and four medical attendants 2500km (1350nm).

**Weights:** Empty equipped 15,700kg (34,610lb), max takeoff 28,000kg (61,730lb).

**Dimensions:** Wing span 28.70m (94ft 2in), length 22.70m (74ft 6in), height 10.57m (34ft 8in). Wing area 82.0m$^2$ (882.6sq ft).

**Accommodation:** Flightcrew of two with provision for a loadmaster. Typical accommodation for 46 fully equipped troops, or 40 fully equipped paratroops. Can carry a 9000kg (18,840lb) payload incl light vehicles and artillery.

**Armament:** None

**Operators:** Argentina, Italy, Libya, Nigeria, Thailand, Tunisia, Venezuela.

**History:** The G222 can be traced back to an early 1960s NATO requirement for a V/STOL tactical transport.

The NATO requirement spawned a number of exotic V/STOL concepts, none of which were practical. The Italian air force contracted Fiat to develop its G222 V/STOL concept, but the contract was later extended to cover a conventionally configured STOL development, which laid the ground work for the definitive G222 transport. The V/STOL and planned anti submarine warfare and civil versions were subsequently dropped. The Italian air force placed a contract for two prototype G222s in 1968. After a number of delays caused by external factors, the first G222 made its first flight on July 18 1970.

The two prototypes were unpressurised but otherwise the prototype and production aircraft were similar. Design features of the G222 include its good short field performance, large double slotted flaps, barrel shaped fuselage, rear freight ramp and tandem main undercarriage wheels with levered suspension and low pressure tyres. The G222 was also designed with provision for JATO rockets to improve takeoff performance.

Much of the Italian aerospace industry was involved in the construction of the G222, with Aermacchi building the outer wings, Piaggio the wing centre sections and SIAI-Marchetti responsible for the tail.

The first of 44 production G222s for Italy flew on December 23 1975, with deliveries from April 1978.

Almost all G222s built were the basic transport, although 20 G222Ts built for Libya are powered by 3635kW (4860shp) Rolls-Royce Tynes. Other variants are the Chrysler C-27A Spartan, procured via Chrysler in 1990 from Alenia to fulfil transport duties with the US Air Force in South America; the Elint configured G222VS; firefighting G222SAA; and the radio/radar calibration G222R/M.

Production ended in 1999.

The ultimate G222 development is the Rolls-Royce AE 2100 powered C-27J Spartan, described under LMATTS.

**Photo:** An Italian air force G222. (Paul Merritt)

# AMX International AMX

**Countries of origin:** Italy and Brazil

**Type:** Light attack aircraft

**Powerplant:** One 49.1kN (11,030lb) Rolls-Royce Spey Mk 807 non afterburning turbofan licence built by Fiat, Piaggio and Alfa Romeo Avio, in cooperation with CELMA in Brazil.

**Performance:** Max speed 915km/h (493kt) at 36,000ft. Max initial rate of climb 10,250ft/min. Service ceiling 42,650ft. Combat radius at max takeoff weight with 2720kg (6000lb) of external payload lo-lo-lo 528km (285nm), hi-lo-hi 925km (500nm); combat radius at typical mission takeoff weight with 910kg (2000lb) of external stores lo-lo-lo 555km (300nm), hi-lo-hi 890km (480nm).

**Weights:** Op empty 6730kg (14,837lb), max takeoff 13,000kg (28,660lb).

**Dimensions:** Wing span 8.87m (29ft 2in), length 13.23m (43ft 5in), height 4.55m (14ft 11in). Wing area 21.0m$^2$ (226.1sq ft).

**Accommodation:** Pilot only, seating for two in tandem in AMX-T.

**Armament:** One 20mm GE M61A1 Vulcan cannon in Italian aircraft, two 30mm DEFA cannons in Brazilian aircraft. External armament of up to 3800kg (8375lb) on four underwing, one centreline and two wingtip stations. Options include wingtip mounted AIM-9 or MAA-1 Piranha AAMs, unguided bombs, LGBs, rockets and cluster munitions.

**Operators:** Brazil, Italy, Venezuela*.

**History:** The AMX resulted from similar air force specifications for a replacement for the G91 and F-104 (in ground attack roles) in Italian service and the AT-26 Xavante (MB-326) in Brazilian use.

Initial work on the AMX began in 1978 when Aeritalia (now Alenia) teamed with Aermacchi. Embraer joined in 1980.

With an initial agreement for 266 production aircraft (79 for Brazil, 187 for Italy) reached in 1981, development of the AMX gathered pace and the first development prototype first flew on May 15 1984. Construction of the first batch of 30 production aircraft and the design of a two seat AMX-T trainer began in mid 1986, while the first production aircraft, for Italy, first flew in May 1988.

AMX design features include HOTAS controls and HUD, multifunction displays, INS navigation and ECM, with provision in the nose for FLIR or a radar. In addition, three different Aeroelectronica of Brazil developed reconnaissance pallets can be fitted in the forward fuselage, while recce pods can be fitted on the external hardpoints.

Alenia was AMX program leader with a 46.7% share of production, Aermacchi has 23.6% and Embraer 29.7%. Component manufacture was not duplicated, however there were separate final assembly lines in Italy and Brazil. Delivery of 136 for Italy wound up in 1998, with deliveries of the 56 for Brazil (Brazil designates the AMX the A-1) continuing through until 1999.

Production is being restarted for Venezuela which has ordered eight AMX-ATAs (Advanced Trainer Attack), with Elbit avionics. Meanwhile a HARM firing two seat EW version (the AMX-E) has been studied, as has an upgraded AMX powered by the Eurojet EJ200.

The AMX-MLU mid life update for both Brazil and Italy is under development. Features will include new radar, NVG compatible glass cockpit, FLIR and new avionics.

**Photo:** An Italian AMX-T. (Lassi Tolvanen)

## Antonov/PZL Mielec An-2

**Countries of origin:** Ukraine and Poland

**Type:** General purpose utility biplane

**Powerplant:** An-2P – One 745kW (1000hp) PZL Kalisz ASz-61IR nine cylinder radial piston engine driving an AW-2 four blade variable pitch propeller.

**Performance:** An-2P – Max speed 258km/h (139kt) at 5740ft, economical cruising speed 185km/h (100kt). Max initial rate of climb 690ft/min. Range at 3280ft with a 500kg (1100lb) cargo 900km (485nm).

**Weights:** An-2P – Empty 3450kg (7605lb), MTOW 5500kg (12,125lb).

**Dimensions:** Upper wing span 18.18m (59ft 8in), lower 14.24m (46ft 9in), length (tail down) 12.40m (40ft 8in). Upper wing area 43.5m² (468.7sq ft), lower 28.0m² (301.2sq ft).

**Accommodation:** Flightcrew of one or two pilots. Passenger accommodation for 12 at three abreast.

**Armament:** None, although some modified to carry bombs.

**Operators:** An-2 – Angola, Armenia, Croatia, Cuba, Georgia, Laos, Latvia, Lithuania, Macedonia, Mali, Mongolia, Nicaragua, North Korea, Poland, Romania, Russia, Ukraine. Y-5 – Albania, China, North Korea.

**History:** The An-2 was originally designed to a USSR Ministry of Agriculture and Forestry requirement. As well as large scale civil use it was adopted in significant numbers by air arms of numerous Soviet aligned countries for a multitude of utility roles.

The An-2 first flew on August 31 1947 and entered production and service the following year. The biplane configuration was chosen for its good takeoff performance, docile low speed handling and excellent climb rates, and the wings were fitted with leading edge slats and double slotted flaps, further improving performance. Power was supplied by a 745kW (1000hp) ASh-62 radial.

Soviet production continued through until 1960, by which time a number of variants had been developed, including the base model An-2P, An-2S and -2M crop sprayers, An-2VA water bomber, An-2M floatplane and the high altitude meteorological research An-2ZA.

Production was transferred to Poland's PZL Mielec in 1960, with the first Polish An-2 flying on October 23 1960. Aside from the An-2P, Polish versions include the An-2PK VIP transport, An-2PR for TV relay work, An-2S ambulance, An-2TD paratroop transport, An-2P cargo/passenger version, An-2 Geofiz geophysical survey version, An-2T utility and An-2TP passenger aircraft.

Chinese production as the Y-5 commenced with Nanchang in 1957, before being transferred to Shijiazhuang Aircraft. The main Chinese version is the standard Y-5N, while the latest development is the Y-5C paratroop carrier for the PLA-AF with distinctive wingtip vanes. Nanchang built over 700 Y-5s, Shijiazhuang has built over 80.

An Antonov turboprop powered version, the An-3, was developed in the late 1980s, but initially did not enter production. Polyot at Omsk in Russia began production conversions from An-2s in 2000.

In military service the An-2 is used in a wide variety of missions including paratroop transport, special forces insertion, navigation training and general utility work. North Korea is one of the largest An-2 operator, with almost 300 in service (both Russian and Chinese built).

**Photo:** A Polish An-2. (Sebastian Zacharias)

## Antonov An-12 & SAC Y-8

**Country of origin:** Ukraine (An-12), China (Y-8)

**Type:** Tactical transport

**Powerplants:** An-12BP – Four 2985kW (4000ehp) Ivchenko (now Progress) AI-20K turboprops driving four blade propellers.

**Performance:** An-12BP – Max speed 777km/h (420kt), max cruising speed 670km/h (360kt). Max initial rate of climb 1970ft/min. Service ceiling 33,465ft. Takeoff run at MTOW 700m (2296ft). Range with max fuel 5700km (3075nm), range with max payload 3600km (1940nm).

**Weights:** An-12BP – Empty 28,000kg (61,728lb), max takeoff 61,000kg (134,480lb).

**Dimensions:** An-12BP – Wing span 38.00m (124ft 8in), length 33.10m (108ft 7in), height 10.53m (34ft 7in). Wing area 121.7m² (1310sq ft).

**Accommodation:** Flightcrew of two pilots, flight engineer, navigator (in glazed nose) and radio operator, plus loadmasters. Can carry up to 20 tonnes (44,060lb) of freight such as artillery, light armoured vehicles and missile carriers, or alternatively up to 90 equipped troops or paratroopers.

**Armament:** Two tail mounted 23mm cannons (not on all aircraft).

**Operators:** Ethiopia, Iraq, Russia, Ukraine, Yemen. Y-8 – China, Myanmar, Sudan.

**History:** For many years the An-12 (NATO codename 'Cub') provided the backbone of Soviet and Warsaw Pact air forces' medium lift transport capabilities.

The origins of the An-12 lie in the An-8, a twin turboprop powered military transport which featured a high wing and rear loading ramp. About 100 An-8s were built and the type formed the basis for the stretched, four engined An-10 airliner for Aeroflot. The An-10 in turn formed the basis for the An-12, the main differences between the two being the latter's redesigned rear fuselage with rear loading ramp.

The An-12 first flew in 1958, powered by Kuznetsov NK-4 turboprops. The definitive production transport, the An-12BP, is powered by Ivchenko AI-20s. The An-12 remained in production until 1973, with a number also delivered to Aeroflot and Soviet aligned airlines. Its replacement in Russian service was the Il-76.

Various special missions variants of the An-12 have been developed, but details on these aircraft are sketchy. Many aircraft have been converted for Elint, festooned with various antennas, and these are covered by the NATO designations 'Cub-A' and 'Cub-B', while the 'Cub-C' and more recent 'Cub-D' are ECM aircraft. Unconfirmed reports have suggested the development of a command post variant, while others have been used for research and development tasks.

Xian in China meanwhile developed the improved Y-8 from 1968. A number of variants have been developed (all built by Shaanxi Aircraft Company), including the Y-8A helicopter carrier, pressurised Y-8C (developed with assistance from Lockheed), Y-8D export aircraft with Western avionics and Y-8E drone carrier. A single Y-8X maritime patrol and ASW aircraft has also flown, while an AEW version with radar in a bulbous nose radome has been developed.

The Y-8 remains in production with various pressurised and Westernised variants under development.

Sri Lanka operated two Y-8s modified as bombers, but both were lost in action against Tamil guerilas.

**Photo:** A Chinese air force Y-8A. (Sebastian Zacharias)

# Antonov An-26 & An-32 & Xian Y-7

**Country of origin:** Ukraine

**Type:** Tactical transport

**Powerplants:** An-26B – Two 2075kW (2780ehp) ZMKB Progress (formerly Ivchenko) AI-24VT turboprops and one auxiliary 7.85kN (1765lb) Soyuz (formerly Tumansky) RU-19A-300 turbojet. An-32 – Two 3760kW (5042ehp) ZMKB Progress AI-20D Series 5 turboprops.

**Performance:** An-26B – Cruising speed 435km/h (235kt). Max initial rate of climb 1575ft/min. Takeoff run sealed runway 870m (2855ft). Range with max payload no reserves 1240km (670nm), range with max fuel no reserves 2660km (1435nm). An-32 – Max cruising speed 530km/h (285kt), econ cruising speed 470km/h (254kt). Service ceiling 30,840ft. Takeoff run sealed runway 760m (2495ft/min). Range with max payload 1200km (645nm), range with max fuel 2520km (1360nm).

**Weights:** An-26B – Empty 15,850kg (34,943lb), MTOW 24,000kg (52,910lb). An-32 – Empty 16,800kg (37,038lb), MTOW 27,000kg (59,525lb).

**Dimensions:** An-26B – Wing span 29.20m (95ft 2in), length 23.80m (78ft 1in), height 8.58m (28ft 2in). Wing area 75.0m² (807.1sq ft). An-32 – same except height 8.75m (28ft 9in).

**Accommodation:** An-26B – Flightcrew of two pilots, flight engineer, navigator and radio operator, plus loadmaster. Seating for up to 40 troops. An-32 – Flightcrew of two pilots and navigator.

**Armament:** None, although some have been fitted with bomb racks.

**Operators:** An-26 – Operators incl Angola, Armenia, Bangladesh, Bulgaria, China, Cuba, Czech Rep, Hungary, Iraq, Laos, Libya, Mongolia, Poland, Romania, Russia, Serbia, Slovakia, Ukraine, Vietnam, Yemen, Zambia. An-32 – Cuba, Czech Rep, India, Mongolia, Peru, Tanzania.

**History:** The An-26 has been the standard light tactical transport aircraft of almost every former Soviet bloc country since the 1970s.

The An-26 (NATO reporting name 'Curl') is a militarised development of the An-24 airliner, which first flew in April 1960. The pressurised An-26 (first flight in 1968) introduced a rear loading freight ramp, more powerful Ivchenko turboprops and a turbojet APU which can serve as an auxiliary engine for takeoff. More than 1400 An-26s and An-26Bs (with improved freight handling system) were built until 1985 when the type was replaced in production by the improved An-32 (NATO reporting name 'Cline'). The An-26D conversion has external fuel tanks on the fuselage sides for extra fuel, while other An-26s have been used for Elint, Sigint, VIP and ambulance work.

The An-32 first flew in 1976 and has much more powerful engines for improved hot and high performance. The An-32 features improved systems and above wing mounted engines, which give greater ground clearance for the increased diameter propellers.

The An-32B has a 500kg (1100lb) increased takeoff weight, the An-32B-100 and An-32V-200 have upgraded engines with six blade propellers. In 2001 Antonov offered Poland the An-32M powered by Pratt & Whitney Canada PW150A turboprops.

Xian in China has developed the Y7 and the Y7H from the An-24, and some are in Chinese military service, while others have been exported. Xian has further developed the design into the MA-60 with P&WC PW127J engines and Western avionics, and has proposed a maritime patrol variant, the MA-MPA Fearless Albatross.

**Photo:** An Indian Air Force An-32. (Sebastian Zacharias)

# Antonov An-70

**Country of origin:** Ukraine

**Type:** Strategic and tactical transport

**Powerplants:** Four 10,290kW (13,800hp) Progress D-27 propfans driving contra rotating Aerosyla Stupino SV-27 14 blade propellers.

**Performance:** Max short range cruising speed 800km/h (432kt), long range cruising speed 750km/h (405kt). STOL takeoff required runway length with 30t payload 600m (1970ft). Range with 20,000kg (44,100lb) of cargo 7400km (3995nm) (3000km/1620nm with STOL takeoff and landing), or 3800km (2050nm) with a 35,000kg (77,161lb) payload.

**Weights:** Empty 72,800kg (160,500lb), max takeoff 130,000kg (286,600lb).

**Dimensions:** Wing span 44.06m (144ft 7in), length 40.73m (133ft 8in), height 16.38m (53ft 9in).

**Accommodation:** Flightcrew of two pilots and a flight engineer, plus accommodation for a loadmaster and optional navigator. Designed to accept a large percentage of NATO and CIS military equipment. Standard payload 35 tonnes (77,161lb), or up to 300 troops.

**Operators:** Russia*, Ukraine*

**Armament:** None

**History:** Antonov has developed the An-70 as a replacement for its An-12. Originally designed to be in production in 1988, delays mean service entry is still to come.

The An-70 incorporates a range of modern technology design concepts. The most prominent feature of the An-70 is its four Russian designed propfans consisting of 14 blade Stupino counter rotating, all composite, scimitar propellers and the Progress turboprops. Combined, these are designed to offer high speed performance combined with low fuel consumption.

Composite materials are widely used, including the horizontal and vertical tails which are all composite. The An-70 also incorporates fly-by-wire and a modern flightdeck with six full colour digital displays and a head-up display used for landings on short strips. The digital avionics are also linked via a databus equivalent to US 1553B standard, believed to be another first for a CIS aircraft, and allowing far easier future integration of Western avionics.

The An-70 program was delayed when in February 1995 the first prototype collided with its An-72 chase plane while on a test flight. The second prototype first flew on April 24 1997, but it too crashed, crash landing soon after takeoff during cold weather trials at Omsk in January 2001. A third prototype is under construction.

Production aircraft will be built at Kiev – Russia now requires 164 (revised from up to 500), the Ukraine 65 (down from 100).

An-70 models include the basic An-70 military freighter, two crew An-70-100, export An-77, commercial An-70T and An-70T-100, twin NK-93 turboprop powered An-70T-200, twin CFM56 powered An-70T-300, four CFM56 powered An-70T-400, An-70TK convertible passenger/freight aircraft, and heavylift An-170.

Germany gave serious consideration to buying the An-70 before committing to the Airbus A400M.

**Photo:** The second An-70 prototype. This aircraft crashed in January 2001. (Paul Merritt)

## Antonov An-72 & An-74

**Country of origin:** Ukraine

**Type:** STOL transport

**Powerplants:** Two 63.7kN (14,330lb) ZMKB Progress D-36 turbofans.

**Performance:** An-72 – Max speed 705km/h (380kt), cruising speed at 32,800ft 550 to 600km/h (295 to 325kt). Service ceiling 38,715ft. Range with max fuel and reserves 4800km (2590nm), with a 7500kg (16,535lb) payload 2000km (1080nm). An-74 – Range with a 1500kg (3310lb) payload 5300km (2860nm). An-72P – Patrol speed 300 to 350km/h (162 to 189kt). Ceiling 33,135ft. Max endurance 7hr 18min.

**Weights:** An-72 – Empty 19,050kg (41,997lb), MTOW from a 1800m (5900ft) runway 34,500kg (76,060lb), MTOW from a 1000m (3280ft) runway 27,500kg (60,625lb). An-72P – MTOW 37,500kg (82,670lb).

**Dimensions:** An-72 – Wing span 31.89m (104ft 8in), length 28.07m (92ft 1in), height 8.65m (28ft 5in). Wing area 98.6m$^2$ (1062sq ft).

**Accommodation:** An-72 flightcrew of two pilots and a flight engineer, An-74 has provision for a radio operator. Can carry a payload of 10 tonnes (22,045lb). An-72 can also seat 68 on removable seats. An-72P – Crew of five.

**Armament:** An-72P – One 23mm gun pod, a UB-23M rocket launcher under each wing and four 100kg (220lb) bombs carried internally. IAI version can carry the Griffin laser guided bomb.

**Operators:** Iran, Moldova, Peru, Russia, Ukraine.

**History:** The An-72 (NATO name 'Coaler') was designed as a replacement for the An-26 tactical transport in Soviet service.

The first of two An-72 prototypes first flew on December 22 1977, although the first of eight extensively revised preproduction An-72s did not fly until 1985. Included in this preproduction batch were two An-74s, which differed from the An-72s in their improved avionics suite for harsh weather conditions in polar regions. The most significant design feature of the An-72 and An-74 is the use of engine exhaust gases blown over the wing's upper surface to improve STOL performance and lift.

Transport versions of the An-72 include the An-72A base model with extended wings and fuselage compared to the prototypes, the An-72AT which can carry international standard containers, and the An-72S VIP transport. An-74 versions include the base An-74A with enlarged nose radome, the An-74T freighter, the An-74TK convertible passenger/freighter model, and the An-74P Salon VIP transport. A prototype AEW An-71 ('Madcap') has also flown.

The An-72P maritime patrol aircraft meanwhile is based on the basic An-72 fuselage with a 23mm gun, rocket pods, four light bombs carried internally, day and night downward looking and oblique optical cameras and an optical TV sight. In service with Ukraine, the An-72P is designed for close-in coastal surveillance. Antonov offers an improved development of the An-72P in conjunction with Israel Aircraft Industries. Changes include a glass cockpit, Elta EL/M 2022A radar, Electro Optical day and night long range observation system and Elisra electronic warfare suite.

Under development are the stretched An-74-400 and the re-engined, conventional under wing mounted D-436 turbofan powered An-74TK-300 and stretched An-174 for passengers or cargo.

**Photo:** An An-72P demonstrator, note rocket launcher. (Paul Merritt)

## Antonov An-124 Ruslan

**Country of origin:** Ukraine

**Type:** Heavylift strategic transport

**Powerplants:** Four 229.5kN (51,590lb) ZMKB Progress (Lotarev) D-18T turbofans.

**Performance:** Max cruising speed 865km/h (468kt), typical cruising speed between 800 and 850km/h (430 to 460kt). Range with max payload 4500km (2430nm), ferry range with max fuel 15,700km (8475nm).

**Weights:** Operating empty 175,000kg (385,800lb), max takeoff 405,000kg (892,875lb).

**Dimensions:** Wing span 73.30m (240ft 6in), length 69.10m (226ft 9in), height 20.78m (68ft 2in). Wing area 628.0m$^2$ (6760sq ft).

**Accommodation:** Flightcrew of six consisting of two pilots, two flight engineers, navigator and communications operator. Upper deck area behind the flightdeck area comprises a galley, rest room and two relief crew cabins. Upper deck area behind the wing can accommodate up to 88 passengers. Main deck cargo compartment is designed to carry an extremely large range of bulky and oversized cargo including 12 ISO standard containers, heavy artillery, main battle tanks, SAM systems, helicopters, SS-20 mobile IRBM, etc. Max payload 150,000kg (330,695lb).

**Armament:** None

**Operators:** Russia.

**History:** The massive An-124 for a time held the mantle of the world's largest aircraft before the arrival of the An-225, a stretched six engine derivative. It is the largest aircraft in the world to achieve series production and enter operational service.

The An-124 was developed primarily as a strategic military freighter to replace the turboprop powered An-22 (described separately) but also for use by the Soviet state airline Aeroflot for carriage of bulky and oversize cargo. The first prototype An-124 flew on December 26 1982, while a second prototype, named Ruslan after Pushkin's mythical giant, made the type's first Western public appearance at the Paris Airshow in mid 1985, preceding the type's first commercial operations in January 1986. Since that time the An-124 has set a range of payload records.

Except for its low set tail, the An-124's configuration is similar to the Lockheed C-5 Galaxy (described separately), which, with a maximum takeoff weight of 350 tonnes, is measurably smaller. Notable features include nose and tail cargo doors which allow simultaneous loading and unloading, 24 wheel undercarriage allowing operations from semi prepared strips, the ability to 'kneel' for easier front loading and a fly-by-wire control system.

An-124 models include the basic An-124, the commercial An-124-100 certificated in Russia in 1992, the An-124-100M with Western avionics, and the EFIS equipped An-124-102.

Almost all An-124s built were delivered with Aeroflot markings, but commonly performed military tasks, while a smaller number of Ruslans were assigned directly to the Russian air force (deliveries began in 1987). Today about 20 are in Russian military service, but many of these wear civilian markings. Others are in civilian use.

**Photo:** A Russian air force An-124. (Lassi Tolvanen)

## Avioane IAR-99 Soim

**Country of origin:** Romania

**Type:** Two seat basic and advanced trainer

**Powerplant:** IAR-99 – One 17.8kN (4000lb) Turbomecanica licence built Rolls-Royce Viper Mk 632-41M turbojet.

**Performance:** IAR-99 – Max speed at sea level 865km/h (467kt). Max initial rate of climb 6890ft/min. Service ceiling 42,325ft. Max range with internal fuel (trainer) 1100km (593nm), ground attack 967km (522nm). Combat radius with pilot only, ventral gun and four rocket pods lo-lo-lo 350km (190nm); with ventral gun, two rocket pods and 500kg (1100lb) of bombs hi-lo-hi 345km (185nm); with ventral gun and four 250kg (550lb) bombs hi-hi-hi 385km (208nm). Max endurance trainer mission 2hr 40min, ground attack 1hr 45min.

**Weights:** IAR-99 – Empty equipped 3200kg (7055lb), max takeoff (trainer) 4400kg (9700lb), (ground attack) 5560kg (12,258lb).

**Dimensions:** IAR-99 – Wing span 9.85m (32ft 4in), length 11.01m (36ft 2in), height 3.90m (12ft 10in). Wing area 18.7m$^2$ (201.4sq ft).

**Accommodation:** Two in tandem, pilot only for ground attack missions.

**Armament:** Removable ventral gun pod contains a 23mm GSh-23 two barrel cannon. Four underwing hardpoints can carry a combined load of 1000kg (2205lb), including light bombs and rocket pods.

**Operators:** Romania

**History:** Romania's IAR-99 Soim (Falcon) is a two seat advanced trainer and light attack aircraft.

Development of the Soim began at Romania's Institute de Aviate at Bucharest in the early 1980s, while the program's existence was revealed at the 1983 Paris Airshow. Romania's state aviation enterprise IAv Croavia (renamed Avioane in 1991) was entrusted with Soim production, and IAv built the first prototype which flew on December 21 1985.

Soim production began in 1987 against an initial Romanian air force order for 20. The Soim replaced the Romanian air force's Aero L-29 Delfins. They are used for basic and advanced training, and have a secondary close air support/ground attack role, supplementing IAR-93s.

The IAR-109 Swift was an upgraded development of the Soim, aimed at export orders. The Swift differed from the Soim in having advanced Israeli developed nav/attack avionics and modern cockpit (including HUD and multifunction displays), and expanded weapons carrying capability. It was offered in IAR-109T basic trainer configuration and IAR-109TF armed combat trainer form.

Avioane announced development of the Swift in 1993, a converted IAR-99 served as the first prototype, while the first new build Swift first flew in November 1993. None were ordered.

IAI has developed an upgrade for Romanian IAR-99s to a similar standard for lead-in fighter training. The first upgraded IAR-99 flew in May 1997. Features include a HUD, multifunction displays and a data transfer system allowing a simulated radar display. Romania ordered 24 IAR-99s to this standard in September 1998, with four in production in mid 2001.

**Photo:** The IAI upgraded IAR-99 demonstrator. Romania has 24 improved IAR-99s on order. (Sebastian Zacharias)

## BAC Strikemaster

**Country of origin:** United Kingdom

**Type:** Advanced jet trainer and light attack aircraft

**Powerplant:** Mk 80 – One 14.0kN (3140lb) Rolls-Royce Viper Mk 535 turbojet.

**Performance:** Mk 80 – Max speed at 18,000ft 775km/h (418kt), at sea level 725km/h (320kt). Max initial rate of climb 5250ft/min. Time to 30,000ft 8min 45sec. Service ceiling 40,000ft. Combat radius on a hi-lo-hi attack mission with 1360kg (3000lb) payload 397km (215nm), with a 455kg (1000lb) payload 925km (500nm). Combat radius on a lo-lo-lo attack mission with 455kg (1000lb) payload 445km (240nm).

**Weights:** Mk 80 – Operating empty 2810kg (6195lb), max takeoff 5215kg (11,500lb).

**Dimensions:** Mk 80 – Wing span 11.23m (36ft 10in), length 10.27m (33ft 9in), height 3.10m (10ft 2in). Wing area 19.9m$^2$ (213.7sq ft).

**Accommodation:** Seating for two, side by side.

**Armament:** Mk 80 – Two internal 7.62mm FN machine guns. Max permissible external stores load 1360kg (3000lb) on four underwing hardpoints, including rockets, bombs, practice bombs, gun and cannon pods, plus reconnaissance pods.

**Operators:** Sudan.

**History:** The Strikemaster is the ultimate and most potent development of a family of two seat trainers that began with the radial piston engine powered Percival Provost.

The Strikemaster is a direct development of the Hunting Percival (later BAC) Jet Provost. The Jet Provost began life as a low cost, minimum change development of the piston engined Provost, although the metamorphosis to jet power involved a much greater redesign than first planned. The Jet Provost (or JP) established the basic configuration of the Strikemaster, and first flew on June 26 1954.

The first major production JP was the T.3, the T.4 introduced two Martin-Baker ejection seats and wingtip tanks. The definitive Jet Provost model, the T.5, featured a redesigned, longer nose with a larger canopy, and formed the basis for the Strikemaster.

The development of an armed Jet Provost T.5 followed the Jet Provost's reasonable success with export customers. The resulting private venture BAC 167 Strikemaster was based closely on the Jet Provost T.5, but introduced a more powerful Viper turbojet, structural strengthening and four underwing hardpoints. The first Strikemaster first flew in October 1967 and production of the Mk 80 began a year later. All but 10 of the 146 built were Mk 80s, with Sudan taking delivery of 10 similar Mk 90s (the last Strikemasters built) in 1984.

An upgraded Strikemaster with more powerful Viper 632 engine was considered in the 1970s but was not developed.

The Strikemaster's appeal lay in its ability to conduct advanced pilot training and light attack missions. Significant operators included Saudi Arabia, New Zealand (its Strikemasters were nicknamed Bluntys), Kenya, Kuwait and Singapore.

In 2001 just one nation operated Strikemasters – Sudan with three Strikemaster 90s used for counter insurgency missions nominally on strength. Others fly in private hands as warbirds.

**Photo:** Kuwait replaced its Strikemasters with Hawk 64s.

## BAE Systems Hawk

**Country of origin:** United Kingdom

**Type:** Two seat advanced trainer and light attack aircraft

**Powerplant:** 60 – One 25.4kN (5700lb) Rolls-Royce Adour 861 turbofan. 100 – One 26.0kN (5845lb) Adour 871.

**Performance:** 60 – Max level speed at sea level 1010km/h (545kt). Max initial rate of climb 11,800ft/min. Service ceiling 46,000ft. Combat radius with 907kg (2000lb) external load 1448km (781nm), with a 2270kg (5000lb) external load 1000km (538nm). 100 – Max speed 1038km/h (560kt) at 36,000ft, at sea level 1001km/h (540kt). Max initial rate of climb 11,800ft/min. Service ceiling 44,500ft. Combat radius hi-lo-hi with seven BL755 cluster bombs 510km (275nm).

**Weights:** 60 – Empty 4012kg (8845lb), max TOW 9100kg (20,060lb). 100 – Empty 4400kg (9700lb), max takeoff 9100kg (20,060lb).

**Dimensions:** 60 – Span 9.39m (30ft 10in), fuselage length 10.78m (35ft 4in), height 3.98m (13ft 1in). Wing area 16.7m² (179.6sq ft). 100 – Span 9.94m (32ft 8in) with wingtip AIM-9s, length incl probe 12.10m (39ft 8in), height 3.99m (12ft 1in). Wing area 16.7m² (179.6sq ft).

**Accommodation:** Seating for two in tandem.

**Armament:** 60 & 100 – Up to 3000kg (6615lb) of external ordnance, including rocket pods, bombs and cluster bombs, AIM-9 Sidewinder AAMs and a centreline 30mm Aden cannon.

**Operators:** Australia, Canada, Finland, Indonesia, Kenya, Kuwait, Malaysia, Oman, Saudi Arabia, Switzerland, South Africa*, South Korea, UAE (Abu Dhabi & Dubai), UK, Zimbabwe.

**History:** The Hawk has proven to be a highly popular advanced jet trainer, and has been progressively developed over three decades.

Hawker Siddeley's P.1182 design was formally adopted by the RAF as its new advanced trainer in 1970. First flight was on August 21 1971.

The RAF took delivery of 176 Hawk T.1s from 1976. In the mid 1980s 89 were modified as T.1As, wired to accept AIM-9s for emergency wartime use as air defence fighters. A small number of rewinged RAF T.1Ws can carry stores on two underwing pylons.

The first export Hawk was the Mk 50 with more powerful engine, a higher max takeoff weight and greater stores carriage on four underwing pylons. The Mk 60 features a further increase in engine power, an improved wing with leading edge fences and a revised flap layout, and Sidewinder and Matra AAM capability.

The improved Hawk 100 introduced a more powerful Adour 871 turbofan; a revised wing with fixed leading edge droop to improve manoeuvrability, full width flaps and optional wingtip missile rails; an extended nose optionally housing FLIR and/or a laser ranger; and revised avionics, including MFDs, plus HUD and HOTAS controls.

Australia's 33 Hawk 127 LIFs delivered in 2000/01 feature three colour CRT displays in each cockpit, 1553B databus, new HUD and HOTAS and other improvements. Bombardier ordered 19 similar Hawk 115s for NATO Flying Training in Canada. These are designated CT-115s and are used for advanced training of Canadian and other NATO pilots.

The Hawk 127 forms the basis for the similar Hawk LIFT (Lead-in Fighter Trainer) with optional inflight refuelling probe. South Africa is the launch customer, with 12 ordered for delivery from 2005.

**Photo:** An Australian Hawk 127. (Paul Sadler)

## BAE Systems Hawk 200

**Country of origin:** United Kingdom

**Type:** Light multirole fighter

**Powerplant:** One 26.0kN (5845lb) Rolls-Royce Adour Mk 871 turbofan.

**Performance:** Max speed at sea level 1000km/h (540kt), economical cruising speed 795km/h (430kt). Max initial rate of climb 11,510ft/min. Service ceiling 45,000ft. Ferry range with two drop tanks 2390km (1365nm). Combat radius with a recce pod and two drop tanks, hi-hi-hi 1600km (862nm); combat radius with 1360kg (3000lb) ordnance hi-lo-hi 945km (510nm); combat radius on a hi-hi-hi intercept with two AIM-9s and two drop tanks 1335km (720nm).

**Weights:** Basic empty 4450kg (9810lb), max takeoff 9100kg (20,060lb).

**Dimensions:** Wing span 9.94m (32ft 8in) with wingtip missiles, normal wingspan 9.39m (30ft 10in), fuselage length 10.95m (35ft 11in), height 4.13m (13ft 7in). Wing area 16.7m² (179.6sq ft).

**Accommodation:** Pilot only.

**Armament:** Up to 3000kg (6615lb) of ordnance on one centreline, four underwing and two wingtip stations. Options include up to four AIM-9 AAMs, Maverick AGMs, a centreline Aden 30mm cannon, bombs and rockets.

**Operators:** Indonesia*, Malaysia, Oman.

**History:** The most potent development of the Hawk family so far, the single seat Hawk 200 fighter has found a small but ready market from three existing two seat Hawk customers.

The original two seat Hawk first flew on August 21 1971, since which time over 570 of all models have been ordered. This commercial success in part contributed to British Aerospace's announcement in 1984 that it was to build a single seat light fighter development known as the Hawk 200. A demonstrator first flew on May 19 1986.

The first Hawk 200 demonstrator crashed two months after its first flight (through g-induced loss of consciousness). A preproduction 200 flew in April 1987, and a production representative, radar equipped Hawk 200RDA demonstrator flew in February 1992.

Compared with the two seater Hawks, the Hawk 200 differs mainly in the redesigned forward fuselage and nose to accommodate the single seat cockpit. Otherwise the Hawk 200 and equivalent Hawk 100 two seater retain 80% commonality. Like the 100, the single seater features the advanced combat wing with leading edge droop for improved manoeuvrability, full span flaps and wingtip rails for air-to-air missiles (typically the Sidewinder). The wingtip rails, centreline and four underwing stations can carry between them three tonnes of ordnance. An inflight refuelling probe is optional.

The redesigned nose houses a Lockheed Martin (formerly Westinghouse) APG-66H multimode radar (similar to that fitted to the F-16). The FLIR/laser rangefinder nose of the Hawk 100 was also offered as an option for the single seater for a time, but was dropped. In the cockpit the 200 features modern avionics, a single colour multifunction display, a HUD and optional HOTAS controls.

So far all Hawk 200 orders have been placed by two seater customers. Oman was the first customer, its initial 200 first flew in September 1993. So far 62 production Hawk 200s have been built.

**Photo:** A Royal Malaysian Air Force Hawk 208. (BAE Systems)

## BAE Systems Nimrod MRA.4

**Country of origin:** United Kingdom

**Type:** Maritime patrol aircraft

**Powerplant:** Four 68.9kN (15,500lb) Rolls-Royce BR710 Mk 101 turbofans.

**Performance:** Max operating Mach number Mach 0.77. Service ceiling 42,000ft. Range with max internal fuel over 11,110km (6000nm). Endurance over 15hr.

**Weights:** Empty 46,500kg (102,515lb), max takeoff 105,376kg (232,315lb). Internal fuel 50,122kg (110,500lb).

**Dimensions:** Wing span over tip pods 38.71m (127ft 0in), length excluding refuelling probe 38.63m (126ft 9in), height 9.45m (31ft 0in). Wing area 235.8m² (2538.0sq ft).

**Accommodation:** Flightcrew of two, with seven tactical mission crew (two taccos, radar, communications, ESM and two acoustics operators), and optionally two observers and a sonobuoy loader, with accommodation for up to 13 relief crew or support personnel.

**Armament:** Will be able to carry a wide variety of current and planned anti ship and anti submarine weapons (such as ASMs, torpedoes and mines) in the internal weapons bay and four underwing hardpoints. External hardpoints will also carry Sidewinder or ASRAAM AAMs for self defence.

**Operators:** UK*

**History:** The Nimrod MRA.4 is a substantial rebuild of the Nimrod, with airframe, engines, cockpit, mission systems and radar changes.

The Nimrod 2000 was British Aerospace (now BAE System)'s response to the Royal Air Force's Nimrod replacement program. The RAF selected BAe's bid of a re-engined and rebuilt Nimrod ahead of offerings from Lockheed Martin (with its Orion 2000), Dassault (Atlantique 3) and Loral (P-3 Valkyrie – rebuilt, upgraded and re-engined ex USN P-3A/Bs). The selection of the Nimrod 2000 was announced on July 25 1996. The designation MRA.4 was subsequently adopted.

The MRA.4 upgrade involves refurbishing the existing fuselage and fitting new build larger area wings and wing box (60% of the structure will be new build), new undercarriage, new hydraulic, fuel and electrical systems, four new, more powerful and 20% more fuel efficient Rolls-Royce BR710 turbofans, a two crew seven-screen EFIS flightdeck and a fully integrated mission system.

The BAE Systems integrated mission system will comprise a Boeing supplied tactical command sensor subsystem, Telephonics communication subsystem, Lockheed Martin Defensive Aids Sub-System and a Smiths Aerospace Armaments Control System. Sensors will include a Racal Searchwater 2000MR radar, Elta ESM, FLIR and the current Nimrod's MAD. The current UYS-503 processor is also retained.

The flightdeck will feature seven Thales colour liquid crystal displays compatible with NVGs, EICAS, a ring laser gyro INS with GPS nav system and a microwave landing system.

Work began on the first three of 21 Nimrods to be rebuilt in early 1997. Program delays (including an overweight wing) mean the in-service date has been pushed from 2003 to 2005.

**Photo:** An artist's impression of the Nimrod 2000. The Nimrod's buried engine configuration significantly reduces radar cross-section.

## Beechcraft T-34 Mentor & Turbo Mentor

**Country of origin:** United States of America

**Type:** Two seat primary trainer

**Powerplant:** T-34A & B – One 170kW (225hp) Continental O-470 flat six piston engine driving a two blade propeller. T-34C – One 535kW (715shp) Pratt & Whitney Canada PT6A-25 turboprop derated to 300kW (400shp) driving a three blade prop.

**Performance:** T-34A & B – Max speed 302km/h (163kt), max cruising speed 270km/h (145kt). Max initial rate of climb 1210ft/min. Service ceiling 21,200ft. Range 1240km (667nm). T-34C – Max speed 414km/h (224kt), max cruising speed 398km/h (215kt). Max initial rate of climb 1480ft/min. Service ceiling 30,000ft plus. Range 1310km (708nm) at 333km/h (180kt) cruising speed.

**Weights:** T-34A & B – Empty 932kg (2055lb), max takeoff 1315kg (2900lb). T-34C – Empty 1193kg (2630lb), MTOW 1938kg (4274lb).

**Dimensions:** T-34A & B – Wing span 10.01m (32ft 10in), length 7.87m (25ft 10in), height 2.92m (9ft 7in). Wing area 16.5m² (177.6sq ft). T-34C – Wing span 10.16m (33ft 4in), length 8.75m (28ft 9in), height 3.02m (9ft 11in). Wing area 16.71m² (179.9sq ft).

**Accommodation:** Seating for two in tandem.

**Armament:** T-34C-1 – Four underwing hardpoints can carry up to 545kg (1200lb) of practice and light bombs, rockets, miniguns, AGM-22A anti tank missiles or towed target equipment.

**Operators:** Mentor – Colombia, Dominican Republic, Uruguay. Turbo Mentor – Argentina, Ecuador, Indonesia, Morocco, Peru, Taiwan, Uruguay, USA.

**History:** Perhaps the West's most successful postwar basic trainer, the T-34 is based on one of civil aviation's most successful light aircraft types, the Beech 35 Bonanza.

The prototype four seat Beech Bonanza first flew on December 22 1945, predating a production run that began in 1947 and continues today. In 1948 Beech took the Bonanza design as the basis for a military basic trainer. The private venture Model 45 Mentor differed from the Bonanza in having seating for two in tandem and a conventional tail unit (the Model 35 Bonanza is famous for its V-tail). The Model 45 Mentor first flew on December 2 1948, arousing the interest of the newly formed US Air Force which ordered three evaluation examples.

The three evaluation YT-34s were delivered in 1950, and successful testing led the USAF to order the first of 450 T-34As in 1953. That year the USN evaluated the T-34 and ordered 290 similar T-34Bs in mid 1954. Mentors were also built under licence in Canada and Japan (as the Fuji T-3) and assembled in Argentina. In all over 1300 were built. USAF Mentors were retired in 1960.

In 1973 the US Navy requested Beech build a turboprop powered development to replace the T-34B and the North American T-28 Trojan. The resulting Pratt & Whitney Canada PT6A powered T-34C Turbo Mentor (dubbed Tormentor) flew for the first time on September 21 1973. Some 352 T-34Cs were built (the last of which, attrition replacements for the USN, were delivered in 1990). Most were for the US Navy, but 129 armed T-34C-1s were exported. T-34Cs will be replaced by T-6s.

**Photo:** An Argentine Turbo Mentor. (Santiago Rivas)

# Bell/Agusta AB139 Military

**Countries of origin:** Italy & USA

**Type:** Medium lift battlefield and utility helicopter

**Powerplants:** Two 1252kW (1679shp) takeoff rated Pratt & Whitney Canada PT6C-67C turboshafts driving a five blade main rotor and four blade tail rotor.

**Performance:** Max cruising speed 155kt (287km/h). Initial rate of climb 2000ft/min. Hovering ceiling out of ground effect 12,000ft. Max range with no reserves 750km (400nm). Endurance with no reserves 3.9hr.

**Weights:** Max takeoff 6000kg (13,227lb). Useful load (external) 2700kg (6000lb).

**Dimensions:** Main rotor diameter 13.80m (45ft 3in), length overall rotors turning 16.65m (54ft 8in), height overall rotors turning 4.95m (16ft 3in). Main rotor disc area 149.6m$^2$ (1610.0sq ft).

**Accommodation:** Flightcrew of one or two. Main cabin seating for up to 15 troops on crashworthy seats. In medevac configuration can carry six stretcher patients and four medical attendants.

**Armament:** Provision for pintle mounted doorway guns, and removable stub wings for weapons such as gun and rocket pods.

**Operators:** None

**History:** The all new AB139 medium lift helicopter is the second product of the Bell/Agusta Aerospace Company (BAAC) joint venture.

The new six tonne class AB139 is being developed in civil and military forms and will complement the Bell 212/412, as it is slightly larger with significantly improved performance.

The joint venture company publicly announced details of the AB139 on September 8 1999 at the Farnborough Airshow, while a mockup was displayed at the following year's Paris Airshow. Three development AB139s have been built, with the first flying on February 3 2001. Certification and first civil deliveries are due in 2002.

Features of the new helicopter include a 287km/h (155kt) cruising speed, delivered courtesy of the twin PT6C engines and the five blade fully articulated main rotor and four bladed canted tail rotor, plus a Honeywell Primus Epic integrated glass cockpit, and a large, unobstructed main cabin with seating for 15.

BellAgusta is marketing a military AB139 for trooplift, SAR, CSAR and utility roles. It would feature armoured and crashworthy crew seats, electronic warfare suite, infrared suppressors on the exhaust, provision for pintle mounted doorway guns, and removable stub wings for weapons such as gun and rocket pods, and sensors such as a FLIR turret.

AgustaWestland is the lead partner on the AB139, responsible for the new helicopter's design and development and production, while the manufacturing workshare is split 75:25 to the Italian manufacturer's benefit. Engine manufacturer Pratt & Whitney Canada and avionics provider Honeywell are risk sharing partners in the program, along with Kawasaki, for the transmission input module, Poland's PZL Swidnik, which is supplying airframe components, and landing gear and air-conditioning system supplier Liebherr of Germany. Final assembly will be undertaken at AgustaWestland's Vergiate plant, while Bell will establish a second line to build AB139s for North American customers.

**Photo:** An artist's impression of the AB139 Military. (BellAgusta)

# Bell 47G/H-13 Sioux

**Country of origin:** United States of America

**Type:** Light utility, training and observation helicopter

**Powerplant:** 47G-3B-2A – One 200kW (270hp) Lycoming TVO-435-F1A supercharged flat six piston engine driving a two blade main rotor and two blade tail rotor.

**Performance:** 47G-3B-2A – Max speed 170km/h (91kt), cruising speed 135km/h (73kt) at 5000ft. Max initial rate of climb 990ft/min. Service ceiling 19,000ft. Hovering ceiling in ground effect 17,700ft, out of ground effect 12,700ft. Range with max fuel 395km (215nm) at 6000ft.

**Weights:** 47G-3B-2A – Empty 877kg (1935lb), max takeoff 1340kg (2950lb).

**Dimensions:** 47G-3B-2A – Main rotor diameter 11.32m (37ft 2in), length overall rotors turning 13.30m (43ft 8in), fuselage length 9.63m (31ft 7in), height 2.83m (9ft 4in). Main rotor disc area 100.8m$^2$ (1085sq ft).

**Accommodation:** Seating for two or three occupants, side-by-side. Can carry two stretchers, one on each skid.

**Armament:** None

**Operators:** Greece, Indonesia, Malta, New Zealand, Pakistan, Zambia.

**History:** The Bell 47 is recognised as being one of the first practical helicopters, and was the first to see widespread military use. Today it soldiers on in use for helicopter pilot training and liaison work.

The 47's lineage dates back to 1943 Bell Model 30, an experimental helicopter the US Army ordered for evaluation. The service ordered 10 Model 30s for evaluation, and the type formed the basis for the improved Model 47. The Model 47's first flight was on December 8 1945. The prototype 47 featured seating for two side-by-side, with car style cabin doors and was powered by a Franklin piston engine, and in this initial form the 47 became the first helicopter to be certificated by the USA's Civil Aeronautics Administration.

The promise the Bell helicopter showed soon translated into military orders from the US services, the US Army Air Force ordering 28 as YR-13s in 1947 for evaluation, some of which went to the US Navy as HTL-1 trainers. In 1948 the US Army ordered 65, designated H-13Bs. The Sioux name was adopted later.

By 1953 Bell was building the definitive 47G, which featured progressively more powerful engines, plus the previously introduced goldfish bowl canopy and uncovered tail, the two features which make the Bell 47 probably the most recognised helicopter in the world. The 47G remained in production through to 1974, with more than 5000 built. It was also licence built by Agusta in Italy (as the AB 47G) and Kawasaki in Japan.

The H-13 saw widespread US military service during the Korean War, where it was used for a range of roles including medevac (fitted with stretchers on either skid), observation and transport, and proved beyond doubt the utility of the helicopter.

Today the Bell 47 remains only in limited military service, as it has largely been replaced by more modern and capable types, with most in use as trainers or for light utility work.

**Photo:** The New Zealand Air Force's five 47G-3B-2 Sioux are used for pilot training. (Peter Clark)

# Bell 204, UH-1B & UH-1C Iroquois

**Country of origin:** United States of America

**Type:** Troop transport and utility helicopter

**Powerplant:** UH-1B & UH-1C – One 820kW (1100shp) Lycoming T53-L-9 or L-11 turboshaft driving two blade main and tail rotors.

**Performance:** UH-1B – Max speed 222km/h (120kt), normal cruising speed 193km/h (104kt). Max initial rate of climb 1900ft/min. Service ceiling 16,700ft. Hovering ceiling out of ground effect 11,800ft. Range 463km (250nm). UH-1C – Max speed and max cruising speed 238km/h (130kt), normal cruising speed 230km/h (124kt). Max initial rate of climb 1400ft/min. Service ceiling 11,500ft. Hovering ceiling in ground effect 10,600ft, out of ground effect 10,000ft. Range with auxiliary fuel 615km (332nm).

**Weights:** UH-1B – Empty 2050kg (4520lb), MTOW 3855kg (8500lb). UH-1C – Empty 2300kg (5070lb), MTOW 4310kg (9500lb).

**Dimensions:** Main rotor diameter 13.41m (44ft 0in), length overall rotors turning 16.15m (53ft 0in), fuselage length 11.70m (38ft 5in), height 3.84m (12ft 7in). Main rotor disc area 141.3m² (1520sq ft).

**Accommodation:** Pilot and copilot or passenger side-by-side, with six troops in main cabin. Alternatively main cabin can accommodate three stretchers and a medical attendant.

**Armament:** UH-1B/C – Can be fitted with a variety of weaponry including a 7.62mm minigun. AB 204AS – Two Mark 44 torpedoes.

**Operators:** Colombia, Ecuador, Indonesia, Singapore, South Korea, Sweden, Turkey, Yemen.

**History:** The Iroquois has a special place in modern military history. Built in greater numbers than any other Western military aircraft since WW2, it is indelibly linked with the Vietnam War, where it proved beyond doubt the importance and value of helicopter air mobility to land warfare.

The Iroquois, or Huey, began life in response to a 1954 US Army requirement for a turbine utility helicopter, primarily for medevac. Bell responded to the request with its Lycoming T53 powered Model 204, which was selected for development, and the first of the XH-40 prototypes flew on October 22 1956. The XH-40s were followed by six larger, preproduction YH-40s, representative of early production aircraft which up until 1962 were designated HU-1A, hence 'Huey'.

The HU-1B or UH-1B introduced a further enlarged cabin and a modified main rotor, and it was this model which was the first to see widespread service in Vietnam, both as a transport and fitted out as a gunship. War experience with gunship configured UH-1Bs led to the UH-1C with an improved rotor system and higher top speed. The UH-1E was similar but developed for the USMC as an assault helicopter and was also built in TH-1E (USMC) and TH-1L (USN) trainer versions. The UH-1F was developed for the USAF and used for missile range support duties and was powered by a General Electric T58 and featured the tailboom of the larger UH-1D (described separately).

Aside from Bell production, short fuselage UH-1s were built in Japan (Fuji) and Italy (by Agusta). Aside from the T53, Agusta built AB 204Bs were powered with the Bristol Siddeley Gnome or GE's T58. The T58 powered AB 204AS was developed for ASW and was fitted with radar and sonar and could carry Mk 44 torpedoes.

**Photo:** An Austrian AB 204B. (Austrian Armed Forces)

# Bell 205, UH-1D & UH-1H Iroquois

**Country of origin:** United States of America

**Type:** Utility and battlefield helicopters

**Powerplant:** UH-1H – One 1045kW (1400shp) Lycoming T53-L-13 turboshaft driving two blade main and tail rotors.

**Performance:** UH-1H – Max speed and max cruising speed 205km/h (110kt). Max initial rate of climb 1600ft/min. Service ceiling 12,600ft. Hovering ceiling out of ground effect 4000ft. Range with max fuel and typical payload 420km (225nm).

**Weights:** UH-1H – Empty equipped 2363kg (5210lb), normal takeoff 4100kg (9040lb), max takeoff 4310kg (9500lb).

**Dimensions:** UH-1H – Main rotor diameter 14.63m (48ft 0in), length overall rotors turning 17.62m (57ft 10in), fuselage length 12.77m (41ft 10in), height overall 4.41m (14ft 6in). Main rotor disc area 168.1m² (1809.6sq ft).

**Accommodation:** UH-1H – Flightcrew of one or two pilots, plus up to 14 equipped troops in the main cabin.

**Armament:** UH-1H – Pintle mounted machines guns, plus miniguns and rockets mounted on fuselage stub wings.

**Operators:** 205, UH-1D/H & AB 205 – Argentina, Australia, Bolivia, Brazil, Chile, Dominican Rep, Ecuador, El Salvador, Germany, Greece, Guatemala, Honduras, Indonesia, Iran, Italy, Japan, Macedonia, Mexico, Morocco, Myanmar, New Zealand, Oman, Pakistan, Panama, Peru, Philippines, Singapore, South Korea, Spain, Taiwan, Thailand, Tunisia, Turkey, UAE (Dubai), USA, Uruguay, Zambia.

**History:** With production of the UH-1B Huey in full swing in 1960, Bell approached the US Army about developing a larger and more powerful model.

The US Army ordered seven improved YUH-1D Iroquois (Bell model number 205), for trials and evaluation in July 1960. First flight of the improved Huey was on August 16 1961 and the type was subsequently ordered into production as the UH-1D.

Compared with the UH-1B and C, the D model featured an 820kW (1100shp) T53-L-11 turboshaft and an enlarged fuselage capable of seating 14 fully equipped troops, twice that of the earlier models. Deliveries of the first of 2008 UH-1Ds for the US Army began in August 1963. In Germany Dornier licence built 352 UH-1Ds.

The definitive UH-1H introduced a more powerful T53-L-13 turboshaft, but otherwise was basically unchanged from the UH-1D. UH-1H deliveries to the US Army began in September 1967, while the final Bell built UH-1H was delivered almost two decades later in 1986. UH-1Hs were licence built in Italy (by Agusta as the AB 205), Taiwan (by AIDC) and Japan where Fuji continues low rate production of the improved UH-1J with uprated engine and transmission from the AH-1S, Bell 212 main rotor and 212 style longer nose and wider fuselage.

The UH-1D and UH-1H both saw widespread service with the US military (and Australia) in Vietnam.

Bell offers an upgrade of the UH-1H, the Honeywell (nee Lycoming) T53-L-703 powered Huey II. Colombia is the launch customer. The US Army dropped plans to re-engine 131 ANG UH-1Hs with the LHTEC T800 due to funding constraints.

**Photo:** A New Zealand UH-1H in East Timor. (Peter Clark)

## Bell 212, UH-1N, AB 212 & UH-1Y

**Countries of origin:** USA & Canada

**Type:** Battlefield/utility helicopter and ASW helo (AB 212ASW)

**Powerplants:** 212 – One 1340kW (1800shp) takeoff rated Pratt & Whitney Canada PT6T-3 or PT6T-3B Turbo Twin-Pac (two coupled PT6 turboshafts) driving two blade main and tail rotors.

**Performance:** 212 – Max cruising speed 206km/h (111kt), long range cruising speed 193km/h (104kt). Max initial rate of climb 1320ft/min. Range with standard fuel at long range cruising speed 457km (247nm).

**Weights:** 212 – Empty 2765kg (6097lb), MTOW 5080kg (11,200lb).

**Dimensions:** 212 – Main rotor diameter 14.63m (48ft 0in), length rotors turning 17.46m (57ft 2in), fuselage length 12.92m (42ft 5in), height overall 4.48m (14ft 8in). Main rotor disc area 168.1m$^2$ (1809.6sq ft).

**Accommodation:** 212 – Total seating for 15, including one or two pilots. In medevac role can house six stretchers and two medical attendants. AB 212ASW – Typical crew of three or four.

**Armament:** 212 – Can be fitted with pintle mounted machine guns in main cabin doors. AB 212ASW – Two Mk 44, Mk 46 or MQ 44 torpedoes, or AS 12 or Sea Killer ASMs.

**Operators:** Argentina, Austria, Bangladesh, Colombia, Ecuador, El Salvador, Greece, Iran, Israel, Italy, Lebanon, Libya, Mexico, Morocco, Panama, Saudi Arabia, Singapore, South Korea, Spain, Sri Lanka, Sudan, Thailand, Tunisia, Turkey, UAE (Dubai) Uganda, USA, Venezuela, Yemen, Zambia.

**History:** Development of the Bell 212 was initiated after Bell, Pratt & Whitney Canada and the Canadian Government agreed to jointly fund development of a twin engine version of the Iroquois.

The early 1968 three way agreement paved the way to mate the basic UH-1H/205 fuselage with a Pratt & Whitney Canada PT6T Turbo Twin-Pac to significantly boost performance. The Twin-Pac mated two PT6 turboshafts through a single combining gearbox and single output shaft, and was fitted with torque sensors so that if one of the engines failed the other could be throttled up to compensate for the power loss. The resulting 212's first flight was in 1968.

When the 1968 agreement was announced, Bell said it held orders for the new helicopter from the Canadian Armed Forces for 50 CUH-1Ns (later CH-135 Twin Hueys) and 141 for the US military as UH-1Ns. The US Navy and Marines were ultimately the largest UH-1N operators, taking delivery of 221 between them.

The 212 was sold commercially as the Twin Two-Twelve, with the last built in 1998. About 950 212s and UH-1Ns were built.

In Italy, Agusta licence built the 212 as the AB 212, and developed the anti submarine warfare AB 212ASW. This unique 212 variant is the Italian navy's primary shipborne helicopter. It is equipped with MM/APS-705 search radar, sonar and ESM and can be armed with homing torpedoes or anti ship missiles.

The USMC has contracted Bell to upgrade its UH-1Ns to UH-1Ys to feature a glass cockpit, four blade main rotor and twin GE T700 turboshafts under the H-1 upgrade program. These will have a high degree of commonality with upgraded USMC AH-1Ws (as AH-1Z), and will remain in service to 2020. First flight was on December 20 2001.

**Photo:** The first UH-1Y rolled out in December 2001. (Bell).

## Bell 412, AB 412 & CH-146 Griffon

**Countries of origin:** USA & Canada

**Type:** Battlefield and utility helicopter

**Powerplants:** CH-146 – One 1425kW (1910shp) Pratt & Whitney Canada PT6T-3D Turbo Twin-Pac (two coupled PT6s) driving a four blade main rotor and two blade tail rotor.

**Performance:** CH-146 – Max cruising speed 240km/h (130kt), long range cruising speed 230km/h (124kt). Hovering ceiling in ground effect 10,200ft, out of ground effect 5200ft. Range at long range cruising speed with standard fuel and no reserves 745km (402nm).

**Weights:** CH-146 – Empty equipped 3065kg (6760lb), max takeoff 5397kg (11,900lb).

**Dimensions:** CH-146 – Main rotor diameter 14.02m (46ft 0in), length overall rotors turning 17.12m (56ft 2in), fuselage length 12.92m (42ft 5in), height overall 4.57m (15ft 0in). Main rotor disc area 154.4m$^2$ (1661.9sq ft).

**Accommodation:** Total seating for 15, including one or two pilots. In medevac role six stretcher patients and two medical attendants.

**Armament:** Military 412 – Offered with removable nose mounted turret gun, 7.62mm machine gun, 20mm cannon and rocket pods and pintle mounted machine guns in the main cabin doors.

**Operators:** 412 – Botswana, Canada, Chile*, Honduras, Indonesia, Norway, Philippines, Poland, Slovenia, Sri Lanka, Sweden, UK, Venezuela. AB 412 – Ghana, Italy, Netherlands, Saudi Arabia, Sweden, UAE (Dubai), Uganda, Venezuela*, Zimbabwe.

**History:** Bell's 412 is a four bladed main rotor development of the 212.

The mating of the Pratt & Whitney Canada PT6T Turbo Twin-Pac with the Bell 205 to produce the Bell 212 was a significant commercial success for Bell. However, by the mid 1970s Bell was looking at further improving the breed, and in particular improving the 212's speed and range performance.

Not wanting to re-engine the 212 or make any major structural changes, Bell instead decided to increase performance by developing a four bladed main rotor for the 212, resulting in the 412. The 412's shorter diameter four blade main rotor is of composite construction except between the leading edge and spar, and has a longer fatigue life and produces less vibration than Bell's earlier two bladed units. First flight of the 412 was in August 1979, while production was transferred to Canada in 1989.

Progressive development of the 412, spurred mainly by growing civil orders, led to the 412SP (Special Performance), 412HP (High Performance) and the current production 412EP (Enhanced Performance). The 412EP also forms the basis for the CH-146 Griffon (412CF), 100 of which were built for the Canadian Forces. In the UK nine 412EPs fly with the civilian operated Defence Helicopter Flying School as Griffin HT.1s. Venezuela has ordered four Helidyne 412 Sentinels with chin mounted search radar and removable dunking sonar.

The 412 is also licence built in Italy by Agusta as the AB 412. The military AB 412 Griffon features strengthened undercarriage skids to increase crash survivability, crew crash absorbing and armoured crew seats and can be fitted with impact absorbing seats for passengers. It is in service with the Italian army as a battlefield transport and the Italian navy for SAR.

**Photo:** A Canadian CH-146. (Bell)

# Bell 214 Huey Plus, Isfahan & BigLifter

**Country of origin:** United States of America

**Type:** Utility and battlefield helicopter

**Powerplant:** 214A – One 2185kW (2930shp) Lycoming LTC4B-8D turboshaft driving two blade main and tail rotors.

**Performance:** 214A – Max cruising speed clean 260km/h (140kt), max cruising speed with sling load 185km/h (100kt). Service ceiling clean 16,400ft, with sling load 12,400ft. Hovering ceiling out of ground effect clean 12,200ft, out of ground effect with sling load 5400ft. Range with reserves 475km (255nm), range with sling load 167km (90nm). Endurance 2hr 35min.

**Weights:** 214A – Empty 3442kg (7588lb), normal takeoff 6260kg (13,800lb), max takeoff with slung load 6805kg (15,000lb).

**Dimensions:** 214A – Main rotor diameter 15.24m (50ft 0in), fuselage length 14.63m (48ft 0in), height overall 3.90m (12ft 10in). Main rotor disc area 182.4m² (1963.5sq ft).

**Accommodation:** 214A – Flightcrew of two pilots plus 14 equipped troops. In medevac role can carry six stretcher patients and two medical attendants.

**Armament:** Usually none.

**Operators:** Ecuador, Iran, Oman, UAE (Dubai).

**History:** A further development of the ubiquitous Bell Iroquois, the Bell 214 remains the most powerful single engined helicopter in military service.

Bell announced it was developing the 214 Huey Plus on October 12 1970. The private development 214 was based on the basic airframe of the UH-1H Iroquois, but introduced a significantly more powerful 1415kW (1900shp) T53-L-702 turboshaft, a new, longer diameter main rotor and a strengthened fuselage to cope with the new rotor and increased torque. A prototype 214 flew for the first time in 1970 and it demonstrated a number of performance improvements such as a top speed at max weight of 306km/h (165kt), but the type failed to attract orders from the US Army.

The 214 did however arouse the interest of Iran, who saw the 214 as being able to meet its requirement for a troop and supply transport able to operate in its hot environment. Iran ordered 287 Bell 214As, which featured the even more powerful 2185kW (2930shp) Lycoming LTC4B-8 turboshaft, on December 22 1972. In addition to the 214As, which were named Isfahan after the town near the Iranian army's helicopter school, Iran also took delivery of 39 search and rescue configured 214Cs.

Plans to establish a production line in Iran for the 214 and the larger 214ST (described separately) were terminated with the fall of the Shah in 1979 and the severing of diplomatic ties with the USA. The cutting of ties with the US also put an end to Bell's support for Iran's large fleet of 214s, and many may no longer be serviceable. Around 100 are nominally on strength.

Bell commercially marketed the 214 as the 214B BigLifter and promoted the helicopter's ability to lift large sling loads. Several countries purchased 214Bs for military use.

**Photo:** One of 287 Bell 214As delivered to Iran during the reign of the Shah. The 214 has a different air intake and exhaust arrangement compared with the 205/UH-1H.

# Bell 214ST

**Country of origin:** United States of America

**Type:** Medium transport helicopter

**Powerplants:** 214ST – Two 1215kW (1625shp) General Electric CT7-2A turboshafts linked through a combining gearbox driving two blade main and tail rotors.

**Performance:** 214ST – Max cruising speed 259km/h (140kt) at 4000ft, or 265km/h (143kt) at sea level. Max initial rate of climb 1780ft/min. Service ceiling with one engine out 4800ft. Hovering ceiling in ground effect 6400ft. Ferry range with auxiliary fuel 1020km (550nm), range with standard fuel and no reserves 805km (435nm).

**Weights:** 214ST – Empty 4300kg (9481lb), max takeoff 7938kg (17,500lb).

**Dimensions:** 214ST – Main rotor diameter 15.85m (52ft 0in), length overall rotors turning 18.95m (62ft 2in), fuselage length 15.03m (49ft 4in), height overall 4.84m (15ft 11in). Main rotor disc area 197.3m² (2124sq ft).

**Accommodation:** 214ST – Pilot and copilot and up to 16 or 17 passengers. Freight volume of 8.95m³ (316cu ft). Can carry an external sling load of 3630kg (8000lb).

**Armament:** Typically none, but can be fitted with pintle mounted machine guns in main cabin door.

**Operators:** Brunei, Iraq, Peru, Thailand, Venezuela.

**History:** Despite sharing a common model number with the 214 Huey Plus and BigLifter (described separately), the Bell 214ST is a much larger helicopter.

Bell developed its biggest helicopter (excluding the V-22) in response to an Iranian requirement for a larger transport helicopter with better performance in its hot and high environment than its 214 Isfahans. Bell based its proposal on the 214 but made substantial design changes, resulting in what is essentially an all new helicopter with little commonality with the smaller 214 series.

The 214ST features two General Electric CT7 turboshafts (the commercial equivalent of the military T700 which powers the AH-64, AH-1W/Z and H-60 series), a stretched fuselage seating up to 17 in the main cabin and stretched main rotor blades from the 214 with composite construction. The 214ST designation originally stood for Stretched Twin, reflecting the changes over the 214, but Bell later changed this to stand for Super Transporter.

The 214ST was to have been built under licence in Iran as part of that country's plans to establish a large army air wing (other aircraft ordered in large numbers under this plan were the 214A Isfahan and AH-1J SeaCobra, both described separately), but Iran's Islamic revolution and fall of the Shah in 1979 put paid to these plans.

Undeterred, Bell continued development of the 214ST for civil and military customers. The 214ST first flew on July 21 1979 and 100 production aircraft were built through to 1990.

Most 214ST sales were to military customers. Iraq was the 214ST's largest customer, taking delivery of 45 during 1987 and 1988, with some most likely seeing service in the Gulf War. Other customers included Peru, Thailand and Venezuela.

**Photo:** The 214ST, Bell's biggest helicopter, differs considerably from the 214A and 214B.

## Bell 206, OH-58, TH-67 & TH-57

**Country of origin:** United States of America

**Type:** Light observation (OH-58), utility transport and training helicopter (TH-67 & TH-57)

**Powerplant:** OH-58A – One 237kW (317shp) Allison T63-A-700 (Allison 250) turboshaft driving two blade main and tail rotors.

**Performance:** OH-58A – Max cruising speed at sea level 196km/h (106kt), economical cruising speed 188km/h (102kt), loiter speed for max endurance 91km/h (49kt). Max initial rate of climb 1780ft/min. Service ceiling 19,000ft. Hovering ceiling in ground effect 13,750ft, out of ground effect 9000ft. Max range at sea level with reserves 480km (260nm). Endurance at sea level with no reserves 3hrs 30mins.

**Weights:** OH-58A – Empty equipped 718kg (1582lb), max takeoff 1360kg (3000lb).

**Dimensions:** OH-58A – Main rotor disc diameter 10.77m (35ft 4in), length overall with rotors turning 12.49m (41ft 0in), fuselage length 9.84m (32ft 4in), height overall rotors turning 2.91m (9ft 7in). Main rotor disc area 91.1m² (980.5sq ft).

**Accommodation:** Total seating for five including pilot.

**Armament:** Usually none, but can be fitted with pintle mounted MGs.

**Operators:** 206 – Includes Brazil, Brunei, Bulgaria, Canada, Chile, Colombia, Cyprus, Ecuador, Guatemala, Guyana, Indonesia, Israel, Italy, Mexico, Myanmar, Pakistan, Peru, South Korea, Sri Lanka, Thailand, UAE (Abu Dhabi & Dubai), Venezuela. OH-58 – Australia, Austria, USA. TH-67 – Bulgaria, Taiwan, USA. TH-57 – USA. 206L – Includes Bangladesh, Mexico, UAE (Dubai), Venezuela.

**History:** The world's most successful light turbine helicopter grew out of Bell's unsuccessful OH-4 bid to meet a 1960 US Army requirement for a four seat light observation helicopter.

While Bell lost that contract to Hughes with what became the OH-6 Cayuse (described separately), the company set about developing a five seat commercial light helicopter based on the general OH-4 design (the first of four OH-4 prototypes first flew in December 1962). The civil Bell 206 JetRanger first flew on January 10 1966, and production aircraft were delivered from later that year. Since then the JetRanger has been in continuous production in progressively modernised forms and has seen widespread military use, as has, to a lesser extent, the stretched 206L LongRanger. In Italy, Agusta has built the 206 under licence as the AB 206.

The wheel turned full circle for Bell when in 1967 the US Army reopened the Light Observation Helicopter competition because of the rising costs and late deliveries of the OH-6, and ordered the 206A into production as the OH-58A Kiowa. In all, 2200 Kiowas were delivered to the US Army from May 1968. Many were upgraded to OH-58C standard with an uprated engine. Canada ordered 72 COH-58A Kiowas (subsequently redesignated CH-139), while Austria acquired 12 similar OH-58Bs. Finally Australia's Commonwealth Aircraft Corporation assembled 57 206B-1 Kiowas locally.

The US Navy and Army also use the 206 for pilot training, the former's aircraft (delivered from 1968) designated TH-57 SeaRangers, the latter's, TH-67 Creeks (137 delivered from 1993). Further TH-67s have been delivered to Taiwan and Bulgaria.

**Photo:** Italy flies over 100 AB 206s for reconnaissance and training.

## Bell Kiowa Warrior & Combat Scout

**Country of origin:** United States of America

**Type:** Armed reconnaissance and light attack helicopters

**Powerplant:** OH-58D – One 485kW (650shp) intermediate rating Allison T703-AD-700 (Allison 250-C30R) turboshaft driving a four blade main rotor and two blade tail rotor.

**Performance:** OH-58D Kiowa Warrior – Max level speed at 4000ft 237km/h (128kt), max cruising speed at mission weight 211km/h (114kt), economical cruising speed 204km/h (110kt). Max initial rate of climb 1540ft/min. Service ceiling 15,000ft. Hovering ceiling out of ground effect 4000ft. Range 413km (223nm). Endurance 2hr 24min.

**Weights:** OH-58D Kiowa Warrior – Empty 1492kg (3289lb), max takeoff 2495kg (5500lb).

**Dimensions:** OH-58D – Main rotor diameter 10.67m (35ft 0in), length overall rotors turning 12.85m (42ft 2in), fuselage length 10.48m (34ft 5in), height overall 3.93m (7ft 10in). Main rotor disc area 89.4m² (962.0sq ft).

**Accommodation:** Seating for pilot and observer side-by-side in OH-58D Kiowa and Kiowa Warrior. Seating for five in Combat Scout.

**Armament:** OH-58D Kiowa Warrior – Four Stinger AAMs, or four AGM-114C Hellfire anti armour missiles, two seven round rocket pods, or podded 7.62mm or 0.50in machine guns.

**Operators:** OH-58D – Taiwan, USA. Combat Scout – Saudi Arabia.

**History:** The OH-58D resulted from the US Army's Army Helicopter Improvement Program of 1979 for a relatively low cost scout and observation helicopter to support attack AH-64 Apaches.

The contract for the AHIP was awarded to Bell for a development of the OH-58 Kiowa. The resulting OH-58D Kiowa first flew on October 6 1983. Unlike the fairly basic Kiowa, the OH-58D introduced the McDonnell Douglas Astronautics developed mast mounted sight which features TV and infrared sensors, plus a new, four blade main rotor to enhance performance.

OH-58D deliveries began in December 1985. Initially the US Army planned to convert 592 OH-58A/Cs to OH-58D standard, but the last of 424 conversions were ordered in 1998.

Originally the OH-58D was to be unarmed, but 188 were upgraded to OH-58D Kiowa Warrior status, capable of carrying Stinger AAMs, Hellfire ASMs, rockets and gun pods. The Kiowa Warrior also features uprated transmission, higher max takeoff weight, RWR, IR jammer, laser warning receiver and lightened structure.

The Multi Purpose Light Helicopter (MPLH) modifications which can be fitted to each OH-58D include squatting landing gear and quick folding rotors allowing it to fit into the cargo holds of C-130s and C-141s and be ready to fly 10 minutes after unloading, cargo hook, six outward facing external troop seats or two external medical stretchers.

The abandoned OH-58X with night flying chin turret, colour digital maps, GPS and other improvements flew in 1992. One had some stealth features.

The 406CS Combat Scout is an export version of the OH-58D without the mast mounted sight (instead, Saudi aircraft are fitted with a Saab-Emerson HeliTOW sight) and lacking some sensitive avionics.

**Photo:** A US Army OH-58D Kiowa Warrior. OH-58Ds will eventually be replaced by RAH-66 Comanches.

# Bell AH-1F & AH-1S HueyCobra

**Country of origin:** United States of America

**Type:** Attack helicopter

**Powerplant:** AH-1F – One 1340kW (1800shp) Textron Lycoming T53-L-703 turboshaft driving two blade main and tail rotors.

**Performance:** AH-1F – Max level speed 227km/h (123kt). Max initial rate of climb 1620ft/min. Service ceiling 12,200ft. Hovering ceiling in ground effect 12,200ft. Range 507km (275nm).

**Weights:** AH-1F – Operating empty 2993kg (6598lb), normal takeoff 4525kg (9975lb), max takeoff 4535kg (10,000lb).

**Dimensions:** AH-1F – Main rotor diameter 13.41m (44ft 0in), length overall rotors turning 16.18m (53ft 1in), fuselage length 13.59m (44ft 7in), height to top of rotor head 4.09m (13ft 5in). Main rotor disc area 141.3m² (1520.2sq ft).

**Accommodation:** Copilot/gunner (in front cockpit) and pilot in tandem.

**Armament:** Eight Hughes TOW anti armour missiles on the outboard stations of two stub wings. Can carry rockets and machine gun pods. General Electric nose mounted three barrel 20mm gun.

**Operators:** Bahrain, Israel, Japan, Jordan, Pakistan, South Korea, Thailand, Turkey, USA.

**History:** The HueyCobra was the world's first operational dedicated two seat attack helicopter, initially intended to be an interim design pending the subsequently cancelled Lockheed AH-56 Cheyenne.

The HueyCobra began life as the Bell 209 private venture when in 1965 Bell took the powerplant, transmission and rotor system of the UH-1B/C Iroquois and matched them to a new fuselage featuring seating for two in tandem, stub wings to carry weapons and a nose gun. The prototype first flew on September 7 1965, just six months after design work had begun. The US Army subsequently ordered the 209 into production as the AH-1G HueyCobra to fulfil an urgent need for an attack helicopter primarily to escort troop carrying UH-1 Iroquois in Vietnam, pending delivery of the troubled AH-56. In all 1078 AH-1Gs were built, many of which saw service in Vietnam, while the AH-56 program was cancelled.

The AH-1G was followed up by the AH-1Q, an interim anti armour version capable of firing Hughes TOW anti tank missiles. The Q first flew in 1973, and 92 AH-1Gs were converted to AH-1Q standard. Combat experience found the AH-1Q's hot and high performance lacking, and resulted in the AH-1S. The AH-1S designation covers staged improvements to the AH-1's powerplant and transmission, armament, avionics and cockpit. New build production AH-1Ss and conversions of AH-1Qs and AH-1Gs resulted in four separate AH-1S subvariants, the AH-1S(MC) being the definitive standard incorporating all the planned improvements.

In 1989 the US Army redesignated the AH-1S to reflect the different variants. Thus AH-1F covers the AH-1S(MC), while the AH-1S designation covers AH-1S(MOD) aircraft (converted AH-1Qs), AH-1P covers early build AH-1Ss, and AH-1E covers AH-1Ss with improved weapon systems. AH-1s remain in US service with the National Guard and Army Reserve.

In Japan Fuji built 91 AH-1S models (equivalent to the AH-1F) under licence between 1984 and 2000.

**Photo:** Pakistan's army flies 20 AH-1F Cobras.

# Bell AH-1J & AH-1W SuperCobra

**Country of origin:** United States of America

**Type:** Attack helicopter

**Powerplants:** AH-1W – Two 1285kW (1723shp) General Electric T700-GE-401 turboshafts driving two blade main and tail rotors.

**Performance:** AH-1W – Max level speed 282km/h (152kt), max cruising speed 278km/h (150kt). Max initial rate of climb on one engine 800ft/min. Service ceiling 14,000ft plus. Hovering ceiling in ground effect 14,750ft, out of ground effect 3000ft. Range with standard fuel and no reserves 587km (317nm). Max endurance 2hr 48min.

**Weights:** AH-1W – Empty 4953kg (10,920kg), MTOW 6690kg (14,750lb).

**Dimensions:** AH-1W – Main rotor diameter 14.63m (48ft 0in), length overall rotors turning 17.68m (58ft 0in), fuselage length 13.87m (45ft 6in), height to top of rotor head 4.11m (13ft 6in), height overall 4.44m (14ft 7in). Main rotor disc area 168.1m² (1809.6sq ft).

**Accommodation:** Copilot/gunner (front cockpit) and pilot in tandem.

**Armament:** AH-1W – GE nose turret houses three barrel 20mm M197 gun. Up to eight Hughes TOW or AGM-114 Hellfire anti armour missiles on outboard stations of stub wings, plus rocket or gun pods on inboard stations. Other armament options include fuel air explosives, iron bombs, two AIM-9L AAMs or AGM-122A Sidearm ASMs.

**Operators:** AH-1J – Iran. AH-1W – Taiwan, Turkey, USA.

**History:** The AH-1J and AH-1W are twin engine variants of the Cobra developed originally specifically for the US Marine Corps.

The AH-1 HueyCobra aroused USMC interest early on in its career, and that service's evaluation of the US Army's AH-1G led to a 1968 order for 49 similar AH-1J SeaCobras. The AH-1J was similar to the AH-1G except for the powerplant, the Marines specifying the 1340kW (1800shp) (flat rated to 820kW/1100shp) Pratt & Whitney Canada T400-CP-400, the military version of the PT6T Turbo Twin-Pac, an installation that coupled two PT6 turboshafts through a combining transmission. The AH-1J also introduced the three barrel M197 20mm cannon in the nose turret. Iran also ordered 202 AH-1Js.

The improved AH-1T (initially known as the Improved SeaCobra) was first ordered in 1974 and differed from the J in having a 1470kW (1970shp) T400-WV-402, a new rotor system based on that for the Bell 214, uprated transmission and lengthened fuselage and tail.

The AH-1W started life as a proposal to Iran for an AH-1T powered by two General Electric T700s. A T700 powered demonstrator flew in 1983 designated AH-1T+, and the type, with further improvements, was ordered into production for the USMC as the AH-1W SuperCobra, dubbed Whiskey Cobra.

Aside from new build AH-1Ws, some AH-1Ts were converted to the new configuration. In all the US Marines took delivery of 179 new build AH-1Ws (delivered between 1986 and 1998) and 32 AH-1Ws upgraded from AH-1Ts. New build AH-1Ws have also been exported to Taiwan and Turkey.

Apart from the AH-1Z upgrade described separately, the AH-1Z has also formed the basis of the proposed AH-1RO Dracula and MH-1W variants. The AH-1RO Dracula program for Romania was abandoned in 1999, while the MH-1W is a 'multimission' version offered to South American nations.

**Photo:** A USMC AH-1W. (Robert Wiseman)

# Bell AH-1Z Super Cobra

**Country of origin:** United States of America

**Type:** Attack helicopter

**Powerplants:** Two 1343kW (1800shp) General Electric T700-GE-401C turboshafts driving four blade main and tail rotors.

**Performance:** Max cruising speed 291km/h (157kt). Range with standard fuel and no reserves 685km (370nm). Max endurance 3hr 30min.

**Weights:** Empty 5579kg (12,300lb), max takeoff 8390kg (18,500lb).

**Dimensions:** Fuselage length 13.87m (45ft 6in).

**Accommodation:** Pilot (front cockpit) and gunner/copilot in tandem.

**Armament:** GE nose turret houses three barrel 20mm M197 gun. Up to eight Hughes TOW or AGM-114 Hellfire anti armour missiles on outboard stations of stub wings, plus rocket or gun pods on inboard stations. Other armament options include fuel air explosives, iron bombs, two AIM-9L AAMs or AGM-122A Sidearm ASMs.

**Operators:** USA*

**History:** The AH-1Z is the ultimate development of the long running AH-1 Cobra series of attack helicopters. Bell is developing the AH-1Z upgrade of the AH-1W to extend the Super Cobra's service life with the US Marine Corps.

The US Marine Corps is upgrading its AH-1Ws to four blade AH-1Z Viper configuration under the H-1 upgrade program which also involves upgrading UH-1Ns to four blade and twin T700 powered UH-1Y standard. Compared with the AH-1W the Z (for a time dubbed Viper) features all new four blade bearlingless composite main and tail rotors, an advanced Litton integrated avionics system, and an all new Lockheed Martin Target Sight System comprising FLIR, TV and infrared sensors. It is powered by slightly more powerful -401C model T700s, allowing higher weights and improved performance.

The new avionics system includes twin large 15 x 20cm Rockwell colour liquid crystal multifunction displays in each cockpit (which are near identical with crew functions interchangeable). The integrated avionics system incorporates a digital map system (DMS) capable of providing moving high fidelity three dimensional colour graphic displays and an integrated mission planning system providing flightpath, navigation data, threat rings and 'intervisibility' information for pre-planned and pop up threats.

The crew's BAE Systems Striker Integrated Helmet Mounted Display & Sighting System helmets feature weapon/sensor slaving, and overlays flight data, sensor information, target cueing and weapons status. The cockpits are similarly configured so the AH-1Z can be flown from either crew station.

First flight was on December 7 2000. The USMC is planning to upgrade 180 AH-1Ws to AH-1Zs, with deliveries beginning in 2005 and continuing to 2013/14.

Turkey has selected a development of the AH-1Z, the AH-1Z King Cobra, for its ATAK program. Turkey's selection of the AH-1Z was announced at the 2000 Farnborough Airshow, although at late 2001 a contract had yet to be signed. Turkey plans to buy 145 which will be assembled locally by TAI at Ankara.

**Photo:** The prototype AH-1Z on its December 7 2000 first flight from Bell's Arlington, Texas facilities. (Bell)

# Bell Boeing V-22 Osprey

**Country of origin:** United States of America

**Type:** Tiltrotor tactical transport

**Powerplants:** Two 4590kW (6150shp) takeoff rated Rolls-Royce T406-AD-400 turboshafts driving three blade proprotors.

**Performance:** Max cruising speed in aeroplane mode at sea level 509km/h (275kt), at sea level in helicopter mode 185km/h (100kt). Service ceiling 26,000ft. Amphibious assault range 953km (515nm) Ferry range 3890km (2100nm). Range with a 4535kg (10,000lb) payload and vertical takeoff over 650km (350nm). Range with a 4535kg (10,000lb) payload and short TO over 1760km (950nm).

**Weights:** Empty 15,032kg (33,140lb), mission weight vertical TO 21,545kg (47,500lb), mission weight short TO 24,947kg (55,000lb), MTOW with short TO for self ferry 27,442kg (60,500lb).

**Dimensions:** Proprotor diameter 11.61m (38ft 1in), wing span including nacelles 15.52m (50ft 11in), fuselage length excluding probe 17.47m (57ft 4in), height overall nacelles vertical 6.73m (22ft 1in), height at top of tail fins 5.38m (17ft 8in). Proprotor disc area each 105.8m$^2$ (1139sq ft), wing area 35.5m$^2$ (392.0sq ft).

**Accommodation:** Flightcrew of two plus loadmaster/crew chief. Seating for up to 24 combat equipped troops in main cabin.

**Armament:** None, although special mission aircraft would be armed.

**Operators:** USA*

**History:** The revolutionary V-22 Osprey for the US Marines combines helicopter utility with fixed wing speeds and ranges.

Development of the Osprey dates back to the early 1980s' joint services program to develop a tiltrotor based on the technology of the successful Bell XV-15 demonstrator. The US Navy awarded a teaming of Bell and Boeing an initial development contract in April 1983, while an order for six flying prototypes (later reduced to five) was signed in May 1986. First flight was on March 19 1989.

Since that time the Osprey program has suffered its share of problems, with two of the prototypes crashing, planned production orders reduced and the whole program coming close to cancellation in 1992 as an economy measure.

The first of four production standard EMD V-22s first flew in February 1997, while the first of four low rate initial production MV-22Bs for the USMC was delivered on May 14 1999 – the first of 360 MV-22s for the USMC (to replace CH-46s and CH-53s).

Two fatal MV-22 crashes in 2000 (April and December) endangered the program once more, but limited production was authorised in May 2001 while software and hydraulics modifications are incorporated into the design.

The V-22 features two Rolls-Royce T400 turboshafts (with FADEC) in tilting nacelles. The engines are also linked via a cross-shaft that allows both proprotors to be powered in the event of an engine failure. Other features include 59% composite construction by weight, digital fly-by-wire, four screen EFIS and AAQ-16 FLIR, while the wings can swivel to be parallel to the fuselage for stowage on ships.

The USAF plans to buy 50 special operations CV-22s fitted with long range tanks and APQ-174 terrain following/avoidance radar. The USN dropped plans for a HV-22 Combat SAR variant in 2001.

**Photo:** The fourth EMD V-22.

# Beriev Be-12 Tchaika

**Country of origin:** Russia

**Type:** Maritime patrol and ASW amphibian

**Powerplants:** Two 3125kW (4190ehp) Ivchenko (now Progress) AI-20D turboprops driving four blade propellers.

**Performance:** Max speed 608km/h (328kt), typical patrol speed 320km/h (173kt). Max initial rate of climb 2990ft/min. Service ceiling 37,000ft. Ferry range 7500km (4050nm), range with combat load 4000km (2160nm).

**Weights:** Empty 21,700kg (47,840lb), max takeoff 31,000kg (68,342lb).

**Dimensions:** Wing span 29.71m (97ft 6in), length 30.17m (99ft 0in), height 7.00m (23ft 0in). Wing area 105.0m² (1130.3sq ft).

**Accommodation:** Five crew complement comprises pilot, copilot, navigator, radar operator and MAD operator.

**Armament:** Internal weapons bay and two underwing hardpoints can carry a variety of weaponry incl torpedoes, depth charges and mines.

**Operators:** Russia, Ukraine.

**History:** One of the few amphibians in military service, the Tchaika (or gull) remains in Russian naval aviation service performing close-in maritime patrol, ASW and SAR work.

The Be-12 (NATO name 'Mail') was developed as a replacement for the earlier piston powered Be-6, which first flew in 1949. The turboprop Be-12 first flew during 1960, and made its public debut at the 1961 Soviet Aviation Day Display at Tushino, Moscow.

The Be-12 was of the same basic configuration as the smaller Be-6, with twin tails and a high cranked wing to give the propellers and engines maximum clearance from the water. Other Be-12 features include the powerful Ivchenko AI-20D turboprops (AI-20s also power the land based Il-38 'May' maritime patrol and ASW aircraft), a stepped hull with spray dams along the nose to minimise engine water ingestion, retractable undercarriage, a nose mounted search radar and tail mounted Magnetic Anomaly Detector (MAD) boom.

The Be-12 was selected for Soviet naval service in 1964 ahead of another Beriev design, the jet powered Be-10. The Be-10 established a number of seaplane world records, but only three or four are thought to have been built, mainly for trials purposes. The Be-12 itself set or broke all 44 FAI (Federation Aeronautique Internationale) records covering turboprop powered amphibians and seaplanes between 1964 and 1983.

Exact production of the Be-12 is unknown, but is thought to have run to around 100 aircraft. The main role of the Be-12 is ASW and maritime patrol within 370km (200nm) of shore bases, however Be-12s have performed a variety of different tasks including Arctic and Siberian exploration and resource exploration, geophysical mapping and search and rescue.

While the brunt of Russian ASW and maritime patrol tasks are now borne by the Il-38 and Tu-142, Be-12s are still in service with the Russian northern fleet. About 12 are on strength. Ukraine has about 14 in service.

Some were also in service in Vietnam until recently.

**Photo:** An ex Russian navy Be-12 used by Beriev to serve as a demonstrator firebomber for civil/government use. (Sebastian Zacharias)

# Beriev A-40 & Be-42 Albatross

**Country of origin:** Russia

**Type:** Maritime patrol & ASW (A-40) and SAR (Be-42) amphibian

**Powerplants:** A-40 – Two 117.7kN (26,455lb) Aviadvigatel D-30KPV turbofans and two 24.5kN (5510lb) RKBM (formerly Klimov) RD-60K booster turbojets.

**Performance:** A-40 – Max level speed 760km/h (410kt), max cruising speed 720km/h (388kt). Max initial rate of climb on one engine 5900ft/min. Service ceiling 31,825ft. Range with max payload 4100km (2210nm), range with max fuel 5500km (2965nm).

**Weights:** A-40 – Max payload 6500kg (14,330lb), max takeoff 86,000kg (189,595lb).

**Dimensions:** A-40 – Wing span 41.62m (136ft 7in), length incl nose probe 43.84m (143ft 10in), fuselage length 38.92m (127ft 8in), height 11.07m (36ft 4in). Wing area 200.0m² (2153sq ft).

**Accommodation:** A-40 – Crew complement of eight consisting of pilot, copilot, flight engineer, radio operator, navigator/observer and three observers. Be-42 – Flightcrew of five, plus three medical attendants, and accommodation for 54 rescued survivors.

**Armament:** A-40 – Internal weapons bay could carry a range of weapons maritime such as torpedoes, mines and depth charges. Be-42 – None.

**Operators:** Russia*

**History:** The Beriev Albatross is the world's largest amphibious aircraft and was designed, initially at least, to replace the Be-12 and Il-38 in maritime patrol and ASW roles.

Design work on the Albatross (NATO identification name 'Mermaid') began in 1983, but it was not publicly known in the West until 1988 when the US announced it had taken satellite photographs of a jet powered amphibian under development in Russia. The Albatross made its first flight in December 1986, while its first public appearance was a fly-by at the 1989 Soviet Aviation Day Display at Tushino, Moscow.

The exact future of the Albatross remains in some doubt. Russia's navy has had a long standing provisional order for 20 maritime patrol A-40 Albatrosses, but a lack of funding has prevented this being converted to a firm order.

Other versions of the aircraft include the Be-42, which is optimised for search and rescue, and the proposed twin propfan powered A-45, Be-40P 105 seat airliner and Be-40PT combi airliner/freighter. The aircraft also forms the basis of the slightly smaller civil Be-200 (first flight September 1998), which is being promoted for various missions including firefighting.

Albatross design features include its unique 'variable rise' single step hull, which is designed to improve stability and controllability in the water, and a unique powerplant combination of two D-30KPV turbofans with a booster turbojet in each of the engine pylons.

The Be-42 SAR aircraft would be able to take 54 survivors of a marine accident and would be equipped with liferafts, powerboats and a range of specialised medical equipment including a transfusion machine, defibrillator and ECG. It would also be equipped with various infrared sensors and a searchlight.

**Photo:** The A-40, the world's largest amphibious aircraft. The project appeared moribund in 2001.

## Beriev/Ilyushin A-50

**Country of origin:** Russia

**Type:** Airborne Early Warning & Control aircraft

**Powerplants:** Four 117.7kN (26,455lb) Aviadvigatel (Soloviev) D-30KP turbofans.

**Performance:** A-50U – Max speed 785km/h (425kt). Service ceiling 34,440ft. Range 5100km (2753nm). Endurance 1000km (540nm) from base 4hr. Generally operates at 33,000ft flying figure-of-eight search tracks, with 100km (54nm) between the centre of each orbit.

**Weights:** A-50U – Empty 119,000kg (262,350lb), max takeoff 190,000kg (418,875lb).

**Dimensions:** Wing span 50.50m (165ft 8in), length 46.59m (152ft 10in), height 14.76m (48ft 5in). Wing area 300.0m$^2$ (3229.2sq ft).

**Accommodation:** Crew of 15, comprising five flightcrew and 10 systems operators.

**Armament:** None

**Operators:** India*, Russia

**History:** Beriev developed the A-50 (NATO name 'Mainstay') to replace Russia's first operational AEW&C aircraft, the Tupolev Tu-126 'Moss' (a conversion of the turboprop powered Tu-114 airliner).

Development of an improved AEW&C aircraft began in 1969, and ultimately resulted in the Liana radar equipped A-50, which first flew on December 19 1978. The A-50 is based on the Ilyushin Il-76MD transport, and features a large E-3 Sentry-style rotating rotodome mounted above the fuselage housing the search radar.

Other external features include a nose mounted refuelling probe (although refuelling is difficult because of buffeting caused by the rotodome in the tanker's slipstream), horizontal blade antennas mounted on each main undercarriage fairing, no nose glazing, a dorsal fin forward of the wing, an intake in the root of the tail to supply air to cool avionics, and a number of smaller antennas.

The A-50 entered service in 1984 and 24 were delivered. These have since been replaced by or upgraded to the improved A-50U standard. The A-50U first appeared in 1995 and features the improved Vega-M Shmel-II radar which can detect fighter sized targets at ranges of 230km (125nm). Inside 10 operators can track up to 50 targets simultaneously.

In 1999 IAI installed an Elta phased array radar in a non rotating, above fuselage radome in an A-50I, which was being developed as a candidate to meet a Chinese requirement for four AEW aircraft. Other features would have included Israeli ESM, Elint and comint systems (as on the IAI Phalcon 707 conversion). However US pressure on Israel saw this program cancelled in mid 2000.

In 2001 Beriev and IAI are understood to have reached agreement to build three A-50EhI aircraft for India. These will feature the Elta phased array radar and be based on new build, PS-90A powered Il-76TDs.

Iraq independently developed two AEW versions of the Il-76. The failed Baghdad 1 featured a Thomson-CSF radar mounted in the lower tail, while the Adnan conversion features a rotodome above the fuselage. Of the three Adnans converted, one was destroyed on the ground during the Gulf War.

**Photo:** A Russian air force A-50U. Twenty-one A-50Us are currently in service at Ivanovo.(Sebastian Zacharias)

## Boeing B-52 Stratofortress

**Country of origin:** United States of America

**Type:** Strategic bomber

**Powerplants:** B-52H – Eight 75.6kN (17,000lb) Pratt & Whitney TF33-P-3 turbofans.

**Performance:** B-52H – Max speed Mach 0.90 or 957km/h (516kt), cruising speed 820km/h (442kt), low level penetration speed 650 to 675km/h (352 to 365kt). Service ceiling 55,000ft. Range with max fuel without inflight refuelling over 16,095km (8685nm).

**Weights:** B-52H – Empty 78,355kg (172,740lb), max takeoff 229,088kg (505,000lb).

**Dimensions:** B-52H – Wing span 56.39m (185ft 0in), length 49.05m (160ft 11in), height 12.40m (40ft 8in). Wing area 371.6m$^2$ (4000sq ft).

**Accommodation:** B-52H – Crew complement of five, comprising aircraft commander, pilot, radar navigator, navigator and electronic warfare officer.

**Armament:** B-52H – In nuclear strike role can be fitted with 20 AGM-86B ALCMs or AGM-129 cruise missiles in the internal bomb bay and two underwing stations. Can be fitted with free fall nuclear bombs. Conventional munitions include up to 12 AGM-84 Harpoon or AGM-142A ASMs, AGM-86C CALCM cruise missiles, JDAMs, or up to 51 750lb (340kg) class bombs or mines.

**Operators:** USA

**History:** The mighty B-52 began life in the 1940s as a proposed replacement for Strategic Air Command's B-36s and B-50s.

Originally the B-52 was to be powered by turboprops as they promised the best compromise between high performance and long range, but the availability of the Pratt & Whitney J57 turbojet (which offered a quantum leap forward in performance and economy over earlier jets) resulted in the definitive eight jet arrangement. The prototype XB-52 first flew on April 15 1952. Successful evaluation of the B-52 led to the first production contracts and an entry into service in March 1955.

In all, 744 B-52s were built through to 1962 in eight major subtypes, the most important numerically being the B-52D (which saw extensive use as a conventional bomber in Vietnam), the B-52G which introduced a shorter vertical tail, remote control tail guns and a wet wing, and the B-52H with turbofan engines.

While all versions of the B-52 were progressively upgraded throughout their service lives to keep pace with new roles, mission profiles and technologies, the only model now in service is the TF33 turbofan powered B-52H (the switch to more economical turbofan engines increased the B-52's range by a third). The B-52H also introduced a tail mounted 20mm cannon, although this is no longer used. B-52H features include a terrain following radar, comprehensive ECM protection and Electro-Optical Viewing System.

About 76 B-52Hs were on strength in 2001, and the USAF intends to keep the type in its fleet until 2045 (when the youngest airframe will be about 80 years old!). ECM and limited avionics (INS, new processors and software) upgrades are underway, while Boeing is studying a glass cockpit. Link 16 datalink and EHF comms upgrades are planned, as is the ability to carry JSOW and JASSM weapons.

B-52s were used extensively against the Taliban in Afghanistan in 2001.

**Photo:** A USAF B-52H – a symbol of US military might. (USAF)

# Boeing KC-135 Stratotanker

**Country of origin:** United States of America

**Type:** Air-to-air refuelling tanker

**Powerplants:** KC-135R – Four 97.9kN (22,000lb) CFM F108 turbofans.

**Performance:** KC-135R – Max speed 982km/h (530kt), cruising speed at 35,000ft 855km/h (462kt). Max initial rate of climb 1290ft/min. Service ceiling 45,000ft. Operational radius 4635km (2500nm).

**Weights:** KC-135R – Operating empty 48,220kg (106,305lb), max takeoff 146,285kg (322,500lb).

**Dimensions:** Wing span 39.88m (130ft 10in), length 41.53m (136ft 3in), height 12.70m (41ft 8in). Wing area 226.0m² (2433.0sq ft).

**Accommodation:** Standard crew complement for tanking of four, comprising pilot, copilot, navigator and boom operator. Fuel capacity 92,210kg (203,288lb). No navigator on Pacer Crag upgraded -135s.

**Armament:** None

**Operators:** France, Singapore, Turkey, USA.

**History:** The KC-135 Stratotanker is a very significant aircraft. It paved the way for Boeing's unparalleled success as the world's premier jet airliner manufacturer, while also considerably boosting the USAF's ability to conduct war by substantially increasing aircraft range through air-to-air refuelling.

In the early 1950s Boeing made the bold decision to build as a private venture a four jet engined transport that could be developed into an airliner, but also meet a USAF requirement for an inflight refuelling tanker with jet aircraft speeds. The resulting 367-80 demonstrator first flew on July 15 1954. Just one month later the USAF ordered it into production as the KC-135 Stratotanker inflight refueller with a Boeing developed flying boom. Features of the KC-135A included four J57 turbojets, fuel in belly and wing tanks and a side loading cargo door for freight on the main deck.

Some 820 KC-135s and C-135 variants were built, giving Boeing considerable experience in building jet transports, with the KC-135 forming the basis for the 707 airliner.

Aside from the KC-135A, 45 C-135 Stratolifter transports were built without tanking equipment, pending the delivery of the Lockheed C-141 Starlifter. A handful survive as transports in support roles with special USAF units. The KC-135Q designation applies to 56 KC-135As modified to refuel SR-71s (later re-engined with F108s as KC-135Ts), while France took delivery of 12 C-135F tankers (also later re-engined with F108s as C-135FRs).

The KC-135 has been the subject of two major re-engining programs. Over 160 Air Force Reserve and Air National Guard KC-135s were re-engined with TF33 turbofans sourced from retired 707 airliners as KC-135Es. The KC-135R designation applies to KC-135s re-engined with CFM International F108 (CFM56) turbofans. Over 440 KC-135Rs have been delivered. The USAF continues to upgrade KC-135s with EFIS and digital avionics under the Pacer Crag program, while 45 were modified with wingtip hose and drogue pods.

Both turbofan re-engining programs significantly increase the KC-135's takeoff performance, range and fuel offload capabilities, and, particularly in the case of the KC-135R, make it significantly quieter. All KC-135As that were not re-engined have been retired.

**Photo:** Singapore operates four KC-135Rs. (Murray Permain)

# Boeing RC-135 Rivet Joint

**Country of origin:** United States of America

**Type:** Intelligence aircraft

**Powerplants:** Four 80.1kN (18,000lb) Pratt & Whitney TF33-P-9 or 97.9kN (22,000lb) CFM F108 turbofans.

**Performance:** Similar to KC-135.

**Weights:** Similar to KC-135.

**Dimensions:** Wingspan 39.88m (130ft 10in), length 42.85m (140ft 6in), height 12.70m (41 ft 8in). Wing area 226.0m² (2433.0sq ft).

**Accommodation:** Rivet Joint crew of up to 30 consists of two pilots, navigators, electronic warfare officers, inflight maintenance technicians and intelligence staff.

**Armament:** None

**Operators:** USA

**History:** The basic C-135 airframe forms the basis of a prolific family of variants, including the command post EC-135 (now retired) and electronic reconnaissance RC-135 Rivet Joint.

The EC-135 was originally developed to serve as an airborne command post for the then Strategic Air Command's B-52 nuclear bomber fleet, and some 40 C-135s were converted as EC-135s at various stages. The last EC-135C 'Looking Glass' command post aircraft retired in 1998, their missions taken over by the US Navy's Boeing E-6B Mercury platform. The EC-135E range instrumentation aircraft was retired in 2000.

The RC-135V and RC-135W Rivet Joint signals intelligence platforms remain a very important part of the USA's intelligence gathering assets. Rivet Joints feature a distinctive thimble (or hog) nose housing sensors, plus slab sided cheek fairings covering the antennas for the Automatic Elint Emitter Locator System (AEELS) which intercepts transmissions on a broad range of frequencies and sorts out those which may be of interest to the aircraft's back end operators.

The USAF is re-engining its Rivet Joints with CFM F108s (as on the KC-135R) to improve fuel economy and extend service life. The first re-engined RC-135V Rivet Joint flew in 1999 and was handed over to its operating unit, the 55th Wing at Offut AFB, Nebraska, in 2001.

The 55th took on its 16 Rivet Joint RC-135s in March 2000. Apart from Offutt, flights are conducted from Kadena AB, Japan; RAF Mildenhall, UK; Souda Bay Naval Support Activity, Crete; and other locations around the world. The Rivet Joints provide direct, near real-time reconnaissance information and electronic warfare support to theatre commanders and combat forces. Its passive sensors gather imagery intelligence (Imint), telemetry intelligence (Telint), and signals intelligence (Sigint).

The RC-135S Cobra Ball records foreign missile launches and testing and may be used tactically for ballistic missile launch detection.

The NC-135 and NKC-135 designations applied to aircraft used for various test and trials purposes, including inflight refuelling tests. An NKC-135B Big Crow has taken on the ARIA airborne telemetry role for missile testing from the retired EC-135E and EC-18 platforms.

Other variants on the C-135 theme include the WC-135M weather research platform and the OC-135 for Open Skies treaty verification reconnaissance with panoramic, oblique and vertical cameras.

**Photo:** An RC-135W Rivet Joint. (Paul Merritt)

# Boeing 707

**Country of origin:** United States of America

**Type:** Strategic & VIP transport, tanker and special mission aircraft

**Powerplants:** 707-320B – Four 80kN (18,000lb) Pratt & Whitney JT3D-3 turbofans or four 84.4kN (19,000lb) P&W JT3D-7s.

**Performance:** 707-320B – Max speed 1010km/h (545kt), max cruising speed 974km/h (525kt), long range cruising speed 885km/h (478kt). Max initial rate of climb 4000ft/min. Range with max passenger load 6920km (3735nm), range with max fuel and 147 passengers and reserves 9265km (5000nm).

**Weights:** 707-320B – Empty 66,408kg (146,400lb), max takeoff 151,315kg (333,600lb).

**Dimensions:** 707-320B – Wing span 44.42m (145ft 9in), length 46.61m (152ft 11in), height 12.94m (42ft 5in). Wing area 283m$^2$ (3050sq ft).

**Accommodation:** Flightcrew of two pilots and flight engineer. In passenger service could seat up to 190 passengers. Alternatively can carry freight on main deck in freighter and combi versions.

**Armament:** None

**Operators:** Angola, Argentina, Australia, Brazil, Chile, Colombia, Germany, India, Indonesia, Israel, Italy, Morocco, NATO, Pakistan, Paraguay, Peru, South Africa, Spain, Togo, Venezuela, Yugoslavia.

**History:** Boeing's first jet airliner, the 707 has been widely adapted for military service.

Boeing's 707 was based on the Model 367-80 jet transport prototype, which first flew on July 15 1954. The 367-80 or Dash 80 demonstrator led to the KC-135 tanker and then the larger 707 airliner. The 707 first flew on December 20 1957 and entered service the next year. Compared with the KC-135, the initial 707-120 featured a wider, longer fuselage. Power was supplied by JT3 turbojets, the commercial equivalent of the J57.

Military 707s are all 707-320Bs or 320Cs. The -320 differs from the original -120 in having four JT3D turbofan engines (equivalent to the TF33) and a stretched fuselage. The passenger 707-320B and the 707-320C convertible passenger/freighter aircraft are the definitive 707 models and were delivered to airlines around the world between 1962 and 1977. Most military 707s are ex civilian aircraft, although Canada, Germany and Iran purchased new build 707s direct from Boeing (the Iranian aircraft were delivered with KC-135 style refuelling booms and Beech probe and drogue wingtip pods).

Aside from Iran, many other 707 operators have fitted their 707s with air-to-air refuelling equipment. Australia, Brazil, Israel, Italy, Morocco, Peru, Spain and Venezuela all operate 707 tankers.

Israel has adopted the 707 for Elint and AEW missions. Some serve as command posts, others combined tanker/Elint aircraft. The AEW Phalcon is the most extensive non US military development of the 707, with Elbit phased array radar mounted in a nose radome and conformal cheeks along the sides of the fuselage. Aside from Israel, Chile operates a single Phalcon.

The USAF retired its two 707 based bulbous nosed range instrumentation EC-18 ARIA platforms in 2000.

Pratt & Whitney offers the 707RE re-engined upgrade with 97kN (21,650lb) JT8D-219s. A demonstrator first flew in August 2001.

**Photo:** A Spanish 707 tanker transport. (Lassi Tolvanen)

# Boeing E-3 Sentry

**Country of origin:** United States of America

**Type:** Airborne Warning & Control System (AWACS) aircraft

**Powerplants:** E-3A/C – Four 93.4kN (21,000lb) Pratt & Whitney TF33-P-100 turbofans. E-3D/F – Four 106.8kN (24,000lb) CFM56-2A-3s.

**Performance:** E-3C – Max speed 853km/h (460kt). Service ceiling over 29,000ft. Operational radius 1610km (870nm) for a 6 hour patrol without inflight refuelling. Endurance without inflight refuelling over 11 hours. E-3D/F – Endurance without refuelling over 10 hours.

**Weights:** E-3C – Operating empty 77,995kg (171,950lb), max takeoff 147,420kg (325,000lb). E-3D – Max takeoff 150,820kg (332,500lb).

**Dimensions:** E-3A/C/F – Wing span 44.42m (145ft 9in), length 46.61m (152ft 11in), height 12.73m (41ft 9in). Wing area 283.4m$^2$ (3050.0sq ft). E-3D – Same except wing span 44.98m (147ft 7in).

**Accommodation:** E-3C/D/F – Total crew complement of 17.

**Armament:** None.

**Operators:** France, NATO, Saudi Arabia, UK, USA.

**History:** The E-3 is a flying command post which detects enemy aircraft and missiles and controls friendly aircraft.

The 707 based Sentry was developed as a replacement for the Lockheed EC-121 Warning Star. Development resulted in the first flight of a prototype EC-137 on February 5 1972. The first operational E-3A Sentry was delivered in March 1977.

The basis of the Sentry's detection abilities is the massive Westinghouse (now Northrop Grumman) APY-1 (first 25 aircraft) or APY-2 radar in the rotodome mounted above the rear fuselage. The rotodome rotates six times per minute and can be operated in various modes such as over the horizon, pulse Doppler scan, passive and maritime. The APY-2 is capable of tracking up to 600 low flying aircraft at one time. The Radar System Improvement Program is enhancing detection abilities against low radar cross section targets.

Internally the E-3 is equipped with operator stations for the radar and comms suite, galley, rest area and bunks for rest/relief crew.

The USAF's original EC-137s and 22 E-3A Core aircraft were upgraded to E-3B Block 20 standard with a maritime surveillance capability, provision for self defence measures, ECM resistant communications equipment, more UHF radios, five more operator stations and a more powerful central computer. A later upgrade was for 10 E-3A Standards to E-3C Block 25 level with more operator consoles, more UHF radios and provision for Have Quick anti jamming radio.

NATO operates 18 E-3A Standard Sentries, while Saudi Arabia took delivery of five E-3A Standards powered by CFM56 engines plus eight KE-3A tankers without AWACS equipment. British E-3D Sentry AEW.1s and French E-3Fs are powered by CFM56s and have a refuelling probe, while E-3Ds have wingtip mounted Loral ESM pods.

Boeing has developed a Multi Stage Improvement Program which involves upgrading the communications suite, fitting GPS, upgrading the radar and the central computer. Additionally, US and NATO E-3s are being fitted with ESM sensors in side mounted canoe type fairings. Boeing is also studying offering the E-3 with the Next Generation 737's modern EFIS two crew cockpit. NATO plans to re-engine its E-3s, either with CFM56s or JT8D-200s.

**Photo:** A NATO E-3. (Paul Merritt)

**Country of origin:** United States of America

**Type:** E-6 – Submarine communications and command post aircraft. EC-18 – Range instrumentation & cruise missile control aircraft

**Powerplants:** E-6A – Four 97.9kN (22,000lb) CFM International F108-CF-100 turbofans.

**Performance:** E-6A – Dash speed 980km/h (530kt), max cruising speed at 40,000ft 842km/h (455kt). Patrol altitude between 25,000 and 30,000ft. Service ceiling 42,000ft. Mission range without inflight refuelling 11,760km (6350nm). Radius 1855km (1000nm) on a 10hr 30min flight without refuelling, or 28hr 55min with one refuelling, or 72hr with multiple refuellings. Unrefuelled endurance 15hr 25min.

**Weights:** E-6A – Operating empty 78,378kg (172,795lb), max takeoff 155,130kg (342,000lb).

**Dimensions:** Wing span 45.16m (148ft 2in), length 46.61m (152ft 11in), height 12.93m (42ft 5in). Wing area 283.4m² (3050.0sq ft).

**Accommodation:** E-6A – Flightcrew of four. Has eight bunks in rest area for relief crew and four communications work stations.

**Armament:** None

**Operators:** USA

**History:** The 707 based E-6 Mercury was developed as a communications relay aircraft for the US Navy, but subsequently also took over the USAF's 'Looking Glass' airborne command post mission.

Boeing developed the E-6 for the US Navy as a replacement for EC-130Q TACAMO (TAke Charge And Move Out) Hercules. Sixteen new build aircraft E-6As were developed to provide a communications link between the US national command structure, other command post aircraft such as the E-4 and the US Navy's submarine fleet – primarily ballistic nuclear missile armed submarines.

The E-6 (initially named Hermes) is powered by CFM F108 turbofans and is equipped with a comprehensive secure communications suite, including HF, VHF and UHF radio comms and UHF satellite comms (two underwing pods house ESM receivers and the UHF satellite antennas). The aircraft is also equipped with two trailing wire antennas. First flight was on February 19 1987 and first delivery in 1989.

The E-6As are currently being upgraded by Raytheon to E-6B standard for the airborne command post role. The E-6B upgrade includes transplanting EC-135 equipment including UHF C3FDM radios and Digital Airborne Intercommunications Switching System, battlestaff operator consoles and an Airborne Launch Control System (ALCS), giving it the capability to launch US land based intercontinental ballistic missiles. The E-6B is easily identified via its large satcom antenna mounted on the fuselage in a bulged fairing.

The USN accepted its first E-6B in December 1997 and the type formally took over the USAF's EC-135 Looking Glass's airborne command post role in September 1998.

A further four 707 airframes are being upgraded to E-6B standard (including two ex USAF EC-18 ARIA airframes) taking the total E-6B fleet to 20. All E-6Bs will also be upgraded to feature new glass cockpits, based on that in Boeing's Next Generation 737 airliner, allowing the aircraft to comply with Global Air Traffic Management (GATM) requirements.

**Photo:** An E-6B Mercury. (Tim Dath)

**Country of origin:** United States of America

**Type:** Passenger and VIP transport

**Powerplants:** C-22B/727-100 – Three 62.3kN (14,000lb) Pratt & Whitney JT8D-7 turbofans.

**Performance:** C-22B/727-100 – Max speed 1017km/h (550kt), max cruising speed 960km/h (518kt). Range with max payload 5000km (2700nm).

**Weights:** C-22B/727-100 – Empty equipped 36,560kg (80,600lb), max takeoff 72,570kg (160,000lb).

**Dimensions:** C-22B/727-100 – Wing span 39.92m (108ft 0in), length 40.59m (133ft 2in), height 10.36m (34ft 0in). Wing area 157.9m² (1700sq ft).

**Accommodation:** C-22B/727-100 – Flightcrew of three (two pilots and flight engineer). Typical two class 727-100 airline seating for 94, max seating for 131. Most are configured with customised VIP/presidential transport interiors. C-22Bs configured to seat 90, including 24 in first class leather seats. All seats face rearwards.

**Armament:** None

**Operators:** 727-100 – Belgium, Congo, Mexico, Panama, New Zealand, Taiwan. 727-200 – Cameroon, Nigeria, Senegal. C-22 – USA.

**History:** Boeing's 727 trijet has been highly successful as an airliner, although only a small number have seen military service.

The 727 began life as a short to medium range medium capacity airliner to slot beneath Boeing's four engined 707 (described separately) and 720. Initial design studies began as early as 1956, and the resulting Model 727, which first flew on February 9 1963, featured three engines (for good field performance), the 707's fuselage cross section but with a redesigned lower fuselage, and limited commonality with the 707 and 720. The first 727 was delivered in February 1964. Relatively slow initial sales led Boeing to develop various sub variants with higher gross weight options, plus the 727-100C Convertible and 727-200QC Quick Change.

The stretched 727-200 was announced in August 1965 in response to demand for a higher capacity model. The 6.10m (20ft) stretch involved equal length plugs fore and aft of the main undercarriage, but no increased fuel capacity, adversely affecting range. This was addressed with the higher gross weight and longer range Advanced 727-200, which entered service in June 1971. The 727-200F freighter flew in 1983 and was the last variant of this highly successful airliner.

While its success as an airliner is almost without parallel (over 1800 were built), only a small number have filtered down into military service. Nevertheless a number of nations use 727-100s for passenger transport, some equipped with customised VIP or presidential/head of state interiors.

The US Air National Guard at Andrews AFB operates three ex airline 727-100s as C-22B staff transports for the National Guard and Air National Guard (a single ex Lufthansa 727-100 C-22A was retired). A single ex Singapore Airlines 727-200 was also operated, designated C-22C.

The USAF is buying Boeing C-40Bs (737-700QCs) to replace the C-22Bs from August 2003.

**Photo:** A US Air National Guard C-22B. (Dave Fraser)

## Boeing 737, CT-43, & Surveiller

**Country of origin:** United States of America

**Type:** 737 – VIP and general transport. CT-43 – Navigation trainer. Surveiller – Maritime reconnaissance/transport

**Powerplants:** 737-200 – Two 64.5kN (14,500lb) Pratt & Whitney JT8D-9A turbofans, or two 69.0kN (15,500lb) JT8D-15s, or two 71.2kN (16,000lb) JT8D-17s, or two 77.4kN (17,400lb) JT8D-17Rs.

**Performance:** 737-200 – Max speed 943km/h (509kt), max cruising speed 927km/h (500kt), economical cruising speed 795km/h (430kt). Max initial rate of climb 3760ft/min. Range with 115 passengers and reserves between 3520km (1900nm) and 4260km (2300nm) depending on weight options and engines.

**Weights:** 737-200 – Operating empty 27,690kg (61,050lb), max take-off 58,105kg (128,100lb).

**Dimensions:** 737-200 – Wing span 28.35m (93ft 0in), length 30.48m (100ft 0in), height 11.28m (37ft 0in). Wing area 91.1m² (980sq ft).

**Accommodation:** Flight crew of two pilots. CT-43 – Configured for 12 students, four advanced students and three instructors. Surveiller – Indonesia's 737s fitted with 14 first class and 88 economy seats.

**Armament:** None

**Operators:** 737 – Brazil, Chile, India, Kuwait, Mexico, Niger, Pakistan, Peru, South Korea, Taiwan, UAE, Venezuela. CT-43 – USA. Surveiller – Indonesia.

**History:** Boeing's 737 is the world's most successful jet airliner in terms of sales, with over 5000 of all variants sold. A small number of these are in military service as transports, while the 737 also forms the basis of the USAF's CT-43 navigation trainer, and is in use for maritime patrol duties with Indonesia.

The 737 was conceived as a short range small capacity airliner. Announcing the project in February 1965, Boeing originally envisaged the 737 as seating 60 to 85, although a 100 seater was settled upon.

The first 737-100 made its first flight on April 9 1967. Further development led to the stretched 737-200, which became the main production model through to the mid 1980s. The -200 was replaced by the CFM International CFM56 powered 110 seat 737-500, 130 seat 737-300 and 145 seat 737-400.

Further development in the mid 1990s led to the similarly sized Next Generation 737s, the 737-600, -700 and -800, plus the further stretched 737-900, with new glass cockpits and other improvements. The BBJ and military developments of the Next Generation 737 – the 737 AEW&C and C-40A – are described separately.

The US Air Force took delivery of 19 T-43 navigation trainers from mid 1973. These aircraft are based on the 737-200 with the specialised trainer featuring accommodation for 12 student navigators, four advanced student navigators and three instructors. Navigation stations are fitted along the starboard side of the fuselage. The T-43 was later redesignated CT-43, reflecting the fact that many of these aircraft also have a secondary passenger transport role.

Indonesia operates three 737-200 Surveillers for maritime reconnaissance, fitted with a Motorola Side Looking Airborne Modular Multi Mission Radar, with antennas fitted in blade fairings on the rear upper fuselage. Other military 737s operate in VIP and staff transport roles.

**Photo:** A Chilean air force 737-500.

## Boeing BBJ & C-40

**Country of origin:** United States of America

**Type:** BBJ – VIP transport. C-40 – Multirole transport

**Powerplants:** Two 117.4kN (26,400lb) CFM International CFM56-7 turbofans.

**Performance:** BBJ – Max cruising speed Mach 0.82, normal cruising speed Mach 0.80, long range cruising speed Mach 0.79. Initial cruise altitude 38,000ft, max certificated altitude 41,000ft. Range with eight passengers 11,480km (6200nm), with 25 passengers 11,075km (5980nm), with 50 passengers 10,205km (5510nm).

**Weights:** BBJ – Typical operating empty 42,895kg (94,570lb), max takeoff 77,560kg (171,000lb).

**Dimensions:** BBJ – Wing span incl winglets 35.79m (117ft 5in), length 33.63m (110ft 4in), height 12.05m (41ft 2in). Wing area 125.0m² (1345.5sq ft).

**Accommodation:** Flightcrew of two. BBJ – Main cabin interiors to customer preference. Typical configuration includes a crew rest area, forward lounge, private suite with double bed and private bathroom facilities including shower, 12 first class sleeper seats at four abreast and 152cm (60in) pitch, and rear galley and bathroom facilities.

**Armament:** None

**Operators:** BBJ – Australia*, South Africa. C-40 – USA*.

**History:** Boeing's BBJ (or Boeing Business Jet) is beginning to find favour as a VIP transport, while the C-40 is a passenger/freight transport development of the 737-700 airframe.

Boeing Business Jets is a joint venture formed by Boeing and General Electric in July 1996 to develop and market a corporate version of the popular 737 airliner, initially focusing on the 737-700 based BBJ (or 737-700BBJ). The first BBJ rolled out from Boeing's Renton plant on August 11 1998 and flew on September 4 that year. On October 30 the US FAA awarded certification to the developed 737-700 airframe on which the BBJ is based. The first completed BBJ was delivered on September 4 1999.

The BBJ combines the Next Generation 737-700's airframe combined with the strengthened wing, fuselage centre section and landing gear of the larger and heavier 737-800, with three to 10 belly auxiliary fuel tanks. It features the Next Generation 737 flightdeck with six LCD screens, equipped with embedded dual GPS, TCAS, enhanced GPWS and head-up displays. Winglets became a standard option following certification in September 2000.

Both Australia and South Africa have ordered BBJs for VIP duties.

The BBJ airframe also forms the basis for the C-40A Clipper ordered by the US Navy (to replace C-9s) and Air National Guard's C-40B (to replace C-22s). The C-40A features a forward main deck freight door, and can be configured for freight or personnel transport. (Boeing's model designation is 737-700QC). The first C-40A delivery to the US Navy was in April 2001. The first Air National Guard C-40B is scheduled to be delivered in August 2003.

The larger BBJ 2 was launched in October 1999 and is based on the stretched 737-800 airframe, offering 25% greater cabin space (and 100% more baggage space) but has slightly reduced range. It is fitted with between three and seven auxiliary belly fuel tanks.

**Photo:** A US Navy C-40A Clipper. (Paul Merritt)

# Boeing 737 AEW&C

**Country of origin:** United States of America

**Type:** Airborne Early Warning & Control platform

**Powerplants:** Two 117.4kN (26,400lb) CFM International CFM56-7 turbofans.

**Performance:** Dash speed 850km/h (460kt), transit/cruising speed 740km/h (400kt), loiter speed 555 to 640km/h (300 to 345kt). Operating altitude 29,000ft. Time on station 555km (300nm) from base 8hr. Range over 5560km (3000nm).

**Weights:** Max takeoff 77,564kg (171,000lb).

**Dimensions:** Wing span 33.63m (110ft 4in), length 31.24m (102ft 6in), height 12.58m (41ft 3in). Wing area 125.0m² (1344sq ft).

**Accommodation:** Flightcrew of two. Six 'common console' operator stations in main cabin.

**Armament:** None

**Operators:** Australia*, Turkey*.

**History:** The 737 AEW&C is a development of the 737-700 airliner, due to enter service with launch customer Australia in 2006.

The 737 AEW&C is based on Boeing's Next Generation 737 family. Compared with earlier 737 models the Next Generation family features more fuel efficient CFM56-7 turbofans, a new wing, larger area tail surfaces and a modern EFIS flightdeck with six flat panel LCDs. The 737 AEW&C itself is based on the airframe of the 737 BBJ (Boeing Business Jet – described separately), which combines the 737-700's fuselage with the stretched 737-800's strengthened wing and undercarriage. The BBJ first flew on September 4 1998.

Boeing developed the 737 AEW&C to meet Australia's Air 5077 Project Wedgetail requirement for an airborne early warning and control aircraft. Australia selected Boeing's proposal over offerings from Lockheed Martin (C-130J-30) and Raytheon (Airbus A310) in July 1999. A firm contract was signed in December 2000.

The heart of the 737 AEW&C is its Northrop Grumman MESA (Multi-role Electronically Scanned Array) radar mounted above the fuselage. On top of the dorsal mounted side looking arrays is the 'top hat' antenna with forward and aft looking arrays, providing the 737 AEW&C 360° coverage out to 350km (190nm). The steerable beam radar operates in the L-band and can track air and sea targets simultaneously, and is integrated with the IFF system.

Other features are an open system architecture mission data processor, six operator consoles (with room for up to 10, depending on customer preference), galley and crew rest area, and optional ESM, EWSP and air-to-air refuelling receptacle or probe (features which will be fitted to Australian aircraft).

Boeing will build four 737 AEW&Cs for Australia with delivery of the first two planned for 2006. Turkey selected the 737 AEW&C in November 2000, and plans to buy six. Boeing is pursuing further export sales (South Korea is a prospect).

Boeing also proposes to develop a maritime patrol version of the 737 to meet a US Navy requirement for a P-3 Orion replacement. This would feature a search radar in an enlarged nose, between five and seven operator stations in the main cabin, internal weapons bay and a rotary sonobuoy launcher.

**Photo:** A BBJ airframe acts as a 737 AEW&C mock-up. (Boeing)

# Boeing 747, E-4, VC-25 & AL-1A

**Country of origin:** United States of America

**Type:** 747 – VIP transport, command post and strategic transport. E-4 – Command post aircraft. VC-25 – Presidential transport. AL-1A – Anti missile aircraft

**Powerplants:** E-4B – Four 233.5kN (52,500lb) GE F103-GE-100 turbofans. VC-25 – Four 252.4kB (56,750lb) F103-GE-102s.

**Performance:** E-4B – Max speed 970km/h (523kt), economical cruising speed 907km/h (490kt). Cruise ceiling 45,000ft. Ferry range 12,600km (6800nm). Mission endurance 12 hours, with refuelling 72 hours. VC-25 – Range 11,490km (6200nm).

**Weights:** E-4B – Max takeoff 362,875kg (800,000lb).

**Dimensions:** E-4B, VC-25 & 747-200 – Span 59.64m (195ft 8in), length 70.51m (231ft 4in), height 19.33m (63ft 5in). Wing area 511m² (5500sq ft).

**Accommodation:** E-4B – Flightcrew of four. Crew rest area in upper deck. Main deck fitted with command area, a conference room, battle staff area and command, control and communications area. VC-25 – Accommodation for the president with 70 passenger seats and accommodation for 23 crew. 747-200/400 – Seating for over 400 troops.

**Armament:** None

**Operators:** 747 – Bahrain, Iran, Israel, Japan, Saudi Arabia. E-4 – USA. VC-25 – USA. AL-1A – USA*.

**History:** Boeing developed the 747, which was over twice the size of any airliner preceding it, as a private venture at enormous financial risk.

The 747 first flew on February 9 1969. Since then it has been built in five basic versions, the initial 747-100, the heavier 747-200, long range, shorter fuselage 747SP, the 747-300 which introduced the stretched upper deck, and the current long range, two crew 747-400.

The USAF selected the 747-200 as the basis for its E-4 Advanced Airborne National Command Post aircraft (alternatively the National Emergency Airborne Command Post – NEACP or Kneecap). Nicknamed the Doomsday Plane, the E-4 is tasked with providing an airborne base from which the US president and senior government officials can operate during war – in particular nuclear war. Three E-4As were delivered from late 1974, while a single E-4B with greatly improved communications and a revised interior was delivered in 1979. The E-4As were later upgraded to E-4B standard.

The VC-25 designation applies to two 747-200s delivered to the USAF in 1990 to serve as presidential transports – Air Force One when the US president is onboard. The VC-25 features a comprehensive communications fit, presidential stateroom, conference room and accommodation for senior staffers, press and flight and cabin crews.

The C-19 designation applies to US 747 airliners which are part of the Civil Reserve Air Fleet, which the military can call upon in crisis.

Japan operates two 747-400s as VIP and troop transports. Iran operates 747-100 tanker/transports and 747-100F Freighters.

The AL-1A is an anti ballistic and cruise missile aircraft based on the 747-400F and equipped with a TRW chemical oxygen iodine long range laser to be mounted in a nose turret. The first YAL-1A green airframe flew in January 2000 and in 2001 was undergoing fitout and modification. The USAF requires seven with deliveries from around 2007.

**Photo:** A Japanese 747-400. (Howard Geary)

## Boeing 757 & C-32

**Country of origin:** United States of America

**Type:** Medium range VIP and government transport

**Powerplants:** 757-200 – Two 166.4kN (37,400lb) Rolls-Royce RB211-535C turbofans, or two 178.4kN (40,100lb) RB211-535E4s, or two 170kN (38,200lb) Pratt & Whitney PW2037s, or two 185.5kN (41,700lb) PW2040s.

**Performance:** 757-200 – Max cruising speed 914km/h (493kt), economical cruising speed 850km/h (460kt). Range with P&W engines and 186 passengers 5522km (2980nm), with RR engines 5226km (2820nm). Range at optional max takeoff weight with P&W engines 7410km (4000nm), with RR engines 6857km (3700nm).

**Weights:** 757-200 – Operating empty with P&W engines 57,040kg (125,750lb), with RR engines 57,180kg (126,050lb). Medium range max takeoff weight 104,325kg (230,000lb), long range max takeoff weight 113,395kg (250,000lb).

**Dimensions:** Wing span 38.05m (124ft 10in), length 47.32m (155ft 3in), height 13.56m (44ft 6in). Wing area 185.25m² (1994sq ft).

**Accommodation:** 757-200 – Flightcrew of two. Typical passenger arrangements vary from 178 to 239 seats. C-32, Argentine and Mexican aircraft have customised interiors.

**Armament:** None

**Operators:** 757 – Argentina, Mexico, Saudi Arabia. C-32 – USA.

**History:** The 757 medium range narrowbody twinjet airliner has so far found a niche military role as a VIP transport with three air arms, including the US Air Force as the C-32.

Boeing considered a number of proposals for a successor to the 727 trijet airliner during the 1970s. In the end Boeing settled on a more conventional design featuring the same fuselage cross section as the 727, but considerably longer in length, with an all new wing, fuel efficient high bypass turbofan engines and a new nose section housing an advanced cockpit. Development of the 757 was launched in 1978 in tandem with the widebody 767. The 767 first flew a few months earlier, but the two types share a number of systems and technologies, including a common flightdeck.

First flight was on February 19 1982, with the 757-200 entering airline service in January the following year. Subsequent versions to appear include the 757-200PF freighter, and the 757-200M Combi. The stretched 240 seat 757-300 first flew in August 1998.

In terms of commercial orders, the 757 has been a great success story for Boeing, with over 1040 ordered by late 2001. However the twinjet is only in limited military service. An example each serves with the air forces of Argentina and Mexico. Both these aircraft are used for VIP and government transport tasks, and are fitted with customised interiors. Another is operated by the Saudi Royal Flight.

In August 1996 the USAF ordered four 757-200s for VIP use to replace aging 707 based VC-137s. Allocated the USAF designation C-32A, the PW2040 powered Boeings were delivered to the 89th Airlift Wing at Andrews AFB from early 1998. The C-32s are used to transport US cabinet and congress members and the vice president. Compared with the 757 they feature auxiliary fuel tanks, an integral air stair and a sophisticated communications suite.

**Photo:** A USAF C-32A. (Craig Murray)

## Boeing E-767 & KC-767

**Country of origin:** United States of America

**Type:** E-767 – AWACS aircraft. KC-767 – Tanker transport

**Powerplants:** E-767 – Two 273.6kN (61,500lb) General Electric CF6-80C2B6FA turbofans.

**Performance:** E-767 – Max cruising speed over 805km/h (434kt). Service ceiling 34,000 to 43,000ft. Unrefuelled range 8335 to 9260km (4500 to 5000nm). Endurance at 1850km (1000nm) patrol radius eight hours, endurance at 555km (300nm) 12 hours. Endurance with inflight refuelling 22 hours. (AAR receptacle not fitted to JASDF aircraft.)

**Weights:** E-767 – Max takeoff 174,635kg (385,000lb).

**Dimensions:** E-767 – Wing span 47.47m (156ft 1in), length 48.51m (159ft 2in), height 15.85m (52ft 0in). Wing area 283.3m² (3050sq ft).

**Accommodation:** E-767 – Full 20 crew complement consists of two pilots, mission director, tactical director, fighter allocator, two weapon controllers, surveillance controller, link manager, seven surveillance operators, communications operator, radar technician, communications technician and computer display technician. Crew rest area and galley in rear of cabin. Reserve crew can also be carried.

**Armament:** None

**Operators:** E-767 – Japan. 767TT – Italy*.

**History:** The Boeing E-767 is an adaptation of the 767-200 airliner fitted with the radar and systems of the E-3 Sentry for Japan.

Development of the E-767 (E-767 is a JASDF designation) was spurred by a Japanese requirement for four AWACS aircraft, with the natural choice being the E-3 Sentry (described separately). However, the closure of the 707/E-3 production line in 1991 led Boeing and Japan to look at developing an AWACS platform using the Sentry's core systems and the airframe of the 767-200ER airliner. Boeing announced it was performing definition studies of such a combination to meet the Japanese requirement in December 1991.

Japan ordered two E-767s in November 1993, and an additional two in October 1994. The first 'green' E-767 airframe flew in October 1994. It was then fitted with a dummy radome for aerodynamic testing and first flew in this configuration on August 9 1996, before being fitted with the AWACS radar and avionics suite. The first two aircraft were delivered in March 1998, the third and fourth aircraft followed in January 1999.

Central to the E-767 is the Northrop Grumman (formerly Westinghouse) APY-2 surveillance radar, as on the E-3. Internally the E-767 is configured with stations for communications, data processing, eight multifunction operator consoles in two rows, equipment bays, galley and crew rest area.

Boeing is also developing the 767-200 and stretched -300 as KC-767 or 767TT tanker transports to replace the large numbers of converted 707s currently in service.

KC-767 features include a forward main deck freight door, optional additional belly fuel tanks, wingtip probe and drogue refuelling pods and a refuelling boom. Launch customer Italy has ordered four in 2001 for delivery 2004-2006. Other potential customers are the UK, Australia and the USAF, which in late 2001 appeared close to leasing 100 to replace its oldest KC-135s.

**Photo:** The E-767. (Boeing)

## Boeing F/A-18 Hornet

**Country of origin:** United States of America

**Type:** Multirole fighter

**Powerplants:** F/A-18C – Two 71.2kN (16,000lb) with afterburning General Electric F404-GE-400 turbofans, or since 1992 two 78.7kN (17,700lb) F404-GE-402 EPEs.

**Performance:** F/A-18C – Max speed over Mach 1.8 or approx 1915km/h (1033kt). Max initial rate of climb 45,000ft/min. Combat ceiling approx 50,000ft. Ferry range over 3335km (1800nm). Interdiction combat radius hi-lo-hi 537km (290nm), attack mission combat radius 1065km (575nm), combat radius on an air-to-air mission 740km (400nm). CAP endurance from a carrier 1hr 45min.

**Weights:** F/A-18C – Empty 10,810kg (23,832lb), max takeoff approx 25,400kg (56,000lb). Internal fuel 4926kg (10,860lb).

**Dimensions:** Wing span 11.43m (37ft 6in), length 17.07m (56ft 0in), height 4.66m (15ft 4in). Wing area 37.2m² (400.0sq ft).

**Accommodation:** Pilot only, or two in tandem in F/A-18B/D.

**Armament:** M61A1 Vulcan 20mm cannon. F/A-18C can carry 7030kg (15,500lb) of ordnance, incl AIM-9, AIM-7 and AIM-120 AAMs, AGM-65, AGM-88, AGM-84 bombs, laser and GPS guided bombs.

**Operators:** Australia, Canada, Finland, Kuwait, Malaysia, Spain, Switzerland, USA.

**History:** The multirole Hornet fighter was designed from the outset for both air-to-air and air-to-ground missions.

When the US Congress cancelled the US Navy's VFAX lightweight multirole fighter program in August 1974, it recommended that the service should study developments of the GD YF-16 and Northrop YF-17 developed for the USAF.

McDonnell Douglas, with Northrop as a major associate (major contractor from 1985), was selected to develop its enlarged YF-17 proposal on May 2 1975. Initially the aircraft was to be built in F-18 fighter and ground attack A-18 versions, but the two roles were combined into the one airframe, resulting in the F/A-18 Hornet. The first of 11 development aircraft flew on November 18 1978.

The F/A-18 is bigger and heavier than the YF-17. Features include fly-by-wire, HUD and HOTAS, a multimode Hughes APG-65 radar, folding wingtips and two GE F404 turbofans.

The improved F/A-18C first flew in 1986. Changes include improved avionics, a new central computer and AIM-120 and AGM-65 compatibility. The US Marines and Navy operate Night Attack F/A-18C/Ds with NVG compatible cockpits with colour MFDs and FLIR and laser designator pods.

Marine and Malaysian F/A-18D two seaters have a dedicated mission capable rear cockpit with two large colour multi function displays and a colour moving map with no flight controls (although these can be added), while USMC F/A-18D(RC)s are wired to carry an Advanced Tactical Airborne Reconnaissance System (ATARS) reconnaissance pod – 31 pods are being delivered through to 2002.

Uprated GE F404-GE-402 engines were introduced from 1992, the improved APG-73 radar from 1994. Australian, Canadian and US Marine Corps F/A-18As are being upgraded with the APG-73.

F/A-18C/D production wound up in 2001.

**Photo:** An Australian F/A-18A. (Paul Sadler)

## Boeing F/A-18E/F Super Hornet

**Country of origin:** United States of America

**Type:** Multirole fighter

**Powerplants:** Two 98.0kN (22,000lb) approx with afterburning General Electric F414-GE-400 turbofans.

**Performance:** F/A-18E – Max level speed more than Mach 1.8 or approx 1915km/h (1033kt). Service ceiling 50,000ft. Combat radius with four 1000lb bombs, external fuel and targeting pods, hi-hi-hi 1230km (665nm). Maritime air superiority combat endurance with six AAMs, external fuel and 278km (150nm) from the carrier, 2hr 15min.

**Weights:** F/A-18E – Empty 13,864kg (30,564lb), takeoff weight attack mission 29,937kg (66,000lb). Internal fuel 6559kg (14,460lb).

**Dimensions:** Span over missiles 13.62m (44ft 9in), length 18.38m (60ft 4in), height 4.88m (16ft 0in). Wing area 46.5m² (500.0sq ft).

**Accommodation:** Pilot only in F/A-18E, two in tandem in F/A-18F.

**Armament:** One M61A1 Vulcan 20mm cannon. Eleven external hardpoints can carry 8028kg (17,700lb) of stores. Armaments include AIM-9 and AIM-120 AAMs and AGM-65, AGM-88, AGM-154 JSOW, GBU-31 & -32 JDAM air-to-ground munitions.

**Operators:** USA*

**History:** The F/A-18E/F Super Hornet is a larger and more capable development of the multirole F/A-18A/C.

McDonnell Douglas (now Boeing) proposed an enlarged Hornet as a successor for the cancelled General Dynamics/McDonnell Douglas A-12 Avenger II in 1991. Official interest was such that a $US3.8bn development contract for the F/A-18E and two seat F/A-18F was signed on December 7 1992. The first of these aircraft rolled out on September 18 1995 (when the Super Hornet name was adopted), with first flight on November 29 that year.

The Super Hornet is significantly larger than the F/A-18A/C. The fuselage is stretched by 86cm (2ft 10in) while the wings are of the same layout but are 1.31m (4ft 4in) longer and 9.3m² (100.0sq ft) greater in area. The LEXes have been enlarged to retain the Hornet's excellent high AoA performance and the horizontal tails are bigger. Increased fuel capacity means that range is up by 40% over the F/A-18C. The re-designed engine intakes allow greater airflow for the more powerful GE F414 engines (a development of the F404).

Initially, the E/F's avionics suite is 90% common with the F/A-18C's, including APG-73 radar, although the cockpit features a large touch panel LCD display, a second LCD colour display and three monochrome displays. It is being delivered with the Raytheon ATFLIR advanced infrared targeting pod and a helmet mounted sight. From 2003 some F/A-18Fs will be built with a combat configured rear cockpit with dual weapon controllers and a large LCD. From 2007, production E/Fs will be fitted with the Raytheon APG-76 active electronically scanned radar.

The USN originally required as many as 1000 F/A-18E/Fs but now plans to buy 448 (204 Es and 244 Fs), equipping each carrier air wing with 12 Es and 14 Fs (some will be used for 'buddy' inflight refuelling). Initial deliveries began in 1998 (63 delivered by Sept 2001), the first carrier deployment is planned for mid 2002.

An electronic warfare variant of the F/A-18F, the EA-18F, has been proposed to replace the EA-6B Prowler.

**Photo:** An F/A-18E. (Neville Dawson)

## Boeing F-15E Eagle

**Country of origin:** United States of America

**Type:** Long range strike fighter

**Powerplants:** F-15E (later aircraft) – Two 79.2kN (17,800lb) dry and 129.4kN (29,100lb) with a/b Pratt & Whitney F100-PW-229 turbofans.

**Performance:** F-15E – Max speed Mach 2.5 or approx 2655km/h (1433kt), cruising speed 917km/h (495kt). Service ceiling 60,000ft. Max range 4445km (2400nm). Combat radius 1270km (685nm).

**Weights:** F-15E – Operating empty 14,515kg (32,000lb), max takeoff 36,740kg (81,000lb). Internal fuel (incl CFTs) 10,207kg (22,482lb).

**Dimensions:** Wing span 13.05m (42ft 10in), length 19.43m (63ft 9in), height 5.63m (18ft 6in). Wing area 56.5m$^2$ (608.0sq ft).

**Accommodation:** Pilot and Weapon Systems Operator in tandem.

**Armament:** One M61A1 20mm Vulcan cannon. Max weapon load of 11,115kg (24,500lb). Options include AIM-9 Sidewinder, AIM-7 Sparrow and AIM-120 Amraam AAMs, GBU-10, GBU-12 and GBU-24 LGBs, electro-optically guided GBU-15 and powered AGM-130 bombs, GBU-31/32 JDAMs, JSOW conventional bombs, cluster munitions, B51 and B61 nuclear bombs and AGM-88 HARM and AGM-65 ASMs.

**Operators:** Israel (F-15I), Saudi Arabia (F-15S), USA (F-15E).

**History:** The multirole F-15E was developed specifically to supplant the long ranging F-111 strike bomber.

McDonnell Douglas (Boeing from 1997) had long promoted the bomb carrying ability of the F-15, even though an official requirement for an air-to-ground capability was dropped in 1975. In the early 1980s the USAF had a requirement for a new multirole fighter, the ETF (Enhanced Tactical Fighter), to supplement the F-111. The USAF selected a two seat development of the F-15, the F-15E, in preference to the F-16XL (an enlarged F-16 featuring a cranked delta wing) in February 1984. First flight was on December 11 1986.

The F-15E features an APG-70 radar with synthetic aperture ground mapping, a wide angle HUD, three colour multifunction CRTs in the front cockpit and four in the rear, permanent CFTs (conformal fuel tanks) fitted with tangential stores stations, more powerful Pratt & Whitney F100-PW-229 engines (-220s in initial aircraft) and removable LANTIRN navigation and target designation pods. The AAQ-13 LANTIRN pod beneath the port intake comprises a wide angle FLIR and terrain following radar. The AAQ-14 (underneath the starboard intake) features FLIR and a laser rangefinder/designator. Current production Es feature enhanced night-vision capability and three new active-matrix liquid crystal displays.

The Saudi F-15S features downgraded avionics, a simplified APG-70 without ground mapping and a Lockheed Martin Sharpshooter targeting pod in place of the AAQ-14. First flight was in June 1995 and the last of 72 on order delivered in 2000.

Twenty-five F-15Is were delivered to Israel (first flight September 1997) through to 1999, differing from the F-15E with Israeli EW suites.

Top up USAF orders will keep F-15 production at a trickle to late 2004, keeping open the possibility of further export sales (Korea is a prospect). In all the US has procured 236 F-15Es.

F-15Es have seen active service during the Gulf War in 1991, over Serbia and Kosovo in 1999, and over Afghanistan in 2001.

**Photo:** The F-15E is nicknamed Beagle (Bomber Eagle). (Paul Sadler)

## Boeing/BAE AV-8B/GR.7 Harrier II

**Countries of origin:** USA and UK

**Type:** STOVL ground attack fighter

**Powerplant:** AV-8B – One 95.4kN (21,450lb) Rolls-Royce F402-RR-406A turbofan, or a 105.9kN (23,800lb) F402-RR-408 from 1990.

**Performance:** AV-8B – Max speed 1065km/h (575kt). Max initial rate of climb 14,715ft/min. Service ceiling over 50,000ft. Short takeoff run at MTOW 435m (1437ft). Ferry range with external fuel 3640km (1965nm). Combat radius from a STO with seven Mk 82 Snakeye bombs and external fuel, hi-lo-hi 1100km (595nm). Endurance with two AIM-9s on a CAP 185km (100nm) from the carrier 3hr.

**Weights:** AV-8B – Operating empty 6336kg (13,968lb), max takeoff (with a STO) 14,060kg (31,000lb).

**Dimensions:** AV-8B – Span 9.25m (30ft 4in), length 14.12m (46ft 4in), height 3.55m (11ft 8in). Wing area with LEXes 22.6m$^2$ (243.4sq ft).

**Accommodation:** Pilot only, or two in tandem in TAV-8B and T.10.

**Armament:** AV-8B – One 25mm GAU-12/A Equaliser five barrel cannon in ventral pod. Max external stores load of 6003kg (13,235lb) can include AIM-9s, AGM-65s and various bombs incl PGMs. Harrier II Plus being develop to carry AIM-120, JDAM and Penguin ASM.

**Operators:** Italy, Spain, UK, USA.

**History:** The Harrier II was developed by McDonnell Douglas with British Aerospace as the junior partner.

Compared to the original Harrier the Harrier II features a much larger supercritical composite wing and new nose and cockpit area. The new wing flew on an AV-8A (designated YAV-8B) on November 9 1978. The first full scale development YAV-8B flew on November 5 1981.

Production AV-8Bs were delivered to the US Marines from January 1984. Two full scale development Harrier GR.5s for the RAF first flew in 1985. AV-8Bs and GR.5s differed in that the British Harriers have two 25mm cannons, rather than one in the AV-8B, and are powered by 95.6kN (21,500lb) RR Pegasus Mk 105s.

Development of the AV-8B Night Attack for the USMC, which introduced a GEC Marconi FLIR mounted in the nose, a head down display and a colour moving map, began in 1984, with deliveries from 1989. Similarly the RAF upgraded all its aircraft to GR.7 standard, with the same nose mounted FLIR for night attack.

The USMC ordered a total of 280 AV-8Bs (including 24 TAV-8Bs two seaters), while the RAF ordered 109 GR.5/GR.7s, including 13 T.10s. The T.10 two seater differs from the TAV-8B in having eight underwing pylons (not two) and a FLIR.

The most advanced Harrier development is the APG-65 radar equipped Harrier II Plus. Spain, Italy and the US Marines have all taken delivery of rebuilt or new build Harrier II Pluses. New build production ceased in 1997 but USMC Harriers are being fitted with new build fuselages through to 2004.

Upgraded software will allow Spanish and Italian Harrier II Pluses to carry AIM-120 Amraams and USMC aircraft JDAM GPS guided bombs. The RAF plans a GR.9 upgrade for its Harriers with new INS/GPS, LCD display in the cockpit and GPWS. The TIALD and Rafael Litening targeting pods have been integrated on UK and US Harriers, respectively.

**Photo:** A USMC AV-8B Harrier. (Paul Merritt)

# Boeing/BAE Systems T-45 Goshawk

**Countries of origin:** UK and USA

**Type:** Advanced carrier-capable trainer.

**Powerplant:** T-45A – One 26.0kN (5845lb) Rolls-Royce Turbomeca F405-RR-401 (navalised Adour).

**Performance:** T-45A – Max speed at 8000ft 1005km/h (543kt). Max initial rate of climb 8000ft/min. Time to 30,000ft clean 7min 40sec. Service ceiling 40,000ft. Ferry range with int fuel 1532km (826nm).

**Weights:** T-45A – Empty 4460kg (9834lb), MTOW 6387kg (14,081lb).

**Dimensions:** T-45A – Wing span 9.39m (30ft 10in), length incl nose probe 11.99m (39ft 4in), fuselage length 10.89m (35ft 9in), height 4.08m (13ft 5in). Wing area 17.7m² (190.1sq ft).

**Accommodation:** Two in tandem.

**Armament:** Usually none. One hardpoint under each wing can be used to carry practice bomb racks, rocket pods or fuel tanks.

**Operators:** USA*

**History:** The Goshawk is a navalised carrier-capable variant of the British Aerospace Hawk (described separately).

The lengthy evolution of the basic Hawk into the Goshawk began in the late 1970s. The US Navy's VTXTS (later T45TS) program to find a replacement for both the TA-4J Skyhawk and T-2 Buckeye evaluated a number of aircraft including the BAe Hawk and the Dassault/Dornier Alpha Jet in 1978. The USN selected the Hawk for further development in November 1981, with McDonnell Douglas (now Boeing) as prime contractor and British Aerospace (now BAE Systems) as principal sub-contractor.

The redesign of the Hawk 60 to make it capable of carrier operations was fairly extensive, and involved strengthening the airframe and undercarriage, with a twin wheel nose gear that retracts into a slightly enlarged forward fuselage, adding a tail arrester hook, two side mounted airbrakes, a ventral fin and US Navy standard cockpit displays and radios. The crew sit on two Martin-Baker Mk 14 NACES ejection seats. The Hawk's Adour turbofan has been modified for operations from carriers and under the US system is designated F405.

The first full scale development T-45 first flew on April 16 1988. Deliveries were originally planned for 1989, but this was delayed when the USN requested further changes to the airframe and engine. Production T-45A aircraft were delivered from January 1992. These aircraft are completed at St Louis, while BAE builds the wings, centre and rear fuselage, tail, canopy and flying controls.

From the 84th production aircraft in late 1997 Goshawks have been fitted with the 'Cockpit 21' glass cockpit, with two Elbit multifunction displays in each cockpit, as the T-45C. From 2004 the T-45As will be upgraded to T-45C standard.

AlliedSignal (now Honeywell) tried unsuccessfully to have its F124 engine replace the Adour. An F124 powered T-45 flew on October 6 1996 (the F124 T-45 was unsuccessfully offered to Australia) but the USN decided against fitting undelivered T-45s with the new engine.

The US Navy plans to acquire 169 production T-45s (down from an originally planned 234). All T-45s are also being fitted with modified engine inlets with top lip extended forward, to improve air flow at high angles of attack.

**Photo:** A T-45C. (Paul Merritt)

# Boeing CH-46 Sea Knight

**Country of origin:** United States of America

**Type:** Medium lift multirole helicopter

**Powerplants:** CH-46E – Two 1395kW (1870shp) General Electric T58-GE-16 turboshafts driving two three-blade rotors.

**Performance:** CH-46E – Max speed at sea level 267km/h (144kt), max cruising speed at sea level 266km/h (143kt). Max initial rate of climb 1715ft/min. Hovering ceiling in ground effect 9500ft, out of ground effect 5750ft. Ferry range 1110km (600nm), range with a 1090kg (2400lb) payload 1020km (550nm).

**Weights:** CH-46E – Empty 5255kg (11,585lb), max takeoff 11,022kg (24,300lb).

**Dimensions:** CH-46E – Rotor diameter each 15.24m (50ft 0in), length overall rotors turning 25.40m (83ft 4in), fuselage length 13.66m (44ft 10in), height to top of rear rotor head 5.09m (16ft 9in). Total rotor disc area 364.8m² (3927.0sq ft).

**Accommodation:** Crew of three, with 25 troops and troop commander. Standard USMC CH-46E load of 17 troops or 15 stretchers. CH-46E max payload 3175kg (7000lb). Can carry external sling loads.

**Armament:** None

**Operators:** Canada, Japan, Sweden, USA.

**History:** The CH-46 Sea Knight is the United States Marine Corps' primary assault troop transport, and began life as a private venture.

In the mid 1950s the Vertol company (later acquired by Boeing) began design studies of a medium lift twin engine transport helicopter, taking advantage of the lifting capabilities offered by turboshaft engines. The resulting Model 107 helicopter first flew in prototype form on April 22 1958. This initial prototype was powered by two 640kW (860shp) Lycoming T53 turboshafts, and featured tandem main rotors (negating the need for an anti torque tail rotor), an unobstructed main cabin and rear ramp.

The Model 107 originally aroused the interest of the US Army, who ordered three as YCH-1As for evaluation, but instead the service went on to order the larger CH-47 Chinook. Instead it was the US Marines who ordered the 107 into production in June 1961, as the HRB-1 (CH-46 after 1962), to replace its UH-34s.

The first of 160 USMC CH-46As entered service in June 1964, these aircraft powered by 935kW (1250shp) General Electric T58-GE-8 turboshafts. The US Navy took delivery of 14 similar UH-46As for vertical replenishment of ships at sea. The USMC's CH-46D and USN's UH-46D introduced 1045kW (1400shp) T58-GE-10s, while the similar CH-46F featured more avionics.

The Marines current CH-46 model is the E, an upgrade of CH-46D and F models with 1395kW (1870shp) T58-GE-16s and improved crash survivability. Deliveries of upgraded Es began in 1977.

Canada took delivery of six CH-46A based CH-113 Labradors for SAR and 12 CH-113A Voyageurs for transport. Sweden's HKP-4s feature Rolls-Royce Gnome engines. In Japan Kawasaki licence built (through to 1990) and further developed the 107 as the KV 107 for military and commercial operators. KV 107 roles include SAR, mine countermeasures and transport. Some were exported to Saudi Arabia and Sweden.

**Photo:** A USMC CH-46E. (Paul Sadler)

# Boeing CH-47 Chinook

**Country of origin:** United States of America

**Type:** Medium lift transport helicopter

**Powerplants:** CH-47D – Two 2795kW (3750shp) takeoff rated Honeywell T55-L-712 turboshafts driving two three-blade rotors.

**Performance:** CH-47D – Max cruising speed at sea level 290km/h (156kt), average cruising speed 256km/h (138kt). Max initial rate of climb 1522ft/min. Service ceiling 8450ft. Hovering ceiling out of ground effect 10,550ft. Range 425km (230nm).

**Weights:** US Army CH-47D – Empty 10,615kg (23,400lb), max takeoff 22,680kg (50,000lb). International CH-47D – Empty 10,578kg (23,231lb), max takeoff 24,495kg (54,000lb).

**Dimensions:** CH-47D – Rotor diameter each 18.29m (60ft 0in), length overall rotors turning 30.18m (99ft 0in), fuselage length 15.55m (51ft 0in), height to top of rear rotor head 5.77m (18ft 11in). Total rotor disc area 525.3m² (5654.9sq ft). International CH-47D – Same except fuselage length 15.87m (52ft 1in).

**Accommodation:** Two pilots and loadmaster/crew chief on jump seat. Standard seating for 37 troops but can carry up to 55 troops, or 24 casualty stretchers and two medical attendants. Underslung load examples include an M198 howitzer, D5 bulldozer or fuel bladders.

**Armament:** Usually none.

**Operators:** Australia, Egypt, Greece*, Iran, Italy Japan*, Libya, Morocco, Netherlands, South Korea, Spain, Taiwan, Thailand, UK, USA.

**History:** The US Army selected the Vertol Model 114 in June 1959 for development as the CH-47 battlefield mobility helicopter.

First flight of the prototype YCH-47A (originally YHC-1B) was on September 21 1961, with service entry of the CH-47A Chinook in August 1962. Features included Vertol's (later Boeing Vertol's) trademark use of tandem counter rotating main rotors above the forward and rear fuselage, with rear mounted Lycoming T55 turboshafts leaving an unobstructed main cabin, and an external cargo hook.

Some 354 CH-47As were built for the US Army, followed by 108 CH-47Bs with uprated engines and larger diameter rotors. Many As and Bs saw service in Vietnam, as did some improved CH-47Cs.

The CH-47C first flew on October 14 1967 and introduced further uprated engines and additional fuel capacity. Many US Army CH-47As and Bs were upgraded to C standard, while new build Cs were widely exported and built in Italy under licence by Elicotteri Meridionali (later Agusta).

The CH-47D first flew in February 1982. It features more powerful T55-L-712s, NVG compatible cockpit and triple external cargo hooks (first introduced on British HC.1s/CH-47Cs). The US Army has procured over 480 CH-47Ds (including 11 modified to special ops MH-47D configuration), most of which were rebuilt CH-47Cs.

The CH-47D has also been widely exported – many of which were upgraded CH-47Cs (incl Britain [as HC.2s], Spain, Australia and the Netherlands). It is marketed for export as the CH-47D International Chinook, with some fitted with EFIS, MH-47E type enlarged fuel tanks and weather radar nose.

Kawasaki in Japan continues to licence build Ds as the CH-47J and weather radar equipped CH-47JA.

**Photo:** An Australian Army CH-47D. (Paul Sadler)

# Boeing MH-47E, CH-47SD & CH-47F

**Country of origin:** United States of America

**Type:** Medium lift transport helicopter

**Powerplants:** MH-47E – Two 3108kW (4168shp) continuous rated Honeywell T55-L-714 turboshafts driving two three-blade rotors.

**Performance:** MH-47E – Max level speed 285km/h (154kt), max cruising speed at sea level 259km/h (140kt). Initial rate of climb 1840ft/min. Service ceiling 10,140ft. Hovering ceiling out of ground effect 5500ft. Operational radius inserting a special forces team 935km (505nm). Ferry range at MTOW 2333km (1260nm).

**Weights:** MH-47E – Empty 12,210kg (26,918lb), max takeoff 24,495kg (54,000lb).

**Dimensions:** MH-47E – Rotor diameter each 18.29m (60ft 0in), length overall rotors turning 30.18m (99ft 0in), fuselage length 15.87m (52ft 1in), height to top of rear rotor head 5.77m (18ft 11in). Total rotor disc area 525.3m² (5654.9sq ft).

**Accommodation:** MH-47E – Two pilots and loadmaster/crew chief on jump seat. Standard seating for 44 special forces troops.

**Armament:** MH-47E – Two window mounted 0.50in M2 machine guns, with provision for Stinger AAMs. Some mount miniguns.

**Operators:** MH-47E – USA. CH-47SD – Singapore*, Taiwan*, UK. CH-47F – USA*.

**History:** The three most recent Chinook developments are the special forces MH-47E, export CH-47SD 'Super D', and the Improved Cargo Helicopter (ICH) CH-47F for the US Army.

The US Army's special operations MH-47Es are used for covert troop insertion and extraction. Features include NVG compatible four screen EFIS flightdeck, GPS, AAQ-16 FLIR in a chin turret, APQ-174 radar with ground mapping and terrain following, refuelling probe, Commercial Chinook weather radar nose, jam resistant radios, radar, laser and missile warning systems, chaff and flares dispensers, greater fuel capacity and uprated T55-L-714 engines. Twenty-five were built.

The most recent export version is the CH-47SD 'Super D'. The CH-47SD first flew on August 25 1999 and features FADEC equipped T55-L-714A engines, the MH-47E's higher max takeoff weight, a simplified structure for maintainability and reliability improvements, night vision goggle compatible EFIS cockpit and radar nose. Singapore was the launch customer, with eight now ordered, while Taiwan is buying nine. The RAF's eight HC.3 special forces Chinooks are based on the SD but with the MH-47E's fuel tanks, weather radar and refuelling probe, plus a unique mission avionics suite.

The US Army plans to upgrade at least 300 CH-47Ds to CH-47F Improved Cargo Helicopter (ICH) standard to extend their service lives beyond 2030, pending the arrival of the Joint Transport Rotorcraft to replace US Army CH-47s and USMC CH-53s. An EMD contract was signed with Boeing in May 1998 and the first CH-47F flew in June 2001. Low rate production is due to start in 2003.

The CH-47F features upgraded T55-GA-714A turboshafts with FADEC, modern avionics including digital comms, modem and Rockwell Collins EFIS, Mil Std 1553B databus, fuselage 'tuning' to reduce vibration and wear, and replacement or repair of systems and structures as required.

**Photo:** The prototype CH-47F on its June 2001 first flight. (Boeing)

## Boeing AH-64 Apache

**Country of origin:** United States of America

**Type:** Attack helicopter

**Powerplants:** AH-64D – Two 1410kW (1890shp) 10min rated, 1238kW (1660shp) max continuous rated General Electric T700-GE-701Cs turboshafts driving four blade main and tail rotors.

**Performance:** AH-64D Apache Longbow – Max speed and max cruising speed 261km/h (141kt). Rate of climb at S/L 2415ft/min. Hovering ceiling OGE 9480ft. Ferry range ext fuel 1900km (1025nm). Max range with int fuel 407km (220nm). Max endurance 3hr 9min.

**Weights:** AH-64D Apache Longbow – Empty 5352kg (11,800lb), max takeoff for ferry mission 10,107kg (22,283lb).

**Dimensions:** AH-64D Apache Longbow – Main rotor diameter 14.63m (48ft 0in), wing span 5.23m (17ft 2in), length overall rotors turning 17.76m (58ft 3in), fuselage length 14.97m (49ft 2in), height overall 4.95m (16ft 3in). Main rotor disc area 168.1m² (1809.1sq ft).

**Accommodation:** Copilot/gunner in front cockpit, with pilot behind.

**Armament:** One M230 Chain Gun 30mm cannon. Four underwing hardpoints can carry up to 16 AGM-114 Hellfire anti armour missiles, or rocket pods, Stinger or Sidewinder AAMs, or Sidearm ARMs.

**Operators:** Egypt, Greece, Israel, Netherlands*, Saudi Arabia, Singapore*, UAE (Abu Dhabi), UK*, USA*.

**History:** The Boeing (nee McDonnell Douglas) Apache was developed to meet the US Army's Advanced Attack Helicopter requirement.

To meet the AAH requirement the US Army sponsored the development of the Bell YAH-63 and the Hughes YAH-64 for a competitive fly-off. Hughes' YAH-64 first flew on September 30 1975, and was selected for further development ahead of the Bell design in December 1976. Apaches were delivered from 1984 and the first unit became operational in 1986.

Apache design features include two shoulder mounted GE T700 turboshafts, crew armour, and the nose mounted AAQ-11 TADS/PNVS (Target Acquisition and Designation Sight/Pilot Night Vision Sensor). TADS comprises a FLIR, TV camera, laser spot tracker and laser rangefinder/designator and is used for target location and designation. The PNVS FLIR allows nap of the earth flying.

Over 800 AH-64As were built for the US Army and export and the type proved very successful in combat in the Gulf War. The interim AH-64B with improvements from combat experience was cancelled.

The improved AH-64D features advanced digital avionics housed in enlarged cheek fairings, the AH-64D Apache Longbow adds the impressive mast mounted Northrop Grumman millimetre wave radar which can guide the radar frequency seeker Hellfire missile.

The US Army is upgrading 501 AH-64As to AH-64D Apache Longbow standard. Deliveries began in March 1997. Planned AH-64D upgrades include colour multifunction displays and Lockheed Martin's Arrowhead advanced TADS/PNVSS system, with advanced FLIR and image intensification television sensor suite.

British Army WAH-64Ds (being assembled by AgustaWestland) feature RTM332 engines. The first WAH-64D rolled out in September 1998 with deliveries to be completed in late 2003. Other D customers are the Netherlands (30), Singapore (20), Egypt (upgrading 35 As) and Israel (9).

**Photo:** A British WAH-64D. (Rolls-Royce)

## Boeing/Sikorsky RAH-66 Comanche

**Country of origin:** United States of America

**Type:** Reconnaissance attack helicopter

**Powerplants:** Two 1165kW (1563shp) LHTEC T800-LHT-801 turboshafts driving a five blade main rotor and eight blade fan-in-fin shrouded tail rotor.

**Performance:** Dash speed 324km/h (175kt) without radar, 308km/h (166kt) with radar, cruise speed 296km/h (160kt) w/o radar, 276km/h (149kt) with radar. Vertical rate of climb 895ft/min w/o radar, 500ft/min with radar. Max range 2224km (1200nm) w/o radar, 1593km (860nm) with radar.

**Weights:** Empty 4222kg (9300lb), primary mission takeoff 5606kg (12,349lb) w/o radar, 5803kg (12,784lb) with radar, max takeoff 7896kg (17,408lb).

**Dimensions:** Main rotor diameter 12.19m (40ft 0in), length overall rotor turning 14.59m (47ft 10in), fuselage length excluding gun 13.20m (43ft 4in), height over tailplane 3.37m (11ft 1in).

**Accommodation:** Pilot (front) and weapon systems operator (rear).

**Armament:** One 20mm, three barrel General Electric cannon in undernose Giat turret. Two weapons bay doors can hold three Hellfire or Stinger missiles each, with four Hellfires or eight Stingers on each optional stub wing.

**Operators:** USA*

**History:** The Comanche is without doubt the most advanced (and most expensive) combat helicopter currently under development.

As early as 1982 the US Army devised the LHX (Light Helicopter Experimental) program to replace 5000 UH-1s, AH-1s, OH-6s and OH-58s. By 1988 when a request for proposals was issued to the Boeing/Sikorsky First Team and the Bell/McDonnell Douglas Super Team, the requirement had been refined to a scout/reconnaissance helicopter, with the requirement brought back to 1292 aircraft.

The Boeing Sikorsky teaming's proposal was selected for development as the RAH-66 Comanche in April 1991. First flight of the first of two YRAH-66 prototypes was on January 4 1996 from West Palm Beach in Florida. The second YRAH-66 flew in March '99. The EMD (Engineering and Manufacturing Development) phase began in June 2000, with five EMD and eight OT&E airframes to be built.

Advanced features of the RAH-66 include stealth with airframe faceting to reduce radar cross section; a five blade, composite main rotor with swept tips and bearingless hub; Sikorsky developed eight blade fan-in-fin shrouded tail rotor; internal weapons bays; retractable undercarriage; two specially developed LHTEC (Honeywell and RR) T800 turboshafts; detachable stub wings; NVG compatible EFIS cockpits with 3D digital moving map displays; triple redundant fly-by-wire flight controls; sidestick cyclics; helmet mounted sights; an electronically scanned development of the Longbow millimetre wave radar; FLIR and laser designator.

The RAH-66 program has suffered from a number of delays and setbacks, mainly because of budget cutbacks. Planning at late 2001 sees the US Army buying 1213 from fiscal year 2010, with a production rate of 62 a year.

**Photo:** The first prototype YRAH-66 prototype, with revised airframe modifications and Comanche fire control radar 'aerodummy'. (Boeing)

# Boeing C-17 Globemaster III

**Country of origin:** United States of America

**Type:** Strategic and intra theatre transport

**Powerplants:** Four 181.0kN (40,700lb) P&W F117-PW-100 turbofans.

**Performance:** Normal cruising speed at 28,000ft Mach 0.74-0.77, max cruising speed at low altitude 648km/h (350kt) CAS. Airdrop speed at sea level 215 to 465km/h (115 to 250kt) CAS. Max ferry range 9432km (5095nm). Operational radius with a 36,785kg (81,000lb) payload and a 975m (3200ft) TO, land in 823m (2700ft), takeoff again with a similar payload in 853m (2800ft) and land in 792m (2600ft) – 925km (500nm). Range with a 68,040kg (150,000lb) payload, a 2320m (7600ft) TO run and a 885m (2900ft) landing – 5185km (2800nm).

**Weights:** Operating empty 126,100kg (278,000lb), max takeoff 265,350kg (585,000lb).

**Dimensions:** Span over winglets 51.76m (169ft 10in), length 53.04m (174ft 0in), height 16.79m (55ft 1in). Wing area 353m² (3800.0sq ft).

**Accommodation:** Flightcrew of two, plus loadmaster. Max payload 77,290kg (170,400lb). Can carry standard freight pallets, air droppable pallets, 100 passengers on seating pallets and 54 along fuselage sides, 48 stretcher patients, or 75 troops on temporary fuselage side and centreline seats, or 102 paratroops, 4WD vehicles, an M1A1 Abrams MBT plus other vehicles, or up to three AH-64s.

**Armament:** None

**Operators:** UK, USA*.

**History:** The C-17 airlifter suffered a controversial and often troublesome development, but in service has proven to be highly reliable and very versatile.

The USAF selected the McDonnell Douglas C-17 to meet its C-X requirement for a heavy airlifter in August 1981. The C-X requirement called for a transport capable of strategic and intra theatre missions, with good short field performance from semi prepared strips, good ground manoeuvrability and a voluminous cargo hold capable of accommodating attack helicopters and the M1 Abrams main battle tank.

The original C-17 full scale development contract was cancelled in 1982 and replaced with low priority development. A new full scale engineering and development contract was signed in late 1985 while the first production contract was signed in January 1988. First flight was on September 15 1991.

The C-17 features a high wing, T-tail, rear loading freight ramp, and four Pratt & Whitney F117 turbofans, developments of the commercial PW2000 (as on the 757). Other design features include fly-by-wire, a two crew glass cockpit with HUDs, externally blown flaps and field performance equivalent to the much smaller C-130's.

The USAF originally required 210 C-17s, but is currently taking delivery of 120 airlifters plus 15 modified for special missions operations. Further airlifter buys are likely. By December 2001 the USAF had taken delivery of 80 C-17s (by which stage the fleet had logged 325,000 flying hours).

Britain's Royal Air Force is leasing four USAF C-17s to meet an airlifter requirement. These were delivered in mid 2001.

Boeing has proposed the KC-17 tanker transport and MD-17 commercial freighter variants.

**Photo:** An RAF C-17. (Ian Doyle)

# Bombardier de Havilland Dash 8 & E-9

**Country of origin:** Canada

**Type:** Utility transport, navigation trainer and range support aircraft

**Powerplants:** 100 – Two 1490kW (2000shp) Pratt & Whitney Canada PW120A turboprops driving four blade propellers.

**Performance:** 100A – Max cruising speed 491km/h (265kt), long range cruising speed 440km/h (237kt). Max initial rate of climb 1560ft/min. Certificated service ceiling 25,000ft. Range with full passenger load, max fuel and reserves 1520km (820nm), range with a 2720kg (6000lb) payload 2040km (1100nm).

**Weights:** 100A – Operating empty 10,251kg (22,600lb), max takeoff 15,650kg (34,500lb).

**Dimensions:** Wing span 25.91m (85ft 0in), length 22.25m (73ft 0in), height 7.49m (24ft 7in). Wing area 54.4m² (585.0sq ft).

**Accommodation:** Flightcrew of two. Typical passenger seating for 37 at four abreast, or max seating for 40.

**Armament:** None

**Operators:** Canada, Kenya, Mexico, USA.

**History:** Bombardier's de Havilland Dash 8 has carved itself a significant slice of the fiercely competitive regional airliner market, but has also found its way into military colours in small numbers.

De Havilland began development of the Dash 8 in the late 1970s in response to what it saw as a considerable market for a new generation 30 to 40 seat commuter airliner. The first flight of the new airliner was on June 20 1983, while the first customer delivery took place on October 23 1984.

The Dash 8 features a high mounted wing and T-tail and has an advanced flight control system and large full length trailing edge flaps. Power is supplied by two Pratt & Whitney Canada PW120 (originally PT7A) turboprops.

The initial Dash 8 production model was the Series 100, built in 100, 100A (with PW120As) and 100B (with PW121s) variants. The Series 200 was delivered from 1994 and features more powerful PW123C engines, and thus has a higher cruising speed, plus greater commonality with the stretched Dash 8-300. The 200B has PW123Ds. The Dash 8-100 and 200 are now marketed as the Dash 8 Q100 and Q200 respectively.

Four Dash 8-200s are fitted with Raytheon SV1022 search radar and FLIR in Australian Customs use (with two more on order).

The stretched, 50 seat Dash 8-300 (now Q300) is powered by PW123s and is greater in length by 3.43m (11ft 3in). A maritime patrol development is marketed as the Triton. A further stretched development is the Dash 8 Q400, a 70 seat regional airliner.

Canada is the largest operator with four modified CT-142 navigation trainers, which feature a mapping radar housed in a bulged nose radome (two CC-142 transports have been sold). Kenya operates three standard Dash 8s as transports. Mexico's navy operates a single Dash 8 Q200 transport.

The US Air Force uses two modified Dash 8s for missile range control, designated E-9As. These feature a large phased array radar mounted along the right hand side of the fuselage, telemetry equipment and an APS-128D surveillance radar in a ventral dome.

**Photo:** A Canadian Forces CC-142 navigation trainer. (Gary Gentle)

## Bombardier Canadair Challenger

*Country of origin:* Canada

*Type:* Special missions and VIP transport

*Powerplants:* 600 – Two 33.6kN (7500lb) Avco Lycoming ALF 502L turbofans. 601 – Two 40.7kN (9140lb) General Electric CF34-3As.

*Performance:* 600 – Max speed 904km/h (488kt), max cruising speed 890km/h (480kt), long range cruising speed 800km/h (432kt). Range with reserves (latter build aircraft) 6300km (3402nm). 601-1A – Max cruising speed 851km/h (460kt), typical cruising speed 820km/h (442kt), long range cruising speed 786km/h (424kt). Range with max fuel and reserves 6208km (3352nm).

*Weights:* 600 latter build aircraft – Empty 8370kg (18,450lb), operating empty 10,285kg (22,675lb), max takeoff 18,200kg (40,125lb). 601-1A – Empty 9050kg (19,950lb), operating empty 11,605kg (25,585lb). Max takeoff 19,550kg (43,100lb).

*Dimensions:* 600 – Wing span 18.85m (61ft 10in), length 20.85m (68ft 5in), height 6.30m (20ft 8in). Wing area 41.8m² (450sq ft). 601 – Same except span 19.61m (64ft 4in). Wing area 48.3m² (520.0sq ft).

*Accommodation:* Flightcrew of two. Various seating options available depending on customer preference, max seating for 19.

*Armament:* None

*Operators:* Australia*, Canada, China, Croatia, Denmark, Germany, Jordan*.

*History:* The Challenger business jet has seen limited military service, largely as a VIP transport.

Canadair purchased the rights to an all new business jet developed by Bill Lear, original designer of the Learjet, in 1976. Known as the LearStar 600 the design featured a large cabin, long range and good operating economics. Canadair launched development of the LearStar design as the CL-600 in October 1976.

The first CL-600 flew on November 8 1978, however the aircraft suffered a number of early problems. A major weight and drag reduction program pared back the CL-600's weight, improving range, but the troubled ALF 502 turbofans failed to meet predicted performance levels.

Problems with the ALF 502 powered CL-600 led Canadair to develop the considerably improved General Electric CF34 powered Challenger 601 (the CF34 also powers the USAF's A-10 Thunderbolt II and USN's S-2 Viking). Other detail changes included winglets, which were also offered as a retrofit to earlier aircraft. The 601 first flew on April 10 1982, the CL-600 was dropped in 1983. The 601 has been offered in progressively improved variants, the latest is the 604 with EFIS avionics and other changes.

Canada is the largest Challenger military operator with six on strength. The Canadian Forces uses CE-144s as high speed, high altitude threat simulators for developing fighter pilot interception skills. One was used as a CX-144 electronics and avionics testbed, while others serve as CC-144 VIP transports. All Canadian CL-600s have been fitted with the winglets of the 601.

Other operators are Malaysia (CL-600), Croatia (601), Denmark (604), Germany (601) and China (601), mostly used as VIP transports. Australia has ordered two 604s for delivery from 2002.

*Photo:* A Canadian Forces CE-144. (Canadian Forces)

## Bombardier Global Express & ASTOR

*Country of origin:* Canada

*Type:* GX – VIP transport. ASTOR – Ground surveillance aircraft

*Powerplants:* GX – Two 65.6kN (14,750lb) Rolls-Royce BR710A2-20 turbofans.

*Performance:* GX – High speed cruise 935km/h (505kt) or Mach 0.88, normal cruising speed 904km/h (488kt) or Mach 0.85, long range cruising speed 850km/h (459kt) or Mach 0.80. Range with eight passengers, four crew and reserves at long range cruising speed 12,038km (6500nm), at normal cruising speed 11,297km (6100nm).

*Weights:* GX – Operating empty 22,135kg (48,800lb), max takeoff 42,410kg (93,500lb) to 43,545kg (96,000lb).

*Dimensions:* GX – Span over winglets 28.65m (94ft 0in), length 30.30m (99ft 5in), height 7.57m (24ft 10in). Wing area 94.95m² (1022sq ft).

*Accommodation:* GX – Flightcrew of two plus one or two flight attendants. Typical arrangements seat from eight to 18 passengers. Can be fitted with a galley, crew rest station, work stations, a conference/lounge/dining area, a stateroom with a fold out bed, toilet, shower and wardrobe. High density 30 seat corporate shuttle configuration offered. ASTOR – Two flightcrew and three backend operators.

*Armament:* None

*Operators:* GX – Malaysia. ASTOR – UK*.

*History:* The Global Express is an ultra long range corporate jet used as a VIP transport by Malaysia and serves as the basis for the Raytheon ASTOR ground surveillance aircraft in development for the UK RAF.

Bombardier's Canadair division announced development of the Global Express business jet in October 1991. Officially launched on December 20 1993, the Global Express first flew on October 13 1996. First customer delivery of a completed aircraft was in July 1999.

The fly-by-wire Global Express shares the CRJ regional airliner's fuselage cross section, but is otherwise an all new design. It features an advanced all new supercritical wing with a 35° sweep and winglets, plus a new T-tail. It is powered by Rolls-Royce BR710s and features an advanced six screen flightdeck with optional head-up displays.

Malaysia is the first military Global Express customer, taking delivery of a single example in 2000 for VIP duties.

In June 1999 the UK Ministry of Defence selected a Raytheon/Bombardier team to meet its Airborne Stand-Off Radar (ASTOR) requirement with a Global Express based platform. The ASTOR Global Express will feature a dual mode SAR/MTI (synthetic aperture radar/moving target indicator) radar based on the U-2's ASARS-2, mounted beneath the forward fuselage in a 4.6m (15ft) long radome. A satcomm antenna is mounted in a fairing on the upper fuselage. Inside the ASTOR Global Express will feature three operator stations, with information transferred by datalink to ground stations for use by battlefield commanders.

The first of five ASTORs will fly in October 2003, with service entry with the RAF in 2005.

In service the ASTOR will fly at 51,000ft where it will have a search range of 300km (160nm). Raytheon is marketing an export version as the GSARS – Ground Surveillance Airborne Radar System.

*Photo:* The Global Express prototype acting as an aerodynamic validation aircraft for the ASTOR program. (Bombardier)

## British Aerospace Bulldog

**Country of origin:** United Kingdom

**Type:** Two seat basic trainer

**Powerplant:** T.1 – One 150kW (200hp) Lycoming IO-360-A1B6 fuel injected flat four piston engine driving a two blade constant speed propeller.

**Performance:** T.1 – Max speed 240km/h (130kt), max cruising speed 222km/h (120kt), economical cruising speed 195km/h (105kt). Max initial rate of climb 1035ft/min. Service ceiling 16,000ft. Range with max fuel at 55% power 1000km (540nm). Endurance with max fuel 5 hours.

**Weights:** T.1 – Empty equipped 650kg (1430lb), normal and semi aerobatic max takeoff 1065kg (2350lb), fully aerobatic max takeoff 1015kg (2238lb).

**Dimensions:** T.1 – Wing span 10.06m (33ft 0in), length 7.09m (23ft 3in), height 2.28m (7ft 6in). Wing area 12.0m² (129.4sq ft).

**Accommodation:** Seating for two side by side, with room for an observer behind them.

**Armament:** Provision for weapons on four optional underwing hardpoints, including rocket and gun pods, practice and live bombs.

**Operators:** Jordan, Kenya, Lebanon, Malta, Sweden, UK.

**History:** The Bulldog two seat primary trainer has its origins in the civil Beagle B.121 Pup light aircraft.

The Beagle Pup first flew time on April 8 1967 and established the Bulldog's basic design and configuration. While the Pup was popular with pilots for its good flying characteristics the Beagle company's continuing financial difficulties forced it to close its doors in January 1970, with Pup production ceasing after 150 had been built, despite the type's promise.

Before its closure Beagle had flown a military trainer variant called the Bulldog on May 19 1969. Based closely on the Pup, features of the Bulldog included a rearward sliding cockpit canopy, seating for two side by side (with room for an observer behind them), a Lycoming IO-360 four cylinder piston engine driving a two blade constant speed prop, and fixed undercarriage.

Following Beagle's collapse, Scottish Aviation (itself since merged into British Aerospace – now BAE Systems) purchased the Bulldog's design rights, and flew its own Bulldog prototype on February 14 1971. The first Series 100 production aircraft flew on June 22 1971 and 98 were built for Kenya, Malaysia and Sweden.

The Series 120 was built in greater numbers, and introduced increased aerobatic capability at maximum weight and full aerobatic capability up to a higher weight. The largest Bulldog customer was the RAF, which took delivery of 130 Model 121s designated the Bulldog T.1. The survivors equip University Air Squadrons to train sponsored undergraduate students but are being replaced by contractor operated Grob 114E Tutors. The 120 was also widely exported, and production ceased in 1981.

A developed version of the Bulldog was the Bullfinch, which featured retractable undercarriage. It flew in 1976 but did not go into production.

**Photo:** A Maltese ex RAF Bulldog. (Harold van Eupen/Sentry Aviation News)

## BAe/Hawker Siddeley HS.748

**Country of origin:** United Kingdom

**Type:** Utility and VIP transport

**Powerplants:** Srs 2A – Two 1700kW (2280ehp) Rolls-Royce Dart RDa.7 Mk 534-2 or 535-2 turboprops driving four blade propellers.

**Performance:** Srs 2A – Cruising speed 452km/h (244kt). Max initial rate of climb 1320ft/min. Service ceiling 25,000ft. Range with max payload and reserves 1360km (735nm), range with max fuel and reserves 3130km (1690nm).

**Weights:** Srs 2A – Operating empty 12,160kg (26,805lb), max takeoff 21,092kg (46,500lb).

**Dimensions:** Srs 2A – Wing span 30.02m (98ft 6in), length 20.42m (67ft 0in), height 7.57m (24ft 10in). Wing area 75.4m² (810.8sq ft).

**Accommodation:** Flightcrew of two. Seating for up to 58 troops in airliner style seating. Can carry 48 paratroopers or 24 stretcher patients and nine medical attendants. Can be fitted with VIP interior. Australian nav trainers fitted with side facing workstation for two students and an instructor, plus passenger seating.

**Armament:** None

**Operators:** Australia, Brazil, India, Nepal, South Korea, Thailand.

**History:** The HS.748 began life as an Avro design effort to re-enter the civil market in anticipation of a decline in military business.

It proved to be a reasonable sales success, mainly as an airliner, but also as a military transport. Of the 382 built, 52 were delivered new to military customers.

The 748 first surfaced in 1958 as the Avro 748 in 1958. The new aircraft first flew on June 24 1960 and became the HS.748 from 1963 (and BAe 748 from 1977).

The improved Series 2 first flew on November 6 1961, and in its 2, 2A and 2C variants, was the most successful of the line. The Series 2 differed from the 1 in having progressively higher weights and more powerful engines. The Series 2B appeared in 1977, with aerodynamic and other improvements, including an increased wing span.

The Super 748 first flew in 1984. It introduced flightdeck improvements, more efficient and hushkitted engines, and a new interior fitout.

Two specific military versions offered were the BAe 748 Military Transport and the Coastguarder. The Military Transport features a large cargo door in the rear fuselage, strengthened floor for freight and optional higher max takeoff weights. Customers included Belgium, Brazil and Ecuador. India licence built 20 similar aircraft.

The Coastguarder was optimised for maritime patrol and SAR and was fitted with a search radar, but none were ordered.

India flew a 748 modified with an AEW style rotodome mounted E-3 style above the fuselage for aerodynamic testing and development of a phased array radar for a possible AEW&C project. It was destroyed in a crash in January 1999.

Australia was a significant 748 operator, originally taking delivery of 12 from 1967. Six survive in RAAF service as navigation trainers but they are due to be replaced in 2002 by modified Raytheon Beech 350 King Airs or Cessna Citations. The Royal Australian Navy operated two configured as EW trainers to simulate an electronic warfare environment for ship crew training.

**Photo:** An Australian HS.748. (Theo van Loon)

## British Aerospace/MDC AV-8S Harrier

**Country of origin:** United Kingdom

**Type:** STOVL light attack aircraft

**Powerplant:** AV-8S – One 95.6kN (21,500lb) Rolls-Royce F402-RR-402 (Pegasus) turbofan.

**Performance:** AV-8S – Max speed 1175km/h (635kt). Max initial rate of climb 29,000ft/min. Time to 40,000ft after vertical takeoff 2min 23sec. Service ceiling 51,000ft. Takeoff run with 2270kg (5000lb) warload 305m (1000ft). Ferry range with external fuel 3430km (1850nm). Combat radius with 1995kg (4400lb) warload, hi-lo-hi, 665km (360nm).

**Weights:** AV-8S – Empty equipped 5530kg (12,190lb), normal VTO 7735kg (17,050lb), max takeoff STO 10,115kg (22,300lb). Internal fuel 2295kg (5060lb).

**Dimensions:** AV-8S – Wing span 7.70m (25ft 3in), length 13.87m (45ft 6in), height 3.63m (11ft 11in). Wing area 18.7m² (201.1sq ft).

**Accommodation:** Pilot only in AV-8S, two in tandem in TAV-8S.

**Armament:** Two 30mm Aden cannons mounted in underfuselage fairings. Four underwing stations can carry up to 2405kg (5300lb) of ordnance, including AIM-9 Sidewinder AAMs, rockets and bombs.

**Operators:** Thailand

**History:** The revolutionary Harrier was the world's first practical V/STOL (vertical/short takeoff and landing) fixed wing aircraft.

The origins of the Harrier lie in the Hawker P.1127, which was designed from 1957 to take advantage of the Bristol BS.53 turbofan engine. The revolutionary BS.53 was able to vector or direct thrust using its four exhaust nozzles which could pivot more than 90° from the horizontal, and evolved into the Rolls-Royce Pegasus.

The first of six P.1127 prototypes successfully made its first hovering flight on October 21 1960, while the first transition from vertical to horizontal flight occurred on September 12 1961. The P.1127s were followed by nine preproduction development aircraft named Kestrel, which were operated for a time by a special tri nation squadron with pilots from the RAF, Germany and the USA. Britain ordered a further six development aircraft in February 1965, which it named Harrier. The first of these original Harriers first flew in August 1966.

While the planned P.1154 multirole supersonic fighter development for the RAF and RN was scrapped, the Harrier entered production for the RAF as a light strike aircraft – the first of these, designated GR.1, flew on December 28 1967. The RAF ordered 132, including T.2 trainers. RAF Harriers were delivered as GR.3s and T.4s from 1976 fitted with a Marconi laser ranger and marked target seeker in a lengthened nose. All have been retired.

The US Marine Corps took delivery of 110 similar AV-8As and two seat TAV-8As. Later upgraded to AV-8C standard, the last was retired in 1987.

The Spanish navy ordered 11 AV-8S single seaters and two TAV-8S two seaters from MDC. Designated VA.1 and VAE.1 respectively and named Matador, these were later replaced by Harrier IIs and Harrier II Pluses and were sold to the Thai navy for service aboard its Spanish built aircraft carrier *Chakri Naruebet*. Thailand took delivery of the AV-8s in 1996 but a lack of spares and funding following the Asian financial crisis has hampered their operation.

**Photo:** A Royal Thai Navy AV-8S. (Royal Thai Navy)

## British Aerospace Sea Harrier

**Country of origin:** UK

**Type:** V/STOL naval multirole fighter

**Powerplant:** One 95.6kN (21,500lb) Rolls-Royce Pegasus Mk 104 turbofan.

**Performance:** FRS.1 – Max speed 1185km/h (640kt) plus at low level, cruising speed at 36,000ft 850km/h (460kt), cruising speed at low level 640 to 835km/h (350 to 450kt). Combat radius on a high altitude intercept mission 750km (405nm), combat radius on a low level attack mission 565km (305nm).

**Weights:** FRS.1 – Operating empty 6375kg (14,052lb), max takeoff 11,880kg (26,200lb). Internal fuel 2295kg (5060lb).

**Dimensions:** FRS.1 – Wing span 7.70m (25ft 3in), length overall 14.50m (47ft 7in), height 3.71m (12ft 2in). Wing area 18.7m² (201.1sq ft).

**Accommodation:** Pilot only.

**Armament:** FRS.1 – Two underfuselage pod mounted 30mm Aden cannons. Four underwing pylons can carry up to 3630kg (8000lb) but cleared for 2270kg (5000lb) of armament including AIM-9 Sidewinders, bombs, rockets and BAe Sea Eagle anti shipping missiles. Indian FRS.51s wired for Matra AAMs.

**Operators:** India

**History:** The Sea Harrier has one of the best air-to-air combat records in recent military history, shooting down 28 Argentine warplanes in the Falklands War for no loss.

The suitability of the basic Harrier design for use from small aircraft carriers was obvious from the program's inception. A P.1127 (Harrier predecessor) first demonstrated the type's suitability for carrier operations by flying off HMS *Ark Royal* in 1963, although official Royal Navy interest was not forthcoming until the early/mid 1970s when the Phantom and Buccaneer equipped *Ark Royal* was nearing retirement without a planned replacement. Thus the RN sanctioned development of a navalised Harrier for operation off the forthcoming ASW helicopter carriers (fitted with ski jump ramps), with 24 Sea Harrier FRS.1s ordered in May 1975.

This far sighted decision was to pay huge dividends as the Sea Harrier came into its own during the 1982 Falklands War, providing vital air cover for British ground forces and ships, and consistently outclassing Argentine Daggers in air-to-air engagements.

The FRS.1 Harrier is similar to the RAF GR.3 except for the forward fuselage. The cockpit was raised, increasing room for additional avionics in the forward fuselage and giving the pilot much greater all round vision, while the FRS.1's nose contains an oblique reconnaissance camera and a Ferranti Blue Fox multimode radar (a development of the Lynx helicopter's Sea Spray radar). The FRS.1's Pegasus Mk 104 engine is a navalised version of the GR.3's Mk 103.

The RN took delivery of a total of 57 FRS.1s plus four T.4N two seat conversion trainers (without Blue Fox radar). Surviving FRS.1s were retired from RN service in 1995 to be upgraded to F/A.2 standard.

India is the only Sea Harrier export customer, ordering the first of 21 Sea Harrier FRS.51s and four T.60 trainers in 1978. Two refurbished ex RAF T.4 two seaters were delivered in 1999. So far upgrade plans remain unfulfilled.

**Photo:** A Indian FRS.51. (BAE Systems)

# British Aerospace Sea Harrier F/A.2

**Country of origin:** United Kingdom

**Type:** Multirole V/STOL fighter

**Powerplant:** One 95.6kN (21,500lb) Rolls-Royce Pegasus Mk 106 turbofan.

**Performance:** F/A.2 – Max speed 1185km/h (640kt) plus, cruising speed at 36,000ft 850km/h (460kt). Max initial rate of climb 50,000ft/min. Service ceiling 51,000ft. Takeoff run without ski ramp approx 305m (1000ft). Combat radius on a 90min time on station CAP with four AIM-120s and two drop tanks 185km (100nm). Hi-lo-hi combat radius with two Sea Eagle missiles and two 30mm cannons 370km (200nm). Hi-lo-hi reconnaissance mission radius with two drop tanks 970km (525nm).

**Weights:** Max takeoff 9843kg (21,700lb). Internal fuel 2351kg (5182lb).

**Dimensions:** F/A.2 – Wing span 7.70m (25ft 3in), length overall 14.17m (46ft 6in), height 3.71m (12ft 2in). Wing area 18.7m² (201.1sq ft).

**Accommodation:** Pilot only.

**Armament:** Cleared for 2270kg (5000lb) on four underwing and two underfuselage hardpoints. Can carry up to four AIM-120 Amraams on outboard and underfuselage stations, or two AIM-120s and four AIM-9s. Underfuselage stations can also carry two 30mm Aden cannons. Other weapons include bombs, rockets and Sea Eagle anti ship missiles.

**Operators:** UK

**History:** The F/A.2 upgrade of the Sea Harrier FRS.1 involved changes to the airframe, cockpit, avionics, radar and armament.

Work on a midlife upgrade of the Sea Harrier first began in January 1985 when BAe was contracted to do a project definition study. British Aerospace initially proposed a number of aerodynamic refinements plus wingtip Sidewinder missile rails that were not adopted, with changes instead focusing around a new radar and modernised cockpit.

The first modified Sea Harrier, designated FRS.2, was an aerodynamic prototype without radar installed and it flew for the first time in its new configuration on September 19 1988. In all, British Aerospace converted 32 FRS.1s to the new standard (the FRS.2 designation was dropped in favour of F/A.2), while 18 new build F/A.2s were ordered to cover attrition losses. The first production conversions were delivered from April 1993, the last in 1997, while the last new build F/A.2 was delivered in December 1998.

The most obvious change with the F/A.2 is the Blue Vixen radar mounted in a new radome. The BAE Systems Blue Vixen is a pulse Doppler multimode radar featuring all weather lookdown/shootdown capability, track-while-scan, multiple target tracking and improved surface target detection abilities. The F/A.2's nose contains an additional avionics bay, while the upgrade to the cockpit involves fitting HOTAS controls and multifunction CRT displays. The fuselage is also stretched slightly, with a 35cm (1ft 2in) plug behind the wing.

The F/A.2 upgrade has greatly boosted the Sea Harrier's capabilities. The F/A.2 is due to be equipped with the ASRAAM in place of the AIM-9 and colour multifunction displays and JTIDS, while further upgrades could include the Harrier II's more powerful Pegasus 11-61.

**Photo:** An F/A.2. (Paul Sadler)

# British Aerospace 146 & Avro RJ

**Country of origin:** United Kingdom

**Type:** VIP transport

**Powerplants:** BAe 146-100 – Four 30.0kN (6700lb) Textron Lycoming ALF 502R-3s or four 31.0kN (6970lb) ALF 502R-5 turbofans.

**Performance:** BAe 146-100 – Cruising speed 767km/h (414kt), long range cruising speed 670km/h (361kt). Range with standard fuel 3000km (1620nm), range with max payload 1630km (880nm).

**Weights:** 146-100 – Operating empty 23,288kg (51,342lb), max takeoff 38,100kg (84,000lb).

**Dimensions:** 146-100 – Wing span 26.21m (86ft 0in), length 26.20m (86ft 0in), height 8.61m (28ft 3in). Wing area 77.3m² (832.0sq ft).

**Accommodation:** 146-100 – Flightcrew of two, plus seating for up to 94 passengers six abreast in an airliner configuration. RAF CC.Mk 2s and Saudi Statesman aircraft fitted with VIP interiors.

**Armament:** None

**Operators:** Bahrain*, Saudi Arabia, UAE (Abu Dhabi), UK.

**History:** The BAe 146 regional jet is only in limited military service as a VIP transport.

The origins of the 146 date to August 1973 when the then Hawker Siddeley Aviation announced it was designing a short range quiet airliner powered by four small turbofans. Designated HS.146, development of the new airliner stalled a few months when a worsening economic recession made the risk of the project seem unjustifiable. Limited development continued before the project was relaunched in 1978, by which time Hawker Siddeley had been absorbed into the newly created British Aerospace.

The renamed BAe 146 made its first flight on September 3 1981. Certification was granted in early 1983, with first deliveries following shortly afterwards in May 1983. Initial deliveries were of the 146-100, later versions included the stretched, 85 to 100 seat 146-200 and further stretched, 100 to 112 seat 146-300. Because of the type's low noise characteristics the 146 series has been quite successful as a freighter, designated QT – Quiet Trader.

The 146QT also formed the basis of the 146STA Small Tactical Airlifter, which featured a cargo door in the rear fuselage. Payloads included up to 60 fully equipped paratroops, or 24 stretchers. A demonstrator 146STA flew in the late 1980s but none were ordered.

The 146 evolved into the Avro RJ series in the early 1990s, with improved engines and other systems. The 146-100 became the RJ70, the 146-200 the RJ85 and the 146-300 the RJ100. Further development has led to the Honeywell AS977 powered RJX series, which first flew in early 2001. BAE cancelled the RJX late that year.

Military use of the 146 is limited to the UK, UAE and Saudi Arabia. The RAF leased three BAe 146-100s as CC.1s for evaluation as replacement for Andovers for the Queen's Flight. Two 146-100s were then ordered as CC.2s for service with the Queen's Flight. These were delivered from 1986 and were later fitted with Loral Matador infrared jamming equipment. A third was delivered in 1990.

Saudi Arabia operates four 146s, named Statesman, as VIP transports with its Royal Flight. Bahrain's royal flight operates one 146-100. Bahrain has also ordered two Avro RJ85s.

**Photo:** A Royal Air Force BAe 146 CC.2. (Dave Fraser)

## British Aerospace Nimrod

**Country of origin:** United Kingdom

**Type:** Maritime patrol and Elint aircraft

**Powerplants:** Four 54.0kN (12,140lb) Rolls-Royce RB.168-20 Spey Mk 250 turbofans.

**Performance:** MR.2 – Max cruising speed 880km/h (475kt), economical cruising speed 787km/h (425kt), typical patrol speed at low level on two engines 370km/h (200kt). Service ceiling 42,000ft. Typical endurance 12 hours. Max endurance without refuelling 15 hours, with one refuelling 19 hours. Ferry range 9265km (5000nm).

**Weights:** MR.2 – Typical empty 39,010kg (86,000lb), max normal takeoff 80,515kg (177,500lb), max overload takeoff 87,090kg (192,000lb). Internal fuel 38,940kg (85,840lb).

**Dimensions:** Wing span 35.00m (114ft 10in), length 38.63m (126ft 9in), height 9.08m (29ft 9in). Wing area 197.0m² (2121.0sq ft).

**Accommodation:** Normal crew of 12 comprising two pilots and flight engineer on flightdeck with navigator, tactical navigator, radio operator, two sonic system operators, ESM/MAD operator and two observers/stores loaders in main cabin.

**Armament:** Total of 6125kg (13,500lb) of ordnance can be carried in the internal weapons bay and on two underwing hardpoints. Options include AGM-84 Harpoon ASMs, Stingray torpedoes, bombs and depth charges, plus up to four AIM-9 Sidewinders for self defence.

**Operators:** UK

**History:** The Nimrod was developed to replace the RAF's aging Avro Shackleton maritime patrol aircraft.

In 1964 two unsold Comet 4 airliners were selected as prototype airframes for the new maritime patrol aircraft. These two prototypes were given the Hawker Siddeley model number 801, and the first flew in converted form on May 23 1967. Changes to the Comet included the replacement of the RR Avon turbojets with Spey turbofans (increasing fuel efficiency, and thus range – the Nimrod can cruise while on patrol on two of its four Speys) and a new lower fuselage with an internal weapons bay and extended nose to house a search radar. Other changes included a magnetic anomaly detector (MAD) mounted in a boom extending from the rear fuselage, and ESM sensors mounted in a fairing on top of the tail. The first of 46 Nimrod MR.1s entered RAF service in October 1969.

The MR.2 designation applies to 32 Nimrods upgraded from 1975. The upgrade involved a new central tactical system with a new computer and processors, new communications suite and EMI Searchwater radar. Subsequently the fleet was modified to MR.2P standard with the addition of an inflight refuelling probe, and more recently Nimrods have been fitted with Loral wingtip ESM pods.

A mid 1980s program to develop a Nimrod based AEW aircraft (designated AEW.3 and fitted with nose and tail mounted radomes) was cancelled due to technical problems.

Three Nimrods serve as R.1P Elint platforms. Identifiable by the lack of MAD boom, the R.1Ps are fitted with sensors to detect and record electronic emissions. A previously stored Nimrod airframe was converted to R.1P configuration after an R.1P made a successful ditching off the coast of Scotland in May 1995.

**Photo:** A Nimrod MR.2P. (Paul Sadler)

## Britten-Norman Islander/Defender

**Country of origin:** United Kingdom

**Type:** STOL utility transport

**Powerplants:** BN-2B-20 – Two 225kW (300hp) Textron Lycoming IO-540K1B5 flat six piston engines driving two blade props.

**Performance:** BN-2B-20 – Max speed 280km/h (151kt), max cruising speed 264km/h (142kt), economical cruising speed 245km/h (132kt). Max initial rate of climb 1130ft/min. Service ceiling 17,200ft. Takeoff run at sea level 352m (1155ft). Range at economical cruising speed with standard fuel 1136km (613nm), with optional fuel 1965km (1061nm).

**Weights:** BN-2B-20 – Empty equipped 1925kg (4244lb), max takeoff 2993kg (6600lb).

**Dimensions:** Wing span 14.94m (49ft 0in), length 10.86m (35ft 8in), height 4.18m (13ft 9in). Wing area 30.2m² (325.0sq ft).

**Accommodation:** Flightcrew of one or two, and eight in main cabin.

**Armament:** Defender fitted with four underwing hardpoints for bombs, rockets and gun pods.

**Operators:** Includes Angola, Belgium, Belize, Botswana, Cyprus, Guyana, India, Jamaica, Mauritania, Panama, Senegal, Seychelles, UK, Venezuela, Zimbabwe.

**History:** More than 1200 Islanders, Defenders and Turbine Islander/Defenders have been built for civil and military customers.

The BN-2 Islander was Britten-Norman's second original design, work on which began during 1963. Design emphasis was on producing a rugged and durable aircraft that had good field performance and operating economics and was easy to maintain.

One unusual feature was that there was no centre aisle between seats in the main cabin, instead there were three doors along each side of the fuselage for passenger boarding. The prototype BN-2 Islander (powered by two 155kW/210hp Continental IO-360s) first flew on June 13 1965.

The first production machines were powered by 195kW (260hp) Lycoming O-540s and were simply designated the BN-2, the first flew in 1967. Since then it has been built in improved BN-2A and BN-2B forms, with the BN-2B still in production. The military specific Defender has four underwing hardpoints.

The BN-2T Turbine Islander/Defender is powered by two RR Allison 250 turboprops, and first flew in August 1980. The BN-2T is not in as wide scale service as its piston powered brothers, but has spawned a range of military special mission derivatives.

The maritime patrol ASW/ASV Islander flew in demonstrator form in 1984, but did not enter production. The CASTOR Islander battlefield surveillance platform was intended for the British Army, the MASTOR featured the Searchwater 2 radar.

Various AEW Defenders have also been marketed including the MSSA (Multi Sensor Surveillance Aircraft) or BN-2T-4R, fitted with an APG-66 radar in a bulbous radome, plus FLIR and GPS.

The Defender 4000 features the larger wing of the Islander's three engined brother, the Trislander, plus an enlarged nose for a search radar, more powerful engines and increased weights. It first flew in August 1994.

**Photo:** The Defender 4000. (Britten-Norman)

# Canadair CT-114 Tutor

**Country of origin:** Canada

**Type:** Two seat advanced jet trainer

**Powerplant:** CL-41A – One 13.1kN (2950lb) Orenda licence built General Electric J85-CAN-J4 turbojet.

**Performance:** CL-41A – Max speed at 28,500ft 801km/h (432kt). Service ceiling 43,000ft. Range 1000km (540nm).

**Weights:** Empty equipped 2220kg (4895lb), max takeoff 3532kg (7788lb).

**Dimensions:** Wing span 11.13m (36ft 6in), length 9.75m (32ft 0in), height 2.84m (9ft 4in). Wing area 20.4m² (220.0sq ft).

**Accommodation:** Seating for two, side by side.

**Armament:** Usually none in Canadian service. Malaysian CL-41Gs were fitted with six hardpoints which could carry a total 1815kg (4000lb) of ordnance, including bombs, rockets, gun pods and air-to-air missiles.

**Operators:** Canada

**History:** The Canadair Tutor served for almost four decades as Canada's advanced pilot trainer, and is the mount of the renowned Snowbirds demonstration team.

The Tutor was initially developed as a private venture due to a lack of official Canadian government interest in the project. Regardless of the lack of support, development continued, resulting in a first flight on January 13 1960. This first prototype CL-41 was powered by a 10.8kN (2400lb) Pratt & Whitney JT12A-5 turbojet. The Tutor design differed from most of its contemporaries in having side by side seating and a T-tail. Another design feature is the two airbrakes on either side of the rear fuselage.

The Canadian government ordered 190 production CL-41s for the then Royal Canadian Air Force in September 1961 after an evaluation of contemporary trainers. Unlike the prototype these production aircraft are powered by a General Electric J85 turbojet, built under licence in Canada by Orenda. In Canadian service the CL-41 is designated the CT-114 Tutor.

The 190 production Tutors were delivered between December 1963 and September 1966.

The principle operator of the Tutor was 2 Canadian Forces Flying Training School (2CFFTS) at Moose Jaw in Saskatchewan, where pilots were trained up to wings standard. Those pilots bound for fast jets then had further Tutor training. However, Canada is transitioning its advanced pilot training to the Bombardier operated NATO Flying Training in Canada program, which became operational in 2000 (and is also based at Moose Jaw). This has resulted in the retirement of most of Canada's Tutors, and leaving the famous Snowbirds aerobatic display team (431 Air Demonstration Squadron) as the major Tutor operator.

The only country outside Canada to operate the Tutor was Malaysia. The Royal Malaysian Air Force took delivery of 20 CL-41Gs, which compared with the basic CL-41 were equipped with six hardpoints capable of carrying a range of armaments including rockets and bombs. Named the Tebuan (or wasp) the CL-41Gs were delivered in 1967-68, but were retired in the mid 1980s.

**Photo:** Canada's Snowbirds are the last Tutor operators apart from a small number used for test and development work.

# Canadair CL-215 & CL-415

**Country of origin:** Canada

**Type:** Firefighting, SAR and multirole transport amphibian

**Powerplants:** CL-215 – Two 1565kW (2100hp) Pratt & Whitney R-2800-CA3 18 cylinder radial piston engines driving three blade constant speed propellers.

**Performance:** CL-215 – Max cruising speed 290km/h (157kt). Max initial rate of climb 1000ft/min. Takeoff run from water at 17,100kg (37,700lb) all up weight 800m (2625ft). Range with a 1590kg (3500lb) payload at max cruising speed 1715km (925nm), or 2095km (1130nm) at long range cruise power.

**Weights:** CL-215 – Empty 12,220kg (26,940lb), typical operating empty 12,740kg (28,080lb), max takeoff from water 17,100kg (37,700lb), max takeoff from land 19,730kg (43,500lb).

**Dimensions:** CL-215 – Wing span 28.60m (93ft 10in), length 19.82m (65ft 1in), height 8.98m (29ft 6in) on land or 6.88m (22ft 7in) on water. Wing area 100.3m² (1080sq ft).

**Accommodation:** Flightcrew of two, plus accommodation in special missions variants for a third flightdeck member, a mission specialist and two observers. Passenger configuration for 30, or in a combi configuration for 11, with firebombing tanks retained and freight in forward fuselage. Fire retardant capacity of 6125kg (13,500lb).

**Armament:** None

**Operators:** Greece*, Spain, Thailand, Venezuela.

**History:** While most production CL-215 amphibians have been for civilian/government agency work where they serve as firebombers, a number have also been acquired for a range of military roles including maritime patrol, search and rescue, and transport.

The CL-215 first flew on October 23 1967, and 125 were built in different batches through to 1990. Primary customers were government agencies, including various Canadian province governments and France, plus the air forces of Greece, Spain, Italy and Yugoslavia. The Italian AF CL-215s were later transferred to a government agency.

In the firefighting role the CL-215's capabilities are impressive – it can scoop up 5455 litres (1200 Imp gal/1440 US gal) of water from a flat water source such as a lake in 12 seconds.

Spain took delivery of a total of 20 CL-215s, of which eight were configured for maritime patrol and search and rescue work, while the Royal Thai Navy operated two CL-215s, also configured for SAR. Another military CL-215 operator is Venezuela, its two aircraft are configured as passenger transports.

Bombardier offers retrofit kits for CL-215s to Pratt & Whitney Canada PW123 turboprop powered CL-215T standard. Spain ordered 15 retrofit kits for its aircraft.

The improved, new build CL-415 SuperScooper features the PW123s, an EFIS cockpit, higher weights and an increased capacity firebombing system. Its principle mission is that of a firebomber, but various special mission (including SAR and maritime patrol) and transport configurations are offered. The first CL-415 flew on December 6 1993. The new CL-415GR ordered by Greece has higher operating weights.

**Photo:** Greece is the largest military CL-215 operator, and is ordering CL-415s. (Greek MoD)

## CAP Aviation CAP 10, 20, 21, 230, 231 & 232

**Country of origin:** France

**Type:** Basic trainer and aerobatics aircraft

**Powerplant:** CAP 10B – One 135kW (180hp) Lycoming AEIO-360-B2F fuel injected flat four piston engine driving a two blade propeller.

**Performance:** CAP 10B – Max speed 270km/h (146kt), max cruising speed at 75% power 250km/h (135kt). Initial rate of climb 1575ft/min. Service ceiling 16,400ft. Range with max fuel 1000km (540nm).

**Weights:** 10B – Empty equipped 550kg (1213lb), max takeoff in aerobatic category 760kg (1675lb), or 830kg (1829lb) in utility category.

**Dimensions:** 10B – Wing span 8.06m (26ft 5in), length 7.16m (23ft 6in), height 2.55m (8ft 5in). Wing area 10.9m² (116.8sq ft).

**Accommodation:** Two side by side in CAP 10, pilot only in other models.

**Armament:** None

**Operators:** CAP 10 – France, Morocco. CAP 230 – Morocco. CAP 231 – France. CAP 232 – France, Morocco*.

**History:** The CAP Aviation (formerly Mudry CAP) CAP series serves as an initial flight screener/basic trainer with the French and Mexican air forces and as an aerobatic display mount for a Moroccan air force team.

The successful CAP series dates back to the Piel C.P.30 Emeraude of the early 1960s. More than 200 two seat Emeraudes (first flight 1962) were built in four different factories across Europe.

One of the companies to build the Emeraude was CAARP, a company owned by Auguste Mudry. CAARP used the basic Emeraude design as the basis for the CAP 10, which was a similar aircraft other than its 135kW (180hp) Lycoming IO-360 engine and stressing for aerobatic flight. The prototype CAP 10 first flew in August 1968. CAARP built 30 CAP 10s for the French air force before Mudry started CAP 10 production for civil orders in 1972 at his other aviation company, Avions Mudry.

The CAP 10 remains in production in 10B form with an enlarged tail. Twenty-six CAP 10Bs were delivered to the French Armée de l'Air.

Other CAP 10 military operators are Morocco, the Mexican air force which took delivery of 20 for aerobatic training, and the French navy, which operates 10 for pilot screening and grading.

The CAP 20 meanwhile is a single seat development with a 150kW (200hp) AEIO-360 engine designed for civil aerobatic competition. The Armée de l'Air took delivery of six CAP 20s for its Equipe de Voltige aerobatic team.

The revised CAP 21 replaced the CAP 20 in 1981. The CAP 21 is of the same basic overall configuration to the CAP 20 but introduced a new wing and undercarriage. The following CAP 230 was heavier, stronger and powered by an uprated AEIO-540 flat six. Four were delivered to the French Equipe de Voltige team. The 230 was followed by the 231, which first flew in April 1990. Seven CAP 231s were delivered to the Moroccan air force's aerobatic display team, Marche Verte (Green March). The CAP 231 EX introduced a carbonfibre wing, while production has switched to the further improved CAP 232, which first flew in July 1994. The French air force bought two 232s, Morocco nine to re-equip its Marche Verte display team.

**Photo:** A French Armée de l'Air CAP 10. (Armée de l'Air)

## CASA C-101 Aviojet

**Country of origin:** Spain

**Type:** Two seat basic and advanced trainer and light attack aircraft

**Powerplant:** C-101CC/DD – One 20.9kN (4700lb) with max reserve power or 19.1kN (4300lb) without reserve Garrett TFE731-5-IJ turbofan.

**Performance:** C-101CC/DD – Max speed with max reserve power 835km/h (450kt) at 15,000ft, max speed at sea level 785km/h (423kt), economical cruising speed 612km/h (330kt). Max initial rate of climb 6360ft/min (with max reserve power), normal max initial rate of climb 4975ft/min. Time to 25,000ft 6min 30sec. Service ceiling 44,000ft. Lo-lo-lo attack radius with four 250kg bombs and 30mm cannon with 5min over target and reserves 482km (260nm). Ferry range with reserves 3705km (2000nm). Max endurance 7 hours.

**Weights:** C-101CC – Empty equipped 3470kg (7650lb), max takeoff 6300kg (13,890lb).

**Dimensions:** Wing span 10.60m (34ft 10in), length 12.50m (41ft 0in), height 4.25m (14ft 0in). Wing area 20.0m² (215.3sq ft).

**Accommodation:** Two in tandem.

**Armament:** C-101CC – Can carry a 30mm DEFA 533 cannon or twin 12.7mm Browning M3 machine gun pod in lower fuselage. Six underwing hardpoints can carry up to 2250kg (4960lb) of ordnance, including bombs, rocket pods. Up to two AGM-65 Maverick ASMs, or two AIM-9 Sidewinder or Matra Magic AAMs on C-101DD.

**Operators:** Chile, Jordan, Spain.

**History:** CASA's C-101 Aviojet has proved to be a relatively inexpensive and capable trainer and light attack aircraft.

Design of the Aviojet began in 1975 to replace the Hispano Saeta after CASA signed a development contract with the Spanish Air Ministry. As CASA's first foray into the jet engined trainer field, the company enrolled the help of Northrop of the USA and Germany's MBB (now Northrop Grumman and EADS Germany respectively). Northrop designed the unswept wing and inlet area, but CASA assumed all design responsibility after the first flight of the first of four prototypes on June 27 1977.

Notable features of the Aviojet include modular construction, the Garrett (now Honeywell) TFE731 high bypass turbofan, an engine widely used on business jets and known for its reliability and fuel efficiency (conversely the high bypass contributes to less than ideal high altitude performance), and a weapons bay in the forward fuselage which can house cannon or gun packs, a reconnaissance pod, an ECM package or a laser designator.

Initial production of the C-101 was for Spain, whose C-101EB trainers are designated E.25 Mirlo, or Blackbird. The C-101BB features a more powerful engine and was sold to Chile as the T-36 (subsequently fitted with a ranging radar) and Honduras.

The C-101CC introduced a more powerful engine with a five minute military reserve power thrust rating of 20.9kN (4700lb). It sold to Chile as the A-36 Halcón (Hawk) and Jordan.

The C-101DD featured nav/attack avionics improvements, including a HUD, HOTAS controls, weapon aiming controls and AGM-65 compatibility. First flight was in May 1985 but, none were ordered.

CASA built 149 C-101s before production wound up.

**Photo:** A Spanish C-101. (Lassi Tolvanen).

# Cessna O-1 Bird Dog

**Country of origin:** United States of America

**Type:** Observation, liaison and forward air control aircraft

**Powerplant:** O-1E – One 159kW (213hp) Continental O-470-11 flat six piston engine driving a two blade constant speed propeller.

**Performance:** O-1E – Max speed at sea level 243km/h (131kt), economical cruising speed 167km/h (90kt). Max initial rate of climb 1150ft/min. Service ceiling 18,500ft. Range 853km (460nm).

**Weights:** O-1E – Empty 732kg (1614lb), max takeoff 1102kg (2430lb).

**Dimensions:** O-1E – Wing span 10.97m (36ft 0in), length 7.85m (25ft 9in), height 2.22m (7ft 4in). Wing area 16.2m² (174.0sq ft).

**Accommodation:** Pilot and observer in tandem. Alternatively stretcher patient (with no observer) can be carried.

**Armament:** O-1E – None. O-1C – Two underwing hardpoints for a 113kg (250lb) bomb each, or unguided rockets.

**Operators:** Chile, Libya, Pakistan, South Korea, Thailand.

**History:** Of the more than 3500 Bird Dogs built from 1950, over 100 remain in military service, testament to the utility of this Korean and Vietnam wars veteran.

During WW2 the US Army successfully employed many thousands of light aircraft, mainly Piper L-4s and Taylorcraft L-2 'Grasshoppers', for observation, artillery direction, tactical reconnaissance and liaison duties. Both the L-2 and L-4 were simple conversions of existing civil aircraft, and their success in their many roles led the US Army postwar to seek a standard observation aircraft, tailored closely to its specific needs.

Cessna developed its Model 305 as a private venture anticipating such a requirement, and this first flew in December 1949. In April 1950 the official US Army competition for an observation aircraft saw Cessna's 305 selected over designs from a number of other manufacturers. The US Army ordered an initial 418 Model 305s as L-19As (redesignated O-1A from 1962).

The 305 was based loosely on the Cessna 170, a taildragger that formed the basis for the Cessna 172 (from which was developed the T-41 Mescalero – described separately). Compared with the 170, for the Model 305 Cessna cut down the rear fuselage, giving 360° vision, while a transparency was fitted in the wing centre section above the cabin. Seating was for two in tandem. At the US Army's request the 305 was also fitted with electrically operated, slotted trailing edge flaps (later fitted to civil Cessnas) to improve short field performance.

Bird Dog variants included the instrument trainer L-19A-ITs and TL-19Ds (TO-1D – many of these were later converted to O-2D and O-2F standards), the US Marine Corps' OE-1 (O-1B) and improved OE-2 (O-1C), the TL-19A (TO-1A) dual control trainer (many of which were converted to O-1G FAC standard), and the definitive L-19E/O-1E, an improved L-19A/O-1A with more modern equipment. L-19E production initially ceased in 1959, but a further batch was built from 1961. Fuji in Japan built 22 L-19Es under licence.

The O-1A saw service in the Korean War, while the O-1E was used extensively by the USAF in Vietnam, primarily directing air strikes (some were flown by Australian and New Zealand exchange personnel).

**Photo:** A Bird Dog in Austrian markings. Note the cut down rear fuselage. Austria has recently retired its Bird Dogs. (Sebastian Zacharias)

# Cessna T-41 Mescalero & 172

**Country of origin:** United States of America

**Type:** Basic trainer, liaison and observation aircraft

**Powerplant:** T-41A – One 108kW (145hp) Continental O-300-C flat six piston engine driving a two blade fixed pitch propeller.

**Performance:** T-41A – Max speed 224km/h (121kt), max cruising speed at 9000ft 211km/h (114kt). Max initial rate of climb 645ft/min. Service ceiling 13,100ft. Ferry range 1030km (555nm), standard range 990km (535nm).

**Weights:** T-41A – Operating empty 565kg (1245lb), max takeoff 1043kg (2300lb).

**Dimensions:** T-41A – Wing span 10.92m (35ft 10in), length 8.20m (26ft 11in), height 2.68m (8ft 10in). Wing area 16.2m² (174.0sq ft).

**Accommodation:** Seating for pilot and instructor side by side, with seats for two passengers behind them.

**Armament:** None

**Operators:** Includes Chile, Colombia, Dominican Republic, Ecuador, El Salvador, Greece, Guatemala, Honduras, Indonesia, Ireland, Liberia, Pakistan, Peru, Philippines, Saudi Arabia, South Korea, Trinidad and Tobago, Turkey.

**History:** The Cessna 172 is by far and away the world's most successful light aircraft. A significant portion of the nearly 44,000 172s have built found their way into military service.

The 172 began life as a tricycle undercarriage development of the four place Cessna 170, the aircraft that also formed the basis for the O-1 Bird Dog (described separately). The prototype 170 flew in September 1947, the prototype 172 in November 1955. The type was a success almost instantly, and through to 1986 the 172 was built in successively improved variants. An improved 172, the 172R, aimed principally at civil customers, entered production in 1996. It has been joined by the improved performance 172SP

US military interest resulted in a July 1964 US Air Force order for Cessna 172Fs for pilot flight screening performed by civil firms under contract, designated the T-41A Mescalero. These aircraft differed little from the civil 172F, and were built between 1964 and 1967. The US Army also ordered 172s for pilot training, its T-41Bs based on the R172E with a 155kW (210hp) Continental IO-360 driving a constant speed prop. The USAF's T-41C was similar to the T-41B except for its fixed pitch propeller, and 52 were built for the USAF Academy. The T-41D, based on the T-41C but with a 28 volt electrical system, was procured for a number of countries under the US Military Assistance Program (MAP). Some 311 T-41Ds were built between 1968 and 1978.

Replacement of the USAF's Mescaleros with Slingsby T-3 Fireflies (described separately) was completed in 1995.

Apart from 172s built as T-41s, several other countries bought civil 172s direct from Cessna or from Reims-Cessna in France (which built several thousand FR172s under licence). In all, over 30 countries have operated military 172s or T-41s.

Apart from basic pilot training, the 172 is also widely used for a number of secondary duties such as observation, liaison and border patrol.

**Photo:** The Greek air force operates 20 T-41Ds in the initial pilot training role. (MAP)

## Cessna T-37 Tweet

**Country of origin:** United States of America

**Type:** Two seat basic and advanced trainer

**Powerplants:** T-37B/C – Two 4.56kN (1025lb) Continental J69-T-25 turbojets.

**Performance:** T-37B – Max speed 684km/h (370kt) at 25,000ft, cruising speed 612km/h (330kt). Max initial rate of climb 3370ft/min. Service ceiling 39,200ft. Range 1500km (810nm). T-37C – Max speed 650km/h (350kt), cruising speed 575km/h (310kt). Max initial rate of climb 2390ft/min. Service ceiling 29,900ft. Ferry range 1517km (820nm) with tip tanks, range with standard fuel 1367km (738nm).

**Weights:** T-37B – Empty 1755kg (3870lb), max takeoff 2993kg (6600lb). T-37C – Max takeoff 3402kg (7500lb).

**Dimensions:** Wing span 10.30m (33ft 9in), length 8.92m (29ft 3in), height 2.80m (9ft 2in). Wing area 17.1m² (183.9sq ft).

**Accommodation:** Seating for two, side by side.

**Armament:** T-37C – Up to 227kg (500lb) of armament on two underwing hardpoints, comprising two 113kg (250lb) bombs or rockets.

**Operators:** Colombia, Germany, Greece, Pakistan, Turkey, USA.

**History:** Cessna's viceless T-37 Tweet has over four decades of service behind it, and seems likely to remain in use with a number of operators for many years yet.

In 1952 the US Air Force formulated a requirement for an 'all through' jet trainer that would train pilots from basic through to wings standard. Cessna won this contest with its Model 318, which featured seating for two side by side, two small turbojets and a straight wing. The first of two prototype Model 318s, designated XT-37, first flew on October 12 1954.

The initial production model was the 4.1kN (920lb) Continental J69-T-9 turbojet (licence built Turbomeca Mabore) powered T-37A, which first flew in September 1955, although some problems with the aircraft delayed service entry until 1957. In all 534 T-37As were built, all for the USAF. In 1959 production switched to the T-37B, which introduced more powerful J69-T-25s, improved avionics and optional wingtip tanks. In all 449 T-37Bs were built. Surviving T-37As were subsequently upgraded to T-37B standard.

The final production Tweet or 'Tweetie Bird' (named after the cartoon character) model was the T-37C, with 269 built for export. It differs from the T-37B in having a higher max takeoff weight and two underwing hardpoints for bombs or rockets.

The US Air Force began all through jet training with the T-37 in 1961, however the cost of operations saw the service reintroduce piston engined T-41 Mescaleros for initial training in 1965.

Plans to replace the USAF's T-37s with an all new jet trainer faltered when the Fairchild T-46 Eaglet was cancelled in 1986 due to program management problems. Cessna then proposed substantially upgrading the T-37 to Garrett turbofan powered T-48 standard, but instead the aircraft's replacement is the long awaited JPATS winner, the Pilatus PC-9 based Raytheon T-6 Texan II (deliveries began in 2000).

In the meantime, USAF T-37s were put through a service life extension program (SLEP) developed by Sabreliner.

**Photo:** Over 400 T-37s are in USAF service, although replacement is in sight with the T-6 Texan II. (USAF)

## Cessna A-37 Dragonfly

**Country of origin:** United States of America

**Type:** Two seat light attack aircraft

**Powerplants:** A-37B/OA-37B – Two 12.7kN (2850lb) General Electric J85-GE-17A turbojets.

**Performance:** A-37/OA-37B – Max speed 816km/h (440kt) at 16,000ft, max cruising speed 787km/h (425kt). Max initial rate of climb 6990ft/min. Service ceiling 41,765ft. Range with max fuel and reserves 1630km (880nm), range with max payload including 1860kg (4100lb) of external ordnance 740km (400nm).

**Weights:** A-37B – Empty equipped 2817kg (6211lb), max takeoff 6350kg (14,000lb).

**Dimensions:** Wing span 10.93m (35ft 11in), length excluding refuelling probe 8.93m (29ft 4in), height 2.71m (8ft 11in). Wing area 17.1m² (183.9sq ft).

**Accommodation:** Seating for two, side by side.

**Armament:** One 7.62mm GAU-2 minigun in forward fuselage. Eight underwing hardpoints can carry a total ordnance load of 1860kg (4100lb), including bombs, rockets and gun pods.

**Operators:** Chile, Colombia, Ecuador, El Salvador, Guatemala, Honduras, Peru, South Korea, Uruguay.

**History:** The US Air Force's decision to evaluate the suitability of an armed version of the T-37 Tweet jet trainer for light attack/counter insurgency work proved fruitful, resulting in the A-37 which saw widespread service in Vietnam.

In 1962 the USAF's Special Air Warfare centre began evaluating two T-37Bs to test the type's suitability for the counter insurgency (COIN) light attack role. After initial testing the two T-37Bs were modified to YAT-37D standard (first flight October 22 1963) and fitted with two 10.7kN (2400lb) General Electric J85-GE-5 turbojets. The trials were positive but initially nothing came of the concept until the Vietnam War intensified.

In 1966 the USAF contracted Cessna to convert 39 T-37Bs to light attack A-37A Dragonfly standard. Apart from the GE J85 turbojets, the A-37As introduced eight underwing hardpoints, extra fuel capacity in wingtip tanks, armour protection, attack avionics, larger wheels and tyres and an internal 7.62mm minigun.

Twenty-five A-37As proved successful in evaluation trials in operational conditions in Vietnam from mid 1967. These A-37As were later upgraded to full operational service, and were transferred to the South Vietnamese air force in 1970.

The major production model was the A-37B, with uprated engines, an inflight refuelling probe and increased internal fuel capacity, and the airframe stressed for 6g rather than 5g. In all 577 A-37Bs were delivered to the USAF and export customers between May 1968 and 1975. A-37Bs saw widespread service with the US and South Vietnamese air forces during the Vietnam War, and captured examples even saw brief service with the North Vietnamese air force during the closing stages of that conflict.

The USAF converted 130 A-37Bs to OA-37Bs with avionics for forward air control work, with the last of these retired in 1992. Ex USAF A-37 and OA-37s serve widely in South America.

**Photo:** A Uruguayan A-37B Dragonfly. (Santiago Rivas)

# Cessna Citation I, II, V, OT-47 & UC-35

**Country of origin:** United States of America

**Type:** VIP and utility transports

**Powerplants:** S/II – Two 11.1kN (2500lb) Pratt & Whitney Canada JT15D-4Bs turbofans. Ultra – Two 13.6kN (3045lb) JT15D-5Ds.

**Performance:** S/II – Cruising speed 746km/h (403kt). Initial rate of climb 3040ft/min. Range with two crew and four passengers 3223km (1739nm). Range with max fuel 3700km (1998nm). Ultra – Max cruising speed 796km/h (430kt). Initial rate of climb 4100ft/min. Ceiling 45,000ft. Range with five passengers 3630km (1960nm).

**Weights:** S/II – Empty equipped 3655kg (8060lb), max takeoff 6850kg (15,100lb). Ultra – Empty 4196kg (9250lb), operating empty 4377kg (9650lb), max takeoff 7393kg (16,300lb).

**Dimensions:** S/II – Wing span 15.91m (52ft 3in), length 14.39m (47ft 3in), height 4.57m (15ft 0in). Wing area 31.8m² (342.6sq ft). V & Ultra – Wing span 15.91m (52ft 3in), length 14.90m (48ft 11in), height 4.57m (15ft 0in). Wing area 31.8m² (342.6sq ft).

**Accommodation:** S/II – Flightcrew of two. Main cabin can be configured to seat 10, but standard interior layout for six. Ultra – Standard seating arrangements for seven or eight passengers.

**Armament:** None

**Operators:** Ecuador, Nigeria, Pakistan, Paraguay, Spain, South Africa, Turkey, USA, Venezuela

**History:** Several nations operate various variants of Cessna's successful straight wing Citation business jet range in military colours.

The original Cessna Citation first flew on September 15 1969 and the type pioneered the small business jet market. Features included two JT15D turbofans, seating for five passengers and a straight wing. Almost 700 Citations and similar Citation Is were built through until 1985, firmly establishing Cessna as a business jet manufacturer. Argentina, Ecuador, China, Mexico and Venezuela have operated military Citation Is.

Cessna used the Citation/Citation I as the basis for a family of business jets, which have been progressively improved over time. The stretched Citation II, with standard seating for six, first flew in 1977 and more than 730 were built through to 1994. It was replaced in production by the Citation Bravo, with P&WC PW530 engines and EFIS. Spain operates Citation IIs with a survey camera mounted in a wing root fairing, while Turkey and Venezuela also operate Citation IIs.

The US Navy bought 15 Citation IIs as T-47A radar trainers but these were replaced in service by T-39 Sabreliners.

The Citation V is a stretched development of the Citation II. Still powered by JT15Ds, the V has standard seating for eight passengers. It first flew in August 1987 and over 260 were built through to 1994. The V's replacement was the EFIS equipped Citation Ultra, with more powerful engines and EFIS avionics.

The Ultra forms the basis for the USAF's OT-47B surveillance platforms fitted with an APG-66 radar (as on the F-16). Five were built. The Ultra also met the US Army's C-XX transport requirement as the UC-35. The Army wants 35 UC-35s and deliveries began in late 1996. The last 18 are due to be UC-35Bs, based on the Citation Ultra Encore, with PW535 engines and other improvements.

**Photo:** One of two South African AF VIP Citation IIs. (Keith Gaskell)

# Chengdu J-7 & F-7

**Country of origin:** China (based on Russian designed MiG-21)

**Type:** Single seat fighter

**Powerplant:** F-7M – One 43.2kN (9700lb) dry and 64.7kN (14,550lb) with afterburner Liyang WP7BM turbojet.

**Performance:** F-7M – Max speed 2175km/h (1175kt). Max initial rate of climb 35,433ft/min. Service ceiling 59,700ft. Max ferry range with external fuel 2230km (1203nm). Combat radius with two 150kg (330lb) bombs and drop tanks hi-lo-hi 600km (325nm), combat radius with two AAMs and three drop tanks 650km (350nm).

**Weights:** F-7M – Empty 5275kg (11,630lb), max takeoff 8888kg (19,577lb).

**Dimensions:** F-7M – Wing span 7.15m (23ft 6in), length (excl probe) 13.95m (45ft 9in), height 4.10m (13ft 6in). Wing area 23.0m² (247.6sq ft).

**Accommodation:** Pilot only, except for two in tandem in JJ-7/FT-7.

**Armament:** F-7M – Two Type 30-1 30mm cannons. Max external ordnance of 1000kg (2205lb) on four underwing hardpoints and on centreline fuel tank station. Inner hardpoints can carry PL-2, -2A or -7 or Matra R550 Magic AAMs. Can carry rockets and bombs.

**Operators:** Albania, Bangladesh, China, Egypt, Iran, Iraq, Myanmar, North Korea, Pakistan, Sri Lanka, Tanzania, Zimbabwe.

**History:** China's copy of the MiG-21 forms an integral part of the People's Liberation Army Air Force inventory and has been widely exported to a number of non aligned countries.

China acquired a licence to build the MiG-21F-13 ('Fishbed C') and its Tumansky R-11F-300 turbojet in 1961. However, the subsequent severing of ties with Russia left the Chinese with incomplete technical drawings, and they instead were forced to reverse engineer pattern aircraft. As a consequence, the first Chinese built MiG-21, designated J-7, didn't fly until January 17 1966. The J-7 entered production the following year with Shenyang despite the turmoil of the cultural revolution. Some were exported to Albania and Tanzania as the F-7A.

Production was subsequently transferred to Chengdu as the J-7I. In 1975 development work began on the improved J-7II, which introduced a more powerful engine with double the time between overhaul. It was exported to Egypt and Iraq in the early 1980s as the F-7B.

The export F-7M Airguard features a GEC-Marconi HUD and weapons aiming computer, an improved ranging radar, radar altimeter, IFF and an improved engine. It has been exported to Bangladesh, Iran and Zimbabwe. The F-7P and F-7MP are similar, but with a number of minor modifications (including Martin-Baker ejection seat and Sidewinder compatibility) and were built for Pakistan.

Other variants include the J-7E, thought to have first flown in 1990 and featuring a cranked delta wing, more powerful engine and extra hardpoints; and the J-7III, loosely equivalent to the MiG-21MF and featuring an all weather radar in an enlarged radome. Two seater JJ-7s and FT-7s meanwhile are built by Guizhou.

The F-7MG features the J-7E's cranked delta wing fitted with leading and trailing edge flaps, upgraded engine and avionics. The F-7MF, which was revealed at the November 2000 Airshow China, features a multi mode pulse Doppler radar in a larger, solid nose, small canards, chin intake, HUD and optional GPS.

**Photo:** An F-7MG demonstrator. (Sebastian Zacharias)

## Chengdu FC-1

**Country of origin:** China

**Type:** Multirole fighter

**Powerplants:** One 81.4kN (18,300lb) with afterburning Klimov RD-93 turbofan.

**Performance:** Max speed at altitude Mach 1.6 to 1.8. Service ceiling 52,000ft. Fighter mission combat radius 1200km (650nm), ground attack combat radius 700km (378nm), max range on internal fuel 1600km (864nm).

**Weights:** Normal takeoff 9100kg (20,062lb), max takeoff 12,700kg (27,998lb).

**Dimensions:** Wing span over wingtip missiles 9.50m (31ft 2in), length 14.00m (45ft 11in), height 5.10m (16ft 9in).

**Accommodation:** Pilot only, two seat conversion trainer planned.

**Armament:** Four underwing, two wingtip and one centreline hardpoints for a variety of air-to-air and air-to-ground weapons, including a GSh-23-2 23mm twin barrel cannon pod on the centreline station, PL-7 and PL-10 AAMs, rockets, bombs and missiles.

**Operators:** None ordered at the time of writing.

**History:** Chengdu Aircraft Corporation's FC-1 has been under development as a replacement for China's big fleet of aging J-7s and for Pakistan in lieu of its suspended F-16 order.

The FC-1 (Fighter China) program began in 1991, following the USA's withdrawal from Super-7 development. The aircraft has been designed with the assistance of Mikoyan, possibly using the MiG designer's experience on the original 1980s MiG-33, a single engine version of the MiG-29.

China publicly revealed the FC-1 at the 1995 Paris Airshow. At the time the FC-1's first flight was planned for early 1997 with first deliveries of production aircraft in 1999. However first flight has been delayed and in late 2001 a prototype had not yet flown.

The FC-1 is a tailed delta design and will be of conventional construction. It will have conventional flight controls with a backup analog fly-by-wire system. Power will be from a single Klimov RD-93 turbofan, a development of the RD-33 which powers the MiG-29. The delta wing will carry AAMs on wingtip stations in addition to the four underwing hardpoints and one centreline station.

Pakistan was participating in the FC-1 program in lieu of the USA's suspension of its F-16 order (rescinded in late 2001) and to replace F-6s and early model F-7s. Subassemblies may be made at Pakistan's Aeronautical Complex at Kamra. If Pakistan orders the FC-1 a final assembly line may also be set up in that country.

Chinese and Pakistani FC-1s would likely be fitted with Western origin avionics built on a Mil Std 1553B databus. Fiar has been pitching its Grifo S7 radar for the FC-1, Thales the RC-400. Another radar option is the Russian Phazoton Kopyo. Other Western features are likely to include a HUD and multifunction displays, a mission computer and inertial navigation system. Western concerns over supplying military technology to China and Pakistan's military coup have contributed to delays to the FC-1 program.

**Photo:** An airshow model of the FC-1. Apart from China and Pakistan, potential FC-1 customers could include current F-7 operators such as Myanmar, Bangladesh and Iran.

## Chengdu J-10 & IAI Lavi

**Countries of origin:** Israel (Lavi) and China (J-10)

**Type:** Multirole fighters

**Powerplant:** Lavi – One 55.5kN (12,500lb) dry and 82.7kN (18,600lb) with afterburning (approx ratings) Pratt & Whitney PW1120 turbojet (a turbojet development of the F100).

**Performance:** Lavi estimated – Max speed above 36,000ft 1969km/h (1063kt) or Mach 1.85. Low level penetration speed with two AAMs and eight 340kg/750lb bombs 997km/h (538kt). Combat radius on an air-to-ground mission, lo-lo-lo 1110km (600nm), or hi-lo-hi with six 113kg/250lb bombs 2130km (1150nm). Combat air patrol radius 1850km (1000nm).

**Weights:** Lavi – Empty approx 7030kg (15,500lb), max takeoff 18,370kg (40,500lb).

**Dimensions:** Lavi – Wing span 8.78m (28ft 10in), length 14.57m (47ft 10in), height 4.78m (15ft 8in). Wing area 33.1m² (355.8sq ft).

**Armament:** Lavi – One internal 30mm cannon. Two wingtip pylons for AAMs. Four underwing and seven underfuselage hardpoints can carry air-to-surface missiles, bombs, laser guided bombs and rockets.

**Accommodation:** Pilot only or two in tandem in Lavi TD.

**Operators:** None

**History:** The Lavi (Young Lion) was originally developed as a multirole fighter for the Israeli air force before program cancellation saw the prototypes used as technology demonstrator airframes. However the Lavi allegedly forms the basis for China's Chengdu J-10 multirole fighter due to enter service mid decade.

Lavi program go-ahead was given in 1980, while full scale development began in October 1982. The first prototype (B-1) first flew on December 31 1986, the second (B-2) flew on March 30 1987. Both were two seaters. However, despite promising results, the Lavi was cancelled in August 1987, mainly due to budget restrictions.

Design features of the Lavi include F-16 style ventral air intake, canard delta configuration, a single PW1120 turbojet, an Elta multimode radar, HUD, HOTAS and three multifunction displays.

Following cancellation IAI elected to use the Lavi as a technology demonstrator and testbed for Israeli developed avionics and systems. To this end the third prototype (B-3) was completed as the Lavi TD. Another two seater, it first flew on September 25 1989.

In the mid 1990s a number of reports surfaced suggesting that IAI was cooperating with China to develop the J-10, a new multirole fighter that strongly resembles the Lavi in configuration and allegedly based on Lavi developed technologies.

The J-10 is believed to be powered by a 122.6kN (27,650lb) with afterburning Saturn AL-31F turbofan (which powers the Su-27). Russian, Chinese and Israeli radars are under evaluation, as are Russian and Israeli armaments.

A prototype J-10 is understood to have flown for the first time on March 24 1998. Four or five are reported to have flown since, with one crashing due to a fly-by-wire failure.

The PLA-AF reportedly requires around 300 J-10s, with service entry in 2005. Chinese licence production of the Su-27 may have some impact on production buys.

**Photo:** IAI's Lavi TD technology demonstrator. (IAI)

# Dassault/Dornier Alpha Jet

**Countries of origin:** France and Germany

**Type:** Advanced trainer and close support aircraft

**Powerplants:** Alpha Jet A – Two 14.1kN (3175lb) SNECMA/Turbomeca Larzac 04-C20 turbofans. E – Two 13.2kN (2975lb) Larzac 04-C6s.

**Performance:** A – Max speed Mach 0.86. Max initial rate of climb 12,000ft/min. Time to 30,000ft less than 5.5min. Service ceiling 48,000ft. Ferry range with four external tanks over 3500km (1900nm). Combat radius with gun pod and two 400kg (1015lb) bombs hi-lo-lo-hi 1075km (580nm), or lo-lo-lo-lo 630km (340nm). E – Same except max speed 1000km/h (540kt). Radius on a lo-lo-lo-lo training mission with two drop tanks 670km (360nm). Endurance with internal fuel over 3hr 30min.

**Weights:** A – Empty equipped 3570kg (7870lb), max takeoff 7600kg (16,750lb). E – Empty equipped 3535kg (7800lb), max takeoff same.

**Dimensions:** A – Wing span 9.11m (29ft 11in), length 13.23m (43ft 5in), height 4.19m (13ft 9in). Wing area 17.5m² (188.4sq ft). E – Same except length 11.75m (38ft 7in).

**Accommodation:** Two in tandem.

**Armament:** More than 2500kg (5510lb) of external ordnance, including centreline 30mm DEFA or 27mm Mauser cannon pod, bombs and rockets, AAMs (such as AIM-9 or Magic) and ASMs (such as AGM-65).

**Operators:** Belgium, Cameroon, Egypt, France, Ivory Coast, Morocco, Nigeria, Portugal, Qatar, Thailand, Togo, UK.

**History:** France and Germany agreed to jointly develop a new subsonic advanced trainer in the late 1960s.

The TA501 design, which was submitted by Dassault, Breguet (the two French companies merged in 1971) and Dornier, was chosen in 1970 over two other competing concepts. The TA501 was named Alpha Jet, and a change in Germany's requirement for the aircraft saw it developed in advanced trainer and close support/battlefield reconnaissance forms.

Official development go-ahead for the program was given in February 1972, with the first flight of a prototype on October 26 1973. French Alpha Jet E (Ecole – school) deliveries to replace Magisters began in 1978, while Germany's first Alpha Jet A (Appui-tactique) first flew in April 1978. Most new build export customers took delivery of aircraft similar to the French standard.

Germany's were fitted with a comprehensive nav/attack suite including twin gyro INS and a Doppler navigation radar. Germany took delivery of 175 Alpha Jets which primarily replaced G91s for close air support. These aircraft were later re-engined with uprated engines. Germany retired all its Alpha Jets in the mid 1990s (50 went to Portugal while more recent customers for stored examples are Thailand, which is upgrading 25, the UK, which has bought six for the Defence Evaluation and Research Agency, and the UAE, although this deal has not been finalised). Belgium is upgrading its Alpha Jet Es with HUD and INS/GPS.

The Alpha Jet NGEA (new generation attack/trainer) was launched in 1980 and features a HUD, cockpit CRTs, laser rangefinder and compatibility with the Matra Magic AAM. It was sold to Cameroon and Egypt.

In all 522 Alpha Jets were built.

**Photo:** A Portuguese Alpha Jet A. (Harold van Eupen)

# Dassault Atlantic & Atlantique 2

**Country of origin:** France

**Type:** Maritime patrol aircraft

**Powerplants:** ATL2 – Two 4225kW (5665shp) Rolls-Royce Tyne RTy.20 Mk 21 turboprops driving four blade propellers.

**Performance:** ATL2 – Max level speed 648km/h (350kt) at altitude or 592km/h (320kt) at sea level, max cruising speed 555km/h (300kt), normal patrol speed 315km/h (170kt). Max initial rate of climb at 30,000kg (66,140lb) AUW 1200ft/min, or at 40,000kg (88,185lb) AUW 700ft/min. Service ceiling 30,000ft. Ferry range with max fuel 9075km (4900nm). Combat radius with two hours on station on anti shipping mission with one AM 39 Exocet missile 3333km (1800nm). Radius with 8hr patrol and four torpedoes 1110km (600nm), or with 5hr patrol 1850km (1000nm). Max endurance 18hr.

**Weights:** ATL2 – Empty equipped standard mission 25,700kg (56,660lb), max takeoff 46,200kg (101,850lb).

**Dimensions:** Span incl wingtip pods 37.42m (122ft 9in), length 33.63m (110ft 4in), height 10.89m (35ft 9in). Wing area 120.3m² (1295.3sq ft).

**Accommodation:** Normal crew complement of 10 to 12, comprising pilot, copilot, flight engineer, nose observer, radio navigator, ESM/ECM/MAD operator, radar & IFF operator, tactical coordinator, two acoustic operators and optionally two observers in rear fuselage.

**Armament:** ATL2 – Up to eight Mk 46 torpedoes, or seven Murène torpedoes or two AM 39 Exocet or AS 37 Martel ASMs (typical load three torpedoes and one missile), or NATO standard bombs in weapons bay. Four underwing hardpoints for ASMs and AAMs.

**Operators:** France, Germany, Italy, Pakistan.

**History:** The Atlantic resulted from a NATO requirement issued in 1958 to find a replacement for the Lockheed P-2 Neptune.

Breguet (who merged with Dassault in 1971) was the successful bidder, with its Br 1150 design selected over 24 other designs submitted from nine countries.

The prototype Atlantic first flew on October 21 1961 and entered service with the French and German navies in 1965. In all, 87 production Atlantics were built through to 1974 by a European consortium led by Breguet. Other customers were Italy and the Netherlands while three ex French navy Atlantics were delivered to Pakistan in the mid 1970s.

Atlantic features include a double bubble fuselage, the lower portion of which is unpressurised and includes the weapons bay, US sourced ASW equipment and a Thomson-CSF (now Thales) search radar in a retractable radome. Germany also operates five Atlantics modified for Elint.

Dassault built 28 new build Atlantique 2s for the French navy, with modern avionics and systems including a Thomson-CSF Iguane radar, a pod mounted FLIR in the nose, a new MAD, new ESM equipment, processors and navigation equipment. First flight was in 1981, with deliveries beginning in 1988 and concluding in 1998.

The proposed Rolls-Royce AE 2100H powered Atlantic 3 would feature a two crew cockpit and new EFIS avionics and systems and sensors. It is being offered to Germany and Italy (for delivery from 2007).

**Photo:** The Atlantic 3 would feature RR AE 2100s. (Dassault)

## Dassault Mystère/Falcon 200 & Gardian

**Country of origin:** France

**Type:** VIP transport, ECM trainer, maritime patrol and utility transport.

**Powerplants:** 200 – Two 23.1kN (5200lb) Garrett ATF 3-6A-4C turbofans.

**Performance:** 200 – Max cruising speed 870km/h (470kt) at 30,000ft, economical cruising speed 780km/h (420kt). Service ceiling 45,000ft. Range with max fuel, eight passengers and reserves 4650km (2510nm).

**Weights:** 200 – Empty 8250kg (18,290lb), max takeoff 14,515kg (32,000lb).

**Dimensions:** Wing span 16.32m (53ft 7in), length 17.15m (56ft 3in), height 5.32m (17ft 6in). Wing area 41.0m² (441.3sq ft).

**Accommodation:** Flightcrew of two. Typical main cabin seating for between eight and 10 passengers, or up to 14 in a high density configuration. Aerial ambulance can be fitted with three stretchers.

**Armament:** The Gardian was offered with the capability of carrying two AM 39 Exocet anti shipping missiles.

**Operators:** Belgium, France, Iran, Morocco, Norway, Pakistan, Peru, Portugal, Spain, Sudan, Syria.

**History:** The Mystère (or Falcon) 20/200 remains Dassault's most successful business jet series thus far, with more than 500 built. Many serve as VIP transports with others used in a variety of special missions roles.

Development of the original Mystère 20 traces back to joint collaboration between Sud Aviation (which later merged into Aerospatiale) and Dassault in the late 1950s. Prototype construction began in January 1962, with a first flight on May 4 1963. This prototype shared the overall configuration of production aircraft, but differed in that it was powered by 14.8kN (3300lb) Pratt & Whitney JT12A-8 turbojets, whereas production Mystère 20s (called Falcon 20s outside France) were powered with General Electric CF-700 turbofans.

The 200, or initially the 20H, features Garrett turbofans, greater fuel tankage and much longer range. This version remained in production until 1988, while production of the 20 ceased in 1983.

The majority of military Falcon 20 and 200 operators use them as VIP transports. However, France's sizeable fleet is an exception. The French navy operates five maritime patrol Gardians from its New Caledonia and Tahiti territories in the Pacific. These aircraft are fitted with a Thomson-CSF (now Thales) Varan radar and large observation windows. Chile has also upgraded two ex civil Falcon 200s to a similar standard.

The French Armée de l'Air meanwhile operates a variety of combat radar and navigation system equipped Mystère 20NAs to train crews bound for Mirage IVs and 2000s. A single Mystère 20NR trained pilots bound for the reconnaissance Mirage F1CR.

Other military applications include target towing, aerial ambulance and EW training aircraft. In the USA the Coast Guard operates a number of HU-25s Guardians for search and rescue. A number are equipped with SLAR and linescan for maritime pollution detection, while others are fitted with an APG-66 radar (as on the F-16) and FLIR and used for tracking suspicious sea and air traffic.

**Photo:** France uses Falcon 20s in a variety of roles. (Dassault)

## Dassault Falcon 50

**Country of origin:** France

**Type:** VIP and government transport, and maritime surveillance

**Powerplants:** 50 – Three 16.5kN (3700lb) AlliedSignal (Honeywell) TFE731-3 turbofans.

**Performance:** 50 – Max cruising speed 880km/h (475kt), long range cruising speed 797km/h (430kt). Max operating altitude 45,000ft. Range at Mach 0.75 with eight passengers 6480km (3500nm). 50 Surmar – Endurance 4hr on station 740km (400nm) at 370km/h (200kt) at 3000ft.

**Weights:** 50 – Empty equipped 9150kg (20,170lb), standard max takeoff 17,600kg (38,800lb), or optionally 18,500kg (40,780lb).

**Dimensions:** Wing span 18.86m (61ft 11in), length 18.52m (61ft 9in), height 6.97m (22ft 11in). Wing area 46.8m² (504.1sq ft).

**Accommodation:** Flightcrew of two pilots. In VIP layout number of cabin seating arrangements are available, depending on the toilet location. Seating for eight or nine with aft toilet, or for up to 12 with forward toilet. Can accommodate three stretchers, two doctors or attendants and medical equipment in a medevac role.

**Armament:** None

**Operators:** Djibouti, France, Iran, Italy, Morocco, Portugal, South Africa, Spain, Sudan.

**History:** The long range trijet Falcon 50 is based loosely on the earlier twinjet Mystère/Falcon 20 and 200 family, and like the 20 and 200, has found a military market as a VIP transport.

The Dassault Falcon 50 was developed for long range trans Atlantic and transcontinental flight sectors. Dassault based the 50 on the Falcon 20, but the required 6440km (3475nm) range requirement meant significant changes, effectively making the Falcon 50 an all new aircraft.

Falcon 50 design features include three 16.5kN (3700lb) Garrett (now Honeywell) TFE731 turbofans mounted on a new rear tail section, plus a new supercritical wing of greater area than that on the 20 and 200. Many Falcon 20 features and components were retained, including the nose and fuselage cross section.

The prototype Falcon 50 first flew on November 7 1976 but production deliveries didn't begin until 1979. In the meantime the wing was redesigned to become a supercritical unit but retained the original wing's planform. A second prototype flew in February 1978 and the first preproduction aircraft flew in June 1978.

The first major Falcon 50 development is the extended range 50EX. It first flew in 1996 and features a new four screen EFIS flightdeck based on that in the Falcon 2000. It is now the current production model.

Most military operated Falcon 50s serve as VIP and government transports, fitted with four or five seats in the main cabin. Italy's Falcon 50s are also convertible to an air ambulance configuration.

The French navy ordered four maritime surveillance Falcon 50 Surmars, with Thales (Thomson-CSF) Ocean Master 100 search radar, Chlio FLIR, two observation windows, the ability to drop SAR equipment, and three operator stations. The first two were delivered in 1999, with the remainder in 2001.

**Photo:** A French navy Falcon 50 Surmar. (Dassault)

# Dassault Falcon 900

**Country of origin:** France

**Type:** VIP transport and maritime patrol aircraft

**Powerplants:** 900 – Three 20.0kN (4500lb) Garrett (now Honeywell) TFE731-5AR-1C turbofans. 900B – Three 21.1kN (4750lb) TFE731-5BRs.

**Performance:** 900 – Max cruising speed 927km/h (500kt), economical cruising speed Mach 0.75. Max cruising altitude 51,000ft. Range with max payload and reserves 6412km (3460nm), range with 15 passengers and reserves 6968km (3760nm), with eight pax and reserves 7227km (3900nm). 900B – Same except for range with 15 pax and reserves 7115km (3840nm).

**Weights:** 900 – Empty equipped 10,545kg (23,248lb), max takeoff 20,640kg (45,500lb). 900B – Empty equipped 10,240kg (22,575kg), max takeoff 20,640kg (45,500lb).

**Dimensions:** Wing span 19.33m (63ft 5in), length 20.21m (66ft 4in), height 7.55m (24ft 9in). Wing area 49.0m² (527.4sq ft).

**Accommodation:** Flightcrew of two. Main passenger cabin accommodation for between eight and 15 passengers, or as many as 18 in a high density configuration.

**Armament:** None

**Operators:** Algeria, Australia, Belgium, Eq Guinea, France, Gabon, Japan, Malaysia, Nigeria, South Africa, Spain, UAE (Abu Dhabi).

**History:** The intercontinental range Falcon 900 serves widely as a military VIP transport.

Dassault announced it was developing a new intercontinental range large size business jet based on its Falcon 50 trijet at the 1983 Paris Airshow. The prototype first flew on September 21 1984, a second prototype flew on August 30 1985.

While of similar overall configuration to the Falcon 50, the Falcon 900 features an all new, wider fuselage, which can seat three passengers abreast, and is also considerably longer. The main commonality with the Falcon 50 is the wing, which despite being originally designed for a considerably lighter aircraft, was adapted almost directly unchanged (and incidentally also appears on the Falcon 2000 twin). In developing the Falcon 900 Dassault made extensive use of computer aided design, while the aircraft's structure incorporates same composite materials.

From 1991 the standard production model was the Falcon 900B, which differed from the earlier 900 in having more powerful engines, increased range, the ability to operate from unprepared strips and Category II visibility approach clearance. A further improved development is the 8335km (4500nm) range 900EX with a five screen EFIS avionics suite and other improvements and delivered from late 1996. The 900C is an update of 900B with the EX's avionics. From 2003 900EXs will be fitted with Dassault's EASy advanced avionics suite.

Like the smaller Falcons (Mystères in France), the 900 has proven popular with a number of countries as military VIP transports. Japan operates a unique maritime surveillance version of the Falcon 900 with a US sourced search radar, HU-25 Guardian/Gardian-like large observation windows, a dedicated operator station and a hatch for dropping sonobuoys, markers and flares.

**Photo:** A Belgium air force Falcon 900. (Belgium SID)

# Dassault Super Etendard

**Country of origin:** France

**Type:** Carrier borne strike fighter

**Powerplant:** One 49.0kN (11,025lb) SNECMA Atar 8K-50 turbojet.

**Performance:** Max speed 1118km/h (604kt), max speed at sea level 1180km/h (637kt). Max initial rate of climb 19,685ft/min. Service ceiling over 45,000ft. Combat radius with one AM 39 Exocet and two drop tanks, hi-lo-lo-hi 910km (490nm).

**Weights:** Empty equipped 6910kg (15,320lb), max takeoff 12,000kg (26,455lb).

**Dimensions:** Wing span 9.60m (31ft 6in), length 14.31m (47ft 0in), height 3.86m (12ft 8in). Wing area 28.4m² (305.7sq ft).

**Accommodation:** Pilot only

**Armament:** Two internal 30mm DEFA cannons. Up to 4500kg (5400lb) of ordnance on two under fuselage and four underwing hardpoints, including rocket pods, bombs, laser guided bombs, Magic AAMs, one Exocet, or one ASMP stand-off nuclear missile.

**Operators:** Argentina, France.

**History:** As its name suggests, the Super Etendard strike fighter is a developed version of the smaller Etendard IV.

The original Etendard (meaning standard, as in flag) was designed in response to the same NATO requirement for a light attack fighter won by the Fiat G91. Dassault, convinced of the Etendard's potential, launched the Etendard IV powered by a SNECMA Atar 8 turbojet (first flight July 24 1956). The IV attracted the attention of the French navy, who, after some delays, took delivery of the attack IVM (ff May 25 1958) and reconnaissance IVR.

The early 1970s Etendard replacement requirement was originally to be met by about 100 navalised SEPECAT Jaguar Ms. Politics and cost interfered, and instead, after evaluation of the Skyhawk and Corsair, the French navy ordered Dassault's proposed Super Etendard.

The Super Etendard introduced a more powerful Atar 8K-50 turbojet, a non afterburning version of the Mirage F1's 9K-50, a strengthened and revised structure for operations at higher speeds and weights, a Thomson-CSF/Dassault Agave radar, inertial navigation, improved avionics and a retractable inflight refuelling probe.

The first of three converted Etendard IVM Super Etendard prototypes first flew on October 28 1974, while the first of 71 production Super Etendards were delivered from 1977.

In the mid 1980s France's Super Etendards were subjected to an upgrade that featured a life extension out to 2008, the ability to launch the ASMP standoff nuclear missile, a new Dassault Electronique Anemone radar, new cockpit instruments, HUD, HOTAS and other systems. More recently they have been fitted with a Thales self protection system.

To replace the last reconnaissance Etendard IVPs retired in May 2000, some Super Etendards have been modified with reconnaissance sensors in place of the internal guns.

Iraq leased five Super Etendards pending the delivery of Mirage F1EQs from 1983. The only other export customer was Argentina. Argentine navy Super Etendards gained some notoriety when they sunk HMS *Sheffield* and the *Atlantic Conveyer* with Exocets during the Falklands War in 1982. Eleven remain in service.

**Photo:** An Argentine navy Super Etendard. (Santiago Rivas)

## Dassault Mirage III

***Country of origin:*** France

***Type:*** Multirole fighter

***Powerplant:*** IIIE – One 43.2kN (9700lb) dry and 60.8kN (13,670lb) with afterburning SNECMA Atar 9C-3 turbojet, plus optional (although rarely used) 14.7kN (3305lb) SEPR jettisonable booster rocket.

***Performance:*** IIIE – Max speed 2120km/h (1145kt), cruising speed at 36,100ft 955km/h (516kt). Time to 26,090ft 3min 0sec. Service ceiling 55,775ft, or 75,460ft with booster rocket. Ferry range with three drop tanks 2600km (1400nm). Combat radius hi-lo-hi with two 500lb bombs and two fuel tanks 1200km (650nm).

***Weights:*** IIIE – Empty 7260kg (16,000lb), max takeoff 13,700kg (30,200lb). Internal fuel 2940 litres.

***Dimensions:*** Wing span 8.22m (27ft 0in), length 15.03m (49ft 4in), height 4.50m (14ft 9in). Wing area 35.0m² (376.8sq ft).

***Accommodation:*** Pilot only, or two in tandem in IIIB and IIID.

***Armament:*** Two 30mm DEFA 552A cannons in lower fuselage. IIIE has four underwing and one centreline hardpoints capable of carrying up to 4700kg (9000lb) of armaments, including one radar guided Matra R.530 AAM, Matra R.550 Magic or AIM-9 Sidewinder infrared guided AAMs, AS 30 and AS 37 ASMs, bombs and rockets.

***Operators:*** Argentina, Brazil, Pakistan, Switzerland.

***History:*** The Mirage III propelled France to the forefront of combat aircraft design, and was the first of Dassault's famous Mirage series of fighters to enter production.

The Mirage name first applied to a design to meet a 1952 French Armée de l'Air requirement for a light, high speed interceptor. The Mirage I was a small delta wing design powered by two Armstrong Siddeley Viper turbojets and first flew on June 25 1955. While the Mirage I was too small to be practical, test experience gained was applied to the much larger SNECMA Atar powered Mirage III.

The prototype Mirage III-001 first flew on November 17 1956 and later became the first western European aircraft to reach Mach 2 in level flight. Ten preproduction Mirage IIIAs were built before the first Mirage IIICs were delivered to the Armée de l'Air in October 1960. IIICs were also built for South Africa (IIICZ) and Israel (IIICJ – used in the 1967 and 1973 Arab-Israel wars, 19 survivors were sold to Argentina in 1982). The equivalent two seater is the IIIB.

The multirole Mirage IIIE retains the Thomson-CSF Cyrano II radar but has nav/attack avionics and Doppler navigation radar (in a bulge beneath the cockpit), while French aircraft had the ability to carry an AN 52 nuclear bomb. The two seat IIID does not have the Cyrano radar.

The IIIE was a significant export success, and was built under licence in Australia (IIIO) and Switzerland (as the IIIS with a Hughes TARAN 18 radar). The reconnaissance Mirage IIIR is based on the IIIE, but features cameras (and no radar) in a modified nose (four South African IIIR2Zs were delivered with Atar 9K-50s).

France retired its Mirage IIIs in the mid 1990s, other Mirage III operators have upgraded their aircraft. IAI has proposed a re-engining program with the GE F404. South Africa's Denel Cheetah and Israel's IAI Kfir developments are described separately. Brazil has upgraded its Mirages with canards and new avionics.

***Photo:*** An Argentine Mirage IIIEA over the Andes. (Santiago Rivas)

## Dassault Mirage 5 & 50

***Country of origin:*** France

***Type:*** 5 – Ground attack and day fighter. 50 – Multirole fighter.

***Powerplant:*** 50 – One 49.0kN (11,025lb) dry and 70.8kN (15,875lb) with afterburning SNECMA Atar 9K-50 turbojet.

***Performance:*** 50 – Max speed 2338km/h (1262kt) at 39,370ft, cruising speed at 36,100ft 955km/h (516kt). Max initial rate of climb 36,615ft/min. Time to 45,000ft 4min 42sec. Service ceiling 59,055ft. Interception combat radius with two AAMs and three drop tanks, hi-hi-hi 1315km (710nm). Combat radius with two 400kg (880lb) bombs and three drop tanks, hi-lo-lo-hi 1260km (680nm), or with same load and lo-lo-lo 650km (340nm).

***Weights:*** 50 – Empty equipped 7150kg (15,763lb), max takeoff 14,700kg (32,407lb).

***Dimensions:*** 50 – Wing span 8.22m (27ft 0in), length 15.36m (50ft 4in), height 4.50m (14ft 9in). Wing area 35.0m² (376.8sq ft).

***Accommodation:*** Pilot only, except two in tandem in two seaters.

***Armament:*** 5 – Two 30mm DEFA 552A cannons in lower fuselage. Can carry up to 3700kg (8150lb) of armament on four underwing and three underfuselage hardpoints, comprising rockets, bombs and infrared guided missiles. Cyrano radar equipped 50s can fire the radar guided Matra R.530. Venezuelan and some Pakistani aircraft can fire AM 39 Exocet anti shipping missiles.

***Operators:*** Argentina, Chile, Colombia, Egypt, Gabon, Libya, Pakistan, Peru, UAE (Abu Dhabi), Venezuela.

***History:*** Dassault developed the Mirage 5 to meet an Israeli requirement for a low cost, day ground attack fighter-bomber.

The Mirage 5 first flew on May 15 1967, and originally differed from the Mirage IIIE on which it is based in the deletion of the Cyrano radar, which allowed a slimmer and longer nose, and also created space for extra internal fuel; and the addition of two extra hardpoints under the fuselage. Variants other than the basic single seater were the two seat 5D and reconnaissance 5R.

France's then president Charles de Gaulle embargoed the delivery of the 50 Mirage 5Js on order for Israel, and these aircraft were delivered to the Armée de l'Air as Mirage 5Fs. Israel instead built an unlicensed copy of the 5 (including its Atar engine), the IAI Nesher. About 60 were built, and many saw active service. Argentina took delivery of 39 ex Israeli Neshers, called Daggers, and many of these saw service in the 1982 Falklands War. The survivors have been upgraded to Finger standard with Israeli avionics in a Kfir nose cone.

The Mirage 5 was offered with increasingly more sophisticated avionics and systems (including ranging radar and laser rangefinders) as production progressed, and a number were fitted with lightweight Cyrano IV, Agave or Aida 2 radars.

The last major production was the Mirage 50, which features a 20% more powerful Atar 9K-50 turbojet, as fitted on the Mirage F1. First flown on May 15 1979, customers were Chile and Venezuela. Dassault also offered the 50 as an upgrade of existing Mirage IIIs and 5s.

Several nations have Mirage 5 upgrade programs, typically including modern avionics and canards. In all, 532 Mirage 5/50s were built, with the last 50 delivered in 1995.

***Photo:*** An Argentine IAI Finger (upgraded Dagger/Nesher). (Santiago Rivas)

# Dassault Mirage IV

**Country of origin:** France

**Type:** Reconnaissance aircraft

**Powerplants:** Two 47.6kN (10,700lb) dry and 67.7kN (15,200lb) with afterburning SNECMA Atar 9K-14 turbojets.

**Performance:** Max speed 2338km/h (1262kt) at 36,100ft, max speed at sea level approx 1350km/h (728kt), normal penetration speed 1913km/h (1033kt). Time to 36,100ft 4min 14sec. Service ceiling 65,615ft. Ferry range with drop tanks 4000km (2158nm). Typical combat radius 1240km (668nm).

**Weights:** Empty equipped 15,200kg (33,500lb), max takeoff 33,800kg (74,800lb).

**Dimensions:** Wing span 11.85m (38ft 11in), length 23.50m (77ft 1in), height 5.65m (18ft 6in). Wing area 78.0m² (839.6sq ft).

**Accommodation:** Crew of two in tandem.

**Armament:** Nuclear capability removed. Can carry up to 7700kg (17,000lb) of conventional ordnance on underwing and underfuselage hardpoints.

**Operators:** France

**History:** The Mirage IV bomber resulted from France's 1954 decision to field a nuclear deterrent force.

Dassault looked at a number of proposals for a strategic nuclear bomber before settling on the Mirage IVA, including developments of the Vautour through to a design approaching the B-58 Hustler in size and powered by two Pratt & Whitney J75 turbojets. In the end the much smaller Mirage IVA design was settled upon, to be powered by two SNECMA Atar turbojets and unable to launch a strike to the Soviet Union and returning without the aid of inflight refuelling. First flight was on June 17 1959.

Resembling a scaled up Mirage III, the Mirage IV features a delta wing, a crew of two in tandem, an inflight refuelling probe extending from the nose (for refuelling from C-135FRs), surveillance and Doppler radars for navigation later augmented by dual INS, while the original 60kT nuclear bomb would be carried semi recessed under fuselage. Twelve booster rockets (six under each wing) can be used to improve field performance.

The successful flight trials of one prototype and three revised preproduction Mirage IVs led to an Armée de l'Air order for 50 production aircraft. In all France took delivery of 62 production Mirage IVAs, and these were subjected to numerous upgrades and modifications throughout their service lives. Twelve IVs were modified for reconnaissance with the fitment of semi recessed cameras and SLAR.

In the late 1980s 19 Mirage IVs were modified to IVP standard, which involved fitting modern avionics including dual INS, plus radar warning receivers and the ability to launch the Aerospatiale ASMP stand-off nuclear missile (which has a range of 80km/43nm at low level, or 250km/135nm from high altitude).

In 1996 all but five of the surviving IVPs were retired, with the survivors relinquishing their nuclear role (to the ASMP nuclear missile armed Mirage 2000N) and instead used to provide a reconnaissance capability.

**Photo:** One of five surviving Mirage IVPs used for reconnaissance. (Paul Merritt)

# Dassault Mirage F1

**Country of origin:** France

**Type:** Multirole fighter

**Powerplant:** F1C – One 49.0kN (11,025lb) dry and 70.6kN (15,900lb) afterburning SNECMA Atar 9K-50 turbojet.

**Performance:** F1C – Max speed 2120km/h (1145kt). Max initial rate of climb 33,000ft/min. Service ceiling 50,000ft. Combat radius with 14 250kg (550lb) bombs hi-lo-hi 425km (230nm), or lo-lo-lo with one AM 39 Exocet ASM and two drop tanks 660km (355nm). Combat air patrol endurance at 150km (80nm) with two Super 350 AAMs, one underfuselage tank and one combat engagement 2hr 15min.

**Weights:** F1C – Empty 8100kg (17,850lb), max takeoff 16,200kg (35,715lb). Internal fuel 4300 litres.

**Dimensions:** F1C – Wing span without wingtip missiles 8.44m (27ft 8in), length 15.25m (50ft 0in), height 4.50m (14ft 9in). Wing area 25.0m² (269.1sq ft). F1C-200 – Same except length 15.30m (50ft 3in).

**Accommodation:** Pilot only, or two in tandem in F1B.

**Armament:** F1C – Two 30mm DEFA 553 cannons can carry 4700kg (10,360lb) of ordnance on four underwing, one centreline and two wingtip hardpoints including wingtip AIM-9 or Magic infrared guided AAMs, R.530 or Super 530F radar guided AAMs, rockets, bombs and ASMs, including the Exocet, or Armat ARM.

**Operators:** Ecuador, France, Greece, Iraq, Jordan, Libya, Morocco, Spain.

**History:** Dassault's Mirage F1 is unlike previous and subsequent Mirages in that it features a conventional swept wing.

In 1964 the French government awarded Dassault a contract to develop an all weather interceptor. Initial work was on the Mirage F2, a 20 tonne class fighter powered by a TF306 turbofan. At the same time Dassault worked on a smaller overall but similarly configured design powered by an Atar turbojet. This design was the Mirage F1, which first flew as a privately funded prototype on December 23 1966. The program was officially backed in 1967.

The Mirage F1 offered significant performance improvements over the Mirage III with its considerably more powerful Atar 9K-50, 43% more internal fuel (doubling the ground attack radius), improved manoeuvrability, 30% better field performance, slower approach speed and improved Cyrano IV radar.

F1 production began with 100 F1C interceptors for the Armée de l'Air which were delivered from March 1973. From 1977 deliveries to the Armée de l'Air were of the F1C-200 which introduced a fixed refuelling probe and a minor fuselage stretch. Fifty-five F1Cs were later modified for ground attack as F1CTs. France also took delivery of 64 reconnaissance F1CRs with infrared linescan in place of the cannons, cameras in a small nose fairing and various centreline recce pods. French two seat F1Bs have less external fuel and a slight fuselage stretch.

Most export F1s have been F1Cs. The F1A is simplified for day ground attack and lacks radar, while the multirole F1E and equivalent F1D two seater achieved some success. In all 725 F1s were built.

South Africa's Aerosud and Marvotech and Rosoboronexport of Russia displayed a demonstrator of their Russian SMR-95 powered Super Mirage F1 upgrade at the August 2001 Moscow Airshow. The SMR-95 is a derivative of the MiG-29's RD-33 engine.

**Photo:** A Spanish F1. (Lassi Tolvanen)

## Dassault Mirage 2000

**Country of origin:** France

**Type:** Multirole fighter

**Powerplant:** 2000C – One 64.3kN (14,500lb) dry and 95.1kN (21,400lb) with afterburning SNECMA M53-P2 turbofan.

**Performance:** 2000C – Max speed over 2338km/h (1262kt). Max initial rate of climb 52,000ft/min. Service ceiling 58,000ft. Time to 50,000ft 4min. Ferry range with drop tanks 3335km (1800nm). Combat range with four 250kg (550lb) bombs 1340km (725nm) without drop tanks, or over 1550km (840nm) with drop tanks.

**Weights:** 2000C – Empty 7800kg (17,200lb), max takeoff 17,500kg (38,600lb). Internal fuel 3145kg (6933lb).

**Dimensions:** 2000C – Wing span 9.13m (30ft 0in), length 14.36m (47ft 1in), height 5.15m (16ft 11in). Wing area 41.0m$^2$ (441.3sq ft).

**Accommodation:** Pilot only, or two in tandem in 2000B.

**Armament:** 2000C – Two 30mm DEFA 554 cannons. Up to 8440kg (14,200lb) of ordnance on four underwing and five underfuselage hardpoints, including Magic 2 and Super 530D AAMs, laser guided bombs, dumb bombs, anti runway bombs, cluster bombs, two AS 30L ASMs, two Armat ARMs or two AM 39 Exocet ASMs.

**Operators:** Egypt, France, Greece*, India*, Peru, Qatar, Taiwan, UAE*.

**History:** The Mirage 2000 combined the benefits of the delta wing layout with technological improvements such as fly-by-wire.

A delta wing configuration boasts a number of advantages such as a large wing area and large internal fuel volume, but has also a number of shortcomings including poor field performance and manoeuvrability due to wing sweep angle. However the Mirage 2000's use of fly-by-wire with inherent instability and leading edge slats dramatically improves manoeuvrability compared with the Mirage III.

Development work on the Mirage 2000 began when a lack of funding forced the cancellation of the larger, twin engined Super Mirage in 1975. Even though the Mirage 2000 was intended as a smaller and simpler fighter than the Super Mirage, the program was still ambitious, as the aircraft was to incorporate advances in radar, cockpit, armament, airframe and powerplant technologies. The official specification written for the Mirage 2000 was issued in 1976, with the first prototype flying for the first time on March 10 1978 and with deliveries of production 2000Cs (and later two seat 2000Bs) occurring from April 1983, only a year behind the original schedule.

Apart from FBW, the 2000 introduced the new SNECMA M53 turbofan, a Thomson-CSF RDM multimode radar, a CRT, HUD and HOTAS.

Initial export customers have ordered the 2000E (and recce pod carrying 2000R), a multirole development powered by the M53-P2. Taiwan and Qatar have ordered the 2000-5, a modernised multirole development and France has upgraded 37 Mirage 2000s to similar 2000-5F standard, delivered from late 1997.

The 2000-5 features five LCD cockpit displays (as developed for Rafale), a multimode Thales RDY radar and Matra Mica AAM compatibility. Abu Dhabi's 2000-9 (30 new 2000-9s and 33 upgrades) and the export 2000-5 Mk2 (ordered by Greece) features a Thales Nahar navigation FLIR and Damocles laser designating pod, upgraded ECM and radar, helmet mounted sight and autopilot terrain following system.

**Photo:** Dassault's 2000-5 Mk 2 demonstrator (a converted 2000B).

## Dassault Mirage 2000N & 2000D

**Country of origin:** France

**Type:** Nuclear and conventional strike fighters

**Powerplant:** 2000D – One 64.3kN (14,500lb) dry and 95.1kN (21,400lb) afterburning SNECMA M53-P2 turbofan.

**Performance:** 2000D – Max speed 1590km/h (860kt). Penetration speed at 195ft 1112km/h (600kt). Max initial rate of climb 59,055ft/min. Service ceiling 38,000ft. Range with max external fuel 3335km (1800nm), combat radius with two Magic 2 AAMs, 1000kg (2205lb) of ordnance and two drop tanks 1200km (650nm).

**Weights:** 2000D – Empty equipped 7750kg (17,085lb), max takeoff 17,500kg (38,600lb). Internal fuel 3100kg (6834lb).

**Dimensions:** 2000D – Wing span 9.13m (30ft 0in), length 14.55m (47ft 9in), height 5.0m (16ft 9in). Wing area 41.0m$^2$ (441.3sq ft).

**Accommodation:** Crew of two in tandem.

**Armament:** Nine hardpoints (one centreline, four underfuselage and four underwing) can carry a total payload of 6200kg (13,700lb). Weapon options include BGL laser guided bombs, AS 30L laser guided ASMs, Armat anti radiation missiles, two AM 39 Exocet anti ship missiles, bombs, cluster bombs, gun pods with two 30mm cannons each and dispensers with anti runway and anti armour munitions. Two Matra Magic 2 AAMs typically carried on outboard wing stations. 2000N can carry a single Aerospatiale 150kT or 300kT yield ASMP 850kg (1875lb) stand-off guided nuclear missile.

**Operators:** France

**History:** The two seat strike variants of Dassault's Mirage 2000 originate from efforts to find a replacement for the Mirage IV.

As early as 1979 Dassault received a contract to build a nuclear attack development of the 2000, designated the 2000P (Pénétration). This designation was subsequently changed to 2000N (Nucléaire), to better reflect its role, and the first of two prototypes first flew on February 3 1983.

The 2000N is based on the airframe of the 2000B conversion trainer, with changes to the airframe restricted mainly to structural strengthening for low level operations. However the 2000N does have a considerably different avionics suite to reflect its offensive roles. The key difference is the Antilope 5 radar, with terrain following (down to 300ft and speeds of 1110km/h/600kt), ground mapping, navigation, air-to-sea and air-to-air modes. The primary weapon of the 2000N is the EADS (Aerospatiale) ASMP stand-off guided nuclear missile which is carried on the centreline station. A typical nuclear attack configuration would be an ASMP, two 2000 litre external fuel tanks and two Magic 2 AAMs.

To augment the Mirage IVP, France ordered 75 2000Ns in two variants, the nuclear only 2000N-K1 and nuclear and conventional capable 2000N-K2. These were delivered between the late 1980s and 1993.

The 2000D (Diversifie) is basically similar to the 2000N-K2 except that it can only carry conventional munitions (it lacks the nose probe). It first flew on February 19 1991, and France has 86 on order, with the last due for delivery in 2001. Finally the 2000S (Strike) was an export version of the 2000D with the Antilope 5 radar, but is no longer marketed.

**Photo:** A Mirage 2000N touches down. (Armée de l'Air)

# Dassault Rafale

**Country of origin:** France

**Type:** Multirole fighter

**Powerplants:** Two 48.7kN (10,950lb) dry and 75kN (16,850lb) with afterburning SNECMA M88-2 turbofans.

**Performance:** Rafale B – Max speed 2125km/h (1147kt), max speed at low level 1390km/h (750kt). Combat radius on a low level penetration mission with 12 250kg (550lb) bombs, four Mica AAMs and three external tanks 1055km (570nm). Air-to-air combat radius with eight Mica AAMs and four tanks 1759km (950nm).

**Weights:** Rafale B – Empty equipped 10,000kg (22,047lb), MTOW initially 19,500kg (47,399lb), developed version 24,500kg (54,013lb). Internal fuel 4300kg (9524lb).

**Dimensions:** Rafale C – Wing span incl wingtip missiles 10.80m (35ft 5in), length 15.27m (50ft 1in), height 5.34m (17ft 6in). Wing area 45.7m² (492sq ft).

**Accommodation:** Pilot in Rafale C & M, pilot & WSO in Rafale B & BM.

**Armament:** One internal 30mm Giat DEFA 791B cannon. Normal external load 6000kg (13,228lb) on six underwing, two wingtip, two centreline and four underfuselage stations. Options include an ASMP nuclear standoff missile, up to eight Mica AAMs, AM 39 Exocets, LGBs, AS 30L laser guided ASMs, or APACHE standoff weapon dispensers with anti armour or anti runway munitions.

**Operators:** France*

**History:** The Mirage 2000 was just entering service in the early 1980s when France began casting its eye on a successor.

When France withdrew as a participant of the EFA (now Eurofighter) consortium, it focused instead on developing Dassault's Avions de Combat Experimentale (ACX) design. The ACX was built in demonstrator form as the Rafale A which first flew on July 4 1986. The Rafale A was used to validate much of the design of the definitive Rafale, including the airframe, fly-by-wire system and SNECMA M88 turbofan.

The definitive Rafale is slightly smaller than the Rafale A, has some stealth measures and greater use of composite materials by weight. It is being built in three versions, the single seat Rafale C (ff May 19 1991) and two seat Rafale B for the Armée de l'Air (the two types are covered by the generic Rafale D designation), and the navalised Rafale M for the French navy. Current plans envisage 234 C and Ds for the air force to replace Jaguars and Mirage F1s and 60 Ms for the navy including 40 two seater BMs to replace F-8 Crusaders and Super Etendards. On top of the 13 production aircraft previously funded, a multi year contract for the first 48 was finally signed in early 1999.

The first production Rafale (a B model) first flew on November 24 1998. The first French navy Rafale squadron was forming in 2001, while French air force deliveries will commence in 2002.

Rafale features include its blended fuselage/wing airframe, comprehensive Spectra fully integrated internal EW system, Thales RBE2 radar (with electronic scanning), LCD cockpit displays, side stick controller, helmet mounted sight, voice controls, wide angle HUD, and front sector optronics (IR, TV and laser rangefinder). An export version would feature more powerful engines and improved radar and avionics. Dassault is also developing shoulder mounted conformal fuel tanks.

**Photo:** The first production Rafale M. (F Robineau, Dassault/Aviaplans)

# De Havilland Canada DHC-6 Twin Otter

**Country of origin:** Canada

**Type:** STOL utility transport

**Powerplants:** 100 – Two 430kW (579shp) Pratt & Whitney Canada PT6A-20 turboprops. 300 – Two 460kW (620shp) PT6A-27s.

**Performance:** 100 – Max cruising speed 297km/h (160kt). Range with max fuel 1427km (770nm), range with a 975kg (2150lb) payload 1344km (727nm). 300 – Max cruising speed at 10,000ft 338km/h (182kt). Max initial rate of climb 1600ft/min. STOL takeoff run 104m (304ft). Range with 1135kg (2500lb) payload 1297km (700nm), range with a 860kg (1900lb) payload and wing tanks 1705km (920nm).

**Weights:** 100 – Basic operating empty 2653kg (5850lb), max takeoff 4765kg (10,500lb). 300 – Operating empty 3363kg (7415lb), max takeoff 5670kg (12,500lb).

**Dimensions:** 100 – Wing span 19.81m (65ft 0in), length 15.09m (49ft 6in), height 5.94m (19ft 6in). Wing area 39.0m² (420sq ft). 300 – Same except for length 15.77m (51ft 9in), or 15.09m (49ft 6in) for floatplane variants.

**Accommodation:** Flightcrew of two. Standard airliner interior seats 20 at three abreast.

**Armament:** None, though DHC-6-300M(COIN) was offered with a cabin mounted machine gun and capability to carry underwing ordnance.

**Operators:** Argentina, Australia, Canada, Chile, Ecuador, Ethiopia, France, Paraguay, Peru, USA.

**History:** The Twin Otter sold widely to the world's military air arms due to its rugged construction and STOL performance, and became de Havilland Canada's best selling design.

Twin Otter development dates to January 1964 when de Havilland Canada started design work on a new STOL twin turboprop commuter airliner (seating between 13 and 18) and utility transport. Designated the DHC-6, construction of the prototype began in November that year, resulting in the type's first flight on May 20 1965. Design features included double slotted trailing edge flaps and ailerons that can act in unison to boost STOL performance.

The first production aircraft were Series 100s. In comparison with the later Series 200 and 300s, the 100s are distinguishable by their blunt noses, while in common with the later aircraft skis and floats can be fitted. Canada was the only military customer for the Series 100, taking delivery of eight CC-138s for search and rescue.

The Series 200, which was introduced in April 1968, incorporated the extended nose, which together with a reconfigured storage compartment in the rear cabin greatly increased baggage stowage area. The Series 300 was introduced from the 231st production aircraft in 1969. It too features the lengthened nose, but introduced more powerful engines, allowing a 450kg (1000lb) increase in takeoff weight. Production ceased in 1988 and comprised 115 Series 100 aircraft, 115 Series 200s and 614 Series 300s.

Dedicated military variants of the 300 were offered in 1982: the DHC-6-200M 15 seat troop transport with optional air ambulance and paratroop configurations; armed and armoured DHC-6-300M(COIN) for counter insurgency missions; and the DHC-6-300MR maritime patrol variant fitted with searchlight and radar.

**Photo:** An Australian Army operated Twin Otter. (Les Bushell)

# De Havilland Canada DHC-4 Caribou

**Country of origin:** Canada

**Type:** STOL tactical transport

**Powerplants:** DHC-4A – Two 1080kW (1450shp) Pratt & Whitney R-2000-7M2 14 cylinder twin row radial piston engines driving three blade propellers.

**Performance:** DHC-4A – Max speed 347km/h (187kt), normal cruising speed 293km/h (158kt). Max initial rate of climb 1355ft/min. Service ceiling 24,800ft. Takeoff run to 50ft at MTOW 360m (1185ft). Range with max payload 390km (210nm), range with max fuel 2105km (1135nm).

**Weights:** DHC-4A – Basic operating 8293kg (18,260lb), standard max takeoff 12,930kg (28,500lb), military overload max takeoff 14,195kg (31,300lb).

**Dimensions:** DHC-4A – Wing span 29.15m (95ft 8in), length 22.13m (72ft 7in), height 9.68m (31ft 9in). Wing area 84.7m² (912.0sq ft).

**Accommodation:** Crew of two and a loadmaster. Can carry almost 4 tonnes (8000lb) of cargo (including two 4WDs or Land Rovers, or light artillery pieces). Can seat 32 equipped troops, or 22 stretcher patients plus medical attendants in air ambulance configuration.

**Armament:** None

**Operators:** Australia, Costa Rica, Liberia, Malaysia.

**History:** De Havilland Canada's fourth design combines DC-3 payload capabilities with excellent STOL performance.

De Havilland Canada (DHC) originally designed the DHC-4 as a private venture with an eye on Canadian and US military requirements. DHC built a prototype demonstrator (with assistance from Canada's Department of Defence Production) that first flew on July 30 1958. Impressed with the DHC-4's STOL capabilities and potential, the US Army ordered five for evaluation as the YAC-1 to meet its requirement for a tactical airlifter to supply the battlefront with troops and supplies and evacuate casualties on the return journey.

The US Army went on to become the largest Caribou operator, taking delivery of 159. The initial AC-1 designation was later changed to CV-2, and then C-7 when the US Army's CV-2s were transferred to the US Air Force in 1966 (the Caribou was the largest aircraft ever operated by the US Army up to that time). Caribou production ended in 1973 after 307 had been built, mostly for military customers.

US Army CV-2s, Air Force C-7s and Australian DHC-4A Caribou saw extensive service during the Vietnam conflict, where the type came into its own. The Caribou was well suited to Vietnam's demanding conditions and its STOL performance (unmatched by few types before or since) saw it operate into areas otherwise restricted to helicopters. Interestingly many US Caribou were captured by North Vietnamese forces in 1975 and remained in service with that country through the late 1970s.

Other former military operators include Canada, Colombia, India, Spain and Tanzania.

Today a dwindling number of Caribou survive in military service, notably with Australia and Malaysia. In 1999 and 2000 Australian Caribou were being used in support of UN peacekeeping in East Timor. Australia intends to keep its Caribou in service through to 2010.

**Photo:** An Australian Caribou. (Paul Sadler)

# De Havilland Canada DHC-5 Buffalo

**Country of origin:** Canada

**Type:** STOL tactical transport

**Powerplants:** DHC-5D – Two 2335kW (3133shp) General Electric CT64-820-4 turboprops driving three blade propellers.

**Performance:** DHC-5D – Max cruising speed 467km/h (252kt). Max initial rate of climb 2330ft/min. Service ceiling 31,000ft. Takeoff run with a 5445kg (12,000lb) payload 290m (950ft). Max range with ferry tanks 6115km (3300nm).

**Weights:** DHC-5D – Operating empty 11,410kg (25,160lb), max takeoff weight from an unprepared strip 18,597kg (41,000lb), max takeoff from prepared strip 22,315kg (49,200lb).

**Dimensions:** DHC-5D – Wing span 29.26m (96ft 0in), length 24.08m (79ft 0in), height 8.73m (28ft 8in). Wing area 87.8m² (945sq ft).

**Accommodation:** Crew of two pilots plus loadmaster. Cabin can seat 41 equipped troops, or 35 paratroops, or 24 stretcher patients and six medical attendants. Max payload 8165kg (18,000lb). Max air droppable unit 2720kg (6000lb).

**Armament:** None

**Operators:** Cameroon, Canada, Congo, Ecuador, Indonesia, Kenya, Mauritania, Mexico, Sudan, Tanzania, Togo, Zambia.

**History:** De Havilland Canada's Buffalo is a turboprop powered development of the Caribou, and was designed specifically to meet a 1962 US Army requirement.

The US Army selected the Buffalo for development ahead of 24 other contenders for a STOL transport requirement. Funding for the development of the DHC-5 (initially called Caribou II) was split equally between de Havilland Canada, the Canadian Government and the US Army. The resulting aircraft was closely based on the Caribou, but introduced two significantly more powerful General Electric CT64 turboprops, an increased maximum lift coefficient, a T-tail and a significantly higher max takeoff weight.

The US Army funded the development of four CV-7A evaluation Buffalos, the first of which first flew on April 9 1964. Unfortunately for de Havilland Canada, the same change of US policy that saw the US Army transfer its CV-2s to the US Air Force saw the cancellation of plans to procure production CV-7s. The four CV-7As were thus transferred to the USAF as C-8s.

A Canadian Armed Forces order for 15 CC-115 Buffalos for search and rescue saved the program from an uncertain future, and export orders soon followed in (the first coming from Brazil). In all 59 Buffalos were built through to 1972 when production ceased for the first time.

Unbuilt Buffalo variants were the DHC-5B with CT64-P4Cs and the DHC-5C with either CT64-P4Cs or Rolls-Royce Darts.

DHC reopened the Buffalo line in 1974 when it introduced the improved DHC-5D. The DHC-5D features more powerful CT64-820-4s (in place of the DHC-5A's 3055ehp CT64-820-1s), increasing payload range. DHC-5D production continued for a number of overseas customers through to 1986, by which time total Buffalo production reached 126.

**Photo:** Canada's six surviving CC-115 Buffalos are used for search and rescue and transport. Note the nose mounted weather radar. (Paul Merritt)

## Denel AH-2 Rooivalk

**Country of origin:** South Africa

**Type:** Attack helicopter

**Powerplants:** Two 1376kW (1845shp) takeoff rated Turbomeca Makila 1K2 turboshafts driving a four blade main rotor and five blade tail rotor.

**Performance:** (ISA at S/L) – Max cruising speed 278km/h (150kt). Max initial rate of climb 2620ft/min. Service ceiling 20,000ft. Hovering ceiling out of ground effect 17,900ft. Range with max internal fuel and no reserves 705km (380nm), range at max takeoff weight with external fuel 1260km (680nm). Endurance with max internal fuel 3hr 35min, endurance with external fuel 6hr 50min.

**Weights:** Empty 5730kg (12,632lb), typical mission takeoff 7500kg (16,535lb), max takeoff 8750kg (19,290lb).

**Dimensions:** Main rotor diameter 15.58m (51ft 2in), length overall 18.73m (61ft 5in), fuselage length (incl tail rotor, excl gun) 16.39m (53ft 9in), height 5.19m (17ft 0in). Main rotor disc area 190.6m² (2051sq ft).

**Accommodation:** Copilot/weapons operator and pilot in tandem.

**Armament:** Steerable chin mounted 20mm Armscor F2 cannon. Six underwing stores pylons (three a side) can carry 70mm rocket launchers, or up to 16 ZT6 Mokopa anti tank missiles on inner four pylons. Outboard stations can carry two or four Mistral infrared AAMs.

**Operators:** South Africa*

**History:** The AH-2 Rooivalk (or Red Kestrel) attack helicopter was designed in response to a South African Air Force requirement.

The Rooivalk is based on experience Denel (then Atlas) gained from building and flying the XH-1 Alpha concept demonstrator, a one-off attack helicopter testbed based on the Alouette III. XH-1 development began in 1981, resulting in a first flight on February 27 1986. The XH-1 retained the Alouette's engine, rotor and transmission systems combined with a new tandem two seat fuselage.

Design of the Rooivalk began in 1984, and subsequent experience with the XH-1, plus two Puma testbeds modified as gunships and designated XTP-1 Beta, allowed a first flight of the XH-2 Rooivalk prototype on February 11 1990. The XH-2 was later redesignated XDM (Experimental Development Model). It was joined by a second flying prototype, the ADM (Advanced Development Model) for avionics and weapons development and the production representative EDM (Engineering Development Model).

The first production Rooivalk flew in 1998 and was handed over to the South African Air Force in January 1999. The SAAF has ordered 12 Rooivalks for one squadron with deliveries continuing to June 2002.

The Rooivalk (the AH-2 designation replaced CSH-2 in 1998) features Turbomeca Makila 1K2 turboshafts, while its transmission and rotor system is based on the SA 330 Puma's. Otherwise the Rooivalk is an all new aircraft, featuring stepped cockpits, extensive armouring, and a gyro stabilised nose mounted turret with FLIR and TV sensors and laser rangefinder which make up an automatic target detection and tracking system.

Production AH-2s feature cheeks on the side of the fuselage which house ammunition and avionics, two colour LCDs in each cockpit, helmet mounted sights and a laser ring gyro nav system. Denel has also considered a naval version.

**Photo:** South Africa is taking delivery of 12 Rooivalks. (Keith Gaskell)

## Denel Cheetah

**Countries of origin:** South Africa and France

**Type:** Multirole fighter

**Powerplant:** One 49.0kN (11,025lb) dry and 70.6kN (15,875lb) with afterburning SNECMA Atar 9K-50 turbojet.

**Performance:** C (approx) – Max speed Mach 2.2. Combat radius with external fuel (dropped when empty), two Mk 82 bombs and two IR AAMs hi-lo-lo-hi 995km (537nm).

**Weights:** C – Max takeoff 16,200kg (35,683lb). Internal fuel 3000kg (6614lb).

**Dimensions:** C (approx) – Wing span 8.78m (28ft 10in), length 16.00m (52ft 6in), height 4.78m (15ft 8in). Wing area 33.1m² (355.7sq ft).

**Accommodation:** Pilot only in Cheetah C, two in Cheetah D.

**Armament:** Two 30mm DEFA cannons. Four underwing and three underfuselage stations for Armscor V3B Kukri and V3C Darter AAMs, ASMs, bombs, cluster bombs and rockets.

**Operators:** South Africa

**History:** The Denel Cheetah is a comprehensive upgrade of the Mirage III, with improvements to the airframe, avionics and powerplant.

Prevented from buying weapons on the world market by a 1977 United Nations arms embargo, in the mid 1980s South Africa instigated its own Mirage mid life update program, with assistance from IAI in Israel (although this was not officially confirmed).

The Cheetah upgrade was announced in 1985. On July 16 1986 Atlas (now Denel) publicly unveiled the Cheetah D, an upgraded Mirage two seater. The Cheetah D resembled the Kfir TC7, with canards, dog tooth leading edge extensions on the wings, a stretched, drooped nose housing avionics and an Elta EL/M-2001B ranging radar, strakes along the lower fuselage below the cockpit, small strakes on the nose and small fences on the wing replacing leading edge slats.

Internally the Cheetah D introduced new Israeli avionics, including a Mil Std 1553B databus, a head-up display, HOTAS (Hands On Throttle And Stick) controls and a new nav/attack system with inertial navigation. The upgrade also incorporated zero-lifing the airframe to extend fatigue life, a fixed inflight refuelling probe, and adding two additional external hardpoints under the engine intakes.

The single seat Cheetah E was first identified in 1989 and resembled the Kfir C7 with Kfir style pointed nose with ranging radar and the avionics and airframe improvements introduced on the B. The last E was withdrawn from service in 1995.

The ultimate Cheetah is the single seat Cheetah C, similar to the proposed IAI Nammer upgrade for the Mirage III/5. The C features a more powerful Atar 9K-50 turbojet (for which Denel has a manufacturing licence) and an Elta EL/M-2035 pulse Doppler radar, plus an advanced EW suite, helmet mounted sight, single piece windscreen, and redesigned refuelling probe. Cheetah C conversions began in the early 1990s and continued through to 1995. Cheetah Ds are also being upgraded with the 9K-50 and new windscreen.

A modified Mirage IIIR2Z served as a prototype with an advanced combat wing with wingtip AAM hardpoints from 1992 but despite successful flight testing the wing was not adopted for production Cheetahs.

**Photo:** A single seat Cheetah C at Waterkloof. (Keith Gaskell)

## Dornier Do 28 & 128

**Country of origin:** Germany

**Type:** STOL utility transport and liaison aircraft

**Powerplants:** Do 28 D-2 – Two 285kW (380hp) Lycoming IGSO-540-A1E flat six piston engines driving three blade constant speed props. 128-6 – Two 300kW (400shp) Pratt & Whitney Canada PT6A-110 turboprops.

**Performance:** Do 28 D-2 – Max speed 325km/h (175kt), max cruising speed 306km/h (165kt), economical cruising speed 241km/h (130kt). Max initial rate of climb 1160ft/min. Service ceiling 25,200ft. Takeoff run 280m (920ft). Range with max payload 1050km (566nm). 128-6 – Max speed 340km/h (183kt), max cruising speed 330km/h (178kt), economical cruising speed 256km/h (138kt). Max initial rate of climb 1260ft/min. Service ceiling 32,600ft. Takeoff run to 50ft altitude 554m (1820ft). Range with max fuel 1825km (985nm), with a 805kg (1774lb) payload 1460km (788nm).

**Weights:** Do 28 D-2 – Empty 2328kg (5132lb), max takeoff 3842kg (8470lb). 128-6 – Empty 2540kg (5600lb), max takeoff 4350kg (9590lb).

**Dimensions:** Do 28 D-2 – Wing span 15.55m (51ft 0in), length 11.41m (37ft 5in), height 3.90m (12ft 10in). Wing area 29.0m² (312sq ft). 128-6 – Same except for wing span 15.85m (52ft 0in).

**Accommodation:** One or two pilots on flightdeck and up to 13 troops on inward facing folding seats. In air ambulance configuration can accommodate five stretchers. Also used to carry freight.

**Armament:** Usually none.

**Operators:** Do 28 – Croatia, Greece, Israel, Kenya, Morocco, Niger, Nigeria, Zambia. Do 128 – Cameroon, Nigeria.

**History:** The Do 28 Skyservant followed from Dornier's successful Do 27 single in the liaison and light transport roles. Dornier built 200, almost all for military customers.

The Skyservant was the second aircraft to bear the Do 28 designation, but is similar only in configuration to the original Do 28 (the first Do 28 flew in 1959 and was a twin engine development of the Do 27). The Skyservant first flew on February 23 1966, and while it retained the earlier Do 28's high wing and side mounted engine configuration, was an all new and much larger aircraft. Other design features were the fixed tailwheel undercarriage and the faired mainwheels mounted beneath the engines.

The Do 28 was developed into a number of progressively improved variants, from the original D, through the D-1 and D-2, to the 128-2, introduced in 1980. Most Do 28 production was for military customers, with Germany the biggest buyer, although small numbers were sold to commercial operators.

A turboprop version of the Do 28, designated the Do 28 D-5X, first flew in April 1978, powered by two Avco Lycoming LTP 101-600-1As derated to 300kW (400shp). Production turboprop Dornier 128-6s feature Pratt & Whitney Canada PT6As, the first such configured aircraft flying in March 1980. Only a small number were built between then and 1986, including examples for Peru, which ordered 16, and Cameroon, whose three Do 128s were fitted with the MEL Marec search radar for maritime patrol.

**Photo:** A Greek Skyservant. (Greek MoD)

## Dornier 228

**Countries of origin:** Germany and India

**Type:** Utility transport and maritime patrol aircraft

**Powerplants:** 100 – Two 535kW (715shp) Garrett TPE331-5 turboprops. 212 – Two 560kW (776shp) TPE331-5-252Ds.

**Performance:** 100 – Max cruising speed 432km/h (233kt). Max initial rate of climb 2050ft/min. Service ceiling 29,600ft. Range at max cruising speed 1730km (935nm), or 1970km (1065nm) at long range cruising speed. Patrol time close to base 7hr 45min, or at 740km (400nm) from base 3hr 45min. 212 – Max cruising speed 434km/h (234kt), cruising speed 408km/h (220kt). Max initial rate of climb 1870ft/min. Service ceiling 28,000ft. Range with 19 passengers at max cruising speed 1037km (560nm), range with a 775kg (1710lb) payload at long range cruising speed 2445km (1320nm).

**Weights:** 100 – Operating empty 3235kg (7132lb), max takeoff 5700kg (12,570lb). 212 – Operating empty 3739kg (8243lb), max takeoff 6400kg (14,110lb).

**Dimensions:** 100 – Wing span 16.97m (55ft 7in), length 15.03m (49ft 3in), height 4.86m (15ft 9in). Wing area 32.0m² (345sq ft). 212 – Same except for length 16.56m (54ft 4in).

**Accommodation:** Flightcrew of two. 100 – Seating for 15. Maritime patrol configuration crew of three with a radar operator. 212 – Typical passenger seating for 19. 228-212 based 228 Cargo has a max payload of 2340kg (5159lb).

**Armament:** None

**Operators:** Germany, India*, Iran, Italy, Malawi, Niger, Nigeria, Oman, Thailand.

**History:** The Dornier 228 was developed as a regional airliner but also serves as a light military transport and in various maritime patrol configurations.

The Dornier 228 incorporates the fuselage cross section of the earlier Do 28 and 128, combined with a new supercritical wing and Garrett (now Honeywell) turboprops. Two fuselage length versions, the 100 and 200, were developed concurrently, the 100 offering better range, the 200 more payload. The 100 was the first to fly, on March 28 1981. The first 200 followed on May 9 1981.

Dornier 228 developments include the 228-101 with reinforced structure and landing gear for higher weights, the corresponding 228-201 version of the -200, the 228-202 version under licence production in India with HAL (over 50 are being acquired for all three military services), and the 228-212. The -212 was the definitive Dornier production model with higher operating weights, improvements to enhance short field performance and modern avionics.

In 1996 Fairchild acquired Dornier, announcing that all future 228 production would be undertaken by HAL, who has been building the type under licence in India since 1991, although none appear to have been built since 1997.

India is by far the largest military 228 operator, with several maritime patrol configured aircraft in service with its air force, navy and coast guard. These aircraft are fitted with a MEL Marec II search radar and linescan equipment, while the Royal Thai Navy operates 228s fitted with a Bendix 1500 radar.

**Photo:** A German navy 228. (Paul Merritt)

# Douglas C-47 Skytrain/Dakota

**Country of origin:** United States of America

**Type:** Tactical transport, gunship and utility transport

**Powerplants:** C-47A – Two 895kW (1200hp) Pratt & Whitney R-1830-92 14 cylinder two row radial piston engines driving three blade propellers. Jet Prop DC-3 – Two 1060kW (1425shp) Pratt & Whitney Canada PT6A-65AR turboprops driving five blade props.

**Performance:** C-47A – Max speed 346km/h (187kt), max cruising speed 298km/h (161kt), economical cruising speed 280km/h (151kt). Max initial rate of climb 1160ft/min. Service ceiling 24,000ft. Range 2415km (1305nm). Jet Prop DC-3 – Max cruising speed 343km/h (185kt). Max initial rate of climb 1000ft/min. Range with max payload 648km (350nm), max range 3705km (2000nm). Max endurance 14hr.

**Weights:** C-47A – Empty equipped 8250kg (18,190lb), max takeoff 13,290kg (29,300lb). Jet Prop DC-3 – Empty 7257kg (16,000lb), max takeoff 12,202kg (26,900lb).

**Dimensions:** C-47A – Wing span 28.95m (95ft 0in), length 19.62m (64ft 6in), height 5.15m (16ft 11in). Wing area 91.7m² (987sq ft). Jet Prop DC-3 – Same except length 20.68m (67ft 10in).

**Accommodation:** C-47 – Flightcrew of two. Up to 28 troops on inward facing seats. Jet Prop DC-3 – Up to 40 troops.

**Armament:** AC-47 – Three 7.62mm MGs through left side windows.

**Operators:** Bolivia, Colombia, El Salvador, Greece, Honduras, Madagascar, Paraguay, South Africa, Taiwan, Thailand.

**History:** The C-47 was the most important military transport of WW2. Even today, six decades later, it remains in service with several air arms around the world.

The C-47 is a militarised DC-3 airliner, which was an improved development of the earlier DC-2 (first flight in 1934). The DC-3 first flew on December 17 1935 and went on to become the mainstay of the US domestic airline fleet prior to World War 2.

The USA's entry into WW2 in December 1941 had a profound effect on the fortunes of the already successful DC-3 (more than 400 had been built by then). The US Army Air Force's requirements for transport aircraft were well met by the in-production DC-3, with the result that as the C-47 Skytrain it became the standard USAAF transport during the war. More than 10,000 were built for service with US and foreign air arms. In British and Commonwealth service it was named Dakota.

Postwar, surplus C-47s became the standard equipment of almost all the world's major airlines, while many US surplus C-47s were also sold or donated to the world's air forces. In the USSR it was built in quantity as the Lisunov Li-2.

The USAF used converted AC-47 gunships over Vietnam.

The C-47's remarkable longevity has resulted in a number of turboprop conversion programs to improve its performance. Two notable conversions are the Basler Turbo-67 and Professional Aviation's Jet Prop DC-3, both of which feature a small fuselage stretch and two Pratt & Whitney Canada PT6A turboprops. A small number of operators have converted their C-47s to Turbo-67 configuration, while South Africa has converted a number to C-47TP Jet Prop standard. These are used for transport and maritime patrol.

**Photo:** A 14 Squadron South African Air Force C-47TP turboprop converted C-47. (Keith Gaskell)

# Douglas DC-8 & EC-24

**Country of origin:** United States of America

**Type:** Strategic and VIP transport, ECM and Elint aircraft

**Powerplants:** Series 50 – Four 80.6kN (18,000lb) Pratt & Whitney JT3D-3 turbofans. Super 70 Series – Four 97.9kN (22,000lb) CFM International CFM56-2-C5 turbofans.

**Performance:** Series 50 – Max recommended cruising speed 933km/h (504kt). Range with max payload 9205km (4970nm), max range 11,260km (6078nm). Super 70 – Max cruising speed 887km/h (479kt), economical cruising speed 850km/h (460kt). Range with max payload (Super 73) 8950km (4830nm).

**Weights:** Series 50 – Operating empty 60,020kg (132,325lb), max takeoff 147,415kg (325,000lb). Super 73 – Operating empty 75,500kg (166,500lb), max takeoff 162,025kg (355,000lb).

**Dimensions:** Wing span 43.41m (142ft 5in), length 45.87m (150ft 6in), height 12.91m (42ft 4in). Wing area 257.6m² (2773sq ft) on early aircraft, or 266.5m² (2868sq ft) on later aircraft. Super 63 & 73 – Wing span 45.23m (148ft 5in), length 57.12m (187ft 5in), height 12.92m (42ft 5in). Wing area 271.9m² (2927sq ft).

**Accommodation:** Flightcrew of three. Series 50 can seat up to 179, and Series 71 and 73 can seat up to 220 in high density passenger configurations.

**Armament:** None

**Operators:** Bolivia, France, Gabon, Peru, USA.

**History:** The DC-8 was Douglas' first jet powered airliner, and arch rival of the more successful Boeing 707. Unlike the 707, only a small number have seen military service.

Douglas was more cautious than Boeing to move into the then radical field of jet powered transports, announcing the DC-8 project in 1955, the year after Boeing had flown its Dash 80 707/KC-135 predecessor. The first DC-8 flew on May 30 1958, and after a concentrated certification program the first production aircraft entered airliner service in September 1959, a year later than the 707.

Over 550 DC-8s were in built in a number of different variants. Original short fuselage models included the turbojet powered Series 10, 20, 30 and 40, and the turbofan powered 40 and 50 series, the latter a direct competitor to the 707-320.

The stretched Super 60 series was built from the late 1960s, and comprised the long range 47.98m (157ft 5in) length 62, and the 57.12m (187ft 5in) length 61 and 63. In the early 1980s McDonnell Douglas initiated a re-engining program for Super 60s with the CFM56. Known as Super 70s, CFM powered DC-8s are quieter, with better fuel economy and range.

France remains the largest military operator, with three Series 72s currently in service. Two are used for strategic and VIP transport, while a third is modified for ECM/Elint reconnaissance. All current French Armée de l'Air DC-8s are ex civil airliners, as are Peru's two DC-8-62CFs which are used as VIP transports.

In the USA the US Navy utilises a single converted DC-8-54F freighter for ECM training. Designated EC-24, the Douglas jet is used to simulate a realistic Electronic Warfare (EW) environment for fleet training exercises.

**Photo:** A French air force DC-8-72CF transport. (Armée de l'Air)

# EADS CASA C-212 Aviocar & Patrullero

**Country of origin:** Spain

**Type:** Aviocar – STOL utility transport. Patrullero – Maritime patrol and Elint/ECM platform

**Powerplants:** 200 – Two 670kW (900shp) Garrett TPE311-10-501C turboprops driving four blade constant speed propellers. 400M – Two 690kW (925shp) Honeywell TPE331-12JR-701Cs.

**Performance:** 200 – Max cruising speed 365km/h (197kt), cruising speed 346km/h (187kt). Range with max payload 410km (220nm), range with max fuel 1760km (950nm). 400M – Max cruising speed 361km/h (195kt), economical cruising speed 302km/h (163kt). Takeoff run to 50ft 520m (1710ft). Range with max payload 430km (233nm), with 2120kg (4674lb) payload and max fuel 1525km (824nm).

**Weights:** 200 – Empty 3780kg (8333lb), MTOW 7450kg (16,424lb). 400 – Empty 3780kg (8333lb), max takeoff 8100kg (17,857lb).

**Dimensions:** 200 – Wing span 19.00m (62ft 4in), length 15.16m (49ft 9in), height 6.30m (20ft 8in). Wing area 40.0m² (430.6sq ft). 400 – Wing span 20.28m (66ft 7in), length 16.15m (53ft 0in), height 6.60m (21ft 8in). Wing area 41.0m² (441.3sq ft).

**Accommodation:** Aviocar – Flightcrew of two. Max passenger seating for 26 troops or 12 stretchers and four medical attendants. Patrullero – Four systems operators in maritime patrol configuration, or radar operator and two observers in ASW configuration.

**Armament:** Aviocar – Two underwing hardpoints of 250kg (550lb) capacity each can carry light gun or rocket pods. Patrullero – Can carry torpedoes (such as Mk 46s or Stingray), rockets and anti shipping missiles (including Aerospatiale AS 15TT and Sea Skua).

**Operators:** Angola, Bolivia, Chile, Colombia, Dominica, Indonesia, Jordan, Mexico, Panama, Paraguay, Portugal, South Africa, Surinam, Thailand, UAE (Abu Dhabi), Uruguay, Venezuela, Zimbabwe.

**History:** The C-212 was designed to replace the Spanish air force's mixed fleet of Douglas C-47 Dakotas and Junkers Ju 52s.

Design work began in the late 1960s with features including good STOL performance and a rear cargo ramp. The first prototype flew on March 26 1971 and the type entered air force service in 1974.

The initial civil version was designated the C-212C, the military version the C-212-5. Production of these models ceased in 1978 when CASA switched to the Series 200 with more powerful engines and higher operating weights. The Series 200 first flew in converted C-212C prototype form on April 30 1978. IPTN/IAe in Indonesia has continued to build small numbers of -200s under licence.

A third development of the Aviocar is the Series 300 which first flew in 1984. Enhancements are improved engines and winglets.

The Series 300 was offered in special mission Patrullero form – as the nose or under belly search radar and sonobuoy equipped maritime patrol 300MP, anti submarine 300ASU, and signal interception, classification, identification and jamming equipped ECM/Elint 300DE.

The latest development is the 400, which first flew on April 4 1997, It features EFIS avionics and improved TPE331-12JR engines which maintain their power output to a higher altitude for improved hot and high performance. Deliveries began in 1998 and it is available in the same model variants as the 300.

**Photo:** A Dominican air force C-212-400 Patrullero. (EADS CASA)

# EADS CASA CN-235

**Countries of origin:** Spain and Indonesia

**Type:** Tactical transport and maritime patrol aircraft

**Powerplants:** Two 1305kW (1750shp) General Electric CT7-9C turboprops driving four blade Hamilton Standard propellers.

**Performance:** CN-235 M – Max cruising speed at 15,000ft 460km/h (248kt). Max initial rate of climb 1900ft/min. Service ceiling 26,600ft. Takeoff distance to 50ft at MTOW 1290m (4235ft). Range (srs 200) with max payload 1500km (810nm), with a 3550kg (7825lb) payload 4445km (2400nm).

**Weights:** CN-235 M – Operating empty 8800kg (19,400lb), max takeoff 16,500kg (36,375lb).

**Dimensions:** CN-235 M – Wing span 25.81m (84ft 8in), length 21.40m (70ft 3in), height 8.18m (26ft 10in). Wing area 59.1m² (636.1sq ft).

**Accommodation:** CN-235 M – Flightcrew of two, plus typically a loadmaster. Can accommodate 48 equipped troops or 46 paratroopers.

**Armament:** CN-235 MP – Six underwing hardpoints allow the carriage of anti shipping missiles such as Exocet and Harpoon.

**Operators:** Botswana, Chile, Croatia*, Ecuador, France, Gabon, Ireland, Morocco, Papua New Guinea, Saudi Arabia, South Africa, South Korea, Spain, Turkey*.

**History:** CASA of Spain (now part of EADS) and Indonesia's IPTN (now Dirgantara or Indonesian Aerospace) jointly developed the CN-235 under the Airtech banner, but since 1992 both companies have developed their own variants of the aircraft separately.

Initial development was shared equally between the two companies, and one prototype in each country was rolled out simultaneously on September 10 1983. The Spanish built prototype was the first to fly, on November 11 1983, while the Indonesian prototype first flew on December 30 that year.

CN-235 final assembly lines are located in both Indonesia and Spain, but all other construction is not duplicated. EADS CASA builds the centre and forward fuselage, wing centre section, inboard flaps and engine nacelles, while Dirgantara is responsible for the outer wings and flaps, ailerons, rear fuselage and tail.

Initial production was of the CN-235-10, subsequent and improved developments include the CN-235-100 and the current production -200, with more powerful engines and structural improvements, respectively. EADS CASA's latest CN-235-300 features an NVG compatible EFIS flightdeck with four LCDs and HUDs, plus inflight refuelling compatibility

While commercial developments of the CN-235 (including the QC – quick change) have sold in modest numbers, the military CN-235 M transport has been quite successful with over 170 in service with over 20 countries, most built by EADS CASA. Features of the CN-235 include its high mounted wing and twin GE CT7 turboprops, good field performance, a rear loading ramp and spacious interior.

EADS CASA's CN-235 MP Persuader maritime patrol variant has been sold to Ireland, Spain and Turkey and features a belly mounted Litton APS-504 search radar, under nose mounted FLIR and Litton ESM.

EADS CASA's stretched and Pratt & Whitney Canada PW127 powered C-295 is described separately.

**Photo:** A Colombian air force CN-235. (EADS CASA)

## EADS CASA C-295

**Country of origin:** Spain

**Type:** Tactical transport

**Powerplants:** Two 1972kW (2645shp) Pratt & Whitney Canada PW127G turboprops driving six blade Hamilton Standard propellers.

**Performance:** Max cruising speed 474km/h (256kt). Absolute ceiling 30,000ft. Takeoff run (ISA, at sea level) 843m (2765ft). Landing run 420m (1380ft). Range with max payload 1455km (785nm), range with max fuel and a 4000kg (8818lb) payload 4969km (2683nm), range with a 6000kg (13,228lb) payload 4165km (2250nm).

**Weights:** Max takeoff 21,000kg (46,297lb), max overload takeoff 23,200kg (51,147lb).

**Dimensions:** Wing span 25.81m (84ft 8in), length 24.45m (80ft 3in), height 8.66m (28ft 5in). Wing area 59.1m² (636.1sq ft).

**Accommodation:** Flightcrew of two. Typical accommodation for 69 fully equipped troops, or 78 troops in a high density configuration, or 48 paratroops, or 27 stretcher patients and four attendants. Max payload 7500kg (16,535lb), max overload payload 9700kg (21,385lb). Can carry up to five 2.24 x 2.74m (88 x 108in) pallets including one on the rear ramp, or three 4WDs.

**Armament:** Provision for three hardpoints under each wing to carry up to 1800kg of ordnance on MPA version.

**Operators:** Poland*, Spain*, Switzerland*, UAE*.

**History:** The EADS CASA C-295 is a stretched and re-engined development of the successful CN-235 tactical transport.

The CN-235 transport was developed jointly by CASA of Spain and IPTN of Indonesia, but since 1992 each company has pursued development of the basic aircraft independently. CASA began studies of a stretched and re-engined CN-235 in 1995.

Development of the C-295 began in November 1996 and was announced at the 1997 Paris Airshow. The prototype, a converted CN-235, made its first flight on November 28 1997, while the first production C-295 flew in December 1998. Civil and military certification was awarded in late 1999, with deliveries to launch customer Spain (which has ordered nine) beginning in November 2001 (although crew training with EADS CASA began mid that year).

Compared with the CN-235, the C-295's fuselage is stretched by six fuselage frames (three forward and three aft of the wing) taking length from 21.40m (70ft 3in) to 24.45m (80ft 3in), increasing the aircraft's payload. The C-295 is powered by two P&WC PW127 turboprops driving six blade composite propellers, increasing cruising speed and reducing the takeoff run required. The basic CN-235 wing is strengthened with increased fuel capacity, while the undercarriage is also strengthened for the increased weights with a dual wheel nosewheel. Other changes include a higher pressurisation differential and a four LCD screen NVG compatible EFIS flightdeck with provision for HUDs.

In March 2001 the UAE ordered the C-295MPA maritime patrol variant with EADS CASA's FITS (Fully Integrated Tactical System) developed for an upgrade to Spain's P-3s. The latest customer is Poland, which ordered eight transports in August 2001.

**Photo:** The second C-295. The C-295 entered service with launch customer Spain in November 2001. (Paul Merritt)

## EADS Socata TBM 700

**Country of origin:** France

**Type:** Light liaison transport

**Powerplant:** One 520kW (700shp) flat rated Pratt & Whitney Canada PT6A-64 turboprop driving a four blade constant speed propeller.

**Performance:** Max cruising speed 555km/h (300kt), economical cruising speed 450km/h (243kt). Initial rate of climb 2380ft/min. Max certificated altitude 30,000ft. Range with max payload and reserves at max cruising speed 1666km (900nm), at economical cruising speed 1853km (1000nm). Range with max fuel at max cruising speed 2500km (1350nm), at econ cruising speed 2870km (1550nm).

**Weights:** Empty equipped 1860kg (4101lb), max takeoff 2984kg (6578lb).

**Dimensions:** Wing span 12.68m (41ft 7in), length 10.64m (34ft 11in), height 4.35m (14ft 3in). Wing area 18.0m² (193.8sq ft).

**Accommodation:** Pilot and one passenger (or copilot) on flightdeck. Main cabin seating for up to five, or typical accommodation for four in a club arrangement.

**Armament:** None

**Operators:** France*

**History:** The TBM 700 is a high performance single engine turboprop powered light corporate transport which the French army and air force have adopted as a liaison transport.

The TBM 700 is mainly optimised as a business transport in competition with twin turboprop designs, mainly Raytheon Beech's C90 King Air series. Unlike the similarly sized C90 King Air, the TBM 700's single engine layout is a major conceptual difference. With its single PT6 turboprop, rather than two on the King Air, the TBM 700 offers lower operating costs yet comparable performance.

The TBM 700 was originally developed in partnership between Socata (Aerospatiale's light aircraft division) in France and Mooney in the USA, hence the TBM designation. The two companies formed TBM SA to build and market the TBM 700, with development responsibility for the project divided on a 70/30 basis between Socata and Mooney respectively.

The TBM 700 first flew on July 14 1988. French certification was granted in January 1990. Shortly after the delivery of the first production aircraft in December 1990, Mooney withdrew from the program, leaving Socata with full responsibility for the aircraft.

The pressurised TBM 700 is of conventional design and construction, with a small amount of composite materials used in some areas. Flight controls, flaps and most of the empennage and fin are made from Nomex honeycomb and metal sheets. Leading edges and undercarriage doors meanwhile are made from a carbon and fibreglass composite.

Apart from the base aircraft the TBM 700 is offered as the TBM 700B with 1.19m x 1.07m rear door, and the TBM 700C freighter with the freight door and separate port side cockpit door. Development of the stretched TBM 700S ceased in 1995.

TBM 700 deliveries to the French air force began in 1992. The French air force requires 22 TBM 700s, while the French army has taken delivery of eight, including three TBM 700Bs delivered from 2000.

**Photo:** A French army TBM 700B with large freight door. (Dave Fraser)

## Embraer EMB-110 & EMB-111

**Country of origin:** Brazil

**Type:** Light utility transport and maritime patrol aircraft (EMB-111)

**Powerplants:** Two 560kW (750shp) Pratt & Whitney Canada PT6A-34 turboprops driving three blade Hartzell propellers.

**Performance:** EMB-111 – Max cruising speed 360km/h (194kt), econ cruising speed 347km/h (187kt). Max initial rate of climb 1190ft/min. Service ceiling 25,500ft. Range 2945km (1590nm).

**Weights:** EMB-111 – Empty equipped 3760kg (8289lb), max takeoff 7000kg (15,432lb).

**Dimensions:** EMB-111 – Span over tip tanks 15.95m (52ft 4in), length 14.91m (48ft 11in), height 4.91m (16ft 2in). Wing area 29.1m² (313sq ft).

**Accommodation:** Flightcrew of two. Can carry up to 18 troops or six stretchers.

**Armament:** EMB-111 – Four underwing pylons can carry rockets, smoke bombs, flares, chaff dispenser and a searchlight.

**Operators:** EMB-110 – Brazil, Cape Verde, Chile, Colombia, Gabon, Uruguay. EMB-111 – Angola, Brazil, Chile, Gabon, Peru.

**History:** The EMB-110 Bandeirante (often dubbed 'Bandit'), was Embraer's first successful indigenous aircraft program and is in widespread civil and military service.

EMB-110 design was undertaken by Brazil's Institute of Research and Development in response to a Ministry of Aeronautics specification for a general purpose light transport suitable for military and civilian duties. The new design was developed with the assistance of well known French designer Max Holste, and the first of three prototypes, designated YC-95, first flew on October 26 1968.

Embraer (or Empresa Brasilera de Aeronáutica SA) was established the following year, and development and production of the YC-95 became one of the company's first responsibilities.

The first of the larger production standard EMB-110 Bandeirantes (Bandeirante is Portuguese for Pioneer) flew on August 9 1972 and the type entered Brazilian air force service in February 1973.

Brazilian military transport versions of the basic EMB-110 are designated C-95, including 60 early build, 12 seat C-95s and 31 stretched C-95Bs, equivalent to the EMB-110P, the definitive civil version. Brazil also operates a small number of navigation aid calibration EC-95s and photographic survey RC-95s.

The most heavily modified Bandeirante is the EMB-111 maritime patrol variant, which features an Eaton-AIL APS-128 Sea Patrol radar mounted in a nose radome, ESM, wingtip tanks and four underwing hardpoints. The last 10 EMB-111s built for Brazil feature improved avionics including a MEL Super Searchmaster radar and EFIS. Brazil's EMB-111s are designated P-95s and are nicknamed Bandeirulha, a contraction of Bandeirante Patrulha.

The definitive commercial production models were the EMB-110P1 convertible passenger/freighter and P2 passenger versions.

Production of the Bandeirante ceased in May 1990, the final aircraft being delivered to the Brazilian air force, with a further two completed in 1992 for the Colombian air force. In all over 500 Bandeirantes were built, including 29 EMB-111s.

**Photo:** A Brazilian air force EMB-111 (P-95). Note radome and wingtip tanks. (Embraer)

## Embraer EMB-120 Brasilia

**Country of origin:** Brazil

**Type:** Twin turboprop VIP transport

**Powerplants:** Two 1340kW (1800shp) Pratt & Whitney Canada PW118 or PW118A turboprops driving four blade Hamilton Standard propellers.

**Performance:** EMB-120 with PW118As – Max cruising speed 574km/h (310kt), long range cruising speed 482km/h (260kt). Max initial rate of climb 2120ft/min. Service ceiling 32,000ft. Range with max passengers and reserves 926km (500nm). EMB-120ER with PW118As – Max cruising speed 580km/h (313kt), long range cruising speed 500km/h (270kt). Max initial rate of climb 2500ft/min. Service ceiling 32,000ft. Range with max pax and reserves 1500km (810nm).

**Weights:** EMB-120 – Empty equipped 7100kg (15,655lb), max takeoff 11,500kg (25,353lb). EMB-120ER – Empty equipped 7140kg (15,741lb), max takeoff 11,990kg (26,433lb).

**Dimensions:** EMB-120 – Wing span 19.78m (64ft 11in), length 20.00m (65ft 8in), height 6.35m (20ft 10in). Wing area 39.4m² (424.42sq ft). EMB-120ER – Same except for length 20.07m (65ft 10in).

**Accommodation:** Flightcrew of two. Standard main cabin seating for 30 at three abreast. Brazil's VC-97s configured as VIP transports.

**Armament:** None

**Operators:** Brazil

**History:** Although in only limited military service, the Brasilia regional turboprop airliner has proven to be a considerable commercial sales success, following in the highly successful footsteps of the earlier and smaller Bandeirante.

Design work of the Brasilia dates back to the late 1970s when Embraer investigated stretching its EMB-121 Xingu corporate turboprop to a 25 seat regional airliner. While this was the first aircraft to bear the EMB-120 designation (it was named the Araguia), the resulting EMB-120 is an all new aircraft. Design studies began in September 1979, first flight of a PW115 powered prototype took place on July 27 1983, and entry into service was in October 1985.

Models include the basic EMB-120, the extended range EMB-120ER, EMB-120 Combi, EMB-120 Convertible, and current production EMB-120ER Advanced with various improvements and an increased max takeoff weight. Hot and high models are powered by two PW118As. Over 350 have been built.

Brazil operates 10 VIP transport configured Brasilias, designated VC-97. These were delivered to the Brazilian air force from 1987.

Brazil also ordered five airborne early warning and three synthetic aperture radar configured Brasilias for its Amazon Surveillance System program. The EMB-120AEWs would have been fitted with an Ericsson Erieye phased array surveillance radar and three multifunction operator work stations and an onboard command and control system. The EMB-120SRs would have been fitted with a synthetic aperture radar, an ultraviolet/visible/infrared line scanner and a high sensitivity TV/FLIR.

First deliveries were planned for 1997 but in 1996 the EMB-145 regional jet airliner (described separately) was chosen as the platform for the two systems in place of the Brasilia. An EMB-120K maritime patrol variant for Brazil was studied in 1999.

**Photo:** A Brazilian air force VC-97 (EMB-120RT) VIP transport.

## Embraer EMB-121 Xingu

**Country of origin:** Brazil

**Type:** Liaison, VIP transport and multi engine trainer aircraft

**Powerplants:** Xingu I – Two 505kW (600shp) Pratt & Whitney Canada PT6A-28 turboprops driving three blade props. Xingu II – Two 635kW (850shp) PT6A-42s driving four blade props.

**Performance:** Xingu I – Max cruising speed 450km/h (243kt), economical cruising speed 365km/h (197kt). Max initial rate of climb 1400ft/min. Service ceiling 26,000ft. Range with max fuel 2352km (1270nm). Xingu II – Max cruising speed 465km/h (251kt), economical cruising speed 380km/h (205kt). Max initial rate of climb 1800ft/min. Range with max fuel 2278km (1230nm), with max payload 1630km (880nm).

**Weights:** Xingu I – Empty equipped 3620kg (7984lb), max takeoff 5670kg (12,500lb). Xingu II – Empty equipped 3500kg (7716lb), max takeoff 6140kg (13,536lb).

**Dimensions:** Xingu I – Wing span 14.45m (47ft 5in), length 12.25m (40ft 2in), height 4.74m (15ft 7in). Wing area 27.5m$^2$ (296.0sq ft).

**Accommodation:** Xingu I – Flightcrew of one or two, plus typical main cabin seating for five or six passengers. Xingu II – Flightcrew of two. Main cabin seating for seven, eight or nine passengers.

**Armament:** None

**Operators:** Brazil, France.

**History:** The EMB-121 Xingu was intended as a fast corporate transport for the civil market, but in the end almost half of all EMB-121 production was for the Brazilian and French militaries.

The sleek looking Xingu combined the EMB-110P2 Bandeirante's wing (but with shortened span and modified tips) with PT6A engines and an all new fuselage. It first flew on October 10 1976, with a production aircraft following on May 20 1977 and customer deliveries starting later that year (the first was delivered to the Copersucar-Fittipaldi Formula One racing team).

Several derivatives of the Xingu design were proposed that did not see the light of day, including the original EMB-120 – the Araguia – a commuter airliner which would have seated 25, and the EMB-123 Tapajós. The Tapajós would have had more powerful 835kW (1120shp) PT6A-45 engines (which also would have powered the Araguia), increased wing span and lengthened fuselage.

A more modest development did enter production, the EMB-121B Xingu II, which is similar in size and performance to the Raytheon Beech King Air 200. The EMB-121B features more powerful engines, four blade props, and increased fuel tankage. The Xingu II made its first flight on September 4 1981. Xingu production ceased in August 1987 after 105 had been built.

The first six production Xingus were delivered to the Brazilian air force in late 1977, designated VU-9 and used for VIP transport. Brazil later acquired a further six EMB-121s second hand, and these were designated EC-9.

Some 41 EMB-121s, almost half of all Xingu production, were delivered to the French Armée de l'Air and navy where they are used for aircrew training and liaison duties. They were ordered in September 1980 and the last was delivered in 1983.

**Photo:** A French air force Xingu. (Ian Doyle)

## Embraer EMB-145 SA, RS & MP

**Country of origin:** Brazil

**Type:** EMB-145 SA – AEW platform. EMB-145 RS – Remote sensing surveillance aircraft. EMB-145 MP – Maritime patrol platform

**Powerplants:** ERJ 145LR – Two 33.1kN (7430lb) Rolls-Royce AE 3007A1 turbofans.

**Performance:** ERJ 145LR – Max cruising speed 797km/h (430kt), econ cruising speed 667km/h (360kt). Service ceiling 37,000ft. Range with 50 passengers 2445km (1320nm). EMB-145 SA – Endurance 9hr.

**Weights:** EMB-145 SA/RS – Max takeoff approx 24,000kg (52,865lb).

**Dimensions:** Wing span 20.04m (65ft 9in), length 29.87m (98ft 0in), height 6.75m (22ft 2in). Wing area 51.2m$^2$ (550.9sq ft).

**Accommodation:** Flightcrew of two. Brazil's EMB-145 SA has three 'back end' operators – a tactical control officer, electronic warfare operator and an intercept operator – with provision for a fourth, and accommodation for three relief operators.

**Armament:** None

**Operators:** Brazil*, Greece*, Mexico*.

**History:** Embraer's 50 seat ERJ 145 regional jet forms the basis for the EMB-145 SA AEW and EMB-145 RS remote sensing platforms being developed for Brazil's SIVAM Amazon surveillance program.

The SIVAM (SIstema de Vigilancia da AMazonia) program seeks to provide surveillance of illegal air and ground activities in the Amazon basin using AEW and remote sensing aircraft, plus ground based radars and light attack ALXs (Super Tucanos). The AEW and remote sensing requirement was originally going to be met by modified EMB-120 Brasilias, before the ERJ 145 jet was adopted in late 1996.

The ERJ 145 had first flown on August 11 1995 and customer deliveries began in December 1996. It is offered in ERJ 145ER, LR and XR forms. The EMB-145 SA and RS are based on the ERJ 145LR airframe, but with an increased max takeoff weight, additional fuel cells in the rear fuselage, modified landing gear, and uprated Rolls-Royce AE 3007A1P engines.

The airborne early warning EMB-145 SA is fitted with an Ericsson PS-890 Erieye phased array radar mounted above the fuselage which at altitude can detect targets up to 450km (243nm) away, or out to 350km (189nm) from low altitude. Inside it features three forward facing operator consoles, with provision for a fourth.

The EMB-145 RS meanwhile is fitted with a Canadian MacDonald Dettwiler IRIS (Integrated Radar Imaging System) synthetic aperture radar (SAR) in a belly mounted radome, nose mounted AAQ-12 FLIR, and Comint and Elint sensors. With the SAR the RS will be able to strip map swaths 100km (54nm) wide.

The SA and RS will be operated by the Brazilian air force, designated the R-99A and R-99B respectively. The service is buying five SAs and three RSs, for delivery from 2001. Apart from SIVAM duties the Brazilian air force will also be able to use its R-99s for more traditional military surveillance tasks.

Greece is buying five EMB-145 SAs fitted with five operator stations, ESM, Thales EWSP and NATO standard data links.

Mexico has ordered the EMB-145 MP maritime patrol variant with FLIR and a Raytheon search radar.

**Photo:** The EMB-145 SA. (Embraer)

# Embraer EMB-312 Tucano

**Country of origin:** Brazil

**Type:** Two seat basic/advanced trainer

**Powerplant:** EMB-312 – One 560kW (750shp) Pratt & Whitney Canada PT6A-25C turboprop driving a three blade propeller. S312 – One 820kW (1100shp) Garrett TPE331-12B driving a four blade prop.

**Performance:** EMB-312 – Max speed 448km/h (242kt), max cruising speed 411km/h (222kt), economical cruising speed 319km/h (172kt). Max initial rate of climb 2330ft/min. Service ceiling 30,000ft. Ferry range with two underwing tanks 3330km (1797nm), typical range on internal fuel 1845km (995nm). Endurance on internal fuel approx 5hr. S312 – Max speed/max cruising speed 507km/h (274kt), economical cruising speed 391km/h (211kt). Max initial rate of climb 3510ft/min. Practical service ceiling 25,000ft. Range with internal fuel 1835km (990nm).

**Weights:** EMB-312 – Basic empty 1810kg (3990lb), max takeoff 3175kg (7000lb). S312 – Basic empty 2138kg (4713lb), max takeoff 3600kg (7937lb).

**Dimensions:** EMB-312 – Wing span 11.14 (36ft 7in), length 9.86m (32ft 4in), height 3.40m (11ft 2in). Wing area 19.4m² (208.8sq ft). S312 – Same as EMB-312 except span 11.28m (37ft 0in).

**Accommodation:** Two in tandem.

**Armament:** Up to 1000kg (2205lb) on four underwing pylons, including bombs, rockets, gun pods and practice bombs.

**Operators:** Argentina, Brazil, Colombia, Egypt, France, Honduras, Iran, Iraq, Kenya, Kuwait, Paraguay, Peru, Venezuela, UK.

**History:** What started as a replacement program for Brazil's T-37 trainers has resulted in South America's most successful military aircraft program, with over 600 Tucano trainers sold to 14 different nations.

Development of the Tucano (Toucan) began in late 1978 when the Brazilian Ministry of Aeronautics awarded Embraer a development contract to design and fly a turboprop powered trainer to replace the Brazilian air force's Cessna T-37s. What resulted was the Tucano, a tandem two seater (with ejection seats) powered by a Pratt & Whitney Canada PT6A turboprop, featuring four underwing hardpoints for light armament or practice bombs. First flight was on August 16 1980.

Brazil originally ordered 133 Tucanos (designated T-27) which were delivered between 1983 and 1986. Egypt became the first export customer when in 1983 it ordered 134, all but 10 of which were to be assembled by Helwan in Egypt. Of those 134, 80 were built for Iraq.

In 1985 Britain's Royal Air Force selected a Garrett TPE331 powered variant of the Tucano to replace its Jet Provosts. These aircraft were licence built by Shorts in Northern Ireland as the S312 (Tucano T.1 in RAF service), and feature a significantly more powerful 820kW (1100shp) TPE331-12B engine, improved systems and structural strengthening for improved fatigue life. Kuwait and Kenya also ordered Shorts built, Garrett powered Tucanos.

France ordered 80 Embraer built EMB-312F Tucanos in 1991 to replace Magisters. Delivered from 1993, EMB-312Fs feature structural strengthening, a ventral air brake and French avionics with LCDs.

A total of 622 Tucanos were delivered through to the late 1990s.

**Photo:** A French AF Tucano. (Armee de l'Air)

# Embraer Super Tucano & ALX

**Country of origin:** Brazil

**Type:** Advanced trainer and ground attack aircraft

**Powerplants:** One 930kW (1250shp) Pratt & Whitney Canada PT6A-68 turboprop driving a five blade propeller.

**Performance:** Max speed 557km/h (301kt), max cruising speed 530km/h (286kt), economical cruising speed 422km/h (228kt). Max initial rate of climb 2925ft/min. Service ceiling 35,000ft. Range with max fuel and reserves 1568km (847nm), ferry range with external fuel 2768km (1495nm). Endurance on internal fuel 6hr 30min.

**Weights:** Basic empty 2420kg (5335lb), max takeoff 3600kg (7936lb).

**Dimensions:** Wing span 11.14m (36ft 7in), length 11.42m (37ft 6in), height 3.90m (12ft 10in). Wing area 19.4m² (208.8sq ft).

**Accommodation:** Two in tandem, pilot only in A-29.

**Armament:** Four underwing and one centreline hardpoints of 225kg (495lb) capacity each for a range of light weaponry including light bombs, rockets, gun pods and AAMs including the MAA-1 Piranha.

**Operators:** Brazil*

**History:** The Super Tucano and ALX are more powerful developments of the basic EMB-312 Tucano.

Embraer first looked at an upgraded Tucano in the late 1980s when it investigated the feasibility of using an armed Tucano development to intercept helicopters and slow flying light aircraft. These design studies evolved into the EMB-312H (later EMB-314) Super Tucano, which Embraer offered to meet the US Air Force/Navy JPATS requirement (won by a Raytheon development of the PC-9).

The Super Tucano features a more powerful engine, a stretched fuselage, reprofiled canopy, new wing, larger tail and ventral strakes. No basic EMB-314s have been sold.

Work on the armed Super Tucano based ALX began in 1993, and the Brazilian air force committed to order 99 in August 1995. The order comprises 49 single seaters, designated A-29, and 50 two seaters, designated AT-29. Thirty of the AT-29s will be used for advanced training (replacing AT-26 Xavantes), 20 for night time Amazon basin surveillance. The A-29s will be used for day policing.

Embraer rolled out the first prototype A-29 alongside the AEW EMB-145 SA on May 28 1999.

The ALX is powered by a 930kW (1250shp) Pratt & Whitney Canada PT6A-68 turboprop. The wing houses two 12mm/.50cal internal machine guns while one underfuselage and four underwing 225kg capacity hardpoints can carry a variety of light weaponry comprising bombs (including laser guided bombs when fitted with a laser designator), rockets, gun pods and air-to-air missiles (such as the infrared guided MAA-1 Piranha).

Internally the ALX features Israeli Elbit avionics on a 1553B databus with two central mission computers, two 15x20cm liquid crystal displays which are night vision goggle compatible, HOTAS controls, a HUD, and INS with imbedded GPS. The two seater will be able to carry a ventrally mounted FLIR, for its night surveillance and attack missions.

Other ALX features include a radar warning receiver, missile approach warning system, and chaff and flare dispenser.

**Photo:** The first YA-29 prototype. (Embraer)

## ENAER T-35 Pillán

**Countries of origin:** Chile and USA

**Type:** Two seat basic trainer

**Powerplant:** T-35A – One 225kW (300hp) Textron Lycoming IO-540-K1K5 fuel injected flat six piston engine driving a three blade constant speed propeller. T-35TD – One 315kW (420shp) Allison 250-B17D turboprop driving a three blade propeller.

**Performance:** T-35A – Max speed 311km/h (268kt), max cruising speed 266km/h (144kt). Max initial rate of climb 1525ft/min. Time to 10,000ft 8min 48sec. Service ceiling 19,160ft. Range at 55% power 1205km (650nm), range at 75% power 1095km (590nm). Endurance at 55% power 5hr 35min, endurance at 75% power 4hr 25min. T-35DT – Max speed 425km/h (230kt), 75% power cruising speed 337km/h (182kt), 55% power cruising speed 313km/h (170kt). Max initial rate of climb 2850ft/min. Time to 9850ft 5min 36sec. Service ceiling 25,000ft. Range at 55% power 760km (410nm), range at 75% power 648km (350nm).

**Weights:** T-35A – Empty equipped 930kg (2050lb), max takeoff 1338kg (2950lb). T-35DT – Empty 943kg (2080lb), max takeoff 1338kg (2950lb).

**Dimensions:** T-35A – Wing span 8.84m (29ft 0in), length 8.00m (26ft 3in), height 2.64m (8ft 8in). Wing area 13.7m² (147.3sq ft). T-35DT – Same except length 8.60m (28ft 3in).

**Accommodation:** Seating for two in tandem.

**Armament:** Usually none.

**Operators:** Chile, Guatemala, Panama, Paraguay, Spain.

**History:** The Pillán (devil) basic trainer resulted from a Chilean air force requirement for a two seat, aerobatic basic trainer.

Piper responded to the requirement with a new trainer based on its PA-28R Saratoga, a six seater with retractable undercarriage (itself based on the PA-28 four seater family). Piper designated its new two seater the PA-28R-300, and while based on the Saratoga it featured a new fuselage centre section and structural strengthening for aerobatics. Like the Saratoga it featured a 225kW (300hp) six cylinder Lycoming IO-540 engine.

Piper built two prototypes, the first flying on March 6 1981, while the first of three ENAER assembled prototypes flew in January 1982. From 1979 ENAER (Empresa Nacional de Aeronáutic de Chile) had assembled under licence 27 Piper PA-28 Dakota four seat light aircraft for the Chilean air force and various local flying clubs and so was already experienced in building Piper aircraft.

ENAER production of the T-35 began in 1985. In all ENAER built 80 for Chile, comprising 60 T-35As and 20 IFR equipped T-35Bs. The most significant export customer for the T-35 was Spain, who ordered 41 T-35Cs. Designated the E.26 Tamiz in Spanish service, these aircraft were assembled in Spain by CASA from ENAER built kits. Other customers were Panama (10 IFR equipped T-35Ds) and Paraguay (15 T-35Ds). Final T-35 deliveries were in 1991.

The turboprop T-35DT Turbo Pillán was a development of the original T-35TX Aucán which first flew in February 1986. The T-35DT featured a new one piece canopy, oxygen system and improved instrumentation. None were sold.

**Photo:** A Pillán in Chilean markings. (Fuerza Aerea de Chile)

## English Electric Canberra

**Country of origin:** United Kingdom

**Type:** Strike, target tug and reconnaissance aircraft

**Powerplants:** B(I).8 – Two 33.2kN (7400lb) Rolls-Royce Avon 109 turbojets.

**Performance:** B(I).8 – Max speed 871km/h (470kt) at 40,000ft, max speed at sea level 827km/h (447kt). Max initial rate of climb 3400ft/min. Service ceiling 48,000ft. Range with max fuel 5840km (3155nm), range with max load and 10 minutes over target 1295km (700nm).

**Weights:** B(I).8 – Basic operating 12,678kg (27,950lb), max takeoff 24,925kg (54,950lb).

**Dimensions:** B(I).8 – Wing span over tip tanks 19.96m (65ft 6in), wing span 19.51m (64ft 0in), length 19.96m (65ft 6in), height 4.77m (15ft 8in). Wing area 89.2m² (960sq ft).

**Accommodation:** B(I).8 – Flightcrew of two. Pilot seated under fighter style canopy, navigator in nose.

**Armament:** Up to six 1000lb (455kg) bombs in weapons bay, or alternatively one 4000lb (1815kg) and four 1000lb (455kg) bombs, or eight 500lb (227kg) bombs, or three 1000lb (455kg) bombs and four Hispano cannons. Two underwing wingtip stations can carry 455kg (1000lb) each.

**Operators:** Argentina, India, Peru, UK.

**History:** The Canberra was Britain's primary medium bomber during the 1950s and into the 1960s, and was widely exported. Dwindling numbers survive in service.

As far back as 1944 English Electric (a large British industrial company that had built Halifax bombers in WW2) was shortlisted along with a number of higher profile British aircraft manufacturers to design the RAF's first jet bomber. English Electric's design was selected and it first flew on Friday May 13 1949.

Features of the Canberra included its very large, broad wing which was designed for high altitude operations but gave the aircraft fighter like agility, its two Rolls-Royce Avon turbojets (one in each wing) and an internal bomb bay. In all, 27 variants were built, including those built under licence in the USA by Martin as the B-57 Canberra, and 48 in Australia by GAF (Australian and US Canberras saw combat in Vietnam). Total Canberra production was 1352.

Significant Canberra models include the B.2 bomber, PR.3 and PR.7 reconnaissance aircraft, and the B.6 bomber. In October 1994 the RAF retired its last T.17s, originally built as conversion trainers but later used for EW training.

The Shorts developed PR.9 remains in RAF service as a reconnaissance platform (they were used over Afghanistan in 2001). Features of this aircraft include more powerful engines, an offset fighter-style tear drop canopy under which sits the pilot (with the navigator in the nose) and increased span wings.

The B(I).8 Interdictor also featured the offset fighter-style canopy. India is still an important Canberra operator with a fleet of 10 including B(I).58s (based on the B(I).8) used as target tugs. Argentina (seven) and Peru (10) also operate Canberras as bombers, while until recently Germany operated two PR.9s.

**Photo:** An RAF Canberra PR.9.

## Eurocopter/Aerospatiale SA 330 Puma

**Country of origin:** France

**Type:** Multirole medium lift helicopter

**Powerplants:** SA 330L – Two 1175kW (1575shp) Turbomeca Turmo IVC turboshafts driving a four blade main rotor and five blade tail rotor.

**Performance:** SA 330L – Max cruising speed 271km/h (146kt). Max initial rate of climb 1810ft/min. Service ceiling 19,685ft. Hovering ceiling in ground effect 13,940ft, out of ground effect 13,940ft. Range 572km (309nm).

**Weights:** SA 330L – Empty 3615kg (7970lb), normal MTOW 7405kg (16,315lb), max takeoff with sling load 7500kg (16,534lb).

**Dimensions:** SA 330L – Main rotor diameter 15.00m (49ft 3in), length overall rotors turning 18.15m (59ft 7in), fuselage length 14.06m (46ft 2in), height overall 5.14m (16ft 11in). Main rotor disc area 176.7m² (1902.2sq ft).

**Accommodation:** Flightcrew of two. Up to 20 troops or six stretchers and six seated patients or medical attendants in main cabin.

**Armament:** Options include 7.62mm gun pods, rockets and ASMs mounted on the fuselage sides, and pintle mounted machine guns in cabin doors.

**Operators:** Puma operators include Argentina, Chile, Ecuador, France, Gabon, Indonesia, Kuwait, Lebanon, Malawi, Morocco, Nepal, Nigeria, Portugal, Romania, Senegal, South Africa (Oryx) Spain, UAE (Abu Dhabi, Dubai), UK.

**History:** The Puma was designed to meet a French army requirement for an all weather medium lift helicopter.

The first of two SA 330 prototypes first flew on April 15 1965, with the first production aircraft flying in September 1968. A 1967 Royal Air Force decision to order the Puma as its new tactical helicopter transport resulted in substantial Westland participation in design and construction. This was a result of the Westland/Sud Aviation helicopter cooperation agreement covering the Puma, Gazelle and Lynx signed in 1967.

Early military versions of the Puma were the French army SA 330B, export SA 330C, SA 330E Puma HC.1 transport for the RAF, and the hot and high Turmo IVC powered SA 330H (designated SA 330Ba in French service). The initial civil variants were the SA 330F passenger and SA 330G freight versions. The SA 330L is the definitive military Puma, and compared to the earlier models has composite main rotors and an increased maximum takeoff weight. The SA 330J is the civil equivalent of the L.

IPTN of Indonesia assembled a small number of SA 330Js as the NSA-330 before switching to the Super Puma. When Aerospatiale ceased production in 1987, the sole source for the Puma became IAR in Romania.

UN arms embargoed South Africa developed its own Puma derivatives. Two Makila powered, armed XTP-1 Beta prototypes were used as testbeds during the 1980s for the Rooivalk attack helicopter program, while the Oryx is a Makila powered development. The Oryx was originally named Gemsbok, and entered service in 1988. Other changes include single pilot operation, weather radar and Super Puma style tail. The SAAF took delivery of 50 Oryxs.

**Photo:** A South African Air Force Oryx at Waterkloof. (Keith Gaskell)

## Eurocopter Super Puma, Cougar & EC 725

**Country of origin:** France

**Type:** Multirole medium lift helicopter

**Powerplants:** AS 532U2 – Two 1375kW (1845shp) t/o rated Turbomeca Makila 1A2 turboshafts driving four blade main and tail rotors.

**Performance:** AS 532U2 – Fast cruising speed 273km/h (147kt), economical cruising speed 242km/h (131kt). Rate of climb 1260ft/min. Service ceiling 13,450ft. Hovering ceiling out of ground effect 6235ft. Range with standard fuel 795km (430nm), with max fuel 1175km (635nm). Endurance 4hr 12min.

**Weights:** AS 535U2 – Empty 4945kg (10,902lb), max takeoff 9750kg (21,495lb).

**Dimensions:** AS 532U2 – Main rotor diameter 16.20m (53ft 2in), length overall 19.50m (63ft 11in), length overall main rotor folded 16.79m (55ft 1in), height overall 4.97m (16ft 4in). Main rotor disc area 206.0m² (2217.4sq ft).

**Accommodation:** AS 532U2 – One pilot for VFR or two pilots for IFR operations. Seats up to 29 troops. Max slung load 4500kg (9920lb).

**Armament:** Options include 7.62mm gun pods, rockets and ASMs (including AM 39 Exocet anti ship missiles) mounted on the fuselage sides, and pintle mounted machine guns in cabin doors.

**Operators:** Argentina, Brazil, Cameroon, Chile, China, Ecuador, France, Germany, Indonesia, Japan, Jordan, Kuwait, Mexico, Nepal, Netherlands, Nigeria, Qatar, Saudi Arabia, Singapore, Sth Korea, Spain, Sweden, Switzerland, Thailand, Togo, Turkey, UAE (Abu Dhabi), Venezuela.

**History:** The Super Puma and Cougar are stretched and re-engined developments of the Puma.

The original Super Puma first flew in September 1978 and was simply a more powerful version of the SA 330 Puma, featuring 1270kW (1700shp) Turbomeca Makila turboshafts, new avionics and composite rotor blades. Military versions were designated AS 332Bs, commercial versions AS 332Cs.

The AS 332M Super Puma (and civil AS 332L) introduced the stretched fuselage and first flew on October 10 1980. Uprated Makila 1A1 engines were introduced in 1986. Indonesia's IPTN has licence built a small number of AS 332Ls for that country's military.

In 1990 Aerospatiale (Eurocopter from 1992) renamed military Super Pumas the AS 532 Cougar Mk I series. Various suffixes denote the different military versions – U for unarmed, A for armed, C for the shorter version, L for the slightly stretched fuselage variant. Further variants are the SAR/surveillance AS 532MC and ASW AS 532SC – both feature the shorter fuselage.

Current production is of the AS 532U2 Cougar Mk II (although the Cougar Mk I remains available). The unarmed U2, armed A2 (France is buying them for Combat SAR) and civil L2, available since 1993, feature a further fuselage stretch allowing an extra row of seats (and making them the longest members of the Super Puma/Cougar family), four screen EFIS cockpit and longer main rotor blades with parabolic tips. The AS 532 Cougar 100 is simplified with fixed landing gear.

The improved EC 725 (EC 225 in civil guise) flew in November 2000. It features a five blade main rotor, increased cabin volume, Makila 1A4 engines with FADEC, 11 tonne MTOW and new EFIS avionics.

**Photo:** The EC 725. (Eurocopter)

# Eurocopter Dauphin 2 & Panther

**Country of origin:** France

**Type:** Multirole helicopter

**Powerplants:** AS 565SB – Two 635kW (851shp) Turbomeca Arriel 2C turboshafts driving a four blade main rotor and shrouded tail rotor.

**Performance:** AS 565SB – Max cruising speed at sea level 278km/h (150kt). Max initial rate of climb 1535ft/min. Hovering ceiling out of ground effect 8200ft. Radius of action with two anti shipping missiles 278km (150nm). Range with max standard fuel 820km (443nm).

**Weights:** AS 565SB – Empty 2312kg (5097lb), MTOW 4250kg (9040lb).

**Dimensions:** AS 565SB/UB – Main rotor diameter 11.94m (39ft 2in), length overall 13.68m (44ft 11in), fuselage length 12.11m (39ft 9in), height 3.98m (13ft 1in). Main rotor disc area 111.9m² (1204.5sq ft).

**Accommodation:** AS 565UB – Two pilots and eight to 10 troops in assault transport role. AS 565SB – Two crew. Up to 10 passengers.

**Armament:** AS 565AA – Two rocket packs, or 20mm Giat M621 gun pods, or up to eight Matra Mistral AAMs in four two-round packs, on two fuselage outriggers. AS 565SB – Can carry four side mounted AS 15TT radar guided ASMs.

**Operators:** Angola, Brazil, Cameroon, China, Dominican Rep, France, Ireland, Israel, Ivory Coast, Saudi Arabia, UAE (Dubai), Uruguay.

**History:** The Panther is a family of military derivatives of the Dauphin 2, which is a twin engined development of the original single Turbomeca Astazou powered SA 360 and SA 361 Dauphin.

A dedicated military anti tank variant of the SA 361 was offered – the HOT anti tank missile equipped SA 361F – but none were sold.

Compared with the SA 360, the SA 365 Dauphin 2 introduced twin Turbomeca Arriel turboshafts and a new engine fairing, Starflex main rotor hub and higher max takeoff weight, but retained the same basic fuselage. The Dauphin 2's first flight was on January 24 1975, while production deliveries of SA 365Cs began in early 1978. Few SA 365Cs are in military service.

The SA 365 was soon replaced by the AS 365N, with more powerful Arriel 1C turboshafts, enlarged tail surfaces, revised transmission and main rotor, new rotor mast fairing and engine cowling, and retractable tricycle undercarriage. The US Coast Guard took delivery of 99 AS 365N based HH-65 Dolphins, optimised for search and rescue. These aircraft are powered by two Lycoming LTS 101s.

The civil AS 365N2 forms the basis for the military AS 565 Panther family. Released in 1990, features of the AS 365N2 and Panther include upgraded Arriel engines, increased max takeoff weights, redesigned cabin doors and optional EFIS displays. The improved N3 and equivalent Panthers feature Arriel 2Cs, while the latest civil version is the 'widebody' EC 155 (previously the AS 365N4).

Current Panther models are based on the AS 365N3 and include the AS 565UB unarmed transport and AS 565AB armed transport. Naval variants comprise the unarmed AS 565MB and armed AS 565SB (which replaced the AS 565MA and SA respectively). Equipment options include sonar, MAD, searchlight, and search radar.

Eurocopter's improved EC 155B development, with larger cabin area, Arriel 2C1 engines and five blade main rotor. Deliveries to first customer the German border guard began in 1999.

**Photo:** A French navy AS 565SB. (Eurocopter)

# Eurocopter Ecureuil & Fennec

**Country of origin:** France

**Type:** Multirole light helicopter

**Powerplants:** AS 555N – Two 340kW (455shp) takeoff rated Turbomeca TM 319 Arrius turboshafts driving a three blade main rotor and two blade tail rotor.

**Performance:** AS 555N – Max cruising speed 225km/h (121kt). Max initial rate of climb 1340ft/min. Service ceiling 13,125ft. Hovering ceiling in ground effect 8530ft, out of ground effect 5085ft. Range 722km (390nm). Endurance with one torpedo 2hr 20min.

**Weights:** AS 555N – Empty 1382kg (3046lb), MTOW 2600kg (5732lb).

**Dimensions:** AS 555N – Main rotor diameter 10.69m (35ft 1in), length overall 12.94m (42ft 6in), fuselage length 10.93m (35ft 11in), height overall 3.34m (11ft 0in). Main rotor disc area 89.8m² (966.1sq ft).

**Accommodation:** Seating for up to six.

**Armament:** Options include a pintle mounted 7.62mm machine gun, a 20mm Giat gun pod, twin 7.62mm gun pods, rockets, HeliTOW anti tank missiles and up to two torpedoes on naval variants.

**Operators:** Algeria, Australia, Botswana, Brazil, Central African Rep, China, Colombia, Denmark, Djibouti, Ecuador, France, Jamaica, Malawi, Mali, Malaysia*, Mexico, Paraguay, Peru, Singapore, Tunisia, UAE (Abu Dhabi), UK.

**History:** The Ecureuil (or Squirrel) light helicopter was conceived as a replacement for the Alouette II and is offered in twin and single engine variants.

Development in the early 1970s culminated in the first flights of the Lycoming LTS 101 powered prototype on June 27 1974 and the Turbomeca Arriel powered prototype on February 14 1975. Customer deliveries began in April 1978.

Initial models offered were the Arriel powered AS 350B, which was marketed outside North America, and the LTS 101 powered AS 350C and A350D Astar sold in the USA. Developments include the AS 350BA fitted with the larger main rotors of the AS 350B2, the AS 350B2 with a more powerful Arriel 1D1 turboshaft and the main and tail rotors developed for the AS 355F Ecureuil 2, and most recently the Arriel 2 powered AS 350B3.

The twin engined Ecureuil 2 first flew on September 28 1979. Powered by two Allison (now RR) 250-C20F turboshafts, the Ecureuil 2 entered production as the AS 355E. In common with the AS 350, the AS 355 features the maintenance free Starflex main rotor hub and main rotor blades of composite construction. The AS 355F replaced the AS 355E from early 1982, while the current production model is the AS 350N (TwinStar in the US) with Turbomeca Arrius turboshafts.

Aerospatiale adopted the name Fennec for dedicated military Ecureuils in 1990. Single engine AS 350B2 based military versions include the utility AS 550U2, gun and rocket armed AS 550A2, HeliTOW missile armed AS 550C2, unarmed maritime AS 350M2 and armed anti shipping AS 550S2. The AS 350B3 based models are the utility AS 550U2, armed A2 and missile firing C2.

Twin engine Fennec variants include the AS 555UN utility, armed AS 555AN, missile armed AS 555CN, unarmed maritime AS 555MN (with optional chin mounted radar) and armed maritime AS 555SN with Honeywell RDR-1500B 360° radar (ordered by Malaysia in 2001).

**Photo:** A Colombian navy AS 555SN. (Eurocopter)

## Eurocopter BO 105

**Country of origin:** Germany

**Type:** Observation, utility and anti tank helicopter

**Powerplants:** BO 105 CB – Two 320kW (429shp) Allison 250-C20B turboshafts driving a four blade main rotor and two blade tail rotor.

**Performance:** BO 105 CB – Max cruising speed 245km/h (137kt), cruising speed 232km/h (125kt). Max initial rate of climb 1773ft/min. Service ceiling 17,000ft. Hovering ceiling out of ground effect 6500ft, in ground effect 9515ft. Range with max payload 655km (354nm), ferry range 1110km (600nm).

**Weights:** BO 105 CB – Empty equipped 1280kg (2820lb), max takeoff 2400kg (5290lb).

**Dimensions:** BO 105 CB – Main rotor diameter 9.84m (32ft 4in), length overall 11.86m (38ft 11in), fuselage length 8.56m (28ft 1in), height 3.00m (9ft 10in). Main rotor disc area 76.1m² (818.6sq ft).

**Accommodation:** Pilot and observer/copilot side by side, with three passengers or two stretchers behind them. Behind the rear seats and below the engine is a cargo compartment, accessible by two clamshell doors in the rear fuselage.

**Armament:** PAH-1 – Six Euromissile HOT anti tank missiles in two three-tube launchers mounted on fuselage outriggers. Majority have been modified to fire HOT 2. Swedish BO 105 CBS can fire ESCO HeliTow anti tank missiles.

**Operators:** Bahrain, Brunei, Chile, Colombia, Germany, Indonesia, Iraq, Kenya, Mexico, Netherlands, Papua New Guinea, Peru, Philippines. South Korea*, Spain, Sweden, UAE (Abu Dhabi & Dubai).

**History:** The BO 105 serves widely as a multirole observation and anti tank attack helicopter, and is well regarded for its agility, twin engine safety and performance.

The first of three BO 105 prototypes made the type's maiden flight on February 16 1967. This helicopter was powered by two 236kW (317shp) Allison 250-C18 turboshafts and featured a conventional main rotor hub, but the subsequent prototypes incorporated a new rigid hub with feathering hinges, composite blades and MAN-Turbo 6022 engines. The BO 105 reverted to Allison 250 power with the second of two preproduction aircraft flying in this form in January 1971. Initial production was of the BO 105 C, available from 1970, while Allison 250-C20 turboshafts became standard from 1973.

The BO 105 CB was introduced in 1975 with uprated engines and a strengthened transmission. The BO 105 CBS has a slight 25cm (10in) fuselage stretch and an additional window, allowing an extra passenger to be carried. The BO 105 L has more powerful engines and a higher takeoff weight. The BO 105 LS is a hot and high version with Rolls-Royce (Allison) 250-C28C engines built exclusively in Canada by Eurocopter Canada, while the BO 105 LSA Super Lifter is designed to carry external loads.

The Germany army is easily the largest BO 105 operator, taking delivery of 212 HOT armed BO 105 Ps as PAH-1s and 100 BO 105 M scouts as VBHs. Both these models are similar to the BO 105 CB, and were upgraded with new rotor blades and other improvements. These modifications also formed the basis of the civil EC Super Five, now BO 105 CBS, which is the primary current production model.

**Photo:** A Bahrain navy BO 105 CBS with search radar and hoist.

## Eurocopter/Kawasaki BK 117

**Countries of origin:** Germany and Japan

**Type:** Multirole helicopter

**Powerplants:** BK 117 B-2 – Two 410kW (550shp) Textron Lycoming LTS 101-750B-1 turboshafts driving four blade main and two blade tail rotors.

**Performance:** BK 117 B-2 – Max cruising speed 248km/h (134kt). Max initial rate of climb 1900ft/min. Hovering ceiling in ground effect 7000ft, out of ground effect 7500ft. Range with internal long range tank 706km (381nm).

**Weights:** BK 117 B-2 – Empty 1745kg (3846lb), MTOW 3350kg (7385lb).

**Dimensions:** Main rotor diameter 11.00m (36ft 1in), length overall 13.00m (42ft 8in), fuselage length 9.98m (32ft 9in), height rotors turning 3.85m (12ft 8in). Main rotor disc area 95.0m² (1023sq ft).

**Accommodation:** One pilot and maximum seating for 10 passengers.

**Armament:** Usually none, although the BK 117 A-3M was offered with eight HOT 2 or four TOW anti tank missiles.

**Operators:** Chile, Iraq, South Africa.

**History:** The BK 117 was developed under a collaborative effort between MBB (now part of Eurocopter) and Kawasaki.

The BK 117 replaced the separate MBB BO 107 and Kawasaki KH-7 design studies. The BK 117 retains the former's overall configuration, with Eurocopter responsible for the rotor system (which uses a scaled up version of the BO 105's four blade rigid main rotor), tail unit, hydraulic system and power controls, while Kawasaki is in charge of the fuselage, transmission and undercarriage.

Development led to the BK 117's first flight on June 13 1979, the first production aircraft (built in Japan) flew in December 1981, civil certification was awarded in December 1982, and first deliveries took place early in 1983. Initial production was of the BK 117 A-1, while the BK 117 A-3 with higher max takeoff weight and enlarged tail rotor with twisted blades was certificated in March 1985.

The BK 117 A-3 also formed the basis of the only specific military development offered, the BK 117 A-3M. It was offered with a roof mounted sight, either TOW or HOT 2 anti tank missiles, a trainable nose mounted machine gun, rocket pods, RWR and ECM. However, the BK 117 A-3M was dropped in 1988 due to a lack of interest.

The BK 117 A-4 introduced from 1987 features enhanced performance through an increased transmission limit at takeoff power, improved tail rotor head and on German built aircraft increased fuel. The BK 117 B-1 (certificated in 1987) has more powerful engines and better performance, the current production BK 117 B-2 has an increased max takeoff weight, while the BK 117 C-1 is a German development with Turbomeca Arriel engines. Indonesia's three licence built aircraft are known as NBK-117s.

The BK 117 has not emulated the military sales success of its smaller BO 105 brother, and is only in limited military service. The largest operator is Iraq, which took delivery of 16 SAR configured BK 117 B-1s. Others are in government and quasi military service.

Eurocopter and Kawasaki are now working on the further improved EC 145 development of the 117, which first flew on June 12 2000. It features an EC 135 style nose, reprofiled main rotor blades and redesigned tail rotor.

**Photo:** MBB's BK 117 A-3M armed with four TOW anti tank missiles.

# Eurocopter EC 120 Colibri

**Countries of origin:** France, Germany, China and Singapore

**Type:** Light utility helicopter

**Powerplants:** One 376kW (504shp) takeoff rated Turbomeca TM 319 Arrius 2F turboshaft driving a three blade main rotor and eight blade Fenestron shrouded tail rotor.

**Performance:** Max cruising speed 226km/h (122kt). Initial rate of climb 1300ft/min. Service ceiling 17,024ft. Range with no reserves 731km (3954nm). Endurance at 120km/h (65kt) 4hr 10min.

**Weights:** Empty 960kg (2116lb), max takeoff 1715kg (3781lb), max takeoff with a sling load 1800kg (3968lb).

**Dimensions:** Main rotor diameter 10.00m (32ft 9in), length overall rotor turning 11.52m (37ft 10in), fuselage length 9.60m (31ft 6in), height 3.40m (11ft 2in). Main rotor disc area 78.6m$^2$ (845.4sq ft).

**Accommodation:** Typical seating for five, with pilot and passenger side by side with three passengers on rear bench seat. Could be configured for special missions roles. Max sling load 700kg (1543lb).

**Armament:** None

**Operators:** Indonesia*, Spain*.

**History:** Eurocopter's solution to develop a new light helicopter lay in forming a partnership with CATIC (Harbin) of China and Singapore Technologies Aerospace of Singapore.

Eurocopter (then Aerospatiale), CATIC and STA launched definition development of a new light helicopter, then designated P120L, in February 1990. The teaming arrangements for the helicopter saw Aerospatiale/Eurocopter take a 61% program share and leadership, CATIC with 24% and STAe with 15%. A development go-ahead contract for the new aircraft was signed in October 1992 (by which time Aerospatiale's helicopter activities had been merged into Eurocopter) and the EC 120 designation was announced in January 1993 (the Colibri [or Hummingbird] name came later).

Within the Eurocopter/CATIC/STAe partnership, Eurocopter is responsible for the design and manufacture of the rotor system and transmission, final assembly (at Marignane in France), flight testing and certification. CATIC builds the EC 120's fuselage, landing gear and fuel system, while STAe's areas of responsibility covers the tailboom, fin and doors.

Notable Colibri design features include a three blade main rotor with a Spheriflex hub integrated with the driveshaft and transmission, composite main and tail rotor blades and skid landing gear, Turbomeca TM 319 Arrius 1F turboshaft, a metal construction fuselage and a new eight blade Fenestron shrouded tail rotor.

The first of two EC 120 prototypes first flew on June 9 1995 from Eurocopter France's Marignane facility. French DGAC certification was awarded in June 1997, while the first production Colibri first flew in December that year. First delivery was in January 1998, the 100th was delivered in May 2000.

The first EC 120 military customer was Spain, which ordered 15 in 1999. These were delivered from mid 2000 and have replaced Hughes 300s in the pilot training role. Indonesia has also ordered EC 120s for helicopter pilot training. Twelve are on order for the air force, three for the navy.

**Photo:** Spain is taking delivery of 15 EC 120s. (Eurocopter)

# Eurocopter EC 135 & EC 635

**Countries of origin:** Germany and France

**Type:** Light twin utility helicopter

**Powerplants:** EC 135 – Either two 500kW (670shp) takeoff rated Turbomeca Arrius 2B1s (EC 135T1) or two 463kW (621shp) max continuous rated P&WC PW206B turboshafts (EC 135P1) driving a four blade main rotor and 10 blade shrouded Fenestron tail rotor.

**Performance:** EC 135 – Max cruising speed 257km/h (139kt). Max initial rate of climb 1653ft/min. Service ceiling 20,000ft. Hovering ceiling out of ground effect 13,450ft. Range with standard fuel 745km (402nm), ferry range with long range tank 878km (474nm).

**Weights:** EC 135 – Empty with Arrius 2Bs 1465kg (3230lb), empty with PW206s 1480kg (3263lb), max takeoff 2720kg (5997lb) or 2900kg (6393lb) with an external load. EC 635 – Empty 1740kg (3826lb).

**Dimensions:** Main rotor diameter 10.20m (33ft 5in), length overall 12.16m (39ft 11in), fuselage length 10.20m (33ft 5in), height to top of rotor head 3.35m (11ft 0in). Main rotor disc area 81.7m$^2$ (879.5sq ft).

**Accommodation:** Designed for single pilot operation (including IFR ops). Alternative cabin layouts are for five or seven in passenger roles. Alternative medevac layouts for one stretcher, three medical attendants and pilot, or two stretchers two attendants and pilot. Stretchers loaded through rear freight door.

**Armament:** None for German training aircraft.

**Operators:** Germany*, Portugal*.

**History:** The EC 135 was designed as a replacement for Eurocopter's successful BO 105 light twin, and is developed from the BO 108 technology demonstrator. The German army is the first military customer, ordering it for advanced training.

The original MBB BO 108 was intended as a high technology helicopter demonstrator, and as such incorporated a range of advanced features including a hingeless main rotor, all composite bearingless tail rotor, shallow transmission (allowing greater cabin height) with special vibration absorbers, composite structures, improved aerodynamics, modern avionics and EFIS instrumentation. The first BO 108 was powered by Allison 250-C20R-3 turboshafts and flew on October 15 1988.

The success of the BO 108 test program led to MBB's announcement in January 1991 that it would develop the 108 with Arrius or PW206 engines as a replacement for the BO 105, with certification planned for 1994, and deliveries in 1995.

However, the formation of Eurocopter gave the program access to Aerospatiale's Fenestron shrouded tail rotor technology. The combination of the BO 108 and the Fenestron led to the definitive EC 135, which first flew on February 15 1994. German certification was granted on June 14 1996.

Germany was the first military EC 135 customer, ordering 15 to replace Alouette IIs in the pilot training role. They were delivered from 1998 to the Army Aviation Weapons Systems School in Buckeburg, and feature NVG compatible cockpit lighting and raised skid landing gear. The German border guard has ordered nine.

Portugal meanwhile is the launch customer for the EC 635 military variant. It is buying nine for its army air corp.

**Photo:** An EC 635 mockup. (Sebastian Zacharias)

# Eurocopter Tiger

**Countries of origin:** France and Germany

**Type:** Anti tank and battlefield reconnaissance helicopter

**Powerplants:** Two 960kW (1285shp) TO rated MTU-Turbomeca-Rolls-Royce MTR 390 turboshafts driving a four blade main rotor and three blade tail rotor.

**Performance:** UHT – Max speed 269km/h (145kt), cruising speed 230km/h (124kt). Max vertical rate of climb 1023ft/min. Hovering ceiling out of ground effect 10,500ft. Range on internal fuel 800km (432nm). Endurance, operational mission 2hr 50min.

**Weights:** Basic empty 3400kg (7496lb), mission takeoff 5300 to 6000kg (11,685 to 13,225lb), max overload takeoff 6100kg (13,448lb).

**Dimensions:** Main rotor diameter 13.00m (42ft 8in), fuselage length 14.08m (46ft 2in), height overall 4.32m (14ft 2in). Main rotor disc area 132.7m² (1428.7sq ft).

**Accommodation:** Pilot (front) & weapon systems operator in tandem.

**Armament:** UHT – Up to eight HOT 2 or Trigat anti tank missiles and four Mistrals or Stingers on two wing pylons, plus rocket and gun pods. HAD – One 30mm Giat cannon in chin turret, four Matra Mistral AAMs and four HOT 3, or later eight Trigat anti tank missiles and four Stinger/Mistral AAMs, or combinations of rockets and missiles.

**Operators:** Australia*, France*, Germany*.

**History:** Europe's most advanced combat helicopter, the Tiger has its genesis in similar German and French army programs.

In the early 1980s the German and French armies separately began studying replacing their PAH-1 (BO 105) and Gazelle anti tank helicopters. In 1984 the two countries signed a MoU covering the joint development of such a helicopter, with an amended MoU signed in 1987. Full scale development was approved in December 1987, while the main development contract was awarded and the name Tiger (or Tigre in French) adopted in late 1989. That year also saw Aerospatiale and MBB form the jointly owned Eurocopter to cover Tiger development.

The Tiger first flew on April 22 1993, and five development aircraft were built (one crashed during an over-enthusiastic demonstration flight in 1998). Production contracts were signed in June 1999, covering an initial 80 Tigers each for France and Germany, out of requirements for 215 and 212 respectively. Deliveries are due to begin in 2003.

Tiger features include redundant electrical, fuel and hydraulic systems, two MTR 390 turboshafts, advanced cockpit displays and composite construction (including fibre elastomer main rotor).

The Tiger will be built in two main production versions. The German army's UHT (nee UHU) is a multirole anti tank/support helicopter (replacing the previously planned PAH-2) with mast mounted sight. The French originally planned to procure the HAP escort/fire support version (called Gerfaut until 1993) with roof mounted sight, and the HAC anti tank version with mast mounted sight. However in 2001 France elected to buy the multirole HAD which is based closely on the HAP, with the roof mounted sight, GIAT 30mm gun, and HOT and later Trigat anti tank missiles. The UHT's and HAD's sights will contain FLIR and TV sensors.

The Tiger scored its first export customer – Australia – in 2001. Its 22 will be similar to the HAD, but with slightly uprated engines.

**Photo:** The HAP configured second prototype. (Eurocopter)

# Eurofighter Typhoon

**Countries of origin:** Germany, Italy, Spain and the UK

**Type:** Advanced multirole fighter

**Powerplants:** Two 60.0kN (13,490lb) dry and 90.0kN (20,250lb) with afterburning Eurojet EJ200 turbofans.

**Performance:** Max speed approx Mach 2.0. Limited supercruise capability. Radius with a 3hr CAP over 185km (100nm). Hi-lo-hi radius with external fuel, three LGBs and seven AAMs 1390km (750nm), lo-lo-lo over 600km (325nm).

**Weights:** Empty 10,995kg (24,250lb), max takeoff 23,000kg (50,706lb). Internal fuel 4500kg (9920lb).

**Dimensions:** Wing span 10.95m (35ft 11in), length 15.96m (52ft 4in), height 5.28m (17ft 7in). Wing area 50.0m² (538.2sq ft).

**Accommodation:** Pilot only, or two in tandem in conversion trainer.

**Armament:** One 27mm Mauser cannon. 13 hardpoints for weapons incl ASRAAM, IRIS-T, AMRAAM and Meteor AAMs, Storm Shadow and KEPD350 stand-off missiles, ALARM ARM, and GBU-10/12 LGBs.

**Operators:** Italy*, Germany*, Spain*, UK*.

**History:** The Eurofighter Typhoon is an advanced multirole fighter entering production for Germany, Italy, Spain and the UK.

The concept of a jointly developed European fighter was already some years old when in June 1986 the Eurofighter consortium was formed to manage the European Fighter Aircraft (or EFA) program. Development workshare was split between the four partner nations according to planned buy numbers. The specific EFA concept was formalised in December 1987.

By then BAe had flown its EAP technology demonstrator with canard delta configuration and fly-by-wire. EAP flight test results played an important part in EFA/Eurofighter/Typhoon development.

German budget constraints forced a program review in 1992, before Germany settled on buying the relaunched Eurofighter EF 2000 with some equipment deleted. More name changes saw the program renamed Eurofighter 2000, and then Eurofighter Typhoon in 1998.

The Eurofighter's first flight occurred on March 29 1994, after much delay, with another six development aircraft following.

Despite its protracted development and controversy over costs, the Typhoon is a highly capable fighter. Features include carbon fibre construction, EJ200 engines, multimode pulse Doppler Captor (formerly ECR90) radar, an infrared search and tracking system (IRST), an advanced Defensive Aids SubSystems or DASS with wingtip mounted ESM pods (and laser warning receiver on UK and Italian aircraft), and an advanced cockpit with wide angle HUD, three LCDs, helmet mounted sight and Direct Voice Input (DVI) controls (hence VTAS controls – Voice, Throttle and Stick).

Future Typhoons could feature conformal fuel tanks, thrust vectoring nozzles, electronically scanned radar and uprated engines.

Britain requires 232 Eurofighters, Germany 180, Italy 121 and Spain 87. The partner nations signed a production contract for an initial 148 aircraft in September 1998. First deliveries are planned for 2002. Initial aircraft will be air-to-air capable only, multirole Typhoons will be delivered from 2004. Eurofighter partners BAE Systems, EADS Germany, Alenia and EADS CASA each have final assembly lines.

**Photo:** BAE built DA2 prototype in black paint for trials. (Eurofighter)

# Fairchild A-10A Thunderbolt II

**Country of origin:** United States of America

**Type:** Anti armour/close air support attack aircraft

**Powerplants:** Two 40.3kN (9065lb) General Electric TF34-GE-100 non afterburning turbofans.

**Performance:** Max speed 835km/h (450kt). Max initial rate of climb 6000ft/min. Ferry range with drop tanks 3950km (2130nm), combat radius on a deep strike mission 1000km (540nm), combat radius on a close air support mission with 1hr 42min loiter 465km (250nm).

**Weights:** Basic empty 9770kg (21,540lb), MTOW 22,680kg (50,000lb).

**Dimensions:** Wing span 17.53m (57ft 6in), length 16.26m (53ft 4in), height 4.47m (14ft 8in). Wing area 47.0m² (506.0sq ft).

**Accommodation:** Pilot only.

**Armament:** One 30mm GE GAU-8 Avenger cannon. Eleven underwing and underfuselage hardpoints can carry 7257kg (16,000lb) of ordnance, including AGM-65, cluster bombs, LGBs and AIM-9s.

**Operators:** USA

**History:** The concept for the A-10 Thunderbolt II was conceived during the Vietnam War for a close support aircraft for low intensity conflicts, but grew into a dedicated anti armour platform.

The US Air Force formulated its AX specification following the un-suitability of its supersonic tactical fighters in close air support roles in the Vietnam War. The AX program sought an aircraft that could carry heavy weapons payloads, loiter for long periods and withstand damage from ground fire. Originally a twin turboprop design was envisaged, but the concept grew to a larger, aircraft powered by twin turbofans.

In the early 1970s designs from Northrop and Fairchild Republic were selected for a competitive fly-off, which occurred in late 1972. The YA-10 (first flight April 5 1972) was selected over Northrop's YA-9, with the result that 707 production A-10A Thunderbolts were built.

The A-10's design layout was dictated by survivability. The large, low straight wing provides good agility and some shielding for the two high mounted engines. The engines themselves are separated by the fuse-lage so a hit to one will not necessarily damage the other, while the A-10 can fly with substantial damage to one of its twin vertical tails. The pilot is protected in a titanium armour bathtub. The A-10's massive GE GAU-8 seven barrel 30mm cannon is the most powerful gun to be fitted to an aircraft in this class.

Debate has surrounded the subsonic A-10's survivability in the mod-ern battlefield, although during the Gulf War the A-10 was ideally suited to operations there where Iraqi air opposition was minimal. It again saw widespread action over Kosovo in 1999.

Some A-10s have been redesignated OA-10 for the Forward Air Control role. These aircraft differ from the A-10 in designation only and carry smoke rockets and Sidewinder AAMs for self defence.

The USAF contracted Northrop Grumman (which took over responsi-bility for managing the A-10 in 1987) in February 2001 to upgrade the A-10 fleet with a digital stores management system and JDAM com-patibility among other changes. The USAF also remains interested in re-engining, possibly with 49kN (11,000lb) CF34-8s (the CF34 is based on the TF34). Over 350 A-10s remain in USAF, USAF Reserve and ANG service. They will eventually be replaced by the F-35 JSF.

**Photo:** The A-10 is nicknamed Warthog. (Paul Merritt)

# Fairchild C-26 & Metro

**Country of origin:** United States of America

**Type:** Light utility transport

**Powerplants:** C-26A/B – Two 835kW (1120shp) Garrett (now Honeywell) TFE331-121UAR turboprops driving four blade propellers.

**Performance:** C-26A/B – Max cruising speed 517km/h (280kt), eco-nomical cruising speed 467km/h (252kt). Max initial rate of climb 2370ft/min. Service ceiling 27,500ft. Range at optional MTOW 1970km (1063nm), range at standard MTOW 710km (385nm).

**Weights:** C-26A/B – Operating empty 4165kg (9180lb), max takeoff 6577kg (14,500lb), or optionally 7257kg (16,000lb).

**Dimensions:** C-26A/B – Wing span 17.37m (57ft 0in), length 18.09m (59ft 4in), height 5.08m (16ft 8in). Wing area 28.7m² (309.0sq ft).

**Accommodation:** Flightcrew of two. Main cabin can be configured to seat 19 passengers, or less with a VIP interior.

**Armament:** None

**Operators:** Argentina, Colombia, El Salvador, Mexico, Peru, Thailand, USA.

**History:** The popular Metro series of commuter airliners has found its way into military service in a variety of utility roles.

Design work on Swearingen's first complete in house design began in the late 1960s, culminating in the SA-226TC Metro's first flight on August 26 1969. The design was similar in appearance and layout to the earlier Merlins, and featured a pressurised fuselage, Garrett TPE331 turboprop engines and double slotted trailing edge flaps on the wings. It entered commercial service in 1973.

The Metro II superseded the I from 1975, with improvements focus-ing on reducing cabin noise levels, plus changes to the flightdeck. The equivalent executive aircraft to the Metro II is the Merlin IV. Following the Metro II from 1981 was the III (by which time Fairchild had taken over Swearingen), which was certificated to a higher standard and allowed greater takeoff weights, while more efficient engines and greater wing span made the III more economical to operate. The Expe-diter civil freighter is based on the III.

Argentina operates three VIP equipped Merlins IVAs and three Merlin IIIs, and Thailand three IVAs. Sweden operated two VIP configured Merlin IVCs (designated Tp 88), while a Metro III served as the testbed for the Ericsson Erieye phased array AEW radar mounted above the aircraft's fuselage.

The USA is the largest military Metro customer. The first of 13 C-26As was ordered in 1988 for the US Air National Guard for use as a general transport/VIP aircraft. Thirty-six C-26Bs (with TCAS, GPS and MLS) were delivered to the Army and Air National Guard. Some were sold off from 1996.

A single UC-26C meanwhile was fitted with an APG-66 radar (as on the F-16) and FLIR, for use in anti drug missions. All C-26 models are based on the Metro III, but with some changes.

The last Metro model was the 23, with higher takeoff weights, more powerful engines and systems improvements first introduced on the C-26. Merlin and Expediter models were offered, while Fairchild offered the 23 as its Multi Mission Surveillance Aircraft (MMSA) platform, fitted with a reconnaissance pod jointly developed with Lockheed Martin. The Metro 23E has EFIS. Metro production wound up in 2000.

**Photo:** A California Air National Guard C-26A. (John Sise)

# FFA AS 202 Bravo

**Country of origin:** Switzerland

**Type:** Two seat basic trainer

**Powerplants:** AS 202/15 – One 110kW (150hp) Lycoming O-320-E2A flat four piston engine driving a two blade fixed pitch propeller. AS 202/18A4 – One 135kW (180hp) Textron Lycoming AEIO-360-B1F fuel injected flat four driving a two blade constant speed propeller, or optionally a three blade prop.

**Performance:** 15 – Max cruising speed 210km/h (114kt), economical cruising speed 203km/h (110kt). Max initial rate of climb 633ft/min. Service ceiling 14,000ft. Range with max fuel and no reserves 890km (480nm). 18A4 – Max speed 240km/h (130kt), max cruising speed 226km/h (122kt), economical cruising speed 205km/h (110kt). Max initial rate of climb 800ft/min. Service ceiling 17,000ft. Range with max fuel and no reserves 1140km (615nm).

**Weights:** 15 – Empty equipped 630kg (1388lb), max takeoff 999kg (2202lb) for Utility, 885kg (1951lb) for Acrobatic. 18AF – Operating empty 710kg (1565lb), max takeoff 1080kg (2380lb) for Utility, 1050kg (2315lb) for Acrobatic.

**Dimensions:** Wing span 9.95m (31ft 12in), length 7.50m (24ft 7in), height 2.81m (9ft 3in). Wing area 13.9m$^2$ (149.2sq ft).

**Accommodation:** Student and instructor side by side, with room for one passenger/observer behind them.

**Armament:** Usually none.

**Operators:** Iraq, Morocco, Oman, Uganda.

**History:** The Bravo basic trainer is in service with a small number of air arms around the world.

Design of the Bravo dates back to the late 1960s, with original design work undertaken by SIAI Marchetti of Italy as the S.202, but with production and subsequent development work the responsibility of FFA (originally established by Dornier as its Swiss subsidiary). The first prototype to fly was Swiss built, it took to the air for the first time on March 7 1969. An Italian built prototype followed soon after on May 7, while the first production standard aircraft flew on December 22 1971.

The first production model was the AS 202/15 and 34 were built through to the early 1980s. The definitive production model was the AS 202/18AF, which first flew in August 1974 and received certification in late 1975. This version differs from the original 15 principally in having a more powerful 135kW (180hp) engine. The AS 202/18 is operated by all the countries listed above. Iraq and Indonesia, with 48 and 40 delivered respectively, were the largest customers. A significant civil operator was BAE Systems Flight Training in Scotland which operated 11 as the Wren.

Two other models have been developed, although single examples of each have flown only. The first was the 195kW (260hp) Textron Lycoming AEIO-540 powered Bravo 26A1, which first flew in 1979. The second was the 240kW (320shp) Allison 250-B17C turbine powered Bravo 32TP which flew in 1991.

The last Bravo was delivered in 1989 and subsequent sales promotion efforts have since ceased. In all 180 were

**Photo:** An Indonesian air force AS 202/18. The Bravo is capable of aerobatics. (Robert Wiseman)

# FMA IA-58 Pucará

**Country of origin:** Argentina

**Type:** Counter insurgency/light ground attack aircraft

**Powerplants:** IA-58A – Two 730kW (978shp) Turbomeca Astazou XVIG turboprops driving three blade propellers.

**Performance:** Max speed 500km/h (270kt), max cruising speed 480km/h (260kt), economical cruising speed 430km/h (232kt). Max initial rate of climb 3545ft/min. Service ceiling 32,800ft. Ferry range with three drop tanks 3710km (2002nm). Combat radius with a 1500kg (3307lb) warload, lo-lo-lo 225km (120nm), hi-lo-hi 350km (190nm). Combat radius with a 1000kg (2205lb) warload lo-lo-lo 400km (215nm), hi-lo-hi 650km (350nm).

**Weights:** IA-58A – Empty equipped 4020kg (8862lb), max takeoff 6800kg (14,990lb).

**Dimensions:** IA-58A – Wing span 14.50m (47ft 7in), length 14.25m (46ft 9in), height 5.36m (17ft 7in). Wing area 30.3m$^2$ (326.2sq ft).

**Accommodation:** Pilot and observer in tandem.

**Armament:** IA-58A – Two 20mm Hispano HS-284 cannons and four 7.62mm Browning machine guns in the forward fuselage. One under fuselage and two underwing hardpoints can carry a total of 1500kg (3307lb) of external ordnance, including bombs and rocket pods.

**Operators:** Argentina, Colombia, Sri Lanka, Uruguay.

**History:** The Pucará was developed to meet a 1960s Argentine requirement for a counter insurgency aircraft, and was made famous by its participation in the Falklands War in 1982.

Design and production responsibility fell to Argentina's government controlled Fabrica Militar de Aviones (FMA), with work culminating in the prototype's first flight on August 20 1969. This prototype was powered by two AiResearch TPE331 turboprops, whereas production Pucarás feature Turbomeca Astazous. A second prototype, the first to be powered by Astazous, first flew in September 1970, while the first production Pucará flew in November 1974. Production deliveries not begin until 1976.

That year the Pucará had its baptism of fire against rebel guerrillas in Argentina's northwest. However the Pucará is better known for its participation in the Falklands War against the British in 1982. In these actions it was less than successful, and all 24 deployed were either destroyed by ground fire, sabotaged by the SAS, or captured when Argentina was evicted from the islands. One captured example was subsequently evaluated by the RAF before it was placed on display at the Imperial War Museum.

The Pucará was built to be manoeuvrable, survivable and carry an effective offensive punch. However its poor showing in the Falklands meant that the type fell out of favour in Argentina, and 40 of the survivors were made surplus in 1986.

Two planned Pucará variants were flown in prototype form but failed to see production. The IA-58B featured improved avionics and twin 30mm DEFA cannons, and first flew in May 1979. The single seat IA-58C had a faired over front cockpit, improved avionics and two 30mm cannons, and could carry Matra Magic AAMs and Martin Pescador ASMs. The prototype flew in December 1985.

**Photo:** A Uruguayan Pucará. Uruguay's air force has five on strength. (Santiago Rivas)

## Fokker F27, Maritime & Troopship

**Country of origin:** Netherlands

**Type:** Tactical transport and maritime patrol aircraft

**Powerplants:** Maritime – Two 1730kW (2320shp) takeoff rated Rolls-Royce Dart RDa7 Mk 536-7R turboprops driving four blade propellers.

**Performance:** Maritime – Normal cruising speed 463km/h (250kt), typical search speed range 277 to 333km/h (150 to 180kt) at 2000ft. Service ceiling 29,500ft. Max range with 30min loiter 5000km (2700nm), time on station 370km (200nm) from base 8hr, or 740km (400nm) from base 6hr, or 1205km (650nm) from base 4hr.

**Weights:** Maritime – Empty 12,520kg (27,600lb), max takeoff 20,410kg (45,000lb).

**Dimensions:** Maritime – Wing span 29.00m (95ft 2in), length 23.56m (77ft 4in), height 8.70m (28ft 7in). Wing area 70.0m² (754sq ft).

**Accommodation:** Maritime – Flightcrew of two. Crew complement would usually include a tactical commander/navigator, a radar operator and two observers. Troopship – Up to 46 troops, or alternatively 24 stretchers and nine medical attendants.

**Armament:** None, although the armed Maritime Enforcer was offered.

**Operators:** Argentina, Bolivia, Finland, Ghana, Guatemala, Indonesia, Iran, Myanmar, Pakistan, Philippines, Senegal, Thailand, Uruguay. Maritime – Philippines, Spain, Thailand.

**History:** The Fokker F27 series, including the Fairchild built F-27 and FH-227, was ordered in greater numbers than any other Western turboprop airliner. Military derivatives serve in tactical transport and maritime patrol roles.

The Fokker F27 began life in 1950 as a 32 seat design study known as the P.275. A prototype first flew on November 24 1955, while a larger prototype representative of production aircraft flew in January 1957. By this stage Fokker had signed an agreement with Fairchild that would see F27s, as F-27s, built in the USA, and later the stretched, 52 seat FH-227.

Friendship developments included the Mk 200/F-27A with more powerful engines, the Mk 300/F-27B, the Mk 400 Combiplane and military Mk 400M Troopship tactical transport. The Troopship first flew in 1965 and features a large freight door and enlarged parachuting doors. The definitive Mk 500 airliner has a 1.50m (4ft 11in) fuselage stretch taking seating to 52, and also forms the basis for the Mk 600 quick change freight/passenger aircraft.

The 400M (the Troopship name was subsequently dropped) was particularly successful, and accounted for the majority of military sales with over 110 built. Other air arms acquired ex civil examples.

The most developed Friendship military variant was the maritime patrol Maritime, which provided a low cost alternative to the likes of the Atlantic and Orion. It features a Litton APS-504 search radar, bulged observation windows, a crew rest area and comprehensive navigation equipment. The armed Maritime Enforcer would also have featured sonobuoys, ESM, an infrared searcher and a MAD, although none were ordered.

F27 production ceased in 1986, replaced by the Fokker 50 (described opposite).

**Photo:** A Philippines air force F27. (Richard Hall)

## Fokker 50 & 60

**Country of origin:** Netherlands

**Type:** Multirole twin turboprop transports

**Powerplants:** 50 – Two 1865kW (2500shp) Pratt & Whitney Canada PW125B turboprops driving six blade propellers. 60 Utility – Two 2050kW (2750shp) P&WC PW127Bs.

**Performance:** 50 – Normal cruising speed 480km/h (260kt), typical search speed 277km/h (150kt) at 2000ft. Service ceiling 25,000ft. Maritime Enforcer 2 – Max radius of action with pylon tanks 3150km (1700nm). Max time on station with pylon tanks 14hr 20min. 60 Utility – Typical cruising speed 520km/h (280kt). Max operating altitude 25,000ft. Range with 50 troops 2965km (1600nm).

**Weights:** 50 Maritime Enforcer 2 – Operating empty 13,560kg (29,895lb), max takeoff 21,545kg (47,500lb). 60 Utility – Typical operating empty 12,500kg (27,855lb), max takeoff 21,950kg (48,390lb), or optionally 22,950kg (50,595lb).

**Dimensions:** 50 – Wing span 29.00m (95ft 2in), length 25.25m (82ft 10in), height 8.32m (27ft 4in). Wing area 70.0m² (753.5sq ft). 60 Utility – Same except length 26.87m (88ft 2in).

**Accommodation:** 50 Utility – Seating for 40 troops. Maritime Enforcer 2 – Crew complement of two flightcrew, tactical coordinator, acoustic sensor operator, sensor operators and two observers. 60 Utility – Seating for up to 50 troops.

**Armament:** Maritime Enforcer 2 – Two fuselage and six underwing hardpoints can carry a range of armaments including mines, torpedoes, depth charges and up to four anti ship missiles such as Harpoon, Exocet, Sea Eagle or Sea Skua.

**Operators:** 50 – Singapore, Taiwan. 60 – Netherlands.

**History:** The Fokker 50 and 60 modernised developments of the F27 were offered in a range of military configurations.

Fokker announced development of the Fokker 50 airliner in November 1983. Based on the F27-500, the 50 introduced Pratt & Whitney Canada PW120 series engines with six blade props, EFIS flightdeck, small winglets, square main cabin windows and some use of composites. First flight was on December 28 1985.

In all 205 Fokker 50s were built, almost all for airlines. Nevertheless, Fokker offered numerous military variants before its March 1996 financial collapse, including the unarmed Fokker 50 Maritime Mk 2 and armed Fokker 50 Maritime Enforcer Mk 2 offered with an APS-134 search radar, FLIR, MAD and sonobuoys. The Enforcer can carry torpedoes, mines and anti ship missiles such as Exocet and Harpoon. Singapore bought five.

Other models offered included the Kingbird Mk 2 AEW variant with the Ericsson Erieye phased array radar, Sentinel Mk 2 reconnaissance aircraft with either sideways looking or synthetic aperture radar, and the Elint/communications Black Crow Mk 2. Finally transport versions were covered by the Utility title.

The Fokker 60 Utility (first flight November 2 1995) is a 1.62m (5ft 4in) stretched version with a large cargo door whose development was launched by a Royal Netherlands Air Force order. All four were delivered before Fokker ceased aircraft manufacturing in 1997 (after its March 15 1996 financial collapse).

**Photo:** One of five Singaporean Fokker 50 Enforcers. (Lenn Bayliss)

## Fokker F28 Fellowship

**Country of origin:** Netherlands

**Type:** VIP and government transport

**Powerplants:** Mk 3000 & 4000 – Two 44kN (9900lb) Rolls-Royce RB183-2 Spey Mk 555-15P turbofans.

**Performance:** Mk 3000 – Max cruising speed 843km/h (455kt), economical cruising speed 678km/h (366kt). Max cruising altitude 35,000ft. Range at high speed cruise with 65 passengers 2743km (1480nm), at long range cruise with 65 passengers 3170km (1710nm). Mk 4000 – Range at high speed cruise with 85 passengers 1900km (1025nm), at long range cruising speed with 85 pax 2085km (1125nm).

**Weights:** Mk 3000 – Operating empty 16,965kg (37,400lb), max takeoff 33,110kg (73,000lb). Mk 4000 – Operating empty 17,645kg (38,900lb), max takeoff 33,110kg (73,000lb).

**Dimensions:** Mk 3000 – Wing span 25.07m (82ft 3in), length 27.40m (89ft 11in), height 8.47m (27ft 10in). Wing area 79.00m² (850sq ft). Mk 4000 – Same except for length 29.61m (97ft 2in).

**Accommodation:** Flightcrew of two. Max passenger seating for 85 at five abreast in Mk 4000, or 65 in Mk 3000. Both marks offered with a 15-20 seat VIP interior.

**Armament:** None

**Operators:** Argentina, Cambodia, Colombia, Ghana, Indonesia, Peru, Tanzania, Togo.

**History:** The commercially successful F28 Fellowship airliner was Fokker's first jet engined design. Small numbers have seen military service, mainly as VIP and government transports.

Fokker began development of the F28 in 1960 after perceiving a market requirement for a jet engined and greater capacity airliner to complement its turboprop powered F27. The first of three F28 prototypes first flew on May 9 1967 with the first customer delivery on February 24 1969.

The initial production F28 was the Mk 1000. The 1000 would typically seat between 55 and 65, and was powered by 44kN (9850lb) Spey Mk 555-15 turbofans. The Mk 2000 introduced a 2.21m (7ft 3in) fuselage stretch, increasing maximum seating to 79.

The longer span 5000 and 6000 were based on the 1000 and 2000 respectively, but attracted little sales interest and no 5000s and just two 6000s were built. Another version that did not come to fruition was the Mk 6600, which would have been stretched by a further 2.21m (7ft 3in), allowing for seating for 100 in a high density layout. However the F28 does form the basis for the 100 seat Rolls-Royce Tay powered Fokker 100, one of which serves in the Ivory Coast, and the smaller Fokker 70, similar in size to the F28-4000.

The final production models were the 3000 and 4000, again based on the 1000 and 2000 respectively. Both introduced a number of improvements, while the addition of two extra above wing emergency exits on the 4000 increased max permissible seating to 85. Freight door equipped convertible versions of each model are identified by a C suffix.

Given its size and performance the F28 has been a popular choice as a VIP, presidential and government transport, and several remain in military and government service in these roles.

**Photo:** An Argentine F28-1000. (Santiago Rivas)

## GAF Nomad & Searchmaster

**Country of origin:** Australia

**Type:** STOL multirole light transport

**Powerplants:** Two 315kW (420shp) Allison 250-B17C turboprops driving three blade propellers.

**Performance:** N22B – Typical cruising speed 311km/h (165kt). Takeoff run at max takeoff weight 225m (730ft). Max initial rate of climb 1460ft/min. Service ceiling 21,000ft. Range with standard fuel at 90% power 1350km (730nm). Searchmaster – Mission endurance at 260km/h (140kt) at 5000ft up to 8 hours.

**Weights:** N22B – Operating empty 2150kg (4741lb), max takeoff 3855kg (8500lb). N24A – Operating empty 2377kg (5241lb), max takeoff 4173kg (9200lb).

**Dimensions:** N22B – Wing span 16.52m (54ft 2in), length 12.56m (41ft 2in), height 5.52m (18ft 1.5in). Wing area 30.1m² (324.0sq ft). N22A – Same except length 14.36m (47ft 1in).

**Accommodation:** Flightcrew of one or two pilots. Seating in main cabin at two abreast for 12 (N22) or 16 (N24). Searchmaster B – Normal crew complement of one or two pilots, a tactical navigator and one or two observers.

**Armament:** Four underwing hardpoints can carry up to 910kg (2000lb) between them, although this capability is rarely used. Thai aircraft may be armed with machine guns as mini gunships.

**Operators:** Indonesia, Papua New Guinea, Philippines, Thailand.

**History:** Australia's Government Aircraft Factory developed the Nomad to provide its facilities with work after construction of licence built Mirage III fighters wound up and to allow it to offer a new rugged STOL utility transport for military and civil operators.

Developed as project N, first flight of the prototype Nomad N2 occurred on July 23 1971. A second prototype flew on December 5 that year. First deliveries of the production N22 aircraft (to the Philippines military) occurred in 1975. The N22 was followed up by the N22B with an increased max takeoff weight, which was certificated in 1975. The military utility transport version was marketed as the Missionmaster, although most are usually just called Nomads.

The N22 also formed the basis for the Searchmaster coastal patrol aircraft. It was offered in two variants, the Searchmaster B with a nose mounted forward looking Bendix RDR 1400 search radar, and the more sophisticated Searchmaster L, with a more capable chin mounted Litton LASR (APS-504) with 360° coverage. Papua New Guinea, Indonesia and the Philippines all operate Searchmasters in the coastal patrol role.

Stretching of the N22 fuselage by 1.14m (3ft 9in) led to the N24. Aimed mainly at regional airlines (as the Commuterliner), the N24 has increased passenger capacity for 16. The N24 was also marketed as the Cargomaster freighter and the Medicmaster aerial ambulance. Both the Australian Army and RAAF operated N24s.

Nomad production ceased in late 1984 after 172 had been built.

The largest military Nomad operator was the Australian Army. However its fleet of N22Bs and N24As was permanently grounded in mid 1995 due to concerns over the type's safety and suitability.

**Photo:** One of the 20 ex Australian Army Nomads transferred to the Indonesian navy. (LAC Ian Hurlock, RAAF)

# General Dynamics F-111 Aardvark

**Country of origin:** United States of America

**Type:** Long range strategic and tactical strike aircraft

**Powerplants:** F-111C – Two 82.3kN (18,500lb) with afterburning Pratt & Whitney TF30-P-103 turbofans.

**Performance:** F-111C – Max speed Mach 2.4 or 2550km/h (1377kt) at altitude, long range cruising speed 780km/h (420kt). Range with internal fuel over 5950km (3215nm).

**Weights:** F-111C – Typical empty 21,456kg (47,303lb), max takeoff 49,895kg (110,000lb).

**Dimensions:** F-111C – Wing span wings fully extended 21.33m (70ft 0in), wing span fully swept 10.35m (31ft 11in), length 22.40m (73ft 6in), height 5.22m (17ft 1in). Wing area wings extended 51.1m² (550sq ft).

**Accommodation:** Pilot and navigator side by side.

**Armament:** F-111C – GBU-12/-10 LGBs, AGM-84s, TV guided GBU-15s, AGM-142s, conventional bombs, and AIM-9s.

**Operators:** Australia

**History:** Highly controversial and expensive during its development, the F-111 (officially named Aardvark at its USAF retirement in 1996) evolved into perhaps the world's most capable strike bomber.

The F-111 was conceived in the early 1960s as the TFX, an ill-fated attempt to meet a US Air Force requirement for a new fighter-bomber and the US Navy's need for a new air defence fighter with a single platform. First flight was on December 21 1964. The USN's overweight F-111B interceptor was cancelled in 1968.

The Air Force's F-111 showed considerably more promise. The F-111 was the first operational aircraft to feature swing wings and afterburning turbofans, while in a clean configuration it could cruise supersonically without afterburner. Other design features include a small internal bomb bay, a cockpit escape capsule and terrain following radar. Initially problems persisted with the complex swing wing mechanism and air inlets, but these were eventually resolved.

USAF F-111 models comprised the F-111A, the F-111E with revised air inlets, the F-111D with digital avionics (a first for a tactical fighter), the F-111F with more powerful engines and improved analog avionics, and the nuclear FB-111 strategic bomber (with longer span wings and strengthened undercarriage). In the early 1990s the FB-111s had their nuclear role removed, and were redesignated the F-111G (they subsequently went through a digital avionics upgrade). The Gulf War veteran F-111F (with upgraded digital avionics and Pave Tack laser designator) was retired in July 1996, while the EW EF-111 Raven jammer bowed out in 1998.

Australia operates 22 F-111Cs. The C combined the engines and avionics of the F-111A with the FB-111B's heavier undercarriage and longer span wings. Four were modified as RF-111C reconnaissance aircraft, with a similar equipment fit in the bomb bay as in the F-14's TARP pod. The F-111Cs carry the Pave Tack pod and the R/F-111C fleet underwent a comprehensive digital avionics upgrade program, completed in 1999. They were re-engined with 93.4kN (20,840lb) TF30-P-109s (from retired USAF F-111s) in the late 1990s.

Australia bought 15 ex USAF F-111Gs which were delivered from 1993. They will help to extend the RAAF F-111 fleet life to 2020.

**Photo:** A RAAF F-111G. (Paul Sadler)

# Grumman S-2 Tracker

**Country of origin:** United States of America

**Type:** Maritime patrol and anti submarine patrol aircraft

**Powerplants:** S-2E – Two 1135kW (1525hp) Pratt & Whitney R-1820-82WA radial piston engines driving three blade propellers. TS-2F – Two 1225kW (1645shp) Honeywell TPE331-15 turboprops driving five blade props.

**Performance:** S-2E – Max speed 425km/h (230kt), cruising speed 333km/h (180kt), patrol speed at 1500ft 240km/h (130kt). Max initial rate of climb 1390ft/min. Service ceiling 21,000ft. Ferry range 2095km (1130nm), range 1855km (1000nm). Endurance 9hr. TS-2F – Max speed 482km/h (260kt), cruising speed 467km/h (252kt). Service ceiling 24,000ft. Range 1200km (648nm).

**Weights:** S-2E – Empty 8505kg (18,750lb), MTOW 13,222kg (29,150lb). TS-2F – Empty 6278kg (13,840lb), MTOW 13,155kg (29,000lb).

**Dimensions:** S-2E – Wing span 22.13m (72ft 7in), span wings folded 8.33m (27ft 4in), length 13.26m (43ft 6in), height 5.06m (16ft 7in). Wing area 46.1m² (496.0sq ft).

**Accommodation:** Normal crew complement of four comprising pilot, copilot, radar operator and MAD operator.

**Armament:** Internal weapons bay can hold two homing torpedoes, depth charges or mines. Six underwing pylons for bombs and rockets.

**Operators:** Argentina, Brazil, Taiwan, Thailand, Uruguay.

**History:** The veteran S-2 Tracker still provides a number of nations with a useful maritime patrol and ASW capability.

The origins of the Tracker date back to the late 1940s when the US Navy devised a requirement to replace the hunter/killer team of Grumman TBM-3W and TBM-3S Avengers then used for anti submarine warfare. Responding to the requirement, Grumman proposed its G-89, featuring a high wing, large cabin area for four crew and avionics, a search radar, extendable MAD, sonobuoys stored in the rear of each engine nacelle and an internal weapons bay.

The G-89 was selected for development in June 1950, resulting in the first flight of the prototype XS2F-1 on December 4 1952. Initial production S2F Trackers entered service in February 1954. The S2F also formed the basis for the WF Tracer AEW aircraft and the TF Trader carrier onboard delivery (COD) aircraft. With the rationalisation of US designations in 1962 the S2F became the S-2, the WF the E-1 and the TF the C-1.

More than 600 Trackers were built in progressively improved variants including the S-2C with an enlarged bomb bay and the S-2D and S-2E with various equipment improvements. The S-2B was an upgrade of the S-2A, the S-2G a rebuilt S-2E. The last USN Trackers were retired from 1976.

A number of turboprop upgrades have flown, using either Honeywell TFE331s (Marsh Aviation's TFE331 program is detailed in the specs above) or Pratt & Whitney Canada PT6As. Israel's IAI offers a comprehensive S-2UP upgrade with modern systems and avionics, plus Marsh Aviation's TFE331 re-engine.

Most surviving Trackers are S-2As and S-2Es. Argentina and Taiwan have upgraded their aircraft with turboprops, improving performance and endurance.

**Photo:** An IAI re-engined Argentine navy S-2E. (IAI)

# Grumman OV-1 Mohawk

**Country of origin:** United States of America

**Type:** Battlefield surveillance aircraft

**Powerplants:** OV-1D – Two 820kW (1100shp) Lycoming T53-L-15 turboprops driving three blade propellers.

**Performance:** OV-1D – Max speed 478km/h (258kt), max cruising speed 444km/h (240kt), economical cruising speed 334km/h (180kt). Max initial rate of climb 2350ft/min. Service ceiling 30,300ft. Takeoff distance to 50ft 268m (880ft). Ferry range with drop tanks 1980km (1068nm). Max endurance 4hr plus.

**Weights:** OV-1D – Empty equipped 5020kg (11,067lb), max takeoff 8722kg (19,230lb).

**Dimensions:** OV-1D – Wing span 14.63m (48ft 0in), length 12.50m (41ft 0in), height 3.86m (12ft 8in). Wing area 33.5m² (360.0sq ft).

**Accommodation:** Crew of two (pilot and observer) side by side.

**Armament:** Usually none, although guns and rocket pods occasionally have been carried on the two underwing hardpoints.

**Operators:** Argentina

**History:** The Mohawk resulted from simultaneous requirements from the US Army and US Marines for a battlefield surveillance aircraft.

The similarity of the two services' requirements – rough field STOL performance and the ability to carry a range of reconnaissance sensors – led to the creation of a joint program. The US Navy acted as program manager for the new aircraft and Grumman's G-134 design was selected for development. Nine G-134s were ordered for evaluation, and the first of these first flew on April 14 1959. Initially the evaluation aircraft were designated YAO-1, but this was changed to YOV-1.

Early experience with the G-134 proved its suitability for the battlefield surveillance role, but despite this the US Marines pulled out from the program (USMC aircraft would have been designated OF-1 pre 1962). Regardless, the US Army placed contracts for what would become the OV-1A and OV-1B in 1959.

The Mohawk became the first twin turboprop powered aircraft to enter US Army service. Other notable design features include considerable crew armouring including bullet resistant glass, a mid set wing and a three tail unit (with horizontal tailplane dihedral). The side cockpit glass is bulged outwards to improve downwards visibility.

The basic OV-1A was equipped for day and night visual reconnaissance using conventional reconnaissance cameras. The OV-1B was similar except for its SLAR (side looking airborne radar) which was carried in a large pod carried under the fuselage, while it lacked optical cameras. The OV-1C was similar to the OV-1B but with an AAS-24 infrared surveillance system.

The definitive OV-1D features more powerful engines, and a side loading door to accept a pallet with optical (KS-80), IR (AAS-24), or SLAR (APD-7) reconnaissance sensors. Aside from new build OV-1Ds, over 110 OV-1B and OV-1C Mohawks were converted to D status. RV-1Cs and RV-1Ds were Mohawks permanently converted to electronic surveillance configurations. Other RV-1D Quick Look II aircraft were converted for Elint, while the US Army denied the existence of EV-1D Quick Look III Mohawks.

Today Argentina is the sole Mohawk operator, with ex US OV-1Ds.

**Photo:** Argentine army OV-1Ds..(Juan Carlos Cicalesi)

# Grumman EA-6B Prowler

**Country of origin:** United States of America

**Type:** Electronic warfare aircraft

**Powerplants:** EA-6B – Two 49.8kN (11,200lb) Pratt & Whitney J52-P-408 turbojets.

**Performance:** EA-6B – Max speed with five jammer pods 982km/h (530kt), cruising speed at optimum altitude 774km/h (418kt). Max initial rate of climb with five jammer pods 10,030ft/min. Service ceiling with five jammer pods 38,000ft. Max ferry range 3860km (2085nm), range with max external load 1770km (955nm).

**Weights:** EA-6B – Empty 14,320kg (31,572lb), normal takeoff from carrier in standard jammer configuration 24,705kg (54,460lb), max takeoff 29,895kg (65,000lb).

**Dimensions:** EA-6B – Wing span 16.15m (53ft 0in), span wings folded 7.87m (25ft 10in), length 18.24m (59ft 10in), height 4.95m (16ft 3in). Wing area 49.1m² (528.9sq ft).

**Accommodation:** Pilot and three EW (electronic warfare) officers.

**Armament:** EA-6B – Up to four (usually two) AGM-88 HARM anti radar missiles on four inboard (of six) underwing hardpoints.

**Operators:** USA

**History:** The Prowler is the USA's sole tactical electronic warfare jammer aircraft, and is based on the retired A-6 Intruder.

The original EA-6A Intruder was developed for the US Marine Corps in the early 1960s to replace Douglas EF-10B Skynights. The EA-6A was based on the A-6A and had a crew of two. A fin top bulge housed a series of antennas, while jammers were carried in underwing pods. Of the 27 built, 15 were new build aircraft. After seeing service over Vietnam, most were retired in the late 1970s.

The definitive EW Intruder development is the EA-6B Prowler. Grumman developed the Prowler from 1966 to replace Douglas EKA-3B Skywarriors on US carrier decks. The EA-6B is based on the A-6, but with a stretched forward fuselage and a four seat cockpit for the pilot and three electronic warfare officers. Another airframe mod is the bulbous fin tip antenna housing, while the jammers are carried in underwing pods. First flight was on May 25 1968, with service entry from 1971. In all, 170 were built for the USN and USMC through to 1991.

The Prowler's EW systems are collectively called the TJS (Tactical Jamming System). The TJS incorporates antennas, processing computer and the jammers, which have been progressively updated under a number of programs, with software and hardware changes.

Update programs were: EXCAP (Expanded Capability); ICAP-1 (Improved Capability 1); ICAP-2; ICAP-2/Block 86 which gave the Prowler the ability to carry HARMs, a capability put to good use in the Gulf War; ADVCAP, or Advanced Capability; ADVCAP/Block 91 with improvements to the jamming system plus GPS; and the current ICAP-3 program with reactive jamming, additional processors and new displays for the EW operators. All EA-6Bs will eventually be upgraded to ICAP-3 standard (the first conversion flew on November 19 2001).

With the 1998 retirement of the USAF's EF-111s, the Prowler is the US military's sole dedicated EW jammer. They are responsible for all US Navy and Air Force EW jamming missions. Prowlers played a critical role in NATO's air campaign against Yugoslavia in 1999.

**Photo:** About 120 Prowlers are in USN/MC service. (Nick Sayer)

# Grumman F-14A Tomcat

**Country of origin:** United States of America

**Type:** Carrier borne air defence/air superiority fighter

**Powerplants:** Two 93.0kN (20,900lb) with afterburning Pratt & Whitney TF30-P-412 or -414A turbofans.

**Performance:** Max speed at altitude Mach 2.4 or 2485km/h (1342kt), max speed at low level 1468km/h (792kt). Max initial rate of climb over 30,000ft/min. Service ceiling over 50,000ft. Max range with internal and external fuel 3220km (1735nm). Radius on a combat air patrol mission with six AIM-7s and four AIM-9s 1233km (665nm).

**Weights:** Empty (with -414A engines) 18,190kg (40,105lb), max takeoff (with six AIM-54 Phoenix) 32,098kg (70,764lb), max overload 33,724kg (74,349lb). Internal fuel 7348kg (16,200lb).

**Dimensions:** Wing span wings extended 19.54m (64ft 2in), span wings swept 11.65m (38ft 3in), length 19.10m (62ft 8in), height 4.88m (16ft 0in). Gross wing area 52.5m$^2$ (565.0sq ft).

**Accommodation:** Pilot and radar intercept officer (RIO) in tandem.

**Armament:** One GE M61A1 Vulcan 20mm cannon. Typical intercept configuration of two AIM-54 Phoenix (the world's longest ranging air-to-air missile), two AIM-7 Sparrows and two AIM-9 Sidewinders, or combinations thereof. Can carry up to 6577kg (14,500lb) of bombs including LGBs. Can self designate when fitted with Lantirn.

**Operators:** Iran, USA.

**History:** Grumman's swing wing F-14 Tomcat air defence fighter emerged from the embers of the failed F-111B.

The cancellation of the overweight F-111B left the US Navy without a successor for the F-4 Phantom, which it flew primarily in the air defence role. Grumman acted as the lead contractor for the US Navy's version of General Dynamics' F-111, but had begun design studies on a new naval air defence fighter even before the F-111B's cancellation.

One of Grumman's design concepts, the G-303, was selected in January 1969 under the VFX program to fill the gap left by the demise of the F-111B. The two crew G-303 was designed from the outset for carrier operations, although it retained many of the features of the F-111, including the powerful AWG-9 radar system and AIM-54 Phoenix missile, the P&W TF30 afterburning turbofans, and swing wings. Other design features included the twin tails and moveable foreplanes, or glove vanes (since removed).

The first prototype F-14 first flew on December 12 1970 (this aircraft subsequently crashed due to hydraulic failure), while 556 production aircraft were delivered to the USN from 1972. Pre-revolutionary Iran was the only Tomcat export customer (buying 79). About 20 of the survivors are believed to be airworthy.

Apart from air defence and an expanding ground attack capability, the F-14 is also used for reconnaissance, carrying a Tactical Air Reconnaissance Pod System (TARPS) camera pod under the fuselage.

The F-14's TF30 turbofans proved troublesome early on, and a number of blade failures caused F-14 loses. Problems with the engines were largely overcome with the TF30-P-414A, which was adapted as standard. The re-engined GE F110 powered F-14B and F-14D are described separately.

The US Navy intends to retire its last F-14As in 2003.

**Photo:** US Navy F-14As in flight. (Nick Sayer)

# Grumman F-14B & F-14D Tomcat

**Country of origin:** United States of America

**Type:** Carrier borne air defence/air superiority fighter

**Powerplants:** F-14D – Two 62.3kN (14,000lb) dry and 102.8kN (23,100lb) with afterburning General Electric F110-GE-400 turbofans.

**Performance:** F-14D – Max speed at altitude Mach 1.88 or 1997km/h (1078kt), cruising speed 764km/h (413kt). Max initial rate of climb over 30,000ft/min. Ceiling over 53,000ft. Max range with internal and external fuel approximately 2965km (1600nm). Combat radius on a CAP with four AIM-7s and four AIM-9s 1995km (1075nm).

**Weights:** F-14D – Empty 18,950kg (41,780lb), max takeoff 33,725kg (74,350lb). Internal fuel 7348kg (16,200lb).

**Dimensions:** F-14D – Wing span wings extended 19.54m (64ft 2in), span wings swept 11.65m (38ft 3in), length 19.10m (62ft 8in), height 4.88m (16ft 0in). Gross wing area 52.5m$^2$ (565.0sq ft).

**Accommodation:** Pilot and radar intercept officer (RIO) in tandem.

**Armament:** One GE M61A1 Vulcan 20mm cannon. Typical intercept configuration of two AIM-54 Phoenix, two AIM-7 Sparrows and two AIM-9 Sidewinders. Can carry conventional and laser guided bombs. Can self designate LGBs when fitted with Lantirn.

**Operators:** USA

**History:** The Grumman F-14B and F-14D are re-engined variants of the F-14A Tomcat.

The F-14A's TF30 turbofan had its problems – it suffered from a number of catastrophic blade failures and was not considered powerful enough for the Tomcat's substantial 30 tonne plus max weight. As early as 1973 a prototype F-14 flew powered by two Pratt & Whitney F401-PW-400 turbofans as the F-14B. However this original F-14B program was cancelled due to technical and budgetary problems.

Consequently development of a re-engined Tomcat was suspended until 1984 when Grumman was contracted to develop the F-14A (Plus) Interim, basically a General Electric F110-GE-400 (with extended jetpipes) powered F-14A intended as an interim aircraft until the arrival of the F-14D. The F-14A (Plus) first flew in September 1986. Redesignated the F-14B, and featuring some minor avionics improvements, 38 new build F-14Bs and 32 F-14As converted to B standard were delivered from 1988.

The F-14D features two GE F110s like the F-14B, but also significant equipment changes. The primary changes are digital avionics with digital radar processing linked to the AWG-9 radar, which is redesignated APG-71, the twin IRST/TV pods under the nose, NACES ejection seats and improved radar warning receiver. Only 37 of a planned total of 127 new build F-14Ds were funded, while plans to convert the remainder of the USN's F-14A fleet to D standard were dropped due to budget cuts, with only 18 being rebuilt.

Other proposed but unfunded Tomcat variants/programs have included Quickstrike, with enhanced air-to-ground capability; the Super Tomcat-21 naval ATF alternative; Attack Super Tomcat-21 an interim A-12 replacement; and ASF-14 naval ATF alternative.

Tomcats are now used widely in air-to-ground missions with the retirement of the Intruder, and can carry the Lantirn designator pod.

The F-14B will be retired in 2006, the F-14D in 2007.

**Photo:** An F-14D. (Paul Merritt)

## Grumman C-2 Greyhound

**Country of origin:** United States of America

**Type:** Carrier onboard delivery aircraft

**Powerplants:** C-2A – Two 3665kW (4912ehp) Allison T56-A-425 turboprops driving four blade propellers.

**Performance:** C-2A – Max speed 575km/h (310kt), max cruising speed 482km/h (260kt). Max initial rate of climb 2610ft/min. Service ceiling 33,500ft. Ferry range 2890km (1560nm), range with a 4535kg (10,000lb) payload over 1930km (1040nm).

**Weights:** C-2A – Empty 16,485kg (36,345lb), max takeoff 26,080kg (57,500lb).

**Dimensions:** C-2A – Wing span 24.56m (80ft 7in), span wings folded 8.94m (29ft 4in), length 17.32m (56ft 10in), height 4.84m (15ft 11in). Wing area 65.0m² (700.0sq ft).

**Accommodation:** Flightcrew of two. Can carry 39 passengers, or 20 stretcher patients plus medical attendants, or up to 4540kg (10,000lb) of freight.

**Armament:** None

**Operators:** USA

**History:** The US Navy's small fleet of C-2 Greyhounds plays a very important but unsung role in supplying the service's aircraft carriers while they are at sea.

The Greyhound is probably the last in a line of Grumman aircraft adapted for the carrier onboard delivery (COD) role since WW2. Immediately after WW2 this role fell to conversions of the Avenger, while the Greyhound's immediate predecessor was the C-1 Trader, a development of the S-2 Tracker.

The Greyhound is an adaptation of existing Grumman's E-2 Hawkeye (described under Northrop Grumman). Unlike the earlier two aircraft, the Greyhound differs significantly from its donor airframe. The C-2 retains the Hawkeye's Allison T56 powerplants and wing, but features a new, much broader fuselage with an upturned tail and rear loading cargo ramp. Apart from passengers the fuselage can carry a range of cargo, including jet engines. Another change is to the tailplane, the Greyhound's unit lacks dihedral (as it does not have to contend with unusual airflows caused by the Hawkeye's radome).

Two converted Hawkeyes served as YC-2A prototypes, the first of these first flew on November 18 1964. An initial batch of 17 production C-2As was built, delivered between early 1966 and 1968. At that time the USN had planned to acquire a further 12 C-2s, but this order was cancelled due to budget cuts. The survivors of the 17 C-2As and two prototypes underwent a Service Life Extension Program (SLEP) from 1978.

To replace its remaining C-1 Traders and to make good C-2 attrition losses the US Navy ordered an additional 39 Greyhounds in 1982. The first of these (dubbed 'Reprocured C-2As') were delivered in 1985, the last rolled off the line in 1989. These aircraft featured improved avionics and aircraft systems.

The C-2 fleet is split between three operational units which provide detachments to carriers at sea, while other examples are on strength with the two E-2 training units.

From 2002 the C-2 fleet (as well as E-2s) will be upgraded with new eight bladed Hamilton Standard propellers.

**Photo:** A C-2 Greyhound. (Peter Woolley)

## Gulfstream II & III, C-20 & SRA-1

**Country of origin:** United States of America

**Type:** VIP transport and reconnaissance platform (SRA-1)

**Powerplants:** Gulfstream II & III – Two 51.1kN (11,400lb) Rolls-Royce Spey turbofans.

**Performance:** GII – Max cruising speed 936km/h (505kt), economical cruising speed 796km/h (430kt). Max initial rate of climb 4350ft/min. Range with max fuel 6880km (3715nm). GIII – Max cruising speed 928km/h (501kt), economical cruising speed 818km/h (442kt). Max initial rate of climb 3800ft/min. Max operating ceiling 45,000ft. Range with eight passengers 7600km (4100nm).

**Weights:** GII – Operating empty 16,740kg (36,900lb), max takeoff 29,710kg (65,500lb). GIII – Empty 14,515kg (32,000lb), operating empty 17,235kg (38,000lb), max takeoff 31,615kg (69,700lb).

**Dimensions:** GII – Wing span 20.98m (68ft 10in), length 24.36m (79ft 11in), height 7.47m (24ft 6in). Wing area 75.2m² (809.6sq ft). GIII – Wing span 23.72m (77ft 10in), length 25.32m (83ft 1in), height 7.43m (24ft 5in). Wing area 86.8m² (934.3sq ft).

**Accommodation:** Flightcrew of two. Main cabin seating for up to 19 in GII or 21 in GIII in a high density configuration, or eight to 12 in a typical corporate/VIP configuration. SRA-1 seats five to 10 operators depending on equipment fit.

**Armament:** None

**Operators:** Denmark, Egypt, India, Ivory Coast, Mexico, Morocco, Saudi Arabia, USA, Venezuela.

**History:** The popular Gulfstream series of business jets is widely used for VIP and government transport, while a number operate in special mission roles.

The Gulfstream II is a jet powered evolution of the original turboprop powered Gulfstream I. The Rolls-Royce Dart turboprop powered Grumman Gulfstream I proved quite successful as a large long range corporate transport, and a number have seen military service. The availability of the Rolls-Royce Spey turbofan allowed the development of a jet successor, which Grumman launched as the Gulfstream II, or GII, in May 1965.

While based on the original Gulfstream I – the GII shares the same forward fuselage and cross section – there are more differences than similarities. Apart from the two Spey turbofans, the GII also has a new swept wing and T-tail. The GII's first flight was on October 2 1966.

The improved Gulfstream III followed Gulfstream American's purchase of Grumman's civil aircraft lines in 1978. The Gulfstream III first flew on December 2 1979. Changes include a greater span and area wing with drag reducing winglets, more fuel tankage and thus range, and a 97cm (3ft 2in) fuselage stretch. Gulfstream IIBs meanwhile are GIIs retrofitted with the GIII's wing.

GIII deliveries began in late 1980 and continued until 1986 when production ceased in preference to the Gulfstream IV.

The Gulfstream III in particular has been popular as a military VIP transport (designated C-20 in US service). Gulfstream also used the GIII as the basis of its SRA-1 (Surveillance and Reconnaissance Aircraft), which was offered in a variety of Elint, reconnaissance and maritime patrol configurations.

**Photo:** The USAF flies 10 C-20A/Bs. (Paul Merritt)

## Gulfstream IV, C-20, SRA-4, V & C-37

**Country of origin:** United States of America

**Type:** VIP and utility transport and multirole surveillance platform

**Powerplants:** IV – Two 61.6kN (13,850lb) Rolls-Royce Tay Mk 611-8 turbofans.

**Performance:** IV – Normal cruising speed 850km/h (460kt). Max initial rate of climb 4000ft/min. Range with max payload 6730km (3633nm), range with eight pax 7820km (4220nm). IV-SP – Normal cruising speed 850km/h (460kt). Max initial rate of climb 3970ft/min. Range with max payload and reserves 6186km (3338nm), range with eight pax and reserves 7820km (4220nm). SRA-4 (maritime patrol) – Time on station 1110km (600nm) from base 6hr. Anti ship radius with two missiles, hi-lo-hi 2500km (1350nm).

**Weights:** IV – Empty 16,102kg (35,500lb), max takeoff 33,203kg (73,200lb). IV-SP – Same except for max takeoff 33,838kg (74,600lb).

**Dimensions:** Wing span 23.72m (77ft 10in), length 26.92m (88ft 4in), height 7.45m (24ft 5in). Wing area 88.3m$^2$ (950.39sq ft).

**Accommodation:** Flightcrew of two. Main cabin seating for between 14 and 19, plus attendant. SRA-4 – Five to 10 operators depending on configuration, or 15 stretchers plus medical attendants.

**Armament:** SRA-4 ASW – Two anti ship missiles on two underwing hardpoints.

**Operators:** IV – Algeria, Egypt, Chile, Gabon, Ireland, Ivory Coast, Japan, Netherlands, Sweden, Turkey, USA. V – Brunei, USA.

**History:** The Gulfstream IV is a significantly improved and advanced development of the earlier Spey powered Gulfstream II and III.

The most significant improvement over the earlier Gulfstream models are the more efficient and quieter Rolls-Royce Tay turbofans. Other changes include a stretched fuselage, structurally revised wing with 30% fewer parts, greater fuel capacity (and hence range), increased span tailplane and modern EFIS glass cockpit.

Design work on the IV began in early 1983, and the first of four production prototypes first flew on September 19 1985. The improved Gulfstream IV-SP, with higher weights and improved payload range performance, replaced the IV from September 1992.

Like earlier Gulfstreams, the GIV has been ordered for the US services. A single C-20F is in US Army use, while the USAF operates two C-20H transports. The US Navy operates four C-20G Operational Support Aircraft (a USMC C-20G was destroyed by a hurricane in 1998), with a convertible interior for passengers or freight, with a large freight door. Meanwhile two of Sweden's three GIVs are equipped for Elint.

Gulfstream offers the GIV for a variety of military roles, under the designation SRA-4. The SRA-4 is offered in a variety of configurations, including electronic warfare support, ASW and maritime patrol (can be armed with two anti shipping missiles), Elint and medical evacuation. Japan has ordered three maritime patrol IV-MPAs and also has utility U-4 transports in service.

The GIV forms the basis for the 2.49m (8ft 2in) stretched, re-winged, ultra long range Rolls-Royce BR710 powered Gulfstream V (first flight was on November 28 1995). The USAF is buying five for VIP transport as C-37As, with one operated by the US Army.

The improved Gulfstream V-SP was due to fly in late 2001.

**Photo:** A Swedish Elint GIV-SP. (Gulfstream)

## Harbin H-5

**Countries of origin:** Russia and China

**Type:** Tactical bomber

**Powerplants:** Il-28 – Two 26.5kN (5950lb) Klimov VK-1A turbojets.

**Performance:** Il-28 – Max speed at 14,765ft 900km/h (485kt), max speed at sea level 800km/h (432kt), typical cruising speed at altitude 875km/h (472kt). Max initial rate of climb 2950ft/min. Service ceiling 40,350ft. Range at 32,810ft 2400km (1295nm), range at 3280ft 1135km (612nm).

**Weights:** Il-28 – Empty equipped 11,890kg (28,415lb), max takeoff 21,200kg (46,738lb).

**Dimensions:** Il-28 – Wing span without tip tanks 21.45m (70ft 5in), fuselage length 17.65m (57ft 11in), height 6.70m (22ft 0in). Wing area 60.8m$^2$ (654.4sq ft).

**Accommodation:** Crew of three – pilot under fighter style canopy, bombardier/navigator in nose and rear gunner/radio operator in tail.

**Armament:** Two NR-23 23mm cannons in lower forward fuselage, two NR-23 cannons in rear turret and up to 3000kg (6615lb) of bombs or two torpedoes in internal weapons bay.

**Operators:** H-5 – China, North Korea, Romania.

**History:** The Harbin H-5 is China's unlicenced copy of the Ilyushin Il-28 'Beagle' light tactical jet bomber.

Ilyushin first began design work on the Il-28 in December 1947 as a private study. The first of three prototypes, powered by two Rolls-Royce Nenes (at the time the most powerful turbojets in the world and donated to the USSR by the UK Government during the late 1940s as 'technical aid'), first flew on July 8 1948. After competitive evaluation against Tupolev's larger but similarly powered Tu-73 the Il-28 was selected for production to meet a Russian air force need for a medium sized jet bomber.

Several thousand Il-28s were built for the Soviet air force and various Warsaw Pact nations, with deliveries beginning in 1950. Over 500 were exported to China in the 1950s, while other Il-28 operators included Egypt, Indonesia, Iraq, North Korea, North Vietnam, Syria and Yemen. Small numbers were also built in Czechoslovakia as the B-228.

Il-28 variants include the basic Il-28 bomber, Il-28T torpedo bomber, reconnaissance Il-28R and the Il-28U trainer with a second cockpit in the nose (forward of the standard cockpit). Several served through to the late 1980s as target tugs and ECM platforms.

After Russia and China severed ties in the 1960s China began a program to build an unlicenced copy of the Il-28. The Harbin Aircraft Factory was responsible for reverse engineering the Il-28 and consequently the first Chinese built 'Beagle', the H-5, first flew on September 25 1966.

H-5 production began the following year and continued into the 1980s (although late production was at a low rate and primarily for attrition replacements). As many as 2000 H-5s may have been built (including HJ-5 trainers and H-5R or HZ-5 reconnaissance platforms) for China's air force and navy. Several hundred still serve, despite their obsolescence. North Korea and Romania also operate Chinese H-5s, with the export designation B-5.

**Photo:** Poland was one of the many nations to operate the Il-28, on which the H-5 is based. (MAP)

# Harbin Z-5

**Countries of origin:** Russia & China

**Type:** Utility helicopter

**Powerplant:** Mi-4 – One 1270kW (1700hp) Shvetsov ASh-82V 18 cylinder radial piston engine driving a four blade main rotor and three blade tail rotor.

**Performance:** Mi-4 – Max speed at 4920ft 210km/h (113kt), economical cruising speed 160km/h (86kt). Service ceiling 18,000ft. Hovering ceiling out of ground effect 2295ft. Range with eight passengers 400km (217km), with 11 passengers 250km (134nm).

**Weights:** Mi-4 – Empty 4900kg (10,802lb), MTOW 7800kg (17,200lb).

**Dimensions:** Mi-4 – Main rotor diameter 21.00m (68ft 11in), length overall rotors turning 25.02m (82ft 1in), fuselage length 16.80m (55ft 1in), height overall 5.18m (17ft 0in). Main rotor disc area 346m² (3724sq ft).

**Accommodation:** Two pilots in flightdeck. Main cabin can accommodate up to 12 combat equipped troops or 1740kg (3835lb) of freight.

**Armament:** Some army assault Mi-4s were fitted with a fixed or movable machine gun in a ventral gondola designed to accommodate a navigator/observer. Optional weapons pylons could carry gun and rocket pods.

**Operators:** Albania, China, North Korea.

**History:** The Mi-4 ('Hound' to NATO) was one of Russia's first effective and useful helicopters with over 3500 built. Harbin of China built several hundred more as the Z-5 and these still form the backbone of China's helicopter force.

Development of the Mi-4 began at the direct request of Soviet Premier Josef Stalin in 1951. Hurried development resulted in the prototype Mi-4 making its first flight in August 1951, while production deliveries began the following year, initially to the state airline Aeroflot (as the passenger carrying Mi-4P). Early production Mi-4s were fitted with wooden rotor blades.

The Mi-4 is close in appearance and configuration to Sikorsky's S-55 (H-19) but larger overall and closer in weights and size to the later S-58 (described under the Westland Wessex entry). Like the S-58 the Mi-4 is powered by a radial piston engine mounted in the nose which drives the four blade main rotor via a shaft which passes between the raised cockpit and the main cabin. The cabin can accommodate 12 fully equipped troops, while the rear fuselage is formed by two clamshell doors.

Apart from the basic troop transport Mi-4 'Hound-A', the Mi-4 was also built in ASW 'Hound-B' form fitted with a search radar, and the 'Hound-C' ECM platform. Soviet production continued until 1969. By 2001 all Mi-4s had been retired.

The first Chinese built Mi-4 had its maiden flight on December 14 1959, with deliveries of Harbin built H-5s commencing in the mid 1960s. Over 500 were built through to 1979 and around 300 remain in Chinese army service. Albania is a large operator with 40 Z-5s on strength. Similarly, North Korea has almost 50 in use.

The Z-6 designation applies to at least one Z-5 fitted with two Pratt & Whitney PT6T turboshafts. It flew in 1979.

**Photo:** Hungary was one of the more than 25 nations to have operated the Mi-4 at some stage. (MAP)

# HAIG K-8 Karakorum

**Countries of origin:** China and Pakistan

**Type:** Two seat basic/advanced trainer

**Powerplant:** One 16kN (3600lb) Honeywell TFE731-2A-2A turbofan.

**Performance:** Max speed at sea level 807km/h (435kt). Max initial rate of climb 5315ft/min. Service ceiling 42,650ft. Range with max internal fuel 1400km (755nm), range with max internal and external fuel 2250km (1215nm). Endurance with max internal fuel 3hr, endurance with max internal and external fuel 4hr 25min.

**Weights:** Empty equipped 2687kg (5924lb), max takeoff with external stores 4330kg (9545lb).

**Dimensions:** Wing span 9.63m (31ft 7in), length incl probe 11.60m (38ft 1in), height 4.21m (13ft 10in). Wing area 17.0m² (183.2sq ft).

**Accommodation:** Two in tandem.

**Armament:** One centreline and four underwing hardpoints can carry a max weapons load of 945kg (2080lb). Centreline hardpoint can carry a 23mm gun pod, other weapon options include light bombs and rockets. Two outboard pylons can carry a PL-7 AAM each.

**Operators:** China, Egypt, Myanmar, Namibia, Pakistan, Sri Lanka, Zambia.

**History:** The Karakorum is China's first locally designed jet trainer and has been developed in cooperation with Pakistan.

Development of the Karakorum, initially designated L-8, was announced at the 1987 Paris Airshow. At the time of the new trainer's launch Nanchang (part of the Hongdu Aviation Industry Group – HAIG) sought international partners to develop the aircraft for export. Subsequently a development and co-production deal was signed with Pakistan, which took a 25% share in the program.

When Pakistan joined the trainer project the aircraft was redesignated K-8 and named Karakorum, after the mountain range that forms part of the China/Pakistan border. Pakistan, through PAC (Pakistan Aeronautical Complex), had some design input into the K-8 and is responsible for the manufacture of the K-8's fin and tailplane. However, Pakistan decided not to establish its own K-8 assembly line.

The first of three flying Karakorum prototypes first flew on November 21 1990. Fifteen preproduction development aircraft followed, the first of these flying in 1993.

The K-8 features a straight wing and tandem seating. Initial and export aircraft are powered by a Honeywell TFE731 turbofan with FADEC, while Chinese production K-8Js would be powered by a 16.9kN (3792lb) Progress ZMKB AI-25TL turbofan.

Other Western equipment in the K-8 includes the two Collins CRTs in each cockpit while the crew sits on two Martin-Baker zero/zero ejection seats. Five hardpoints, one centreline and four under the wings, give the K-8 a light ground attack/weapons training capability.

Pakistan has a total requirement for up to 100 K-8s to replace T-37s – but has only accepted an initial batch of six, delivered by late 1996. The Chinese K-8 requirement for several hundred airframes seems to have been abandoned due to the K-8's high degree of foreign content. The Chinese Flight Test Establishment flies a fly-by-wire K-8VSA testbed.

K-8 export customers include Egypt (80 on order, making it the biggest customer), Myanmar, Namibia, Sri Lanka and Zambia.

**Photo:** A Zambian air force Karakorum. (Keith Gaskell)

# Hawker Hunter

**Country of origin:** United Kingdom

**Type:** Multirole fighter

**Powerplant:** FGA.9 – One 48.7kN (10,150lb) Rolls-Royce Avon 207 turbojet.

**Performance:** FGA.9 – Max speed at sea level 1150km/h (622kt), max speed at 36,000ft 1010km/h (545kt), economical cruising speed 740km/h (400kt). Max initial rate of climb 16,500ft/min. Time to 40,000ft 5min 30sec clean or 12min 30sec loaded. Service ceiling 50,000ft. Combat radius with two drop tanks and rockets 875km (472nm), combat radius with two 455kg/1000lb bombs and two drop tanks 352km (190nm). Max ferry range 2955km (1595nm).

**Weights:** FGA.9 – Empty 6610kg (14,572lb), max takeoff 11,078kg (24,422lb).

**Dimensions:** FGA.9 – Wing span 10.26m (33ft 8in), length 13.98m (45ft 11in), height 4.01m (13ft 2in). Wing area 32.4m² (349sq ft).

**Accommodation:** Pilot only, or two side by side in trainers.

**Armament:** Four 30mm Aden cannons in lower forward fuselage. Four underwing pylons can carry a total of 3355kg (7400lb) of ordnance, including rockets and bombs. Some wired for AAMs.

**Operators:** Lebanon, Zimbabwe.

**History:** Perhaps the most famous British jet fighter, the Hawker Hunter has seen four decades of frontline service and is still a useful ground attack platform.

The Hunter's origins lie in the Hawker P.1067 design penned by Sydney Camm to meet an RAF requirement to replace the Gloster Meteor. Three P.1067 Hunter prototypes (two powered by the Rolls-Royce Avon and one by the Armstrong Siddeley Sapphire) were ordered in May 1948 for evaluation, and the first of these flew for the first time on July 20 1951.

Production Hunter F.1s were delivered from 1953, although these early aircraft suffered from a chronic lack of range and engine surge when the four cannons were fired. Nevertheless, the problems with early production Hunter models were resolved in time, leaving a very capable fighter.

Early Hunter models, including the Sapphire powered F.2 and F.5, served primarily as interceptors. Most went to the RAF, although the Avon powered F.4 and 'large bore' Avon 200 powered F.6 were the subject of significant export orders, and were built under licence in the Netherlands and Belgium. The T.7 and T.8 were two seat side by side trainers for the RAF and RN respectively.

The definitive Hunter model, and the basis for all single seaters remaining in service, was the FGA.9, a multirole aircraft with strengthened structure and substantially greater payload. All FGA.9s were in fact conversions of earlier aircraft (almost 400 in all), with significant operators including the RAF, India and Switzerland (whose aircraft were retired in 1994). The first FGA.9 conversion flew in July 1959, the last was delivered in 1975.

In 2001 Zimbabwe and Lebanon were the only countries with Hunters on strength (Lebanon's are not airworthy). Other nations which have retired their Hunters in recent years include Chile, India and the UK. In all 1972 Hunters were built.

**Photo:** A Sidewinder armed Hunter FGA.9.

# Hindustan HPT-32 Deepak

**Country of origin:** India

**Type:** Two seat basic trainer

**Powerplants:** One 195kW (260hp) Textron Lycoming AEIO-540-D4B5 flat six piston engine driving a two blade constant speed propeller.

**Performance:** Max speed at sea level 265km/h (143kt), max cruising speed 213km/h (115kt), economical cruising speed 176km/h (95kt). Max initial rate of climb 1100ft/min. Service ceiling 18,045ft. Range at 10,000ft and economical cruising power 745km (400nm).

**Weights:** Basic empty 890kg (1962lb), max takeoff weight 1250kg (2756lb).

**Dimensions:** Wing span 9.50m (31ft 2in), length 7.72m (25ft 4in), height 2.88m (9ft 6in). Wing area 15.0m² (161.5sq ft).

**Accommodation:** Seating for two side by side, with provision for a third seat behind.

**Armament:** None

**Operators:** India

**History:** India's indigenous HAL HPT-32 Deepak is used for initial pilot training, plus a number of utility tasks.

HAL developed the Deepak for the Indian Air Force to replace the tandem two seat HT-2 basic trainer and to undertake a range of utility roles including armed patrol, observation, liaison work, supply dropping, search and rescue, reconnaissance, glider and target tug towing, and even weapons training and light strike.

The prototype Deepak first flew on January 6 1977, followed by a second in March 1979. However these early prototypes failed to meet the specified requirements and so the aircraft was redesigned with numerous aerodynamic changes and underwent a weight reduction program.

A third prototype built to the definitive production standard flew in July 1981, although production deliveries did not start until 1984, with 12 aircraft officially handed over to the Indian Air Force's Bidar based Elementary Flying School.

The initial Indian Air Force requirement was for 160 Deepaks. The first production batch of 24 Deepaks was followed by subsequent re-orders which took total deliveries to 134, delivered through to 1997. Eight were built for the Indian Navy.

The Deepak design is conventional. It features a semi monocoque structure with stressed skin, fixed tricycle undercarriage, and a rearwards sliding canopy above the two side by side seats. Behind these seats is room for a third. Power is supplied by a six cylinder Lycoming AEIO-540 and the aircraft is fully aerobatic.

The only development of the Deepak was the turboprop powered HTT-34, which HAL developed as a private venture. The 313kW (420shp) Allison 250-B17D powered HTT-34 first flew in converted HTP-32 prototype form on June 17 1984. A second preproduction HTT-34 was unveiled in 1989. Apart from the engine other changes included a 35cm (1ft 2in) stretch and smaller tail.

The Allison 250 turboprop significantly boosted performance of the basic aircraft but the new variant did not attract official interest and none were ordered.

In 2001 around 125 Deepak's remained in Indian air force service.

**Photo:** The HPT-32 Deepak. (Sebastian Zacharias)

# Hindustan HJT-16 Kiran

**Country of origin:** India

**Type:** Advanced trainer and light attack aircraft

**Powerplant:** Mk II – One 18.4kN (4130lb) HAL licence built Rolls-Royce Orpheus 701-01 turbojet.

**Performance:** Mk II – Max speed at sea level 704km/h (380kt), max cruising speed at 15,000ft 620km/h (335kt), economical cruising speed 417km/h (225kt). Max initial rate of climb 5250ft/min. Service ceiling 39,375ft. Range with standard fuel 615km (332nm).

**Weights:** Mk II – Empty equipped 2965kg (6540lb), max takeoff 4950kg (10,913lb).

**Dimensions:** Mk II – Wing span 10.70m (35ft 1in), length 10.25m (33ft 8in), height 3.64m (11ft 11in). Wing area 19.0m² (204.5sq ft).

**Accommodation:** Two side by side.

**Armament:** Mk II – Two 7.62mm Aden guns in nose. Four underwing pylons can carry rocket pods, a single 250kg (550lb) bomb each, various practice bombs or fuel tanks.

**Operators:** India

**History:** The Hindustan Kiran (Ray of Light) was first developed in the early 1960s to replace India's sizeable fleet of licence built de Havilland Vampire two seat advanced trainers.

Design of the Kiran began in 1961 at Hindustan's Bangalore facilities under the leadership of Dr V M Chatage. Dr Chatage's team came up with a design similar in some respects to the contemporary Jet Provost, as the Kiran featured a straight wing, side by side seating and a Bristol (now Rolls-Royce) Viper turbojet. The first prototype Kiran first flew on September 4 1964, the second followed in August 1965.

HAL built a batch of 24 preproduction Kiran Mk Is, with the first of these delivered to the Indian Air Force from 1968. In addition, 118 production Kiran Is were built, some as Kiran IAs with two underwing hardpoints for weapons training. The Kiran Mk I entered service with the Indian Air Force Academy in 1973, while a small number were also transferred to the Indian Navy.

The improved Kiran Mk II first flew on July 30 1976. Compared with the Kiran I, the Mk II introduced a more powerful Rolls-Royce Orpheus turbojet in place of the Viper, four underwing hardpoints for light ground attack/COIN work, two 7.62mm Aden guns in the forward fuselage, and an improved hydraulic system.

The Mk II featured performance and payload improvements over the Kiran Mk I, but the Indian Air Force initially deemed it unsuitable for night flying and it had poor payload range. These shortfalls delayed Kiran Mk II production by many years and it was not until 1983 that official development work was completed. Deliveries of the first of 61 production Kiran Mk IIs began in March 1985, with the line closing in 1989. Aside from the Indian Air Force, six Kiran Mk IIs were also delivered to the Indian Navy.

In 1998 HAL revealed a mockup of the HJT-36 two seat jet trainer which is being developed as the Kiran's replacement. This Snecma Larzac powered low wing tandem two seater will feature modern avionics including HUD and LCDs and will be able to carry weaponry on one underfuselage and four underwing hardpoints. First flight is planned for 2002. Up to 200 are required.

**Photo:** India is the only Kiran operator. (Sebastian Zacharias)

# Hindustan Advanced Light Helicopter

**Country of origin:** India

**Type:** Troop transport/ship borne multirole helicopter

**Powerplants:** In four of five prototypes – Two 745kW (1000shp) take-off rated Turbomeca TM 333-2B turboshafts driving four blade main and tail rotors.

**Performance:** Max level speed 290km/h (157kt), max cruising speed 245km/h (132kt). Max initial rate of climb 2362ft/min. Service ceiling 19,680ft. Hovering ceiling in ground effect over 9840ft. Range with max fuel 800km (430nm), range with a 700kg (1543lb) payload 400km (215nm). Endurance 4hr.

**Weights:** Army version – Empty equipped 2450kg (5401lb), max take-off 4500kg (9920lb). Naval version – Empty equipped 2450kg (5501lb), max takeoff 5500kg (12,125lb).

**Dimensions:** Main rotor diameter 13.20m (43ft 4in), length overall rotors turning 15.87m (52ft 1in), fuselage length tail rotor turning 13.43m (44ft 1in), height overall tail rotor turning army version 4.98m (16ft 4in), naval version 4.91m (16ft 2in). Main rotor disc area 136.9m² (1473.0sq ft).

**Accommodation:** Flightcrew of two. Main cabin seating for 10 to 14, depending on configuration. Max external sling load army variant 1000kg (2205lb), naval variant 1500kg (3307lb).

**Armament:** Two stub wings on army variants for eight anti tank missiles, four rocket pods or two pairs of air-to-air missiles. Navy variant can mount two torpedoes or up to four anti ship missiles on cabin side pylons. Army versions can carry a ventral 20mm gun pod.

**Operators:** India*

**History:** The Advanced Light Helicopter is India's first indigenous helicopter program. It will be built in different versions for the Indian Army, Navy, Coast Guard and Air Force, plus civil customers.

In the early 1980s India approached Germany's MBB (now Eurocopter) to help it design and build a mid size multirole helicopter for both military and civil use. Subsequently a cooperation agreement was signed in July 1984, covering design support, development and production. Design work began in November that year, while the first flight of the first of four prototypes was on August 20 1992.

The ALH features a hingeless four blade main rotor with swept back tips connected to a Eurocopter fibre elastomer rotor heard. The main and tail rotors are made from composites.

The Advanced Light Helicopter will be built in two military versions, one for the Indian Air Force and Army, and one for the Navy. Army and air force versions will feature skids, and will be used for a number missions including ground attack, troop transport and SAR. Naval versions will be fitted with retractable tricycle undercarriage and a folding tail boom and could be fitted with sonar, radar, ESM, torpedoes, depth charges and anti ship missiles. A coast guard variant will feature a search radar and FLIR. A civil version will be powered by LHTEC CTS800s.

The Indian Government has signed a letter of intent for 300 ALHs for its military, of which 100 were covered by a firm contract signed in 1996.

**Photo:** The fourth prototype ALH, powered by the LHTEC CTS800. (Sebastian Hindustan)

# Hughes/MD Helicopters OH-6 & MD 500

**Country of origin:** United States of America

**Type:** Observation, light attack, training and utility helicopter

**Powerplant:** OH-6A – One 189kW (253shp) takeoff rated Allison T63-A-5A turboshaft driving a five blade main rotor and two blade tail rotor.

**Performance:** OH-6A – Econ cruising speed 215km/h (116kt). Max initial rate of climb with mil power 1840ft/min. Service ceiling 15,800ft. Hovering ceiling in ground effect 11,800ft, out of ground effect 7300ft. Range at 5000ft 610km (330nm). Ferry range 2510km (1355nm).

**Weights:** OH-6A – Empty equipped 557kg (1229lb), max takeoff 1090kg (2400lb), max overload takeoff 1225kg (2700lb).

**Dimensions:** OH-6A – Main rotor diameter 8.03m (26ft 4in), length overall rotors turning 9.24m (30ft 4in), fuselage length 7.01m (23ft 0in), height to top of rotor head 2.48m (8ft 2in). Main rotor disc area 50.6m² (544.6sq ft).

**Accommodation:** OH-6A – Typical seating for four, but rear two seats can be removed to make room for four troops to sit on the floor.

**Armament:** OH-6A – Provision for machine guns and rocket pods.

**Operators:** OH-6 – Brazil, Dominican Republic, USA. 500 – Argentina, Colombia, Costa Rica, Cyprus, El Salvador, Finland, Italy, Japan, Jordan, Kenya, Mexico, North Korea, Philippines, South Korea, Spain.

**History:** The highly successful Hughes, McDonnell Douglas, Boeing and now MD Helicopters 500 series began life in response to a US Army requirement for an observation helicopter.

Hughes won the US Army observation helicopter contest against competition from Bell and Hiller, resulting in the Allison 250 powered OH-6 Cayuse, which first flew in February 1963. Several thousand OH-6s (or Loaches) have served widely with the US Army in observation and special mission roles since the mid 1960s (including in Vietnam). The OH-6 was marketed in civil guise as the Hughes 500, which formed the basis for a number of export military variants.

The first Hughes 500 export military variant was the 500M Defender, which was delivered to Colombia and built under licence by Kawasaki in Japan as the OH-6J. The 500M was followed by the 500MD Defender in 1976, an improved variant with a more powerful engine, small T-tail and new five blade main rotor. Apart from the basic Defender, it was offered in 500D Scout Defender, anti tank 500MD/TOW Defender and torpedo carrying 500MD/ASW Defender (with search radar and towed MAD) variants.

The 500MG Defender is the military variant of the 500E (with a recontoured nose and a RR/Allison 250-C20B). The military equivalent of the more powerful, hot and high 530F is the 530MG Defender. Current models are the 500MG and 530MGs offered with a FLIR, mast mounted TOW sight and a laser rangefinder.

Built alongside these models is the revolutionary NOTAR equipped MD 520N, and while none are in military service, small numbers of US Army special ops MH-6Js and machine gun and rocket armed AH-6Js have been fitted with NOTAR tails (these may have been refitted with conventional tail rotors).

Boeing is upgrading AH/MH-6Js under the Mission Enhanced Little Bird program. About 40 are in service.

**Photo:** An Argentine 500D. (Santiago Rivas)

# IAI Arava

**Country of origin:** Israel

**Type:** STOL utility transport

**Powerplants:** 201 – Two 560kW (750shp) Pratt & Whitney Canada PT6A-34 turboprops driving three blade propellers.

**Performance:** 201 – Max speed 326km/h (176kt), max cruising speed 320km/h (172kt), economical cruising speed 311km/h (168kt). Initial rate of climb 1290ft/min. Service ceiling 25,000ft. Takeoff run at MTOW 295m (960ft). Range with max payload 260km (140nm), range with a 1585kg (3500lb) payload 1000km (540nm).

**Weights:** 201 – Operating empty 4000kg (8816lb), max takeoff 6804kg (15,000lb).

**Dimensions:** 201 – Wing span 20.96m (68ft 9in), length 13.03m (42ft 9in), height 5.21m (17ft 1in). Wing area 43.7m² (470.2sq ft).

**Accommodation:** Flightcrew of two. Seating for 24 passengers at four abreast in 201. Configurations offered included freighter, aerial ambulance, Elint and maritime patrol.

**Armament:** Can be fitted with fuselage mounted 12.7mm gun pods or up to 12 rockets.

**Operators:** Bolivia, Cameroon, Colombia, Ecuador, El Salvador, Guatemala, Honduras, Israel, Papua New Guinea, Swaziland, Thailand, Venezuela.

**History:** The IAI Arava STOL utility transport was developed to meet an Israeli requirement to replace Douglas DC-3s, but it also proved popular with export customers in underdeveloped and rugged regions of the world.

IAI began design work on the Arava in 1966. Design objectives included STOL performance, the ability to operate from rough strips and room for 25 troops or bulky payloads. To achieve this the Arava design is fairly unusual, featuring a barrel-like short but wide fuselage, the rear of which is hinged and swings open for easy loading and unloading; plus long span wings, twin tails (to compensate for the loss of moment arm due to the short fuselage) mounted on booms that run from the engine nacelles, and two Pratt & Whitney Canada PT6A turboprops.

The Arava first flew on November 27 1969, while a second prototype flew on May 8 1971. The initial Arava 101 was not put into production, but it formed the basis for the 101B, 102 and 201 production models. The 101B differed from the 101 in having an improved 19 seat interior and more powerful PT6A-36s. The 102 had a 20 seat passenger interior.

The 201 is the primary military version, and sold in the most numbers. More than 70 were built, mainly for Israel and customers in Latin America. Israeli aircraft have been used for a variety of roles other than transport, including maritime patrol (fitted with a search radar) and Elint. Thailand uses its Aravas for Elint/border surveillance.

The final Arava development is the 202, which is easily recognised by its large Whitcomb winglets, boundary layer fences inboard of each wingtip and slightly stretched fuselage. The winglets and boundary layer fences were offered as a retrofit kit for existing Aravas.

More than 90 Aravas were built through to mid 1987.

**Photo:** A Papua New Guinea Defence Force Arava, one of three used for transport and surveillance.

# IAI Kfir

**Country of origin:** Israel

**Type:** Multirole fighter

**Powerplant:** C7 – One 52.9kN (11,890lb) dry and 79.4kN (17,860lb) with afterburning IAI licence built General Electric J79-JIE turbojet.

**Performance:** C7 – Max speed over 2440km/h (1315kt) or Mach 2.3, max sustained speed Mach 2.0, max speed at sea level 1390km/h (750kt). Max initial rate of climb 45,930ft/min. Interception radius with two Shafrir AAMs and three drop tanks (total 3425 l/904 US gal) 775km (420nm). Radius with two 363kg/800lb and three 180kg/400lb bombs, two Shafrir AAMs and three drop tanks (total 4700 l/1241 US gal) hi-lo-hi 1185km (640nm). Ferry range with three drop tanks 2990km (1615nm).

**Weights:** C7 – Empty approx 7285kg (16,060lb), max takeoff 16,500kg (36,375lb). Internal fuel 2572kg (5670lb).

**Dimensions:** C7 – Wing span 8.22m (27ft 0in), length overall 15.65m (51ft 4in), height 4.55m (14ft 11in). Wing area 34.8m² (374.6sq ft).

**Accommodation:** Pilot only, or two in tandem in trainer variants.

**Armament:** Two IAI built DEFA 30mm cannons. Five under fuselage and four underwing hardpoints can carry two AIM-9 Sidewinder, Python 3 or Shafrir 2 AAMs on outer wing stations, bombs, rockets, Shrike and Maverick ASMs, or GBU-15 laser guided bombs.

**Operators:** Colombia, Ecuador, Israel, Sri Lanka.

**History:** The Israeli developed Kfir is arguably the most potent member of the basic Dassault Mirage III/5 fighter series.

In 1967 France cancelled deliveries of paid for Mirage 5Js to Israel, leading IAI to develop and build the Nesher, an unlicensed Mirage 5 copy. After building 100 or so Neshers (some of which were subsequently sold to Argentina as the Dagger and used in the 1982 Falklands War), IAI switched to building the Kfir.

With the Kfir (Lion Cub) IAI was able to make major improvements over the basic Mirage, the most important of which was the use of the significantly more powerful General Electric J79 turbojet (necessitating larger intakes and a dorsal airscoop, the latter for afterburner cooling), plus Israeli developed avionics (but no radar) in an extended nose. The first Kfir, a converted French built Mirage, first flew in October 1970. The first IAI built Kfir flew in September 1971.

Initial production Kfirs were delivered from April 1975, but these were soon followed by the Kfir C2, the first major production model and the first to introduce canards. Early Kfirs meanwhile were subsequently upgraded to C1 standard, fitted with small canards. Between 1985 and 1989 some leased examples were operated by the US Navy and Marines as the F-21 for aggressor training.

The C2 introduced modifications to improve manoeuvrability, including larger canards, nose strakes and dogtooth wing leading edges, as well as improved avionics and a HUD. 185 C2s and two seat TC2s were built, with small numbers delivered to Ecuador and Colombia in the 1980s. Most Israeli C2s were upgraded to C7 standard during the 1980s with upgraded cockpit including HOTAS controls.

Surplus Israeli Kfir C2s and C7s have been offered for export. IAI has also offered the Kfir 2000 (or C10) upgrade for these aircraft, with new avionics, including the multimode radar developed for the Lavi.

**Photo:** Israeli Kfir C7s. (IAI)

# Ilyushin Il-18, Il-20, Il-22 & Il-38

**Country of origin:** Russia

**Type:** Il-18 – VIP and general transport. Il-20 – Elint platform. Il-22 – Command Post. Il-38 – Maritime patrol and ASW aircraft.

**Powerplants:** Il-38 – Four 3125kW (4190ehp) ZMKB Progress (Ivchenko) AI-20M turboprops driving four blade propellers.

**Performance:** Il-38 – Max speed at 21,000ft 722km/h (390kt), max cruising speed at 27,000ft 610km/h (330kt), patrol speed at 2000ft 400km/h (216kt). Range with max fuel 7200km (3887nm). Patrol endurance with max fuel 12hr.

**Weights:** Il-38 – Empty 36,000kg (79,367lb), max takeoff 63,500kg (140,000lb).

**Dimensions:** Il-38 – Wing span 37.42m (122ft 9in), length overall 36.90m (129ft 10in), height 10.17m (33ft 4in). Wing area 140.0m² (1506.9sq ft).

**Accommodation:** Il-38 – Flightcrew of two pilots and flight engineer. Operational crew believed to be nine, which would include a tactical coordinator, sensor operators, MAD operator and observers.

**Armament:** Il-38 – Forward and aft internal weapons bays can carry homing torpedoes, sonobuoys and nuclear and conventional depth charges.

**Operators:** Il-18 – China, North Korea. Il-20 & -22 – Russia. Il-38 – India, Russia.

**History:** Ilyushin's Il-18 turboprop airliner played a significant role in developing the USSR's air services in the 1960s and 1970s, and was also been adopted for a variety of military roles, ranging from transport, to command post, Elint and maritime patrol.

The Il-18 was originally developed against a mid 1950s Aeroflot requirement for an economical 75 to 100 seat airliner. The Il-18 first flew on June 4 1957, and entered airline service with Aeroflot in 1959. Some 600 were built, mainly for Aeroflot and Soviet client state airlines, with a smaller number delivered for military service as VIP and general transports. Given the NATO reporting name 'Coot', a small number remain in military service.

The Il-18 airframe also serves as the basis of the Il-20 Elint/reconnaissance platform. The Il-20M ('Coot-A') first flew in March 1968 and features a variety of antennas, with a large ventral mounted side looking radar. Blisters on either side of the forward fuselage are another obvious external feature.

Several Il-22M ('Coot-B') airborne command post aircraft were converted from surplus Il-18 airliners, and again feature a variety of antennas and external protuberances.

The most well known military adaptation of the Il-18 is the maritime patrol/ASW Il-38 'May'. The Il-38 prototype first flew on September 28 1961. Service entry was in 1967 and about three dozen serve with Russian naval aviation. Fifty-seven were built to 1972, with five later delivered to India in 1975.

The Il-38's airframe is stretched by 4m (13ft) over the Il-18 and the wings are moved forward. The tail contains a magnetic anomaly detector (MAD), while under the forward fuselage a Berkut search radar (named 'Wet Eye' by NATO) is housed in a bulged radome. There are two internal weapons bays, one forward and one rear of the wing.

**Photo:** A Russian navy Il-38.

# Ilyushin Il-76 & Il-78

**Country of origin:** Russia

**Type:** Strategic transport. Il-78 – Aerial refueller.

**Powerplants:** Four 117.7kN (26,455lb) Aviadvigatel D-30KP turbofans. Il-76MF – Four 156.9kN (35,275lb) Aviadvigatel PS-90AN turbofans.

**Performance:** Il-76M – Max speed 850km/h (460kt), cruising speed 750 to 800km/h (405 to 432kt). Max range 6700km (3617nm), range with a 40 tonne (88,185lb) payload 5000km (2700nm). Il-76MD – Speeds same. Range with max payload 3650km (1970nm), range with 20 tonne (44,090lb) payload 7300km (3940nm). Il-76MF – Range with 40 tonne (88,185lb) payload 5200km (2805nm).

**Weights:** Il-76M – Max takeoff 170,000kg (374,785lb). Il-78 – Empty 98,000kg (216,050lb), max takeoff 190,000kg (418,875lb).

**Dimensions:** Il-76M – Wing span 50.50m (165ft 8in), length 46.59m (152ft 10in), height 14.76m (48ft 5in). Wing area 300.0m² (3229.2sq ft). Il-76MF – Same except length approx 53m (174ft).

**Accommodation:** Il-76M & Il-76MF – Crew of seven comprising two pilots, flight engineer, navigator and radio operator, plus two freight handlers. Can carry up to 140 troops or 120 paratroops.

**Armament:** Il-76 – Provision for two 23mm twin barrel GSh-23L guns in the tail.

**Operators:** Algeria, Belarus, India, Libya, North Korea, Russia, Syria, Ukraine, Uzbekistan, Yemen.

**History:** The Ilyushin Il-76 (NATO name 'Candid') was developed as a replacement for the turboprop powered Antonov An-12.

Il-76 development under the leadership of G V Novozhilov began in the late 1960s, resulting in the type's first flight on March 25 1971. Series production commenced in 1975.

The Il-76 features a high mounted wing, four engines, a T-tail, rear loading ramp and freight doors. For enhanced short field performance the Il-76 features wide span triple slotted trailing edge flaps, upper surface spoilers and near full span leading edge slats. The aircraft rides on a total of 20 low pressure tyres – the front nose unit features four wheels, the main wheel bogies having two rows of four tyres each.

Military versions developed from the basic Il-76 include the Il-76M with additional fuel and the Il-76MD with increased takeoff and payload weights and D-30KP-2s which retain their power output to higher altitudes. Civil variants include the Il-76T and Il-76TD. The A-50 AEW&C development is described under Beriev.

The stretched PS-90 powered Il-76MF first flew on August 1 1995. The Russian air force requires over 100 but has lack of funding has prevented it placing firm orders. The Uzbekistan government is buying five Il-76MFs, re-engined with the CFM56

The Il-78 'Midas' is an air-to-air refuelling development of the Il-76, built to replace tanker conversions of the Myasischev 'Bison' bomber. The Il-78 is based on the Il-76MD and features two internal fuel tanks which can be removed, allowing the aircraft to revert to a freighter configuration. The more developed Il-78M features three permanent tanks capable of holding up to 35 tonnes of fuel. Fuel is transferred via three hose drum units, one under each wing and one on the rear starboard fuselage. A rangefinding radar is built into the rear fuselage and an observer sits in the tail. Service entry was in 1987.

**Photo:** An Algerian air force Il-76 transport. (Keith Gaskell)

# IAe CN-235

**Countries of origin:** Indonesia and Spain

**Type:** Tactical transport and maritime patrol aircraft

**Powerplants:** Two 1305kW (1750shp) General Electric CT7-9C turboprops driving four blade Hamilton Standard propellers.

**Performance:** CN-235 M – Max cruising speed at 15,000ft 460km/h (248kt). Max initial rate of climb 1900ft/min. Service ceiling 26,600ft. Takeoff distance to 50ft at MTOW 1290m (4235ft). Range (srs 200) with max payload 1500km (810nm), with a 3550kg (7825lb) payload 4445km (2400nm).

**Weights:** CN-235 M – Operating empty 8800kg (19,400lb), max takeoff 16,500kg (36,375lb).

**Dimensions:** CN-235 M – Wing span 25.81m (84ft 8in), length 21.40m (70ft 3in), height 8.18m (26ft 10in). Wing area 59.1m² (636.1sq ft).

**Accommodation:** CN-235 M – Flightcrew of two, plus typically a loadmaster. Can accommodate 48 equipped troops or 46 paratroopers. CN-235 MPA – Typical arrangement features two observer stations, two operator consoles and six passenger seats.

**Armament:** CN-235 MPA – Six underwing hardpoints. Can carry anti ship missiles such as Exocet and Harpoon, plus two Mk 46 torpedoes.

**Operators:** Brunei, Indonesia*, Malaysia, Nigeria*, Pakistan*, South Korea*, UAE (Abu Dhabi).

**History:** Indonesia's IPTN and CASA of Spain jointly developed the CN-235 under the Airtech banner, but since 1992 both companies have developed their own variants of the aircraft separately.

Initial development was shared equally between the two companies, and one prototype in each country was rolled out simultaneously on September 10 1983. The Spanish built prototype was the first to fly, on November 11 1983, while the Indonesian prototype first flew on December 30 that year.

CN-235 final assembly lines are located in both Indonesia and Spain, but all other construction is not duplicated. EADS CASA builds the centre and forward fuselage, wing centre section, inboard flaps and engine nacelles, while IAe is responsible for the outer wings and flaps, ailerons, rear fuselage and tail.

Initial production was of the CN-235-10. Subsequent and improved joint IPTN/CASA developments include the CN-235-100 and the current production -200, with more powerful engines and structural improvements respectively. Military versions are also designated CN-235 M.

IPTN (since August 2000 Indonesian Aerospace, of PT Dirgantara Indonesia) offers the CN-235 MPA maritime patrol aircraft with a range of equipment including either a BAE Systems Seaspray 4000 or Raytheon APS-134 search radar mounted in a nose or under fuselage radome. Brunei and Indonesia have ordered MPAs.

The Indonesian air force has also shown interest in buying an Ericsson Erieye equipped AEW variant, primarily for maritime surveillance. Development has not been funded.

The CN-235-330 Phoenix was an improved transport offered to Australia, with Honeywell avionics, including a Mil Std 1553B databus. IPTN withdrew from the bidding in 1998.

IPTN has also studied, but not built, the stretched CN-245 development

**Photo:** An Indonesian navy CN-235 MPA. (Robert Wiseman)

# KAI T-50 & A-50 Golden Eagle

**Countries of origin:** South Korea and USA

**Type:** Advanced/lead-in fighter trainer (T-50) and light fighter (A-50)

**Powerplants:** One 78.7kN (17,700lb) with afterburning General Electric F404-GE-402 turbofan.

**Performance:** Max speed Mach 1.4. Max initial rate of climb 33,000ft/min. Service ceiling 48,000ft.

**Weights:** Empty 6263kg (13,808lb), max takeoff 11,974kg (26,400lb).

**Dimensions:** Wing span 9.11m (29ft 11in), length 12.98m (42ft 0in), height 4.78m (15ft 9in).

**Accommodation:** Two in tandem.

**Armament:** An internal 20mm gun. Two wingtip, one centreline, and four underwing hardpoints for a variety of weaponry including AIM-9 Sidewinder AAMs and AGM-65 Maverick ASMs (wingtip stations can carry AAMs only), rockets and bombs.

**Operators:** South Korea*

**History:** The T-50 Golden Eagle advanced trainer and lead-fighter is being developed jointly by Korean Aerospace and Lockheed Martin to meet a South Korean requirement, but is also marketed internationally.

Initial design of the T-50 (KTX-2 until early 2000) dates to 1992. Samsung was assisted with preliminary design work by Lockheed as part of offset work arising from Korea's F-16 purchase. By mid 1995 the basic design had been finalised (one early design configuration envisaged a mid mounted wing and twin tail configuration).

However the program had to bide its time for the next two years while the Korean government decided whether or not to proceed with the project. Finally on July 3 1997 Korea elected to go ahead with the KTX-2 project (in favour of a rival offering from Daewoo with DASA's proposed AT2000). Subsequently Samsung signed a cooperation agreement with Lockheed Martin covering joint development of the aircraft. Samsung is now part of Korean Aerospace Industries (KAI).

The South Korean government is funding 70% of the T-50 program's $US1.8-2bn pricetag and has a requirement for 94 T-50s for the RoKAF for delivery from 2003. KAI is funding 17% and Lockheed Martin the remaining 13%.

Full scale T-50 development began in late 1997. The prototype was rolled out on October 31 2001 and is due to fly in mid 2002. Deliveries to the RoKAF are due to begin in 2004 and continue through to 2009. All production aircraft will be built at KAI's modern Sachon plant (where KAI/Samsung builds F-16Cs under licence).

The T-50 features seating for two in tandem, a shoulder mounted wing with wingtip AAM stations, a GE F404-GE-402 turbofan and fly-by-wire flight controls.

Lockheed Martin is responsible for developing the T-50's avionics system, flight control system and wings at its Fort Worth facilities. The T-50's cockpit displays will feature similar symbology and switchology as LM's F-16, F-22 and F-35 fighters.

The A-50 light fighter version of the T-50 will be fitted with a radar, and is pitched as an F-5 replacement. As well as further Korean air force orders, KAI and Lockheed Martin forecast a world market for 600 to 800 T-50s/A-50s.

**Photo:** The T-50 rolled out on October 31 2001. First flight is due in mid 2002.

# Kaman SH-2 Seasprite

**Country of origin:** United States of America

**Type:** Shipborne ASW, ASuW and surveillance helicopter

**Powerplants:** SH-2G – Two 1285kW (1723shp) General Electric T700-GE-401 turboshafts driving four blade main and tail rotors.

**Performance:** SH-2G – Max speed 256km/h (138kt), normal cruising speed 222km/h (120kt). Max initial rate of climb 2500ft/min. Service ceiling 23,900ft. Hovering ceiling in ground effect 20,800ft, out of ground effect 18,000ft. Max range with two external tanks 885km (478nm). Time on station 65km (35nm) from ship with two torpedoes 1hr 30min. Max endurance with two external tanks 5hr.

**Weights:** SH-2G – Empty 4173kg (9200lb), MTOW 6125kg (13,500lb).

**Dimensions:** SH-2G – Main rotor diameter 13.41m (44ft 0in), length overall rotors turning 16.00m (52ft 6in), fuselage length 12.34m (40ft 6in), height overall rotors turning 4.62m (15ft 2in), height blades folded 4.14m (13ft 7in). Main rotor disc area 141.3m$^2$ (1521.1sq ft).

**Accommodation:** Crew of three, comprising pilot, copilot/tactical coordinator and sensor operator in NZ and Egyptian aircraft. Crew of two in Australian SH-2G(A)s (pilot and TACCO/observer).

**Armament:** SH-2G – Options include one or two Mk 46 or Mk 50 torpedoes. Australian Gs will carry Penguin ASMs, NZ Gs AGM-65s.

**Operators:** Australia*, Egypt, New Zealand*.

**History:** The Seasprite was designed to meet a 1956 US Navy requirement for a long range, all weather multirole utility helicopter.

Kaman's K-20 was selected for development as the HU2K-1 (UH-2A from 1962), and it flew in prototype form on July 2 1959. The UH-2A and improved UH-2B were powered by a single GE T58 turboshaft, and could carry up to 11 passengers or a 1815kg (4000lb) sling load. In all 190 were built for utility transport, SAR and Vertrep. From 1968 surviving UH-2s were re-engined with two T58s.

The UH-2 was selected as the basis for an interim ASW LAMPS (Light Airborne Multi-Purpose System) helicopter in October 1970 as the SH-2D. Twenty Seasprites were converted to SH-2D standard with a Litton search radar, MAD on the starboard fuselage pylon and a removable sonobuoy launcher.

From May 1973 Kaman converted 88 Seasprites to LAMPS 2 SH-2F standard, with uprated engines, Marconi radar and towed MAD. Kaman delivered 52 new build SH-2Fs from 1981.

The SH-2G Super Seasprite is powered by two General Electric T700s, and has multifunction displays, a new acoustic processor and a new tactical management system. The first YSH-2G prototype first flew on April 2 1985. Six new build SH-2Gs were delivered from 1991, alongside 18 converted from SH-2Fs. These aircraft equipped two US Navy Reserve units, while Egypt took delivery of 10 similar SH-2G(E)s.

In 1997 the Australian and New Zealand navies selected the SH-2G to meet similar intermediate naval helicopter requirements. Australia's 11 SH-2G(A)s (rebuilt from SH-2Fs) feature advanced two crew glass cockpits, APS-143 radar, FLIR, ESM, composite rotor blades and will carry the Kongsberg Penguin anti ship missile. Development problems have delayed delivery by more than two years. New Zealand's five new build SH-2G(NZ)s are similar, but without the advanced avionics, and carry the AGM-65 ASM. Delivery began in mid 2001.

**Photo:** An Egyptian SH-2G. (Kaman)

# Kamov Ka-25

**Country of origin:** Russia

**Type:** ASW and multirole shipborne helicopter

**Powerplants:** Ka-25PL – Two 670kW (900shp) Glushenkov (OMKB Mars) GTD-3F turboshafts driving two three-blade coaxial rotors.

**Performance:** Ka-25PL – Max speed 209km/h (113kt), normal cruising speed 193km/h (104kt). Service ceiling 11,000ft. Range with standard fuel 400km (217nm), range with external tanks 650km (350nm).

**Weights:** Ka-25PL – Empty 4765kg (10,505lb), max takeoff 7500kg (16,535lb).

**Dimensions:** Ka-25PL – Rotor diameter (each) 15.74m (51ft 8in), fuselage length 9.75m (32ft 0in), height to top of rotor head 5.37m (17ft 8in). Rotor disc area (each) 194.6m² (2095sq ft).

**Accommodation:** Pilot and copilot side by side. Main cabin can carry up to 12 passengers on folding seats when so equipped.

**Armament:** Some equipped with internal weapons bay which can contain two torpedoes or nuclear or conventional depth charges.

**Operators:** India, Russia, Syria, Ukraine.

**History:** The Kamov Ka-25 was built in large numbers for the Soviet navy and export customers as a ship based ASW and utility helicopter, but has largely been replaced by the Ka-32.

The Ka-25 was the end result of a 1957 Soviet navy requirement for a shipborne anti submarine warfare helicopter. In response Kamov developed the Ka-20 which first flew during 1960. The Ka-20 was displayed in the 1961 Soviet Aviation Day flypast at Tushino carrying two dummy air-to-surface missiles. The Ka-20 formed the basis for the production Ka-25 (NATO name 'Hormone'), with 460 or so production helicopters delivered between 1966 and 1975. In the Soviet navy the Ka-25 replaced the Mil Mi-4 as the service's primary shipborne helicopter.

The most prominent design feature of the Ka-25 is Kamov's trademark counter rotating coaxial main rotors, which do away with the need for a tail rotor, and means the tail can be kept short and thus saving space, an important consideration for naval operations. Other features include a search radar mounted beneath the nose, a downward looking electro optical sensor in the tailboom, and a MAD which can be mounted either in the fuselage or tail. The Ka-25 is usually flown unarmed, but can be fitted with an underfuselage weapons bay that can carry torpedoes and mines.

Up to 25 separate Ka-25 variants may have been built. Major identified variants include the Ka-25PL 'Hormone-A', the Ka-25Ts 'Hormone-B', the Ka-25PS 'Hormone-C', and the Ka-25BShZ. The Ka-25BSh is the primary ASW variant. The Ka-25Ts was used for target acquisition and mid course guidance for ship launched missiles, with most now retired.

The Ka-24PS is a dedicated search and rescue variant. It is stripped of all ASW equipment and can also be used for troop transport (carrying up to 12 passengers), Vertrep and utility transport. Many Ka-25PSs were fitted with a searchlight and a rescue winch. The Ka-25BShZ was developed to tow minesweeping gear.

In 2001 more than 60 Ka-25s remained in Russian navy service.

**Photo:** A Russian navy Ka-25. Aside from Russia, Ukraine, India and Syria have the Ka-25 on strength. (Sebastian Zacharias)

# Kamov Ka-27, Ka-28 & Ka-32

**Country of origin:** Russia

**Type:** ASW and multirole shipborne helicopter

**Powerplants:** Ka-27PL – Two 1645kW (2205shp) Klimov (Isotov) TV3-117V turboshafts driving two three-blade counter rotating coaxial main rotors.

**Performance:** Ka-27PL – Max speed 250km/h (135kt), max cruising speed 230km/h (124kt). Max initial rate of climb 2460ft/min. Service ceiling 16,405ft. Hovering ceiling out of ground effect 11,485ft. Ferry range with auxiliary fuel 800km (432nm). Radius of action tracking a submarine moving at up to 75km/h (40kt) at a depth of 500m (1640ft) 200km (108nm). Endurance 4hr 30min.

**Weights:** Ka-27PL – Basic empty 6100kg (13,338lb), operating empty 6500kg (14,330lb), max takeoff 12,600kg (27,778lb).

**Dimensions:** Ka-27PL – Rotor diameter (each) 15.90m (52ft 2in), length rotors folded 12.25m (40ft 2in), fuselage length 11.30m (37ft 1in), height to top of rotor head 5.40m (17ft 9in). Rotor disc area (each) 198.5m² (2138sq ft).

**Accommodation:** Ka-27PL – Normal crew complement of three, comprising pilot, tactical coordinator and ASW systems operator. Ka-32 – Main cabin can accommodate up to 16 passengers or freight.

**Armament:** Torpedoes or depth charges carried in a ventral weapons bay.

**Operators:** Ka-27 – Algeria, Russia, Ukraine. Ka-28 – China, India, Vietnam.

**History:** The Kamov Ka-27 was developed to replace the Ka-25, and is the Russian navy's standard ship based ASW helicopter.

The Kamov design bureau began work on a successor for its Ka-25 in 1967, when Sergei Mikheyev became chief designer following Nikolai Kamov's death. The Soviet navy required a replacement for its Ka-25s as they could not operate dunking sonar at night or in poor weather. The result was the Ka-27 (NATO name 'Helix'), an all new helicopter of similar overall dimensions to the Ka-25 and featuring Kamov's signature counter rotating coaxial main rotors. The Ka-27 first flew in 1973.

The Ka-27's similar overall dimensions to the Ka-25 means it requires only the same amount of deck space to operate from as the older helicopter. However the Ka-27 features more powerful Isotov turboshafts which turn redesigned, although similar diameter rotors, giving greater performance and allowing higher weights.

The basic Ka-27PL anti submarine warfare helicopter features an under nose mounted search radar, dipping sonar and disposable sonobuoys. The Ka-27PL usually operates in 'hunter killer' teams, with one aircraft tracking the target sub, the other dropping depth charges. The Ka-28 is a downgraded export version of the Ka-27PL, while the Ka-27PS is a naval SAR helicopter with some ASW equipment deleted, an external winch and fuselage side mounted fuel tanks. The proposed Ka-29PK would be an armed variant with the Kh-35 anti ship missile. The Ka-29 assault transport derivative is described separately.

The planned Ka-27PLM upgrade of the PL will feature a new sensor system and more powerful TV3-117MVA-SB3 turboshafts.

The Ka-32 is the civil version of the Ka-27, although none have been sold to military operators.

**Photo:** An Indian navy Ka-28. (Sebastian Zacharias)

## Kamov Ka-29 & Ka-31

**Country of origin:** Russia

**Type:** Assault transport and radar picket helicopter

**Powerplants:** Ka-29 – Two 1635kW (2190shp) Klimov (Isotov) TV3-117V turboshafts driving two three-blade counter rotating coaxial main rotors.

**Performance:** Ka-29 – Max level speed at s/l 280km/h (151kt), cruising speed 235km/h (127kt). Initial rate of climb 3050ft/min. Service ceiling 14,100ft. Hovering ceiling OGE 12,140ft. Ferry range 740km (400nm), range with max std fuel 460km (248nm). Combat radius with six to eight attack passes 100km (54nm). Ka-31 – Max level speed 250km/h (135kt). Range 600km (324nm). Loiter endurance 2hr 30min.

**Weights:** Ka-29 – Empty 5520kg (12,170lb), max takeoff 12,600kg (27,775lb).

**Dimensions:** Ka-29 – Main rotor diameter (each) 15.90m (52ft 2in), length overall excluding nose probes and rotors 11.30m (37ft 1in), height to top of rotor hub 5.40m (17ft 9in). Main rotor disc area (each) 198.5m² (2138sq ft).

**Accommodation:** Ka-29 – Crew of two. Main cabin can accommodate up to 16 combat equipped troops, or four stretcher patients and six seated patients in medevac configuration.

**Armament:** One 7.62mm four barrel Gatling type machine gun mounted underneath right side door. Two pylons on each stub wing can carry rocket pods, or two four-round clusters of 9M114 Shturm (AT-6 Spiral) ASMs and two rocket pods. Can carry a 30mm gun above left side stub wing.

**Operators:** Ka-29 – Russia, Ukraine. Ka-31 – India*, Russia.

**History:** The Ka-29 development of the Ka-27 was designed for fire support of Russian navy amphibious landing operations, while the Ka-31 is an AEW variant.

The Ka-29 'Helix-B' was initially thought to be a non radar equipped transport version of the ASW Ka-27, an observation later proven untrue. The basic Ka-29 variant is the Ka-29TB attack helicopter, with around 45 entering Soviet navy service from 1985.

While the Ka-29 is based on the Ka-27, there are a number of substantial changes. The Ka-29's forward fuselage is widened, with changes to the nose profile including a five piece flat windscreen and blunt nose. Armament is carried on two stub wings with two hardpoints each, typically carrying rocket pods or air-to-surface missiles. The Ka-29 also features an electro optical sensor under the nose, thought to be a combined TV/FLIR unit.

The Ka-31 (formerly Ka-29RLD – radiolokatsyonnogo dozora) is a radar picket development of the Ka-29 and features an E-801E Oko radar mounted beneath the fuselage. The radar (which has a 100-150km detection range against fighter sized targets) folds flat against the fuselage bottom for transit flight and stowage, and extends and rotates beneath the fuselage in operation, while the undercarriage retracts upwards, so it doesn't interfere with the radar. The Ka-31 first flew in October 1987 and was first noted in 1988 when two were observed operating off the carrier *Admiral of the Fleet Kuznetsov* (then *Tbilsi*).

India is the first export customer, buying 10, while Russian acquisition intentions are unclear. Production began in 1999.

**Photo:** The Ka-29.

## Kamov Ka-50 & Ka-52

**Country of origin:** Russia

**Type:** Attack helicopter

**Powerplants:** Ka-50/-52 – Two 1635kW (2190shp) Klimov TV3-117VMA turboshafts driving two three-blade counter rotating co-axial main rotors.

**Performance:** Ka-50 – Max speed 310km/h (167kt). Hovering ceiling OGE 13,125ft. Combat range 520km (280nm). Endurance with standard fuel 1hr 40min, endurance with aux fuel 4hr. Ka-52 – Max speed 300km/h (162kt). Max rate of climb 1575ft/min. Hovering ceiling OGE 11,820ft. Range 450km (243nm), ferry range 1200km (647nm).

**Weights:** Ka-50 – Normal takeoff 9800kg (21,605lb), max takeoff 10,800kg (23,810lb). Ka-52 – Normal takeoff 10,400kg (22,925lb).

**Dimensions:** Ka-50 – Rotor diameter (each) 14.50m (47ft 7in), length overall rotors turning 16.00m (52ft 6in), height overall 4.93m (16ft 2in). Rotor disc area (each) 165.1m² (1777.4sq ft).

**Accommodation:** Pilot only in Ka-50, or crew of two in Ka-52.

**Armament:** One single barrel 30mm 2A42 gun on right side of the fuselage. Two hardpoints on each stub wing for rockets, tube launched laser guided Vikhr-M ASMs, gun pods or AAMs.

**Operators:** No production aircraft ordered.

**History:** The Ka-50 Black Shark (or 'Hokum' to NATO), along with the Mi-28, was developed to meet a Russian army requirement for a new close air support helicopter.

Ka-50 design work began in 1977, and the first prototype, the V.80, first flew on July 27 1982. Like other Kamovs, the Ka-50 features two counter rotating coaxial main rotors, but it is unique among attack helicopters for its single seat configuration. To compensate for the higher workload, Kamov incorporated some advanced autohover systems, while another unique feature is the ejection seat – the rotors are jettisoned before the pilot's seat is ejected. Over 35% of the Ka-50's structure by weight is of composites.

The Ka-50 was reportedly selected over the Mil Mi-28 in 1986, although in early 1994 new competitive evaluation trials between the two types began. Further delays mean production funding for either type has been postponed, with only small number of each built.

The Ka-50N is a night capable version with FLIR, electro-optic sight and Russian or French avionics.

The two seat Ka-52 Alligator was originally developed because of Russian army concerns of pilot workload in the Ka-50. The all weather, day and night capability Ka-52 is unique among dedicated attack helicopters in that it seats two side by side in a redesigned nose. About 85% of the airframe remains unchanged from the Ka-50. First flight was on June 25 1997. It features a turreted FLIR and TV sensor above the cockpit, nose mounted radar, IR sensor and laser rangefinder, and Thales avionics, including helmet mounted sights.

The Ka-50-2 designation covers three proposed export variants of the Ka-52. Israel's IAI and Kamov jointly proposed the tandem two seat Ka-50-2 Erdogan to meet a Turkish attack helicopter requirement (won by the AH-1Z). It would have featured IAI developed glass cockpits and other systems. The other proposed Ka-50-2 variants are a single seater and a side-by-side two seater.

**Photo:** The Ka-50. (Ian Moy)

## Kamov Ka-60 Kasatka

**Country of origin:** Russia

**Type:** Battlefield and utility helicopter

**Powerplant:** Two 970kW (1300shp) max continuous rated RKBM Rybinsk RD-600V turboshafts driving a four blade main rotor and shrouded 11 blade tail rotor.

**Performance:** Max speed 300km/h (162kt), cruising speed 265km/h (143kt). Max rate of climb 2050ft/min. Hovering ceiling out of ground effect 6880ft. Range 700km (378nm).

**Weights:** Max takeoff 6500kg (14,317lb). Max external payload 2750kg (6062lb).

**Dimensions:** Main rotor diameter 13.50m (44ft 4in), length overall rotors turning 15.60m (51ft 2in), fuselage length 13.47m (44ft 2in), height overall 4.60m (15ft 1in). Main rotor disc area 143.1m² (1540.3sq ft)

**Accommodation:** Pilot and copilot side-by-side, seating for up to 16 troops in main cabin. Six stretchers and three attendants in medevac configuration. A VIP configuration could seat five to nine.

**Armament:** Could carry 80mm rockets, 7.62 or 12.7mm gun pods and missiles on detachable pylons.

**Operators:** None

**History:** Kamov has been developing the Ka-60 Kasatka (Killer Whale) as a replacement for the Russian army's Mi-8, but a lack of funding has slowed progress.

The predecessor to the Ka-60 was the single engined, coaxial main rotor equipped V.60, which won a Russian army evaluation against the Mil Mi-36 for the Mi-8 replacement in 1982. Kamov subsequently substantially redesigned the V.60 into the Ka-60, which, with a conventional tail rotor, shrouded tail rotor and twin engines, promised to be faster than the V.60. Originally the Ka-60 was scheduled to first fly in 1993, but development has been slowed by a lack of funding and firm orders from the Russian army, plus a decision to place emphasis on the civil Ka-62 variant.

The Ka-60 was officially rolled out at Lyubertsy in July 1997, the prototype first flew on December 10 1998 (official first flight was on December 24). The Russian army has yet to order the helicopter.

Ka-60 design features include 60% composite construction by weight, including the main rotor blades and fuselage, Russian avionics and RD-600 engines, run dry gearboxes, retractable undercarriage, Fenestron style shrouded tail rotor and dual systems redundancy. The main rotor blades feature swept tips and are designed to be resistant to 23mm shells. The transmission is designed to be resistant to 12.7mm bullets. Kamov says the Ka-60 has been designed with minimised IR, optical and radar signatures. Defensive systems include a Pastel radar warning receiver and Otklik laser warning system.

Various Ka-60 models have been proposed. The basic troop transport Ka-60 could be joined by the Ka-60U trainer, naval Ka-60K for utility missions and over the horizon targeting, and the reconnaissance Ka-60R. The Ka-62 civil variant is also being developed in Westernised Ka-62M form with GE T700s and five blade main rotor.

The Russian army requires the Ka-60U trainer first, production could start in 2003.

**Photo:** The Ka-60 prototype. (Sebastian Zacharias)

## Kawasaki C-1

**Country of origin:** Japan

**Type:** Tactical transport

**Powerplants:** Two 64.5kN (14,500lb) Pratt & Whitney JT8D-M-9 turbofans, licence built in Japan by Mitsubishi.

**Performance:** Max speed 805km/h (435kt), max cruising speed 704km/h (380kt), economical cruising speed 658km/h (355kt). Max initial rate of climb 3495ft/min. Takeoff run at MTOW 640m (2100ft). Range with max fuel and a 2200kg (4500lb) payload 3355km (1810nm), range with a 7900kg (17,415lb) payload 1295km (700nm).

**Weights:** Empty equipped 24,300kg (53,570lb), max takeoff 45,000kg (99,205lb).

**Dimensions:** Wing span 30.60m (100ft 5in), length 29.00m (95ft 2in), height 9.99m (32ft 9in). Wing area 120.5m² (1297.1sq ft).

**Accommodation:** Flightcrew of four, comprising two pilots, flight engineer and navigator. Can carry up to 60 equipped troops, or 45 paratroops or 36 stretchers plus medical attendants.

**Armament:** None

**Operators:** Japan

**History:** Japan's first large jet powered transport was developed for the Japan Air Self Defence Force (JASDF) to replace an aging fleet of Curtiss C-46 Commandos.

The JASDF formulated its C-X specification for a Japanese developed tactical transport for its C-46 replacement requirement. NAMC, a consortium of Japanese aerospace companies which had developed the YS-11 turboprop powered airliner, began work on the C-X in 1966. Kawasaki was responsible for the construction of the first three prototype XC-1 aircraft (one was a static test article), with a first flight on November 12 1970.

Kawasaki subsequently assumed overall responsibility for the C-1, although production remained a collaborative venture. Fuji built the outer wings, Mitsubishi the centre and rear fuselage and tail, Nihon the control surfaces and engine pods. Kawasaki built the forward fuselage and the wing centre section, as well as being responsible for final assembly and flight testing.

Just 31 C-1s were built, including prototypes and two preproduction aircraft. The first C-1 production delivery to the JASDF was in February 1974, while the last production aircraft was delivered in 1981.

The C-1 is of conventional military freighter configuration, with a T-tail, rear loading ramp and a high wing that does not obstruct the fuselage. Power is supplied by Mitsubishi licence built JT8D turbofans. The last five production C-1s had an additional fuel tank in the wing centre section.

Two notable C-1 conversions are the C-1Kai and the Asuka STOL research platform. The C-1Kai is a one-off ECM trainer and features flat bulbous nose and tail radomes, plus various antennas underneath the fuselage. The Asuka was fitted with four above wing turbofans and blown flaps.

The C-1 was not developed beyond its basic form and no export sales were sought. A number of variants were proposed, including an air-to-air inflight refueller, weather reconnaissance and electronic warfare versions, but none of these left the drawing board.

**Photo:** A Japan Air Self Defence Force C-1. (John Adlard)

## Kawasaki T-4

*Country of origin:* Japan

*Type:* Two seat advanced jet trainer

*Powerplants:* Two 16.4kN (3680lb) Ishikawajima-Harima F3-IHI-30 turbofans.

*Performance:* Max speed at altitude 1038km/h (560kt), max speed at sea level 1038km/h (560kt), cruising speed 797km/h (430kt). Max initial rate of climb 10,240ft/min. Service ceiling 50,000ft. Ferry range with drop tanks 1667km (900nm), range with standard fuel 1295km (700nm).

*Weights:* Empty 3790kg (8356lb), max takeoff 7500kg (16,535lb).

*Dimensions:* Wing span 9.94m (32ft 8in), length 13.00m (42ft 8in), height 4.60m (15ft 1in). Wing area 21.0m² (226.1sq ft).

*Accommodation:* Two in tandem.

*Armament:* Usually none, although theoretically can carry up to 2000kg (4410lb) of external ordnance. Two underwing pylons designed to carry fuel tanks.

*Operators:* Japan

*History:* The Kawasaki T-4 is the Japan Air Self Defence Force's intermediate and advanced pilot trainer, replacing the Fuji T-1 and Lockheed T-33 in service.

Kawasaki headed up a design team of Japanese aerospace companies to develop a new advanced trainer from the early 1980s. Kawasaki was selected as the prime contractor to develop the new trainer in September 1981. The T-4 was designed by a team led by Kohki Isozaki. Four XT-4 prototypes were built, and the first of these first flew on July 29 1985.

The T-4 features as much Japanese content as possible, including the engines, which are locally designed and built Ishikawajima-Harima F3 turbofans. The T-4's ailerons, fin, rudder and airbrakes are made from carbon fibre. Other design features are the high mounted supercritical wing with dogtooth leading edges and two hardpoints for drop tanks, stepped tandem cockpits with excellent visibility from the rear seat, Japanese ejection seats and a small rear baggage compartment for liaison duties. A centreline hardpoint beneath the fuselage can carry a target towing winch, an air sampling pod or an ECM pod, reflecting the T-4's secondary utility roles.

T-4 manufacture is a collaborative venture. Fuji constructs the rear fuselage, wings and tail unit, while Mitsubishi builds the centre fuselage including the air intakes. Fuji and Mitsubishi each have a 30% share of the T-4 production program. Prime contractor Kawasaki builds the forward fuselage and is responsible for final assembly and flight testing.

The Japanese Air Self Defence Force has so far ordered 212 T-4s to replace Fuji T-1s and Lockheed T-33s. T-4 production began in 1986 with deliveries from late 1988. Since the mid 1990s production has been running at about 10 aircraft a year. Export orders have not been sought.

Aside from training units, a small number serve with operational squadrons as liaison/currency aircraft, with some of these painted in a camouflage scheme. T-4s also service with the JASDF's Blue Impulse aerobatic display team.

*Photo:* A Kawasaki T-4. (MAP)

## Kawasaki OH-1

*Country of origin:* Japan

*Type:* Armed reconnaissance helicopter

*Powerplant:* Two 662kW (888shp) Mitsubishi TS1-10QT turboshafts driving a four blade main rotor and shrouded eight blade tail rotor.

*Performance:* Max speed 277km/h (150kt). Combat radius 200km (108nm). Range 550km (297nm).

*Weights:* Empty 2450kg (5400lb), max takeoff 3550kg (7826lb).

*Dimensions:* Main rotor diameter 11.6m (38ft 1in), fuselage length 12.0m (39ft 5in), height overall 3.8m (12ft 6in). Main rotor disc area

*Accommodation:* Pilot and gunner in tandem.

*Armament:* Four Toshiba Type 91 short range, lightweight infrared guided air-to-air missiles for self defence carried on stub wings.

*Operators:* Japan

*History:* Kawasaki has developed the OH-1 armed scout to replace the Japan Ground Self Defence Force's OH-6D.

The Japan Defence Agency's Technical Research and Development Institute (TRDI) issued request for proposals for a new scout helicopter to Japan's aerospace industry in April 1992. Kawasaki was selected as prime contractor to develop the new helicopter in September 1992, teaming with Fuji and Mitsubishi (with 20% program stakes each) as the Observation Helicopter Engineering Team.

A mockup of the provisionally designated OH-X was unveiled on September 2 1994. Six development helicopters were built (two were ground test articles), with the first prototype first flying on August 6 1996 (after being rolled out that March). Later in 1996 the OH-X was redesignated OH-1.

Kawasaki handed over the first XOH-1 prototype to the Japan Defence Agency on May 26 1997, in 1998 this helicopter's XTS1-10 turboshafts were replaced by the production TS1-10QT. The last of the four flying prototypes was handed over to the JDA in August 1997.

The first three production OH-1s were ordered in 1998. The first of these flew in June 1999 and was delivered to the JGSDF in January 2000. In all the JGSDF requires between 150 and 200 OH-1s.

The OH-1 features a number of advanced technologies. By weight, 37% of the OH-1's airframe is made from composite materials. The rotor blades and hingeless, bearingless hub are also made from composites, and the blades are designed to be resistant to 20mm shells. The Fenestron style shrouded tail rotor features eight unevenly spaced blades, the transmission can run dry for 30 minutes. The OH-1 is powered by specifically developed Mitsubishi TS1-10 turboshafts. Stub wings can carry air-to-air missiles for self defence or 235 litre external fuel tanks.

The cockpits feature twin liquid crystal displays, a Mil-Std 1553B databus, and dual HOCAS controls, while the pilot's station features a HUD. A roof mounted turret sight features a Fujitsu thermal imager, NEC colour TV camera and NEC rangefinder and designator. An ALQ-144 infrared jammer is mounted above and between the engine exhausts.

A growth version of the OH-1 has been studied which would feature more powerful engines. The OH-1 was also offered to meet the JGSDF's AH-X attack helicopter requirement, won by the AH-64D Apache.

*Photo:* The OH-1 entered service in 2000.

## LMAASA (FMA) IA-63 Pampa

**Country of origin:** Argentina

**Type:** Trainer and light ground attack aircraft

**Powerplant:** One 15.6kN (3500lb) Honeywell TFE731-2-2N turbofan.

**Performance:** Max speed 750km/h (405kt). Max initial rate of climb 5120ft/min. Service ceiling 42,325ft. Air-to-air gunnery training mission radius with 250kg (550lb) of external ordnance 440km (237nm). Air-to-ground combat radius with 1000kg (2205lb) external load 360km (195nm). Ferry range with max internal and external fuel 1000km (1850nm). Max endurance at 555km/h (300kt) 3hr 48min.

**Weights:** Empty 2820kg (6220lb), max takeoff 5000kg (11,025lb).

**Dimensions:** Wing span 9.69m (32ft 10in), length 10.90m (35ft 10in), height 4.29m (14ft 1in). Wing area 15.6m² (168.3sq ft).

**Accommodation:** Student and instructor in tandem.

**Armament:** Four underwing and one underfuselage hardpoints can carry a combined ordnance load of 1550kg (3415lb), including a 30mm DEFA cannon pod on the centreline station, and light bombs.

**Operators:** Argentina

**History:** The IA-63 Pampa was developed against an Argentine air force requirement for a modern armed trainer, and is so far South America's only locally developed jet trainer.

FMA (Fabrica Militar de Aviones) began development work on what would result in the Pampa in 1979, to met the Argentine air force's requirement for a new aircraft to replace its Morane-Saulnier MS.760 four place jets (described separately). To design the new trainer FMA teamed with Dornier of Germany, who had considerable experience in developing and building jet trainers through its co-development of the Alpha Jet with Dassault. The FMA/Dornier teaming came up with seven joint designs, with the selected configuration resembling the Alpha Jet.

Like the Alpha Jet, the IA-63 Pampa features a high wing, stepped tandem cockpits and side mounted air intakes. The Pampa differs in having a single turbofan (a Garrett, now Honeywell TFE731) and unswept wing and tailplane. For its secondary ground attack role the Pampa is equipped with five hardpoints and was upgraded with a HUD and an Elbit weapon delivery and navigation system.

The first prototype (EX-01) first flew on October 6 1984, while the first production aircraft's flew in October 1987. The Argentine air force ordered 18 Pampas, the first of which was delivered in April 1988.

Development of a navalised Pampa capable of operating off Argentina's aircraft carrier lapsed due to a lack of funding, although Argentina's navy remains interested in the aircraft.

Since 1995 FMA has been under Lockheed Martin Aircraft Argentina SA (LMAASA, originally LAASA) control. In 1997 LMAASA announced it was offering the Pampa NG (New Generation) with updated avionics. The Pampa NG A would be a trainer, the NG B a combat capable model with an uprated engine. The Pampa 2000 International version was also offered (unsuccessfully) in the USAF/USN JPATS program.

LMAASA built a new Pampa from spares and new components in 1999, demonstrating that it could still build the aircraft. An Argentine air force follow on order for 12 was announced in June 2000, with deliveries planned from 2003. Existing Pampas are being upgraded with IAI avionics.

**Photo:** Argentina's Pampas are based at El Plumerillo. (Santiago Rivas)

## Learjet 35, 36 & C-21

**Country of origin:** United States of America

**Type:** Multirole utility and VIP transport

**Powerplants:** Two 15.6kN (3500lb) Garrett TFE731-2-2B turbofans.

**Performance:** 35A/36A – Max speed 872km/h (471kt), max cruising speed 852km/h (460kt), economical cruising speed 774km/h (418kt). Max initial rate of climb 4350ft/min. Service ceiling 41,000ft. Range with four passengers and max fuel 4070km (2195nm) for 35A; 4673km (2522nm) for 36A.

**Weights:** 35A/36A – Empty equipped 4590kg (10,119lb), max takeoff 8300kg (18,300lb).

**Dimensions:** 35/36 – Wing span over tip tanks 12.04m (39ft 6in), length 14.83m (48ft 8in), height 3.73m (12ft 3in). Wing area 23.5m² (253.3sq ft).

**Accommodation:** Flightcrew of two. Seating for up to eight in main cabin in 35 and 31, or up to six in 36A. Can carry light freight.

**Armament:** None

**Operators:** Bolivia, Brazil, Chile, Finland, Japan, Saudi Arabia, Switzerland, Thailand, USA.

**History:** The Learjet series of business jets serves widely with a number of military air arms as utility and VIP transports.

The original six to eight seat turbojet powered Learjet 23 first flew on October 7 1963. It was replaced by the Lear 24 in 1966, while the Learjet 25 introduced a 1.27m (4ft 2in) fuselage stretch allowing seating for up to eight passengers. The Learjet 28 and 29 Longhorns were based on the 25 but introduced a new increased span wing with drag reducing winglets.

The Learjet 35 and 36 are larger, turbofan powered developments of the initial Learjet models. The availability of the Garrett AiResearch TFE731 turbofan in the late 1960s led to the development of the stretched Learjet 35, which first flew on August 22 1973. The Learjet 36 is similar, but sacrifices seating capacity for range. The improved 35A and 36A appeared in 1976.

Further development of the 35 and 36 resulted in the 31, which combines the 35/36's fuselage and powerplants with the wing (including winglets) of the Learjet 55. It replaced the 35/36 in production.

A small number of Lear 24s and 25s survive in military service, although most military Lears are 35s and 36s. They are used for a variety of missions ranging from VIP transport, to photo survey and reconnaissance, light transport, staff transport, medevac, target towing and EW training.

The US Air Force and Air National Guard acquired 85 Learjet 35As as the C-21. These are used as Operational Support Aircraft transporting priority freight and for medevac and staff transport.

Learjet also marketed a range of military developments of the 35 and 36. The PC-35A maritime patrol aircraft was offered with a search radar, ESM, FLIR, MAD and sonobuoys; the RC-35A and RC-36A reconnaissance platforms were offered with a variety of sensors; while the UC-35A is a utility transport. Japan's navy operates five modified U-36As for target towing, electronic warfare training and anti ship missile simulation.

**Photo:** A Finnish air force Learjet 35A used for electronic warfare training. (Lassi Tolvanen)

## Let L 410 Turbolet

*Country of origin:* Czech Republic

*Type:* Light tactical and utility transport

*Powerplants:* 410 UVP-E – Two 560kW (751shp) Motorlet M 601 E turboprops driving five blade propellers.

*Performance:* 410 UVP-E – Max cruising speed 380km/h (205kt), economical cruising speed 365km/h (197kt). Max initial rate of climb 1420ft/min. Service ceiling 19,700ft. Takeoff run at max takeoff weight 445m (1460ft). Range with max fuel (including wingtip tanks), a 920kg (2030lb) payload and reserves 1318km (707nm).

*Weights:* 410 UVP-E – Empty (without tip tanks) 4020kg (8662lb), max takeoff 6400kg (14,109lb).

*Dimensions:* 410 UVP-E – Wing span (with tip tanks) 19.98m (65ft 7in), length 14.42m (47ft 4in), height 5.83m (19ft 2in). Wing area 34.9m² (375.2sq ft).

*Accommodation:* Flightcrew of one or two. Standard seating for 15 at three abreast. Alternatively seats 12 paratroops and loadmaster. Can be configured for freight. Air ambulance version configured for six stretcher patients and six seated injured or medical attendants.

*Armament:* None

*Operators:* Bulgaria, Czech Republic, Germany, Latvia, Libya, Lithuania, Russia, Slovakia, Slovenia.

*History:* This very successful Czech regional airliner was first built in response to an Aeroflot requirement, but has also seen military service with a number of Eastern European countries.

Let began initial design studies of the 15 seat L 410 in 1966. The resulting design, named the Turbolet, was conventional, but was designed to be capable of operating from unprepared strips. The all new Czech designed Walter (now Motorlet) M 601 engine was selected, but was not available in time to power the prototypes and so Pratt & Whitney Canada PT6A-27s were fitted in their place. First flight occurred on April 16 1969 and series production began in 1970. Initial production L 410s were also powered by the PT6A and production aircraft were not fitted with the M 601 until 1973.

The L 410 was replaced from 1979 by the L 410 UVP with a 0.47m (1ft 7in) fuselage stretch, M 601B engines and detail refinements. The UVP was in turn replaced by the UVP-E which featured a reconfigured interior to allow seating for up to 19 passengers and M 601E powerplants.

The L 410 proved to be quite popular as a regional airliner, and over 1000 have been built. While most of those aircraft were for Aeroflot and various east European state owned airlines, others were delivered for military use as utility transports. Military duties include freight and troop transport, communications and paradropping.

The L 420 is an improved civil variant with more powerful M 601F engines, higher weights and improved performance, designed to meet Western certification requirements. It first flew in November 1993 and has US civil certification.

US company Ayres bought Let in 1998 and planned to develop the L 410/420 line, however the company filed for bankruptcy in mid 2000, leaving Let's future in doubt, and aircraft manufacture suspended.

*Photo:* A Lithuanian air force L 410. (Joris van Boven/Sentry)

## Lockheed T-33 Shooting Star

*Country of origin:* United States of America

*Type:* Advanced trainer, light attack, liaison aircraft and EW trainer

*Powerplant:* T-33A – One 24.0kN (5400lb) Allison J33-A-35 turbojet.

*Performance:* T-33A – Max speed 965km/h (520kt), cruising speed 732km/h (395kt). Max initial rate of climb 4870ft/min. Service ceiling 48,000ft. Ferry range with tip tanks 2050km (1105nm), range with internal fuel 1650km (890nm).

*Weights:* T-33A – Empty equipped 3795kg (8365lb), max takeoff 6830kg (15,060lb).

*Dimensions:* T-33A – Wing span 11.85m (38ft 11in), length 11.51m (37ft 9in), height 3.55m (11ft 8in). Wing area 21.8m² (234.0sq ft).

*Accommodation:* Two in tandem. Pilot only in RT-33.

*Armament:* Can be fitted with two 12.7mm (0.50in) M-3 machine guns mounted in the nose. Can carry up to 910kg (2000lb) of external armament including bombs or rockets.

*Operators:* Bolivia, Canada, Ecuador, Mexico, Paraguay.

*History:* The T-33 is the most successful jet trainer in history, with more than 6000 built. Today significant numbers survive in service more than half a century after its first flight.

The T-33 is a development of the F-80 Shooting Star, the USAAF's first operational jet fighter. The F-80 first flew in prototype form on January 8 1944 and saw combat in Korea. The T-33 arose from a USAF requirement for an advanced two seat jet trainer, which Lockheed was easily able to meet by stretching the F-80 and adding a second seat under a lengthened canopy. The first prototype, designated TF-80C, first flew on March 22 1948.

Lockheed built 5691 T-33s between 1948 and 1959. The largest T-33, or T-bird, operator was the USAF, while just under 700 modified examples were delivered to the US Navy as TV-2 SeaStars (or T-33B from 1962). Several thousand T-birds were built under the USA's MAP (Military Assistance Program) and were delivered to friendly nations around the world.

Lockheed built variants of the T-33 included the AT-33, an armed close air support T-bird delivered to various nations under MAP, and the RT-33, a single seat variant with reconnaissance sensors in the nose.

The Shooting Star was built under licence in Japan by Kawasaki (210 built) and in Canada. Canadair built 656 Rolls-Royce Nene powered CL-30 Silver Stars, designated the CT-133 in Canadian Forces service.

Twenty-seven CT-133s survive in CF service, providing electronic warfare training and target/adversary training to Canada's CF-18s, army anti-aircraft defence systems and navy. The CT-133 fleet is due to be phased out beginning March 31 2002, although four will be retained for test support use.

Bolivia, Ecuador and Mexico both operate large T-33 fleets. Bolivia's T-33s and AT-33s are its only frontline fighters, while Mexico uses its 30 AT-33s for counter-insurgency and advanced training roles.

The Skyfox was a substantially reworked development of the T-33 with two Garrett TFE731 turbofans designed by Skyfox in the USA. A demonstrator flew in 1983, but no customers were found.

*Photo:* A Canadian CT-133. The basic P-80/T-33 family has been in military service longer than any other jet aircraft. (Paul Merritt)

# Lockheed F-104 Starfighter

**Country of origin:** United States of America

**Type:** Multirole fighter

**Powerplant:** F-104ASA – One 52.8kN (11,870lb) dry and 79.6kN (17,900lb) with afterburning General Electric J79-GE-19 turbojet.

**Performance:** F-104ASA – Max speed at 36,000ft Mach 2.2 or 2333km/h (1260kt), max speed at sea level 1465km/h (790kt), max cruising speed at 36,000ft 980km/h (530kt). Max initial rate of climb 55,000ft/min. Service ceiling 58,000ft. Ferry range with drop tanks 2920km (1575nm), combat radius with max fuel 1247km (673nm).

**Weights:** F-104ASA – Empty 6760kg (14,903lb), max takeoff 14,060kg (30,995lb). Internal fuel 2641kg (5824lb).

**Dimensions:** F-104ASA – Wing span without tip tanks 6.68m (21ft 11in), length 16.69m (54ft 9in), height 4.11m (13ft 6in). Wing area 18.2m² (196.1sq ft).

**Accommodation:** Pilot only, or two in tandem in TF-104.

**Armament:** F-104ASA – One 20mm T171ES Vulcan six barrel cannon. Can carry up to 3400kg (7495lb) of ordnance including AIM-9L Sidewinders, Selenia Aspide medium range AAMs, conventional bombs and rockets.

**Operators:** Italy.

**History:** Lockheed's Starfighter was intended as a day fighter, but grew into a capable fighter-bomber, with 2406 built.

Lockheed's Kelly Johnson led Skunk Works began work on the F-104 in 1952 after evaluating the experiences of American fighter pilots in Korea. In designing the new fighter performance was considered the overriding driver.

The resulting aircraft was remarkable in that it featured incredibly small, straight wings (only 10cm/4in deep at their thickest points) with blown flaps and a single J79 turbojet engine (the most advanced engine of the day) giving a max speed of Mach 2.2. The small size and powerful single engine allowed Mach 2 performance in an aircraft that defied the trends of greater complexity, weight and hence cost.

The XF-104 prototype first flew on February 7 1954 powered by a Wright XJ65 (Sapphire) turbojet. Service entry was in 1958, although the USAF had transferred the survivors of its F-104A/B/C/D fleet to the Air National Guard by 1968. USAF experience with the F-104 was less than favourable, with high attrition.

The F-104 gained a new lease of life with the F-104G model, which was redesigned as a fighter-bomber. The F-104G first flew on October 5 1960 and introduced a more powerful engine and a multirole nav/attack system. In what was termed the 'Sale of the Century', in 1959 Belgium, Germany, Italy and the Netherlands selected the F-104 for a joint production program. Germany was the largest customer, taking delivery of 750, although Luftwaffe attrition was very high. The F-104G was also built under licence in Japan as the F-104J and in Canada as the CF-104G.

Aeritalia (now Alenia) in Italy built 246 (including 40 for Turkey) AIM-7 Sparrow capable F-104S Starfighters through to 1979. As the F-104ASA, 147 Italian Starfighters were further upgraded with FIAR Setter radar and Selenia Aspide compatibility through to 1993. Around 100 remain in service, due to be replaced by the Eurofighter Typhoon.

**Photo:** An Italian F-104ASA. (Paul Merritt)

# Lockheed U-2

**Country of origin:** United States of America

**Type:** High altitude electronic and optical reconnaissance aircraft

**Powerplant:** U-2S – One 84.5kN (19,000lb) General Electric F118-GE-101 turbofan.

**Performance:** U-2S – Max cruising speed 690km/h (373kt). Operational ceiling 85,000ft. Range over 12,260km (5566nm). Endurance 12hr.

**Weights:** U-2S – Operating empty 6487kg (14,288lb), max takeoff 18,144kg (39,965lb).

**Dimensions:** U-2S – Wing span 31.39m (103ft 0in), length 19.13m (62ft 9in), height 4.88m (16ft 0in). Wing area approx 92.9m² (1000sq ft).

**Accommodation:** Pilot only, except two in tandem in U-2ST.

**Armament:** None

**Operators:** USA

**History:** The high flying U-2 remains an important part of the USA's intelligence gathering capabilities.

In 1954 the US began development of a purpose built high altitude spyplane. Development was entrusted to Lockheed's Skunk Works, with the black nature of the program responsible for the U-2 designation (U for utility) to hide the aircraft's true role.

The U-2 first flew in August 1955. Subsequent production comprised 48 U-2A/B/C single seaters and five two seat U-2Ds. These had outstanding high altitude performance and were successfully used by the USAF and CIA for a number of years. One such CIA operated aircraft, piloted by Gary Powers, gained infamy when it was shot down by a SAM while operating over the USSR in April 1960.

The early U-2s were airframe hour limited, so Lockheed developed the larger U-2R. The U-2R first flew on August 28 1967 and 12 initial production aircraft were operated by the USAF and the CIA. The U-2R featured a larger airframe, allowing the carriage of more sensors and fuel. Two seaters were designated U-2RT.

The U-2 line was reopened again in 1979, this time to build 37 new TR-1As (including two TR-1Bs and a U-2RT – both two seaters). The TR-1 was designed for tactical reconnaissance (hence the TR prefix), and combined the U-2R's airframe with the ASARS-2 battlefield surveillance radar. The TR-1 was later redesignated U-2R in recognition of the fact that the two aircraft were basically identical. NASA operates three similar ER-2s.

From 1992 to 1998 Lockheed re-engined surviving U-2Rs to U-2S standard with a more powerful yet more efficient General Electric F118-101 turbofan, extending service life to 2020. The two seaters have been redesignated U-2ST.

U-2 sensors are carried in detachable noses, in the forward fuselage and in underwing pods, while some aircraft carry Senior Span satellite communications equipment for real time global data transmission in a teardrop shaped dorsal mounted pod.

The ASARS-2 Radar Improvement Program is upgrading the ASARS-2 radar, enhancing real time targeting, broad area coverage and ground moving target indication, with a computer for onboard image processing. The U-2 fleet is also being upgraded with modern avionics including three liquid crystal multifunction displays, and an upfront control and display unit.

**Photo:** U-2s are operated from Beale AFB in California. (USAF)

# Lockheed C-130 Hercules

**Country of origin:** United States of America

**Type:** Tactical and multirole transport

**Powerplants:** C-130E – Four 3020kW (4050shp) Allison T56-A-17 turboprops driving four blade propellers.

**Performance:** C-130E – Max cruising speed 592km/h (320kt), econ cruising speed 547km/h (295kt). Max initial rate of climb 1830ft/min. Service ceiling 23,000ft. Takeoff run over a 15m (50ft) obstacle 1700m (5580ft). Range with max fuel and a 9080kg (20,000lb) payload 7565km (4085nm), range with max payload 3895km (2105nm).

**Weights:** C-130E – Operating empty 33,064kg (72,892lb), max normal TOW 70,310kg (155,000lb), max overload TOW 79,380kg (175,000lb).

**Dimensions:** C-130E/H – Wing span 40.41m (132ft 7in), length 29.79m (97ft 9in), height 11.66m (38ft 3in). Wing area 162.1m² (1745.0sq ft).

**Accommodation:** Typical crew of five comprising two pilots, flight engineer, navigator and loadmaster. Standard layouts seat 92 troops, or 64 paratroops, or 74 stretcher patients and two medical attendants. Can carry light armoured vehicles, artillery pieces and 4WDs.

**Armament:** None, except on AC-130, described separately.

**Operators:** In service with over 60 countries incl Australia, Brazil, Canada, Israel, Japan, Saudi Arabia, Taiwan, Thailand, Turkey, UK, USA.

**History:** The C-130 Hercules is the world's most successful and prolific postwar military transport, with over 2200 built over four decades.

The Hercules was developed against a 1951 US Air Force requirement for a new tactical transport to equip the Military Air Transport Service (MATS). The USAF ordered two YC-130 prototypes from Lockheed in July 1951 and the first of these flew for the first time on August 23 1954. The first production C-130A flew in April 1955.

The Hercules established the basic military transport configuration, with a high wing with minimal obstruction of the fuselage and a rear loading freight ramp. Other features included Allison T56 turboprops, pressurisation and limited STOL performance. Apart from the blunt, radar-less nose of early production C-130As, the Hercules' external configuration has remained largely unchanged.

The improved C-130B entered service in mid 1959. Compared with the C-130A, the B introduced more powerful engines driving four blade props, strengthened undercarriage and greater fuel capacity. In 1961 production switched to the C-130E with more powerful engines with greater hot and high performance, increased max takeoff weight, some structural strengthening and larger external tanks, mounted between the engines (rather than outboard of them).

The C-130H was introduced in 1965. Early C-130Hs featured more powerful engines, while changes introduced to the H over the following two decades included structural strengthening and updated avionics. The C-130H-30 is stretched by 4.57m (15ft).

Civil standard Hercules are designated L-100 and have been built in standard length L-100, stretched L-100-20 and further stretched L-100-30 (equivalent to the C-130H-30) versions.

The last T56 powered C-130 (a USAF C-130H) was delivered in January 1998. The USAF meanwhile has contracted Boeing to perform the C-130 Avionics Modification Program, which will see about 500 C-130E/H upgraded with a common cockpit (based on the 737-700's).

**Photo:** An Israeli C-130. (Lassi Tolvanen)

# Lockheed Martin C-130J Hercules II

**Country of origin:** United States of America

**Type:** Tactical and multirole transport

**Powerplants:** Four 3458kW (4637shp) Rolls-Royce AE 2100D3 turboprops rated at 3424kW (4591shp) driving six blade propellers.

**Performance:** C-130J – Max cruising speed 645km/h (348kt), economical cruising speed 628km/h (339kt). Max initial rate of climb 2100ft/min. Time to 20,000ft 14min. Max effort takeoff run 550m (1800ft), normal takeoff run 930m (3050ft). Range with a 18,155kg (40,000lb) payload 5250km (2835nm).

**Weights:** C-130J – Operating empty 34,274kg (75,562lb), max takeoff 70,305kg (155,000lb), max overload 79,380kg (175,000lb). C-130J-30 – Same except operating empty 35,966kg (79,291lb).

**Dimensions:** Wing span 40.41m (132ft 7in), length 29.79m (97ft 9in), height 11.84m (38ft 10in). Wing area 162.1m² (1745.0sq ft). J-30 – Same except length 34.37m (112ft 9in), height 11.81m (38ft 9in).

**Accommodation:** Flightcrew of two pilots. C-130J can seat 92 troops, or 64 paratroops, or 74 stretcher patients and two medical attendants. C-130J-30 can seat 128 troops.

**Armament:** None

**Operators:** Australia, Denmark*, Italy*, UK, USA*.

**History:** The C-130J Hercules II is a comprehensive update of the C-130, with new cockpit, engines and systems.

Lockheed began development of the C-130J primarily to offer the US Air Force a replacement for its aging fleet of C-130E Hercules. The USAF was unprepared to fund the development of a new Hercules variant, so Lockheed Martin developed an improved C-130 as a private venture, aimed at both USAF and export requirements.

The C-130J and stretched C-130J-30 airframes differ little from their predecessor C-130H and C-130H-30 donors. The J features composite flaps and leading edge surfaces, and the external fuel tanks are deleted (although they can be added to extend range), but the airframe is otherwise unchanged. New generation Rolls-Royce AE 2100 turboprops drive six blade, swept Dowty propellers. The J can be optionally fitted with a refuelling probe and underwing hose and drogue air-to-air refuelling pods.

Big changes inside the Hercules II include simplified wiring and systems and the new two crew flightdeck. The flightdeck features two HUDs, four large multifunction displays, five monochrome displays and fighter style controls on the control columns.

The first C-130J (a RAF C-130J-30/C.4) after some delays first flew on April 5 1996. Unexpected problems delayed first customer deliveries by over 18 months to August 1998 (the first to the UK's Defence Evaluation Research Agency for further trials of RAF Js). The definitive Block 5.3 software standard for the J was released in September 2001.

C-130J customers include the UK (12 C-130J-30s/C.5s & 10 C-130Js/C.4s), Australia (12 C-130J-30s), Denmark (three J-30s), the USA with 49 so far (including 10 WC-130J weather reconnaissance aircraft, five EC-130J Command Solo psychological warfare platforms, and 11 KC-130Js for the USMC – out of a total requirement for 79), and Italy (18 C-130Js, some of which will be used as tankers).

In 1999 Australia rejected an AEW&C variant of the C-130J-30.

**Photo:** A RAAF C-130J-30 Hercules II. (Paul Sadler)

# Lockheed C-130 Special Missions Variants

**Country of origin:** United States of America

**Type:** Special missions adaptations of the C-130 Hercules

**Powerplants:** MC-130E – Four 3020kW (4050shp) Allison T56-A-7 turboprops. AC-130H – Four 3362kW (4508shp) T56-A-15s.

**Performance:** MC-130E – Max speed 590km/h (318kt). Max initial rate of climb 1600ft/min. Range 3705km (2000nm). AC-130H – Max speed 612km/h (330kt), cruising speed 592km/h (320kt). Max initial rate of climb 1830ft/min. Endurance 5hr.

**Weights:** MC-130E – Empty 33,065kg (72,892lb), max takeoff 70,310kg (155,000lb). AC-130H – Empty 33,065kg (72,892lb), max takeoff 70,310kg (155,000lb).

**Dimensions:** Wing span 40.41m (132ft 7in), length 29.79m (97ft 9in), height 11.66m (38ft 3in). Wing area 162.1m² (1745.0sq ft).

**Accommodation:** Basic flightcrew of four.

**Armament:** AC-130H – Two M61 Vulcan 20mm cannons, two 7.62mm miniguns (not usually carried), two 40mm Bofors cannons and a 105mm Howitzer.

**Operators:** Special Missions – USA. KC-130 – Argentina, Brazil, Canada, Indonesia, Israel, Saudi Arabia, Singapore, Spain, UK, USA.

**History:** The versatility and longevity of the basic Hercules airframe is reflected in the multitude of special missions adaptations.

The USAF began modification work on a C-130A to gunship configuration in 1965. A further 17 were modified to AC-130As (equipment fit included two 7.62mm miniguns, two 20mm cannons and two 40mm Bofors cannons, plus a beacon tracker and radar). Their combat success in Vietnam led to the procurement of 11 similar AC-130Es. From 1973 the 10 survivors were upgraded to AC-130H standard with T56-A-15s, and then subsequently fitted with a 105mm Howitzer. Rockwell AC-130U Spectres have modern sensors and a 25mm GAU-12 cannon in place of the M61s.

The US Navy operates drone carrying DC-130s, while the USAF operates the similar NC-130H. The EC-130 designation covers a number of EW Hercules adaptations. EC-130E variants include the ABCCC (Airborne Command & Control Centre); the Elint EC-130E(CL); and the EC-130E(RR) 'Rivet Rider', which apart from comint and sigint, can be used for TV and radio broadcasts. The EC-130H Compass Call is a stand-off jammer.

The HC-130 designation covers USAF SAR aircraft. Forty-three HC-130Hs were delivered with the ARD-117 Cook Aerial Tracker in a blunt radome. The HC-130N is similar but equipped for inflight refuelling (hose & drogue). New build HC-130H(N)s have modern avionics.

The KC-130 is a tanker variant. The USMC is the largest operator, with KC-130Fs, KC-130Rs, KC-130Ts and stretched KC-130T-30s (with replacement by KC-130Js underway). Ski equipped US Navy LC-130s were used for Antarctic support operations, until replaced by ANG C-130Hs.

The USAF's MC-130 Combat Talons are used in support of special forces operations. MC-130Es are fitted with a weather/nav radar with a terrain following function in a blunt nose, Fulton STAR personnel recovery nose forks and a retractable FLIR pod. The MC-130H has an APQ-170 radar in a reprofiled nose.

**Photo:** An AC-130H. (USAF)

# LMATTS C-27J Spartan

**Countries of origin:** Italy and the United States of America

**Type:** Tactical transport

**Powerplants:** Two 3460kW (4640shp) Rolls-Royce AE 2100D2 turboprops driving six blade Dowty propellers.

**Performance:** Max speed 602km/h (325kt). Service ceiling 30,000ft. Takeoff run 410m (1345ft). Range with max payload 2148km (1160nm), with 6000kg (13,228lb) payload 4630km (2500nm). Radius with 46 paratroops 2037km (1100nm).

**Weights:** Operating empty 17,000kg (37,479lb), max takeoff 31,800kg (66,138lb).

**Dimensions:** Wing span 28.70m (94ft 2in), length 22.70m (74ft 6in), height overall unloaded 10.57m (34ft 8in), loaded height overall 9.70m (31ft 10in). Wing area 82.0m² (882.7sq ft).

**Accommodation:** Flightcrew of two with provision for a loadmaster. Typical accommodation for 46 fully equipped troops, or 40 fully equipped paratroops. Can carry an approx 10 tonne payload comprising light vehicles and artillery among others.

**Armament:** None

**Operators:** Italy*.

**History:** The LMATTS (Lockheed Martin Alenia Tactical Transport Systems) C-27J Spartan is an advanced and improved development of the Alenia G222 with significant commonality with the C-130J Hercules II.

The concept of an improved G222 arose from Lockheed Martin and Alenia discussions in 1995 on industrial offsets following from Italy's then mooted purchase of C-130Js for its air force. Initially discussions focused on fitting the G222 with the C-130J's advanced EFIS cockpit displays and improved T64G variants of the G222's existing powerplant driving four (rather than three) blade propellers. This improved transport was dubbed the G222J.

The updated G222 concept evolved to the stage where in February 1996 Lockheed Martin and Alenia jointly launched the C-27J project (the US style C-27J designation is unofficial, but reflects that the aircraft is a C-130J style upgrade of the G222, which saw limited USAF service as the C-27A Spartan). With the new designation came the most important change to the G222, the Allison (now Rolls-Royce) AE 2100 turboprops, driving swept six blade Dowty propellers (as on the C-130J).

The joint LMATTS company was formed in 1997. The C-27J prototype, converted from Alenia's G222 demonstrator, first flew on September 25 1999. The second C-27J, the first new build aircraft, flew on May 12 2000. The C-27J is assembled in Italy but features some Lockheed Martin made components.

Key C-27J features include Rolls-Royce AE 2100D2 engines (which are significantly more powerful than the G222's T64s but are 5% more fuel efficient), a two crew flightdeck with Honeywell avionics including five colour LCDs, new APU and undercarriage, and the C-130J's internal loading systems. Performance improvements over the G222 include 15% faster cruising speed and 35% greater range payload range, plus significantly lower operating costs.

Italy is the launch customer for the C-27J, buying 12 (plus six options) for delivery from 2002.

**Photo:** The first two C-27Js. (LMATTS)

## Lockheed Electra

*Country of origin:* United States of America

*Type:* Maritime patrol and transport aircraft

*Powerplants:* Four 2800kW (3750shp) Allison 501-D13 turboprops driving four blade propellers.

*Performance:* L-188C – Max speed 720km/h (390kt), max cruising speed 652km/h (352kt), economical cruising speed 602km/h (325kt). Service ceiling 27,000ft. Range with max payload 3450km (1910nm), with max fuel 4023km (2180nm).

*Weights:* L-188C – Operating empty 27,895kg (61,500lb), max takeoff 52,664kg (116,000lb).

*Dimensions:* Wing span 30.18m (99ft 0in), length 31.90m (104ft 6in), height 10.01m (32ft 10in). Wing area 120.8m² (1300sq ft).

*Accommodation:* Flightcrew of two pilots and flight engineer. Max payload in freighter configuration is approximately 12 tonnes (26,000lb). Seating for up to 98 in passenger configuration.

*Armament:* None

*Operators:* Argentina, Bolivia, Honduras.

*History:* The Electra is one of the world's first turboprop airliners. Ex civil examples are in service with Argentina, Bolivia and Honduras.

The L-188 Electra resulted from an American Airlines requirement for a domestic airliner. In June 1955 Lockheed was awarded an order for 35 such aircraft. Lockheed's design, designated the L-188, featured a low wing and four turboprops – Allison 501s, the civil equivalent of the C-130's T-56). By the time the first prototype flew on December 6 1957 airlines had placed 144 orders. However, any optimism Lockheed felt about a strong sales future would have been short lived, as the arrival of jet airliners and two mysterious Electra crashes (later found to be the fault of a faulty engine mount design) soon after the type had entered service contributed to orders drying up.

As an interim measure following the crashes speed restrictions were imposed on Electras while the problem was resolved. Strengthened nacelles, nacelle mountings and a stronger wing structure overcame the problems, but it was not until 1961 that the speed restrictions were lifted.

Two versions of the Electra were built. The L-188A was the basic production aircraft and accounted for most Electra sales. The L-188C also entered service in 1959 and had more fuel and higher weights. From 1967 Lockheed converted 41 Electras to freighters or convertible freighter/passenger aircraft, fitting a strengthened floor and a large cargo door forward of the wing on the left side. Other companies have also converted Electras to freighters. In all 170 production Electras were built.

In the early 1980s the Argentine navy acquired four L-188A Electras which it converted for maritime patrol, with the primary change being the installation of an APS-705 search radar in an underfuselage radome. Subsequently IAI converted one of these for Elint and Sigint reconnaissance. The two surviving maritime patrol aircraft were augmented by eight ex USN P-3B Orions from late 1997.

Bolivia and Honduras are the only other current military Electra operators, with a single example in service each. Bolivia's is stored, while Honduras' Electra is used for VIP transport.

*Photo:* One of the Argentine navy's converted Electras.

## Lockheed Martin P-3 Orion

*Country of origin:* United States of America

*Type:* Maritime patrol aircraft

*Powerplants:* P-3C – Four 3660kW (4910ehp) Allison T56-A-14 turboprops driving four blade propellers.

*Performance:* P-3C – Max speed 760km/h (411kt), econ cruising speed 608km/h (328kt), patrol speed at 1500ft 380km/h (206kt). Ceiling 28,300ft. Ferry range 8945km (4830nm). Mission radius 3hr on station at 1500ft 2495km (1345nm). Max endurance on four engines 12hr 20min, on two engines 17hr 10min.

*Weights:* P-3C – Empty 27,890kg (61,490lb), max normal takeoff 61,235kg (135,000lb), max permissible weight 64,610kg (142,000lb).

*Dimensions:* P-3B/C – Wing span 30.37m (99ft 8in), length 35.61m (116ft 10in), height 10.27m (33ft 9in). Wing area 120.8m² (1300.0sq ft).

*Accommodation:* Normal crew complement of 10 comprises two pilots, flight engineer and navigator on flightdeck, with a tactical coordinator, two acoustic sensor operators, a MAD operator and two observers/sonobuoy loaders. Has seating/bunks for a relief crew.

*Armament:* Internal weapons bay can carry eight torpedoes or eight depth bombs. A total of 10 underwing hardpoints can carry up to eight AGM-86 Harpoons, or 10 torpedoes, or 10 mines.

*Operators:* Argentina, Australia, Brazil, Chile, Greece, Japan, Netherlands, New Zealand, Norway, Pakistan, Portugal, Sth Korea, Spain, Thailand.

*History:* The Orion was developed against a 1957 US Navy requirement to replace the Lockheed P2V/SP-2 Neptune.

Lockheed's submission was based on a shortened Electra airliner and was selected for development in April 1958. The first Orion prototype (converted from an Electra) first flew on November 25 1959.

Features of the Orion (which entered service in 1962) include a MAD mounted in a boom extending from the tail, search radar and an internal weapons bay forward of the wing.

Initial production was of the P-3A. The P-3B, with more powerful engines, was delivered from 1965. The definitive P-3C was introduced in 1969 and featured a new APS-115 radar, MAD and processing equipment. The P-3C was built in improved Update I, II, II.5 and III forms.

The US Navy also employs a number of special missions P-3 developments. The VP-3 is a VIP/staff transport conversion of early P-3A/Bs, the EP-3E 'Aries' is an Elint platform, the TP-3A is a crew trainer, the UP-3A a utility transport, WP-3As perform weather reconnaissance, RP-3As are designed for oceanographic reconnaissance and NP-3As are used for trials work. The EP-3J is an EW trainer. The US Customs service operates AEW configured Orions fitted with APS-138 radar.

Three significant US Orion upgrades/developments have all been cancelled or dropped for budgetary reasons. USN Orions are instead being fitted with a new radar (APS-134). Lockheed Martin plans to offer its Orion 21 to meet the USN's Multi-Mission Aircraft (MMA) requirement to replace its P-3s from 2015.

Australia is upgrading its P-3Cs to AP-3C standard with new Elta radar, MAD and processing equipment. Over 700 Orions have been built, including 100 under licence by Kawasaki in Japan. US production ceased in 1995, but the line could be reopened.

*Photo:* A Norwegian P-3C. (Lockheed Martin)

# Lockheed CP-140 Aurora & Arcturus

**Country of origin:** United States of America

**Type:** Maritime patrol aircraft

**Powerplants:** Four 3660kW (4910ehp) Allison T56-A-14 turboprops driving four blade propellers.

**Performance:** CP-140 – Max cruising speed 732km/h (395kt). Max initial rate of climb 2980ft/min. Service ceiling 28,250ft. Ferry range 8340km (4500nm). Operational radius for an 8hr 10min patrol 1850km (1000nm).

**Weights:** CP-140 – Empty 27,892kg (61,491lb), max permissible load 64,610kg (142,000lb).

**Dimensions:** Wing span 30.37m (99ft 8in), length 35.61m (116ft 10in), height 10.27m (33ft 9in). Wing area 120.8m$^2$ (1300.0sq ft).

**Accommodation:** Crew complement of 11, including flightcrew of four comprising two pilots, a flight engineer and navigator.

**Armament:** Theoretical armament as for P-3C, including eight torpedoes or eight depth bombs in internal weapons bay. A total of 10 underwing hardpoints can carry up to eight AGM-86 Harpoons, or 10 torpedoes, or 10 mines. Can be fitted with two AIM-9 Sidewinder AAMs for self defence.

**Operators:** Canada

**History:** The CP-140 Aurora is a unique development of the Orion which combines the P-3's airframe with the electronic systems of the US Navy S-3 Viking, while the CP-140A Arcturus is a down spec Aurora optimised for training and fishery patrols.

In 1976 the Canadian Armed Forces ordered the Aurora to replace the CP-107 Argus. While the resulting aircraft closely resembles the P-3 Orion externally, internal changes have made the Aurora a significantly different aircraft. The Aurora was fitted with the Texas Instruments APS-116 search radar, a Texas Instruments ASQ-501 MAD and an AYK-10 processing computer, all equipment featured on the S-3A Viking (described separately).

Other equipment allows the Aurora to fly a number of secondary missions including pollution patrol, aerial survey, shipping, fishing and Arctic surveillance, and search and rescue. The Aurora also carries a crew of 11, rather than 10 on the Orion.

Canada ordered 18 Auroras and the first of these first flew on March 22 1979. The last example was delivered in July 1981. They currently serve at CFB Greenwood, Nova Scotia (13) and at CFB Comox, British Colombia (five).

The CP-140A Arcturus is a stripped down development of the Aurora and has the twin roles of Aurora crew training (thus increasing the amount of patrol hours Auroras can fly, and increasing their service lives) and environmental, drug interdiction, Arctic sovereignty and fishery patrols. The Arcturus feature no ASW equipment, but are fitted with the APS-134 radar.

Canada ordered the three CP-140As in 1989. These were the last Orion family aircraft to be built at Lockheed's Burbank, California, assembly line before production was transferred to Marietta, Georgia, alongside the C-130. The final CP-140A was delivered in September 1991.

**Photo:** A Canadian Forces CP-140 Aurora. Externally the aircraft is near identical to the P-3 Orion. (Gary Gentle)

# Lockheed S-3 Viking

**Country of origin:** United States of America

**Type:** Carrier borne ASW and tanker aircraft

**Powerplants:** Two 41.3kN (9275lb) General Electric TF34-GE-2 turbofans.

**Performance:** S-3A – Max speed 815km/h (440kt), patrol speed at optimum altitude 295km/h (160kt). Max initial rate of climb 4200ft/min. Service ceiling 40,000ft. Max ferry range 6085km (3230nm), range with max payload 3705km (2000nm). Operational radius over 1750km (945nm). Endurance 7hr 30min.

**Weights:** S-3A – Empty 12,088kg (26,650lb), MTOW 23,832kg (52,540lb).

**Dimensions:** Wing span 20.93m (68ft 8in), length 16.26m (53ft 4in), height 6.93m (22ft 9in). Wing area 55.6m$^2$ (598.0sq ft).

**Accommodation:** Crew of four, consisting of two pilots, a tactical coordinator and a sensor operator.

**Armament:** The internal weapons bay can house four torpedoes, or four Mk 36 Destructors, or four Mk 82 bombs, or four Mk 53 mines. Two underwing hardpoints can carry a torpedo each, or an AGM-84 Harpoon or AGM-65 Maverick each (S-3B only), or rocket pods.

**Operators:** USA

**History:** The Viking was developed to replace the S-2 Tracker and to counter increasingly difficult to detect Soviet missile submarines.

In 1967 the USN invited US manufacturers to submit designs for its consideration, with Convair, Grumman, McDonnell Douglas, North American Rockwell and Lockheed/Ling Temco Vought responding. In 1969 the USN selected Lockheed's proposal, and the first of eight service evaluation YS-3As first flew on January 21 1972.

Lockheed developed the Viking in cooperation with Vought, who was responsible for the design and manufacture of the aircraft's wings, tail unit, landing gear and engine nacelles. The S-3A Viking's design features a high wing, two TF34 turbofan engines, an internal weapons bay, seating for four crew, a Univac AYK-10 digital computer, Texas Instruments APS-116 search radar and a retractable FLIR pod. ASW systems comprise an extendable tail MAD boom and sonobuoys. The S-3A entered service in July 1974 and 187 were built.

Development of the improved S-3B upgrade was initiated in 1980. The S-3B gained an improved acoustic processing suite, expanded ESM coverage, better radar processing, a new sonobuoy receiver system and the ability to carry and fire the AGM-84 Harpoon anti ship missile. The first converted S-3B development aircraft flew in September 1984. Almost all S-3As were converted to S-3B configuration.

The USN also operated four US-3A carrier onboard delivery (COD) aircraft, stripped of ASW equipment. A single KS-3A dedicated tanker was evaluated. None were ordered, but S-3s regularly buddy tank.

With the diminished submarine threat carriers embark fewer S-3s and buddy tanking is now a prime role. S-3s are being fitted with new radios, INS/GPS, digital flight data computer, liquid crystal displays and a 1553 databus. Sixty-six are also being fitted with the AYK-23 data processor/mission computer (replacing the AYK-10).

The ES-3A 'Shadow' Elint variant first flew in 1991 and replaced the EA-3B Skywarrior, which was retired in 1987. Sixteen were converted but they were retired in 1998.

**Photos:** S-3 is due to remain in US Navy service to 2015. (Paul Merritt)

# Lockheed C-141 Starlifter

**Country of origin:** United States of America

**Type:** Strategic transport

**Powerplants:** C-141B – Four 93.4kN (21,000lb) Pratt & Whitney TF33-P-7 turbofans.

**Performance:** C-141B – Max cruising speed at altitude 910km/h (492kt), economical cruising speed at altitude 795km/h (430kt). Max initial rate of climb 2920ft/min. Service ceiling 41,600ft. Takeoff distance to 50ft at MTOW 1770m (5800ft). Ferry range 10,280km (5550nm), range with max payload 4725km (2550nm).

**Weights:** C-141B – Operating empty 67,185kg (148,120lb), max takeoff 155,580kg (343,000lb).

**Dimensions:** C-141B – Wing span 48.74m (159ft 11in), length 51.29m (168ft 4in), height 11.96m (39ft 3in). Wing area 299.8m² (3228.0sq ft).

**Accommodation:** Flightcrew of four comprising two pilots, a flight engineer and navigator. Can be configured to seat 205 equipped troops, or 168 paratroops or 103 stretchers. Max payload 41,220kg (90,880lb). Can carry a variety of cargoes including five HMMWV 4WDs, or a single light tank, or 13 standard pallets.

**Armament:** None

**Operators:** USA

**History:** The Lockheed C-141 Starlifter was the USA's first jet powered strategic transport, designed to give the US military the capability to airlift large amounts of equipment to a war zone in as short a time as possible.

The Starlifter was designed against Specific Operational Requirement 182 for a turbofan powered strategic transport for Military Airlift Command. Lockheed was selected to develop the new airlifter ahead of Boeing, Douglas and General Dynamics. Lockheed's design took the basic cross section of the C-130 Hercules combined with swept, high mounted wings with high lift devices for good field performance, four TF33 turbofans and a rear loading ramp.

The first C-141A first flew on December 17 1963 (there was no C-141 prototype). Service entry was in 1965, replacing C-124s, C-97s and C-135s. Some 285 C-141As were built through to 1968.

The Starlifter was soon used for trans Pacific transport flights to Vietnam and the type has been used in support of almost every US military deployment since. In service use the USAF soon found that the C-141A's cargo volume could easily be filled (or bulked out) without reaching the aircraft's maximum payload limit, thus prompting development of the stretched C-141B.

The prototype YC-141B conversion first flew on March 24 1977, and through to May 1982 271 Starlifters were converted to C-141B standard. Apart from the fuselage stretch the C-141B also gained an inflight refuelling receptacle above the flightdeck.

Aside from standard transport C-141Bs, the USAF also operates 13 C-141Bs equipped for special missions support, with defensive countermeasures and a retractable FLIR pod, while four short fuselage NC-141As are used for various test duties.

Raytheon is upgrading C-141Bs with EFIS displays and a digital autopilot.

**Photo:** A USAF C-141B. In 2001 the average age of the USAF's Starlifters was 34 years. (Doug Mackay)

# Lockheed C-5 Galaxy

**Country of origin:** United States of America

**Type:** Heavylift strategic transport

**Powerplants:** C-5B – Four 191.3kN (43,000lb) General Electric TF39-GE-1C turbofans.

**Performance:** C-5B – Max speed 920km/h (496kt), max cruising speed at 25,000ft 890 to 910km/h (460 to 480kt). Max initial rate of climb 1725ft/min. Service ceiling at 278,960kg (615,000lb) 35,750ft. Takeoff distance to 15m (50ft) obstacle at MTOW 2985m (9800ft). Range with max fuel 10,410km (5618nm), with max payload 5525km (2982nm).

**Weights:** C-5B – Operating empty 169,643kg (374,000lb), max takeoff 379,655kg (837,000lb).

**Dimensions:** Wing span 67.88m (222ft 9in), length 75.54m (247ft 10in), height 19.85m (65ft 2in). Wing area 576.0m² (6200.0sq ft).

**Accommodation:** Five crew: two pilots, flight engineer and two loadmasters. Can carry 15 relief crew on upper deck rear of flightdeck. C-5 can carry up to 350 troops, with 75 on upper deck. Max payload on C-5B 118,385kg (261,000lb), can carry two M1A1 Abrams tanks, or one CH-47, or four lights tanks and five HMMVW 4WDs, or 10 LAV 25s.

**Armament:** None

**Operators:** USA

**History:** The C-5 Galaxy was the world's largest aircraft for over a decade and was a remarkable engineering accomplishment.

The Galaxy was born out of the US Air Force's Cargo Experimental Heavy Logistics System (CX-HLS) requirement, which called for an enormous transport (for the day) capable of airlifting payloads of 113,400kg (250,000lb) over 4830km (2605nm) without inflight refuelling. Boeing, McDonnell Douglas and Lockheed were awarded initial contracts for the airframe, while Pratt & Whitney and GE were awarded initial contracts to develop a suitable engine.

In August 1965 GE's TF39 high bypass turbofan was selected, while Lockheed was selected as the C-5 prime contractor two months later. The Galaxy first flew on June 30 1968 and entered service in December 1969, although cost overruns earned the C-5 the nickname FRED – Fantastic Ridiculous Economic Disaster.

C-5 features include the high wing, T-tail, rear ramp and upward lifting nose freight door, allowing roll-on, roll-off loading and unloading. The Galaxy also features a complex four leg main undercarriage system, allowing operations from semi prepared runways.

In all, 81 C-5As were delivered between 1969 and 1973 (structural problems meant 77 C-5As were rewinged in the 1980s), while the production line was reopened for 50 new build C-5Bs delivered between 1986 and 1989. The B features simplified landing gear and an improved automatic flight control system. Two Galaxies modified for satellite carriage were designated C-5C.

Lockheed Martin and Honeywell are undertaking the C-5's Avionics Modernization Program, upgrading the flightdeck with six liquid crystal displays, a digital flight control system, and a new comms/nav suite.

In 2000 the USAF selected the GE CF6-80C2L1F, derated to (50,000lb), for the planned C-5 Reliability and Re-engining Program (RERP) upgrade, which will also involve structural repairs and systems improvements. The USAF plans to keep the C-5 in service to 2040.

**Photo:** A USAF C-5. (Wayne Grant)

## Lockheed L-1011 TriStar

**Country of origin:** United States of America

**Type:** Strategic transport and tanker

**Powerplants:** K.1 – Three 222.4kN (50,000lb) Rolls-Royce RB211-524B or -525B4 turbofans.

**Performance:** K.1 – Max cruising speed 964km/h (520kt), economical cruising speed 890km/h (480kt). Max initial rate of climb 2820ft/min. Service ceiling 43,000ft. Range with max pax payload 7785km (4200nm).

**Weights:** K.1 – Operating empty 110,165kg (242,684lb), max takeoff 244,955kg (540,000lb).

**Dimensions:** K.1/KC.1/C.2 – Span 50.09m (164ft 4in), length 50.05m (164ft 3in), height 16.87m (55ft 4in). Wing area 329.0m² (3540sq ft).

**Accommodation:** Flightcrew of three. Total fuel capacity in K.1 136,080kg (300,000lb).

**Armament:** None

**Operators:** Jordan, Saudi Arabia, UK.

**History:** The TriStar was the third widebody commercial airliner to be launched and the UK successfully adapted and modified it as a strategic tanker transport.

The L-1011 TriStar was Lockheed's last commercial airliner, and was launched in 1968 in response to an American Airlines requirement (that also resulted in the DC-10) for a large capacity medium range airliner. Lockheed initially studied a twin engined layout, but felt that three engines would be necessary to ensure the aircraft could takeoff at max weights from existing runways. The engine choice was Rolls-Royce's advanced three-shaft design RB211, which after initial troubles (which contributed to bankrupting RR) eventually proved to be extremely reliable and efficient in service.

The TriStar flew on November 16 1970 and entered airline service in 1972. The basic L-1011-1 was followed by progressively improved models, the most significant being the shortened L-1011-500. The L-1011-500 was developed for long range missions and sacrificed seating capacity for range. The first L-1011-500 flew on October 16 1978 and entered service in May 1979. Only 50 L-1011-500s were built from a total TriStar production run of 250.

In the early 1980s the UK Ministry of Defence acquired six ex British Airways and three ex PanAm L-1011-500s for conversion into tanker transports. Marshall of Cambridge converted four of the BA aircraft to TriStar K.1s with extra fuel tanks in the cargo holds, a refuelling probe and twin retractable refuelling drogues mounted under the rear fuselage. The first K.1 conversion flew in July 1985.

Two K.1s and two additional L-1011-500s were converted to KC.1 configuration, gaining a forward freight door, structural strengthening of the main cabin door and a freight handling system allowing the carriage of palletised cargo and 35 passengers.

Two of the ex PanAm aircraft serve as C.2 troop transports without any refuelling capability, while the third is a C.2A, which is identical save for some military avionics and a new interior. All RAF TriStars have been fitted with radar warning receivers.

TriStars equip Jordanian and Saudi royal flights.

**Photo:** The RAF's nine TriStars equip 216 Squadron. This is a K.1 without refuelling probe. (Sgt Rick Brewell RAF, UK Crown Copyright)

## Lockheed F-117 Nighthawk

**Country of origin:** United States of America

**Type:** Low observable precision strike fighter

**Powerplants:** Two 48.0kN (10,800lb) non afterburning General Electric F404-GE-F1D2 turbofans.

**Performance:** Max level speed 1040km/h (560kt), normal max operating speed Mach 0.9. Unrefuelled mission radius with a 2270kg (5000lb) weapon load 1055km (570nm).

**Weights:** Estimated empty 13,380kg (29,500lb), max takeoff 23,815kg (52,500lb).

**Dimensions:** Wing span 13.20m (43ft 4in), length overall 20.08m (65ft 11in), height 3.78m (12ft 5in). Wing area 84.8m² (913.0sq ft).

**Accommodation:** Pilot only.

**Armament:** Usually two 910kg/2000lb bombs, either BLU-109B low level laser guided bombs or GBU-10 or GBU-27 laser guided bombs, in internal weapons bay. Can also carry AGM-65 Maverick or AGM-88 HARM ASMs and AIM-9 Sidewinder AAMs. No provision for external stores carriage.

**Operators:** USA

**History:** Lockheed's 'Black Jet', the F-117 Nighthawk was designed in utmost secrecy from the ground up as a stealthy attack fighter.

F-117 development traces back to the mid 1970s when the US Air Force awarded Lockheed's Advanced Development Company – the Skunk Works – a contract under the Have Blue program to develop an attack aircraft that would be very difficult to detect with radar. Two XST (Experimental Stealth Technology) Have Blue prototypes were built, and the first of these flew from Groom Lake in Nevada in December 1977. The two Have Blue demonstrators were powered by two small General Electric CJ610 turbojets and were similar in overall configuration to the ensuing F-117 except for inward canted tailplanes. Both XSTs had crashed by 1980.

Development of the operational F-117A began in November 1978 under the Senior Trend program, with the first of five preproduction F-117s flying on June 18 1981, while the first of an eventual 60 production F-117As was delivered in August 1982.

The F-117s were operated by the 4450th Tactical Group in complete secrecy at the remote Tonopah Test Range and all flights were undertaken at night. It was not until late 1988 that the veil of secrecy was lifted when the US DoD confirmed the aircraft's existence and the F-117 began flying daylight missions. Today they equip the 37th Fighter Wing, based at Holloman AFB, New Mexico.

The F-117 uses a range of features to evade radar and to remain undetected, or to minimise detection ranges. The most obvious feature is the Nighthawk's faceted airframe construction and the avoidance of straight lines on doors and panels, so that radar energy is reflected in all directions. The airframe is also covered in a range of radar absorbent material (RAM) coatings. The two non afterburning F404 engines' exhaust gases mix with bypass air and exit through platypus exhausts to reduce their infrared signature.

The USAF's surviving F-117s are being fitted with an upgraded navigation system and are expected to remain in service to 2015.

**Photo:** Nighthawks are based at Holloman AFB in New Mexico. They have seen active combat service over Iraq and Yugoslavia. (USAF)

# Lockheed Martin F-16A/B Fighting Falcon

**Country of origin:** United States of America

**Type:** Multirole fighter

**Powerplant:** F-16A – One 65.3kN (14,670lb) dry and 106.0kN (23,830lb) with afterburning Pratt & Whitney F100-PW-200 turbofan.

**Performance:** F-16A – Max speed at 40,000ft over Mach 2.0 or 2125km/h (1145kt), at sea level 1472km/h (795kt). Max initial rate of climb over 50,000ft/min. Service ceiling above 50,000ft. Combat radius with six 1000lb (454kg) bombs, hi-lo-hi 545km (295nm).

**Weights:** F-16A – Operating empty 6607kg (14,567lb), max takeoff 14,968kg (33,000lb).

**Dimensions:** F-16A – Span with AAMs 10.00m (32ft 10in), length 15.03m (49ft 4in), height 5.01m (16ft 5in). Wing area 28.9m$^2$ (300.0sq ft).

**Accommodation:** Pilot only in F-16A, two in tandem in F-16B.

**Armament:** One internal M61A1 20mm cannon. Up to 5435kg (12,000lb) of ordnance, incl AIM-9 & AIM-120 AAMs (can be mounted on wingtip stations), bombs, AGM-65s and Penguin anti ship missiles.

**Operators:** Belgium, Denmark, Egypt, Indonesia, Israel, Italy*, Netherlands, Norway, Pakistan, Portugal, Singapore, Taiwan*, Thailand, USA, Venezuela.

**History:** The F-16 (or 'Viper' as it's nicknamed) was conceived as a lightweight, highly agile and relatively inexpensive multirole fighter to complement the F-15.

The F-16 evolved from the USAF's Lightweight Fighter (LWF) program to evaluate the concept of a small and manoeuvrable fighter. In April 1972 General Dynamics and Northrop were selected ahead of Boeing, LTV and Lockheed to build two prototypes each of their respective designs for a competitive fly-off. The first General Dynamics YF-16 first flew on January 20 1974, and the type was selected for further development after almost a year of evaluation against the twin engine Northrop YF-17. The first production F-16A flew in 1978.

The F-16 was the first production fighter to feature fly-by-wire and relaxed stability. It also features wing/fuselage blending, a Westinghouse (now Northrop Grumman) APG-66 radar, an advanced (for the time) cockpit with sidestick controller and a 30° reclined seat.

The USAF selected the F-16 for production in early 1975. Later that year Belgium, Denmark, the Netherlands and Norway jointly selected the F-16 to build under licence in Europe.

The inferior GE J79 turbojet powered F-16/79 was offered for international sales until the F100 powered F-16A was released for wider export. Production F-16As (and two seat Bs) were built to Block 1, 5, 10, 15, 15OCU and 20 (for Taiwan) standards. Block 15 introduced many changes including the extended horizontal stabilator and a track while scan mode for the radar.

The USAF had 272 Block 15s converted to ADF (Air Defense Fighter) standard. The F-16A ADFs are air defence interceptors and feature upgraded radar, AIM-120 and AIM-7 compatibility and a searchlight, and can be identified by their bulged fin/fuselage fairing.

Belgium, Denmark, Portugal, the Netherlands and Norway are upgrading their F-16s under the MLU (mid life update) program with two colour LCDs, wide angle HUD, NVG compatible cockpit, upgraded APG-66(V2A) radar, GPS and a modular mission computer.

**Photo:** Portuguese F-16As.

# Lockheed Martin F-16C/D Fighting Falcon

**Country of origin:** United States of America

**Type:** Multirole fighter

**Powerplant:** F-16C Block 50 – One 131.6kN (29,588lb) with afterburning General Electric F110-GE-129 turbofan.

**Performance:** F-16C Block 50 – Max speed at 40,000ft above Mach 2.0 or 2125km/h (1145kt), at sea level 1472km/h (795kt). Service ceiling above 50,000ft. Ferry range with drop tanks 4215km (2276nm). Radius with two AIM-9s, two 910kg/2000lb bombs and external fuel, hi-lo-lo-hi 1485km (802nm).

**Weights:** F-16C Block 50 – Empty 8665kg (18,917lb), max takeoff 19,190kg (42,300lb). Internal fuel 3104kg (6846lb).

**Dimensions:** Span with wingtip AAMs 10.00m (32ft 10in), length 15.03m (49ft 4in), height 5.01m (16ft 8in). Wing area 28.9m$^2$ (300.0sq ft).

**Accommodation:** Pilot only in F-16C, two in tandem in F-16D.

**Armament:** One M61A1 20mm cannon. Six underwing, two fuselage, one centreline and two wingtip hardpoints for 5435kg (12,000lb) of ordnance. Options include AIM-9 or AIM-120 AAMs (can be mounted on wingtips), bombs, rockets, AGM-65, GBU-10 and GBU-12 LGBs, AGM-88, AGM-84 , AGM-154 JSOW, GBU-31/32 JDAM and CBU-103/4/5.

**Operators:** Bahrain, Egypt*, Greece*, Israel, Oman*, Singapore*, South Korea*, Turkey*, USA*.

**History:** Various avionics, radar and cockpit changes mark the evolution of the F-16A into the more capable and heavier F-16C/D.

The F-16C first flew on June 19 1984. Changes to the F-16C and two seat D came under the Multinational Staged Improvement Program (MSIP), which aimed to increase the F-16's ground attack and all weather capabilities and introduce BVR missile compatibility. Initial production F-16C Block 25s introduced the F-16C's APG-68 radar, an improved cockpit with a wide angle HUD, and compatibility with AGM-65D and AIM-120 missiles. The F-16C's fin is extended forward.

Subsequent F-16C/D block models include: the General Electric F110-GE-100 powered Block 30 and the PW F100-PW-220 powered Block 32; the GE powered Block 40 and PW powered Block 42 Night Falcon with upgraded APG-68(V) radar and compatibility with LANTIRN pods (sometimes called F-16CG & DG); the more powerful increased Performance Engine (IPE) F110-GE-229 Block 50 and F100-PW-220 Block 52 both with APG-68(V5); and the Block 50D and 52D with AGM-88 HARM compatibility (unofficially designated F-16CJ and DJ).

Since 1997 production USAF Block 50s/52s have the F-16A MLU's modular mission computer and twin colour LCDs. Singaporean and Israeli F-16Ds feature a weapon system operator station in the rear cockpit and unique avionics in a dorsal spine.

The F-16N and TF-16N designations applied to 26 Block 30s modified for aggressor training for the US Navy.

The USAF's Common Configuration Implementation Program (CCIP) will see almost 700 Block 40/42s and 50/52s fitted with common avionics (plus PGM targeting pods for the 50/52s).

Greece has ordered 50 Block 52s with conformal fuel tanks, upgraded APG-68(V)XM radar, F100-PW-229 engine, modular mission computer, colour displays and helmet mounted cueing system.

The 4000th F-16 was delivered in May 2000.

**Photo:** A Singaporean F-16D. (Lenn Bayliss)

# Lockheed Martin F-16I & Block 60

**Country of origin:** United States of America

**Type:** Multirole strike fighter

**Powerplant:** F-16I – One 129.4kN (29,100lb) with afterburning Pratt & Whitney F100-PW-229 turbofan. Block 60 – One 142.3kN (32,000lb) General Electric F129-GE-132.

**Performance:** F-16C Block 60 – Max speed at 40,000ft above Mach 2.0 or 2125km/h (1145kt). Service ceiling above 50,000ft. Combat radius with conformal and external fuel tanks 1480km (800nm).

**Weights:** Block 60 – Empty 9170kg (20,200lb), max takeoff 22,700kg (50,000lb).

**Dimensions:** Span with wingtip AAMs 10.00m (32ft 10in), length 15.03m (49ft 4in), height 5.01m (16ft 8in). Wing area 28.9m² (300.0sq ft).

**Accommodation:** F-16I – Two in tandem. UAE Block 60 – Will be delivered in single and two seat forms.

**Armament:** One M61A1 20mm cannon. Six underwing, two fuselage, one centreline and two wingtip hardpoints. F-16I – Various Israeli weaponry. Block 60 – Options include AIM-9 or AIM-120B AAMs (can be mounted on wingtips), bombs, rockets, and GBU-31/32 JDAM.

**Operators:** Israel*, UAE (Abu Dhabi)*.

**History:** The F-16C Block 60 and F-16I are advanced developments of the popular F-16 fighter, ordered by the United Arab Emirates and Israel respectively.

The F-16I and F-16 Block 60 are the result of continual evolution of the F-16 line. Israel selected the two seat F-16I in July 1999 following a competitive evaluation against the F-15I (already in Israeli service) for a long range strike fighter. Israel signed a contract for 50 F-16D Block 52+ or F-16I jets in January 2000, and then exercised an option for 52 more in September 2001.

F-16Is (covered by the Peace Marble V program) will be delivered from 2003 through to 2008. This evolution of the F-16C Block 50 will feature conformal fuel tanks (with 1893 litres of additional fuel), Pratt Whitney F100-PW-229 turbofan, Northrop Grumman APG-68(V)XM radar, and significant Israeli avionics content.

Israeli content on the F-16I will include its Elisra electronic warfare suite, Elbit helmet mounted sight, central mission computer, cockpit displays and stores management system. Like earlier Israeli F-16Ds, the F-16I will feature a weapon systems operator station in the rear cockpit, dorsal spine housing avionics, and the Rafael Litening II targeting pod.

The ultimate development of the F-16 so far is the F-16 Block 60, selected by the UAE in May 1998 (with a firm contract covering 80 aircraft signed in March 2000). The Block 60 "Desert Falcon" configuration will include an active electronically scanned array (AESA) Northrop Grumman APG-80 radar, an infrared targeting system with sensor turrets mounted above the nose and below the intake, advanced cockpit with three liquid crystal displays, fibre optic databus, conformal fuel tanks (as on the F-16I) internal electronic countermeasures, and 142.3kN (32,000lb) F110-GE-132 engine (the most powerful engine on an F-16 variant so far).

The UAE's Desert Falcons will be delivered from 2004 through to 2006. Some will be single seaters, others (an undisclosed number) two seaters with missionised rear cockpits and dorsal spine.

**Photo:** An artist's impression of the F-16I. (Lockheed Martin)

# Lockheed Martin/Boeing F-22 Raptor

**Country of origin:** United States of America

**Type:** Air dominance fighter

**Powerplants:** F-22A – Two 155kN (35,000lb) class Pratt & Whitney F119-PW-100 afterburning turbofans.

**Performance:** F-22A – Estimated max speed at sea level 1480km/h (800kt). No other figures released.

**Weights:** F-22A – Target empty 14,365kg (31,760lb), max takeoff approx 27,215kg (60,000lb).

**Dimensions:** F-22A – Wing span 13.56m (44ft 6in), length 18.92m (62ft 1in), height 5.02m (16ft 5in). Wing area 78.0m² (840.0sq ft).

**Accommodation:** Pilot only.

**Armament:** Internal long barrel GE M61A1 Vulcan 20mm cannon. Two side weapons bays can carry two AIM-9 Sidewinders each. Ventral weapons bay can carry four AIM-120A Amraams, or six AIM-120Cs, or GBU-32 JDAM PGMs. Four underwing hardpoints can carry 2270kg (5000lb) of weaponry each or fuel tanks.

**Operators:** US*

**History:** The Lockheed Martin/Boeing F-22 Raptor air dominance fighter is due to replace the USAF's F-15C Eagles.

The F-22 resulted from the USAF's Advanced Tactical Fighter (ATF) program to develop a replacement for the F-15 Eagle. In October 1986 the USAF selected Lockheed and Northrop to build two prototypes each of their respective ATF designs for evaluation. At the same time competing engines for the ATF from General Electric (YF120) and Pratt & Whitney (YF119) would be compared.

Lockheed teamed with General Dynamics and Boeing and their YF-22 first flew on September 29 1990. The rival Northrop McDonnell Douglas YF-23 had flown on August 27. The USAF selected the P&W F119 powered F-22 for development in April 1991.

The first of 11 F-22A development aircraft first flew on September 7 1997, the second on June 28 1998. The USAF's first production Raptor is due to be delivered to the USAF in early 2003, with the first unit becoming operational in 2005. The US DoD approved F-22 Low Rate Initial Production in August 2001, authorising production of 295.

The F-22 is designed to defeat all current and projected fighters in air-to-air combat (first look first kill), while it will have a secondary precision ground attack function with JDAM GPS guided bombs. It is designed to be extremely agile and incorporates low observable (stealth) technology (including radar absorbent material and serrated edges on doors and panels) as an integral part of the design. The low bypass two shaft F119 engines give the F-22 a thrust to weight ratio of 1.4 to 1 and the aircraft can cruise at supersonic speeds without afterburner (supercruise) with the exhaust exiting through two-dimensional vectoring nozzles.

The avionics system integrates data from the Northrop Grumman APG-77 low probability of intercept electronically scanned radar, comms system and RWR for presentation on the HUD and four large colour LCDs. The cockpit also features a sidestick controller and the aircraft has triplex fly-by-wire flight controls.

The two seat F-22B was cancelled in mid 1996. Strike versions could be developed in the future to replace the F-15E and F-117.

**Photo:** Two EMD Raptors. (Lockheed Martin)

# Lockheed Martin F-35 JSF

**Country of origin:** United States of America

**Type:** Advanced multirole fighter

**Powerplants:** One 180kN (40,000lb) class with afterburning Pratt & Whitney F135 turbofan.

**Performance:** No data publicly released at late 2001.

**Weights:** Empty approx 13.5 tonnes. Internal fuel CTOL 8.4 tonnes, STOVL 6 tonnes, CV 8.6 tonnes. Max takeoff approx 30 tonnes.

**Dimensions:** Provisional – CTOL & STOVL – Wing span 10.7m (35ft 1in), length 15.5m (50ft 10in). CV – Span 13.1m (43ft), length same.

**Accommodation:** Pilot only.

**Armament:** Boeing/Mauser 27mm cannon for CTOL aircraft. Two internal weapons bays and underwing hardpoints for a variety of weaponry, including AIM-9X, AIM-120 and JDAM.

**Operators:** Planned buys: USAF 1763, USN 480, USMC 609, RN & RAF 150 worth $US200bn. Significant exports expected.

**History:** Lockheed Martin's F-35 stealthy multirole fighter is the winner of the lucrative Joint Strike Fighter program to replace USAF F-16s and A-10s, USN F/A-18s and USMC and UK Harriers.

JSF is potentially the world's biggest arms program, and aims to develop a common aircraft in conventional (CTOL), carrier capable (CV) and short takeoff and vertical landing (STOVL) variants for the USAF, USN, USMC, UK and export. It grew out of the late 1994 merger of programs to replace USAF F-16s and USN F/A-18s and USMC AV-8s.

By June 1996 Lockheed Martin, Boeing and McDonnell Douglas had submitted JSF design proposals, with Boeing and Lockheed Martin then being selected to build two JSF Weapon System Concept Demonstrator aircraft each to validate their design proposals.

Lockheed Martin's X-35A first flew on October 24 2000, followed by the STOVL X-35B in June 23 2001. The X-35A was converted to act as the CV X-35C demonstrator, first flying in this configuration on December 16 2000. The US DoD selected Lockheed Martin to develop its JSF proposal as the F-35 on October 26 2001.

Lockheed Martin's F-35 effort is based in Fort Worth, Texas, where production F-35s will be built. LM is partnered with Northrop Grumman (centre fuselage and wingbox) and BAE Systems (rear fuselage).

The F-35 features a mid mounted trapezoidal wing, diverter-less inlets, twin outward canted tail fins, huge internal fuel volume, Northrop Grumman phased array radar and IR sensor, helmet mounted cueing system, and advanced avionics. Initial F-35s will be powered by the P&W F135, a development of the F-22's F119. GE is developing its JSF-F120 which will compete with the F135 for F-35 production contracts from 2011. CTOL and CV F-35s will have thrust vectoring nozzles.

The CV F-35 will feature a larger wing and tail and tailhook, beefier undercarriage and structural strengthening for carrier ops. The STOVL F-35 will have a Rolls-Royce lift fan (mounted behind the cockpit) with two contra-rotating fans driven by a shaft from the engine, a swivel duct nozzle on the engine, and off-take ducts and roll post nozzles.

Under the $US25bn System Development and Demonstration Phase, Lockheed will build 14 flying development F-35s. Low rate initial production is due to begin in 2006, with first deliveries to the Marines in 2008. IOC for the USAF will be in 2010, USN and UK in 2011.

**Photo:** The X-35C carrier demonstrator. (Lockheed Martin)

# McDonnell Douglas F-4 Phantom II

**Country of origin:** United States of America

**Type:** Multirole fighter

**Powerplants:** F-4E – Two 52.5kN (11,810lb) dry and 79.6kN (17,900lb) with afterburning General Electric J79-GE-17A turbojets.

**Performance:** F-4E – Max speed at 36,000ft Mach 2.2 or 2390km/h (1290kt), cruising speed at MTOW 920km/h (495kt). Max initial rate of climb 61,400ft/min, intercept mission rate of climb 49,800ft/min. Service ceiling 62,250ft. Ferry range 3185km (1720nm). Intercept combat radius 1265km (683nm), interdiction combat radius 1145km (618nm).

**Weights:** F-4E – Empty 13,757kg (30,328lb), MTOW 28,030kg (61,795lb). Internal fuel 7022 litres.

**Dimensions:** F-4E – Wing span 11.77m (38ft 8in), length 19.20m (63ft 0in), height 5.02m (16ft 6in). Wing area 49.2m² (530.0sq ft).

**Accommodation:** Pilot and weapons system operator in tandem.

**Armament:** F-4E – One M61A1 20mm cannon. One centreline and four underwing hardpoints can carry 7255kg (16,000lb) of ordnance including AIM-9 AAMs, bombs, rockets and LGBs. Four AIM-7s can be carried in semi recessed underfuselage stations.

**Operators:** Egypt, Germany, Greece, Iran, Israel, Japan, Sth Korea, Turkey.

**History:** More than 5000 F-4 Phantoms were built between 1957 and 1981 and it remains the West's most significant postwar fighter.

The Phantom began life as a company study, the F3H-G naval strike fighter, which would have been powered by Wright J65s. In 1954 the US Navy issued a letter of intent for two F3Hs for evaluation as the AH-1, to be powered by General Electric's promising J79 turbojet. Later in 1955 the AH-1 was adapted to meet a Navy requirement for a fleet defence fighter, and with suitable changes the AH-1 became the F4H Phantom II. Development go-ahead was given in mid 1955.

The first prototype F4H-1 first flew on May 27 1958, and it demonstrated performance levels far above anything then flying. Indeed Navy Phantoms set a dramatic series of speed, altitude and time to height records in the late 1950s and early 1960s.

Initial production was of the Navy's F-4B fleet defence fighter. In 1961 the USAF took the unprecedented step of buying a USN fighter when it ordered the F-4C (originally F-110A). Subsequent USN and USMC F-4s comprised the F-4J, F-4N and F-4S. These models, the USAF's F-4Cs, F-4Ds and SEAD F-4Gs, and British Spey powered FG.1/F-4Ks and FGR.2/F-4Ms have been retired. F-4Ds survive with South Korea and Iran.

The definitive Phantom variant is the APQ-120 radar and gun equipped F-4E. It first flew on August 7 1965, and almost 1500 were built. The 5057th and last US built Phantom was an F-4E for Korea, handed over in October 1979.

About 50 Israeli F-4Es were upgraded to Kurnass 2000 standard with Elbit avionics and multifunction displays and Norden APG-76 radar. IAI is updating 54 Turkish F-4Es with a structural upgrade and Elta radar. Most of Japan's 158 F-4EJs were built under licence by Mitsubishi (the last delivered in May 1981), 96 are being upgraded to F-4EJ Kai standard with an APG-66J radar. Germany's Improved Combat Efficiency (ICE) upgrade to its F-4Fs added APG-65 radar and AIM-120 compatibility. EADS is performing a similar upgrade for 39 Greek F-4Es.

**Photo:** A Turkish F-4E Phantom. (Joris van Boven/Sentry Aviation News)

## McDonnell Douglas RF-4 Phantom II

**Country of origin:** United States of America

**Type:** Tactical reconnaissance fighter

**Powerplants:** RF-4C – Two 48.5kN (10,900lb) dry and 75.6kN (17,000lb) with afterburning General Electric J79-GE-15 turbojets.

**Performance:** RF-4C – Max speed at 40,000ft 2348km/h (1267kt), max speed at sea level 1445km/h (780kt). Max initial rate of climb 48,000ft/min. Service ceiling 59,400ft. Ferry range with external fuel 2815km (1520nm). Combat radius 1355km (730nm).

**Weights:** RF-4C – Empty 12,825kg (28,275lb), max takeoff 26,308kg (58,000lb).

**Dimensions:** RF-4C – Wing span 11.77m (38ft 8in), length 19.17m (62ft 11in), height 5.03m (16ft 6in). Wing area 49.2m$^2$ (530.0sq ft).

**Accommodation:** Pilot and reconnaissance officer in tandem.

**Armament:** None, although max theoretical external load is 7255kg (16,000lb). Many RF-4s wired to carry two AIM-9s for self defence.

**Operators:** Greece, Japan, Israel, South Korea, Spain, Turkey.

**History:** A number of factors made the F-4 Phantom suitable for conversion as a reconnaissance platform, including its speed (and hence survivability), range and availability.

Development of the reconnaissance Phantom was done at the request of the US Air Force, who ordered the RF-4C in 1965 to replace the RF-101 Voodoo (also a McDonnell product). The RF-4C retained the basic airframe and systems of the F-4C fighter but introduced a lengthened nose containing an APQ-99 forward looking radar for mapping and terrain clearance plus an APQ-102 side looking radar and various optical cameras.

Cameras fitted to RF-4Cs included the KS-72 and KS-87 forward looking oblique cameras, the KA-56A low altitude camera, the KA-55A high altitude panoramic camera and the 167cm (66in) focal length KS-127. Other systems fitted to the RF-4 include the ARN-101 digital navigation and reconnaissance system, infrared linescan cameras, Elint and ESM sensors.

The YRF-4C prototype first flew on August 9 1963, and production RF-4Cs were delivered from the following year. In all McDonnell built 505 RF-4C Phantoms for the USAF through to December 1973, and these have served widely including during the Vietnam and Gulf wars. Despite the RF-4C's utility, the type was retired from US service in 1996, leaving the USAF without a dedicated tactical reconnaissance aircraft. Surplus USAF RF-4Cs were supplied to Spain in the early 1970s and to South Korea from 1988. Spain's have been fitted with fixed refuelling probes for hose and drogue refuelling.

The US Marines took delivery of 46 RF-4Bs from 1965. The survivors were retired in the early 1990s. These were similar to the RF-4C but based on the naval F-4B.

The export RF-4E was developed initially for Germany and first flew in September 1970. Compared with the RF-4C, the RF-4E was based on the F-4E and did not feature some of the RF-4C's more sensitive systems. New build RF-4Es were delivered to Germany, Japan, Israel, Greece and Turkey (the latter two now also operate ex Luftwaffe RF-4Es). Israeli RF-4Es are fitted with indigenous sensors and avionics and can fire Shafir and Python air-to-air missiles.

**Photo:** A Greek ex German air force RF-4E. (Lassi Tolvanen)

## McDonnell Douglas F-15 Eagle

**Country of origin:** United States of America

**Type:** Air superiority fighter

**Powerplants:** F-15C – Two 65.3kN (14,670lb) dry and 105.7kN (23,770lb) with afterburning Pratt & Whitney F100-PW-220 turbofans.

**Performance:** F-15C – Max level speed over Mach 2.5, or approx 2655km/h (1433kt). Max initial rate of climb over 50,000ft/min. Service ceiling 60,000ft. Ferry range with external fuel and conformal fuel tanks over 5745km (3100nm). Combat radius on an intercept mission 1965km (1060nm). Endurance with conformal fuel tanks 5hr 15min.

**Weights:** F-15C – Operating empty 12,793kg (28,600lb), max takeoff 30,845kg (68,000lb). Internal fuel 6103kg (13,455lb).

**Dimensions:** Wing span 13.05m (42ft 10in), length 19.43m (63ft 9in), height 5.63m (18ft 6in). Wing area 56.5m$^2$ (608.0sq ft).

**Accommodation:** Pilot only, or two in tandem in F-15B/D.

**Armament:** One M61A1 20mm cannon. Can carry total external ordnance load of 7257kg (16,000lb). Typical CAP fit of four AIM-7s on fuselage stations and two AIM-9s or AIM-120s on each wing pylon.

**Operators:** Israel, Japan, Saudi Arabia, USA.

**History:** The impressive F-15 air superiority fighter replaced the F-4 Phantom in USAF service as its premier fighter.

Design work on a new fighter for the USAF first began in the mid 1960s, and the program gained fresh impetus later that decade when US satellites revealed the existence of the Soviet MiG-23 and MiG-25. The FX requirement took in lessons from Vietnam and called for a fighter with a thrust to weight ratio in excess of unity and the ability to out turn any adversary to bring its missiles to bear first.

McDonnell Douglas' design was chosen ahead of proposals from Fairchild-Republic and North American Rockwell, and the first development F-15 Eagle first flew on July 27 1972. Design features include the specifically developed P&W F100 turbofans, Hughes APG-63 radar, a high wing of great area, and advanced (for the time) cockpit displays, including a HUD.

The F-15 entered service in January 1976, and 355 F-15As and 57 two seat F-15Bs were built. Israel was the first F-15 export customer, and its Eagles were the first to be used in combat.

Production switched to the improved F-15C/D in 1979. Changes are minor but include the ability to carry the conformal fuel tanks (CFTs) on each fuselage side, uprated engines and improved radar. The C/D was exported to Israel and Saudi Arabia and Mitsubishi built 204 under licence in Japan until late 1999 as the F-15J (and DJ two seater). US F-15C/D production ceased in 1992 (622 built). Japan intends to upgrade its F-15Js with features developed for the Mitsubishi F-2, including a new radar and EW suite, and possibly GE F110-GE-129s.

During the 1991 Gulf War Saudi and US F-15s claimed 32 Iraqi aircraft without loss. USAF F-15Cs also flew CAP and escort missions during the Kosovo conflict in 1999.

USAF F-15C/Ds were upgraded from 1985 to 1997 under the Multi Stage Improvement Program (MSIP) to feature the Hughes APG-70 radar, a colour CRT in the cockpit and AIM-120 compatibility. Eighteen F-15Cs have been upgraded with the active array APG-63V(2) radar.

The F-15E strike fighter is described under Boeing.

**Photo:** Rear view of a USAF F-15C. (Paul Sadler)

## McDonnell Douglas A-4 Skyhawk

**Country of origin:** United States of America

**Type:** Light attack/multirole fighter

**Powerplant:** A-4M – One 50kN (11,200lb) non afterburning Pratt & Whitney J52-P-408 turbojet.

**Performance:** A-4M – Max speed with a 1815kg (4000lb) bomb load 1038km/h (560kt), at sea level 1100km/h (595kt). Initial rate of climb 10,300ft/min. Ceiling 38,700ft. Ferry range 3305km (1785nm), combat radius with a 1815kg (4000lb) bomb load 545km (295nm).

**Weights:** A-4M – Empty 4747kg (10,465lb), normal takeoff 11,115kg (24,500lb). Internal fuel 3028 litres.

**Dimensions:** A-4M – Wing span 8.38m (27ft 6in), length 12.27m (40ft 4in), height 4.57m (15ft 0in). Wing area 24.2m² (260.0sq ft).

**Accommodation:** Pilot only, or two in tandem in TA-4.

**Armament:** Two 20mm Colt Mk 12 cannons in wing roots. A-4M max ordnance of 4155kg (9155lb) on one centreline and four underwing hardpoints including bombs, AIM-9s, Bullpup and Maverick ASMs.

**Operators:** Argentina, Brazil, Indonesia, Israel, Malaysia.

**History:** Affectionately dubbed the Scooter and Heinemann's Hot Rod, the A-4 Skyhawk enjoyed a three decade, 2960 unit production run.

In the early 1950s Douglas had been working on its turboprop powered A2D Skyshark to replace the piston powered AD (A-1) Skyraider, but development was terminated due to problems with the powerplant. At the same time Douglas' Ed Heinemann had been working on a compact jet powered light attack aircraft and in early 1952 the US Navy ordered this aircraft for further development. The first of nine XA4D-1 development aircraft first flew on August 14 1954. Deliveries of production A4D-1s began in September 1956.

The Skyhawk's dimensions were such that it could fit on an aircraft carrier lift without the need for folding wings. Power for initial A-4A, A-4B and A-4C Skyhawks was from a Wright J65, a licence built Armstrong Siddeley Sapphire.

The A-4C was followed into USN service by the much improved A-4E, a heavier development powered by a Pratt & Whitney J52. The final Skyhawk for the US Navy was the A-4F, characterised by its dorsal avionics hump. The ultimate production Skyhawk was the USMC's A-4M Skyhawk II, which introduced a larger canopy for better pilot vision, a more powerful J52-P-408 and a max takeoff weight double that of initial A-4A's. It first flew in 1970 and remained in production until 1979. The USN used two seat TA-4Fs as advanced trainers.

The Skyhawk was widely exported. Argentina was the first export customer, taking delivery of A-4Ps and A-4Qs (modified A-4Bs and Cs respectively) in the mid 1960s. More recently in 2000 it took delivery of the last of 36 Lockheed Martin refurbished A-4Ms as A-4AR Fightinghawks with ARG-1 (APG-66) radar, HUD and new avionics. Israel operates A-4E based A-4Hs and A-4M based A-4Ns. Malaysia has modified ex USN A-4Es, while Singapore's A-4S is described separately. New Zealand's upgraded A-4Ks (with HUD, HOTAS, two CRTs and APG-66 radar, and AIM-9L, AGM-65 and laser guided bomb compatibility) were retired in December 2001 and were offered for sale. Brazil is the latest Skyhawk operator with 23 ex Kuwaiti T/A-4KUs for service on the ex French navy carrier *Foch*, renamed *Sao Paulo*.

**Photo:** An Argentine A-4AR. (Santiago Rivas)

## McDonnell Douglas C-9 & DC-9

**Country of origin:** United States of America

**Type:** Multirole transport and medical evacuation aircraft

**Powerplants:** C-9A – Two 64.5kN (14,500lb) Pratt & Whitney JT8D-9 turbofans.

**Performance:** C-9A – Max speed 935km/h (505kt), typical cruising speed 810km/h (437kt). Max initial rate of climb 2900ft/min. Time to 35,000ft 25min. Service ceiling 35,820ft. Range with max payload 1690km (913nm), ferry range 4700km (2538nm).

**Weights:** C-9A – Basic equipped 28,235kg (62,247lb), max takeoff 48,990kg (108,000lb).

**Dimensions:** C-9A – Wing span 28.47m (93ft 5in), length 36.37m (119ft 4in), height 8.38m (27ft 6in). Wing area 93.0m² (1000.7sq ft).

**Accommodation:** Crew on C-9A comprises two flightcrew, flight observer, senior flight nurse, nurse, senior medical technician and two medical attendants. Can carry 40 ambulatory patients or 30 stretcher patients, or combinations thereof. DC-9-30 has max seating in passenger configuration for 115.

**Armament:** None

**Operators:** Kuwait, USA.

**History:** The DC-9 was a highly successful family of twinjet airliners (2400 built) ranging in size from 80 to 150 seats. In its DC-9-30 form it has been adopted for military use as an aeromedical transport (C-9A) and staff and utility transport (C-9B/C-9C).

Douglas developed the DC-9 as a short range airliner to complement its much larger DC-8 and fill a market sector that at the time Boeing did not fill. Development was launched on April 8 1963.

The DC-9 was an all new design, featuring rear fuselage mounted engines, a T-tail, moderately swept wings and seats for up to 80 passengers. Prototype construction began in July 1963 with first flight on February 25 1965. Certification and service entry occurred on November 23 1965 and December 8 1965 respectively.

The DC-9 had been designed with stretched and larger capacity developments in mind, and such versions of the basic DC-9-10 soon followed. The first stretch resulted in the 4.54m (14ft 11in) longer DC-9-30, which entered service in February 1967. Subsequent stretched versions are the DC-9-40, DC-9-50, JT8D-200 powered MD-80 series, the V2500 powered, 150 seat MD-90, and RR BR710, powered, DC-9-30 sized Boeing 717.

The DC-9-30 is the major DC-9 development adopted for military use. In August 1967 the USAF selected the DC-9-30 to meet its requirement for an off the shelf airliner suitable for development as an aeromedical transport. Designated C-9A, USAF aeromedical DC-9s are appropriately named Nightingale. The 21 C-9As delivered feature a large forward freight door, provision for a therapeutic oxygen supply and an isolated care section. In addition, the USAF acquired three DC-9-30s as C-9C VIP/staff transports.

The US Navy and Marines acquired a total of 15 freight door equipped staff/logistical transport C-9B Skytrain IIs from 1972. The Skytrain II name honours the legendary Douglas C-47/DC-3.

Italy operated two DC-9-30s as VIP transports, which have been replaced by Airbus A319CJs.

**Photo:** A USAF C-9A Nightingale. (Paul Merritt)

# MDC KC-10 Extender & KDC-10

*Country of origin:* United States of America

*Type:* Strategic tanker transport

*Powerplants:* KC-10 – Three 233.5kN (52,500lb) General Electric F103-GE-100 (CF6-50C2) turbofans.

*Performance:* KC-10 – Max speed at 25,000ft 982km/h (530kt), max cruising speed at 30,000ft 908km/h (490kt), long range cruising speed 870km/h (470kt). Max initial rate of climb 2900ft/min. Range with max payload 7030km (3797nm). Max ferry range unrefuelled 18,505km (9990nm). Can transfer 90,720kg (200,000lb) of fuel 3540km (1910nm) from base.

*Weights:* KC-10 – Operating empty 108,890kg (240,065lb), max take-off 267,620kg (590,000lb).

*Dimensions:* Wing span 47.34m (155ft 4in), length 55.35m (181ft 7in), height 17.70m (58ft 1in). Wing area 358.7m² (3861.0sq ft).

*Accommodation:* KC-10 – Crew complement of five, with six seats provided for a relief crew. Can be configured with 75 passenger seats. Max payload 76,845kg (169,410lb), design fuel capacity 161,510kg (356,065lb).

*Armament:* None

*Operators:* KC-10 – USA. KDC-10 – Netherlands.

*History:* The KC-10 Extender tanker transport is a military development of the DC-10 widebody airliner.

McDonnell Douglas launched DC-10 development in February 1968 with orders from American and United Airlines. The second widebody (twin aisle) airliner to fly (behind the 747), the DC-10 began life as a twinjet, but gained a third engine to meet American Airlines' field performance requirements. The prototype first flew on August 29 1970.

DC-10 variants include the initial production DC-10-10, the intercontinental range DC-10-30 (with extra fuel and a third main undercarriage unit) and the P&W JT9D powered DC-10-40.

In December 1977 the US Air Force selected the DC-10 as its Advanced Tanker Cargo Aircraft (ATCA), ahead of the Boeing 747. The ATCA program aimed to procure an off the shelf jet transport for use as both a strategic transport and an air-to-air refueller.

The USAF initially ordered 16 modified DC-10s as the KC-10A Extender. The KC-10 first flew on July 12 1980. In May 1982 the total KC-10 order was increased to 60. The final KC-10 was delivered in 1988.

The KC-10 is based on the DC-10-30CF (convertible freighter) and features a large forward freight door, an air-to-air boom receptacle above the cockpit, a McDonnell Douglas Advanced Aerial Refuelling Boom and a hose and reel refuelling unit, both beneath the rear fuselage. In addition 20 KC-10s feature two underwing hose and reel refuelling units. As well as the basic fuel tanks, fuel is stored in seven bladder tanks in the lower cargo holds. The main deck accommodates freight and up to 75 passengers.

The only DC-10 military operator is the Royal Netherlands Air Force, which in 1995 took delivery of the first of two ex Martinair DC-10-30CFs that KLM and McDonnell Douglas had converted with refuelling boom to KDC-10 configuration. They feature a telerobotic refuelling system with TV cameras which provide three dimensional displays of refuelling operations to the refuelling operator.

*Photo:* A USAF KC-10. (Gerard Williamson)

# Mikoyan MiG-AT

*Country of origin:* Russia

*Type:* Two seat advanced trainer

*Powerplants:* Two 14.1kN (3175lb) Turbomeca-SNECMA Larzac 04-R20 turbofans. Series production aircraft for Russia planned to have two 16.7kN (3750lb) Chernyshev built Soyuz RD 1700s.

*Performance:* Estimated – Max speed at 8200ft 1000km/h (540kt), max speed at sea level 850km/h (460kt). Service ceiling 50,860ft. Ferry range approx 2600km (1405nm).

*Weights:* Normal takeoff 4610kg (10,155lb), MTOW 7000kg (15,420lb).

*Dimensions:* Wing span 10.16m (33ft 4in), length overall including nose probe 12.01m (39ft 5in), height 4.42m (14ft 6in). Wing area 17.7m² (190.2sq ft).

*Accommodation:* Two in tandem.

*Armament:* Six underwing and one centreline hardpoints on armed models can carry a max external load of 2000kg (4410lb), including missiles and bombs.

*Operators:* No firm orders placed at late 2001.

*History:* The Mikoyan MiG-AT is one of two competitors for a long running Russian air force requirement for a new advanced jet trainer to replace the Czech designed L-39 Albatros.

The MiG-AT and Yak-130 were shortlisted for further development and competitive evaluation from a number of design proposals from Russian aircraft designers. In 1992 Mikoyan reached an agreement with engine manufacturer SNECMA of France that the first two prototypes would be powered by two Larzac turbofans.

The MiG-AT is of conventional configuration and features a large degree of composite construction and reconfigurable fly-by-wire flight controls (which allows the flying characteristics of different front line aircraft to be emulated). The wing is straight and the two engines are mounted either side of the fuselage. One early design change was the repositioning of the tailplane from the top of the fin to lower down on the vertical tail.

Any MiG-ATs ordered by Russia would feature Russian avionics and engines. Mikoyan is also offering the MiG-AT for export with either Russian or French avionics. In Westernised form the MiG-AT features Thales' Topflight advanced avionics and cockpit displays including LCD colour displays, a wide angle HUD and HOTAS controls, with a Mil Std 1553B databus, allowing future integration of further Western equipment and weaponry. The French government is providing a line of credit to Mikoyan to cover the purchase of the French engines and avionics.

Series production aircraft for the Russian air force would be powered by the 16.7kN (3570lb) Aviadvigatel designed RD 1700 turbofan.

The first prototype MiG-AT first flew on March 21 1996 (following a 5min hop on March 16) and is equipped with Thales avionics. The second prototype is equipped with Russian avionics and revised inlet arrangement was unveiled in late 1997. It was displayed at the 2001 Paris Airshow with the original inlet configuration, which is cheaper to manufacture.

A single seat attack version of the MiG-AT is also planned, designated MiG-AS. Features could include an internal gun and radar.

*Photo:* The second MiG-AT prototype. (Paul Merritt)

# Mikoyan-Gurevich MiG-15 & MiG-15UTI

**Country of origin:** Russia

**Type:** Lead-in fighter and advanced trainer

**Powerplant:** MiG-15UTI – One 22.2kN (5000lb) Klimov RD-45F turbojet.

**Performance:** MiG-15UTI – Max speed at sea level 1015km/h (549kt), max speed at 9600ft 1010km/h (547kt). Time to 16,400ft 2min 35sec, time to 32,800ft 6min 48sec. Service ceiling 48,640ft. Max range with external fuel 1425km (770nm), range with internal fuel 950km (513nm). Max endurance 2hr 30min.

**Weights:** MiG-15UTI – Empty 3720kg (8200lb), max takeoff 5415kg (11,938lb).

**Dimensions:** MiG-15UTI – Wing span 10.13m (33ft 3in), length 11.15m (36ft 7in), height 3.39m (11ft 2in). Wing area 20.6m$^2$ (221.8sq ft).

**Accommodation:** Pilot only in MiG-15, or two in tandem in MiG-15UTI.

**Armament:** None usually carried, but can be fitted with one 23mm NR-23 cannon or one 12.4mm UBK-E machine gun, or one 12.7mm A-12.7 machine gun.

**Operators:** MiG-15 – Albania. MiG-15UTI – Albania, Congo, Syria, Tanzania, Yemen.

**History:** The MiG-15 shattered complacent Western beliefs of the standard of Russian aircraft design when it appeared in combat during the Korean War. Today it survives in service in single and two seat forms.

The MiG-15 (NATO reporting name 'Fagot') resulted from Project S – a 1946 requirement for a new jet powered high altitude day fighter capable of speeds over 1000km/h (540kt) with a ceiling of 46,000ft. The Lavochkin, Yakovlev and Mikoyan-Gurevich design bureaus responded with fairly similar aircraft, all with swept wings and tail surfaces, a stubby fuselage with nose air intake, and, probably most important of all, a Klimov RD-45 turbojet. The RD-45 was an unlicenced copy of the Rolls-Royce Nene centrifugal turbojet and was far more advanced than contemporary Russian turbojets.

Mikoyan-Gurevich's design, the I-310, first flew on December 30 1947. Following evaluation both the Mikoyan-Gurevich and Lavochkin designs were ordered into production, as the MiG-15 and La-15 respectively. Around 500 La-15s were built, compared with at least 3000 single seat MiG-15s (many under licence in Poland and Czechoslovakia).

Chinese MiG-15s flown by Russian pilots were used widely in combat during the Korean War. The MiG's excellent performance came as something of a shock to the West, although it was ably countered by experienced and well trained US pilots flying North American F-86 Sabres.

The basic single seater MiG-15 was in production only a year before it was replaced by the improved MiG-15bis in 1950. MiG-15bis improvements included a more powerful and reliable engine (redesignated VK-1), lower empty weight, greater fuel capacity and aerodynamic changes.

Over 5000 two seat MiG-15UTIs (or 'Midgets') were built for operational conversion and advanced training from 1949.

Today just five nations have MiG-15s (or Chinese built FT-2s) on strength – Albania, Tanzania, Syria, Yemen and Congo. Albania's are Chinese built F-2s/FT-2s. At least 7500 MiG-15s of all models were built.

**Photo:** Russia has long retired its MiG-15UTIs. (Robert Wiseman)

# Mikoyan-Gurevich MiG-17 & Chengdu J-5

**Country of origin:** Russia

**Type:** Light attack fighter

**Powerplant:** MiG-17F – One 25.5kN (5732lb) dry and 33.1kN (7450lb) with afterburning Klimov VK-1F turbojet.

**Performance:** MiG-17F – Max speed at 16,400ft Mach 0.98 or 1130km/h (610kt), max speed at 32,810ft Mach 0.93 or 1071km/h (578kt). Max initial rate of climb 12,795ft/min. Service ceiling 54,460ft. Range with external fuel at 32,810ft 1470km (794nm), range with internal fuel at 32,810ft 970km (524nm).

**Weights:** MiG-17F – Empty equipped 3930kg (8665lb), max takeoff 6070kg (13,380lb).

**Dimensions:** MiG-17F – Wing span 9.63m (31ft 7in), length 11.26m (37ft 0in), height 3.80m (12ft 6in). Wing area 22.6m$^2$ (243.3sq ft).

**Accommodation:** Pilot only, or two in tandem in JJ-5/FT-5.

**Armament:** MiG-17F – Three 23mm NR-23 cannons. Four underwing hardpoints can carry a single 250kg (550lb) bomb each, or a UV-16-57 rocket pod (with 16 x 50mm rockets) each.

**Operators:** MiG-17 – Congo, Cuba, Guinea-Bissau, Guinea, Madagascar, Mali, Syria. J-5/F-5/JJ-5/FT-5 – Albania, China, Sudan.

**History:** The MiG-17 was designed to overcome some of the performance and design shortcomings of the MiG-15.

Design work on the improved MiG-15 began in early 1949 under the designation I-330. The developed MiG-15 (Mikoyan-Gurevich's Project SI) aimed in particular to overcome the MiG-15's poor high Mach number handling characteristics (a lack of directional control limited the MiG-15's top speed to Mach 0.92).

While the MiG-17 looks very similar to the MiG-15, the -17 introduced a new increased area, wider chord wing with greater sweepback angle, and a redesigned tailplane. The tail is taller while the horizontal surfaces have greater sweepback.

The prototype MiG-17 first flew on February 1 1950 and the type was ordered into production in August 1951. Initial production was of the MiG-17 (NATO 'Fresco-A'), while the MiG-17F ('Fresco-C') introduced an afterburning VK-1F turbojet. The MiG-17PF featured radar, the MiG-17PFU radar and four radar guided AAMs.

At least 8000 MiG-17s were built in Russia, Poland (as the Lim-6) and China (as the J-5). The MiG-17 served widely with Soviet client state air forces, initially as an interceptor and later as a light attack/close support platform armed with bombs and rockets. Several nations still use it for ground attack and weapons training.

The only two seat MiG-17s were built in China, as the USSR deemed the MiG-15UTI suitable for conversion training for the MiG-17 and MiG-19. The Chinese two seat MiG-17, the JJ-5, was built by Chengdu. Design changes include the two cockpits in tandem under a similar canopy as that on the MiG-15UTI and a slightly stretched fuselage. The JJ-5 first flew on May 8 1966 and Chengdu built more than 1060 through to 1986. The JJ-5 was exported widely as the FT-5 and Albania and Sudan continue to operate it as an advanced trainer. Single seat equivalents are the J-5 and export F-5.

In 2001, China operated as many as 500 J-5s (MiG-17Fs) and 500 JJ-5 trainers.

**Photo:** A Chengdu J-5 in a museum. (Steve Allsopp)

# Mikoyan MiG-21

**Country of origin:** Russia

**Type:** Light fighter

**Powerplant:** MiG-21MF – One 39.1kN (8792lb) dry and 63.6kN (14,307lb) with afterburning Tumansky (now Soyuz) R-13-300 turbojet.

**Performance:** MiG-21MF – Max speed at 36,090ft 2230km/h (1203kt), max speed at sea level 1300km/h (703kt). Max initial rate of climb 23,620ft/min. Service ceiling (theoretical) 59,710ft. Ferry range with three drop tanks 1800km (970nm). Combat radius with four 250kg (550lb) bombs hi-lo-hi 370km (200nm), combat radius with two 250kg (550lb) bombs and external fuel hi-lo-hi 740km (400nm).

**Weights:** MiG-21MF – Empty 5350kg (11,795lb), max takeoff 9400kg (20,723lb).

**Dimensions:** MiG-21MF – Span 7.15m (23ft 6in), length incl probe 15.76m (51ft 9in), height 4.13m (13ft 6in). Wing area 23.0m$^2$ (247.5sq ft).

**Accommodation:** Pilot only, or two in tandem in MiG-21U/UM.

**Armament:** MiG-21MF – One 23mm GSh-23L cannon. Max external ordnance load of 2000kg (4410lb) on four underwing hardpoints.

**Operators:** Algeria, Angola, Bulgaria, Cambodia, Congo, Croatia, Cuba, India, Iraq, Libya, Madagascar, Mali, Mongolia, Nigeria, North Korea, Poland, Romania, Slovakia, Syria, Uganda, Vietnam, Yemen, Yugoslavia.

**History:** More MiG-21s were built (11,000+), served with more nations and fought in more wars than any other jet fighter.

The MiG-21 ('Fishbed' to NATO) was conceived as a lightweight day interceptor, with design emphasis on performance, simplicity, ease of construction and maintainability. Prototype MiG-21s were flown in swept wing 'Faceplate' and tailed delta forms in 1955.

The tailed delta configuration was selected for development. Consequently 40 preproduction MiG-21Fs were built. Initial production was of the MiG-21F-13 ('Fishbed-C'). Primary armament was a cannon and two AA-2 'Atoll' AAMs. The MiG-21F-13 also formed the basis for the MiG-21U ('Mongol') two seater conversion trainer.

Further early model MiG-21s, characterised by their forward opening single piece cockpit canopies, included the gun-less MiG-21P ('Fishbed-D'), the RP-21 Sapfir radar equipped MiG-21PF and export MiG-21FL with down spec radar and less powerful engine. The MiG-21P and MiG-21PF were called 'Fishbed-E' by NATO and later subvariants featured a ventral cannon. The MiG-21PFS and PFM (both 'Fishbed-F') were similar but introduced a two piece canopy, upgraded radar and more powerful engine.

The reconnaissance MiG-21R ('Fishbed-H') was based on the MiG-21PFM and carried a centreline recce pod which could contain a variety of sensors including optical or TV cameras, infrared sensors or a Sideways Looking Airborne Radar (SLAR).

Development of fighter MiG-21s continued with the MiG-21S with a RP-22 radar and ventral gun pod. The export MiG-21MF (and two seat UM) and more powerful R-13-300 powered MiG-21SM re-introduced an internal cannon. Improvement continued with the R-13-300 powered MiG-21MF ('Fishbed-J') with RP-22 radar and AAM missile capability on all four underwing hardpoints, plus the MiG-21SMT with an enlarged dorsal fairing containing fuel.

**Photo:** An upgraded Romanian MiG-21U. (Ian Doyle)

# Mikoyan MiG-21bis

**Country of origin:** Russia

**Type:** Light multirole fighter

**Powerplant:** One 40.2kN (9038lb) dry and 69.7kN (15,653lb) with afterburning Tumansky, with provision for two 24.5kN (5510lb) SPRD-99 rocket boosters.

**Performance:** Max speed at 42,650ft Mach 2.1 or 2175km/h (1177kt), max speed at sea level 1150km/h (620kt). Max initial rate of climb with two AAMs and 50% fuel 45,275ft/min. Service ceiling 57,415ft. Typical combat radius 450 to 500km (245 to 270nm).

**Weights:** Empty 5450kg (12,015lb), max takeoff 9800kg (21,605lb).

**Dimensions:** Wing span 7.15m (23ft 6in), length incl probe 15.76m (51ft 9in), height 4.13m (13ft 6in). Wing area 23.0m$^2$ (247.5sq ft).

**Accommodation:** Pilot only.

**Armament:** One 23mm GSh-23 cannon. One centreline and four underwing hardpoints can carry a total ordnance load of 2000kg (4410lb). Options include four rocket pods, or two 500kg (1100lb) and two 250kg (550lb) bombs, AA-2 'Atoll' and R-60 AA-8 'Aphid' AAMs.

**Operators:** Algeria, Angola, Bulgaria, Cambodia, Croatia, Cuba, Guinea, India, Poland, Romania, Syria, Vietnam, Yemen, Yugoslavia.

**History:** The MiG-21bis was developed as a multirole fighter for the Soviet Union's Frontal Aviation and was the most important and capable MiG-21 variant. Most surviving MiG-21 fighters are MiG-21bis.

The MiG-21bis introduced further improvements to the MiG-21's airframe, engine, avionics (based on those in the MiG-23), radar and weaponry. The MiG-21bis is powered by a Tumansky R-25-300 turbojet with improved after burner, over a third more powerful than the original MiG-21's engine. This increase in power allowed Mikoyan to increase the MiG-21's weights and increase fuel capacity in an enlarged dorsal spine.

The MiG-21bis entered Russian service in early 1972, and was allocated the NATO reporting name 'Fishbed-L'. NATO's 'Fishbed-N' designation covers the later production MiG-21bis-SAU fitted with an undernose ILS antenna and improved avionics.

Some 296 MiG-21s were built under licence by HAL in India between 1980 and 1987. India remains an important operator of MiG-21bis and earlier model MiG-21s with over 400 in service.

With large numbers of MiG-21bis in service the type is the subject of a number of upgrade programs. Various MiG-21 upgrades are on offer, most notably from RSK MiG and Israel's IAI. IAI's MiG-21-2000 upgrade package is offered in varying levels of equipment, including airframe overhaul, avionics upgrades and new radar. The first upgraded MiG-21-2000 first flew in May 1995.

RSK MiG offers its upgraded MiG-21-93 featuring Russian avionics, a new Phazotron Lopyo radar, helmet mounted sight, Elta EW system, Thales INS/GPS and compatibility with Russian R-73 and R-77 AAMs and KAB500 guided bombs. The first conversion flew in October 1998. India HAL began upgrading 123 MiG-21s to this standard in 2000.

The Elbit/Aerostar MiG-21 Lancer upgrade for Romania features new colour cockpit displays, a HUD, HOTAS controls and Elta 2032 radar in air defence fighters and M-2001B radar in those dedicated to ground attack.

**Photo:** A Polish MiG-21bis. Note practice bomb. (Sebastian Zacharias)

## Mikoyan MiG-23

**Country of origin:** Russia

**Type:** Multirole fighter

**Powerplant:** MiG-23ML – One 83.8kN (18,850lb) dry and 127.5kN (28,660lb) with afterburning Tumansky (now Soyuz) R-35-300 turbojet.

**Performance:** MiG-23ML – Max speed with weapons Mach 2.35 or 2500km/h (1349kt). Max initial rate of climb 47,250ft/min. Service ceiling 59,055ft. Combat radius with six AAMs 1150km (620nm), combat radius with 2000kg (4410lb) of bombs 700km (378nm).

**Weights:** MiG-23ML – Empty 10,200kg (22,485lb), max takeoff 17,800kg (39,250lb). Internal fuel 4250 litres.

**Dimensions:** MiG-23ML – Span wings extended 13.97m (45ft 10in), span wings swept 7.78m (25ft 6in), length overall exc probe 15.88m (52ft 1in), height 4.82m (15ft 10in). Wing area wings extended 37.3m² (401.5sq ft), wing area wings swept 34.2m² (368.1sq ft).

**Accommodation:** Pilot only, or two in tandem MiG-23UM and UB.

**Armament:** One twin barrel 23mm GSh-23 cannon. Five external hardpoints (one centreline, two underfuselage and two underwing) can carry a max external load of 2000kg (4410lb) on MiG-23ML. Typical air-to-air configuration of two R-60 (AA-8 'Aphid') and two R-23 (AA-7 'Apex') AAMs.

**Operators:** Algeria, Belarus, Bulgaria, Cuba, Ethiopia, India, Iraq, Libya, North Korea, Romania, Sudan, Syria, Yemen.

**History:** From the mid 1970s and into the 1980s the MiG-23 (NATO name 'Flogger') was the Soviet Union's most capable tactical fighter.

The MiG-23 was developed to replace the MiG-21, with improvements in overall performance and in particular short field performance. Two Mikoyan designed prototypes were built, the swept wing 23-01 'Faithless' and the swing wing 23-11. The 23-11 first flew on April 10 1967 and was ordered into production as the MiG-23S, fitted with the MiG-21S's RP-22 radar. Fifty were built for evaluation.

The MiG-23M ('Flogger-B') was the first model to introduce the specially designed Sapfir-23 pulse Doppler radar in a larger nose radome and also featured a more powerful engine and IRST and R-23 missile compatibility. The down graded spec export MiG-23MS ('Flogger-E') was similar, while the export and further down spec MiG-23MF ('Flogger-B') features the RP-22 radar and smaller nose.

Subsequent fighter MiG-23s were the lightened MiG-23ML ('Flogger-G') with less fuel and no dorsal fin extension, the MiG-23P interceptor that could be automatically guided to its target by ground controllers, and the MiG-23MLD ('Flogger-K') with aerodynamic changes. The MiG-23UB ('Flogger-C') is the two seat conversion trainer.

Various MiG-23 models were also built specifically for ground attack. The first to appear was the MiG-23B with a pointed, radar-less nose and a Lyulka AL-21 turbojet. The improved MiG-23BN returned to the Tumansky turbojet. NATO called both the MiG-23B and MiG-23BN the 'Flogger-F'. Further improved MiG-23 attack variants were the MiG-23BK and MiG-23BM, both of which featured nav attack systems from the MiG-27.

Various MiG-23 upgrades have been proposed.

**Photo:** A Polish MiG-23MF. Poland revived its MiG-23s in 1999. (Sebastian Zacharias)

## Mikoyan MiG-27

**Country of origin:** Russia

**Type:** Ground attack aircraft

**Powerplant:** MiG-27 – One 78.5kN (17,637lb) dry and 112.8kN (25,353lb) with afterburning Tumansky (now Soyuz) R-29B-300 turbojet.

**Performance:** MiG-27 – Max speed at 36,200ft 1885km/h (1017kt), max speed at sea level 1350km/h (728kt). Max initial rate of climb 39,370ft/min. Service ceiling 45,930ft. Combat radius with two Kh-29 ASMs and three drop tanks lo-lo-lo 540km (290nm), radius with two Kh-29s and no external fuel 225km (120nm).

**Weights:** MiG-27 – Empty equipped 11,910kg (26,252lb), max takeoff 20,300kg (44,753lb).

**Dimensions:** MiG-27 – Span wings extended 13.97m (45ft 10in), span wings swept 7.78m (25ft 6in), length 17.08m (56ft 0in), height 5.00m (16ft 5in). Wing area wings extended 37.4m² (402.1sq ft), wings swept 34.2m² (367.7sq ft).

**Accommodation:** Pilot only.

**Armament:** One GSh-6-30 30mm cannon. Max external weapons load of over 4000kg (8820lb). Options include laser, TV and electro optically guided ASMs and PGMs, conventional bombs, rockets, gun and cannon pods and tactical nuclear bombs.

**Operators:** India, Sri Lanka.

**History:** The MiG-27 is a strike and ground attack optimised development of the MiG-23.

The MiG-27 designation originally applied to a range of Mikoyan design studies aimed to meet a requirement for a modern day Shturmovik that was eventually met by the Sukhoi Su-25. Instead the MiG-27 is the definitive strike/ground attack member of the MiG-23/27 'Flogger' family.

The ground attack MiG-23s, as described in the previous entry, were regarded as interim solutions pending the arrival of the optimised MiG-27. Compared with the MiG-23, the MiG-27 features simplified air intakes (as opposed to the F-4 style variable intake ramps of the MiG-23 optimised for high end performance) and a simplified two stage afterburner nozzle. An extra external hardpoint and strengthened main undercarriage permit the carriage of over 4000kg (8820lb) of armaments. The duckbill nose (which it shares with ground attack MiG-23s) houses a laser rangefinder and other sensors. The MiG-27 features nav attack systems allowing all weather operations, and can be used in the tactical reconnaissance role carrying various recce pods.

The MiG-27 first flew in prototype form in 1972. The initial production MiG-27 was soon followed by the MiG-27K ('Flogger-D'). NATO's 'Flogger-J' designation covers the improved MiG-27D, MiG-27M and MiG-27K ('Flogger-J2') with a laser designator.

Outside the CIS India was a major MiG-27 customer, where HAL built it under licence through to 1997. India calls its aircraft MiG-27M Bahadurs, although Mikoyan refers to them as MiG-27Ls. Sri Lanka operates six MiG-27s – a seventh was destroyed in a Tamil Tigers attack on Colombo Airport in July 2001. They were acquired from Ukraine in 2000/01.

**Photo:** The duckbill nose, stronger undercarriage, simpler intakes and a shorter exhaust nozzle differentiate the MiG-27 from the MiG-23. This is an Indian MiG-27M. (Sebastian Zacharias)

## Mikoyan MiG-25

**Country of origin:** Russia

**Type:** Interceptor and reconnaissance aircraft

**Powerplants:** MiG-25PDS – Two 109.8kN (24,690lb) with afterburning Tumansky (now Soyuz) R-15BD-300 turbojets.

**Performance:** MiG-25PDS – Max speed Mach 2.8 or 3000km/h (1620kt), max speed at sea level 1200km/h (647kt). Time to 65,615ft 8min 55sec. Service ceiling 67,915ft. Range with internal fuel 1730km (933nm). Endurance 2hr 5min.

**Weights:** MiG-25PDS – Normal takeoff with four R-40 AAMs and max internal fuel 36,720kg (80,950lb). Internal fuel 17,660 litres.

**Dimensions:** MiG-25PDS – Wing span 14.02m (46ft 0in), length 23.82m (78ft 2in), height 6.10m (20ft 0in). Wing area 61.4m² (660.9sq ft).

**Accommodation:** Pilot only, or two in separate cockpits in MiG-25PU.

**Armament:** Four underwing hardpoints can carry a total ordnance load of 4000kg (9635lb). Typical interceptor configuration of two R-40 (AA-6 'Acrid') and four R-60 (AA-8 'Aphid') AAMs, or alternatively can carry four R-40s, or two R-23s (AA-7 'Apex') and four R-73A (AA-11 'Archer') AAMs. MiG-25BM can carry four Kh-58 (AS-11 'Kilter') anti radiation missiles.

**Operators:** Algeria, India, Iraq, Libya, Russia, Syria.

**History:** The MiG-25 high altitude, high speed interceptor was initially developed to counter the Mach 3 XB-70 Valkyrie bomber under development in the US in the late 1950s and early 1960s.

Although the XB-70 program was cancelled in 1961 (apart from research flying), work on Russia's new high speed interceptor and reconnaissance platform continued. The two main design considerations for the new aircraft were speed and high altitude performance, something attained at the expense of manoeuvrability. Design of the MiG-25 was also a remarkable feat, given that it had to withstand the high temperatures of high speed flight. The airframe is made mainly of nickel steel, with some titanium used in areas such as leading edges.

The first MiG-25 to fly was the Ye-155R-1 reconnaissance prototype and it first flew on March 6 1964. The interceptor Ye-166P-1 first flew that September. Under the designations Ye-266 and Ye-266M, two MiG-25s set a range of speed and altitude records, many of which remain unbroken.

Initial 'Foxbat' production was of the MiG-25P interceptor. Service entry was in 1973. Subsequent MiG-25 interceptors were the new build MiG-25PD 'Foxbat-E' with new look down shoot down radar, more powerful engines and an IRST, and the similar MiG-25PDS to which standard MiG-25Ps were rebuilt from 1979. The MiG-25PU 'Foxbat-C' two seat conversion trainer has stepped separate cockpits.

The initial reconnaissance production variant was the MiG-25R, which was soon replaced by the MiG-25RB 'Foxbat-B', which also had a ground attack capability. Variants with different equipment were the MiG-25RBS, BSh and RBV. The MiG-25RBK is fitted with SLAR rather than optical cameras, as is the MiG-25RBF. The MiG-25RU is a two seater. Finally the MiG-25BM ('Foxbat-F') is a dedicated defence suppression platform that carries up to four Kh-58 (AS-11 'Kilter') anti radiation missiles.

**Photo:** A MiG-25RB.

## Mikoyan MiG-31

**Country of origin:** Russia

**Type:** Interceptor

**Powerplants:** MiG-31 – Two 93.1kN (20,930lb) dry and 151.9kN (34,170lb) with afterburning Aviadvigatel (nee Soloviev) D-30F6 turbofans.

**Performance:** MiG-31 – Max speed Mach 2.83 or 3000km/h (1620kt), max speed at sea level 1500km/h (810kt), max cruising speed Mach 2.35, economical cruising speed Mach 0.85. Time to 32,800ft 3min. Ceiling 67,600ft. Combat radius with four R-33 AAMs and max internal fuel at Mach 2.35 720km (388nm), radius with four R-33s and external fuel at Mach 0.85 1450km (782nm). Ferry range with external fuel 3300km (1780nm). Endurance with external fuel 3hr 35min.

**Weights:** MiG-31 – Empty 21,820kg (48,110lb), max takeoff 46,200kg (101,850lb). Internal fuel 15,500kg (34,170lb).

**Dimensions:** MiG-31 – Wing span 13.46m (44ft 2in), length 22.69m (74ft 5in), height 6.15m (20ft 2in). Wing area 61.6m² (663.0sq ft).

**Accommodation:** Pilot and weapon systems operator in tandem.

**Armament:** One GSh-6-23 23mm cannon. Four R-33 (AA-9 'Amos') long range AAMs carried under the fuselage. Four underwing hardpoints (two earlier) can carry two R-40T (AA-6 'Acrid') AAMs on inner pylons and four R-60 (AA-8 'Aphid') AAMs on outboard pylons.

**Operators:** Russia

**History:** The MiG-31 two seat interceptor is designed to counter low flying strike aircraft and cruise missiles.

Development of this massive interceptor began in the 1970s, although the MiG-31 was first conceived as a single tail swing wing design, and then a tail-less canard delta. In the end a design based on the MiG-25 was settled upon and a development aircraft, the Ye-155MP, first flew on September 16 1975. Production MiG-31 'Foxhound-A's were delivered from 1979 and 280 were built.

While the MiG-31's airframe is based on the MiG-25, it is really a new aircraft. Unlike the MiG-25, the MiG-31 is powered by afterburning turbofans. Its airframe construction is made up of nickel steel (50%), light alloy (33%) and titanium (16%). The MiG-31 is also the first production aircraft to feature an electronically scanned phased array radar – the SBI 16 Zalson ('Flash Dance') – which can track up to 10 targets and engage four simultaneously. Via datalink the MiG-31 can be controlled automatically by a ground controller. Other changes include a retractable inflight refuelling probe (on later production aircraft), an internal gun and tandem main undercarriage.

Production models are the basic MiG-31 and the MiG-31B with radar, ECM and EW upgrades. Strike (MiG-31F), defence suppression (MiG-31BM) and export (MiG-31E and FE) variants have also been proposed, while two anti satellite MiG-31Ds were built.

The improved MiG-31M was developed from 1984. It features a Phazotron phased array radar, retractable IRST, no gun, two centreline hardpoints, R-37 (a derivative of the R-33) and R-77 (AA-12) AAM compatibility, a 52 tonne max takeoff weight and three colour CRTs in the rear cockpit. One has been observed with wingtip ECM pods. Just six MiG-31M prototypes were built due to a lack of funding.

Russia plans to upgrade its existing MiG-31 fleet to MiG-32BM standard with new cockpit displays and improved radar.

**Photo:** A MiG-31M prototype. (Alex Radetski)

## Mikoyan MiG-29

**Country of origin:** Russia

**Type:** Tactical counter-air fighter

**Powerplants:** MiG-29/-29S – Two 49.4kN (11,110lb) dry and 81.4kN (18,300lb) with afterburning Klimov/Sarkisov RD-33 turbofans.

**Performance:** MiG-29S – Max speed at altitude Mach 2.3 or 2445km/h (1320kt), max speed at sea level Mach 1.225 or 1500km/h (810kt). Max initial rate of climb 65,000ft/min. Ceiling 59,060ft. Range with ext fuel 3000km (1565nm), range with int fuel 1430km (772nm).

**Weights:** MiG-29S – Max takeoff 19,700kg (43,430lb). Internal fuel 4550 litres.

**Dimensions:** Span 11.36m (37ft 3in), length incl nose probe 17.32m (56ft 10in), height 4.73m (15ft 6in). Wing area 38.0m² (409.0sq ft).

**Accommodation:** Pilot only, or two in tandem in MiG-29UB.

**Armament:** MiG-29S – One 30mm GSh-301 cannon. Six underwing hardpoints can carry a max weapons load of 3000kg (6615lb), including R-27, R-73 and R-77 AAMs, plus rockets and bombs.

**Operators:** Algeria, Bangladesh, Belarus, Bulgaria, Cuba, Eritrea, Germany, Hungary, India, Iran, Iraq, Nth Korea, Malaysia, Myanmar, Peru, Poland, Romania, Slovakia, Syria, Yemen, Yugoslavia.

**History:** The highly capable MiG-29 is Russia's most important tactical fighter and has been widely exported, with over 1200 built.

Serious development of the MiG-29 began in 1974 against a Soviet air force need for a highly manoeuvrable lightweight fighter to replace a range of aircraft in Frontal Aviation service including the MiG-21, MiG-23 and Su-15. The first of 14 prototypes flew on October 6 1977, although service entry was not until 1984. Some 600 are in Russian service and several hundred have been exported.

The MiG-29 features excellent high angle of attack performance and low speed handling, plus a thrust to weight ratio greater than unity. It is equipped with a RP-29 pulse Doppler look down shoot down radar and an IRST unit which allows it to passively detect, track and engage other aircraft, and a helmet mounted sight which can cue IR guided AAMs to off boresight targets.

Doors seal the main intakes to protect the engines from foreign object damage (FOD) during start-up and taxying, with air drawn from louvred intakes in the wingroots. The intake doors open on takeoff rotation.

The basic MiG-29 'Fulcrum' (and MiG-29UB two seater) was joined in production by the 'Fulcrum-C' with a larger dorsal spine containing extra fuel. The 'Fulcrum-C' was built only for Russia and forms the basis for the MiG-29S with a modified flight control system, improved Phazotron N019M radar, compatibility with the advanced Vympel R-77 (AA-12) radar guided AAM and greater weapons load. The S is offered for export as the MiG-29SE (and SD export upgrade of the 'Fulcrum-A'). The MiG-29SM has greater ASM compatibility.

The MiG-29SMT is an upgrade of the basic MiG-29 incorporating improvements developed for the MiG-29M, including twin liquid crystal displays, upgraded HUD and improved N019MP radar. It also features an enlarged spine with more fuel. The Russian air force wants to upgrade 200 MiG-29s to SMT standard. The SMT-II would incorporate further upgrades, the SMTK would be carrier capable. The two seat UBT features SMT improvements.

**Photo:** A demonstrator for Romania's proposed MiG-29 'Sniper' upgrade.

## Mikoyan MiG-29M & MiG-29K

**Country of origin:** Russia

**Type:** Multirole fighter

**Powerplants:** MiG-29M – Two 86kN (19,355lb) with afterburning Klimov/Sarkisov RD-33K turbofans.

**Performance:** MiG-29M – Max speed Mach 2.35 or 2445km/h (1320kt), max speed at sl Mach 1.22 or 1500km/h (810kt). Max initial rate of climb 64,960ft/min. Service ceiling 55,780ft. Range with external fuel 3200km (1728nm), range with max internal fuel 2000km (1080nm). Combat radius with six AAMs and ext fuel 1400km (755nm), with 3000kg (6615lb) of bombs and ext fuel 1200km (645nm).

**Weights:** MiG-29M – Max takeoff approx 20,000kg (44,050lb).

**Dimensions:** -29M – Wing span 11.36m (37ft 3in), length incl probe 17.37m (57ft 0in), height 4.73m (15ft 6in). Wing area 38.0m² (409.0sq ft).

**Accommodation:** Pilot only.

**Armament:** MiG-29M – One GSh-301 30mm cannon. Max ordnance of 4500kg (9920lb) on eight underwing hardpoints including R-60MK (AA-8), R-27R1 (AA-10A), R-73E (AA-11) and R-77 (AA-12) AAMs, plus laser guided Kh-25ML (AS-10 'Karen'), Kh-29L (AS-14 'Kedge') ASMs, radar homing Kh-31P/A (AS-17 'Krypton') ASMs, TV guided Kh-29T (AS-14 'Kedge') ASMs, TV guided bombs, bombs and rockets.

**Operators:** India* (MiG-29K)

**History:** The MiG-29M is a multirole development of the MiG-29 and forms the basis of the carrier capable MiG-29K ordered by India.

Development of the MiG-29M dates to the mid 1980s. Six prototypes were built and the first of these flew on April 25 1986 (although powered by RD-33s rather than RD-33Ks). The first prototype powered by the definitive, more powerful RD-33K powerplants first flew in late 1989. Funding has prevented the Russian air force ordering the M into production. The MiG-29ME, later MiG-33, would have been an export aircraft, but is no longer marketed.

The MiG-29M features significant changes over the basic MiG-29. The MiG-29M has greatly increased internal fuel capacity courtesy of the bulged dorsal spine (different than that of the 'Fulcrum-C'), a smaller cannon ammunition tank and the deletion of the overwing air intakes (the MiG-29M instead features retractable meshed intake FOD doors). The MiG-29M's chaff and flare dispensers are housed in the spine rather than in the extended fins of earlier models, while the M also features redesigned leading edge root extensions, tail, and, to a lesser extent, wing.

Internally the MiG-29M features an analog fly-by-wire flight control system and a slightly aft centre of gravity for relaxed stability, a new Phazotron N-010 Zhuk radar with vastly improved processing capabilities and new operating modes expanding air-to-ground capabilities, and a revised cockpit with two CRT displays and HOTAS controls. The -29M can also fire a wider range of advanced AAMs and ASMs.

Russia passed over the MiG-29M based navalised MiG-29K for a development of Su-27, but India has ordered 46 for its new carrier (the ex Russian *Baku/Admiral Gorshkov*), plus four two seater MiG-29KUBs.

Mikoyan has also failed to interest the Russian air force in the MiG-35 development, which would have featured a Phazotron RP-35 phased array radar, more powerful engines and thrust vectoring.

**Photo:** India has ordered the MiG-29K. (Sebastian Zacharias)

# Mikoyan 1.42 MFI/1.44

**Country of origin:** Russia

**Type:** Advanced multirole fighter demonstrator

**Powerplants:** Two 175kN (39,350lb) class afterburning Lyulka/Saturn AL-41F turbofans.

**Performance:** Estimated – Max speed 2500km/h (1350kt), max supercruise speed 1700km/h (918kt). Range 4500km (2430nm).

**Weights:** Max takeoff approx 35,000kg (77,160lb).

**Dimensions:** Estimated – Wing span 17.0m (55ft 11in), length 22.8m (74ft 11in), height 5.7m (18ft 9in).

**Accommodation:** Pilot only.

**Armament:** Would likely be able to carry the full range of Russian air-to-air and air-to-ground armaments.

**Operators:** No production aircraft funded.

**History:** Mikoyan's latest fighter, the 1.44 aerodynamic prototype demonstrator for the Article 1.42 MFI (Mnogo-Funktsionalniy Istrebitel or multirole fighter) was unveiled in January 1999.

Mikoyan's 1.42 was selected as Russia's next fighter in 1986 to be developed to supersede the Su-27 and counter the USA's Advanced Tactical Fighter (which became the F-22 Raptor). However development has been slow and fitful, particularly since the collapse of the Soviet Union when funding has been scarce.

In 1999 Mikoyan unveiled a 1.44 aerodynamic demonstrator built for the 1.42 program. Taxi trials of the 1.44 occurred at Zhukovsky in 1994 (already four years behind schedule). At its unveiling in January 1999 a first flight was expected the following month, but this was delayed until February 29 2000.

If the 1.42 lived up to its claims it would prove to be a highly potent aircraft. Mikoyan's general director Mikhail Korzhuyev has claimed the aircraft's performance "... will be equal or superior to the F-22."

The two hugely powerful thrust vectoring Lyulka-Saturn AL-41 engines are designed to give the aircraft a top speed of 2600km/h (1405kt) and the ability to supercruise (cruise at supersonic speeds without afterburner). The engines have been test flown on a Tu-16 and a MiG-25. Range is said to be greater than the Su-27's.

Mikoyan also claims the 1.42 to be a stealthy design with a radar cross section comparable to the F-22, but most Western observers have suggested this claim is optimistic. Mikoyan says the aircraft has internal weapons bays but the 1.44 was fitted with underwing external pylons. The inlet and nose layout resemble's the Eurofighter Typhoon's.

The aircraft's canard delta configuration was selected for high angle of attack performance and low supersonic energy bleed. The canards and 14 other control surfaces are linked to a fly-by-wire flight control system.

The 1.44 does not appear to be fitted with radar, production aircraft would have an active phased array radar.

The Russian government does not have plans to fund further development of the program and it appears work on the production aircraft has ceased. Mikoyan is thought to have approached China about funding further development and production, evidently without any conclusive result.

**Photo:** The 1.44 demonstrator at the time of its unveiling in January 1999. (Mikoyan)

# Mil Mi-6 & Mi-22

**Country of origin:** Russia

**Type:** Heavylift transport helicopter

**Powerplants:** Mi-6T – Two 4045kW (5425shp) Soloviev (now Aviadvigatel) D-25V (TV-2BM) turboshafts driving a five blade main rotor and four blade tail rotor.

**Performance:** Mi-6T – Max speed 300km/h (162kt), max cruising speed 250km/h (135kt). Service ceiling 14,750ft. Hovering ceiling in ground effect 8200ft. Ferry range with auxiliary fuel 1450km (780nm), range with external fuel and a 4500kg (9920lb) payload 1000km (540nm), range with a 8000kg (17,635lb) payload 620km (335nm).

**Weights:** Mi-6T – Empty 27,240kg (60,055lb), max takeoff for a vertical takeoff 42,500kg (93,700lb).

**Dimensions:** Main rotor diameter 35.00m (114ft 10in), wing span 15.30m (50ft 3in), length overall rotors turning 41.74m (137ft 0in), fuselage length exc nose gun 33.18m (108ft 11in), height overall 9.86m (32ft 4in). Main rotor disc area 962.1m² (10,356sq ft).

**Accommodation:** Crew of five comprising two pilots, flight engineer, navigator and radio operator. Main cabin can accommodate 65 to 90 passengers or 70 combat equipped troops, or 41 stretcher patients and two medical attendants in medevac configuration. Max sling load 8000kg (17,637lb), max internal payload 12,000kg (26,450lb).

**Armament:** Mi-6T fitted with a 12.7mm machine gun in the nose.

**Operators:** Algeria, Iraq, Laos, Peru, Russia, Syria, Ukraine.

**History:** The remarkable Mil Mi-6 ('Hook') was the world's largest and fastest helicopter at the time of its first flight.

The Mi-6 was developed against a joint Soviet air force/Aeroflot requirement for a heavylift helicopter. The resulting Mi-6 is a behemoth, its 42 tonne max takeoff weight approaching that of the Lockheed Martin C-130 Hercules. The Mi-6 was also the first turboshaft powered helicopter in the USSR to reach production, and, remarkably for its size, became the first helicopter to break 300km/h (162kt).

The Mi-6 first flew in late 1957 and around 800 production aircraft were built through to 1981. The basic military transport Mi-6T 'Hook-A' was joined by the civilian Mi-6P with square windows, and improved Mi-6A.

Three specialised variants are the Mi-6VKP 'Hook-B', the Mi-22 'Hook-C' and Mi-6AYaSh 'Hook-D'. The Mi-6VKP and Mi-22 are both command support aircraft that seem to act as portable command posts. The Mi-6VKP can be identified by a U shaped antenna under the tailboom and a number of T shaped antennas around the tailboom. The Mi-22 can be distinguished by its single blade antenna on the tailboom and assortment of antennas under the fuselage. Little is known of their precise equipment or roles. The Mi-6AYaSh is another command post model fitted with what is thought to be a SLAR.

The Mi-6TZ tanker version was used to refuel helicopters and aircraft on the ground.

The lack of suitable airfields in the underdeveloped regions of Russia makes the Mi-6 particularly useful. Despite the type's continued utility, the Mi-6 is being retired from service as their wooden tail rotors reach the end of their service lives.

**Photo:** The Mi-6's substantial wings provide 20% of total lift in cruise. (Sebastian Zacharias)

## Mil Mi-8 & Mi-17

**Country of origin:** Russia

**Type:** Multirole transport helicopter

**Powerplants:** Mi-8 – Two 1255kW (1700shp) Klimov (Isotov) TV2-117A turboshafts driving five blade main and three blade tail rotors.

**Performance:** Mi-8 – Max speed 260km/h (140kt), max cruising speed 225km/h (122kt). Service ceiling 14,760ft. Hovering ceiling out of ground effect 2625ft. Range with standard fuel 465km (250nm).

**Weights:** Mi-8 – Empty 7600kg (16,007lb), max takeoff 12,000kg (26,455lb).

**Dimensions:** Mi-8/-17 – Main rotor diameter 21.29m (69ft 11in), length overall rotors turning 25.24m (82ft 10in), fuselage length 18.17m (59ft 7in), height overall 5.65m (18ft 7in). Main rotor disc area 356.0m² (3823.1sq ft).

**Accommodation:** Mi-8 – Two pilots and loadmaster. Main cabin can accommodate 28 troops, or 12 stretcher patients.

**Armament:** Outriggers with two hardpoints each, usually for rockets.

**Operators:** Mi-8/-17 in service with 50+ nations incl Bulgaria, China, Cuba, Czech Rep, Egypt, Hungary, India, Iraq, Nth Korea, Pakistan, Peru, Poland, Romania, Russia, Slovakia, Ukraine, Vietnam, Yugoslavia.

**History:** The rugged and useful Mi-8 and Mi-17 have been built in more numbers (12,000+) than any other Russian helicopter.

Work on the Mi-8 began in 1960 with the aim of finding a successor for the piston engined 14 seat Mi-4 'Hound'. The resulting aircraft featured the Mi-4's dynamic systems coupled to a new fuselage and powered by a turboshaft engine. The first prototype Mi-8 ('Hip-A') flew during June 1961 and was powered by a single 2015kW (2700shp) Soloviev turboshaft, but the Mi-8 was found to be underpowered so two Isotov TV2 turboshafts and a five blade main rotor were substituted instead. The Mi-8 first flew in this configuration in August 1962.

Initial production Mi-8s, including the Mi-8T, are covered by the NATO designation 'Hip-C' and include the basic military transport plus civil versions with square windows. The Mi-8TB 'Hip-E' is a dedicated assault version with three (instead of two) outrigger hardpoints either side of the fuselage for rockets or 9M17 (AT-2 'Swatter') anti armour missiles, while the export Mi-8TBK 'Hip-F' was armed with 9M14M (AT-3 'Sagger') missiles.

There have been numerous Mi-8 special mission variants including the Mi-8PS 'Hip-D' radio relay/command post aircraft, the similar Mi-9 'Hip-G' with hockey stick antennas under the tailboom and fuselage, the Mi-8SMV 'Hip-J' ECM jammer, and the Mi-8PPA 'Hip-K' communications jammer with a unique antenna array either side of the fuselage.

The Mi-17 has uprated TV3 turboshafts and can be identified by its port side tail rotor. Covered by the Mi-8M designation in Russian service, variants include the Mi-8MT 'Hip-H' transport, improved hot and high Mi-8MTV with 1633kW (2190shp) TV3-117VMs, the unarmed Mi-8AMT, and night attack Mi-8MTO. The Mi-8AMT(Sh) (developed from the Mi-8MTV) features an electro optic sight and radar, and can be armed. The Ulan-Ude built Mi-171 and Kazan built Mi-172/Mi-8MTV-3 were export equivalents of the Mi-8AMT. Kazan has also developed the Mi-17MD with rear ramp and 'dolphin' nose for radar, and Mi-17KF with Western avionics. Various upgrade programs are offered.

**Photo:** An Indian Air Force Mi-8. (Sebastian Zacharias)

## Mil Mi-14

**Country of origin:** Russia

**Type:** ASW, mine countermeasures and SAR amphibious helicopter

**Powerplants:** Mi-14PL – Two 1397kW (1874shp) Klimov (Isotov) TV3-117MT turboshafts driving a five blade main rotor and three blade tail rotor.

**Performance:** Mi-14PL – Max speed 230km/h (125kt), max cruising speed 215km/h (116kt), economical cruising speed 205km/h (110kt). Max initial rate of climb 1535ft/min. Service ceiling 11,500ft. Time to 3280ft 2min 18sec. Range with max fuel 1135km (612nm). Endurance 5hr 55min.

**Weights:** Mi-14PL – Empty 8900kg (19,625lb), max takeoff 14,000kg (30,865lb).

**Dimensions:** Mi-14PL – Main rotor diameter 21.29m (69ft 11in), length overall rotors turning 25.30m (83ft 0in), fuselage length 18.38m (60ft 4in), height overall 6.93m (22ft 9in). Main rotor disc area 356.0m² (3832.1sq ft).

**Accommodation:** Mi-14PL has a crew of four. The Mi-14PS has a crew of three and can accommodate 10 rescued survivors in the main cabin including two on stretchers.

**Armament:** The Mi-14PL can carry torpedoes, bombs and depth charges in an enclosed weapons bay in the lower hull.

**Operators:** Cuba, Libya, North Korea, Russia, Syria.

**History:** The Mi-14 is an amphibious development of the Mi-8/Mi-17, used for a variety of maritime tasks including anti submarine warfare, search and rescue and mine countermeasures.

The Mi-8 was a logical replacement for a number of Mi-4 variants in Soviet naval service, and so development on a navalised variant began in 1968. Under the preliminary designation V-14 the first Mi-14 prototype first flew in 1968. This first prototype featured the TV2 turboshafts and right hand side tail rotor of the Mi-8, while production Mi-14s feature the more powerful TV3s and left hand side tail rotor later introduced on the Mi-17. The most notable feature of the Mi-14 (NATO name 'Haze') is the boat-like hull, sponsons, floatation equipment and retractable undercarriage.

The Mi-14 was built in three basic variants. The Mi-14PL 'Haze-A' is the ASW variant and features a large undernose radome, dunking sonar, sonobuoys, an APM-60 towed MAD bird and a weapons bay which can house torpedoes, bombs and depth charges. It is designated Mi-14PW in Polish service. An improved model is designated Mi-14PLM.

The Mi-14BT 'Haze-B' is a dedicated mine countermeasures variant. The Mi-14BT was introduced into service in the early 1980s and can carry three towed sleds to counter magnetic, acoustic or contact mines. The Mi-14BT retains the nose radome but lacks the MAD bird of the Mi-14PL and has a searchlight.

Finally the search and rescue Mi-14PS 'Haze-C' features an enlarged sliding door, a retractable hoist, a searchlight either side of the nose and carries 10 20-place liferafts. The cabin can accommodate 10 rescued survivors, while others can be towed in liferafts.

The Mi-14P and Mi-14GP are civilian conversions. The Mi-14PZh and Mi-14 Helitanker are firefighting conversions.

**Photo:** A Russian navy Mi-14PS. (Sebastian Zacharias)

## Mil Mi-24, Mi-25 & Mi-35

**Country of origin:** Russia

**Type:** Armed assault/attack helicopter

**Powerplants:** Mi-24P – Two 1635kW (2190shp) Klimov TV3-117 turboshafts driving a five blade main rotor and three blade tail rotor.

**Performance:** Mi-24P – Max speed 335km/h (180kt), cruising speed 270km/h (145kt), economical cruising speed 217km/h (117kt). Max initial rate of climb 2460ft/min. Service ceiling 14,750ft. Hovering ceiling out of ground effect 4920ft. Range with auxiliary fuel 1000km (540nm), range with standard internal fuel 500km (270nm). Combat radius with max military load 160km (85nm), radius with two external fuel tanks 225km (120nm), radius with four tanks 288km (155nm).

**Weights:** Mi-24P – Empty 8200kg (18,078lb), max takeoff 12,000kg (26,455lb).

**Dimensions:** Mi-24P – Main rotor diameter 17.30m (56ft 9in), length overall rotors turning 21.35m (70ft 1in), fuselage length exc gun 17.51m (57ft 5in), height to top of rotor head 3.97m (13ft 1in). Main rotor disc area 235.1m² (2530.2sq ft).

**Accommodation:** Weapons operator and pilot in tandem stepped cockpits. Main cabin can accommodate eight troops or four stretchers.

**Armament:** One 12.7mm four barrel YakB machine gun in undernose turret or twin 23mm or 30mm cannons. Two anti tank missiles on each stub wing endplate. Four underwing hardpoints for rockets and guns.

**Operators:** Algeria, Angola, Armenia, Azerbaijan, Bulgaria, Croatia, Cuba, Czech Rep, Hungary, India, Iraq, Libya, Mozambique, Nigeria, Nth Korea, Peru, Poland, Russia, Rwanda, Slovakia, Syria, Ukraine, Yemen.

**History:** Mil's feared 'Devil's Chariot' is unique in that it is a combined armed assault/attack helicopter, although the latter is its primary role.

The Mi-24 was based on the dynamic systems of the Mi-8 transport helicopter, although almost all production aircraft feature the TV3 turboshafts and port side tail rotor of the upgraded Mi-17. First flight of the V-24 prototype was on September 19 1969, while production Mi-24 'Hind-A's entered service in 1973. Early production 'Hind-A's, 'Hind-B's and 'Hind-C's feature a glasshouse style cockpit for the pilot and weapons operator which afforded poor visibility and protection.

The Mi-24D 'Hind-D' and export Mi-25 introduced the definitive stepped and armoured cockpits, plus the four barrel 12.7mm machine gun in an undernose turret plus undernose missile guidance and electro optical pods. The similar Mi-24V 'Hind-E' (or Mi-35 for export) introduced more powerful TV3-117V engines, the stubwing endplates for 9M114 (AT-6 'Spiral') anti armour missiles and a HUD for the pilot. The Mi-24VP introduced a twin barrel GSh-23L cannon on the starboard fuselage side as operational experience in Afghanistan found the original gun ineffective against some targets, while the Mi-24P 'Hind-F' (and export Mi-35P) has a twin 30mm cannon. The Mi-24RKR is a NBC reconnaissance platform, the Mi-24K an artillery spotter. The Mi-24VN is an interim night attack model with NVG compatible cockpit.

Mil is developing the upgraded Mi-35M, featuring the Mi-28's rotors and transmission, 1636kW (2194shp) TV3-117VMA engines, a 23mm cannon and 9K114-9 Attacka advanced anti armour missiles, Thales of France avionics and displays and Chlio FLIR ball. Russia plans to upgrade 200 Mi-24s in a three phased program to Mi-35M standard.

**Photo:** IAI Taman's Mi-24 upgrade. (IAI)

## Mil Mi-26

**Country of origin:** Russia

**Type:** Heavylift helicopter

**Powerplants:** Mi-26 – Two 7460kW (10,000shp) ZMKB Progress (Lotarev) D-136 turboshafts driving an eight blade main rotor and five blade tail rotor.

**Performance:** Mi-26 – Max speed 295km/h (160kt), typical cruising speed 255km/h (137kt). Service ceiling 15,100ft. Hovering ceiling in ground effect 14,765ft. Range with max internal fuel at max takeoff weight with reserves 800km (432nm), range with four auxiliary fuel tanks 1920km (1036nm).

**Weights:** Mi-26 – Empty 28,200kg (62,170lb), normal takeoff 49,600kg (109,350lb), max takeoff 56,000kg (123,450lb).

**Dimensions:** Mi-26 – Main rotor diameter 32.00m (105ft 0in), length overall 40.03m (131ft 4in), fuselage length 33.73m (110ft 8in), height to top of rotor head 8.15m (26ft 9in). Main rotor disc area 804.3m² (8657sq ft).

**Accommodation:** Flightcrew of four with two pilots, flight engineer and navigator, plus loadmaster. Four seat passenger compartment behind flightdeck. Main cabin accommodates freight typically (max payload 20 tonnes/44,090lb), or up to 80 combat equipped troops, or in medevac role 60 stretcher patients and four or five medical attendants. Mi-26MS medical version equipped with operating theatre and accommodation for stretcher patients and medical attendants.

**Armament:** None

**Operators:** India, Mexico, Peru, Russia, Ukraine.

**History:** The largest helicopter in the world by a large margin, the Mi-26 (NATO reporting name 'Halo') has a maximum takeoff weight greater than that of the Transall C-160 and an internal freight hold close in size to that in the C-130 Hercules.

Development of the Mi-26 began in the early 1970s and resulted in a first flight on December 14 1977. The original design requirement called for a helicopter for military and civil use with a maximum takeoff weight one and a half times that of any previous helicopter. Preproduction machines were built from 1980, production machines some time after that. The first Mi-26s are understood to have become operational with the Soviet military during 1983.

The Mi-26 is notable for its eight blade main rotor, powerful turboshaft engines, massive size, rear loading freight doors and twin internal hoists. Several versions have been developed or proposed.

These include the basic Mi-26 'Halo-A' freighter, the equivalent civil Mi-26T and export Mi-26TS, Mi-26MS medevac version, civil Mi-26P 63 passenger airliner, Mi-26TP firebomber, Mi-26TM and PK flying cranes, Mi-26TZ fuel tanker and anti submarine warfare Mi-26NEF-M with undernose radome and towed MAD.

The improved Mi-26M is under development and features new 10,700kW (14,350shp) ZMKB Progress D-127 turboshafts, reprofiled composite main rotor blades, improved aerodynamics, better hot and high performance, 22 tonne max payload and EFIS cockpit displays.

The Mi-26 or Mi-26M could also form the basis of a replacement for command support Mi-6s (possibly designated Mi-27).

Around 280 Mi-26Ts are estimated to have been built so far.

**Photo:** A Mi-26 flying crane. (Sebastian Zacharias)

# Mil Mi-28

**Country of origin:** Russia

**Type:** Two seat attack helicopter

**Powerplants:** Mi-28N – Two 1838kW (2465shp) for takeoff Klimov TV3 turboshafts driving a five blade main rotor and four blade tail rotor.

**Performance:** Mi-28N – Max speed 320km/h (172kt), max cruising speed 265km/h (143kt). Max initial rate of climb 2677ft/min. Service ceiling 10,700ft. Hovering ceiling out of ground effect 14,760ft. Ferry range with reserves 1100km (595nm), max range with standard fuel 460km (250nm). Combat radius with standard fuel, 10min loiter and reserves 200km (110nm). Endurance with max fuel 2hr.

**Weights:** Mi-28N – Empty equipped 8590kg (18,938lb), max takeoff 11,500kg (25,353lb).

**Dimensions:** Main rotor diameter 17.20m (56ft 5in), length exc rotors 17.01m (55ft 9in), height to top of rotor head 3.82m (12ft 7in). Main rotor disc area 232.3m$^2$ (2501sq ft).

**Accommodation:** Navigator/weapons operator and pilot in stepped tandem cockpit with navigator in front cockpit. A rear fuselage compartment can accommodate two or three people – intended for emergency recovery of personnel only.

**Armament:** One NPPU-28 30mm cannon in undernose turret. Four underwing hardpoints can carry a combined ordnance load of 1920kg (4230lb). Typical configuration of two rocket pods and up to 16 9P149 Shturm C (AT-6 'Spiral') radio guided tube launched anti armour missiles.

**Operators:** No production aircraft ordered.

**History:** Manoeuvrable, well armed, armoured and fast, the Mi-28 is Mil's first dedicated two seat attack helicopter, developed in competition with the Kamov Ka-50 to meet a long standing Russian army requirement.

Mi-28 (NATO reporting name 'Havoc') design began in 1980 under Marat Tishchenko. The first of three prototypes first flew on November 10 1982.

The Mi-28 has tandem stepped cockpits with energy absorbing crew seats, an undernose turret containing a 30mm cannon, stubwings with two hardpoints each and twin TV3-117VM turboshafts (the TV3 also powers the Ka-50, plus Mil's Mi-17 and Mi-24). The original three blade tail rotor unit has been replaced by a four blade X shaped unit, similar to that on the AH-64 Apache. The cockpits feature ceramic and titanium armour, while the entire airframe is designed to absorb and survive small arms fire. Countermeasures are carried in the wingtip pods. The thimble nose radome contains a missile guidance radar, beneath are two fixed infrared sensors.

The Mi-28N is an improved night/all weather development featuring a mast mounted millimetre wave radar (either Kinzhal V or Arbalet), a FLIR ball turret under the nose radome, a low light TV, night vision compatible cockpit lighting, EFIS displays, integrated flight/weapon aiming system with automatic terrain following and uprated 1838kW (2465shp) for takeoff TVS-117VK turboshafts and swept main rotor tips.

The Mi-28N first flew on April 30 1997. Production aircraft would be to Mi-28N standard.

**Photo:** The mast mounted sight equipped Mi-28N. (Alex Radetski)

# Morane-Saulnier MS-760 Paris

**Country of origin:** France

**Type:** Basic trainer, light strike, fast liaison/communications and target simulation aircraft.

**Powerplants:** MS-760B – Two 4.74kN (1058lb) Turbomeca Maboré VI turbojets.

**Performance:** MS-760B – Max speed at 25,000ft 695km/h (375kt), max cruising speed at 16,400ft 633km/h (342kt), economical cruising speed 550km/h (297kt). Max initial rate of climb 2460ft/min. Service ceiling 39,370ft. Max range 1740km (940nm).

**Weights:** MS-760B – Empty equipped 2067kg (4557lb), max takeoff 3920kg (8642lb).

**Dimensions:** MS-760B – Wing span 10.15m (33ft 3in), length 10.24m (33ft 7in), height 2.60m (8ft 6in). Wing area 18.0m$^2$ (193.7sq ft).

**Accommodation:** Seating for four.

**Armament:** For weapons training and light strike two underwing hardpoints (one under each wing) can carry 7.5m machine gun pods, rockets or light bombs.

**Operators:** Argentina

**History:** Morane-Saulnier's four seat Paris jet was designed primarily as a high speed military liaison/communications aircraft but was also offered in civil forms. A small number remain in service with the Argentine air force.

The Paris was based on Morane-Saulnier's MS-755 Flueret, a two seat jet trainer which flew in 1953. The larger MS-760 Paris introduced seating for four under a rearwards sliding canopy with dual controls for pilot training, a straight wing, two Turbomeca Maboré turbojets (fed through air inlets in the wingroots) and a T-tail. It can be armed with four 3.5in rockets, gun pods or 50kg (110lb) bombs for weapons training missions.

The prototype Paris, designated MS-760-01, first flew on July 29 1954. The Paris was then subsequently adopted by the French air force for communications and liaison duties. Initial production was of the 3.94kN (880lb) Maboré IIC turbojet powered MS-760A, which first flew on February 7 1958. The production total of 150 MS-760As includes 48 assembled in Argentina by FMA.

About 15 of the MS-760s delivered to Argentina remain in service, upgraded to improved MS-760B standard. The MS-760B flew on December 12 1960 and introduced more powerful Maboré VI turbojets, integral fuel tanks in the wing leading edge and wingtip fuel tanks. Sixty-three new production MS-760Bs were built, including 48 assembled in Brazil for that country's air force.

In all 219 MS-760s were manufactured. A stretched six seat development, the MS 760C Paris III, flew in February 1964 and was offered for civil use as an executive transport.

Until recently about 30 MS-760s remained in service with the French Armée de l'Air where they were used for liaison, continuation training and target simulation. Eight in French navy service have also been recently retired.

Argentina's surviving MS-760s are used by two units for weapons training, while Brazil's MS-760s have long been retired.

**Photo:** The French air force and navy have retired their MS-760s, leaving Argentina (pictured) the only operator. (Santiago Rivas)

## Mitsubishi T-2

**Country of origin:** Japan

**Type:** Two seat advanced trainer and weapons trainer

**Powerplants:** Two 22.8kN (5115lb) dry and 32.5kN (7305lb) with afterburning Ishikawajima-Harima TF40-IHI-801A (licence built Rolls-Royce Turbomeca Adour Mk 801) turbofans.

**Performance:** Max speed at 36,000ft Mach 1.6 or 1700km/h (917kt). Max initial rate of climb 35,000ft. Service ceiling 50,000ft. Ferry range 2595km (1400nm).

**Weights:** Operating empty 6305kg (13,905lb), max takeoff 12,800kg (28,220lb).

**Dimensions:** Wing span 7.88m (25ft 10in), length overall incl probe 17.86m (58ft 7in), fuselage length 17.31m (56ft 10in), height 4.33m (14ft 3in). Wing area 21.2m² (227.9sq ft).

**Accommodation:** Two in tandem.

**Armament:** T-2A – One licence built JM61 Vulcan 20mm cannon in lower fuselage. AIM-9 Sidewinder or Mitsubishi AAM-1 AAMs on wingtips, plus bombs, rocket pods and fuel tanks on one centreline and four underwing hardpoints.

**Operators:** Japan

**History:** The T-2 is Japan's first indigenously developed supersonic aircraft and serves as the Japan Air Self Defence Force's primary advanced trainer and weapons trainer.

The Japanese Defence Ministry selected Mitsubishi as prime contractor to develop a supersonic advanced and weapons trainer in September 1967. The T-2 was designed by a team led by Dr Kenji Ikeda and the resulting aircraft was similar in configuration and philosophy to the Northrop T-38 Talon and the SEPECAT Jaguar. First flight of the first of four flying XT-2 prototypes was on July 20 1971. Service entry was in 1976.

The Mach 1.6 T-2 was designed as a lead-in trainer for F-4EJ and F-104J fighters. It features two afterburning licence built Rolls-Royce Turbomeca Adour 801A turbofans (built under licence in Japan by Ishikawajima-Harima as the TF40-IHI-801A), a shoulder mounted wing (which lacks ailerons, lateral control is instead provided by differential spoilers ahead of the flaps), an airbrake on either side of the fuselage, tandem seating under separate canopies and licence built ejection seats. About 10% of the T-2's structure by weight is titanium, in particular around the engine bays.

Ninety production T-2s were ordered, comprising 28 standard T-2 trainers and 62 T-2A combat trainers. The T-2A features wingtip missile rails for Sidewinder or Mitsubishi AAM-1 infrared guided air-to-air missiles, a JM61 Vulcan 20mm cannon, four underwing hardpoints for weaponry, a HUD and a Mitsubishi Electric J/AWG-11 search and ranging radar.

A single T-2 was converted to act as the T-2CCV control configured vehicle, with a triplex digital fly-by-wire flight control system and canards with test equipment in the rear cockpit. In addition, two T-2s were built as prototypes for the F-1 ground attack fighter (which is described in the next entry).

The last production T-2 was delivered in early 1988 to the 4th Air Wing at Matsushima.

**Photo:** A JASDF T-2 on its landing roll. (John Adlard)

## Mitsubishi F-1

**Country of origin:** Japan

**Type:** Close support/ground attack fighter

**Powerplants:** Two 22.8kN (5115lb) dry and 32.5kN (7305lb) with afterburning Ishikawajima-Harima TF40-IHI-801A (licence built Rolls-Royce Turbomeca Adour Mk 801) turbofans.

**Performance:** Max speed at 36,000ft Mach 1.6 or 1700km/h (917kt). Max initial rate of climb 35,000ft/min. Service ceiling 50,000ft. Combat radius with eight 500lb/227kg bombs, hi-lo-hi 350km (190nm), combat radius with two ASM-1 anti ship missiles and two drop tanks, hi-lo-hi 555km (300nm).

**Weights:** Operating empty 6358kg (14,017lb), max takeoff 13,700kg (30,203lb).

**Dimensions:** Wing span 7.88m (25ft 10in), length overall incl probe 17.85m (58ft 7in), fuselage length 17.31m (56ft 10in), height 4.48m (14ft 8in). Wing area 21.2m² (227.9sq ft).

**Accommodation:** Pilot only.

**Armament:** One licence built JM61 Vulcan 20mm internal cannon. AIM-9L Sidewinder or Mitsubishi AAM-1 AAMs on wingtip and outboard underwing hardpoints. One centreline and four underwing hardpoints for bombs, rocket pods and fuel tanks. Can carry an ASM-1 radar guided anti ship missile on each inboard underwing pylon.

**Operators:** Japan

**History:** The T-2 advanced trainer based Mitsubishi F-1 is the first supersonic fighter built in Japan and is tasked primarily with anti shipping strike.

The Japan Air Self Defence Force ordered the development of a single seat ground attack development of the Mitsubishi T-2 under the provisional designation FS-T2-Kai in 1972. The second and third production T-2 trainers were converted to act as F-1 prototypes, and the first of these flew in modified form on June 3 1975 (the second flew four days later).

The F-1 prototypes were largely unchanged from the T-2 except that the faired over rear cockpit contained a fire control system and test equipment. In mid 1975 they were delivered to the JASDF's Air Proving Wing at Gifu for a year of service testing. Following the successful completion of service trials the F-1 designation was adopted and the type was ordered into production. In all, 77 F-1s were built, delivered between September 1977 and March 1987, replacing elderly F-86 Sabres.

The only major change from the T-2 to the F-1 was the faired over second cockpit which contains the bombing computer, inertial navigation system and radar warning system. From 1982 the Mitsubishi J/AWG-12 search and ranging radar replaced the earlier J/AWG-11, introducing compatibility with the radar guided ASM-1 anti ship air-to-surface missile. With this weapon the F-1 is primarily tasked with anti shipping strike. The F-1 is also cleared to fire the AIM-9L Sidewinder.

The F-1 is due to be replaced by the Mitsubishi F-2 which began entering service in 2000.

**Photo:** Compared with its predecessor the T-2, the F-1 features avionics in the faired over rear cockpit and a higher max takeoff weight. About 60 survive in JASDF service. (John Adlard)

## Mitsubishi F-2

**Countries of origin:** Japan and the USA

**Type:** Ground attack and maritime strike fighter

**Powerplants:** One 131.7kN (29,600lb) with afterburning General Electric F110-GE-129 turbofan.

**Performance:** Max speed approx Mach 2.0. F-2A combat radius over 835km (450nm).

**Weights:** Empty 9525kg (21,000lb), max takeoff 22,100kg (48,722lb). Internal fuel 4637 litres.

**Dimensions:** Wing span over wingtip missile rails 11.13m (36ft 6in), length overall 15.52m (50ft 11in), height 4.96m (16ft 4in). Wing area 34.8m² (375.0sq ft).

**Accommodation:** Pilot only, or two in tandem in F-2B.

**Armament:** One M61A1 Vulcan 20mm internal cannon. AIM-9L Sidewinders or Mitsubishi AAM-3 AAMs on wingtip rails. One centreline and four underwing hardpoints. Weaponry includes Mitsubishi ASM-1 and ASM-2 anti ship missiles and AIM-7M Sparrow AAMs.

**Operators:** Japan*

**History:** The Mitsubishi F-2 is a development of the Lockheed Martin F-16C to replace Japan's F-1s for maritime strike, ground attack and counter air missions.

In the early 1980s Japan's Technical Research and Development Institute had been studying designs for a new fighter for the Japan Air Self Defence Force to replace F-1s. However the USA exerted considerable pressure on Japan to continue to buy US sourced weapons and to reduce the large trade imbalance between the two countries. Thus plans to develop an indigenous fighter were dropped in 1987 with the Japan Defence Agency (JDA) instead compromising on developing an existing US fighter with considerable US industrial participation.

The then General Dynamics F-16 was selected to form the basis of the new FS-X support fighter in October 1987. Mitsubishi was appointed prime contractor in November 1988 while the General Electric F110-GE-129 was selected as the FS-X's powerplant in December 1990. Four FS-X prototypes were built, the first flying on October 7 1995. The FS-X was redesignated F-2 in December that year.

Compared with the F-16 the F-2 features a 25% larger wing constructed of co-cured composites, a longer fuselage, conventional cockpit canopy, a Mitsubishi Electric developed active phased array radar and Japanese avionics including the integrated electronic warfare system, liquid crystal displays and a HUD. In addition the F-2 features a Japanese developed fly-by-wire flight control system (developed on the T-2CCV) because of the USA's refusal to release F-16 fly-by-wire software source codes. Lockheed Martin builds the rear fuselage and parts of the wing.

The JASDF originally required 141 FS-Xs, including some two seat TFS-X conversion trainers, although funding cuts and spiralling development costs (over $US3bn) saw this number reduced, initially to around 80. The JDA now plans to acquire 130 – 83 F-2A fighters and 47 F-2B two seat conversion trainers. Problems with the composite wing delayed first deliveries, until September 2000.

Mitsubishi has proposed a dedicated air superiority version to replace Japan's F-4s.

**Photo:** Early production F-2s cost about $US100m. (Lockheed Martin)

## NAMC YS-11

**Country of origin:** Japan

**Type:** Utility transport, ECM trainer and Elint platform

**Powerplants:** YS-11A-200 – Two 2280kW (3060shp) Rolls-Royce Dart Mk 542-10K turboprops driving four blade propellers.

**Performance:** -200 – Max cruising speed 470km/h (253kt), economical cruising speed 452km/h (244kt). Service ceiling 22,900ft. Range with max payload and no reserves 1090km (590nm), range with max fuel and no reserves 3215km (1736nm).

**Weights:** -200 – Operating empty 15,419kg (33,993lb), max takeoff 24,500kg (54,010lb).

**Dimensions:** Wing span 32.00m (105ft 0in), length 26.30m (86ft 4in), height 8.98m (29ft 6in). Wing area 94.8m² (1020.4sq ft).

**Accommodation:** Flightcrew of two. Typical seating in main cabin for 60. JMSDF YS-11M-As have seating for 48 with a rear cargo compartment. The combi YS-11A-300 was designed for freight in the forward fuselage and seating for 46 in rear fuselage.

**Armament:** None

**Operators:** Greece, Japan.

**History:** The YS-11 is postwar Japan's only locally developed airliner. Several serve with the Japanese military.

The YS-11 was a product of the Nihon Aircraft Manufacturing Company (NAMC), a consortium of Fuji, Kawasaki, Mitsubishi, Nippi, Shin Meiwa and Showa. NAMC was formed on June 1 1959 specifically to design and develop a short to medium range airliner, particularly to meet the requirements of Japanese domestic airlines.

Within NAMC Fuji was given responsibility for the tail unit, Kawasaki the wings and engine nacelles, Mitsubishi the forward fuselage and final assembly, Nippi the ailerons and flaps, Shin Meiwa the rear fuselage and Showa the light alloy honeycomb structural components.

The YS-11 first flew on August 30 1962. Airline service entry was in April 1965. Initial production was of the YS-11-100. The YS-11A-200 was designed for export and had an increased max takeoff weight. The YS-11A-300 was a combi passenger/freight model, while the YS-11A-400 was a pure freighter with a forward freight door. The YS-11A-500, -600 and -700 were equivalent to the -200, -300 and -400, but with a 500kg (1100lb) greater max takeoff weight. Production ceased in February 1974 after 182 were built.

The Japan Air Self Defence Force acquired four YS-11-100s as YS-11Ps for VIP transport, a YS-11-300 combi as the YS-11PC, seven YS-11-400 freighters as YS-11Cs (one subsequently converted to a YS-11NT nav trainer), and a YS-11-200 as a YS-11FC for flight check duties. In 1976 two YS-11Cs were converted to YS-11E ECM trainers (festooned with various antennas and a large chaff/flare dispenser fairing behind the starboard wing). A third YS-11C was converted as a YS-11E(EL) in 1982 for Elint reconnaissance.

The Japanese Maritime Self Defence Force acquired two YS-11-100s as YS-11M transports and two YS-11-400 combis as YS-11M-As. Four YS-11-200s and two YS-11-600s serve as YS-11T-A ASW crew trainers, fitted with a search radar in an underbelly radome, while two transports also remain in service.

Greece has operated ex Olympic Airways YS-11s as transports.

**Photo:** One of Greece's YS-11s. (Greek MoD)

# Nanchang CJ-5 & CJ-6/PT-6

**Country of origin:** China

**Type:** Two seat basic trainer

**Powerplant:** CJ-6A – One 215kW (285hp) Zhuzhou (SMPMC) HS6A nine cylinder radial piston engine (Chinese development of the Ivchenko AI-14R) driving a two blade propeller.

**Performance:** CJ-6A – Max speed 297km/h (160kt), cruising speed 260km/h (160kt). Max initial rate of climb 1250ft/min. Service ceiling 20,500ft. Range with max fuel 690km (372nm). Endurance 3hr 35min.

**Weights:** CJ-6A – Empty 1095kg (2414lb), max takeoff 1400kg (3086lb).

**Dimensions:** CJ-6A – Wing span 10.22m (33ft 7in), length 8.46m (27ft 9in), height 3.25m (10ft 8in).

**Accommodation:** Two in tandem.

**Armament:** CJ-6 – None, although 10 armed CJ-6Bs built could carry light armament.

**Operators:** Albania, Bangladesh, China, North Korea, Sri Lanka, Zambia.

**History:** The Nanchang CJ-6 is a Chinese development of the Yak-18 and is that country's primary basic trainer.

During the 1950s China had built the Yak-18 under licence as the CJ-5. China began development of its own version of the Yak-18/CJ-5 optimised specifically for its requirements and incorporating a number of improvements in the mid 1950s. Design work was carried out at Shenyang during the late 1950s. The first prototype first flew on August 27 1958 and it was powered by a 110kW (145hp) Mikulin M-11ER engine. However the CJ-6 prototype soon proved underpowered and a re-engined aircraft powered by a 195kW (260hp) Ivchenko AI-14R first flew in July 1960.

CJ-6 design and production was subsequently transferred to Nanchang where further design changes were incorporated and a production standard CJ-6 first flew on October 15 1961. Production go-ahead was announced the following year.

Compared with the CJ-5, the CJ-6 differed in its retractable undercarriage and more powerful engine. Initial production CJ-6s were powered by the 195kW (260hp) Chinese HS6 version of the Ivchenko AI-14. The CJ-6 was superseded in production by the definitive CJ-6A in 1965. The CJ-6A introduced the 215kW (285hp) HS6A. In addition, 10 armed CJ-6Bs were built between 1964 and 1966.

The CJ-6 was also considered the basis for a civil agricultural spraying aircraft, and a single prototype flew in this form as the Haiyan-A.

In all, around 1800 CJ-6s were built through to the mid 1980s, with all but 200 for the PLA-AF. It has been exported to several non-aligned nations – Bangladesh, Cambodia, North Korea, Tanzania and Zambia – where it carries the Westernised PT-6A designation, except for Bangladesh, whose aircraft are designated BT-6.

The CJ-6 is easy to fly, rugged, easy to maintain and well suited to its training role. Design features include the two blade constant speed prop, dihedral on the outer wing panels and a framed glasshouse style canopy covering the two occupants and giving good all round visibility. Several fly in the West as warbirds in private hands.

**Photo:** One of the 1800 CJ-6 trainers built. About 1500 remain in Chinese service. CJ stands for Chuji Jiaolanji, which translates to basic training aircraft. (Sebastian Zacharias)

# Nanchang Q-5/A-5

**Country of origin:** China

**Type:** Ground attack aircraft

**Powerplants:** Two 25.5kN (5732lb) dry and 31.9kN (7165lb) with afterburning Shenyang WP6 turbojets.

**Performance:** A-5C – Max speed at 36,000ft Mach 1.12 or 1190km/h (643kt), max speed at sea level 1210km/h (653kt). Max rate of climb at 16,400ft, 16,430 to 20,275ft/min. Service ceiling 52,000ft. Range with max internal and external fuel 2000km (1080nm). Combat radius with max external stores hi-lo-hi 600km (325nm), lo-lo-lo 400km (215nm).

**Weights:** A-5C – Empty 6375kg (14,054lb), max takeoff 12,000kg (26,455lb).

**Dimensions:** A-5C – Wing span 9.70m (31ft 10in), length overall incl nose probe 16.26m (53ft 4in), length exc nose probe 15.42m (50ft 7in), height 4.52m (14ft 10in). Wing area 28.0m² (300.9sq ft).

**Accommodation:** Pilot only.

**Armament:** Q-5 II/A-5C – Two Norinco Type 23 23mm cannons. Ten external hardpoints for a max ordnance load of 2000kg (4410lb) including bombs, rockets, air-to-surface and air-to-air missiles. Some Chinese aircraft believed to be modified to carry a five to 20kT nuclear bomb.

**Operators:** Bangladesh, China, Myanmar, North Korea, Pakistan.

**History:** The Nanchang Q-5 (export designation A-5) is a close air support/ground attack fighter developed from China's MiG-19 copy.

Development of the Q-5 (NATO reporting name 'Fantan') began in 1958, with Shenyang undertaking initial work and mock-up construction and assisting Nanchang with subsequent detail design. Prototype construction began in May 1960 although the Chinese Cultural Revolution intervened and the prototype program was cancelled in 1961. Between then and 1963 when development was officially reinstated a small team continued work on the aircraft. First flight was on June 4 1965 and subsequent testing revealed the need for a number of modifications. The first of two prototypes with the required changes flew in late 1969 and production aircraft were delivered from 1970.

The Q-5 retained the Shenyang J-6's (MiG-19's) rear fuselage and powerplants but features a stretched area-ruled fuselage with an internal weapons bay, side mounted air intakes, a new conical nose and larger wings with less sweepback.

Initial production was of the Q-5. The longer range Q-5 I has extra fuel in place of the internal bomb bay. Chinese navy Q-5 Is may be fitted with a radar and can carry C-801 anti ship missiles and torpedoes. The Q-5 IA gained two extra underwing hardpoints and the Q-5 II is fitted with a radar warning receiver.

The A-5C was developed for Pakistan and is based on the Q-5 I but with upgraded Western avionics and compatibility with Western weapons (including the AIM-9). The export A-5K Kong Yun (Cloud) with Thomson-CSF laser rangefinder was cancelled in 1990.

The A-5M was also intended for export and features improved engines and Alenia avionics based on those in the AMX, including a ranging radar, INS, HUD and RWR. It first flew in 1988, but none were sold and development was later abandoned.

Almost 1000 Q-5/A-5s were built.

**Photo:** The A-5C was exported to Pakistan. (Sebastian Zacharias)

# NH Industries NH 90

**Countries of origin:** France, Germany, Italy and the Netherlands

**Type:** Medium lift tactical transport and naval helicopter

**Powerplants:** Two 1566kW (2100shp) Rolls-Royce Turbomeca RTM 322-01/9 turboshafts or in Italian aircraft two 1521kW (2040shp) General Electric T700-T6Es driving four blade main and tail rotors.

**Performance:** TTH – Max cruising speed 298km/h (160kt), econ cruising speed 259km/h (140kt). Service ceiling 13,940ft, absolute ceiling 19,680ft. Hovering ceiling out of ground effect 7720ft. Ferry range 1213km (655nm). Endurance 4hr 35min. NFH – Max cruising speed 291km/h (157kt), econ cruising speed 244km/h (132kt). Time on station 90km (49nm) from base 3hr 20m. Max endurance 4hr 45min.

**Weights:** TTH – Empty 5400kg (11,905lb), max takeoff 10,600kg (23,369lb). NFH – Empty equipped 6428kg (14,171lb), max takeoff same.

**Dimensions:** Main rotor diameter 16.30m (53ft 6in), length overall rotors turning 19.56m (64ft 2in), fuselage length 16.14m (53ft 0in), height overall tail rotor turning 5.44m (17ft 10in). Main rotor disc area 208.7m² (2246.1sq ft).

**Accommodation:** TTH – One or two pilots and up to 20 combat equipped troops or a two tonne 4WD. NFH – Pilot, copilot/tacco and sensor operator, or two pilots, tacco and sensor operator.

**Armament:** TTH – To be fitted with area suppression and defensive armament. NFH – Anti ship missiles and torpedoes.

**Operators:** Finland*, France*, Germany*, Italy*, Netherlands*, Norway* Sweden*.

**History:** The NH 90 battlefield transport and anti ship and ASW helicopter resulted from a 1985 teaming of five European nations to jointly develop a NATO Helicopter for the '90s (hence NH 90).

The UK withdrew from the program in 1987, leaving France, Germany, Italy and the Netherlands the four partners. The first prototype, built by Eurocopter France, first flew on December 18 1995.

The NH 90 is being developed in two basic versions, the land TTH (tactical transport helicopter) and naval NFH (NATO Frigate Helicopter). The NH 90's EFIS cockpit features LCD screens – five in the NFH, four in the TTH. The NH 90 also features quadruplex fly-by-wire flight control system and composite construction for the entire fuselage and rotor blades (with curved tips).

TTH features include a rear loading ramp to allow it to carry a two tonne vehicle, ECM, NVG and FLIR compatibility and accommodation for up to 20 fully equipped troops. A Combat SAR NH 90 is planned.

The NFH is designed for autonomous anti ship, anti submarine warfare and other general naval helicopter tasks (SAR and vertrep etc). Equipment will include an Ocean Master based search radar in an undernose radome, dipping sonar, FLIR, MAD, an EW suite and Link II datalink, plus a crew of three or four.

NH Industries' partners are Eurocopter France, AgustaWestland, Eurocopter Deutschland and Fokker Aerostructures. A production agreement signed in June 2000 covers an initial 366 aircraft for the partner nations. Production deliveries are planned for 2003. Portugal joined the NH 90 program in June 2001, buying 10, while Finland (20), Norway (14) and Sweden (18) ordered the NH 90 in September 2001.

**Photo:** The fourth NH 90 prototype in TTH configuration. (Eurocopter)

# North American T-6 Texan/Harvard

**Country of origin:** United States of America

**Type:** Advanced piston engined trainer

**Powerplant:** T-6G – One 410kW (550hp) Pratt & Whitney R-1340-AN-1 Wasp nine cylinder radial piston engine driving a two blade prop.

**Performance:** T-6G – Max speed at 5000ft 340km/h (184kt), max cruising speed 274km/h (148kt), economical cruising speed 235km/h (127kt). Max initial rate of climb 1643ft/min. Service ceiling 24,750ft. Normal range 1400km (755nm).

**Weights:** T-6G – Empty 1938kg (4271lb), max takeoff 2546kg (5617lb).

**Dimensions:** Wing span 12.80m (42ft 0in), length 8.99m (29ft 6in), height 3.56m (11ft 9in). Wing area 23.6m² (253.7sq ft).

**Accommodation:** Seating for two in tandem.

**Armament:** Could be fitted with machine guns in the wings, a rearward firing manually operated machine gun in the rear cockpit, and with underwing bomb racks for light bombs.

**Operators:** Paraguay

**History:** North American's Texan/Harvard/SNJ series was the most important Allied trainer of World War 2.

This prolific aircraft family began with the NA-16, which was similar in appearance to subsequent models but featured fixed undercarriage, open cockpits and fabric covering around the fuselage. First flight was in April 1935. The US Army Air Corps adopted the NA-16 as the BT-9 basic trainer. Similar variants included the BT-14, Canada's Yale and the retractable undercarriage BC-1 and British Harvard I. Another development was the Australian built Wirraway, with three blade propeller, fabric covered fuselage and retractable undercarriage. The Wirraway (755 built) saw widespread use in advanced trainer, army cooperation, light bomber, dive bomber and even fighter roles (one shot down a Japanese Zero in December 1942).

The AT-6 Texan (AT = advanced trainer) was introduced in 1939 with retractable undercarriage, a two blade prop and metal fuselage covering. The initial Texan model was the AT-6A, supplied to the US Navy as the SNJ-3 and built in Canada (by Noorduyn) as the Harvard IIB (over 2000 went to Britain). The similar AT-6C/SNJ-4/Harvard III was redesigned to eliminate high value aluminium alloys and high alloy steels, although fears of shortages of these materials proved groundless and they were reintroduced into production.

Other wartime models were the AT-6D/SNJ-5/Harvard III and the AT-6F/SNJ-6. In all 15,000 T-6s/SNJs/Harvards were built through to 1945. In addition, small numbers of single seat AT-6 based fighters were built for Peru and Siam (Thailand).

Cancar in Canada built a further 555 T-6Gs for the US and Canadian air forces between 1951 and 1954, bringing total production of all variants to approximately 20,300.

Postwar, thousands of refurbished surplus Texans (designated T-6 by the USAF from 1948) and Harvards etc served on every continent. By 1980 still more than 20 nations operated T-6s/Harvards for advanced training and light strike. South Africa began replacing its 50 Harvards with Pilatus PC-7 Mk II Astras from 1995 and all are now retired. In 2001 the final operator appeared to be Paraguay (with two).

**Photo:** An ex South African Air Force Harvard. (Alan Scoot)

# Northrop Grumman E-2 Hawkeye

**Country of origin:** United States of America

**Type:** Carrier and land based AEW aircraft

**Powerplants:** E-2C – Two 3805kW (5100ehp) Rolls-Royce (Allison) T56-A-427 turboprops driving four blade propellers.

**Performance:** E-2C – Max speed 626km/h (338kt), max cruising speed 602km/h (325kt), ferry cruising speed 480km/h (260kt). Service ceiling 37,000ft. Ferry range 2855km (1540nm). Time on station 320km (175nm) from base 4hr 24min. Endurance 6hr 15min.

**Weights:** E-2C – Empty 18,363kg (40,484lb), MTOW 24,687kg (54,426lb).

**Dimensions:** Wing span 24.56m (80ft 7in), length 17.60m (57ft 9in), height 5.58m (18ft 4in). Wing area 65.0m² (700.0sq ft).

**Accommodation:** Crew complement of five – pilot, copilot, combat information centre officer, air control operator and radar operator.

**Armament:** None

**Operators:** Egypt, France*, Japan, Singapore, Taiwan*, USA*.

**History:** The Hawkeye was developed to replace another Grumman design, the E-1 Tracer, an AEW development of the S-2 Tracker.

In March 1957 Grumman was announced the winner of a US Navy requirement to develop an AEW aircraft, with a design with twin turbo-props, a crew of five, digital processing computers and a General Electric APS-96 surveillance radar. The resulting W2F (E-2 from 1962) Hawkeye featured the APS-96 in an above fuselage rotodome, two Allison T56 turboprops, a high wing and a wide span tailplane with considerable dihedral with four fins including two rudders (providing the necessary directional control while conforming to carrier hangar height limitations). First flight was on October 21 1960. Production E-2As (59 aircraft in all) saw widespread service in the Vietnam theatre.

From 1969 the E-2As were upgraded to E-2B standard with an improved computer and provision for inflight refuelling. All E-2Bs have been retired from USN service.

The E-2C Hawkeye first flew in January 1970. The main new feature of the E-2C was the APS-125 radar and improved signal processing capability. The C can be identified by its large air intake ahead of the wing and has been continually updated and fitted with increasingly capable radars, in the form of the APS-138, APS-139 and now the APS-145. The APS-145 has greater resistance to jamming, better overground performance and the ability to track up to 2000 targets at one time. Other recent E-2C features include more powerful engines (as described in the specs) and JTIDS software. The TE-2C is a trainer (two converted).

The E-2C patrols at an altitude of 30,000ft and can detect and assess targets out to a range of 555km (300nm).

The latest E-2 development is the E-2C Hawkeye 2000, which features a new mission computer (with 15 times the processing power) and new workstations. The first of 21 for the US Navy was handed over on October 25 2001, although IOC is not scheduled until 2004. Taiwan and France have new build Hawkeye 2000s on order, while Egypt and Japan plan to upgrade their E-2Cs to 2000 standard.

Under a separate program, US Navy E-2s (and C-2s) will be fitted with eight bladed Hamilton Standard propellers from 2002. A further upgrade with a UHF electronically scanned radar is under study.

**Photo:** An E-2C test bed fitted with the new eight blade props.

# Northrop Grumman E-8 Joint STARS

**Country of origin:** United States of America

**Type:** Long range battlefield reconnaissance platform.

**Powerplants:** E-8C – Four 80.1kN (18,000lb) Pratt & Whitney JT8D-3B turbofans.

**Performance:** E-8C – Max speed 1010km/h (545kt), max cruising speed 974km/h (525kt), long range cruising speed 885km/h (478kt). Service ceiling 42,000ft. Endurance with internal fuel 11hr, endurance with one inflight refuelling 20hr.

**Weights:** E-8C – Empty 77,565kg (171,000lb), max takeoff 152,407kg (336,000lb).

**Dimensions:** Wing span 44.42m (145ft 9in), length 44.61m (152ft 11in), height 12.95m (42ft 6in). Wing area 283.4m² (3050.0sq ft).

**Accommodation:** Two pilots and flight engineer. E-8A fitted with consoles for 10 operators. E-8C fitted with 18 operator consoles, one of which is for navigation/self defence.

**Armament:** None

**Operators:** USA*

**History:** The Northrop Grumman developed E-8 Joint STARS is a Joint Strategic Target Attack Radar System, a long range battlefield surveillance platform fitted with a side looking radar.

Grumman was awarded a full scale development Joint STARS contract, covering the conversion of two Boeing 707 airliners to serve as prototypes, in September 1985. The first of these prototypes first flew in converted E-8A configuration on December 22 1988. Originally the USAF planned to acquire 22 new build E-8B production aircraft, powered by F108 turbofans (CFM56s), and one green airframe was built (and flown in 1990) before the US instead opted to convert second hand Boeing 707 airliners into E-8Cs. The two E-8A prototypes will be upgraded to E-8C standard to serve alongside production E-8C conversions. The first production E-8C first flew in March 1994, although it will be used as a permanent testbed. The E-8Cs are operated by the USAF on behalf of the US Army, with first deliveries in 1996.

The heart of the E-8 is the Northrop Grumman (Norden) APY-3 side looking phased array multimode radar, housed in a canoe fairing beneath the fuselage. In synthetic aperture radar mode the APY-3 can image targets up to 175km distant and can survey one million km² in one eight hour sortie. Pulse Doppler modes gather moving target information, allowing the operators to track moving vehicles and convoys.

Joint STARS provides ground commanders with a complete overview of the battlefield and can also be used for specific target reconnaissance and for individual targeting functions. E-8 gathered information is relayed to mobile ground stations via datalink, allowing individual ground commanders to access specific information.

The two E-8As were hastily deployed to the Gulf War in 1991 where they flew 49 operational missions. Joint STARS were also used operationally over Bosnia, Kosovo and Afghanistan.

Under the Radar Technology Insertion Program the radar will be replaced by a two dimensional electronically scanned unit with improved resolution and faster scan rate. The new radar will be fitted to E-8C Block 50s from 2006, earlier staged block upgrades include new networked comms, secure datalinks, processing and enhanced inverse SAR.

**Photo:** An E-8C demonstrates defensive flare firing.

# Northrop T-38 Talon

**Country of origin:** United States of America

**Type:** Two seat advanced trainer

**Powerplants:** Two 11.9kN (2680lb) dry and 17.1kN (3850lb) with afterburning General Electric J85-GE-5 turbojets.

**Performance:** Max speed at 36,000ft Mach 1.22 or 1295km/h (700kt), max cruising speed 930km/h (502kt). Max initial rate of climb 33,600ft/min. Service ceiling 53,600ft. Ferry range 1760km (950nm), typical range 1385km (747nm).

**Weights:** Empty 3255kg (7175lb), max takeoff 5465kg (12,050lb).

**Dimensions:** Wing span 7.70m (25ft 3in), length 14.14m (46ft 5in), height 3.92m (12ft 11in). Wing area 15.8m$^2$ (170.0sq ft).

**Accommodation:** Two in tandem.

**Armament:** Usually none, although Portuguese T-38s (now retired) were equipped to fire AIM-9 AAMs.

**Operators:** Germany, South Korea, Turkey, USA.

**History:** The supersonic Talon is the US Air Force's advanced trainer and is a development of Northrop's N-156 light fighter proposal.

Northrop began private venture development of its N-156 light fighter concept in the mid 1950s. Part of Northrop's N-156 design work was the N-156T two seater which it offered to the USAF as an advanced trainer. In 1956 the USAF ordered three N-156Ts for evaluation and the first of these YT-38s (powered by non afterburning YJ85-GE-1s) first flew on April 10 1959. In all, six YT-38s were built, the final three with afterburning YJ85-GE-5s. Testing of the latter was promising, and the YT-38 was ordered into production as the T-38 Talon. Deliveries began in March 1961 and continued to 1972 after 1187 had been built.

The T-38A was the basic Talon production model. For a time the US Navy operated some QT-38 drones and DT-38 drone controllers and NASA flies T-38A(N)s on astronaut training duties. Finally 132 T-38As were converted to T-38B LIFT configuration, able to carry practice bombs, rockets and a minigun for weapons training. These were unofficially dubbed AT-38Bs.

The USAF now expects its 500 T-38s to remain in service until 2040, when the eldest airframes will approach 80 years of age! The USAF plans to upgrade Talons to T-38C standard. Boeing has developed the T-38C Avionics Upgrade Program (AUP) with an EFIS cockpit (including MFDs and HUD). Northrop Grumman is also developing a new wingbox for a fleet re-wing program which will commence in 2006. General Electric has delivered upgrade kits for the J85 engine, reducing fatigue, and cutting maintenance man hours.

Apart from the USAF's Air Education and Training Command, the Talon is in service with Air Combat Command and Air Mobility Command for the Companion Trainer Program. Others are used as chase aircraft for various test programs. Previous USAF T-38 operators include aggressor squadrons and the Thunderbirds.

The USAF also operates 41 German owned T-38s to train Luftwaffe pilots. Ex USAF aircraft meanwhile were supplied to Turkey and Portugal. Taiwan leased T-38s to make up for a shortfall in fast jet numbers, while the latest operator is South Korea, again leasing USAF aircraft as an interim measure until the T-50 enters service.

**Photo:** A USAF T-38. (Paul Merritt)

# Northrop F-5A/B Freedom Fighter

**Country of origin:** United States of America

**Type:** Light multirole fighter

**Powerplants:** Two 12.1kN (2720lb) dry and 18.2kN (4080lb) with afterburning General Electric J85-GE-13 turbojets.

**Performance:** F-5A – Max speed at 36,000ft Mach 1.4 or 1488km/h (802kt), cruising speed at 36,000ft 1030km/h (556kt). Max initial rate of climb 28,700ft/min. Service ceiling 50,500ft. Ferry range 2595km (1400nm). Combat radius with two 240kg (530lb) bombs and max fuel hi-lo-hi 898km (485nm), radius with max external bomb load (1995kg/4400lb) hi-lo-hi 315km (170nm).

**Weights:** F-5A – Empty equipped 3667kg (8085lb), max takeoff 9380kg (20,677lb). Internal fuel 2207 litres.

**Dimensions:** F-5A – Wing span over tip tanks 7.87m (25ft 10in), span without tip tanks 7.70m (25ft 3in), length 14.38m (47ft 2in), height 4.01m (13ft 2in). Wing area 15.8m$^2$ (170.0sq ft).

**Accommodation:** Pilot only in F-5A, two in tandem in F-5B.

**Armament:** Two M39A2 20mm cannons. Max weapons load of 1995kg (4400lb) including bombs, rockets and AIM-9 Sidewinders on four underwing hardpoints (AIM-9s also on wingtip stations).

**Operators:** Botswana, Morocco, Philippines, Saudi Arabia, South Korea, Spain, Thailand, Turkey, Venezuela.

**History:** The US adopted Northrop's N-156 lightweight fighter as the F-5 Freedom Fighter to supply to friendly European and Asian nations under the Military Assistance Program (MAP).

As early as 1952 Northrop designed its first lightweight jet fighter, the N-102 Fang to be powered by a single GE J79 turbojet. While the USAF rejected the Fang its interest in a lightweight fighter was aroused and in 1954 it conducted a study into the concept of a lightweight yet high performance fighter that could be supplied under MAP. This study prompted Northrop to design a new lightweight fighter to meet such a requirement, resulting in the N-156 powered by two J85 turbojets (an engine originally developed for a drone).

US official interest was initially for the two seat N-156T which became the T-38 Talon, while Northrop continued development of the single seat N-156 and a privately funded prototype first flew on July 30 1959 (Mach 1 was reached on this first flight).

Because of initial USAF disinterest the first production F-5A Freedom Fighter did not fly until May 1963. The USAF operated a squadron of F-5As in Vietnam for combat evaluation (Skoshi Tiger) but it never intended to acquire the F-5 in any numbers.

Northrop built 879 F-5As and two seat F-5Bs for over a dozen MAP customers, while Canadair built 250 (with uprated engines and an inflight refuelling probe as the CF-5A and CF-5D for Canada and NF-5A/B for the Netherlands) and CASA of Spain built 70 under licence. The RF-5A is a reconnaissance variant with four KS-92A cameras in a reprofiled nose.

Several countries upgraded their F-5A/B fleets, including Canada, Venezuela and Norway. Canada's upgrade was the most comprehensive, with an airframe refurbishment, a HUD, advanced avionics and HOTAS controls. However, all have been retired and they were offered for sale, with Botswana a buyer (of 13).

**Photo:** Greece has retired its RF-5As. (Greek MoD)

# Northrop F-5E/F Tiger II

**Country of origin:** United States of America

**Type:** Lightweight multirole fighter

**Powerplants:** Two 15.5kN (3500lb) dry and 22.2kN (5000lb) with afterburning General Electric J85-GE-21B turbojets.

**Performance:** F-5E – Max speed at 37,000ft Mach 1.63 or 1730km/h (935kt), cruising speed at 36,000ft 1040km/h (562kt). Max initial rate of climb 34,300ft/min. Service ceiling 51,800ft. Ferry range with max external fuel and empty tanks dropped 3720km (2010nm). Combat radius with two AIM-9s 1405km (760nm).

**Weights:** F-5E – Empty 4350kg (9558lb), max takeoff 11,187kg (24,664lb). Internal fuel 1996kg (4400lb).

**Dimensions:** F-5E – Wing span with tip mounted AIM-9s 8.53m (28ft 0in), length 14.45m (47ft 5in), height 4.08m (13ft 5in). Wing area 17.3m² (186.0sq ft).

**Accommodation:** Pilot only in F-5E, two in tandem in F-5F.

**Armament:** Two M39A2 20mm cannons. Up to 3178kg (7000lb) of ordnance on two wingtip, one centreline and four underwing hardpoints including AIM-9 Sidewinders, bombs, rockets, cluster bombs and ASMs (including AGM-65 Mavericks).

**Operators:** Bahrain, Brazil, Chile, Honduras, Indonesia, Iran, Jordan, Kenya, Malaysia, Mexico, Morocco, Saudi Arabia, Singapore, South Korea, Switzerland, Taiwan, Thailand, Tunisia, USA, Yemen.

**History:** Northrop's F-5E Tiger II was selected as the US's International Fighter Aircraft (IFA), a lightweight fighter for export.

Northrop began work on an improved F-5 as a private venture. This resulted in the first flight of a converted F-5A prototype powered by two GE J85-GE-21 turbojets in March 1969. This aircraft was submitted for the US Government's International Fighter Aircraft competition (previously Advanced International Fighter), which was managed by the USAF. To comply with government procedures for selecting and procuring a new fighter the F-5E had to be evaluated against other US fighters including versions of the Vought F-8 Crusader, Lockheed F-104 Starfighter and even the F-4 Phantom. The F-5E was officially selected in November 1970.

Compared with the F-5A, the F-5E Tiger II features more powerful engines, enlarged leading edge extensions, permanent wingtip AAM stations and more modern and capable avionics and systems. First flight was on August 11 1972. The F-5F two seater first flew in September 1974. The RF-5E Tigereye features four KS-121A 70mm cameras in a modified nose section.

The F-5E was extremely popular and over 1300 (including two seater F-5Fs) were built through to 1987. Licence production was undertaken in Taiwan, South Korea and Switzerland, while large numbers have seen USAF and USN service as DACT aggressors.

Several companies now offer F-5 upgrades, including IAI which upgraded Chilean aircraft with Elta M-2032 radar, avionics, HUD and HOTAS, and Northrop Grumman who offers a staged upgrade.

The ultimate F-5 development was the F-5G, or F-20 Tigershark, powered by a GE F404 and fitted with a modified APG-66 radar. The relaxation of availability restrictions for the F-16 damaged its sales prospects and the program was cancelled in 1986.

**Photo:** A Brazilian F-5E and F. (Embraer)

# Northrop Grumman B-2 Spirit

**Country of origin:** United States of America

**Type:** Low observables strategic bomber

**Powerplants:** Four 77.0kN (17,300lb) General Electric F118-GE-110 turbofans.

**Performance:** Max speed at sea level approx 915km/h (495kt). Service ceiling 50,000ft. Range with eight AGM-129s and eight B83 bombs (total weapons weight 16,920kg/37,300lb) hi-hi-hi 11,665km (6300nm), hi-lo-hi with 1850km (1000nm) flown at low level 8150km (4400nm). Range with eight AGM-129s and eight B61s (total weapons weight 10,885kg/24,000lb) hi-hi-hi 12,225km (6600nm), hi-lo-hi with 1850km (1000nm) flown at low level 8335km (4500nm).

**Weights:** Empty 69,717kg (153,700lb), typical takeoff 152,635kg (336,500lb). Internal fuel 81,650-90,720kg (180-200,000lb).

**Dimensions:** Wing span 52.43m (172ft 0in), length 21.03m (69ft 0in), height 5.18m (17ft 0in).

**Accommodation:** Crew of two with provision for a third member.

**Armament:** Two Boeing rotary launcher assemblies (RLAs), one in each bomb bay, can carry a total of 16 AGM-129 ACMs, or 16 B61 tactical/strategic or B83 strategic freefall nuclear bombs, or 80 Mk 82 bombs, or 16 JDAMs, or 16 GAMs, or 16 Mk 84 bombs. Planned weapons include EGBU-28, JSOW and JASSM.

**Operators:** USA

**History:** The B-2 Spirit strategic penetration stealth bomber was designed from the outset to be near invisible to radar.

The Advanced Technology Bomber (ATB) program for a new strategic bomber incorporating low observables or stealth technology was launched in 1978. A Northrop design (with Boeing as principal subcontractor) was selected over a rival concept from Lockheed/Rockwell in June 1981. Only the existence of the program and that the aircraft was a flying wing had been officially recognised before the B-2 was publicly rolled out in November 1988. First flight was on July 17 1989.

The USAF originally planned to acquire 133 B-2s, although the aircraft's cost and the end of the Cold War saw this figure reduced to 21, including the refurbished AV-1 development prototype.

The B-2's flying wing design harks back to Northrop's revolutionary postwar XB-35 and XB-49, and features a double W trailing edge with eight flying control surfaces. The flying wing design has an inherently low radar cross section, and the airframe is largely constructed of graphite/epoxy, which forms a honeycomb radar absorbent structure. Exterior surfaces are designed to minimise radar returns and heat radiation. Other features include four GE F118-GE-110 turbofans (modified non afterburning GE F110s), fly-by-wire flight controls, two side by side internal weapons bays, a Hughes APQ-181 low probability of intercept radar (for terrain following and last minute target position updates) behind two dielectric panels beneath the nose, and a 81 to 90 tonne internal fuel capacity.

B-2 production wound up in 1997, with all bar one (a test aircraft) upgraded to full Block 30 standard by early 2001. The B-2 made its combat debut in the Kosovo campaign in 1999 flying nonstop missions from the US, dropping 454 tonnes (in total) of GPS guided bombs (primarily JDAMs). They were also used over Afghanistan in 2001.

**Photo:** B-2 development and production cost $US45bn. (USAF)

## Panavia Tornado IDS & ECR

**Countries of origin:** Germany, Italy and UK

**Type:** Strike/ground attack aircraft

**Powerplants:** IDS (from 1983) – Two 40.5kN (9100lb) dry (downrated to 38.5kN/8650lb for RAF aircraft) and 71.5kN (16,075lb) with afterburning Turbo-Union RB199-34R Mk 103 turbofans.

**Performance:** IDS – Max speed Mach 2.2 (Mach 1.3 for RAF aircraft), max speed with external stores Mach 0.92 or 1112km/h (600kt). Time to 30,000ft less than 2min. Radius with a heavy weapon load hi-lo-lo-hi 1390km (750nm). Ferry range approx 3890km (2100nm).

**Weights:** IDS – Basic empty approx 13,890kg (30,620lb), max takeoff approx 27,950kg (61,620lb). Internal fuel 4663kg (10,280lb).

**Dimensions:** Span wings extended 13.91m (45ft 8in), span wings swept 8.60m (28ft 3in), length 16.72m (54ft 10in), height 5.95m (19ft 6in). Wing area (25° sweepback) 26.6m² (286.3sq ft).

**Accommodation:** Pilot and weapons system operator/navigator.

**Armament:** Two IWKA-Mauser 27mm cannons. Max load over 9000kg (19,840lb), including AIM-9s, bombs, laser guided bombs, ALARM (RAF) and HARM (ECR) anti radiation missiles, WE177B (RAF) and B61 (Luftwaffe) nuclear bombs, JP 233 (RAF) and MW-1 (Luftwaffe) area denial weapons, Sea Eagle (GR.1B) and Kormoran (Marineflieger) anti ship missiles.

**Operators:** Germany, Italy, Saudi Arabia, UK.

**History:** A veteran of combat over Iraq and Kosovo/Yugoslavia, the Tornado is western Europe's most important strike aircraft.

The Tornado resulted from a late 1960s study for a strike aircraft conducted by Belgium, Canada, Germany, Italy, the Netherlands and the UK (Belgium, Canada and the Netherlands subsequently withdrew). Panavia was formed in March 1969 to develop the aircraft, dubbed the MRCA (Multi Role Combat Aircraft), with formal development beginning in mid 1970.

The first of nine prototypes first flew on August 14 1974, production aircraft were delivered from July 1980. A total of 828 production IDSs were built, with the last delivered to Saudi Arabia in 1998.

The Tornado features variable geometry wings, two Turbo-Union RB199 engines (developed specifically by a consortium of Rolls-Royce, MTU and FiatAvio), a Texas Instruments radar with terrain following and ground mapping, fly-by-wire and digital INS.

UK aircraft are designated GR.1 and feature a laser rangefinder in an undernose pod, while their intakes have been fixed and engines downrated. Twelve GR.1As are used for reconnaissance and are fitted with a BAe SLIR (side looking infrared) and Vinten IR linescan. The 24 converted GR.1Bs are used for maritime strike and can carry up to five Sea Eagle anti ship missiles. The GR.4 upgrade (involving 142 GR.1s) comprises a new HUD, undernose FLIR, new avionics and ECM. Redeliveries began in 1997.

Italy and Germany are upgrading their IDS aircraft with the Rafael Litening targeting pod, improved ECM and new avionics.

The Tornado ECR (Electronic Combat Reconnaissance) for Germany and Italy is a dedicated Suppression of Enemy Air Defence (SEAD) variant of the IDS fitted with a Emitter Location System (ELS) and armed with the AGM-88 HARM. Guns are not fitted to the ECRs.

**Photo:** An RAF Tornado GR.4. (RAAF)

## Panavia Tornado ADV

**Countries of origin:** Germany, Italy and UK

**Type:** Air defence fighter/interceptor

**Powerplants:** F.3 – Two 40.5kN (9100lb) dry and 73.5kN (16,520lb) with afterburning Turbo-Union RB199-34R Mk 104 turbofans.

**Performance:** F.3 – Max speed Mach 2.2. Operational ceiling approx 70,000ft. Combat radius supersonic 555km (300nm), subsonic over 1850km (1000nm). CAP endurance 555 to 740km (300 to 400nm) from base with time for interception and 10min combat, 2hr.

**Weights:** F.3 – Operating empty approx 14,500kg (31,970lb), max takeoff 27,895kg (61,700lb). Internal fuel 5263kg (11,603lb).

**Dimensions:** Span wings spread 13.91m (45ft 8in), span wings swept 8.60m (28ft 3in), length 18.68m (61ft 4in), height 5.95m (19ft 6in). Wing area (25° sweepback) 26.6m² (286.3sq ft).

**Accommodation:** Pilot and radar operator in tandem.

**Armament:** One IKMA-Mauser 27mm cannon. Four underfuselage Skyflash AAMs and two AIM-9L Sidewinders on each underwing pylon. Italian F.3s modified to carry Alenia Aspide AAMs under fuselage.

**Operators:** Italy, Saudi Arabia, UK.

**History:** An air-to-air Tornado model had always been envisioned in early planning, and a feasibility study of an air defence variant was first conducted in 1968.

The Tornado was subsequently selected to meet the UK's 1971 requirement for an air defence fighter armed with BAe's Skyflash medium range air-to-air missile and fitted with an advanced radar. Formal development of the Tornado ADV, or Air Defence Variant, as the Tornado fighter was designated, was authorised in March 1976.

The first of three Tornado ADV prototypes first flew on October 27 1979, while the first production Tornado F.2 first flew in March 1984.

Compared with the Tornado IDS, the ADV features a 1.36m (4ft 6in) fuselage stretch, allowing the underfuselage carriage of four Skyflash missiles in semi recessed stations, while also increasing internal fuel capacity to 7143 litres. The ADV features the GEC-Marconi AI.24 Foxhunter radar, which was designed to track up to 20 targets while scanning, with a search range out to 185km (100nm). Development of the Foxhunter however was troubled and early production Tornado F.2s and F.3s were fitted with Foxhunters completed to interim X and Y standards, not meeting the full RAF requirement. AA standard Foxhunters fully meeting the RAF requirement were installed in production aircraft from 1989, and have been upgraded to improved 2G standard with a new data processor.

The RAF ordered 173 Tornado ADVs, the first 18 of which were delivered in interim F.2 standard with less powerful Mk 103 engines, while the definitive F.3 features the RB199 Mk 104. F.2s have been retired from service. F.3s are being fitted with JTIDS and about 100 are being modified to carry ASRAAM and AIM-120 missiles.

Saudi Arabia is the only Tornado ADV export customer, with 24 delivered from 1989. Saudi and RAF Tornados flew patrols during the Gulf War, but without seeing combat. Italy has leased 24 RAF Tornado F.3s (modified to fire the Alenia Aspide) to bolster its fighter force, but these will be replaced by leased F-16s from 2003. In all 197 ADVs were built.

**Photo:** Coningsby based RAF F.3s. (Sgt Jack Pritchard RAF)

# Pacific Aerospace CT-4 Airtrainer

**Country of origin:** New Zealand

**Type:** Two/three seat basic trainer

**Powerplant:** CT-4B – One 155kW (210hp) Teledyne Continental IO-360-D fuel injected flat six piston engine driving a two blade propeller. CT-4E – One 225kW (300hp) Textron Lycoming AEIO-540-L1E5 flat six.

**Performance:** CT-4B – Max speed 267km/h (144kt), cruising speed 260km/h (140kt). Max initial rate of climb 1250ft/min. Range with max fuel at normal cruising speed 1110km (600nm). CT-4E – Max speed 302km/h (163kt), cruising speed 293km/h (158kt). Max initial rate of climb 1830ft/min. Service ceiling 18,500ft. Range at 6000ft with max fuel 982km (530nm).

**Weights:** CT-4B – Max takeoff 1202kg (2650lb). CT-4E – Empty equipped 780kg (1720lb), max takeoff 1179kg (2600lb).

**Dimensions:** CT-4B – Wing span 7.92m (26ft 0in), length 7.06m (23ft 2in), height 2.59m (8ft 6in). Wing area 12.0m² (129.0sq ft). CT-4E – Same except length 7.26m (23ft 10in).

**Accommodation:** Two side by side, with optional third seat behind.

**Armament:** None

**Operators:** New Zealand, Thailand.

**History:** The CT-4 Airtrainer is a two seat basic trainer.

The CT-4 was developed from the Australian Victa Airtourer, a light two seat GA aircraft. The Airtourer was designed in 1953 by Henry Millicer, then chief aerodynamicist at Australia's Government Aircraft Factory. Victa had developed a larger four place Aircruiser, but development work was not continued with and instead the production rights for the Aircruiser were purchased by Aero Engine Services Ltd (or AESL) of New Zealand in 1974, which by then already had the rights to the Airtourer series. AESL developed the Aircruiser into the CT-4 Airtrainer, with a clamshell canopy, structural strengthening for aerobatics and stick controls, making it suitable for military basic training.

The first CT-4A Airtrainer flew on February 23 1972. Primary customers were the Australian (51 aircraft), New Zealand (24) and Thai (26) air forces. Production by NZAI (New Zealand Aircraft Industries), as AESL had become, continued until 1977.

In 1991 Pacific Aerospace Corporation (the successor to NZAI) resumed production of the CT-4B against an order from the then BAe/Ansett Flying College in Tamworth, Australia. Today, the now BAE Systems Flight Training school uses these aircraft and ex RNZAF CT-4Bs for flight screening and basic training for Australian and Papua New Guinean military pilots under contract. The Royal Australian Air Force's own CT-4As were retired in early 1993. Five CT-4Bs were also built for the Royal Thai Air Force, while that service's surviving CT-4As were rewinged to extend their service lives.

Three other CT-4 models have been developed. The turboprop Allison 250 powered T350 (previously CT-4C) flew on January 21 1991, and a retractable version, the CT-4CR, was proposed.

The 225kW (300hp) IO-540 powered CT-4E was aimed at the US Air Force's Enhanced Flight Screening competition. Production of 14 CT-4Es began in 1997 with 13 built for the RNZAF (operated under lease) to replace CT-4Bs.

**Photo:** An RNZAF CT-4E. (FLTSGT P Stein, RNZAF)

# Pilatus PC-6 Porter & Turbo-Porter

**Country of origin:** Switzerland

**Type:** STOL utility transport

**Powerplant:** PC-6/B2-H4 – One 410kW (550shp) flat rated Pratt & Whitney Canada PT6A-27 turboprop driving a three blade propeller.

**Performance:** PC-6/B2-H4 (Utility version) – Economical cruising speed 213km/h (115kt). Max initial rate of climb 940ft/min. Max operating altitude 25,000ft. Takeoff run at sea level 127m (415ft). Range with max payload at economical cruising speed and no reserves 730km (395nm), range with max internal fuel 925km (500nm), with external fuel 1610km (870nm).

**Weights:** PC-6/B2-H4 – Empty equipped 1270kg (2800lb), max takeoff 2800kg (6173lb).

**Dimensions:** PC-6/B2-H4 – Wing span 15.87m (52ft 1in), length 10.90m (35ft 9in), height tail down 3.20m (10ft 6in). Wing area 30.2m² (324.5sq ft).

**Accommodation:** Pilot and passenger on flightdeck, with max seating for nine in main cabin. Standard seating for six in main cabin. Alternative layouts include two stretchers and three medical attendants, or 10 paratroops.

**Armament:** Usually none. Thai AU-23s armed with one XM-197 cannon and two pod mounted 7.62mm machine guns, plus rockets and bombs.

**Operators:** Austria, Chad, Ecuador, France, Iran, Myanmar, Peru, Switzerland, Thailand, USA.

**History:** Highly regarded for their exceptional STOL performance and low speed handling, the Pilatus Porter and Turbo-Porter STOL utilities are used for a number of tasks ranging from paradropping to liaison, reconnaissance and light transport.

The Porter first flew on May 4 1959. The first production aircraft built, delivered from 1960, were powered by a six cylinder Lycoming GSO-480 piston engine, but it was not long after that a turboprop powered development flew. The first PC-6/A Turbo-Porter flew in May 1961, powered by a 390kW (523shp) Turbomeca Astazou II turboprop.

The majority of PC-6s built are PC-6/Bs, powered by the ubiquitous Pratt & Whitney Canada PT6A. PC-6/Cs are powered by a 310kW (575shp) Garrett TPE331 and were first delivered in 1965.

The PC-6/B was first delivered from 1964, and remains in production today. Initial models were powered by the 410kW (550shp) PT6A-6 or -20. The PC-6/B2-H2 first flew in 1970 and introduced the PT6A-27 and an increased maximum takeoff weight. Current production is of the PC-6/B2-H4 with a further increase in max takeoff weight, larger dorsal fin fillet, revised wingtips, strengthened airframe structure and improved undercarriage.

Fairchild in the USA manufactured the PC-6 under licence as the Heli-Porter. The Fairchild AU-23 Peacemaker was an armed COIN variant initially ordered by the US Army for evaluation against the Helio Courier. The 15 evaluation AU-23As were subsequently delivered to the Royal Thai Air Force, plus 20 new production aircraft. About 22 are still in RTAF service.

The US Army operates two PC-6s which are designated UV-20 Chiricahua.

**Photo:** An Argentine police PC-6 Turbo-Porter. (Santiago Rivas)

# Pilatus PC-7 Turbo-Trainer

**Country of origin:** Switzerland

**Type:** Two seat trainer

**Powerplant:** PC-7 – One 410kW (550shp) Pratt & Whitney Canada PT6A-25A turboprop driving a three blade prop. Mk II – One 522kW (700shp) PT6A-25C driving a four blade prop.

**Performance:** PC-7 aerobatic category – Max cruising speed 412km/h (222kt), economical cruising speed 317km/h (171kt). Max initial rate of climb 2150ft/min. Service ceiling 33,000ft, max operating altitude 25,000ft. Max range at cruise power and reserves 1200km (647nm). Mk II – Max cruising speed 465km/h (251kt). Max initial rate of climb 2840ft/min. Max operating altitude 25,000ft. Max range with internal fuel 1500km (810nm).

**Weights:** PC-7 – Basic empty 1330kg (2932lb), max takeoff aerobatic category 1900kg (4188lb), max takeoff utility category 2700kg (5952lb). Mk II – Empty equipped 1670kg (3682lb), max takeoff aerobatic cat 2250kg (4960lb), utility cat 2850kg (6283lb).

**Dimensions:** PC-7 – Wing span 10.40m (34ft 1in), length 9.78m (32ft 1in), height 3.21m (10ft 6in). Wing area 16.6m$^2$ (179.0sq ft). Mk II – Wing span 10.19m (33ft 5in), length 10.18m (33ft 5in), height 3.26m (10ft 8in). Wing area 16.3m$^2$ (175.3sq ft).

**Accommodation:** Two in tandem.

**Armament:** Usually none.

**Operators:** Angola, Austria, Bolivia, Botswana, Brunei, Chad, Chile, Guatemala, Iran, Iraq, Malaysia, Mexico, Myanmar, Netherlands, South Africa, Switzerland, UAE (Abu Dhabi), Uruguay.

**History:** The PC-7 Turbo-Trainer basic trainer is Pilatus' most successful military aircraft program.

The PC-7 is based on the earlier Pilatus P-3, a 195kW (260hp) Lycoming GO-435 flat six powered two seat basic trainer developed for the Swiss air force to replace North American T-6s.

The first PC-7s were converted P-3s and the first prototype flew on April 12 1966. A series of P-3-05 preproduction aircraft were built, however it was not until August 18 1978 that the first production aircraft flew. In that time the PC-7 underwent significant structural redesign (in conjunction with Dornier) to arrive at its current production form. Deliveries of production aircraft (to Myanmar, then Burma) began in December 1978.

Through the early 1980s the PC-7 attracted large orders from a number of air forces. Other than Switzerland, the PC-7 is in service with several air arms including the Netherlands, Abu Dhabi, Malaysia and Myanmar. Optional ejection seats were offered from 1985.

The basic PC-7 has now been joined by the PC-7 Mk II, which Pilatus developed specifically to meet a South African Air Force requirement to replace T-6 Harvards. The Mk II has been substantially revised and features the PC-9's airframe and a more powerful 520kW (700shp) PT6A-25 engine driving a four blade prop. South Africa ordered 60, which it has named Astra, with significant local industrial participation including assembly. The first PC-7 Mk II first flew on September 28 1992. Production of kits for assembly by Atlas began in early 1994 and is now complete. Brunei ordered four.

Over 500 PC-7s were built through to 2000.

**Photo:** A wet Chilean navy PC-7. (Alvaro Romero)

# Pilatus PC-9

**Country of origin:** Switzerland

**Type:** Two seat advanced trainer

**Powerplant:** PC-9 – One 855kW (1150shp) Pratt & Whitney PT6A-62 turboprop (flat rated to 710kW/950shp) driving a four blade propeller.

**Performance:** PC-9 – Max speed at 20,000ft 555km/h (300kt), max speed at sea level 500km/h (270kt). Max initial rate of climb 4090ft/min. Max operating altitude 25,000ft, service ceiling 35,000ft. Max range at cruise power with reserves 1640km (887nm). Endurance at typical mission power settings, two 1hr sorties plus reserves.

**Weights:** PC-9 – Basic empty 1685kg (3715lb), max aerobatic category takeoff 2250kg (4960lb), max utility cat takeoff 3200kg (7055lb).

**Dimensions:** PC-9 – Wing span 10.19m (33ft 5in), length 10.18m (33ft 5in), height 3.26m (10ft 8in). Wing area 16.3m$^2$ (175.3sq ft).

**Accommodation:** Two in tandem.

**Armament:** Usually none.

**Operators:** PC-9 – Angola, Australia, Croatia, Cyprus, Iraq, Myanmar, Saudi Arabia, Slovenia, Switzerland, Thailand.

**History:** Pilatus's PC-9 is a more powerful and higher performing turboprop trainer based on the PC-7, intended for basic and advanced training. The PC-9 was also the successful contender for the USAF/USN's JPATS program.

Design work on the PC-9 began in 1982. Aerodynamic features of the PC-9 were test flown on a modified PC-7 in 1982/3, while the first of two preproduction PC-9s had its first flight on May 7 1984. Swiss civil certification was granted in September 1985.

The PC-9 retains limited structural commonality with the earlier PC-7. Key differences are the more powerful Pratt & Whitney PT6A-62 turboprop driving a four blade prop (when the PC-9 was first in development some reports suggested it would be powered by a Garrett TFE331), stepped tandem cockpits with ejection seats and an airbrake under the centre fuselage.

Major PC-9 operators are Australia, Iraq, Saudi Arabia and Thailand. Australia ordered 67 PC-9/As to replace CT-4 Airtrainers and MB-326s for basic and advanced training. All but the first two were assembled in Australia by Hawker de Havilland and they feature low pressure tyres (as on the PC-7) for grass strip operations and Bendix EFIS displays. Four are used for forward air control (FAC) training.

Saudi Arabia's 30 PC-9s were sold through British Aerospace as part of a comprehensive arms deal, while Thailand's 20 PC-9s have augmented RFB Fantrainers. In Germany a civil firm operates 10 PC-9Bs equipped for target towing under contract to the Luftwaffe. In all sales of the PC-9 exceed 240.

In June 1995 a modified version of the PC-9 was selected to meet the US Air Force and Navy's Joint Primary Aircraft Training System requirement to find a successor for the USAF's T-37s and the USN's T-34s. The PC-9 based T-6 Texan II (described separately) is being built by Raytheon in Kansas and features a new two piece canopy and an upgraded engine, among other changes.

The PC-9M, announced in 1997, features the enlarged dorsal fin fairing from the PC-7 Mark II and other aerodynamic changes.

Pilatus is working on the PC-21 replacement for the PC-7 and PC-9.

**Photo:** An Australian forward air control PC-9. (Robert Wiseman)

# Pilatus PC-12 Eagle

**Country of origin:** Switzerland

**Type:** Special missions and light utility transport

**Powerplant:** One 895kW (1200shp) Pratt & Whitney Canada PT6A-67B turboprop driving a four blade constant speed Hartzell propeller.

**Performance:** PC-12 – Max cruising speed 500km/h (270kt), economical cruising speed 430km/h (232kt). Initial rate of climb 1680ft/min. Max certificated altitude 30,000ft. Max range with VFR reserves 4187km (2261nm). Eagle – Max cruising speed 463km/h (250kt). Max range at 30,000ft and 370km/h (200kt) 3080km (1635nm).

**Weights:** PC-12 – Empty 2600kg (5732lb), max takeoff 4500kg (9920lb). Eagle – Empty 2900kg (6393lb), max takeoff 4500kg (9920lb).

**Dimensions:** PC-12 – Wing span 16.23m (53ft 2in), length 14.40m (47ft 3in), height 4.27m (14ft 0in). Wing area 25.8m$^2$ (277.8sq ft). Eagle – Same except wing span 16.09m (52ft 10in).

**Accommodation:** PC-12 – Flightcrew of one or two pilots. Max seating for nine in commuter airliner configuration. Corporate/executive transport configurations typically seat six. Combi passenger/freight version seats four passengers in main cabin plus freight pallet. Eagle – Has two work stations in main cabin.

**Armament:** None

**Operators:** South Africa

**History:** The latest in a line of single engined PT6 turboprop powered Pilatus products, the PC-12 is a new generation utility aimed at fulfilling commuter, executive and freight transport missions. Although designed primarily for private and corporate customers, Pilatus also offers it for military and police work in the PC-12 Eagle special missions form.

Pilatus announced it was developing a new single engine multipurpose transport at the National Business Aviation Association's annual convention in October 1989. First flight of the first of two prototypes occurred on May 31 1991. This aircraft then entered a flight test program that originally envisaged achieving Swiss certification in mid 1993, with first deliveries later that year. However the development program was delayed somewhat when Pilatus redesigned the wing to feature winglets to meet performance guarantees. The improvements were successful, but the delays meant that the PC-12 was not certificated until mid 1994, with first deliveries following soon after.

The PC-12 is offered in standard nine passenger combi form and in a six seat executive configuration. The South African Air Force operates one basic PC-12 for utility work.

The PC-12 Eagle is a special missions variant, pitched at military and government requirements. It is offered with two workstations in the main cabin and a ventral pannier that can carry a range of sensors, such as a FLIR, search radar, synthetic aperture radar and infrared linescan. The Eagle also has revised wingtips and could be fitted with self protection equipment such as chaff/flare dispensers and a missile approach warning system.

Around 250 PC-12s have been built so far.

**Photo:** The first of two Pilatus PC-12 Eagle demonstrators. Note the ventral pannier with ball turret FLIR. (Pilatus)

# PZL Mielec TS-11 Iskra

**Country or origin:** Poland

**Type:** Two seat advanced trainer

**Powerplant:** One 9.8kN (2205lb) IL SO-1/SO-3 turbojet.

**Performance:** Max speed at 16,400ft 720km/h (390kt), cruising speed 600km/h (324kt). Max initial rate of climb 2915ft/min. Service ceiling 36,100ft. Range with max fuel 1460km (790nm), standard range 1250km (675nm).

**Weights:** Empty 2560kg (5645lb), max takeoff 3840kg (8465lb).

**Dimensions:** Wing span 10.06m (33ft 0in), length 11.17m (36ft 8in), height 3.50m (11ft 6in). Wing area 17.5m$^2$ (188.4sq ft).

**Accommodation:** Two in tandem, or pilot only in Iskra-Bis C.

**Armament:** One 23mm internal cannon in forward starboard fuselage. Four underwing hardpoints (two on Iskra-Bis A) can carry a max external ordnance of 400kg (882lb), mainly practice weapons.

**Operators:** India, Poland.

**History:** The PZL Mielec TS-11 Iskra (or Spark) jet trainer was ordered into production for the Polish air force despite losing a Warsaw Pact competition for an advanced trainer to the Czech Aero L-29 Delfin.

The TS-11 and L-29 (and the Yak-30) were designed against a late 1950s requirement for a standardised basic jet trainer to be adopted by Warsaw Pact nations. The XL-29 Delfin prototype first flew on April 5 1959, while the first Iskra first flew some months later on February 5 1960. Subsequent evaluation saw the L-29 selected for production for the USSR and most other Warsaw Pact nations, however, Poland, in the interests of developing its aviation industry, elected instead to procure the Iskra. The Iskra entered production in 1963, with deliveries to the Polish air force the following year.

The Iskra features a straight, mid mounted wing, tandem seating with lightweight ejection seats and the rear seat slightly raised, a Polish developed SO-1 or SO-3 turbojet, a 23mm internal gun and four underwing hardpoints (except on early production examples) for practice armament. The tailplane is mounted on a boom to keep the control surfaces clear of the engine's exhaust.

Early production Iskras were powered by the interim 7.65kN (1720lb) H-10 Polish designed turbojet, pending the availability of the more powerful SO-1 (designed by the Instytut Lotnictwa/Aviation Institute and built by PZL Rzeszów). Some Iskras are powered by the improved but similarly rated SO-3.

Initial production was of the Iskra-Bis A with the two underwing hardpoints, while the Iskra-Bis B has four. The Iskra-Bis D weapons trainer is basically similar – 50 were delivered to India in 1975 where it remains in service. The Iskra-Bis C or Iskra 200 was a single seater optimised for light ground attack, although it was only built in small numbers. The Iskra-Bis DF is a two seat reconnaissance and combat trainer, while the upgraded TS-11R (six conversions delivered from late 1991) is used by the Polish navy for reconnaissance.

PZL Mielec built 400 Iskras through to 1977. Production resumed at a much lower rate in 1982 for the Iskra-Bis DF, continuing into the late 1980s. Today large numbers (150+) of TS-11s remain in Polish air force and naval air arm service.

**Photo:** An Iskra from the Polish air force's aerobatic display team. (Dave Fraser)

# PZL Swidnik (Mil) Mi-2

*Countries of origin:* Poland and Russia

*Type:* Light utility helicopter

*Powerplants:* Two 300kW (400shp) Isotov designed Polish built GTD-350 turboshafts driving a three blade main rotor and two blade tail rotor.

*Performance:* Max cruising speed 200km/h (108kt), long range cruising speed 190km/h (102kt). Max initial rate of climb 885ft/min. Service ceiling 13,125ft. Hovering ceiling in ground effect 6560ft, out of ground effect 3280ft. Range with max payload and reserves 170km (91nm), range with max fuel 440km (237nm), range with optional fuel 580km (313nm).

*Weights:* Basic operating 2365kg (5213lb), max takeoff 3550kg (7825lb).

*Dimensions:* Main rotor diameter 14.50m (47ft 7in), length overall 17.42m (57ft 2in), fuselage length 11.40m (37ft 5in), height to top of rotor head 3.75m (12ft 4in). Main rotor disc area 166.4m$^2$ (1791.1sq ft).

*Accommodation:* Two pilots or one pilot and passenger on flightdeck, and main cabin seating for seven in passenger configuration. Ambulance configurations can accommodate four stretchers and one medical attendant or two stretchers and two attendants. Can carry 700kg (1540lb) of internal freight.

*Armament:* Mi-2URP – Four 9M14M Malyutka (AT-3 'Sagger') anti armour missiles (with four more in cargo compartment). Mi-2US – One port fuselage side mounted 23mm NS-23m cannon, two 7.62mm gun pods either side of fuselage and two 7.62mm pintle mounted guns in rear cabin. Mi-2URN – As Mi-2US plus two rocket pods.

*Operators:* Algeria, Armenia, Bulgaria, Czech Republic, Indonesia, Latvia, Libya, Mexico, Poland, Russia, Slovakia, Syria, Ukraine.

*History:* Poland's most successful helicopter was originally developed in Russia by Mil. More than 5450 were built.

Mil originally designed the light utility Mi-2 (NATO reporting name 'Hoplite') in Russia during the early 1960s, resulting in a first flight in September 1961. In January 1964 an agreement between the USSR and Poland saw development and manufacture transferred to the latter country, with production commencing in 1965. The Mi-2 has evolved since that time and survived in very low rate production into the 1990s.

Swidnik developed a diverse number of Mi-2 variants apart from the basic civil Mi-2. The Mi-2T is the basic military transport variant, while the Mi-2RM is a naval version. Armed Mi-2 models are the combat support/reconnaissance Mi-2URN, anti tank Mi-2URP and Mi-2US gunship.

The Kania (or Kitty Hawk) is a substantial upgrade of the basic Mi-2, and features Allison 250-C20B turboshafts, Western avionics, composite main and tail rotor blades and US FAR Pt 29 certification. Developed in cooperation with Allison, the Kania first flew on June 3 1979 and US certification was granted in February 1986. The Kania is in limited production while existing Mi-2s can be upgraded to Kania standard. About 30 Kanias have been built or ordered (including two operated by the Cyprus air force).

*Photo:* A Slovak Mi-2T transport. (Sebastian Zacharias)

# PZL Swidnik W-3 Sokol

*Country of origin:* Poland

*Type:* Multirole utility helicopter

*Powerplants:* Two 670kW (900shp) takeoff rated WSK-PZL Rzeszów PZL-10W (Polish built Mars TVD-10) turboshafts driving a four blade main rotor and three blade tail rotor.

*Performance:* W-3A – Max cruising speed 243km/h (131kt). Max initial rate of climb 2008ft/min. Hovering ceiling in ground effect 9200ft, out of ground effect 6220ft. Service ceiling 19,680ft. Range with standard fuel and reserves 680km (367nm).

*Weights:* W-3A – Empty 3300kg (7275lb), operating empty 3850kg (8488lb), max takeoff 6400kg (14,110lb).

*Dimensions:* W-3A – Main rotor diameter 15.70m (51ft 6in), length overall rotors turning 18.79m (61ft 8in), fuselage length 14.21m (46ft 8in), height overall 5.14m (16ft 10in), height to top of rotor mast 4.20m (13ft 10in). Main rotor disc area 193.6m$^2$ (2083.8sq ft).

*Accommodation:* Two pilots or pilot and flight engineer or passenger on flightdeck. Main cabin seating for 12 in passenger configuration, or three medical attendants and eight rescued survivors in SAR Anakonda version, or four stretchers and medical attendants in ambulance configuration, one stretcher and medical attendants in critical care EMS version. Can carry a 2100kg (4630lb) sling load.

*Armament:* W-3W – One 23mm GSz-23 gun, plus rockets.

*Operators:* Czech Republic, Myanmar, Poland.

*History:* The multipurpose W-3 Sokol, or Falcon, was the first helicopter to be fully designed and built in Poland.

The Sokol made its first flight on November 16 1979. Following a fairly protracted development program, low rate production commenced during 1985, since which time 124 had been delivered by late 1999.

The Sokol's two PZL-10W turboshafts are based on the Russian designed TVD-10B turboprops. Composites are used in the tail and main rotor blades.

Sokol variants include the improved W-3A Sokol which was awarded US civil certification in May 1993. Apart from the initial civil/military W-3 transport, military variants include the W-3RM Anakonda offshore search and rescue development in Polish navy service with a watertight cabin, external winch and inflatable flotation bags; the armed W-3 based W-3W and W-3A based W-3WA; float equipped W-3AM; and W-3 based VIP W-3P and W-3T for training. The armed W-3U Salamandra with a roof mounted sight with TV and FLIR was shelved. A single electronic combat reconnaissance S-1RR is in Polish air force service.

The cancelled W-3WB Huzar flew in demonstrator form and was based on the W-3W but with Denel weapons and systems as developed for the Rooivalk. Instead the program was been replaced by the W-3H, which will have IAI avionics and weapons. The Polish air force required 100, but the deal was cancelled in 1998.

A W-3 undertook test firings with HOT-3 anti tank missiles in March 1999.

Other proposed W-3 variants have included the stretched W-3 Sokol-Long and the W-3U-1 Alligator ASW variant.

*Photo:* One of 11 W-3As delivered to the Czech air force. (Sebastian Zacharias)

## PZL Warszawa-Okecie Orlik

**Country of origin:** Poland

**Type:** Two seat basic/advanced trainer

**Powerplant:** PZL-130TC-1 – One 560kW (750shp) Walter M 601 T turboprop driving a five blade propeller. TC – One 710kW (950shp) Pratt & Whitney Canada PT6A-62.

**Performance:** PZL-130TC-1 – Max speed at 19,685ft 500km/h (270kt), max speed at sea level 454km/h (245kt). Max initial rate of climb 2620ft/min. Service ceiling 33,000ft. Range with max fuel 970km (523nm). TC – Max speed at 19,685ft 560km/h (302kt), max speed at sea level 510km/h (274kt). Max initial rate of climb 4055ft/min. Service ceiling 33,000ft. Range with max fuel 930km (500nm), range with two external tanks 2300km (1242nm).

**Weights:** PZL-130TC-1 – Empty 1600kg (3527lb), max takeoff 2700kg (5952lb). TC – Empty 1450kg (3197lb), max takeoff same.

**Dimensions:** Wing span 9.00m (29ft 6in), length 9.00m (29ft 6in), height 3.53m (11ft 7in). Wing area 13.0m² (139.9sq ft).

**Accommodation:** Two in tandem.

**Armament:** Six underwing hardpoints (stressed for 160kg/353lb each) for gun pods, bombs, rockets and 'Strela' air-to-air missiles.

**Operators:** Poland*

**History:** The PZL-130 Orlik (Spotted Eagle) was designed as the aircraft centrepiece of the Polish air force's System 130 pilot training program.

System 130 called for a new trainer aircraft, aircraft diagnostics equipment and an aircraft simulator. Design work on the aircraft began in 1983 under the leadership of Andrej Frydrychewicz. The Orlik trainer originally began life powered by the Russian radial piston Vedneyev M14. Otherwise it was similar to contemporary trainers with tandem seating (with the second seat slightly raised) and retractable undercarriage. First flight was on October 12 1984.

The piston powered PZL-130 was hamstrung by supply problems with the Vedneyev engine and PZL Warszawa-Okecie was forced to look at alternative powerplants. In 1988 a preproduction Orlik made its first flight powered by a Polish Kalisz KS-8A but this aircraft soon proved underpowered and development of the piston powered Orlik was abandoned in 1990.

Development of a turboprop powered Orlik, or Turbo Orlik, dates to 1984 when PZL looked at powering the Orlik with a Pratt & Whitney Canada PT6. A PT6 powered Orlik development aircraft had its first flight on July 13 1986. Subsequent Motorlet M 601 powered and PT6A-25 powered Turbo Orlik development aircraft were designated PZL-130TM and PZL-130T respectively.

The Polish air force ordered the M 601 powered Turbo Orlik (the Turbo prefix was subsequently dropped) as the PZL-130TB. Production switched to the improved PZL-130TC-1 with Martin-Baker zero-zero ejection seats and GPS, while early production TBs were upgraded to TC-1 configuration.

The PT6A-62 powered PZL-130TC was aimed primarily at export markets and features Honeywell avionics and a HUD. The PZL-130TC-2 is similar save for its less powerful 560kW (750shp) PT6A-25C. None were sold.

**Photo:** A production PZL-130TC-1 Orlik. (PZL Warszawa-Okecie)

## Raytheon Beech King Air

**Country of origin:** United States of America

**Type:** Utility, VIP, Elint, ESM, Sigint and maritime patrol aircraft

**Powerplants:** B200T – Two 635kW (850shp) Pratt & Whitney Canada PT6A-42 turboprops driving three blade propellers.

**Performance:** Maritime Patrol B200T – Max cruising speed 490km/h (265kt) at 4990kg (11,000lb) AUW, typical patrolling speed 260km/h (140kt). Range with max fuel, patrolling at 420km/h (227kt) with reserves 3315km (1790nm). Typical endurance at 260km/h (140kt) patrolling speed with reserves 6hr 35min. Max time on station with wingtip fuel tanks fitted 9hr.

**Weights:** B200T – Empty 3745kg (8255lb), max takeoff 5670kg (12,500lb), max takeoff restricted category 6805kg (15,000lb).

**Dimensions:** Wing span over tip tanks 17.25m (56ft 7in), wing span 16.61m (54ft 6in), length 13.34m (43ft 9in), height 4.57m (15ft 0in). Wing area 28.2m² (303.0sq ft).

**Accommodation:** Flightcrew of two. Standard main cabin seating for four in King Air 90 family, seven in 200, and eight in 350 series.

**Armament:** None

**Operators:** 90 series – Includes Algeria, Bolivia, Chile, Japan, Mexico, USA, Venezuela. 200 series – Includes Argentina, Australia, Bolivia, Chile, Colombia, Ecuador, Greece, Guatemala, Israel, Japan, Morocco, Peru, Sweden, USA, Venezuela. RC-12 – Israel, USA. B200T – Algeria, Malaysia, Uruguay.

**History:** A highly successful family of light corporate aircraft in civilian life, Beech's King Air series has also been adopted for a diverse range of military tasks, ranging from transport to Elint gathering.

The King Air series began life as a turboprop powered development of the piston engined Queen Air (which today is in limited military service). The initial 90 series King Air differed from the Queen Air primarily in having two Pratt & Whitney Canada PT6 turboprops and pressurisation. First flown in January 1964 it remains in military service with a number of nations. US military developments of the King Air 90 include the US Army's unpressurised U-21 Ute and the RU-21 Elint aircraft, and the US Navy's T-44 Pegasus trainer.

Beech stretched the King Air 90 in 1969 to come up with the King Air 100, but most military King Airs are based on the 200. The King Air 200 used the stretched 100's fuselage, combined with a T-tail, and first flew in October 1972. Most King Airs are used as transports. King Air 200s are used by the US Air Force and Army as C-12s, by the US Navy and Marines as UC-12s. More than 380 King Airs have been delivered to the US military.

A small number of Maritime Patrol B200Ts are in military service, fitted with a search radar, bubble observation windows and wings that can be fitted with tip tanks. Optional B200T equipment includes ESM, GPS, FLIR, sonobuoys and processor and a tactical navigation computer.

The US Army's RC-12 Guardrail has been progressively improved, and is used for intercepting radio transmissions. Israel ordered five RC-12Ds, designated FWC-12AD

Military developments of the King Air 300 and stretched 350 series are also on offer and are operated by Japan (LR-2) for liason and reconnaissance.

**Photo:** A Chilean air force King Air 200. (Alvaro Romero)

## Raytheon Beech T-1A Jayhawk & T-400

**Country of origin:** United States of America

**Type:** Tanker and transport aircrew trainer

**Powerplants:** Two 12.9kN (2900lb) P&WC JT15D-5 turbofans.

**Performance:** Max level speed 867km/h (468kt) at 27,000ft, typical cruising speed at 12,500ft 835km/h (450kt), long range cruising speed 725km/h (392kt). Service ceiling 41,000ft. Range with max fuel and four pax at long range cruising speed 3575km (1930nm).

**Weights:** Operating empty 4589kg (10,115lb), max takeoff 7157kg (15,780lb).

**Dimensions:** Wing span 13.25m (43ft 6in), length 14.75m (48ft 5in), height 4.24m (13ft 11in). Wing area 22.4m² (241.4sq ft).

**Accommodation:** T-1A – Student pilot and instructor side by side on flightdeck, with observer seated behind them on a jump seat. Main cabin can accommodate four passengers or waiting students.

**Armament:** None

**Operators:** T-1 – USA. T-400 – Japan.

**History:** The Jayhawk is an off-the-shelf development of the Beechjet 400A business jet and was acquired to meet a US Air Force require-ment for a Tanker Transport/Training System (TTTS) aircraft.

The TTTS requirement was formulated as part of the US Air Force's Specialized Undergraduate Pilot Training system which was designed to make USAF pilot training more efficient and to ease strain on the Northrop T-38 Talon fleet. The TTTS requirement was issued in the late 1980s, and the USAF considered proposals from British Aerospace, Learjet, Cessna and Beech. In February 1991 the USAF ordered the first 28 of an eventual 180 Beechjet 400A based T-1A Jayhawks. The first was delivered in January 1992 and an initial operating capability (IOC) was achieved in January 1993. The final Jayhawk was delivered to the USAF on July 23 1997. Pilots training on the T-1 go on to fly transports such as the C-17, C-141, C-5, KC-10 and KC-135.

The Beechjet 400 design began life as the Mitsubishi MU-300 Dia-mond, which first flew in August 1978. The improved Diamond 2 production aircraft flew in June 1984, but only 11 were built before Beech acquired the manufacturing and design rights. Beech replaced the Diamond 2's JT15D-4s with -5s, improved the interior, moved production to the USA and renamed the aircraft the Beechjet 400.

The improved Beechjet 400A, on which the T-1 is based, first flew in September 1989 and introduced a number of improvements including EFIS. Beech also increased the weights and repositioned the rear fuselage fuel tank to increase cabin volume.

The T-1 differs from the 400A in having fewer cabin windows, the avionics relocated from the nose to the cabin, greater fuel capacity, single point refuelling, TACAN, reinforced windscreen protection against birdstrikes, and strengthening of the wing carry through struc-ture and engine pylons to handle increased low-level flight stresses.

The Japanese Air Self Defence Force also selected the Beechjet as the basis for a transport aircrew trainer, designated the T-400. Ten T-400s are fitted with the optional thrust reversers, plus long range inertial navigation and direction finding systems.

In 1997 Raytheon was a awarded a contract to fit 62 Jayhawks with GPS. The contract could be extended to upgrade the remaining T-1s.

**Photo:** A USAF T-1A Jayhawk. (Doug Mackay)

## Raytheon T-6A Texan II

**Countries of origin:** USA and Switzerland

**Type:** Two seat advanced trainer

**Powerplant:** T-6A – One 1274kW (1708shp) Pratt & Whitney Canada PT6A-68 turboprop (flat rated to 820kW/1200shp) driving a four blade propeller.

**Performance:** T-6A – Max speed 574km/h (310kt), max cruising speed 426km/h (230kt). Initial rate of climb 4500ft/min. Service ceiling 35,000ft. Range at altitude 1575km (850nm).

**Weights:** T-6A – Empty 2087kg (4600lb), max takeoff 2858kg (6300lb).

**Dimensions:** T-6A – Wing span 10.18m (33ft 5in), length 10.16m (33ft 4in), height 3.25m (10ft 7in). Wing area 16.3m² (175.3sq ft).

**Accommodation:** Two in tandem.

**Armament:** None

**Operators:** Canada*, Greece*, USA*.

**History:** The T-6A Texan II was the winner of the USAF's and USN's JPATS trainer competition and is a development of the Pilatus PC-9.

The US DoD formed the JPATS (Joint Primary Aircraft Training Sys-tem) program in 1991 to find a replacement for USAF T-37s and US Navy T-34 Turbo Mentors, with the aim of reducing costs through commonality and buying an off-the-shelf design.

Seven jets and turboprops vied for the contract, all non US designs bar one (the all new Cessna 526) with their manufacturers teamed with US partners. The Beech Pilatus PC-9 Mk II development of the PC-9 was selected on June 22 1995.

Earlier in support of its JPATS contest work, Beech (now part of Raytheon) modified two Pilatus built PC-9s. Beech then built two pro-duction prototypes (respective first flights Dec '92 and July '93).

The T-6 Texan II designation (honouring the original North American T-6 Texan) was adopted in June 1997, by which time construction of the first production T-6 was underway. This aircraft first flew in June 1998 and US civil certification was awarded in August 1999, clearing the way for T-6 deliveries.

The first USAF T-6 was handed over on March 1 2000, with deliver-ies of 454 to continue through to 2011. IOC with the USAF was planned for 2001 at Randolph AFB Texas, while IOC with the USN, at NAS Whiting Field, Florida, is planned for 2003. The Navy plans to buy 328 Texans.

So far export customers comprise the Bombardier operated NATO Flying Training in Canada program which has 24 T-6A-1s (designated CT-156 Harvard II in Canada – Harvard was the British Commonwealth name for the original Texan) on order with deliveries beginning in February 2000, and Greece (45 for delivery 2000-03, the last 20 of which will have underwing hardpoints and a fixed sight).

The T-6 features many improvements over the PC-9, with 90% of the structure redesigned and strengthened, a more powerful PT6A-68 with a Power Management Unit for linear power delivery (for easier student transition to jets), a higher max takeoff weight, EFIS, zero-zero Martin-Baker ejection seats, provision for a HUD, and a revised shape cockpit canopy thickened for improved birdstrike protection.

T-6 production is due to reach 43 aircraft a year by 2004.

**Photo:** T-6 deliveries began in 2000. (USAF)

## Raytheon Hawker 800/BAe 125 & Dominie

**Countries of origin:** United Kingdom and United States of America

**Type:** VIP transport, navigation trainer (Dominie) and SAR aircraft

**Powerplants:** 700 – Two 16.6kN (3700lb) Garrett TFE731-3-RH turbofans. 800 – Two 19.1kN (4300lb) TFE731-5R-1Hs.

**Performance:** 700 – Max cruising speed 808km/h (436kt), economical cruising speed 723km/h (390kt). Service ceiling 41,000ft. Range with max payload 4725km (2500nm). 800 – Max cruising speed 845km/h (456kt), economical cruising speed 741km/h (400kt). Max initial rate of climb 3100ft/min. Service ceiling 43,000ft. Range with max payload 5318km (2870nm), range with max fuel 5560km (3000nm).

**Weights:** 700 – Empty 5826kg (12,845lb), max takeoff 11,567kg (25,500lb). 800 – Empty 6676kg (14,720lb), max takeoff 12,430kg (27,400lb).

**Dimensions:** 700 – Wing span 14.33m (47ft 0in), length 15.46m (50ft 9in), height 5.36m (17ft 7in). Wing area 32.8m² (353.0sq ft). 800 – Wing span 15.66m (51ft 5in), length 15.60m (51ft 2in), height 5.36m (17ft 7in). Wing area 34.8m² (374.0sq ft).

**Accommodation:** Flightcrew of two. Typical seating for nine in VIP layout, or max seating for 14. Dominie crew complement of two pilots, instructor and three students.

**Armament:** None

**Operators:** Brazil, Japan, Malawi, Saudi Arabia, South Korea, UK.

**History:** This long running business jet began life as the de Havilland DH.125, was developed by successor companies Hawker Siddeley and BAe, and is now built in the US as the Hawker 800. Hawkers serve as VIP transports, while the original 125 formed the basis for the RAF's Dominie navigation trainer.

What is now the Hawker 800 started life as the de Havilland DH.125, which first flew on August 13 1962. For a time named the Jet Dragon, initial DH.125 production models were the Series 1 and improved Series 1A and 1B. The similar Series 2 was the basis for the Dominie T.1, the Royal Air Force's standard navigator trainer since 1966. Twenty Dominies were built – from 1993 11 were updated with modern systems to make them more representative of current frontline aircraft.

Subsequent Viper powered 125 models were the Series 3; Series 4, or Series 400 when de Havilland merged into Hawker Siddeley; and the Series 600 with a stretched fuselage and seating for eight.

The much improved British Aerospace 125-700 with more fuel efficient Garrett TFE731 turbofans first flew in 1976. The 700 remained in production until replaced by the 125-800 in the early 1980s. The 125-800 first flew in May 1983 and introduced aerodynamic changes including a reprofiled nose and windscreen; a larger ventral fuel tank, more powerful engines and a redesigned interior.

The 125-800 became the Raytheon Hawker 800 from mid 1993 when Raytheon purchased BAe's Corporate Jets division. Production was transferred to the US between 1995 and 1997.

Raytheon delivered the first of 27 required SAR equipped Hawker 800s (U-125A) to Japan from 1995 (deliveries should continue through to 2004). These aircraft feature a search radar, FLIR and observation windows. The USAF's Hawker 800 based C-29 flight inspection platforms (delivered in 1990) were transferred to the FAA in 1991.

**Photo:** A JASDF U-125. (Raytheon)

## Rockwell T-2 Buckeye

**Country of origin:** United States of America

**Type:** Two seat carrier capable advanced trainer

**Powerplants:** T-2C – Two 13.1kN (2950lb) General Electric J85-GE-4 turbojets.

**Performance:** T-2C – Max speed 840km/h (470kt). Initial rate of climb 6200ft/min. Service ceiling 40,415ft. Range 1685km (910nm).

**Weights:** T-2C – Empty 3680kg (8115lb), max takeoff 5977kg (13,179lb). Internal fuel 2616 litres.

**Dimensions:** T-2C – Wing span over tip tanks 11.62m (38ft 2in), length 11.67m (38ft 4in), height 4.51m (14ft 10in). Wing area 23.7m² (255.0sq ft).

**Accommodation:** Two in tandem.

**Armament:** T-2C – Usually none, but has two underwing hardpoints for practice bombs, rockets and gun pods, and target towing equipment. T-2D/T-2E – Six underwing hardpoints can carry a total ordnance load of 1588kg (3500lb).

**Operators:** Greece, USA, Venezuela.

**History:** The T-2 Buckeye advanced trainer was responsible for training and carrier qualifying countless thousands of US Navy fast jet pilots since the early 1960s.

In 1956 the US Navy issued a requirement for a new jet powered trainer for advanced, weapons and combat training and carrier qualification. Later in 1956 North American Aviation, which had already made thousands of SNJ and T-28 Trojan trainers (plus the FJ Fury fighter) for the US Navy, was selected to develop its NA-249 design proposal as the T-2J-1 with an initial order for 26.

The NA-249/T2J-1 design featured a single 15.1kN (3400lb) Westinghouse J34-WE-36 turbojet fed by two undernose intakes, plus tandem seating, a mid mounted straight wing with tip tanks and an arrester hook for carrier operations/training.

The first T2J-1 first flew on January 31 1958 (there was no prototype). Two hundred and seventeen T2J-1 (T-2A from 1962) Buckeyes were built, the first entered service in July 1959. In 1960 two T2J-1s were converted to YT2J-2 standard with two 13.4kN (3000lb) Pratt & Whitney J60-P-6 turbojets. The first of these flew on August 30 1962 as the YT-2B, while the first production T-2B flew on May 21 1966. The 97 production T-2Bs were delivered to the USN from 1966.

The definitive US Navy Buckeye was the T-2C. The T-2C is powered by two General Electric J85-GE-4 turbojets (the J85 also powers the F-5), and first flew in 1968. The T-2C (231 built) was delivered between 1968 and 1975, replacing surviving T-2As and T-2Bs in service.

The T-2C has been replaced in the training role by the T-45 Goshawk, but a small number remain in service in utility roles and with the Naval Test Pilots School at NAS Patuxent River, Maryland.

The Buckeye was exported to Greece and Venezuela. Venezuela ordered 12 T-2Ds (with some avionics changes and no carrier gear) in 1972. A subsequent batch of 12 T-2Ds featured six underwing hardpoints. Greece's T-2E are essentially similar, with the six underwing hardpoints. Forty were delivered through to 1977.

In all, 550 Buckeyes were built through to 1977. Small numbers of T-2B and T-2Cs were converted to DT-2 drone controllers.

**Photo:** A Greek air force T-2E. (Greek MoD)

## Rockwell OV-10 Bronco

**Country of origin:** United States of America

**Type:** Light attack/COIN and FAC aircraft

**Powerplants:** OV-10A – Two 535kW (715ehp) Garrett T76-G-416/417 turboprops driving three blade propellers.

**Performance:** OV-10A – Max speed 452km/h (244kt). Max initial rate of climb 2650ft/min. Service ceiling 24,000ft. Combat radius with max external ordnance 367km (198nm). Ferry range with external fuel 2300km (1240nm).

**Weights:** OV-10A – Empty equipped 3160kg (6970lb), max takeoff 6552kg (14,444lb).

**Dimensions:** OV-10A – Wing span 12.19m (40ft 0in), length 12.67m (41ft 7in), height 4.62m (15ft 2in). Wing area 27.0m² (291.0sq ft).

**Accommodation:** Two crew in tandem, with provision for two stretchers and a medical attendant or five troops in rear fuselage.

**Armament:** Four 7.62mm machine guns in underfuselage sponsons. Two underwing, one centreline and four under sponson hardpoints for light bombs, rockets and gun pods.

**Operators:** Indonesia, Morocco, Philippines, South Korea, Thailand, Venezuela.

**History:** The OV-10 resulted from the US Marines sponsored Light Armed Reconnaissance Aircraft (LARA) program to find a multirole utility aircraft that could perform recce and light attack missions.

North American's NA-300 design was selected in August 1964. Seven YOV-10A prototypes were ordered for evaluation and the first of these first flew on July 16 1965.

The OV-10 has a unique configuration with two crew in tandem under a large canopy, room in the rear fuselage for five troops or two stretchers, a high wing and twin tailbooms extending from the engine nacelles. Power is from two Garret T76s (one YOV-10 was powered by two T74s/PT6s). Sponsons extending either side of the fuselage house four 7.62mm guns and feature weapons hardpoints.

Production OV-10As were delivered to the USAF, Navy and Marines, and many saw operational service in Vietnam where they were used for forward air control (FAC) and light attack.

The OV-10B designation applies to six Broncos delivered to Germany from 1970 for target towing. A further 18 OV-10B(Z)s for Germany were fitted with an above wing mounted J85 auxiliary turbojet. All have been retired.

The Royal Thai Air Force continues to operate 19 survivors of 32 OV-10Cs delivered from 1971, while Venezuela took delivery of 16 OV-10Es (and later ex USAF OV-10As). The OV-10C, OV-10E and Indonesia's OV-10Fs are similar to the OV-10A.

Seventeen OV-10As were converted to OV-10D standard over 1979/80 for the US Marines, the result of the US Navy sponsored OV-10D NOGS (Night Observation/Gunship System) program to give the Bronco an all weather capability. Now retired, the OV-10Ds featured an undernose turret containing a FLIR, laser designator and automatic video tracker, plus uprated engines and extra underwing hardpoints. The OV-10D saw service during the Gulf War and could be armed with a 20mm M197 three barrel cannon in place of the 7.62mm guns.

**Photo:** Indonesian OV-10F Broncos. (Angkasa, via Robert Wiseman)

## Rockwell B-1B Lancer

**Country of origin:** United States of America

**Type:** Strategic bomber

**Powerplants:** Four 136.9kN (30,780lb) with afterburning General Electric F101-GE-102 turbofans.

**Performance:** Max speed Mach 1.25 or 1324km/h (715kt), penetration speed at 200ft over 965km/h (520kt). Service ceiling over 50,000ft. Range with standard fuel approx 12,000km (6475nm).

**Weights:** Empty equipped 87,090kg (192,000lb), max takeoff 216,365kg (477,000lb). Max fuel 87,090kg (192,000lb).

**Dimensions:** Wing span fully extended 41.67m (136ft 9in), span wings swept 23.84m (78ft 3in), length 44.81m (147ft 0in), height 10.36m (34ft 10in). Wing area approx 181m² (1950sq ft).

**Accommodation:** Crew of four comprising pilot, copilot, offensive systems operator (OSO) and defensive systems operator (DSO).

**Armament:** Max internal payload of 34,020kg (75,000lb) in three internal weapons bays. Weapons include B-61 and B-83 thermonuclear bombs or on rotary launchers up to 8 AGM-86B ALCMs, 24 AGM-69A short range attack missiles (SRAM-As), 12 B-28, 28 B-61 or 28 B-93 free fall nuclear bombs. Can carry up to 84 500lb/225kg Mk 82 conventional bombs and CBU-87, -89 & -97 cluster bombs, and JDAM.

**Operators:** USA

**History:** The B-1 had to endure criticisms of its high cost, cancellation, a 20 year gestation period and operational serviceability problems.

The B-1 resulted from the USAF's Advanced Manned Strategic Aircraft (AMSA – or, as it became known, America's Most Studied Airplane) program of 1965 to find a low altitude penetration nuclear bomber to replace the B-52. A North American Rockwell design was eventually selected for further development in 1970.

The first of four B-1A prototypes first flew on December 23 1974. However in 1977 new US President Carter cancelled planned B-1A production (SAC hoped to acquire 250) but test flying continued.

The B-1 was resurrected in 1981 after Ronald Reagan was inaugurated as US President and 100 improved production B-1s, designated B-1B, were ordered. Compared with the B-1A the B-1B (ff Oct 18 '84) features improved avionics and systems, incorporation of some low observable features such as RAM coatings, optional weapons bay fuel tanks, external underfuselage hardpoints for fuel and weapons, ejection seats rather than a crew escape capsule, fixed, rather than variable air inlets (limiting top speed to Mach 1.25 rather than the B-1A's Mach 2.3) with ducting masking the engines from radar. The B-1B's offensive systems are based around the APG-164 radar (based on the APG-66) for navigation and terrain following, with a low observable phased array antenna. The core of the defensive systems is the Eaton ALQ-161 upgradable ECM suite.

All 100 production B-1B Lancers were delivered by April 1988. Block upgrade programs are equipping the Lancer with precision conventional weapons, including JDAM, JSOW and JASSM, plus the ALE-50 Towed Decoy System and GPS navigation. The Defensive System Upgrade Program is adding the ALE-55 fibre optic towed decoy and new RWR and jammer. The B-1 was used operationally over Iraq in 1998, Kosovo/Serbia in 1999, and Afghanistan in 2001.

**Photo:** A B-1B in company with an F-15E. (USAF)

# Saab 105

**Country of origin:** Sweden

**Type:** Basic/advanced trainer, liaison and light attack aircraft

**Powerplants:** Sk 60B – Two 7.3kN (1638lb) Turbomeca Aubisique turbofans. Sk 60W – Two 8.1kN (1812lb) class Williams Rolls FJ44-1C (RMIS) turbofans.

**Performance:** Sk 60B – Max speed at 20,000ft 765km/h (413kt), max speed at sea level 720km/h (388kt), max cruising speed 685km/h (370kt). Max initial rate of climb 3445ft/min. Time to 29,530ft 15min. Service ceiling 39,370ft. Ferry range 1780km (960nm), standard range 1400km (755nm). Sk 60W – Max speed 790km/h (426kt). Service ceiling 36,080ft. Range on internal fuel 2500km (1350nm).

**Weights:** Sk 60B – Empty 2510kg (5535lb), MTOW 4500kg (9920lb). Sk 60W – Empty 2782kg (6134lb), MTOW 4832kg (10,654lb).

**Dimensions:** Wing span 9.50m (31ft 2in), length 10.50m (34ft 5in), height 2.70m (8ft 10in). Wing area 16.3m² (175.5sq ft).

**Accommodation:** Two side by side in all models except Sk 60D, which has seating for four on fixed (non ejection) seats.

**Armament:** Sk 60B – Six underwing hardpoints can carry a total ordnance load of 800kg (1764lb), including rockets and bombs. Austrian 105Ös can carry a 2000kg (4410lb) ordnance load.

**Operators:** Austria, Sweden.

**History:** The Saab 105 light attack, liaison and advanced jet trainer began life as a private venture.

Saab designed the 105 to be capable of diverse roles including ground attack, reconnaissance, basic and advanced pilot training, liaison, target towing and even air ambulance. The first of two Saab 105 prototypes first flew on June 29 1963, while the following year the Swedish air force ordered 130 production aircraft (later increased to 150) designated the Sk 60. The first production Sk 60 flew in August 1965.

The Sk 60A trainer entered Swedish service in 1966. These aircraft were delivered unarmed but were later retrofitted with hardpoints for weapons, allowing a secondary wartime ground attack role. The Sk 60B is primarily tasked with weapons training and ground attack. The Sk 60C has a Fairchild KB-18 reconnaissance camera in the nose, but also retains a secondary ground attack capability. The Sk 60D and four seat Sk 60E (with the two ejection seats replaced by four fixed seats) are used for liaison and check rides.

Ninety-six Swedish Sk 60s were re-engined with Williams Rolls FJ44 turbofans to Sk 60W standard. The prototype conversion first flew in October 1995, the last conversion was completed in 1998. Benefits include lower fuel consumption and maintenance costs and improved reliability.

The only Saab 105 export was Austria's order for 40 Saab 105Ös. The 105Ö is based on the General Electric J85 turbojet powered Saab 105XT, which first flew on April 29 1967. The Saab 105XT was intended for export and apart from the more powerful engines has improved avionics, greater internal fuel capacity and a strengthened wing allowing an increased external ordnance load.

For many years the 105Ös were tasked with air defence until the arrival of Austria's Drakens.

**Photo:** An Austrian Saab 105Ö. (Lassi Tolvanen)

# Saab Safari & Supporter & PAC Mushshak

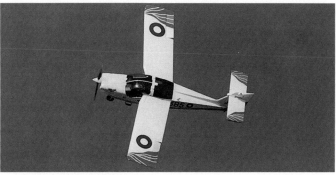

**Country of origin:** Sweden

**Type:** Two seat basic trainer

**Powerplant:** MFI-17 – One 150kW (200hp) Lycoming IO-360-A1B6 flat four piston engine driving a two blade propeller.

**Performance:** MFI-17 – Max speed 236km/h (127kt), cruising speed 208km/h (112kt). Max initial rate of climb 807ft/min. Service ceiling 13,450ft. Endurance 5hr 10min.

**Weights:** MFI-17 – Empty equipped 646kg (1424lb), max takeoff 1200kg (2646lb).

**Dimensions:** MFI-17 – Wing span 8.85m (29ft 1in), length 7.00m (23ft 0in), height 2.60m (8ft 7in). Wing area 11.9m² (128.1sq ft).

**Accommodation:** Standard seating for two side by side, with optional rear facing seat behind them.

**Armament:** Mushshak – Six underwing hardpoints, inner two stressed for 150kg (330lb) each, outer four for 100kg (220lb), for rocket and gun pods and Bofors Bantam anti tank missiles.

**Operators:** Safari – Norway. Supporter – Denmark, Zambia. Mushshak – Iran, Oman, Pakistan, Syria.

**History:** The MFI-15 Safari and MFI-17 Supporter resulted from Saab's adaptation of the MFI-9 Junior/Minicom for basic training for civil and military operators.

The original Swedish two seat tricycle undercarriage Malmö MFI-9 first flew on October 10 1958. MBB of Germany acquired production rights to the MFI-9 and it built locally as the Bo 208 Junior (first flight in 1962). In all over 250 75kW (100hp) Rolls-Royce Continental O-200 powered MFI-9s and Bo 208s were built through to the late 1960s, mostly for civil customers.

In 1968 Saab began work on its MFI-15, based on the MFI-9 but with some design changes. Foremost of the changes in the Saab built MFI-15 prototype was the 120kW (160hp) Lycoming IO-320 piston engine. Like the MFI-9/Bo 208 the MFI-15 retained the unusual braced, mid mounted and slightly forward swept wing and rearward hinging canopy, offering good all round vision.

The prototype Saab MFI-15's maiden flight was on July 11 1969. Following testing the MFI-15 gained a more powerful IO-360, while the horizontal tail was relocated to clear it of damage of thrown up debris. First flight in this modified form was in February 1971.

Sold as the MFI-15 Safari, most went to civil customers, however Sierra Leone and Norway took delivery of Safaris for military pilot training.

To improve the Safari's military appeal, Saab developed the MFI-17 Supporter, fitted with six underwing hardpoints for light and practice weaponry, giving it weapons training and light COIN capabilities. First flight was on July 6 1972. Important customers were Denmark (designated T-17) and Zambia. Production ended in the late 1970s after about 250 Safaris and Supporters had been built. Most were for civil customers.

Pakistan meanwhile took delivery of 18 Saab built Supporters, while PAC assembled 92 from knocked down kits and built a further 149. It is named Mushshak (Proficient) in Pakistani service. Mushshaks have been exported to a number of Muslim nations.

**Photo:** A Pakistani Mushshak. (Paul Merritt)

## Saab 35 Draken

**Country of origin:** Sweden

**Type:** Multirole fighter

**Powerplants:** 35XD – One 56.9kN (12,790lb) dry and 78.5kN (17,650lb) with afterburning Volvo Flygmotor RM6C turbojet (licence built Rolls-Royce Avon 300).

**Performance:** 35XD – Max speed Mach 2 or approx 2125km/h (1145kt). Max initial rate of climb 34,450ft/min. Time to 36,000ft 2min 36sec, time to 49,200ft 5min 0sec. Radius with internal fuel only, hi-lo-hi 635km (345nm), with two 100lb/455kg bombs and two drop tanks hi-lo-hi 1005km (540nm). Ferry range with max internal and external fuel 3250km (1755nm).

**Weights:** 35XD – Empty 8250kg (18,188lb), max takeoff 16,000kg (35,275lb). Internal fuel 4925 litres. J 35J – MTOW 12,500kg (27,557lb).

**Dimensions:** Wing span 9.40m (30ft 10in), length 15.35m (50ft 4in), height 3.89m (12ft 9in). Wing area 49.2m² (529.6sq ft).

**Accommodation:** Pilot only, or two in tandem in Sk 35C and TF-35.

**Armament:** One or two 30mm Aden cannons (one in each wing). Nine stores stations can carry 454kg (1000lb) each including Bofors rockets, 1000lb/455kg and 500lb/225kg bombs, Rb 24 Sidewinder (licence built AIM-9P) and Rb 27 Falcon (licence built AIM-4) AAMs.

**Operators:** Austria.

**History:** The remarkable Draken (Dragon) was developed against a demanding 1949 Swedish air force requirement for an advanced high performance interceptor to replace the Saab J 29 Tunnan.

Among that requirement's specifications was speed 50% greater than any other fighter then entering service. Saab's design team led by Erik Bratt used a unique double delta wing, giving Mach 2 performance and shorter airfield takeoff lengths than contemporaries such as the Mirage III and F-104. The double delta wing configuration was successfully test flown on the Saab 201 research aircraft before the first of three Draken prototypes (powered by an Avon 200) first flew on October 25 1955.

Initial production RM6B powered J 35A fighters were delivered to the Swedish air force from 1960. New build and converted J 35Bs featured Saab's S7 fire control radar and a lengthened rear fuselage, while the J35D was powered by an improved and uprated RM6C turbojet. The final Swedish fighter Draken, the J 35F, introduced a Hughes weapon system comprising a pulse Doppler radar, automatic fire control system and Falcon AAMs. The J 35F-II has a Hughes infrared sensor. Sixty-six J 35Fs were upgraded to J 35J standard for service through to 1999, when the last Swedish Drakens were due to be retired.

Aside from the J 35 fighters the Swedish air force acquired reconnaissance S 35Es with five cameras in the nose, and the Sk 35 two seat conversion trainer.

The export 35X was sold to Denmark (the 35XD as the F-35 fighter, reconnaissance R-35 and two seat TF-35) and Finland which bought 12 J 35XS and later ex Swedish J 35Fs (Finland retired its last Drakens in 2000).

Austria's J 35ÖEs are rebuilt ex Swedish air force J 35Ds (24 were delivered from 1988). They are due to remain in service until 2003/04.

**Photo:** An Austrian Draken.

## Saab 37 Viggen

**Country of origin:** Sweden

**Type:** Multirole fighter

**Powerplant:** JA 37 – One 72.1kN (16,203lb) dry and 125kN (28,108lb) with afterburning Volvo Flygmotor RM8B turbofan.

**Performance:** JA 37 – Max speed above Mach 2, or more than 2125km/h (1145kt), max speed at 330ft Mach 1.2. Time to 32,800ft less than 1min 42sec. Takeoff run approx 400m (1310ft). AJ 37 – Tactical radius with external ordnance hi-lo-hi over 1000km (540nm).

**Weights:** JA-37 – Clean takeoff approx 15,000kg (33,070lb), takeoff with normal armament 17,000kg (37,478lb).

**Dimensions:** Wing span 10.60m (34ft 9in), length overall incl probe 16.40m (53ft 10in), fuselage length 15.58m (51ft 2in), height 5.90m (19ft 4in). Wing area 46.0m² (495.1sq ft).

**Accommodation:** Pilot only, or two in separate cockpits in Sk 37.

**Armament:** JA 37 – One 30mm Oerlikon KCA cannon in permanent underfuselage pack. Four underwing and three under fuselage hardpoints for Rb 74 Sidewinders, Rb 71 Sky Flashes or AIM-120s on each inboard wing pylon, plus rockets. AJ 37 – Weapons include Saab Rb 15F anti ship and Rb 75 Maverick missiles, Rb 27/28 Falcon and Rb 74 Sidewinder AAMs, rockets and bombs.

**Operators:** Sweden

**History:** The Viggen (Thunderbolt) for many years formed the backbone of Sweden's front line fighter force.

The Viggen was developed as the airborne component of Sweden's System 37 air defence network and to replace the Saab Lansen. Design work began in the early 1960s and considerations included Mach 2 speed at altitude, supersonic flight at low level and unprecedented STOL performance. To meet these requirements Saab utilised the then unconventional canard delta configuration. First flight was on February 8 1967.

The Viggen's canards or foreplanes are fixed but have trailing edge flaps. The wing arrangement not only gives good agility but also excellent takeoff performance, allowing operations from damaged runways or sections of freeways. Power is from a modified Volvo Flygmotor RM8 licence built Pratt & Whitney JT8D turbofan with afterburning. Tandem main undercarriage and thrust reversal allows short, non flare landings.

The Initial production model was the AJ 37 (first delivered in June 1971) optimised for ground attack but with a secondary interception role. In all 110 were built and they featured an Ericsson PS-37/A radar, Saab digital nav/attack computer and a HUD. The SF 37 (26 built) and SH 37 (26 built) are reconnaissance variants, the SH 37 with radar is optimised for maritime reconnaissance with a secondary maritime strike role. The Sk 37 (18 built) is a two seater.

Final production was of the JA 37 interceptor with an Ericsson PS-46/A multimode, Doppler, look down/shoot down radar, Sky Flash and Sidewinder missile armament, an uprated RM8B engine and new avionics. The last of 149 built was delivered in June 1990.

About 100 AJ, SH and SF 37s have been modified to multirole AJS 37 standard with expanded weaponry and some new avionics, while 60 JA 37s are being upgraded to JA 37D standard with modified PS-46/A radar, improved avionics and cockpit displays, and AIM-120 compatibility.

**Photo:** A JA 37 Viggen. (Paul Merritt)

# Saab JAS 39 Gripen

**Country of origin:** Sweden

**Type:** Lightweight multirole fighter

**Powerplant:** One 54.0kN (12,140lb) dry and 80.5kN (18,100lb) with afterburning Volvo Aero Corporation RM12 turbofan.

**Performance:** JAS 39A – Supersonic at all altitudes. Takeoff and landing strip length approx 800m (2625ft). Combat radius approx 800km (430nm).

**Weights:** JAS 39A – Operating empty 6622kg (14,600lb), max takeoff approx 13,000kg (28,660lb). Internal fuel 2268kg (5000lb).

**Dimensions:** JAS 39A – Wing span 8.40m (27ft 7in), length 14.10m (46ft 3in), height 4.50m (14ft 9in). JAS 39B – Same except length 14.76m (48ft 5in).

**Accommodation:** Pilot only, two in tandem in JAS 39B.

**Armament:** One 27mm Mauser BK27 cannon. Wingtip stations for Rb 74 (AIM-9) AAMs. One centreline and four underwing hardpoints for rockets, DWS 39 cluster bomb dispensers, Rb 75 (AGM-65) ASMs, RBS 15 anti ship missiles, bombs, AIM-120 or Matra Mica AAMs.

**Operators:** Czech Republic*, Hungary*, South Africa*, Sweden*.

**History:** Saab's sixth jet fighter, the Gripen (Griffin) is an advanced light single seat fighter.

The Gripen was developed to replace the Swedish air force's Viggens and remaining Drakens. Definition studies began in 1980, government program approval and development funding (including for five prototypes and 30 production aircraft) was approved in 1982. Meanwhile in 1981 the IG JAS (Industry Group JAS) teaming of Saab, Volvo Aero Corporation, Ericsson and FFV Aerotech had been formed to develop and build the new aircraft.

The growing cost of new fighters meant that the new fighter would be smaller than the Viggen and that it would be powered by a single engine. The General Electric F404 turbofan was selected for local development and production as the Volvo RM12, other design features include the canard delta configuration, lateral instability with fly-by-wire, an Ericsson/GMAv PS-05/A pulse Doppler multimode look down/shoot down radar with multiple target track while scan and ground mapping capabilities, three multifunction displays, a wide angle HUD and HOTAS controls. Thirty percent of the Gripen by weight is of composites.

The prototype Gripen first flew on December 9 1988 but crashed the following February due to fly-by-wire software problems. The second prototype Gripen flew in May 1990. The first production Gripen delivery was in June 1993 and 204 are on order. The first Swedish air force Gripen squadron was declared operational in 1997, deliveries are due to continue to 2007.

The JAS 39B two seater first flew on April 29 1996. Future deliveries could be to JAS 39C and D standard with helmet mounted sight and IRST, and improved radar and EW. A phased array radar upgrade is also planned from around 2010.

Saab is pursuing Gripen export sales with part owner BAE Systems. South Africa is the launch export customer, signing for 19 in 1999, although deliveries won't start until 2007. In 2001 Hungary agreed to lease 14 Swedish air force Gripens for 12 years from 2004, while the Czech Republic announced it planned to order 24 for delivery from 2005.

**Photo:** A Gripen single seater. (Sebastian Zacharias)

# Saab 340 & Argus

**Country of origin:** Sweden

**Type:** VIP transport (Tp 100) and AEW platform (Argus)

**Powerplants:** 340B – Two 1305kW (1750shp) General Electric CT7-9B turboprops driving four blade propellers.

**Performance:** 340B – Max cruising speed at 15,000ft 523km/h (282kt), long range cruising speed at 25,000ft 467km/h (252kt). Max initial rate of climb 2000ft/min. Service ceiling 31,000ft. Range with 35 passengers at long range cruising speed 1735km (935nm).

**Weights:** 340B – Operating empty 8140kg (17,945lb), max takeoff 13,155kg (29,000lb).

**Dimensions:** Wing span 21.44m (70ft 4in), length 19.73m (64ft 9in), height 6.97m (22ft 11in). Wing area 41.8m² (450sq ft).

**Accommodation:** Flightcrew of two. Main cabin seats up to 37 in passenger configuration. Tp 100 configured for VIPs. AEW S 100B has three multifunction workstations in main cabin.

**Armament:** None

**Operators:** Greece, Sweden.

**History:** The successful Saab 340 regional airliner has been adapted for military service as a VIP transport and as an AEW platform as the S 100B Argus.

In 1979 Saab (which wanted to diversify out of military aviation) and Fairchild reached an agreement to conduct joint feasibility and development studies on a 30 to 40 seat commuter. The resulting SF340 design was powered by two General Electric CT7 turboprops (a commercial development of the T700 turboshaft). Within the 65%/35% Saab-Fairchild partnership Saab was responsible for the fuselage, fin and final assembly, while Fairchild was responsible for the wings, engine nacelles and empennage.

The first of three SF340 prototypes first flew on January 25 1983. Saab assumed total program responsibility on November 1 that year and the SF340 designation was subsequently changed to 340A.

The first improved development of the Saab 340 was the 340B with more powerful engines, while other changes include a higher max takeoff weight and better range. First delivery was in September 1989. The last development of the 340 was the further improved 340BPlus. Saab ceased regional airliner production in 1999, after building 458 340s (plus 63 of the stretched, AE2100 powered Saab 2000).

Sweden operates a single VIP configured Saab 340B which was delivered to the Royal Swedish Air Force's Royal Flight in 1990 and is designated Tp 100.

Sweden also operates the 340 based airborne early warning and control configured S 100B Argus. Six (including the prototype, which first flew in 1994) were built, fitted with an Ericsson PS-890 Erieye side looking phased array radar mounted above the fuselage. The Erieye has a range of 300km (190nm) against fighter sized targets, including against clutter, and also has a sea surveillance mode. The Argus can be fitted with three multifunction workstations, while commands and information can be transmitted to and from ground stations via datalink. Delivery to the Swedish air force took place between 1997 and 1999.

Greece is leasing two Arguses for AEW operating experience (for 2.5 years from August 2001) before its EMB-145 SAs enters service.

**Photo:** The S 100B Argus. (Joris van Boven, Sentry Aviation News)

# Schweizer/Hughes 269, TH-55 Osage & 300

**Country of origin:** United States of America

**Type:** Training and light utility helicopter

**Powerplant:** 300C – One 140kW (190hp) Textron Lycoming HIO-360-D1A fuel injected flat four derated from 170kW (225hp) driving a three blade main rotor and two blade tail rotor.

**Performance:** 300C – Max cruising speed 153km/h (82kt), economical cruising speed 124km/h (67kt). Max initial rate of climb 750ft/min. Hovering ceiling in ground effect 5900ft, out of ground effect 2750ft. Service ceiling 10,200ft. Range with max fuel and no reserves 360km (195nm). Max endurance 3hr 24min.

**Weights:** 300C – Empty 474kg (1046lb), max takeoff 930kg (2050lb), or 975kg (2150lb) with an external sling load.

**Dimensions:** Main rotor diameter 8.18m (26ft 10in), length overall 9.40m (30ft 10in), fuselage length 6.80m (22ft 0in), height to top of rotor head 2.66m (8ft 9in). Main rotor disc area 52.5m² (565.5sq ft).

**Accommodation:** 300C – Typical seating for three (two in 269). Can lift a 475kg (1050lb) payload in an external sling load.

**Armament:** Usually none.

**Operators:** El Salvador, Greece, Nigeria, Pakistan, Paraguay, Spain, Sweden, Thailand.

**History:** The Hughes/Schweizer 260/TH-55/300 series is a highly successful family of two/three seat light helicopters, with over 3500 delivered by two manufacturers over three decades.

Hughes flew the two seat Model 269 for the first time in October 1956. The basic design sparked US Army interest and five were ordered as the YHO-2-HU for evaluation in the scout and observation roles. Deliveries of commercial equivalent Model 269As began in 1961.

The 269A program received a huge boost when Hughes won a US Army contract for a light helicopter primary trainer. Eventually 792 were built as the TH-55A Osage and more than 60,000 US Army helicopter pilots learned to fly in the type.

The Osage has been replaced in US Army service by the Bell TH-67 Creek, but TH-55s survive in service with a number of nations. Japan's Kawasaki built 38 TH-55Js (essentially similar to the TH-55A) under licence, but these have been retired.

The three seat, slightly larger 269B, which Hughes marketed as the Hughes 300, first flew in 1964. The 300 was followed from 1969 by the improved 300C, which introduced a more powerful 140kW (190hp) Lycoming HIO-360 engine and increased diameter main rotor, giving an increase in payload of 45%, plus overall performance improvements. The 300C (or 269C) flew in August 1969 and remains in production, essentially unchanged.

Since 1983 the 300C has been built by Schweizer in the USA. Schweizer built the 300C initially under licence for Hughes, and then acquired all rights to the helicopter in 1986. Under Schweizer's stewardship more than 250 minor improvements have been made to the 300C, but the basic design has been left unchanged.

Both Schweizer and Hughes have delivered 300s to military customers. Schweizer markets the TH-300C for military training (Thailand took delivery of 58 in the late 1980s). The 300C was also built in small numbers under licence in Italy by Breda Nardi as the NH-300C.

**Photo:** A 300C of the Fuerza Aerea Salvadorena. (Santiago Rivas)

# SEPECAT Jaguar

**Countries of Origin:** France and the United Kingdom

**Type:** Ground attack aircraft

**Powerplants:** GR.1A – Two 23.7kN (5320lb) dry and 35.8kN (8040lb) with afterburning Rolls-Royce/Turbomeca Adour Mk 104 turbofans.

**Performance:** GR.1A – Max speed Mach 1.6 or 1700km/h (917kt), max speed at sea level Mach 1.1 or 1350km/h (730kt). Time to 30,000ft 1min 30sec. Service ceiling 45,930ft. Combat radius hi-lo-hi with internal fuel 850km (460nm), or lo-lo-lo 537km (290nm). Combat radius with external fuel hi-lo-hi 1408km (760nm), lo-lo-lo 917km (495nm).

**Weights:** GR.1A – Empty equipped 7700kg (16,975lb), max takeoff 15,700kg (34,612lb). Internal fuel 4200 litres.

**Dimensions:** GR.1A – Wing span 8.69m (28ft 6in), length incl probe 16.83m (55ft 3in), length exc probe 15.52m (50ft 11in), height 4.89m (16ft 1in). Wing area 24.2m² (260.3sq ft).

**Accommodation:** Pilot only, or two in tandem in Jaguar/T.2.

**Armament:** GR.1B – Two 30mm Aden cannons. Two above wing (for AAMs only), four underwing and one centreline hardpoints for 4540kg (10,000lb) of ordnance, including bombs and rockets.

**Operators:** Ecuador, France, India, Nigeria, Oman, UK.

**History:** The world's first binational military aircraft, the Jaguar was the result of a joint British/French requirement for an advanced jet trainer. The British originally required a supersonic jet trainer, the French wanted a subsonic, cheap to build trainer/attack aircraft.

The SEPECAT (Société Européené de Production de l'Avion de Ecole de Combat et Appui Tactique) teaming of Breguet (design leader) and BAC was established in 1966 to build the aircraft, while Rolls-Royce and Turbomeca teamed to develop the Adour engine.

The first of eight prototypes first flew on September 8 1968. Deliveries began to the French in 1972 and to the British in 1974, by which time the Jaguar was viewed solely as a ground attack platform.

The 203 Jaguars delivered to the RAF comprised 165 GR.1 (Jaguar S) single seaters and 38 two seat T.2s (Jaguar B). The GR.1s (since upgraded to GR.1A standard with Adour Mk 104s) feature an advanced nav/attack system and laser rangefinder in a chisel shaped nose. Britain is currently upgrading its Jaguars to GR.3 (and T.4) standard with TIALD pod and ASRAAM compatibility, a helmet mounted sight, improved ECM, a towed decoy system, new LCD screen in the cockpit and up to 25% more powerful Adour Mk 106 turbofans.

France took delivery of 160 single seaters (Jaguar As) and 40 trainers (Jaguar Es). French Jaguar Es were delivered with a less advanced nav/attack system and twin DEFA cannons. Half were delivered with an undernose laser rangefinder and 30 can carry the ATLIS laser designator pod for the AS.30L laser guided missile.

The export Jaguar International had some success. It was marketed and built by BAe, and was based on the GR.1. India is the largest customer, and continues to build Jaguars under licence. Some are fitted with an Agave radar and can fire Sea Eagle anti ship missiles (these will be upgraded with the Elta EL/M-2032 radar). India's latest batch of 17 two seaters (due to be delivered from 2001) will have a DARIN nav/attack system and be used for night attack.

**Photo:** A French Jaguar A. (Joris van Boven/Sentry Aviation News)

# Shenyang J-6/F-6

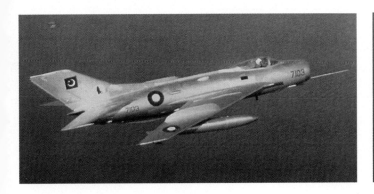

**Countries of origin:** Russia and China

**Type:** Interceptor/ground attack fighter

**Powerplants:** J-6 – Two 24.5kN (5730lb) dry and 31.9kN (7165lb) with afterburning Liming Wopen-6 (Tumansky R-9BF-811) turbojets.

**Performance:** J-6 – Max speed Mach 1.45 or 1540km/h (831kt), cruising speed 950km/h (512kt). Max initial rate of climb over 30,000ft/min. Service ceiling 58,725ft. Combat radius with external fuel 685km (370nm). Normal range 1390km (750nm), ferry range with external fuel 2200km (1187nm).

**Weights:** J-6 – Empty approx 5760kg (12,700lb), max takeoff approx 10,000kg (22,045lb).

**Dimensions:** J-6 – Wing span 9.20m (30ft 2in), length incl probe 14.90m (48ft 11in), length exc probe 12.60m (41ft 4in), height 3.88m (12ft 9in). Wing area 25.0m² (269.1sq ft).

**Accommodation:** Pilot only, or two in tandem in JJ-6/FT-6.

**Armament:** Three 30mm NR-30 cannons (one in each wing root and one in lower forward fuselage). Four underwing hardpoints for 500kg (1100lb) of external ordnance including AAMs (AIM-9 Sidewinders on Pakistani aircraft), rockets and bombs.

**Operators:** Albania, Bangladesh, China, Egypt, Iran, North Korea, Pakistan, Tanzania, Zambia.

**History:** The Shenyang J-6 is a Chinese built development of the 1950s vintage MiG-19 and numerically is still the most important combat aircraft in Chinese air force service.

The MiG-19 (NATO reporting name 'Farmer') was designed as an interceptor and first flew on January 5 1954. Capable of supersonic speeds in level flight, 2500 were built (including in Czechoslovakia) in several variants including the radar equipped MiG-19P. It was not exported widely and all are believed to have been retired from service.

China selected the basic MiG-19 for licence manufacture in the late 1950s. Russia supplied production diagrams for the MiG-19P to the Shenyang Aircraft Factory and the first Chinese assembled MiG-19 flew on December 17 1958, while the first Chinese built MiG-19 flew the following September.

Shenyang and initially Nanchang were assigned to build the MiG-19 (from 1961 the basic MiG-19S 'Farmer-C' dayfighter), however China's political and cultural instability during much of the 1960s meant that production was sporadic and quality often poor.

From 1966 production became more regular of the J-6 (equivalent to the MiG-19S) and the J-6A/B with Chinese developed air intercept radar (equivalent to the MiG-19P). Chinese developments include the JJ-6 tandem two seat trainer with lengthened fuselage and tandem seating (there was no two seat MiG-19), improved J-6C fighter, JZ-6 high altitude reconnaissance variant, and the J-6III with a variable shock cone in the nose – often misidentified as the J-6Xin and as having a radar.

As the F-6 (and two seat FT-6) the J-6 was exported widely and production continued into the 1980s. Pakistan was a big customer, taking delivery of a first batch of 40, from a total of 135, in 1966. Most of these were modified to carry the AIM-9 Sidewinder.

Total J-6/F-6 production is estimated at 3000.

**Photo:** A Pakistani F-6. Note the large wing fences.

# Shenyang J-8

**Country of origin:** China

**Type:** Interceptor

**Powerplants:** J-8 II – Two 42.7kN (9590lb) dry and 65.9kN (14,815lb) with afterburning Liyang (Guizhou) WP13A II turbojets.

**Performance:** J-8 II – Max speed at 36,000ft 2338km/h (1262kt). Max initial rate of climb 39,370ft/min. Service ceiling 66,275ft. Ferry range 2200km (1190nm). Combat radius 800km (432nm).

**Weights:** J-8 II – Empty 9820kg (21,649lb), max takeoff 17,800kg (39,242lb).

**Dimensions:** J-8 II – Wing span 9.34m (30ft 8in), length 21.59m (70ft 10in), height 5.41m (17ft 9in). Wing area 42.2m² (454.3sq ft).

**Accommodation:** Pilot only.

**Armament:** J-8 II – One 23mm Type 23-2 cannon in underfuselage blister fairing. One centreline and six underwing hardpoints for PL-2B infrared guided AAMs, PL-7 medium range semi active radar guided AAMs, unguided air-to-air rockets, air-to-ground rockets and bombs. J-8 IIM – As well as Chinese AAMs can carry Russian R-77s and R-27R1s.

**Operators:** China

**History:** China's J-8 and J-8 II interceptors have suffered from protracted and fitful development.

The J-8 (NATO reporting name 'Finback') resulted from a 1964 requirement for a new interceptor with improved performance compared to the MiG-21. The resulting aircraft was a tailed delta with a nose air intake, ranging radar in the intake centrebody and a single piece forward opening canopy, powered by two engines.

The first of two prototypes first flew on July 5 1969. Because of the upheaval of China's Cultural Revolution initial production was not authorised until 1979. Only small numbers of J-8s were built, although around 100 improved J-8 Is were delivered from the mid 1980s. The J-8 I featured a Sichuan SR-4 radar in an enlarged intake centrebody, conferring some all weather capability, plus some aerodynamic changes. First flight was on April 24 1981.

Development of the much improved J-8 II began in 1981 and it first flew on June 12 1984. The J-8 II introduced lateral air intakes (similar in configuration to the MiG-23's) and a nose mounted radar. It features a ventral folding fin which extends after takeoff and conventional two piece canopy, and has a secondary ground attack role. About 60 have been built and low rate batch production continues. It has been offered for export as the F-8 II. The J-8 IID is modified for inflight refuelling.

The Peace Pearl program to fit the J-8 II with US avionics (integrated by Grumman) including the APG-66 radar and US ejection seat, HUD and INS, as well as a bubble canopy with a frameless windscreen, was suspended following the 1989 Tiananmen Square massacre. Two J-8 IIs had been delivered to Grumman in the US for conversion but were returned unmodified to China in 1993.

Shenyang is currently working on the F-8 IIM which is intended for export. It features more powerful 68.7kN (15,432lb) WP13B turbojets, a Russian Phazotron Zhuk-8 II pulse Doppler radar and a modernised cockpit with a HUD, HOTAS controls, multifunction displays and INS and GPS navigation. First flight was on March 31 1996.

Shenyang flew a fly-by-wire F-8 demonstrator over 1996-99.

**Photo:** The J-8 IIM. (US DoD)

# ShinMaywa US-1

**Country of origin:** Japan

**Type:** Search and rescue amphibian

**Powerplants:** US-1A – Four 2535kW (3400ehp) Ishikawajima T46-IHI-10J turboprops (licence built GE T64s) driving three blade props.

**Performance:** US-1A – Max speed 522km/h (282kt), cruising speed at 10,000ft 426km/h (230kt). Max initial rate of climb, AUW 36,000kg (79,365lb) 2340ft/min. Service ceiling 28,400ft. Max range at 425km/h (230kt) cruising speed 3815km (2060nm).

**Weights:** US-1A – Empty 23,300kg (51,367lb), empty equipped 25,500kg (56,218lb), max takeoff from water 43,000kg (94,800lb), max takeoff from land 45,000kg (99,200lb).

**Dimensions:** Wing span 33.15m (108ft 9in), length 33.46m (109ft 9in), height 9.95m (32ft 8in). Wing area 135.8m² (1462.0sq ft).

**Accommodation:** Flightcrew of two pilots, flight engineer and navigator/radio operator (in main cabin). Main cabin can seat 20 seated survivors or 12 stretcher patients, plus two medical attendants, or alternatively up to 69 passengers.

**Armament:** None

**Operators:** Japan

**History:** ShinMaywa's US-1 is a large four engine amphibian which is used for search and rescue.

The SAR US-1 is a development of the earlier ASW/maritime patrol PS-1 flying boat. The first Shin Miewa (ShinMaywa from 1992, Kawanishi up to 1949) PX-S prototype first flew on October 5 1967, with 23 production PS-1s (SS-2s to Shin Meiwa) delivered to the Japanese Maritime Self Defence Force. The PS-1 was powered by four licence built General Electric T64 turboprops, and was equipped with sonobuoys, a MAD and search radar, and could carry mines, torpedoes and rockets. An auxiliary gas turbine (a GE T58) provided high pressure air for boundary layer control over the flaps, rudder and elevators, allowing the PS-1 to fly at very low speeds and reducing takeoff runs. The last PS-1 was retired from JMSDF service in 1989.

The US-1 (ShinMaywa designation SS-2A) was based closely on the PS-1 and differed mainly in its internal fit and permanent retractable undercarriage. First flight, from water, was on October 16 1974, while the US-1's first flight from land was in December that year. Initially 13 US-1s were built (for the JMSDF), while in 1992 production restarted against a single order with further single aircraft buys placed in the 1990s for attrition and to replace aging earlier US-1s, taking the production total to 19 thus far.

All US-1s have been upgraded to US-1A standard with more powerful T64-IHI-10J engines replacing the original T64-IHI-10s. A single US-1 was evaluated as a firebomber, fitted with a tank system developed by Comair of Canada.

ShinMaywa is now working on the much improved US-1A Kai. The US-1A Kai will feature new Rolls-Royce AE 2100J engines with Dowty six blade propellers, fly-by-wire and glass cockpit, pressurisation, a redesigned empennage and a Thales Ocean Master search radar. Metal cutting began in 1999, first flight is due in August 2003 and service entry planned for 2009. Initially seven existing US-1s will be upgraded to Kai standard.

**Photo:** The US-1 is operated by the JMSDF's 71 SAR Squadron.

# Shorts Skyvan

**Country of origin:** United Kingdom

**Type:** Light STOL utility transport

**Powerplants:** Srs 3 – Two 535kW (715shp) Garrett TPE331-2-201A turboprops driving three blade propellers.

**Performance:** 3M – Max cruising speed 324km/h (175kt), normal cruising speed 311km/h (168kt), economical cruising speed 278km/h (150kt). Max initial rate of climb 1530ft/min. Service ceiling 22,500ft. Takeoff run at MTOW 238m (780ft). Range with max fuel 1075km (582nm), range with a 2270kg (5000lb) payload 385km (208nm).

**Weights:** 3M – Operating empty (in utility configuration) 3355kg (7400lb), max takeoff 6577kg (14,500lb).

**Dimensions:** 3M – Wing span 19.79m (64ft 11in), length 12.21m (40ft 1in), or 12.60m (41ft 4in) with weather radar, height 4.60m (15ft 1in). Wing area 35.1m² (378sq ft).

**Accommodation:** Flightcrew of one or two. Seating for up to 22 combat equipped troops, or 16 paratroopers or 12 stretcher patients.

**Armament:** None

**Operators:** Austria, Ghana, Mexico, Nepal, Oman, Yemen.

**History:** The box like and rugged Shorts Skyvan STOL utility transport links back to the civil postwar Miles Aerovan project.

Shorts began development of the Skyvan, or SC.7, in 1959 as a private venture, with the intention of developing a small multirole transport with good short field performance and a square sided fuselage to accommodate oversize loads. The new design incorporated the results of Miles' research into high aspect ratio wings, with Shorts adopting the Aerovan's wing design for the SC.7. The prototype SC.7 Series 1 first flew powered by two Continental 290kW (390hp) GTSIO-520 piston engines on January 17 1963.

Initial production aircraft were powered by 545kW (730shp) Turbomeca Astazou XII turboprops. The original piston powered Series 1 prototype was the first Astazou powered Skyvan to fly (with 390kW/520shp Astazou IIs), in October 1963. The re-engined prototype was designated the Series 1A, while early Astazou powered production aircraft were designated Series 2.

Early on in the SC.7's production run Shorts switched the powerplant choice to 535kW (715shp) Garrett TPE331-201s, resulting in the definitive Series 3 (which first flew on December 15 1967). Many of the early build Series 2 Skyvans were also converted with Garretts.

The basic civil Series 3 and the higher takeoff weight Series 3A Skyvans can perform a number of utility missions including passenger transport, ambulance, aerial survey and freight work, while the Skyliner was a commuter airliner version.

The definitive military Skyvan models are the Series 3M and the higher max takeoff weight 3M-200 with a rear loading freight ramp. The 3M features a blister window on the port side for the loadmaster, inward facing paratroop seats and anchor cables for parachute static lines.

The Skyvan proved reasonably popular with developing world military customers for operations. Almost 60 of the 150 or so Skyvans built through to the late 1980s were for military customers and many remain in service.

**Photo:** An Austrian Skyvan. (Austrian Armed Forces)

## Shorts 330 & C-23 Sherpa

**Country of origin:** United Kingdom

**Type:** Utility transport

**Powerplants:** C-23A – Two 895kW (1120shp) Pratt & Whitney Canada T101-CP-100 (PT6A-45R) turboprops driving five blade props.

**Performance:** C-23A – Max cruising speed 352km/h (190kt), economical cruising speed 291km/h (157kt). Max initial rate of climb 1180ft/min. Service ceiling 20,000ft. Takeoff run at MTOW 560m (1840ft). Range with a 2270kg (5000lb) payload 1240km (670nm), range with a 3175kg (7000lb) payload 362km (195nm).

**Weights:** C-23A – Empty equipped 6680kg (14,727lb), max takeoff 11,565kg (25,500lb).

**Dimensions:** Wing span 22.76m (74ft 8in), length 17.69m (58ft 1in), height 4.95m (16ft 3in). Wing area 42.1m² (453sq ft).

**Accommodation:** Flightcrew of two. Typical passenger seating configuration for 30. In combi freight/passenger configuration can house freight in the forward fuselage and 18 passengers in the rear.

**Armament:** None

**Operators:** Thailand, USA.

**History:** The Shorts 330 is a stretched and enlarged development of the SC.7 Skyvan.

The 300, which began life designated the SD3-30, retained the Skyvan's overall configuration, including the slab sided fuselage cross section, supercritical above fuselage mounted braced wing (extended by 2.97m/9ft 9in) and twin tails. Compared with the Skyvan the 330's fuselage is stretched by 3.78m (12ft 5in), allowing seating for 10 extra passengers. Improved performance over the fairly slow Skyvan is courtesy of the two Pratt & Whitney PT6A turboprops driving five blade props, a more streamlined nose and retractable undercarriage. More than 60% greater fuel capacity boosts range significantly over the Skyvan.

An engineering prototype of the 330 first flew on August 22 1974, while a production prototype flew on July 8 1975. The first true production aircraft flew that December.

Initial Shorts 330s were powered by PT6A-45As and -45Bs and are known as 330-100s, while the definitive 330-200 features more powerful PT6A-45s, plus a number of detail improvements, while equipment previously available as options were made standard. The 330 also forms the basis for the larger 36 seat Shorts 360, which also features more powerful PT6A-65R (or -67R) engines and a conventional vertical tail.

The 330 has seen only limited military service. Thailand's army took delivery of two Shorts 330-UTs with rear loading freight ramp. The US Air Force ordered 18 similar C-23A Sherpas (lacking side windows) for transport services between its European bases and they operated between 1984 and 1990. Ten C-23Bs (with cabin windows) were delivered to the US Army National Guard and are used in various support and utility transport roles.

Twenty-eight ex airline Shorts 360s were converted to C-23B+ configuration for the US Army National Guard. The conversion involved fitting a rear loading freight ramp and twin tails, plus new avionics. Conversions began in 1994 and were completed in early 1997.

**Photo:** A Thai Shorts 330. (Dave Fraser)

## Sikorsky SH-3 Sea King & S-61R

**Country of origin:** United States of America

**Type:** ASW, SAR and utility maritime helicopter

**Powerplants:** SH-3H – Two 1045kW (1400shp) General Electric T58-GE-10 turboshafts driving five blade main and tail rotors.

**Performance:** SH-3H – Max speed 267km/h (144kt), economical cruising speed 219km/h (118kt). Max initial rate of climb 2200ft/min. Service ceiling 14,700ft. Hovering ceiling in ground effect 10,500ft, out of ground effect 8200ft. Range 1005km (542nm).

**Weights:** SH-3H – Empty 5600kg (12,530lb), max takeoff 9525kg (21,000lb).

**Dimensions:** Main rotor diameter 18.90m (62ft 0in), length overall rotors turning 22.15m (72ft 8in), fuselage length 16.69m (54ft 9in), height overall 5.13m (16ft 10in). Main rotor disc area 280.5m² (3109sq ft).

**Accommodation:** Crew of four, optional seating for 15 in main cabin.

**Armament:** Max external ordnance of 380kg (840lb), typically comprising two torpedoes.

**Operators:** SH-3 – Argentina, Canada, Iran, Italy, Japan, Peru, Spain, USA. AS-61R/S-61R/HH-3 – Argentina, Egypt, Iraq, Italy, Malaysia, Peru, Tunisia.

**History:** For many years the Sea King formed the backbone of the US Navy's ASW helicopter force. While largely replaced by the SH-60 in US service, many other nations rely on the Sea King for ASW, SAR and various maritime utility duties.

The Sikorsky HSS-2 (S-61) Sea King resulted from a US Navy requirement for a single helicopter that could both detect/track and attack submarines. Sikorsky was awarded a development contract in 1957 and the YHSS-2 prototype first flew on March 11 1959. At that time the Sea King represented a significant advance on anything before it, featuring twin turboshafts (GE T58s) mounted above the voluminous main cabin which had space to accommodate bulky ASW gear, including dunking sonar and radar. Other features were a boat hull for amphibious operations and five blade main and tail rotors.

Initial production was of the SH-3A (HSS-2 pre 1962) with 245 built, while the 73 SH-3Ds had improved sonar and radar and uprated engines. Over 100 SH-3As were converted to SAR/transport SH-3G form, with ASW gear deleted. The SH-3H (116 converted) was modified for service from aircraft carriers for inner zone ASW, plane guard and surface surveillance and targeting. Most have been replaced by SH-60Fs. Other US conversions were the UH-3A utility transport, VH-3A/D VIP transport and SAR HH-3A.

Mitsubishi (SH-3A/D/H), Agusta (SH-3D) and Westland (its Rolls-Royce Gnome powered variants are described separately) all built the Sea King under licence. Most of Canada's CHSS-2s/CH-134s were assembled under licence by United Aircraft of Canada.

The stretched S-61R or CH-3C was developed specifically for the USAF and had a stretched fuselage with a rear loading freight ramp. As the HH-3E 'Jolly Green Giant' it gained fame rescuing downed aircrew in Vietnam. All USAF CH/HH-3s have been retired, as have all the US Coast Guard's HH-3F Pelicans. Agusta licence built 35 AS-61Rs for Italy for SAR and combat rescue and 33 remain in use.

**Photo:** An Agusta licence built AS-61R (HH-3F). (Joris van Boven)

# Sikorsky CH-53 Sea Stallion

**Country of origin:** United States of America

**Type:** Medium/heavylift helicopter

**Powerplants:** MH-53J – Two 2935kW (3935shp) General Electric T64-GE-7A turboshafts driving a six blade main rotor and four blade tail rotor.

**Performance:** MH-53J – Max speed at sea level 315km/h (170kt), cruising speed 278km/h (150kt). Max initial rate of climb 2180ft/min. Service ceiling 20,400ft. Hovering ceiling in ground effect 11,700ft, out of ground effect 6500ft. Range 868km (468nm).

**Weights:** MH-53J – Empty 10,691kg (23,569lb), max takeoff 19,050kg (42,000lb).

**Dimensions:** Main rotor diameter 22.02m (72ft 3in), length overall rotors turning 26.90m (88ft 3in), fuselage length 20.47m (67ft 2in), height overall rotors turning 7.60m (24ft 11in), height to top of rotor head 5.22m (17ft 2in). Main rotor disc area 380.9m² (4099.8sq ft).

**Accommodation:** Flightcrew of three. Seating in main cabin for 55 equipped troops or 24 stretcher patients and four medical attendants.

**Armament:** MH-53J – Can be fitted with 12.7mm machine guns and 7.62mm miniguns.

**Operators:** Germany, Iran, Israel, USA.

**History:** The CH-53 Sea Stallion was the result of a 1960 US Marine Corps requirement for a heavylift helicopter for troop transport to replace the Sikorsky CH-37C.

Sikorsky used its CH-54 Tarhe (S-64 Skycrane) as the basis to meet the Marines' requirement. The resulting S-65 used the CH-54's dynamic systems coupled with an all new fuselage, including a watertight hull giving an emergency water landing capability, plus a rear ramp.

Two prototypes were ordered in August 1962, the first of which first flew on October 14 1964. Production deliveries of CH-53As to the Marine Corps commenced in 1966 and by 1967 the type was being used operationally in Vietnam. CH-53As were exported to Austria (two, both sold to Israel in 1980), Germany (112 CH-53Gs, most licence built in Germany) and Israel (45). Israel is upgrading its aircraft with new avionics as the CH-53 Yasur 2000. The USMC's CH-53D has uprated engines and automatic blade folding.

The US Air Force ordered its first combat rescue variants of the CH-53 in 1966. Eight initial HH-53Bs were followed by 44 HH-53Cs with external fuel tanks and an inflight refuelling probe. Some of these were later converted to HH-53H Pave Low III configuration with terrain following radar, Doppler and INS navigation, GPS, nose turret mounted FLIR, and then to MH-53H standard with a night vision goggle compatible cockpit for insertion/extraction missions.

From 1986 39 H-53s were upgraded to MH-53J Pave Low III Enhanced standard. Equipment fit includes terrain following radar, FLIR, GPS, inflight refuelling probe, secure communications, titanium armour, jammers, flare and chaff dispensers, NVG compatible cockpit, searchlight and external hoist. The survivors have undergone a life extension program.

The US Navy's RH-53D minesweepers have been replaced by MH-53E Sea Dragons. Six were delivered to pre-revolutionary Iran.

**Photo:** A German army CH-53G. (Paul Merritt)

# Sikorsky Super Stallion & Sea Dragon

**Country of origin:** United States of America

**Type:** CH-53E – Heavylift assault transport. MH-53E – Mine sweeper

**Powerplants:** CH-53E – Three 3265kW (4380shp) General Electric T64-GE-416 turboshafts driving a seven blade main rotor and four blade tail rotor.

**Performance:** CH-53E – Max speed at sea level 315km/h (170kt), cruising speed at sea level 278km/h (150kt). Max initial rate of climb (with a 11,340kg/25,000lb payload) 2500ft/min. Service ceiling 18,500ft. Hovering ceiling in ground effect 11,550ft, out of ground effect 9500ft. Operational radius with 9070kg (20,000lb) external payload 925km (500nm), with a 14,515kg (32,000lb) external payload 93km (50nm). Ferry range 2075km (1120nm).

**Weights:** CH-53E – Empty 15,072kg (33,338lb), max takeoff 31,640kg (69,750lb), max takeoff with external sling load 33,340kg (73,500lb).

**Dimensions:** CH-53E – Main rotor diameter 24.08m (79ft 0in), length overall rotors turning 30.19m (99ft 1in), fuselage length 22.35m (73ft 4in), height overall rotors turning 8.97m (29ft 5in), height to top of rotor head 5.32m (17ft 6in). Main rotor disc area 455.4m² (4901.4sq ft).

**Accommodation:** Flightcrew of three. Accommodation in main cabin for 55 equipped troops or light artillery pieces or vehicles.

**Armament:** None but has been trialled with AIM-9s for self defence.

**Operators:** CH-53E – Turkey*, USA. MH-53E – Japan, USA.

**History:** The CH-53E (S-80) Super Stallion is a three engined development of the Sea Stallion, with greatly improved lifting capabilities.

The Super Stallion resulted from a US Marine Corps' need for a helicopter with much greater lifting abilities than the already impressive CH-53 able to operate from its amphibious assault ships. Sikorsky met the requirement by adding a third engine and uprated transmission to the CH-53, resulting in the CH-53E (S-80). The third engine (all GE T64-GE-415s) was mounted near the main rotor mast on the aircraft's port side. Other changes introduced on the CH-53E were a lengthened fuselage and enlarged fuselage sponsons housing extra fuel, a removable inflight refuelling probe and a seven blade main rotor.

The first YCH-53E prototype first flew on March 1 1974 (this aircraft was subsequently destroyed during a ground running test). The second YCH-53E introduced a revised tail (the vertical tail is canted 20 degrees to port, while the horizontal tail is braced). Deliveries began in June 1981, with 177 CH-53Es built for the USMC and US Navy. The Marines use them primarily for lifting heavy weapons and equipment (including recovering downed aircraft) alongside CH-53Ds, while the USN's are used for ship supply. Various CH-53E upgrades have been proposed, but so far none have been funded.

In 2000 Turkey ordered eight of the S-80E export version of the CH-53E, with a Rockwell Collins EFIS avionics system with four large LCDs. These will be delivered in 2002.

The MH-53E Sea Dragon mine countermeasures helicopter was developed for the US Navy to replace RH-53Ds. Identifiable by their extra large composite construction sponsons which house extra fuel, the MH-53Es tow a hydrofoil sled carrying mechanical, acoustic and magnetic sensors for mine detection. Eleven similar S-80M-1s (without the inflight refuelling probe) were delivered to Japan from 1989.

**Photo:** A USMC CH-53E. (Paul Merritt)

# Sikorsky UH-60 Black Hawk & MH-60S

**Country of origin:** United States of America

**Type:** Medium lift helicopter

**Powerplants:** UH-60L – Two 1342kW (1800shp) intermediate rated General Electric T700-GE-701C turboshafts driving four blade main and tail rotors.

**Performance:** UH-60L – Max cruising speed 294km/h (159kt). Max vertical rate of climb from 4000ft 1550ft/min. Service ceiling 19,140ft. Hovering ceiling out of ground effect at 35° 7640ft. Range with max internal fuel 584km (315nm). Endurance 2hr 6min.

**Weights:** UH-60L – Empty 5224kg (11,516lb), MTOW 11,113kg (24,500lb).

**Dimensions:** UH-60 – Main rotor diameter 16.36m (53ft 8in), length overall rotors turning 19.76m (64ft 10in), fuselage length 15.26m (50ft 1in), height overall rotors turning 5.13m (16ft 10in), height to top of rotor head 3.76m (12ft 4in). Main rotor disc area 210.1m² (2262sq ft).

**Accommodation:** Flightcrew of two with gunner/crew chief behind them. Accommodation in main cabin for 11 equipped troops, or 14 in a high density configuration, or alternatively six stretcher patients.

**Armament:** Two pintle mounts for machine guns or miniguns, one either side in forward cabin. Four hardpoints on detachable external stores support system (ESSS) usually for fuel but, as on AH-60, can carry Hellfire anti armour missiles and rockets.

**Operators:** Argentina, Australia, Austria, Bahrain, Brazil, Brunei, Chile, China, Colombia, Egypt, Israel, Japan, Jordan, Malaysia, Mexico, Morocco, Philippines, Saudi Arabia, Sth Korea*, Taiwan, Thailand*, Turkey*, USA*.

**History:** The UH-60 is the US Army's standard troop transport helicopter, and has been adopted for a number of special mission roles.

The Black Hawk was developed to replace the Bell UH-1 Iroquois, meeting the US Army's 1972 Utility Tactical Transport Aircraft System (UTTAS) requirement. Three YUH-60A prototypes (first flight October 17 1974) were successfully evaluated against prototype Boeing Vertol YUH-61s. The first production UH-60 Black Hawk first flew in October 1978, with first deliveries in 1979.

Basic US Army Black Hawk transport models are the UH-60A and improved UH-60L (with more powerful T700-GE-401C engines to combat increased weight, first flight 1988). Other US models include the EH-60A ECM jammer; FLIR equipped special missions MH-60A, MH-60L and definitive MH-60K with terrain following radar and inflight refuelling probe; medevac UH-60Q Dustoff; Hellfire and rocket armed AH-60L 'Direct Action Penetrator'; and the command and control UH-60C, currently under development. The US Air Force operates about 100 HH-60G combat rescue Black Hawks. The US Marines operates nine VIP VH-60N White Hawks.

The US Army plans to upgrade up to 1200 UH-60As and Ls to UH-60M standard with new avionics, composite main rotor and strengthened fuselage, with service entry in 2006.

The MH-60S (formerly CH-60) has been developed to meet a USN requirement for a combat SAR and vertrep helicopter. A converted YCH-60S demonstrator first flew on October 6 1997, the first new build CH-60 on January 27 2000. The USN requires 200. It combines the airframe of the UH-60 with the SH-60's automatic flight control system, blade and tail folding mechanisms.

**Photo:** A US Army medevac configured UH-60L. (Paul Merritt)

# Sikorsky SH-60 & MH-60R Seahawk

**Country of origin:** United States of America

**Type:** Shipborne ASW helicopter

**Powerplants:** SH-60B – Two 1415kW (1900shp) General Electric T700-GE-401 turboshafts (1342kW/1800shp -401Cs from 1988) driving four blade main and tail rotors.

**Performance:** SH-60B – Dash speed at 5000ft 235km/h (126kt). Max vertical rate of climb at sea level 700ft/min. Operational radius with 3hr loiter 93km (50nm), or for a 1hr loiter 278km (150nm).

**Weights:** SH-60B – Empty for ASW mission 6190kg (13,648lb), max takeoff 9925kg (21,884lb).

**Dimensions:** SH-60B – Main rotor diameter 16.36m (53ft 8in), length overall rotors turning 19.76m (64ft 10in), fuselage length 15.26m (50ft 1in), height overall rotors turning 5.18m (17ft 10in), height to top of rotor head 3.79m (12ft 6in). Main rotor disc area 210.1m² (2262sq ft).

**Accommodation:** Pilot and airborne tactical officer in cockpit, sensor operator station in main cabin.

**Armament:** SH-60 – Two Mk 46 or Mk 50 torpedoes or AGM-119 Penguin anti ship missiles, plus pintle mounted machine guns.

**Operators:** Aus, Greece, Japan, Spain, Taiwan, Thailand, Turkey*, USA*.

**History:** The Seahawk is the US Navy's standard shipborne anti submarine warfare helicopter.

Sikorsky based its proposal to meet the US Navy's LAMPS (light airborne multipurpose system) Mk III program for a new ASW helicopter on the UH-60 Black Hawk airframe. Sikorsky's bid was selected ahead of a rival proposal from Boeing Vertol. The prototype YSH-60B first flew on December 12 1979.

The SH-60 features navalised General Electric T700 turboshafts, a repositioned tailwheel with twin wheels, lateral pylons for torpedoes or external fuel tanks, an external winch and a sensor station in the main cabin. The SH-60B is operated off USN frigates, destroyers and cruisers, and is fitted with an APS-124 search radar and a 25 tube sonobuoy launcher on the port side of the fuselage and carries a towed MAD. Primary armament is the Mk 46 torpedo and more latterly the Mk 50 torpedo and AGM-119 Penguin anti ship missile.

The SH-60F is the USN's CV Inner Zone ASW helicopter and provides close-in ASW protection for USN aircraft carrier battle groups. It features a dunking sonar, FLIR and ESM, while the search radar is deleted. Eighty-one were delivered to replace SH-3H Sea Kings, while Taiwan has 10 similar S-70C(M)-1 Thunderhawks.

Seahawks have been exported to Australia (S-70B-2, with Thomson Thorn Super Searcher radar and integrated Rockwell Collins avionics), Greece, Japan (SH-60J), Spain, Thailand and Turkey.

Other SH-60 variants include the USN's minigun armed HH-60H Rescue Hawk used for strike rescue (recovery of downed aircrew) and SEAL commando insertion/extraction, the US Coast Guard's HH-60J Jayhawk and the USN's MH-60R (previously SH-60R).

The USN plans to buy 243 new build multimission MH-60Rs with dipping sonar, APS-147 radar, colour displays, FLIR and AGM-119 Hellfire compatibility. The MH-60R prototype (a converted SH-60B) first flew on July 19 2001. The MH-60R will replace SH-60B/Fs and HH-60Hs (the USN had planned to upgrade HH/SH-60s to MH-60R standard).

**Photo:** The prototype MH-60R. (Sikorsky)

## Sikorsky S-76/H-76 Eagle

**Country of origin:** United States of America

**Type:** Utility helicopter

**Powerplants:** H-76 – Two 660kW (885shp) max continuous rated Pratt & Whitney Canada PT6B-36A turboshafts driving four blade main and tail rotors.

**Performance:** H-76 – Max speed 287km/h (155kt), cruising speed 270km/h (145kt). Max initial rate of climb 1650ft/min. Max operating altitude 15,000ft. Range at 257km/h (140kt) cruising speed with no reserves 650km (350nm).

**Weights:** H-76 – Basic empty 2545kg (5610lb), MTOW 5170kg (11,400lb).

**Dimensions:** Main rotor diameter 13.41m (44ft 0in), length overall 16.00m (52ft 6in), fuselage length 13.21m (43ft 4in), height overall 4.41m (14ft 6in). Main rotor disc area 141.3m$^2$ (1520.5sq ft).

**Accommodation:** Flightcrew of two. Accommodation for 10 equipped troops. VIP configurations seat six or eight. Medevac configured aircraft can accommodate three stretchers and two medical attendants.

**Armament:** AUH-76 – Can be fitted with pintle mounted machine guns in main doorways, plus rockets, gun and cannon pods, Hellfire and TOW anti armour missiles and Stinger AAMs. H-76N – Torpedoes and Sea Skua anti ship missiles.

**Operators:** Guatemala, Panama, Philippines, Spain, Thailand.

**History:** Unique among Sikorsky's current helicopter line, the S-76 was designed for civilian use and then adapted for military service, rather than the other way around.

Sikorsky developed the mid sized S-76 to diversify its product lineup away from military work. The S-76 was designed to perform a diverse range of roles including oil rig support and executive transport. Sikorsky began development work on the S-76 (for a time named Spirit) in the mid 1970s and used technologies and knowledge gained from the military H-60/S-70 program. The resulting design featured two Allison 250-C30S turboshafts and a wide cabin with seating for 12. First flight was on March 13 1977.

Civil models comprise the S-76A; the S-76 Mark II (introduced in March 1982) with more powerful Allison engines and numerous detail refinements; the twin Pratt & Whitney Canada PT6T powered S-76B; the S-76C, powered by two Turbomeca Arriel 1S1 engines; the S-76A+ – undelivered S-76As subsequently fitted and delivered with Arriel engines and S-76As converted to Arriel power; and the S-76C+ with more powerful Arriel 2S1 engines. The S-76D utility is a proposed joint development with Mil which would be built in Russia. Since mid 2000 the S-76's fuselage has been built by Aero Vodochy in the Czech Republic.

More than 500 S-76s have been built, but almost all of them have been for civil customers. The Philippines (four AUH-76s and one S-76 Mk II) and Spain (eight S-76Cs designated HE.24 and used for IFR helicopter pilot training and SAR) are among the current operators.

The H-76 Eagle is the dedicated military variant developed from the S-76B. The AUH-76 is a cannon, rocket and missile armed gunship, while the navalised S-76N can be fitted with search radar and armed with torpedoes and anti ship missiles. Thailand has bought six for its navy (but without radar and unarmed).

**Photo:** Thailand has taken delivery of six S-76Ns. (Royal Thai Navy)

## Sikorsky S-92

**Country of origin:** United States of America

**Type:** Medium lift transport helicopter

**Powerplants:** Two 1790kW (2400shp) takeoff rated General Electric CT7-8 turboshafts driving four blade main and tail rotors.

**Performance:** Max cruising speed 287km/h (155kt), economical cruising speed 260km/h (140kt). Hovering ceiling in ground effect (civil aircraft) 11,100ft, out of ground effect 6100ft. Range 890km (480nm).

**Weights:** Military model – Empty 6895kg (15,200lb), max takeoff 11,430kg (25,200lb), with sling load 12,020kg (26,500lb).

**Dimensions:** Main rotor diameter 17.71m (56ft 4in), length overall rotors turning 20.85m (68ft 5in), fuselage length 17.32m (56ft 10in), height overall 6.45m (21ft 2in). Main rotor disc area 231.6m$^2$ (2492.4sq ft).

**Accommodation:** Flightcrew of two. Accommodation in main cabin for 22 combat equipped troops.

**Armament:** None

**Operators:** None

**History:** The Sikorsky S-92 is a new medium lift helicopter being developed as an SH-3/S-61 class replacement.

Development of the S-92 was first announced in 1992 when Sikorsky unveiled a mockup of the new helicopter. In 1993 Sikorsky postponed launching the S-92 due to the international helicopter market downturn and instead began searching for international risk sharing partners. By 1995 Sikorsky had formed its Team S-92 partners and formally launched the S-92 at the 1995 Paris Airshow.

The S-92 combines the dynamic systems of the H-60/S-70 series with a larger cabin. Components based on those from the H-60 series include the rotor head, transmission and powerplants. Otherwise the S-92 is all new with all composite wide chord and drooped tip rotor blades (40% of the aircraft is of composite construction). The main cabin is wider and longer than the H-60's and features a rear ramp, while the cockpit features four liquid crystal displays.

Team S-92 members include risk sharing partners Mitsubishi Heavy Industries (7.5%, – responsible for the main cabin), Gamesa of Spain (7% – cabin interior and transmission housing) and China's Jingdezhen Helicopter Group (2% – tail pylon and tailplane), while Taiwan Aerospace (6.5% – flightdeck) and Embraer (4% – sponsons and fuel system) are fixed price suppliers/partners. Russia's leading helicopter designer Mil is also a program participant.

Sikorsky has initially built five development S-92s (one a ground test article), the first of which first flew on December 23 1998 from Sikorsky's West Palm Beach, Florida, Development Flight Centre. The last S-92 development aircraft flew on October 5 2001, and was the first completed in the production configuration with Rockwell Collins glass cockpit (with four large NVG compatible LCDs presenting flight and navigation data plus a digital map), 41cm (16in) lengthened cabin, reduced height tail pylon and relocated horizontal stabiliser.

The base model S-92A is now offered for both civil and military duties after the military specific S-92IU (International Utility) model was dropped. US civil certification and deliveries to commercial customers are planned for 2002.

**Photo:** S-92 on evaluation in Finland. (Lassi Tolvanen)

# Singapore Aerospace Super Skyhawk

**Countries of origin:** USA and Singapore

**Type:** Light ground attack aircraft

**Powerplant:** One 48.4kN (10,800lb) General Electric F404-GE-100D non afterburning turbofan.

**Performance:** Max speed at sea level 1128km/h (609kt), max cruising speed at 30,000ft 825km/h (445kt), economical cruising speed at 35,000ft 785km/h (424kt). Max initial rate of climb 10,913ft/min. Combat ceiling 40,000ft. Range with max payload 1160km (625nm), range with internal and external fuel 3790km (2045nm).

**Weights:** Operating empty 4650kg (10,250lb), max takeoff 10,205kg (22,500lb).

**Dimensions:** Wing span 8.38m (27ft 6in), length 12.72m (41ft 9in), height 4.57m (15ft 0in). Wing area 24.1m² (259.8sq ft).

**Accommodation:** Pilot only, or two in tandem, separate cockpits in TA-4SU.

**Armament:** One centreline and four underwing hardpoints for rockets, bombs, AIM-9 AAMs, AGM-65 ASMs and gun pods.

**Operators:** Singapore

**History:** Singapore's program to upgrade the A-4 with a non afterburning F404 turbofan and modern avionics has resulted in perhaps the ultimate Skyhawk variant.

Singapore joined the ranks of McDonnell Douglas A-4 Skyhawk operators in 1970 when the first of 40 refurbished ex USN A-4Bs were delivered (as the A-4S). Lockheed upgraded the first eight aircraft, with the remainder modified in Singapore by Singapore Aerospace. The upgrade to A-4S standard involved installing a more powerful Wright J65-W-20 turbojet, spoilers and new nav/attack system. The two seat TA-4S Skyhawk conversion is unique in its installation of separate tandem cockpits. Further ex US Navy Skyhawks were delivered (16 A-4Bs in 1983 and 70 A-4Cs in 1980) and while most of these were broken down for spares, enough were converted to A-4S standard to allow the formation of an additional squadron.

In 1984 Singapore elected to further upgrade its Skyhawks to extend their service lives rather than replace them. Phase one of Singapore Aerospace's two phase Super Skyhawk program was developed with Grumman and General Electric assistance and involved installing a non afterburning General Electric F404-GE-100D turbofan, plus strengthening to accommodate the new and heavier engine and modification to the air intakes.

The 27% more powerful F404 resulted in a 15% higher dash speed, a 35% greater climb rate, and 40% better level acceleration, plus enhanced takeoff performance and sustained turn rate. The first F404 powered Skyhawk first flew on September 19 1986, with production conversions of 52 A-4S Skyhawks to GE powered A-4SU standard completed in 1989.

The separate phase two of the program was the Ferranti (now part of BAE Systems) developed avionics upgrade. Features of the avionics upgrade include a Mil Std 1553B databus, head-up display, a multifunction display, mission computer and ring laser gyro INS.

The first Republic of Singapore Air Force Super Skyhawk squadron became operational in 1992.

**Photo:** An A-4SU Super Skyhawk in France. (Joris van Boven/Sentry)

# Slingsby T67 Firefly

**Country of origin:** United Kingdom

**Type:** Two seat basic trainer

**Powerplant:** T67M260 – One 195kW (260hp) Textron Lycoming AEIO-540-D4A5 flat six piston engine driving a three blade propeller.

**Performance:** T67M260 – Max speed at sea level 280km/h (152kt), max cruising speed 260km/h (140kt). Max initial rate of climb 1380ft/min. Range with max fuel at 65% power 755km (410nm).

**Weights:** T67M260 – Empty 794kg (1750lb), MTOW 1157kg (2550lb).

**Dimensions:** T-3A – Wing span 10.59m (34ft 9in), length 7.57m (24ft 10in), height 2.36m (7ft 9in). Wing area 12.6m² (136.0sq ft).

**Accommodation:** Seating for two side by side.

**Armament:** None

**Operators:** Belize, Jordan*.

**History:** The Firefly two seat trainer is in service with Belize, on order with Jordan and used by private contractors for flight screening and initial training.

The Firefly is a development of the French Fournier RF-6B two seat aerobatic basic trainer which first flew in March 1974. Forty-five were built (with a 75kW/100hp Rolls-Royce Continental O-200) through to the early 1980s. In 1980 Fournier flew the 87kW (116hp) Lycoming O-235 powered RF-6B-120, which would form the basis for Slingsby's T67 Firefly.

Slingsby bought the manufacturing and development rights for the RF-6B in 1981 (before that Slingsby specialised in sailplane construction and composite materials). Slingsby initially built nine T67As, basically RF-6B-120s, before placing into production its own development of the type, the T67B, which is made almost entirely from glassfibre reinforced plastics (GFRPs). Benefits of GFRP include better resistance to fatigue, and less weight and drag.

The definitive civil version of the Firefly is the T67C. The T67C is similar to the T67B except for its more powerful 120kW (160hp) Textron Lycoming O-320 engine. Variants of the T67C are the T67C1 with standard fuselage fuel tankage and one piece canopy, the T67C2 with a two piece canopy and the T67C3 with wing tanks and three piece canopy.

The basic military Firefly is the T67M Mk II, which flew in December 1982. Many are used for initial military pilot training and screening with civil firms under contract (including in the Netherlands, Norway, Canada and the UK's Joint Elementary TS). T67Ms have aerobatic engines and two blade constant speed props, among other changes, compared with the T67C. The T67M200 has a 150kW (200hp) AEIO-360.

In addition 113 T67M260s (powered by a 195kW/260hp AEIO-540) were ordered by the US Air Force as the T-3A Firefly. The Firefly was selected to meet the USAF's Enhanced Flight Screener contract to replace Cessna T-41 Mescaleros. Northrop Grumman assembled the 113 T-3As in Texas and they were delivered between early 1994 and late 1995. However the USAF grounded its Firefly fleet in 1997 following three fatal accidents and then permanently grounded the aircraft in 1999, despite the aircraft being cleared of safety concerns. Their flight screening role has been contracted out.

In late 2001 Jordan ordered 16 T67M200s for delivery in 2002.

**Photo:** Jordan has ordered the T67M200. (Slingsby)

## Soko Galeb & Jastreb

**Country of origin:** Bosnia-Herzegovina

**Type:** Two seat trainer (Galeb) and light strike fighter (Jastreb)

**Powerplant:** G2-A – One 11.1kN (2500lb) Rolls-Royce Viper Mk 22-6 turbojet.

**Performance:** G2-A – Max speed at 20,350ft 812km/h (438kt), max speed at sea level 755km/h (408kt), max cruising speed at 19,685ft 730km/h (395kt). Max initial rate of climb 4500ft/min. Time to 19,685ft 5min 30sec. Service ceiling 39,375ft. Max range with tip tanks full at 29,520ft 1240km (670nm). Max endurance at 23,000ft 2hr 30min.

**Weights:** G2-A – Empty equipped 2620kg (5775lb), max takeoff (strike version) 4300kg (9840lb).

**Dimensions:** G2-A – Wing span over tip tanks 11.62m (38ft 2in), length 10.34m (33ft 11in), height 3.28m (10ft 9in). Wing area 19.4m² (209.1sq ft).

**Accommodation:** Two in tandem in Galeb, pilot only in Jastreb.

**Armament:** G2-A – Two 12.7mm machine guns in nose. Underwing hardpoints for two 50kg (110lb) or 100kg (220lb) bombs and four rockets. J-1 – Three 12.7mm machine guns in nose. Eight underwing hardpoints, innermost for light bombs, outer hardpoints for single rockets.

**Operators:** Croatia, Libya, Yugoslavia.

**History:** The Galeb (Seagull) two seat trainer and subsequent Jastreb (Hawk) single seat attack fighter variant were Soko's first products.

Yugoslavia's VTI (Aeronautical Technical Institute) began design work on the G2-A Galeb in 1957. The first flight of the first of two prototypes was in May 1961. Production began in 1963, making it the first indigenous jet to be built in Yugoslavia. Production lasted through to the early 1980s.

The Galeb is similar to the contemporary Aermacchi MB-326 in configuration and both are powered by a single Rolls-Royce Viper turbojet. The Galeb features a straight wing with tip tanks, Folland Type 1-B lightweight ejector seats, sideways hinging canopy transparencies and underwing hardpoints for light bombs and rockets.

In all, around 270 Galebs were built for the Yugoslav air force, Libya, which took delivery of 120, and Zambia (six).

The J-1 Jastreb is a single seat ground attack development of the Galeb. Changes include a more powerful engine, structural strengthening, extra hardpoints for rockets and three, instead of two, 12.7mm guns in the nose. The RJ-1 is a reconnaissance variant, with one fuselage and two wingtip mounted cameras.

Approximately 250 to 300 Jastrebs were built, including 30 or so RJ-1s, plus around 30 two seat JT-1 trainers (basically the Galeb with the Jastreb's strengthening, extra hardpoints and weaponry and more powerful engine). First flight was in 1974, with deliveries from 1975. In addition 20 J-1Es and RJ-1Es were delivered to the Zambian air force in 1971, today the survivors are probably unserviceable.

Both Galebs and Jastrebs saw service during Yugoslavia's civil war with Serbian forces. Many were destroyed on the ground during NATO's Allied Force bombing campaign of Serbia and Kosovo in 1999.

Today Libya is the biggest operator with over 20 Jastrebs and 80 Galebs still on strength.

**Photo:** The Galeb is used for advanced pilot and weapons training with the Yugoslav air force.

## Soko Super Galeb

**Country of origin:** Bosnia-Herzegovina

**Type:** Advanced trainer and light attack aircraft

**Powerplants:** G-4 – One 17.8kN (4000lb) Rolls-Royce Viper Mk 632-46 turbojet.

**Performance:** G-4 – Max speed at 32,800ft Mach 0.81, max speed at 13,120ft 910km/h (490kt), max cruising speed at 19,700ft 845km/h (455kt), economical cruising speed at 19,700ft 550km/h (297kt). Max initial rate of climb 6100ft/min. Service ceiling 42,160ft. Range with max internal fuel at 36,090ft 1900km (1025nm), range with max external and internal fuel 2500km (1350nm). Range with gun pod and four BL-755 cluster bombs 1300km (700nm).

**Weights:** G-4 – Empty equipped 3172kg (6993lb), max takeoff 6300kg (13,890lb).

**Dimensions:** G-4 – Wing span 9.88m (32ft 5in), length overall 12.25m (40ft 2in), fuselage length 11.02m (36ft 2in), height 4.30m (14ft 0in). Wing area 19.5m² (209.9sq ft).

**Accommodation:** Two in tandem.

**Armament:** Removable ventral gun pod contains a GSh-23L twin barrel cannon. Four underwing hardpoints can carry 1280kg (2820lb) of bombs, cluster bombs and rockets. Croatia armed its aircraft with AAMs and AGM-65s. G-4M has wingtip rails for R-60 AAMs and can also carry AGM-65s on outboard hardpoints.

**Operators:** Croatia, Myanmar, Yugoslavia.

**History:** The Super Galeb advanced trainer and light ground attack aircraft was developed to replace the Galeb and Lockheed T-33 in Yugoslav service.

Design of the new trainer began in 1973 and was undertaken by VTI, the then Yugoslavia's Aeronautical Technical Institute (which also designed the Novi Avion MiG-21 replacement light fighter which was cancelled in 1992). Prototype construction began in 1975, while first flight was on July 17 1978. The prototype and six pre-series Super Galebs were designated G-4 PPP.

The Super Galeb features a swept wing with four underwing hardpoints, stepped cockpits, a Rolls-Royce Viper turbojet and anhedral on the all moving tailplane. The basic version is designated G-4. The improved G-4M would have featured advanced avionics including a HUD and multifunction displays, a greater payload and wingtip rails for AAMs. The G-4M was designed to take over some of the weapons training syllabus of front line combat aircraft. First flight was planned for 1992 but development was abandoned due to the Yugoslav civil war.

About 135 Super Galebs were built for the Yugoslav air force (production aircraft entered service in 1985), while Myanmar took delivery of 12 in the early 1990s. In 1992 during the Yugoslav civil war the Soko plant at Mostar, within Bosnia, was abandoned (including several incomplete aircraft) while Mostar was occupied by Serbian forces. The Super Galeb jigs were transferred to UTVA within the new Yugoslav state, however Super Galeb production did not resume. Super Galebs were used for light ground attack during Yugoslavia's civil war, while many were destroyed during NATO's 1999 Allied Force air strike campaign.

**Photo:** A Super Galeb in old Yugoslav markings. (Les Bushell)

# Soko Orao & Avioane IAR-93

**Countries of origin:** Bosnia-Herzegovina and Romania

**Type:** Ground attack aircraft

**Powerplants:** IAR-93B – Two 17.8kN (4000lb) dry and 22.2kN (5000lb) with afterburning Turbomecanica/Orao licence built Rolls-Royce Viper Mk 633-47 turbojets.

**Performance:** IAR-93B – Max speed at sea level 1085km/h (585kt), max cruising speed at 15,240ft 1090km/h (587kt). Max initial rate of climb 12,800ft. Service ceiling 44,625ft. Radius with four rocket launchers and 5min over target lo-lo-lo 260km (140nm), radius with two rocket launchers, six 100kg (220lb) bombs and one drop tank, with 10min over target, hi-lo-hi 450km (243nm), radius with four 250kg (550lb) bombs and one drop tank with 5min over target hi-hi-hi 530km (285nm).

**Weights:** IAR-93B – Empty equipped 5750kg (12,675lb), max takeoff 10,900kg (24,030lb).

**Dimensions:** Wing span 9.30m (30ft 6in), length overall incl probe 14.90m (48ft 11in), two seater length overall incl probe 15.38m (50ft 6in), height 4.52m (14ft 10in). Wing area 26.0m² (279.9sq ft).

**Accommodation:** Pilot only, or two in tandem in two seaters.

**Armament:** IAR-93 – One GSh-23L 23mm twin barrel cannon in lower forward fuselage. One centreline and four underwing hardpoints can carry a max external stores load of 1500kg (3305lb), for rockets, bombs and AAMs.

**Operators:** Croatia, Romania, Yugoslavia.

**History:** The J-22 Orao (Eagle) and IAR-93 resulted from collaboration between the aircraft industries of the former Yugoslavia and Romania to meet ground attack aircraft requirements.

A joint team of Romanian and Yugoslav designers began work on the J-22/IAR-93 in 1970 under the project name Yurom. Planning called for the new aircraft to be built in single seat ground attack and two seat advanced trainer/conversion trainer versions, with service entry around 1977. Each country built single seat prototypes which both made their first flights on October 31 1974. Similarly two two-seaters, one built in each country, had their maiden flights on January 29 1977. After 30 pre-series prototypes were built (15 in each country), series production began in Romania (with IAv Craiova, now Avioane) in 1979 and with Soko in Yugoslavia in 1980.

Romanian IAR-93s and Yugoslav Oraos are generally similar. Romanian production models comprised the initial non afterburning single and two seat IAR-93A (26 single seaters and 10 two seaters built), and the single and two seater IAR-93B with afterburning engines (first flight 1985, 165 built).

Yugoslav Orao variants are the non afterburning Orao 1 (17 built), which was considered underpowered and was relegated to reconnaissance duties as the IJ-22 (two two-seaters were designated INJ-22), the NJ-22 production two seat reconnaissance variant (35 built, some with afterburning) and the J-22 Orao production single seater (most with afterburning).

Soko built 75 J-22s at Mostar in Bosnia until 1992 when the factory was abandoned and the J-22 jigs were transferred to UTVA within the new Yugoslav state.

**Photo:** Note deployed airbrakes on this Yugoslav Orao. (MAP)

# Sukhoi Su-17/-20/-22

**Country of origin:** Russia

**Type:** Ground attack/strike fighter

**Powerplant:** Su-22M4 – One 76.5kN (17,200lb) dry and 110.3kN (24,800lb) with afterburning Lyulka AL-21F-3 turbojet.

**Performance:** Su-22M4 – Max speed Mach 1.74 or 1850km/h (1000kt). Max initial rate of climb 45,275ft/min. Service ceiling 49,865ft. Range with external fuel at altitude 2550km (1375nm), at low level 1400km (755nm).

**Weights:** Su-22M4 – Empty equipped 10,767kg (23,737lb), max take-off 19,400kg (42,770lb).

**Dimensions:** Wing span extended 13.68m (44ft 11in), span wings swept 10.03m (32ft 11in), length incl probes 19.03m (62ft 5in), fuselage length 15.87m (52ft 1in), height 5.13m (16ft 10in). Wing area wings extended 38.5m² (414.3sq ft), wings swept 34.9m² (375.1sq ft).

**Accommodation:** Pilot only, or two in tandem in Su-17U/Su-22U.

**Armament:** Two 30mm NR-30 guns. Nine hardpoints for 4000kg (8820lb) of armament incl bombs, gun pods, rockets, two R-13M, R-60 or R-73A AAMs, Kh-25ML, Kh-27, Kh-29 and Kh-58 ASMs.

**Operators:** Angola, Azerbaijan, Bulgaria, Czech Republic, Iran, Iraq, Libya, Peru, Poland, Slovakia, Syria, Turkmenistan, Ukraine, Uzbekistan, Vietnam, Yemen.

**History:** The swing wing Su-17 was the result of efforts to improve the Su-7 'Fitter-A's payload range and takeoff performance.

The prototype for the Su-17, designated S-22I or Su-7IG (Izmenyae-maya Geometriya – variable geometry) and designated by NATO 'Fitter-B', first flew on August 2 1966 (the wings pivot midway along their length, outboard of a large wing fence). Similar Lyulka AL-7 powered 'improved Fitter-B' pre-series Su-17s were noted in service in the early 1970s.

Initial production was of the Su-17M 'Fitter-C' with ranging radar, a 110.3kN (24,800lb) AL-21F-3 turbojet and a new nav/attack system. It was exported as the Su-20. In addition small numbers of reconnaissance pod carrying Su-17Rs and Su-20Rs were built.

The improved Su-17M2 and shorter fuselage Su-17M2D (both 'Fitter-D') were built from 1974 and introduced a slightly cut down nose for better pilot visibility, a fixed intake centrebody carrying a laser rangefinder and a Doppler radar in an undernose pod. The 'Fitter-D' was exported as the Tumansky R-29 powered Su-22 'Fitter-F'.

A two seat development of the Su-17M2 is the Tumansky R-29 powered Su-22U 'Fitter-E'.

Lyulka powered two seater Su-17UM3 'Fitter-G' conversion trainers and single seat Su-17M3 'Fitter-Hs' have a deeper spine and modified tail, the Su-17M3 also has an internal Doppler radar. Respective export variants are the Tumansky or Lyulka powered Su-22UM-3K 'Fitter-G' and Tumansky or Lyulka powered Su-22M3 'Fitter-J'. The Lyulka powered Su-17M4 and export Su-22M4 (both 'Fitter-K') have a dorsal air inlet for cooling and were delivered from 1980.

Sukhoi offers an Su-22 upgrade with a GPS, pod mounted FLIR and KAB-500 TV and laser guided bomb compatibility. Israel's Lahav is upgrading Polish Su-22s with an Elta synthetic aperture radar, colour displays, HUD and new mission computer.

**Photo:** A Polish Su-22M4 'Fitter-K'. (Sebastian Zacharias)

# Sukhoi Su-24

**Country of origin:** Russia

**Type:** Long range strike fighter

**Powerplants:** Su-24M – Two 75.0kN (16,864lb) dry and 109.8kN (24,690lb) with afterburning Saturn/Lyulka AL-21F-3A turbojets.

**Performance:** Su-24M – Max speed Mach 1.35. Max initial rate of climb 29,525ft/min. Service ceiling 57,400ft. Combat radius with 2500kg (5500lb) of bombs 950km (515nm), hi-lo-hi with external fuel and 3000kg (6615lb) of bombs 1050km (565nm).

**Weights:** Su-24M – Empty equipped 22,300kg (49,163lb), max takeoff 39,700kg (87,523lb). Max internal fuel 9764kg (21,525lb).

**Dimensions:** Su-24M – Wing span extended 17.64m (57ft 11in), span wings swept 10.37m (34ft 0in), length incl probe 24.60m (80ft 8in), height 6.19m (20ft 4in). Wing area wings extended 55.2m² (593.8sq ft), wing area wings swept 51.0m² (549.2sq ft).

**Accommodation:** Pilot and weapon systems operator side by side.

**Armament:** One 23mm gun. Nine external stores stations for TN-1000 and TN-1200 nuclear weapons, or four TV or laser guided bombs, or Kh-23 (AS-7 'Kerry'), Kh-25ML (AS-10 'Karen'), Kh-58 (AS-11 'Kilter'), Kh-25MP (AS-12 'Kegler'), Kh-59 (AS-13 'Kingbolt'), Kh-29 (AS-14 'Kedge') and Kh-31 (AS-17 'Krypton') ASMs, two R-60 (AA-8 'Aphid') AAMs for self defence, rockets and bombs.

**Operators:** Algeria, Iran, Azerbaijan, Belarus, Libya, Kazakhstan, Russia, Syria, Ukraine, Uzbekistan.

**History:** The formidable Su-24 (NATO name 'Fencer') strike fighter was developed to replace Il-28 and Yak-28 medium bombers.

Sukhoi's original proposal for the new bomber was the delta wing T-6 with four RD-36-35 auxiliary lift jets to improve takeoff performance. A T-6-1 prototype first flew in July 2 1967, but the jet lift configuration was abandoned in favour of using swing wings. A variable geometry T-6-2IG prototype (without lift jets) first flew on January 17 1970. The T-6-2IG was adopted for production as the Su-24, with around 1200 built.

The basic Su-24 was built in three variants, which NATO designated 'Fencer-A', 'Fencer-B' and 'Fencer-C'. The 'Fencer-A' first flew in late 1971 but served only in small numbers with a trials unit. The 'Fencer-B' was the first major production variant while the 'Fencer-C' had improved avionics.

The major production Su-24M 'Fencer-D' has a terrain following radar (rather than terrain avoiding radar), a retractable inflight refuelling probe, a longer nose for new avionics including a Kaira laser/TV weapons guidance system, wing root fences (on Russian aircraft only) and a single nose probe. The export version is the Su-24MK.

The Su-24MR 'Fencer-E' reconnaissance variant has a Shtik side looking radar in a shortened nose (with dielectric panels), infrared and TV sensors, a panoramic camera in the nose and an oblique camera in the lower fuselage (and no wing root fences). The Su-24MR can also carry various reconnaissance and Elint pods.

The final Su-24 variant is the EW, jammer and Sigint Su-24MP 'Fencer-F'. Only 12 are thought to have been built.

In 1999 Russia began flight testing an upgraded Su-24M with HUD, GPS and new processor.

**Photo:** An Su-24 'Fencer-B'.

# Sukhoi Su-25

**Country of origin:** Russia

**Type:** Close support/ground attack aircraft

**Powerplants:** Two 44.2kN (9920lb) Soyuz/Tumansky R-195 turbojets.

**Performance:** Su-25K – Max speed at sea level 975km/h (526kt), max attack speed, air brakes deployed 690km/h (372kt). Service ceiling 22,960ft. Range with a 4400kg (9700lb) warload and two external fuel tanks at sea level 750km (405nm), at altitude 1250km (675nm).

**Weights:** Su-25K – Empty 9500kg (20,950lb), MTOW 17,600kg (38,800lb).

**Dimensions:** Su-25K – Wing span 14.36m (47ft 2in), length 15.53m (51ft 0in), height 4.80m (15ft 9in). Wing area 33.7m² (362.8sq ft).

**Accommodation:** Pilot only, or two in tandem in Su-25UB.

**Armament:** Su-25K – One AO-17A 30mm gun. Eight underwing hardpoints for up to 4400kg (9700lb) – 1400kg (3086lb) normally – of armaments including laser guided rocket boosted bombs, Kh-23 'Kerry'), Kh-25ML (AS-10 'Karen') and Kh-29L (AS-14 'Kedge') ASMs, rockets, bombs, cluster bombs, gun pods, and R-3 and R-60 AAMs.

**Operators:** Angola, Armenia, Azerbaijan, Belarus, Bulgaria, Georgia, Iraq, Kazakhstan, Macedonia, North Korea, Peru, Turkmenistan, Slovakia, Russia, Ukraine.

**History:** The Su-25 ('Frogfoot' to NATO) was designed specifically for close air support missions in support of ground forces.

Su-25 development began in 1968. A prototype, designated T-8-1, first flew on February 22 1975 powered by twin Tumansky RD-9Bs. Between then and 1981 when the first Soviet Su-25 units were declared operational, the Su-25 underwent a number of changes.

A unit of Su-25s, initially preproduction aircraft, saw combat in Afghanistan where experience resulted in a number of modifications including bolt on chaff/flare dispensers, engine exhaust IR signature suppressors and titanium shielding between the engines.

The Su-25 features titanium cockpit armouring and wingtip pod airbrakes. The Su-25's engines can run on kerosene, diesel or petrol if necessary while the aircraft can self deploy its own ground support and maintenance equipment in four underwing pods.

The basic Su-25 and export Su-25K (both 'Frogfoot-A') account for most Su-25 production. The Su-25UB and export Su-25UBK (both 'Frogfoot-B') are two seat conversion trainers with a ground attack capability. The Su-25UT, later Su-28 (both also 'Frogfoot-B'), was offered as a dedicated advanced trainer. Ten carrier capable two seat Su-25UTGs (with arrester hook and strengthened undercarriage) were built for carrier trials while the Su-25UBP conversion of the Su-25UB is similar. Su-25BMs are single seater target tugs.

The Su-25TM (Su-39 to Sukhoi) is a dedicated anti tank variant based on the two seaters but with the rear cockpit faired over for extra fuel and avionics including a new nav system, plus chaff/flare dispenser in the base of the tail and a laser rangefinder and TV camera in the nose and centre line pod mounted radar. A small number of radar less Su-25Ts were built, but Russia has a requirement for 24 TMs.

Russia is to upgrade about 80 Su-25s to Su-25SM standard with Kyopo-25 radar, and two LCDs and HUD in the cockpit. Israel's Lahav offers the Su-25 Scorpion upgrade with HUD, twin LCDs and a weapons delivery and navigation system.

**Photo:** The Lahav upgraded Su-25 Scorpion. (Paul Merritt)

# Sukhoi Su-27, Su-30 & Su-33

**Country of origin:** Russia

**Type:** Air superiority/multirole/carrier based fighter

**Powerplants:** Su-27 – Two 79.4kN (17,857lb) dry and 122.6kN (27,557lb) with afterburning Saturn/Lyulka AL-31F turbofans.

**Performance:** Su-27 – Max speed Mach 2.35 or 2500km/h (1350kt), max speed at sea level Mach 1.1 or 1345km/h (725kt). Initial rate of climb 60,040ft/min. Service ceiling 59,055ft. Range with max fuel 3680km (1985nm). Intercept radius with four AAMs 1500km (810nm).

**Weights:** Su-27 – Empty 16,380kg (36,110lb), max takeoff 33,000kg (72,750lb). Max internal fuel 9400kg (20,723lb).

**Dimensions:** Su-27 – Span 14.70m (48ft 3in), length exc probe 21.94m (72ft 0in), height 5.93m (19ft 6in). Wing area 62.0m² (667.4sq ft).

**Accommodation:** Pilot only, or two in tandem in Su-27UB and Su-30.

**Armament:** Su-27 – One GSh-301 30mm gun. Ten hardpoints for up to 10 AAMs comprising semi active radar guided R-27Rs, IR guided R-27Ts, semi active radar guided R-27ERs, IR guided R-27ETs, R-73s and R-60s.

**Operators:** Belarus, China*, Ethiopia, India*, Kazakhstan, Russia, Syria, Ukraine, Vietnam.

**History:** The Su-27 was designed as a manoeuvrable interceptor and bomber escort with a secondary ground attack capability.

Development work began in 1969, with the first flight of a prototype designated T-10-1 (and powered by two AL-21F-3 turbojets) on May 20 1977. Designated 'Flanker-A' by NATO, the T-10-1 and subsequent T-10 prototypes exhibited serious control problems and so the aircraft was considerably redesigned, resulting in the T-10S-1. The T-10S-1 first flew on April 20 1981 and closely resembled production Su-27s.

Su-27 design features include the blended wing/fuselage design, widely separated AL-31 turbofans, all moving tailplanes, a large F-15 style airbrake, leading edge slats, an IRST and laser rangefinder set which allows passive target detection and engagement, fly-by-wire, HUD and Zhuk look down shoot down and track while scan radar.

The Su-27 'Flanker-B' is a single seat air defence fighter and can carry wingtip EW pods. The similar export multirole Su-27SK can carry a 4000kg (8820lb) bomb load (China has taken delivery of 50 Su-27SKs, and has begun licence production of 80 – by SAC – as the J-11); the similar Su-27SMK has two extra hardpoints and 8t weapon load; while the Su-27UB 'Flanker-C' and export UBK are two seat operational trainers. A modified Su-27, designated P-42, set a series of time to height world records.

The two seat Su-30 (or Su-27PU) air defence fighter can fly up to 10 hour missions and provide targeting information for other Su-27s by datalink. The Su-30M and export Su-30MK are multirole variants, the latter ordered by India (with canards, thrust vectoring, Thales avionics, N011M phased array radar and Israeli EW when fully upgraded). India is buying 50, and plans to build 140 under licence by HAL. China is to build 50 (plus 10 built in Russia) multirole Su-30MKKs with Russian avionics and weapons.

The Russian navy has over 20 carrier capable Su-33 fighters for its carrier *Kuznetsov*. Features include folding wings, canards, strengthened undercarriage, refuelling probe and arrester hook.

**Photo:** Su-30MKK prototype for China. (Paul Merritt)

# Sukhoi Su-35 & Su-37

**Country of origin:** Russia

**Type:** Multirole fighter

**Powerplants:** Su-35 – Two 125.5kN (28,218lb) with afterburning Saturn/Lyulka AL-35F turbofans. Su-37 – Two 142.2kN (31,970lb) with afterburning, thrust vectoring AL-37FUs.

**Performance:** Su-35 – Max speed Mach 2.35 or 2500km/h (1350kt), max speed at sea level Mach 1.14 or 1400km/h (755kt). Service ceiling 59,055ft. Range with max internal fuel over 4000km (2160nm), range with inflight refuelling over 6500km (3510nm). Su-37 – Similar but range with internal fuel 3300km (1780nm).

**Weights:** Su-35 – Empty 17,000kg (37,479lb), max takeoff 34,000kg (74,956lb). Max fuel 13,400kg (29,542lb). Su-37 – Max takeoff 25,670kg (56,592lb) to 34,000kg (74,956lb).

**Dimensions:** Su-35 & Su-37 – Wing span over wingtip ECM pods 15.16m (49ft 9in), length 22.20m (72ft 10in), height 6.36m (20ft 10in). Wing area 62.0m² (667.4sq ft).

**Accommodation:** Pilot only.

**Armament:** Su-35 – One GSh-30 30mm gun. Twelve external hardpoints can carry 8000kg (17,655lb) of weapons, including R-27, R-40, R-60, R-73A and R-77 AAMs, Kh-25ML, Kh-25MP, Kh-29, Kh-31 and Kh-59 ASMs, S-25 IR and laser guided rockets, and laser guided GBU-500 and GBU-1500 laser guided bombs and GBU-500T and -1500T TV guided bombs. Su-37 – Same options plus R-37 and KS-172 AAMs and anti radiation Kh-15P and Kh-65S ASMs.

**Operators:** None

**History:** Development of advanced and more capable Su-27 variants began in the mid 1980s.

A development Su-27 fitted with canards first flew in May 1985, while the first prototype for what would become the Su-35, the T-10S-70, first flew on June 28 1988. For a time the improved Su-27 was designated Su-27M, it has since been redesignated Su-35.

Changes over the basic Su-27 are numerous. Canard foreplanes were added while power is from two upgraded Saturn AL-35F (or AL-31MF) turbofans. Flight control is provided by a digital fly-by-wire system with quadruplex redundancy (the Su-27's fly-by-wire system is analog). The reprofiled nose houses a multimode Phazotron N011 Zhuk 27 radar (with a larger diameter, flat plate antenna) which has a search range of 100km (55nm), can track 24 targets simultaneously and has terrain following/avoidance, while the phased array Zhuk-Ph upgrade has been under development. The tailcone houses a rearwards facing N012 radar. A new IRST set has been repositioned on the nose. The EFIS cockpit features three colour CRTs and a HUD. Other features are a retractable inflight refuelling probe, taller squared off fins each containing an auxiliary fuel tank, and twin nosewheels. Some have been noted with large ECM wingtip pods.

The Su-37 first flew in 1996 and is a further improvement of the Su-35 with two dimensional thrust vectoring nozzles operated through the fly-by-wire flight control system.

The Russian air force had hoped to introduce the Su-35 into service in the late 1990s, but these plans did not come to fruition. Indian Su-30MKIs will feature some Su-35/37 features.

**Photo:** The thrust vectoring Su-37. (Paul Merritt)

# Sukhoi Su-27IB & Su-27KUB

**Country of origin:** Russia

**Type:** Long range fighter bomber

**Powerplants:** Two 74.5kN (16,755lb) dry and 122.6kN (27,577lb) with afterburning Saturn/Lyulka AL-31F turbofans.

**Performance:** Max speed at 36,000ft Mach 1.8 or 1900km/h (1025kt), max speed at sea level Mach 1.14 or 1400km/h (755kt). Combat radius internal fuel hi-hi-hi 1113km (601nm), lo-lo-lo 600km (324nm). Range with max internal fuel 4500km (2450nm).

**Weights:** Max takeoff 45,100kg (99,428lb).

**Dimensions:** Wing span 14.70m (48ft 3in), length 23.34m (76ft 7in), height 6.50m (21ft 4in). Wing area 62.0m² (667.4sq ft).

**Accommodation:** Pilot and weapon systems operator side by side.

**Armament:** One 30mm GSh-301 gun in forward starboard fuselage. Two wingtip stations for self defence AAMs. Twelve hardpoints for R-73 and RVV-AE (R-77) AAMs, KAB-500 LGBs, and ASMs.

**Operators:** Russia*

**History:** The Su-27IB is a side by side two seat development long range strike development of the Su-27. The Su-27KUB two seater is intended for carrier taining.

When the Su-27IB first appeared in 1991 confusion surrounded its intended role, with the first prototype, '42', variously identified as an aircraft carrier trainer designated Su-27KU (Korabelnii Uchebno or shipborne trainer) and a strike fighter as the Su-27IB (Istrebitel Bombardirovschik or fighter bomber).

It later became clear that two distinct variants of the aircraft had been proposed, the air force Su-27IB fighter bomber and the Su-32FN (Sukhoi's designation), a shore based long range maritime strike fighter intended to replace Russian naval aviation Su-24s.

Features of the Su-27IB, which first flew in April 1990, aside from side by side seating, include twin nosewheels and tandem main undercarriage units, canards, AL-35F turbofans, a Leninetz phased array multifunction radar with terrain following/avoidance, a rearwards facing radar in the tailcone (as on the Su-35), a retractable inflight refuelling probe, broader chord tailfins, three multifunction displays in the cockpit and modern avionics.

Access to the cockpit is via an integral ladder aft of the nosewheel, while behind the two crew seats in the forward fuselage is a small galley and toilet. The crew sit on Z-36 zero/zero ejection seats and the cockpit is protected by titanium armour. Reconnaissance and EW variants have been proposed.

Series production for the Russian air force has not yet been funded.

The Su-32FN is similar but would have featured a maritime search radar, sonobuoy launcher, MAD, laser rangefinder, wingtip ECM pods and seven LCD screen EFIS cockpit. The Su-32FN program was reportedly suspended in 1997.

The carrier trainer concept has been resurrected with the Su-27KUB. Sukhoi began flight testing the Su-27KUB side by side two seat Flanker variant in 1999. While a side by side two seater, the Su-27KUB is not based on the Su-27IB and features a more rounded nose. The Su-30K-2 is a two seat interceptor version under development.

**Photo:** The Su-27KUB. (Sebastian Zacharias)

# Sukhoi S-37 Berkut

**Country of origin:** Russia

**Type:** Fighter technology demonstrator

**Powerplants:** Two 93.1kN (20,930lb) dry and 152kN (34,200lb) with afterburning Aviadvigatel D-30F6M turbofans. May later be fitted with thrust vectoring Saturn AL-37FU or AL-41 turbofans.

**Performance:** Max speed at 30,000ft 2200km/h (1190kt), max speed at sea level 1400km/h (756km/h). Service ceiling 59,060ft. Range 3300km (1781nm).

**Weights:** Normal takeoff 25,670kg (56,590lb), max takeoff 34,000kg (74,957lb).

**Dimensions:** Wing span 16.7m (54.7ft), length 22.6m (74ft), height 6.4m (21ft). Wing area approx 56m² (600sq ft).

**Accommodation:** Pilot only

**Armament:** None in the prototype.

**Operators:** Experimental aircraft, not in operational service.

**History:** The S-37 Berkut (Golden Eagle) is an experimental fighter technology demonstrator built to validate and gain experience with various technology advances (particularly the forward swept wings) which could be incorporated into a fifth generation Sukhoi fighter. In particular it was designed to explore post stall manoeuvrability and 'super manoeuvrability'.

The S-37 was initially known as the S-32 and initial reports of the program's existence surfaced in early 1996 when it appeared the aircraft was intended to be a fifth generation fighter, rather than a technology demonstrator.

The S-32 first flew on September 25 1997 (two weeks after the F-22's first flight), with greater details and photographs made public shortly after. The most obvious feature of the new Sukhoi is its forward swept wing, which is made of composite materials to give the necessary structural strength. Benefits of forward sweep include improved manoeuvrability at subsonic speeds, enhanced controllability at high angles of attack, reduced takeoff and landing rolls (also resulting in improved range) and a reduced forward hemisphere radar signature (the S-37 may also be fitted with radar absorbent material).

As well as the forward swept wings, the S-37's flying and control surfaces include canards, conventional horizontal tails and slightly outward canted twin vertical tails. Power for the S-37 is provided by twin Aviadvigatel D-30F6 turbofans, generating 152kN (34,200lb) with afterburner (the D-30F6 also powers the MiG-31). Later on the S-37 may be fitted with thrust vectoring Saturn AL-37FP turbofans. The S-37's inlets are fixed, while air scoops on the wings' leading edge extend to provide the engines with additional airflow at low speeds. The S-37's canopy and cockpit are from the Su-27, the landing gear from the Su-27K.

Both Sukhoi and the Russian air force agree that the S-37 is a fighter technology demonstrator only, and not a prototype for production. The S-37 made its first public appearance at Zhukovsky in August 1999, and flew supersonically for the first time in August 2000.

Sukhoi was able to fund development of the S-37 with proceeds from sales of export Su-27s and has promoted it as the basis of a new fighter for the Russian air force.

**Photo:** The S-37 prototype. (Sebastian Zacharias)

# Transall C-160

**Countries of origin:** France and Germany

**Type:** Tactical transport

**Powerplants:** Two 4550kW (6100ehp) Rolls-Royce Tyne RTy.20 Mk 22 turboprops driving four blade propellers.

**Performance:** Max speed 513km/h (277kt). Max initial rate of climb 1300ft/min. Service ceiling at 45,000kg (99,210lb) AUW 27,000ft. Takeoff run 715m (2345ft). Range with 8 tonne (17,640lb) payload and reserves 5095km (2750nm), range with a 16 tonne (35,275lb) payload and reserves 1853km (1000nm). Max ferry range with centre section wing fuel tank 8850km (4780nm).

**Weights:** Min operating empty 28,000kg (61,730lb), typical operating empty 29,000kg (63,935lb), max takeoff 51,000kg (112,435lb).

**Dimensions:** Wing span 40.00m (13ft 3in), length exc probe 32.40m (106ft 4in), height 11.65m (38ft 3in). Wing area 160.1m² (1722sq ft).

**Accommodation:** Flightcrew of three. Main cabin can seat up to 93 equipped troops, or 61 to 68 paratroops, or 62 stretcher patients and four medical attendants, or armoured vehicles, artillery and 4WD vehicles and trucks. Can airdrop an 8 tonne load.

**Armament:** None

**Operators:** France, Germany, Turkey.

**History:** The Transall C-160 tactical transport forms the backbone of the transport fleets of the German and French air forces.

Germany and France formed Transall Allianz in January 1959 to design and build a tactical transport for each countries' air force, plus for export. Germany and France participated in the program on a 50/50 basis, with program partners comprising Germany's MBB and VFW and France's Aerospatiale. Design features settled upon included a high wing, voluminous fuselage, rear loading freight door and two Rolls-Royce Tyne turboprops.

First flight occurred on February 25 1963. Production lines were established in France (at Toulouse) and Germany and aircraft were delivered from 1967 for the air forces of Germany (110 C-160Ds), France (50 C-160Fs) and South Africa (9 C-160Zs, now retired). Turkey took delivery of 20 C-160Ts, all ex German aircraft.

Transall production initially ceased in 1972, but a French requirement saw a further 33 C-160s (including four for an Indonesian civil operator which were later operated by the air force) built between 1981 and 1985. These aircraft are designated C-160NG (Nouvelle Generation) and feature a fixed inflight refuelling probe. Ten C-160NGs have a secondary tanker role and are fitted with a hose drum unit in the port undercarriage sponson. Five more C-160NGs are plumbed to be converted to tankers.

Two C-160NGs were converted as Sigint platforms before delivery as the C-160 GABRIEL or C-160G. Features include wingtip pods, a blister fairing on the rear port fuselage, a large retractable dome under the forward fuselage and various antennas around the fuselage. Four other French C-160s, designated the C-160H ASTARTE, carry a Collins TACAMO VLF radio for submarine communications.

France and Germany have been upgrading their C-160s to extend their service lives, French C-160s are being fitted with HUDs and four screen EFIS.

**Photo:** A German Transall C-160. (Keith Gaskell)

# Tupolev Tu-134

**Country of origin:** Russia

**Type:** VIP transport

**Powerplants:** Tu-134 – Two 64.5kN (14,490lb) Soloviev D-30 turbofans. Tu-134A – Two 66.7kN (14,990lb) Soloviev D-30 Srs IIs.

**Performance:** Tu-134 – Max cruising speed 900km/h (485kt), economical cruising speed 750km/h (405kt). Normal operating ceiling 39,730ft. Range with 7000kg (15,420lb) payload and reserves 2400km (1295nm), with 3000kg (6600lb) payload 3500km (1890nm). Tu-134A – Max cruising speed 900km/h (485kt), long range cruising speed 750km/h (405kt). Range with 5000kg (11,025lb) payload and reserves 3020km (1630nm).

**Weights:** Tu-134 – Operating empty 27,500kg (60,627lb), max takeoff 44,500kg (98,105lb). Tu-134A – Operating empty 29,050kg (64,045lb), max takeoff 47,000kg (103,600lb).

**Dimensions:** Tu-134 – Wing span 29.00m (95ft 2in), length 34.35m (112ft 8in), height 9.02m (29ft 7in). Wing area 127.3m² (1370.3sq ft). Tu-134A – Same except length 37.05m (121ft 7in), height 9.14m (30ft 0in).

**Accommodation:** Two pilots and a navigator. Tu-134 seats 72, Tu-134A seats up to 84. Most military Tu-134s are fitted with a VIP interior.

**Armament:** None

**Operators:** Azerbaijan, Belarus, Bulgaria, Kazakhstan, Moldova, North Korea, Russia, Syria, Tajikistan, Ukraine.

**History:** For many years the Tupolev Tu-134 was the standard short haul jet airliner in the USSR and eastern Europe, with 700 built. Small numbers are in military service as VIP transports.

The Tupolev design bureau was responsible for the Soviet Union's first jet powered airliner, the Tu-104 (which was based on the Tu-16 bomber), and the Tu-104's smaller brother the Tu-124. Both of these short range jetliners had a number of performance and technology shortfalls, which the Tu-134 was developed to address. Initially the Tu-134 was based fairly closely on the Tu-124, and for a time was designated the Tu-124A. However the decision was instead taken to change the aircraft's overall configuration to feature rear fuselage mounted engines and T-tail.

Flight testing of the Tu-134 began during 1962, with six development aircraft built. Production began in 1964 but Aeroflot did not launch full commercial services until September 1967.

Initial production was of the standard fuselage length Tu-134. The stretched Tu-134A entered Aeroflot service in the second half of 1970 and could seat up to 76 passengers in a single class. Tu-134A features include a 2.10m (6ft 11in) fuselage stretch, a reprofiled nose, more powerful D-30 engines and an APU. Other versions are the Tu-134B with a forward facing position for the third crew member between and behind the pilots, the Tu-134B-1 which has a revised interior to seat up to 90 passengers without a galley, and the Tu-134B-3 which can seat 96 with full galley and toilet facilities.

Apart from converted Tu-134s serving in a military VIP role, Russia operates a small number converted as bomber trainers. The Tu-134BSh was a bombardier trainer and featured the Tu-22M's radar in the nose. The Tu-134UBL is a Tu-160 crew trainer with the bomber's avionics and radar in a Tu-160 shaped nose.

**Photo:** A Bulgarian air force VIP Tu-134A. (Paul Merritt)

# Tupolev Tu-95 & Tu-142

# Tupolev Tu-22

**Country of origin:** Russia

**Type:** Strategic bomber (Tu-95) and maritime patrol platform (Tu-142).

**Powerplants:** Tu-95MS – Four 11,035kW (14,795ehp) KKBM Kuznetsov NK-12MV turboprops driving eight blade counter rotating props.

**Performance:** Tu-95MS – Max speed 925km/h (500kt), at sea level 650km/h (350kt), cruising speed 710km/h (385kt). Ceiling 39,370ft. Radius with a 11,340kg (25,000lb) payload 6400km (3455nm).

**Weights:** Tu-95MS – Empty 94,400kg (208,115lb), max takeoff 185,000kg (407,850lb).

**Dimensions:** Tu-95MS – Wing span 50.04m (164ft 2in), length 49.13m (161ft 2in), height 13.30m (43ft 8in). Wing area 289.9m² (3120sq ft).

**Accommodation:** Tu-95MS – Seven crew: two pilots, comms operator, nav/defensive systems operator, flight engineer, navigator and tail gunner.

**Armament:** Tu-95MS – Up to six Kh-55 (AS-15A 'Kent') cruise missiles on a rotary launcher in the bomb bay.

**Operators:** Tu-95 – Russia. Tu-142 – India, Russia.

**History:** The massive Tu-95 was conceived in the early 1950s when turboprops promised the best compromise between speed and range.

The Tu-95 (NATO reporting name 'Bear') was developed around the 8950kW (12,000shp) Kuznetsov NK-12 turboprop and the fuselage cross section originally introduced on the Tu-4 'Bull', the USSR's unlicenced copy of the B-29 Superfortress. The engines deliver their power through eight blade counter rotating propellers, while the wings, unique for a propeller driven aircraft, are swept. The Tu-95 has a top speed over Mach 0.8, while its massive internal fuel capacity and turboprops give intercontinental range.

The prototype Tu-95 first flew on November 12 1952. Initial production was of the Tu-95M 'Bear-A' high altitude freefall nuclear bomber (now withdrawn from use). Some were converted as Tu-95U crew trainers. Tu-95Ms were converted to Kh-20 (AS-3 'Kangaroo') cruise missile launching Tu-95K-20 'Bear-B' standard with a nose mounted radar. The Tu-95KD was similar but had an inflight refuelling probe. The similar Tu-95KM 'Bear-C' (thought to be new build aircraft) had an inflight refuelling probe, Elint antennas and some reconnaissance sensors. The Tu-95K-22 'Bear-G' had a revised radome profile and carried two Kh-22 (AS-4 'Kitchen') missiles, one under each wing root. The final bomber variant was the Tu-95MS 'Bear-H', developed to carry the Kh-55 (AS-15A 'Kent') and based on the Tu-142's airframe (but shortened), and was built from 1983. It is the key Tu-95 model still in service.

Surplus Tu-95M bombers were converted to maritime reconnaissance Tu-95RT 'Bear-D' and Tu-95MR 'Bear-E' configurations. The Tu-95RT has an undernose radome and was used for missile mid course guidance and reconnaissance duties, while the Tu-95MR has various cameras in the bomb bay.

The Tu-142 is a dedicated maritime reconnaissance/ASW platform developed from the Tu-95. The Tu-142 'Bear-F' features a slight fuselage stretch and a maritime search radar in a ventral radome. It carries sonobuoys, torpedoes and mines. The later Tu-142M 'Bear-F Mod 2' introduced a Magnetic Anomaly Detector (MAD) on top of the tail. The Tu-142MR 'Bear-J' is used as a submarine communications relay.

Tu-95/142 production ended in 1994.

**Photo:** An Indian Tu-142MK-E. (Sebastian Zacharias)

**Country of origin:** Russia

**Type:** Strategic bomber/electronic warfare aircraft

**Powerplants:** Tu-22K – Two 122.6kN (27,560lb) dry and 161.8kN (36,375lb) with afterburning Dobrynin RD-7M-2 turbojets.

**Performance:** Tu-22K – Max speed at 39,350ft Mach 1.52 or 1610km/h (870kt), max speed at sea level 890km/h (480kt). Service ceiling 43,635ft. Combat radius hi-lo-hi with a 400km (215nm) full throttle dash 2200km (1190nm). Ferry range with internal fuel 4900km (2645nm).

**Weights:** Tu-22K – Empty 38,100kg (83,995lb), normal loaded 85,000kg (187,390lb), max rocket assisted takeoff 94,000kg (207,230lb).

**Dimensions:** Tu-22K – Wing span 23.50m (77ft 0in), length 42.60m (139ft 9in), height 10.67m (35ft 0in). Wing area 162.0m² (1744sq ft).

**Accommodation:** Crew of three in tandem, with navigator/systems operator forward of pilot in lower forward nose.

**Armament:** One NR-23 23mm gun in tail for self defence. Weapons bay can hold 8 tonnes (17,600lb) of bombs. Tu-22K can alternatively carry a single Kh-22 (AS-4 'Kitchen') supersonic cruise missile semi recessed in the weapons bay.

**Operators:** Libya, Ukraine.

**History:** The Tu-22 was Russia's first successful attempt at fielding a supersonic bomber.

The Tu-22 ('Blinder' in NATO parlance) dates from a 1955 study to build a supersonic bomber capable of penetrating air defences and carrying a payload similar to the subsonic Tu-16. The new aircraft (Tupolev's own designation was Tu-105) flew for the first time in September 1959 (piloted by Yu I Alasheyev). The Tu-22 remained unknown in the West until two years later when 10 Tu-22s (one with a Kh-22/AS-4 'Kitchen' cruise missile) participated in the Tushino aviation day flypast.

The Tu-22's most unusual feature is the position of the engines at the base of the fin, which had the dual benefits of leaving the fuselage free for fuel (and without the need for long inlet ducts) and giving the two engines (mounted side by side) largely undisturbed airflow. The lips of the intakes move forward for takeoff creating a gap through which extra air is drawn.

The slender, area ruled fuselage houses a bombing/navigation radar in the nose, a crew of three with the navigator in the lower forward fuselage with the pilot and radio operator/gunner in tandem behind him, an internal weapons bay, 45,000 litres internal fuel capacity and a 23mm defensive gun in the tail. The large swept wing features pods which the main undercarriage units retract into.

Some 311 Tu-22s were built. Initial production was of the Tu-22 'Blinder-A' conventional and nuclear bomber. About 150 Tu-22s were Kh-22 cruise missile firing Tu-22K 'Blinder-C's with an enlarged radome for the 2.8m diameter multimode radar. The Tu-22U 'Blinder-D' trainer had a raised second cockpit aft of the normal cockpit, while about 60 of the Tu-22R and -22RD 'Blinder-C's were built, fitted with a range of reconnaissance sensors. Russia also converted some as Tu-22PD 'Blinder-E' EW jammers.

**Photo:** Two Tu-22s soon after takeoff. Ukraine and Libya appeared to be the only Tu-22 operators in 2001.

# Tupolev Tu-22M

**Country of origin:** Russia

**Type:** Strategic and maritime strike/reconnaissance bomber

**Powerplants:** Tu-22M-3 – Two 245.2kN (55,115lb) with afterburning Kuznetsov/KKBM NK-25 turbofans.

**Performance:** Tu-22M-3 – Max speed at high altitude Mach 1.88 or 2000km/h (1080kt), max speed at low level Mach 0.86 or 1050km/h (567kt), normal cruising speed at altitude 900km/h (485kt). Service ceiling 43,650ft. Supersonic combat radius with a 12,000kg (26,455lb) weapons load 1500 to 1850km (810 to 1000nm). Subsonic combat radius with max weapons load hi-hi-hi 2200km (1190nm). Subsonic combat radius with 12,000kg (26,455lb) bomb load lo-lo-lo 1500 to 1665km (810 to 900nm), or hi-lo-hi 2410km (1300nm).

**Weights:** Tu-22M-3 – Empty 54,000kg (119,050lb), max TO 124,000kg (273,370lb), rocket asst TO 126,400kg (278,660lb). Int fuel app 50 tonnes.

**Dimensions:** Tu-22M-3 – Wing span wings extended 34.28m (112ft 6in), span wings swept 23.30m (76ft 6in), length overall 42.46m (139ft 4in), height 11.05m (36ft 3in). Wing area wings extended 183.6m$^2$ (1976.1sq ft), wing area wings swept 175.8m$^2$ (1892.4sq ft).

**Accommodation:** Crew of four with pilot and copilot side by side, with navigator and weapons systems operator behind them.

**Armament:** One GSh-23 twin barrel 23mm cannon in the tail. Can carry 24,000kg (52,910lb) of conventional bombs or mines in bomb bay, or six Kh-15P (AS-16 'Kickback') ASMs on a rotary launcher in bomb bay and four underwing, or three Kh-22 (AS-4 'Kitchen') ASMs, one semi recessed under fuselage and one on each underwing hardpoint.

**Operators:** India*, Russia, Ukraine.

**History:** The Tu-22M was conceived as a swing wing development of the Tu-22 but evolved into essentially an all new aircraft.

Tupolev first looked at fitting the Tu-22 with swing wings in 1961. Design work on this aircraft, designated Tu-22M, began in late 1962, however Tupolev took the opportunity to substantially redesign the basic Tu-22 to even further improve performance. Apart from the swing wings the other key change was the powerplants, two Kuznetsov NK-20 afterburning turbofans mounted in the rear of the fuselage. The engines were fed by two F-4 style intakes with variable splitter plates. The nose was redesigned, while new six wheel main undercarriage units retracted into the fuselage.

The first Tu-22M-0 prototype first flew on August 30 1968, although the West did not identify the new bomber until September 1969. The NATO reporting name 'Backfire-A' was adopted. Production was of the further redesigned Tu-22M-2 (with a new nav/attack radar), which began in 1972.

About 200 Tu-22M-2 'Backfire-Bs' were built before production switched to the Tu-22M-3, which first flew in 1980. The Tu-22M-3 is powered by two increased thrust NK-25 turbofans fed by new wedge shaped air inlets, and introduced a new multimode radar in a reprofiled nose and has an increased max takeoff weight. The Tu-22MR is a reconnaissance version (12 converted for the Russian navy), the Tu-22MP a EW/escort jammer flown in prototype form.

Almost 500 Tu-22Ms of all models have been built, while Tupolev is developing the M5 upgrade with new radar and avionics.

**Photo:** A Ukrainian air force Tu-22M-3. (Paul Merritt)

# Tupolev Tu-160

**Country of origin:** Russia

**Type:** Strategic bomber

**Powerplants:** Four 137.3kN (30,865lb) dry and 245.2kN (55,115lb) with afterburning Samara/Trud NK-231 turbofans

**Performance:** Max speed at 40,000ft Mach 2.05 or 2220km/h (1200kt), cruising speed at 45,000ft 960km/h (518kt). Max initial rate of climb 13,780ft/min. Service ceiling 49,200ft. Radius of action at Mach 1.3 2000km (1080nm). Max range 12,300km (6640nm).

**Weights:** Empty 110,000kg (242,505lb), normal takeoff 267,000kg (589,950lb), max takeoff 275,000kg (606,260lb). Internal fuel 171,000kg (376,990lb).

**Dimensions:** Wing span wings extended 55.70m (182ft 9in), span wings swept 35.60m (116ft 9in), length 54.10m (177ft 6in), height 13.10m (43ft 0in). Wing area wings extended approx 400.0m$^2$ (4305.6sq ft).

**Accommodation:** Crew of four, with two pilots side by side and with navigator/bombardier and electronic systems operator behind them.

**Armament:** Max weapon load 40,000kg (88,185lb), comprising freefall bombs or ASMs in two internal bomb bays. One rotary launcher can be carried in each bay to carry six Kh-55MS (AS-15 'Kent') ALCMs or 12 Kh-15P (AS-16 'Kickback') SRAMs.

**Operators:** Russia

**History:** The massive swing wing Tu-160 ('Blackjack' to NATO) is the heaviest and most powerful bomber ever built and was developed as a direct counter to the Rockwell B-1A.

Tupolev began design work under the leadership of V I Bliznuk of its all new 'Aircraft 70', a direct response to the B-1, in 1973. Although the B-1A was cancelled in 1977, design and development work on the new Tupolev bomber continued, resulting in a first flight on December 19 1981. Production of 100 Tu-160s was authorised in 1985, although only about 30 were built before the line closed in 1992.

The Tu-160 features four NK-231 afterburning turbofans, the most powerful engines fitted to a combat aircraft, mounted in pairs under the inner fixed wings. The variable geometry air inlets are designed for speed (Mach 1 at low level, over Mach 2 at altitude). The Tu-160 has a retractable inflight refuelling probe although it is rarely used due to the aircraft's massive internal fuel capacity.

The variable geometry wings have full span leading edge slats and double slotted trailing edge flaps, while the airframe is free of any protuberances (except for a small video camera window for the pilots). The nav/attack radar is believed to have a terrain following function, while the Tu-160 has a comprehensive ECM jamming system. The four crew sit on their own ejection seats and the pilots have fighter style sticks. The Tu-160 has a fly-by-wire flight control system.

About 15 Tu-160s are in Russia, joined by survivors of 19 left in the Ukraine after the collapse of the USSR. Eight of these were transferred to Russian control in late 1999/early 2000, with the remainder being scrapped.

The Tu-160SK is a commercial variant being offered as a launch vehicle for the Burlak-Diana satellite launching rocket. Three demilitarised ex Ukrainian aircraft were sold in the US in 1999 for use as satellite launchers, but the status of this deal is unclear.

**Photo:** A Zhukovsky based test Tu-160. (Robert Meerding)

# Tupolev Tu-154

**Country of origin:** Russia

**Type:** Medium range airliner

**Powerplants:** Tu-154 – Three 93.2kN (20,950lb) Kuznetsov NK-8-2 turbofans. Tu-154M – Three 106.2kN (23,380lb) Aviadvigatel (Soloviev) D-30KU-154-II turbofans.

**Performance:** Tu-154 – Max cruising speed 975km/h (527kt), economical cruising speed 900km/h (486kt), long range cruising speed 850km/h (460kt). Range with max payload and reserves 3460km (1870nm), range with max fuel and 13,650kg (31,100lb) payload 5280km (2850nm). Tu-154M – Max cruising speed 950km/h (513kt). Range with max payload 3900km (2105nm), range with max fuel and 5450kg (12,015lb) payload 6600km (3563nm).

**Weights:** Tu-154 – Operating empty 43,500kg (95,900lb), max takeoff 90,000kg (198,415lb). Tu-154M – Basic operating empty 55,300kg (121,915lb), max takeoff 100,000kg (220,460lb).

**Dimensions:** Wing span 37.55m (123ft 3in), length 47.90m (157ft 2in), height 11.40m (37ft 5in). Wing area 201.5m² (2169sq ft).

**Accommodation:** Flightcrew of three or four. Typical single class seating for 158 to 164 at six abreast, or 167 in a high density layout for Tu-154; Tu-154M seats a maximum of 180. Most military Tu-154s have been converted with a VIP interior.

**Armament:** None

**Operators:** Belarus, Czech Republic, Kazakhstan, North Korea, Poland.

**History:** The Tu-154 is Tupolev's sixth commercial airliner design and is currently in widespread civil use in Russia as a medium range airliner. Small numbers of the 900 built are in military service, mainly used as VIP transports.

The Tu-154 was developed to replace the turbojet powered Tupolev Tu-104, plus the An-10 and Il-18 turboprops. Design criteria in replacing these three relatively diverse aircraft included the ability to operate from gravel or packed earth airfields, the need to fly at high altitudes above most Soviet Union air traffic, and good field performance. The initial Tu-154 design featured three Kuznetsov (now KKBM) NK-8 turbofans, triple bogey main undercarriage units which retract into wing pods, and a rear engine T-tail configuration.

The Tu-154's first flight occurred on October 4 1968. Regular commercial service began in February 1972. Three Kuznetsov powered variants of the Tu-154 were built, the initial Tu-154, the improved Tu-154A with more powerful engines and a higher max takeoff weight, and the Tu-154B with a further increased max takeoff weight. Tu-154S is a freighter version of the Tu-154B.

Current production is of the Tu-154M, which first flew in 1982. The major change introduced on the M was the far more economical, quieter and reliable Soloviev (now Aviadvigatel) turbofans. The Tu-154M2 is a proposed twin variant powered by two Perm PS-90A turbofans that remains unbuilt.

Most Tu-154s in military service are used for VIP transport, while Germany converted one with various sensors for Open Skies treaty verification flights. One of Germany's two Tu-154s was involved in a mid air collision with a USAF C-141 off Africa during 1997. The other has since been retired.

**Photo:** A Tu-154M in Slovak markings. (Sam Chui)

# Vickers VC10

**Country of origin:** United Kingdom

**Type:** Strategic transport and tanker transport

**Powerplants:** C.1 – Four 97.0kN (21,800lb) Rolls-Royce Conway RCo.43 Mk 301 turbofans.

**Performance:** C.1 – Max cruising speed 935km/h (505kt) at 31,000ft, economical cruising speed 885km/h (478kt). Service ceiling 42,000ft. Max payload range 6275km (3385nm).

**Weights:** C.1 – Empty 66,225kg (146,000lb), max takeoff 146,510kg (323,000lb). K.2 – Max takeoff 142,000kg (313,056lb). K.3 – Max takeoff 151,900kg (334,882lb).

**Dimensions:** C.1 & K.2 – Wing span 44.55m (146ft 2in), length exc probe 48.38m (158ft 8in), height 12.04m (39ft 6in). Wing area 272.4m² (2932sq ft). K.3 – Same except length exc probe 52.32m (171ft 8in).

**Accommodation:** C.1 – Flightcrew of two pilots and flight engineer. Seating for up to 150 in main cabin, or alternatively 76 stretchers and six medical attendants. K.2 – Practical max fuel weight 74,000kg (163,142lb). K.3 – Practical max fuel weight 80,000kg (176,370lb).

**Armament:** None

**Operators:** UK

**History:** The VC10 forms the backbone of the Royal Air Force's tanker/transport fleet.

Work on the VC10 dates back to 1956. Design of the VC10 was mainly against a BOAC (the British long haul international airline) requirement for a jet airliner capable of serving its routes to Africa, the Far East and Australasia, and thus dictated the requirement for good airfield and hot and high performance. BOAC officially selected the VC10 in May 1957, and ordered 35 of the type on January 14 1958.

The VC10 first flew on June 29 1962. Features included four rear mounted Rolls-Royce Conway turbofans, a T-tail and an advanced wing with sophisticated high lift features. Awarded civil certification in April 1964, the VC10 at the time was the largest aircraft to enter production in western Europe.

The VC10 was also selected by the Royal Air Force to meet its 1960 requirement for a strategic transport for the then Transport Command and 14 were ordered as VC10 C.1s. These aircraft differed from standard airliner VC10s in having uprated Conways, a refuelling probe, a large freight door, extra fuel in the fin and rear facing passenger seats. The first flight of an RAF C.1 was in November 1965 and deliveries began early the following year. VC10 C.1s remain in RAF service, and have been fitted with two underwing refuelling pods as C.1(K)s, giving them a secondary tanker role.

The first VC10 tankers were delivered from 1984. Five VC10s and four stretched Super VC10s, all ex airliners, were converted to dedicated tankers, involving fitting fuel tanks on the main deck, closed circuit TV to monitor tanking operations, two underwing refuelling pods, and a rear fuselage mounted refuelling unit. The VC10 tankers are designated K.2, the Super VC10s K.3. The K.4 designation applies to five additional Super VC10s converted to tankers in the late 1980s. The K.4s do not feature main deck fuel tanks.

The VC10s are due to be replaced from 2004. Already all K.2s and some C.1Ks have been retired.

**Photo:** A VC10 K.3 refuels USN F/A-18Cs. (US Navy)

## Vought A-7 Corsair II

**Country of origin:** United States of America

**Type:** Attack aircraft

**Powerplant:** A-7E – One 66.7kN (15,000lb) non afterburning Allison TF41-A-2 (licence built Rolls-Royce Spey) turbofan.

**Performance:** A-7E – Max speed 1112km/h (600kt), max speed at 5000ft 1102km/h (595kt). Ferry range with external fuel 4605km (2485nm), ferry range with max internal fuel 3670km (1980nm).

**Weights:** A-7E – Empty 8668kg (19,111lb), MTOW 19,050kg (42,000lb).

**Dimensions:** A-7E – Wing span 11.80m (38ft 9in), span wings folded 7.24m (23ft 9in), length 14.06m (46ft 2in), height 4.90m (16ft 1in). Wing area 34.8m² (375sq ft).

**Accommodation:** Pilot only, or two in tandem in TA-7.

**Armament:** One M61A1 Vulcan 20mm cannon mounted in port side forward fuselage. Two side fuselage (AIM-9 compatible only) and six underwing hardpoints can carry a total ordnance load of over 6805kg (15,000lb) including AIM-9s, bombs, LGBs, AGM-65s and rockets.

**Operators:** Greece, Thailand.

**History:** The A-7 Corsair attack fighter was one of the very few US Navy aircraft to be ordered and operated by the US Air Force.

The US Navy's 1963 VAL (light attack aircraft) specification aimed to find a 'light' attack aircraft with roughly twice the payload of the A-4 Skyhawk, for an in service date of 1967. Vought's proposal was selected ahead of those from North American, Douglas and Grumman, and seven development aircraft and 35 production A-7As were ordered on March 19 1964.

Vought's design, named Corsair II in honour of the WW2 F4U Corsair fighter, was similar in configuration to its F-8 Crusader fighter, however the A-7 was smaller and shorter, with fixed incidence wings, and was subsonic. The A-7A was powered by a non afterburning 54.7kN (12,200lb) Pratt & Whitney TF30-P-8 turbofan. First flight was on September 27 1965, with production deliveries from October 1966. The A-7B had a more powerful 54.3kN (12,200lb) TF30-P-8.

The USAF ordered its own version of the A-7 in 1966 to fill a requirement for a tactical attack aircraft. The USAF's A-7D (first flight April 5 1968) introduced the Allison TF41 turbofan, a licence built development of the Rolls-Royce Spey. The USN's improved A-7E (first flight November 1968) was also powered by the TF41 (the first 67 were TF30 powered due to problems with the TF41, and were later designated A-7Cs). The A-7K was a two seater for the USAF, while the USN converted 65 A-7A/Bs to two seat TA-7C configuration. The USAF's mid 1980s A-7F close air support upgrade program was cancelled. The 1541st and last A-7 built, an A-7E, was delivered in 1982.

USAF and USN Corsairs were used widely during the Vietnam War, while USN Corsairs were again used in the Gulf War. Both services had retired their A-7s by 1993.

The first Corsair II export customer was Greece, who ordered 60 A-7Hs and five TA-7Hs in the mid 1970s. They can fire AGM-65 Mavericks and are used primarily for anti shipping strike. Portugal until recently operated A-7Ps, refurbished ex USN A-7As upgraded with A-7E avionics (delivered 1981-85). Thailand acquired 18 ex USN A-7Es/TA-7s for service with its navy in the land based maritime strike role.

**Photo:** Thai TA-7s. (Thai Navy)

## Westland Wasp

**Country of origin:** United Kingdom

**Type:** Naval utility helicopter

**Powerplant:** One 785kW (1050shp) derated to 530kW (710shp) Rolls-Royce (Bristol Siddeley) Nimbus Mk 503 turboshaft driving a four blade main rotor and two blade tail rotor.

**Performance:** Max speed at sea level 193km/h (104kt), max and economical cruising speed 180km/h (96kt). Max initial rate of climb 1440ft/min. Hovering ceiling in ground effect 12,500ft, out of ground effect 8800ft. Max range with standard fuel 488km (263nm), range with four passengers 435km (235nm).

**Weights:** Empty 1565kg (3452lb), max takeoff 2495kg (5500lb).

**Dimensions:** Main rotor diameter 9.83m (32ft 3in), length overall rotors turning 12.29m (40ft 4in), fuselage length 9.24m (30ft 4in), height overall tail rotor turning 3.56m (11ft 8in), height to top of rotor head 2.72m (8ft 11in). Main rotor disc area 75.9m² (816.9sq ft).

**Accommodation:** Operational crew of three, or up to four passengers. Rear seats removable for cargo.

**Armament:** Two Mk 44 torpedoes or a single Mk 46 torpedo, or depth charges, or two Aerospatiale AS 12 wire guided anti ship missiles if fitted with a roof mounted sight.

**Operators:** Indonesia, Malaysia.

**History:** The Westland Wasp is a specialised maritime development of the Scout utility and anti tank helicopter which was operated by the British Army for many years.

The helicopter that became the Wasp started life in 1956 as the Saunders Roe P.351. The first of two prototype P.531s first flew on July 20 1958.

The new turboshaft powered helicopter attracted the interest of the British Army Air Corps and a pre-production batch of P.531-2 Mk 2s was ordered for evaluation, which occurred from October 1960. The British Army's initial order for what would become 150 Scout AH.1s was placed in 1960. The AH.1 could be armed with up to four AS 11 anti tank missiles and a number saw service in the Falklands War.

The last Scouts were retired from British Army service in 1994. Two Scouts were exported to the Royal Australian Navy and three to Jordan but these are no longer in service.

Soon after its merger with Saunders Roe, Westland began work on a naval P.531 development. The Royal Navy ordered two naval P.531s, which it designated Sea Scout HAS.1, for trials. The Sea Scout name was subsequently changed to Wasp before the first Wasp/Sea Scout first flew on October 28 1962. The Wasp differs from the Scout primarily in that it has wheels rather than skids. It lacks sensors of its own but can carry up to two torpedoes, launching them with target information provided by the mother ship. Other roles include search and rescue and training.

Westland built 134 Wasps, comprising 98 for the Royal Navy and 35 for export to Brazil, the Netherlands, New Zealand and South Africa.

Today Wasps are still in service with Indonesia (with ex Netherlands aircraft) and Malaysia (ex RN aircraft). Indonesia's aircraft are unlikely to be airworthy.

**Photo:** New Zealand's Wasps were retired in 1998 when they were replaced by SH-2F Seasprites. (Doug Mackay)

# Westland Wessex

**Countries of origin:** USA and UK

**Type:** Utility transport/SAR helicopter

**Powerplants:** HC.2 – Two 1005kW (1350shp) Rolls-Royce (Bristol Siddeley) Gnome Mk 110/111 turboshafts driving a four blade main rotor and four blade tail rotor.

**Performance:** HC.2 – Max speed at sea level 212km/h (115kt), max cruising speed 195km/h (105kt). Max initial rate of climb 1650ft/min. Hovering ceiling out of ground effect 4000ft. Ferry range with auxiliary fuel 1040km (560nm). Range with standard fuel 770km (415nm).

**Weights:** HC.2 – Operating empty 3767kg (8304lb), max takeoff 6123kg (13,500lb).

**Dimensions:** HC.2 – Main rotor diameter 17.07m (56ft 0in), length overall rotors turning 20.04m (65ft 9in), fuselage length 14.74m (48ft 5in), height overall 4.93m (16ft 2in), height to top of rotor head 4.39m (14ft 5in). Main rotor disc area 228.1m² (2643.0sq ft).

**Accommodation:** Two pilots on flightdeck with up to 16 equipped troops in main cabin. In medevac configuration can be fitted for eight stretcher patients, two seated patients and a medical attendant.

**Armament:** None usually.

**Operators:** UK, Uruguay.

**History:** The Wessex is a re-engined and re-engineered development of Sikorsky's S-58, built initially for the Royal Navy as an anti submarine warfare platform.

The Sikorsky S-58 arose from a 1951 US Navy requirement for an ASW helicopter. The Wright R-1820 radial piston engine powered S-58 first flew on March 8 1952 and was adopted by the US Navy as the HSS-1 Seabat (or SH-34G from 1962). Other S-58 variants include the US Army's CH-34 Choctaw and the US Marine Corp's UH-34 Seahorse. All piston powered S-58s have now been retired from military service, although twin Pratt & Whitney Canada PT6T turboshaft S-58T conversions serve in Thailand and Indonesia (operating five and 10 each respectively).

UK interest in the S-58 resulted when the Royal Navy cancelled development of the twin Napier Gazelle turboshaft powered Bristol 191 in 1956. The 191 was being developed to meet an ASW helicopter requirement but instead the RN opted for a single Napier powered development of the S-58. A Westland re-engined Napier powered S-58 first flew on May 17 1957, and the type was ordered into production as the Wessex HAS.1 (with dunking sonar and armed with torpedoes).

Retired Wessex variants include the HAS.1, more powerful HAS.3 with a new automatic flight control system, the Royal Marines' HU.1 troop transport and the RAF's HC.5, a transport conversion of RN HAS.1/HAS.3s.

The RAF's major Wessex variant is the HC.2, which differs significantly from the Royal Navy's Wessexes in that it is powered by two Bristol Siddeley Gnome turboshafts joined through a combining gearbox.

About 14 HC.2s still serve with the RAF for search and rescue and utility transport, while HC.2s exported to Brunei (as the Mk 54), Iran (Mk 52) and Ghana (Mk 53) have all been retired. Uruguay is the only other current Wessex operator.

**Photo:** An RAF Wessex HC.2 utility transport. (Paul Merritt)

# Westland Sea King & Commando

**Countries of origin:** USA and UK

**Type:** ASW, SAR and utility transport helicopter

**Powerplants:** HC.4 – Two 1240kW (1660shp) Rolls-Royce Gnome H.1400-1T turboshafts driving a five blade main rotor and six blade tail rotor.

**Performance:** HC.4 – Cruising speed at sea level 245km/h (132kt). Max initial rate of climb 2030ft/min. Hovering ceiling out of ground effect 4700ft. Ferry range with auxiliary fuel 1740km (940nm). Range with max payload (28 troops) 395km (215nm).

**Weights:** HC.4 – Typical operating empty 5620kg (12,390lb), max takeoff 9752kg (21,500lb).

**Dimensions:** Main rotor diameter 18.90m (62ft 0in), length overall rotors turning 22.15m (72ft 8in), fuselage length 17.02m (55ft 10in), height overall rotors turning 5.13m (16ft 10in), height to top of rotor head 4.72m (15ft 6in). Main rotor disc area 280.6m² (3020.3sq ft).

**Accommodation:** Two pilots with seating for up to 28 in Commando. ASW crew of four (two pilots, radar operator and sonar operator).

**Armament:** Commando – Door mounted machine guns, can be fitted with sponsons for rockets. Sea King – Up to four torpedoes.

**Operators:** Sea King – Australia, Belgium, Germany, India, Norway, Pakistan, UK. Commando – Egypt, Qatar.

**History:** Westland's Sea King and Commando are very different aircraft from Sikorsky's SH-3 Sea King, despite appearances.

Westland developed its own Sea King development in response to a Royal Navy requirement for an advanced long endurance ASW helicopter to replace the Wessex. Changes over the SH-3 included Rolls-Royce Gnome turboshafts and British avionics and ASW systems, including the search radar, dunking sonar and processing equipment. First flight was on May 7 1969.

Initial Westland production was of the Sea King HAS.1 – 56 were delivered to the Royal Navy followed by 21 improved HAS.2s (plus 37 conversions) with uprated engines, six blade tail rotors and air intake deflectors/filters. From 1980 30 improved Sea King HAS.5s with a Sea Searcher radar and ESM were delivered, while the final RN ASW Sea King is the HAS.6 (six new build and 69 conversions delivered from 1990). They feature improved processing and ESM. ASW Sea Kings were also delivered to Australia, India and Pakistan. The last export standard was the Advanced Sea King with uprated engines.

The Royal Navy also operates Sea King AEW.2s with an EMI Searchwater radar mounted in a swivel radome on the starboard side of the fuselage. Development was spurred by the Falklands War. They are being upgraded with Searchwater 2000 radar, JTIDS, colour display, INS/GPS and other changes to AEW.7 standard.

Search and rescue Sea Kings include the RN's HAR.5 and the RAF's HAR.3 and HAR.3A. Germany, Belgium and Norway also operate SAR Westland Sea Kings. The last new build Sea King, an RAF HAR.3, was delivered in May 1997 (328 were built).

The Westland Commando is a troop transport/assault development with seating for 28 troops and no ASW gear or floats. It was sold to Egypt and Qatar (three with full Sea King systems), while the Royal Navy operates the similar Sea King HC.4 for the Royal Marines.

**Photo:** An Indian Navy Sea King. (Sebastian Zacharias)

## Westland Lynx AH.1, AH.7 & AH.9

**Country of origin:** United Kingdom

**Type:** Battlefield transport and anti tank helicopter

**Powerplants:** AH.9 – Two 845kW (1135shp) Rolls-Royce Gem 42-1 turboshafts driving four blade main and tail rotors.

**Performance:** AH.9 – Max continuous cruising speed 255km/h (138kt), max endurance cruising speed 130km/h (70kt). Max initial rate of climb approx 2480ft/min. Hovering ceiling out of ground effect 10,600ft. Range 685km (370nm).

**Weights:** AH.9 – Operating empty in troop transport configuration 3495kg (7707lb), max takeoff 5125kg (11,300lb).

**Dimensions:** AH.9 – Main rotor disc diameter 12.80m (42ft 0in), length overall rotors turning 15.24m (50ft 0in), length rotors folded 13.24m (53ft 5in), height overall rotors turning 3.73m (12ft 3in). Main rotor disc area 128.7m$^2$ (1385.4sq ft).

**Accommodation:** Max seating for pilot and 12 equipped troops, or six stretcher patients and a medical attendant in medevac layout.

**Armament:** Eight TOW anti tank missiles in two fuselage side launchers in anti tank configuration. Can also be fitted with pintle mounted machine guns and 20mm cannon on fuselage sides.

**Operators:** UK

**History:** Westland's Lynx is well regarded for its exceptional agility and good speed. Land based versions serve widely with the British Army for troop transport and anti armour missions.

The origins of the Lynx lie in the Westland WG.13, one of three helicopter designs covered by the February 1967 British/French helicopter coproduction agreement which also included the Gazelle and Puma. The Lynx is entirely of Westland design with Aerospatiale (now Eurocopter) originally responsible for 30% of production (including the forged titanium rotor hub for the semi rigid main rotor, key to the Lynx's agility). The Lynx also features a digital flight control system.

The first of 13 Lynx prototypes first flew on March 21 1971. The Lynx was originally intended as a ship borne ASW/anti surface warfare helicopter for the British and French navies, but its large cabin and excellent performance attracted British Army interest in it for troop transport and anti tank missions to replace Scouts.

The British Army's first Lynx model was the AH.1, which first flew in 1977. Of the 113 AH.1s built 103 were upgraded to AH.7 standard with improved systems and an IR suppressor on the exhaust, while the tail rotor is made from composites and rotates in the opposite direction to reduce noise.

The latest British Army Lynx model is the AH.9, which is equivalent to the export Battlefield Lynx (none ordered). The AH.9 features wheel undercarriage rather than skids, no TOW capability, composite construction main rotor blades with swept tips and an increased max takeoff weight. Sixteen new build AH.9s were ordered plus seven conversions. Five have been outfitted as command posts.

Westland is studying an upgrade program which would see up to 78 AH.7s and all AH.9s upgraded to a common standard with wheel undercarriage, new avionics including GPS, and new defensive aids. As WAH-64D Apaches are delivered, AH.7s will be used in the combat scout role. AH.9s will continue as transports.

**Photo:** A Lynx AH.7. (Paul Merritt)

## Westland Lynx – Naval Models

**Country of origin:** United Kingdom

**Type:** Shipborne ASW, ASuW, SAR and utility helicopter

**Powerplants:** HAS.8 – Two 845kW (1135shp) Rolls-Royce Gem 42-1 turboshafts driving four blade main and tail rotors.

**Performance:** HAS.8 – Max continuous cruising speed 232km/h (125kt), max endurance cruising speed 130km/h (70kt). Max initial rate of climb approx 2170ft/min. Hovering ceiling out of ground effect 8450ft. Max range approx 595km (320nm). Combat radius with four Sea Skua anti ship missiles 275km (148nm). Radius of action for a 140min ASW patrol with one torpedo 37km (20nm). Surveillance mission endurance 140km (75nm) from ship 245min.

**Weights:** HAS.8 – Basic empty 3290kg (7255lb), MTOW 5125kg (11,300lb).

**Dimensions:** HAS.8 – Main rotor disc diameter 12.80m (42ft 0in), length overall rotors turning 15.24m (50ft 0in), length with main rotor blades and tail folded 10.85m (35ft 7in), height overall rotors turning 3.67m (12ft 1in). Main rotor disc area 128.7m$^2$ (1385.4sq ft).

**Accommodation:** Crew of two or three.

**Armament:** Two Mk 44, Mk 46, A244S or Stingray torpedoes, or two Mk 11 depth charges for ASW. Up to four Sea Skua anti ship missiles. French Lynx can carry up to four AS 12 wire guided missiles.

**Operators:** Brazil, Denmark, France, Germany, Malaysia*, Netherlands, Nigeria, Norway, Portugal, South Africa*, South Korea, UK.

**History:** Naval Lynx variants form an important part of the inventories of several NATO navies, performing ASW and ASuW missions.

When the 1967 Anglo/French helicopter production deal was signed covering the Lynx (originally WG.13), Gazelle and Puma, the Lynx had been planned from the outset as a ship based ASW/ASuW helicopter and it was not until later that land based variants for the British Army (described separately) were developed. The first Lynx prototype first flew on March 21 1971, while the first production Lynx HAS.2 for the Royal Navy had its maiden flight in February 1976. All naval Lynx feature wheeled undercarriage, an automatic flight control system and a folding tail and main rotor.

Features of the RN's Lynx HAS.2 include a Ferranti Seaspray search radar and dunking sonar. France's HAS.2(FN) is similar but has a OMERA-Segid search radar. The RN's HAS.3 has uprated RR Gem 42-1 turboshafts and a modified GEC-Marconi (BAE) Seaspray radar. Most export Lynx are of similar standard to the HAS.2/HAS.3.

The Lynx HAS.8 features composite main rotor blades with swept tips, uprated engines, a nose mounted BAE Sea Owl thermal imager and improved ESM and processing equipment. A rear mounted MAD and new 360° coverage Sea Spray 3000 radar were planned, instead the original Sea Spray radar is upgraded to 3000 standard. Forty-four RN Lynx HAS.3s were being upgraded to HMA.8 standard with conversion work due to be completed in 2001.

Naval Lynx are now being offered in three Super Lynx versions – the basic Series 100 equivalent to the HAS.8 but with 360° radar, the Series 200 with LHTEC CTS800 engines, and the Series 300 with CTS800s and a two crew, six screen EFIS cockpit (South Africa is the 300 launch customer – its will have APS-145 radar, while Malaysia ordered six in 1999).

**Photo:** A British Navy upgraded Lynx HMA.8. (Westland)

# Xian JH-7

**Country of origin:** China

**Type:** Strike/ground attack aircraft

**Powerplants:** Two 91.2kN (20,515lb) with afterburning Liming WS6 turbofans (licence built Rolls-Royce Spey Mk 202s).

**Performance:** Max level speed at 36,080ft Mach 1.7 (1807km/h/975kt), cruising speed Mach 0.8-0.85 (850-900km/h-460-490kt). Service ceiling 51,180ft. Combat radius 1650km (890nm). Ferry range 3650km (1970nm).

**Weights:** Max takeoff 28,475kg (62,776lb). Internal fuel 10,050kg (22,156lb).

**Dimensions:** Wing span 12.71m (41ft 8in), length exc probe 21.03m (69ft 0in), height 6.58m (21ft 7in). Wing area 52.3m² (563.0sq ft).

**Accommodation:** Pilot and weapons system operator in tandem.

**Armament:** One 23mm twin barrel gun in starboard lower fuselage. Wingtip, one centreline and four underwing hardpoints can carry a max external stores load of 6500kg (14,330lb). Options include PL-5B and PL-7 air-to-air missiles, C-801 or C-802K sea skimming anti ship missiles, plus rockets and bombs

**Operators:** China

**History:** China's JH-7 is a Tornado class strike fighter in limited service with the PLA Naval Air Force.

Development of the JH-7 is believed to date to the 1970s, although it was not publicly revealed until the 1988 Farnborough Airshow, where a model was displayed. Roll out of the first prototype was reported to be in August 1988, first flight was on December 14 1988. It took a decade from first flight before the JH-7 made its first public appearance, with a prototype making a flypast at the November 1998 Airshow China in Zhuhai.

The JH-7 is a fairly large aircraft, similar to the F-4 and Tornado. Design features include its high mounted wing with dog tooth leading edge and wingtip and underwing hardpoints, twin Xian WS6 turbofans, which are licence built Rolls-Royce Spey Mk 202 turbofans (the Mk 202 powered British Phantoms), a crew of two in tandem, and a JL-10A pulse Doppler fire control radar. So far prototype and production JH-7s have been powered by Rolls-Royce built Speys, but series production aircraft would have the licence built WS6s. At one stage Xian had looked at using the far more powerful AL-31F (from the Su-27) to power the JH-7.

So far JH-7 production appears to be limited to about 20 aircraft, with most in service with two Chinese navy squadrons for use in the maritime strike role. Full series production of the JH-7 has not been authorised, and the project may not be a priority given China's licence manufacture of the Sukhoi Su-30MKK strike fighter.

Various improvements for the JH-7 are understood to be under development, including a LANTIRN style targeting and navigation pod and a helmet mounted sight. Other reported upgrades include extra hardpoints, digital fly-by-wire flight controls and one piece windscreen.

FBC-2 Flying Leopard is the marketing name for a potential export variant, which would have customer selected avionics, radar and weaponry.

**Photo:** A poor quality internet image of the JH-7.

# Yakovlev Yak-130 & Aermacchi M-346

**Countries of origin:** Russia and Italy

**Type:** Two seat advanced trainer and ground attack aircraft

**Powerplants:** Yak-130 – Two 21.6kN (4850lb) Povazske Stojàrne DV-2S (Klimov RD-35) turbofans. M-346 – Two 28.0kN (6300lb) ITEC F124 turbofans.

**Performance:** Yak-130 – Max speed 1038km/h (560kt). Max initial rate of climb 11,000ft/min. Time to 20,000ft 2min. Service ceiling 42,650ft. Range with internal fuel 2547km (1375nm), with external fuel 3334km (1800nm). M-346 – Max speed 1056km/h (570kt). Range with internal fuel 2030km (1100nm), with two external fuel tanks 2590km (1400nm).

**Weights:** Yak-130 – Empty equipped 4600kg (10,132lb), normal take-off 6500kg (14,317kg), max takeoff 9500kg (20,943lb). M-346 – Empty 4627kg (10,200lb), takeoff and max takeoff same.

**Dimensions:** Yak-130 & M-346 – Wing span 9.72m (31ft 10in), length 11.49m (37ft 8in), height 4.76m (15ft 8in). Wing area 23.5m² (253.0sq ft).

**Accommodation:** Two in tandem.

**Armament:** Yak-130 – Seven or nine external hardpoints (wing tip stations optional for up to 3000kg of weapons.

**Operators:** None

**History:** The Yak-130 is aimed at a Russian air force advanced trainer requirement, developed in partnership with Aermacchi. The Italian manufacturer is now developing its own variant, the M-346.

The Yak-130 was developed in competition with the Mikoyan MiG-AT to meet a Russian air force requirement to replace Aero L-29 and L-39 jet trainers. Design work on the Yak-130 began in 1987, the first prototype first flew on April 25 1996. In 1993 Yakovlev signed a collaborative agreement with Aermacchi covering design and marketing. Aermacchi had considerable input into refining the basic Yak-130 design including 5000 hours of wind tunnel testing of various configurations, 3000 hours of rig testing of the Yak-130's fly-by-wire system, and flight testing. Aermacchi and Yakovlev definition of the baseline standard aircraft, which production Yak-130s and M-346s will be based on, was completed in December 1999.

Yak-130 features include twin DV-2S turbofans (Klimov RD-35s, built in Slovakia). Aerodynamic features include inboard wing fences, leading edge slats and LEXs, permitting flight up to 35° angle of attack to be flown. Production aircraft may feature RD-2500 engines and will be slightly smaller than the prototype.

The baseline Russian aircraft features Russian avionics on a Western standard Mil Std 1553 databus (allowing easy integration of Western avionics and weapons), a HUD in the front cockpit and two colour LCD displays in each cockpit. The Yak-130's fly-by-wire system has selectable modes, so the aircraft's flight envelope can be representative of a simpler trainer or a more demanding front line fighter.

Four pre-production aircraft are under construction at Sokol.

Aermacchi's fully Westernised M-346 has superseded the previous Yak/AEM-130 development. The M-346 will be based on the common baseline Yak-130 airframe, but will be powered by ITEC F124 turbofans, with a wide angle HUD, HOTAS controls, and three multifunction LCDs in each cockpit. First flight is planned for mid 2003.

**Photo:** The first Yak-130 prototype in 2001. (Sebastian Zacharias)

## General Atomics RQ-1 Predator

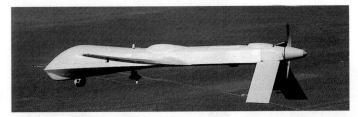

*Type:* Reconnaissance UAV

*Powerplant:* One 75kW (100hp) Rotax 914 four cylinder piston engine

*Performance:* Speed 222km/h (120kt). Max altitude 20,000ft, typical altitude 15,000ft. Endurance 40hr+, endurance 740km (400nm) from base 14+hr.

*Weights:* Takeoff 999kg (2200lb).

*Dimensions:* Span 14.9m (48.7ft), length 8.2m (27ft).

*Armament:* Tested with AGM-114 Hellfire missiles

*Sensors:* Electro optical/infrared turret and synthetic aperture radar.

*Notes:* The highly successful Predator, already a veteran of operational deployments over Bosnia and Afghanistan, first flew in June 1994 and was declared operational with the USAF in 1996. By late 2001 over 60 had been built, although 20 had been lost to accidents or enemy action. EO and IR cameras provide real time streaming video for ground commanders. Has been tested fitted with a laser designator to 'lase' targets for fighters, and armed with two Hellfire missiles (used operationally over Afghanistan). An enhanced capability TPE331 turboprop powered variant is under development and first flew in February 2001.

## Northrop Grumman RQ-4 Global Hawk

*Type:* Reconnaissance UAV

*Powerplant:* One Rolls-Royce AE 3007 turbofan.

*Performance:* Speed 730km/h (394kt). Max range 26,655km (14,395nm). Endurance 42hr. Altitude 65,000ft.

*Weights:* Takeoff 11,622kg (25,600lb).

*Dimensions:* Span 35.4m (116.2ft), length 13.5m (44.4ft).

*Sensors:* Synthetic aperture radar/moving target indicator, electro optical and infrared. Forward fuselage contains satellite datalink dish.

*Notes:* The high altitude long range Global Hawk reconnaissance platform is under engineering and manufacturing development before entering production for the USAF, but has already been used operationally over Afghanistan in 2001. The U-2 sized RQ-4 first flew in February 1998. Deliveries of the first of 51 production RQ-4s is due in 2003.

## Northrop Grumman Firescout

*Notes:* The Rolls-Royce 250 turboprop powered Firescout Vertical Takeoff UAV (VTUAV) is based on the Schweizer 330 helicopter. Northrop Grumman won an engineering and manufacturing development contract for Fire Scout in February 2000. The VTUAV will be able to fly from any "air capable" combat ship for real-time reconnaissance and targeting missions.

## Boeing X-45

*Notes:* Boeing is developing two X-45 UCAV (Unmanned Combat Air Vehicle) demonstrators in conjunction with the US Defense Advanced Research Agency. They will be used to prove the feasibility of UCAVs undertaking dangerous and high priority combat missions, particularly SEAD. Flight testing is due to begin in 2002. The X-45 has a 3630kg (8000lb) empty weight, 10.3m (34ft) wing span and 8.2m (27ft) length.

## Northrop Grumman X-47 Pegasus

*Notes:* Norhrop Grumman began development of the diamond shaped stealthy Pegasus as a private venture. It features a Pratt & Whitney Canada JT15D turbofan, is 8.5m (27.9ft) long with a 8.5m (27.8ft) span. The land based X-47A was due to fly in late 2001 but had not done so at the time of writing. The X-47B will be used to demonstrate the feasibility of aircraft carrier based UCAVs.

# AIRCRAFT CARRIERS

## Nimitz Class (USA)

USS John C Stennis

**Ships:** USS *Nimitz* (CVN 68), USS *Dwight D Eisenhower* (CVN 69), USS *Carl Vinson* (CVN 70), USS *Theodore Roosevelt* (CVN 71), USS *Abraham Lincoln* (CVN 72), USS *George Washington* (CVN 73), USS *John C Stennis* (CVN 74), USS *Harry S Truman* (CVN 75), *Ronald Reagan* (CVN 76 – service entry 2003), CVN 77 (under construction, delivery 2008).

**Powerplants:** Two nuclear reactors, approx total output 193,960kW (260,000shp). Speed 30+kt (56+km/h).

**Displacement:** Approx 98,557 tonnes.

**Dimensions:** Length 333m (1092ft), flight-deck width 76.9m (252ft).

**Aircraft:** Carrier air wing comprises 10 F-14, 36 F/A-18, 4 EA-6B, 8 S-3, 4 E-2, 2 C-2, 6 SH-60.

**Armament:** Sea Sparrow SAMs, three-four 20mm Phalanx CIWS.

**Complement:** Ship's company 3200, air wing 2480.

**Notes:** The nuclear power *Nimitz* class carriers form the backbone of the US Navy carrier force. Two nuclear reactors require less space than *Enterprises*' eight allows 20% greater aviation fuel capacity. Lead ship *Nimitz* commissioned May 1975. CVN 77 (construction began 2001) will feature a new island, an integrated combat system and incorporate commercial ship techonologies.

## Enterprise (USA)

**Ships:** USS *Enterprise* (CVN 65)

**Powerplants:** Eight nuclear reactors, total output 208,880kW (280,000shp). Speed 30+kt (56+km/h).

**Displacement:** Approx 91,038 tonnes.

**Dimensions:** Length 335.8m (1101ft), flight-deck width 76.9m (252ft).

**Aircraft:** Carrier air wing comprises 10 F-14, 36 F/A-18, 4 EA-6B, 8 S-3, 4 E-2, 2 C-2, 6 SH-60.

**Armament:** Sea Sparrow SAMs, three 20mm Phalanx CIWS.

**Complement:** Ship's company 3150, air wing 2480.

**Notes:** The world's first nuclear powered aircraft carrier, fitted with eight nuclear reactors. Completed in 1961. Nuclear power very costly, but benefits include reduced life cycle cost, greater endurance and increased space for aviation fuel. Elimination of need for ship's fuel bunker allows 50% increase in aviation fuel compared to similar sized *Kitty Hawk* class.

## Kitty Hawk Class (USA)

USS Kitty Hawk

**Ships:** USS *Kitty Hawk* (CV 63), USS *Constellation* (CV 64), USS *John F Kennedy* (CV 67).

**Powerplants:** Four steam turbines, total output 208,880kW (280,000shp). Speed 30+kt (56+km/h).

**Displacement:** Approx 82,097 tonnes.

**Dimensions:** Length 324m (1062.5ft), flight-deck width 76.9m (252ft).

**Aircraft:** Carrier air wing comprises 10 F-14, 36 F/A-18, 4 EA-6B, 8 S-3, 4 E-2, 2 C-2, 6 SH-60.

**Armament:** Sea Sparrow SAMs, three 20mm Phalanx CIWS.

**Complement:** Ship's company 3150, air wing 2480.

**Notes:** Improved *Forrestal* design with increased area flightdeck and revised lift design. *Kitty Hawk*, commissioned 1961, is based in Japan, *Constellation* is the US Navy's flagship. Improved *John F Kennedy* similar to *Kitty Hawk* and *Constellation*, changes include canted stack and redesigned forward end of the angled deck. Fourth ship in class, USS *America* (CV 66), decommissioned 1996.

## Kuznetsov (Russia)

**Ships:** *Kuznetsov*

**Powerplants:** Two steam turbines, total output 74,600kW (100,000shp). Speed 29kt (54km/h).

**Displacement:** Approx 55,000 tonnes.

**Dimensions:** Length 302.3m (991ft), beam 72.3m (237ft).

**Aircraft:** Su-27Ks and Ka-27s.

**Armament:** 12 Granit ASMs, 60 anti sub rockets, Klinok SAMs, Kashstan Air Defence Gun/Missile System. Six AK630 AD 30mm guns.

**Complement:** Ship's company approx 2000, 600 air wing.

**Notes:** Russia's only carrier, *Kuznetsov* (ex *Tbsilisi* and *Leonid Brezhnev*) was commissioned in 1991. Based on smaller *Admiral Gorshkov/Baku* (sold to India).

## Invincible Class (UK)

HMS Invincible

**Ships:** HMS *Invincible* (R05), HMS *Illustrious* (R06), HMS *Ark Royal* (R07).

**Powerplants:** Four Rolls-Royce Olympus gas turbines, total output 72,360kW (97,000shp). Speed 30kt (56km/h).

**Displacement:** 20,930 tonnes.

**Dimensions:** Length 210m (686ft), beam 36m (118ft).

**Aircraft:** Sea Harrier F/A.2, Harrier GR.7, Sea King (AEW & ASW).

**Armament:** Two 20mm guns, three Phalanx/Goalkeeper CIWS.

**Notes:** Originally concieved as Through Deck Cruisers capable of operating large ASW helicopters only. Design later modified for V/STOL Sea Harriers with small ski jump at end of flightdeck. Lead ship *Invincible* launched in 1977.

## Charles de Gualle (France)

**Ships:** *Charles de Gualle*

**Powerplants:** Two nuclear reactors.

**Displacement:** 38,000 tonnes.

**Dimensions:** Length 261.5m (857.4ft), flight-deck beam 64m (209.8ft).

**Aircraft:** 40 aircraft including Rafale M, Super Etendard, E-2C Hawkeye, AS 565, and NH 90.

**Armament:** Eight Giat 20F2 20mm guns, AS-TER 15 SAM system.

**Complement:** Ship's company 1150, air wing 600.

**Notes:** The only nuclear powered carrier built in Europe, France's *Charles de Gualle* launched in May 1994 but did not enter service until April 2001. Plans to build a sistership scrapped due to cost.

# THE 2002/03 WORLD AIRPOWER GUIDE
## The inventories of the world's air arms

**ALBANIA**
**Air Force**
22 F-7. 31 F-6. 19 F-5/FT-5. 13 F-2. 10 FT-2. 6 CJ-5. 10 Y-5. 3 AS 350B. 1 Bell 222UT. 11 Harbin Z-5. 4 SA 316/9. Operational status of some of these aircraft unknown.

**ALGERIA**
**Air Force**
33 MiG-29*. 35 Su-24/MR*. 30+ MiG-25/R/U. 29 MiG-23BN/MS/U. 60 MiG-21MF/bis/U. 36 L-39ZA/C. 30 Zlin 142. 6 T-34C. 1 An-12. 9 Il-76. 19 C-130H/H-30. 2 F27-400. 2 Gulfstream IV. 1 Gulfstream III. 2 Falcon 900. 2 King Air 200T. 6 King Air 90. 12 1900D. 47 Mi-24. 4 Mi-6. 68 Mi-8/17. 9 AS 355F. 3 Ka 27. 20 Mi-2.

**ANGOLA**
**Air Force**
26 MiG-23. 20 MiG-21bis/U. 36 Su-22M4/U. 15 Su-25. 6 L-29. 9 PC-7. 2 707. 4 BN-2T. 2 L-100-20. 8 An-26. 17 C-212. 6 BN-2A. 4 PC-6. 29 Mi-25/Mi-35. 18 Mi-8/-17. 8 AS 565. 6 SA 342M. 6 SA 342L. 28 IAR 316. Operational status of some of these aircraft unknown.

**ARGENTINA**
**Air Force**
21 Mirage III. 8 Mirage 5. 24 Dagger A/B. 7 Canberra B.62/T.64. 12 A-4P. 36 A-4AR/TA-4R (A-4M/OA-4M). 60 IA-58A. 30 T-34A. 28 EMB-312. 26 IA-63*. 15 MS-760B. 2 KC-130H. 10 C-130B/H. 1 L-100-30. 4 707-320B/C. 1 757-200. 10 F27-400/600. 4 F28-1000/1000C. 7 DHC-6-200. 1 Sabreliner 75A. 5 Lear 35. 1 PA-31. 7 Commander 560. 17 Cessna A182J. 2 CH-47C. 1 S-70A. 5 Bell 212. 1 Bell 412. 2 UH-1D/H. 14 Hughes 369/500D. 4 SA 315B. 1 S-61R.
**Naval Aviation**
12 Super Etendard. 5 A-4Q. 5 MB-339A. 4 MB-326GB. 12 EMB-326. 10 T-34C. 8 P-3B. 10 S-2E/A. 3 L-188. 3 F28-3000. 9 King Air 200. 5 Queen Air B80. 2 PC-6B. 9 SH-3D/H. 8 UH-1H. 4 AS 555. 4 A 109A. 6 Alouette III.
**Coastguard**
5 C-212. 2 SA 330. 2 AS 365. 2 AS 565. 1 Hughes 300. 1 PA-23. 1 PA-28.
**Army Aviation**
23 OV-1. 6 T-41. 3 G222. 1 C-212. 2 DHC-6. 1 Sabreliner 75A. 1 Citation I. 3 Merlin III. 3 Merlin IV. 1 Queen Air B80. 20 AS 532. 3 AS 332B. 2 SA 330L. 1 Bell 212. 4 Bell 205A1. 40 UH-1H. 5 A 109A. 5 SA 315B. 8 UH-12ET.

**ARMENIA**
1 MiG-25. 5 Su-25. 2 L-39. 1 An-24. 1 An-32. 6 An-2. 10 Iak-52. 12 Mi-24. 9 Mi-8. 2 Mi-2.

**AUSTRALIA**
**Air Force**
17 F-111C. 12 F-111G. 4 RF-111C. 71 F/A-18A/B. 4 737AEW&C*. 19 P-3C/AP-3C. 3 TAP-3. 33 Hawk 127. 65 PC-9. 12 C-130J-30. 12 C-130H. 4 707-320C. 14 DHC-4. 2 737BBJ*. 3 Challenger 604*. 5 Falcon 900. 6 HS.748. 4 King Air 200.
**Navy Fleet Air Arm**
16 S-70B-2. 11 SH-2G(A)*. 7 Sea King 50A. 11 AS 350BA.
**Army Aviation Corps**
22 Tiger*. 36 S-70A-9. 6 CH-47D. 25 UH-1H. 42 Bell 206B-1. 2 DHC-6-300. 3 King Air 200.

**AUSTRIA**
**Air Force**
23 J 35ÖE. 29 Saab 105ÖE. 16 PC-7. 1 CN-235. 2 Skyvan 3M. 12 PC-6. 9 UH-60L*. 23 Bell 212. 8 Bell 204B. 11 OH-58B. 11 Bell 206. 23 Alouette III.

**AZERBAIJAN**
8 MiG-25PD. 14 MiG-25RB. 6 MiG-25U. 5 Su-24. 4 Su-17M. 2 Su-25. 12 L-39. 18 L-29. 3 Il-76. 1 An-24. 1 An-12. 1 Tu-134A. 15 Mi-24. 13 Mi-8. 7 Mi-2. Operational status of some of these aircraft unknown.

**BAHAMAS**
**Defence Force**
1 Cessna 421C. 1 Cessna 404.

**BAHRAIN**
**Air Force**
22 F-16C/D. 12 F-5E/F. 1 747SP. 1 727. 1 Avro RJ. 1 Gulfstream II. 1 Gulfstream III. 12 AH-1E. 2 BO 105. 2 S-70A. 12 AB 212. 4 AB 412.
**Navy Air Arm**
2 BO 105CBS.

**BANGLADESH**
**Air Force**
8 MiG-29. 28 F-7M/FT-7B. 21 A-5C. 10 FT-6. 10 CM 170. 12 T-37C. 8 L-39ZA. 36 CJ-6. 4 Cessna 152. 2 Cessna 337. 4 C-130. 3 An-26. 3 An-32. 1 Mi-8. 15 Mi-17. 12 Bell 212. 3 Bell 206L.

**BELARUS**
**Air Force**
25 Su-27/UB. 65 MiG-29C/UB. 37 MiG-23MLD/UB. 42 Su-24MK/MR. 95 Su-25/UB. 32 Il-76. 9 An-26. 7 An-12. 1 Tu-154. 1 Tu-134. 1 Yak-40. 75 Mi-24. 125 Mi-8. 10 Mi-6. 30 Mi-26.

**BELGIUM**
**Air Force**
90 F-16A/B. 29 Alpha Jet E. 32 SF.260M. 2 A310. 11 C-130H. 4 ERJ 135. 5 Merlin III. 2 Falcon 20. 2 Falcon 900. 5 Sea King 48.
**Naval Aviation**
3 Alouette III.
**Army Aviation**
10 BN-2. 28 A 109HA. 18 A 109HO. 32 Alouette II.

**BELIZE**
**Defence Force**
2 BN-2. 1 T67M-200.

**BENIN**
**Armed Forces**
2 An-26. 2 Dornier 128-2. 1 DHC-6. 1 Commander 500B.

**BHUTAN**
**Army**
1 Dornier 228. 2 Mi-8.

**BOLIVIA**
**Air Force**
19 AT-33/T-33. 19 PC-7. 3 SF.260C. 30 T-33 Uirapuru. 12 Cessna 152. 9 Cessna 172K/T-41D. 1 DC-8-54CF. 9 C-130A/B/H. 5 F27-400. 1 Basler Turbo 67. 5 CV-580. 1 IAI-201. 1 C-212. 1 L-188C. 1 Sabreliner 60. 3 Learjet 25/35A. 3 King Air 90/200. 3 Commander 680/1000. 4 Cessna 402/421. 19 Cessna 185. 31 Cessna 206. 7 Cessna 210. 4

*Argentina has re-engined its S-2 Trackers with TPE331 turboprops. (Santiago Rivas)*

PA-32. 1 Beech B55. 1 Beech B36. 12 Cessna 152. 2 Bell 212. 24 UH-1H. 10 Hughes 500M. 9 SA 315B.

**Army Aviation**
1 C-212. 1 King Air 200.

**Naval Aviation**
1 Cessna 402.

## BOSNIA-HERZEGOVINA
**Army**
1 Citation II. 4 UTVA-75. 15 UH-1H. 6-12 Mi-8/-17. 1 Mi-34.

**Serbian Republic Air Force**
Some Oraos, Jastrebs, Galebs, Super Galebs, Mi-8s and Gazelles operational.

## BOTSWANA
**Air Force**
13 CF-5A/B. 7 PC-7. 3 C-130B. 2 CN-235. 10 BN-2A. 2 C-212. 2 Skyvan 3M. 9 O-2. 1 Gulfstream IV. 2 Cessna 152. 6 Bell 412. 7 AS 350.

## BRAZIL
**Air Force**
14 Mirage IIIE. 4 Mirage IIID. 56 F-5. 27 AMX. 14 AMX-T. 106 EMB-326. 71 EMB-312. 99 EMB-312 ALX*. 98 T-25 Universal. 25 T-23 Uirapuru. 5 EMB-145 SA*. 3 EMB-145 RS. 12 P-3A/B*. 13 S-2E. 21 EMB-111A. 4 707-320C. 3 KC-130H. 2 C-130H. 17 C-130E. 17 DHC-5A. 13 HS.748. 216 EMB-110. 2 737-200. 15 BAe 125. 4 Hawker 800*. 24 Learjet 35/36. 5 EMB-120. 11 EMB-121. 31 EMB-810C (PA-34). 3 Caravan 1. 80 U-27A/L-42. 6 AS 332M. 55 UH-1H. 4 Bell 206A/B. 4 OH-6A. 27 HB 350B Esquilo. 8 AS 355F. 25 OH-13.

**Naval Aviation**
23 A-4MB/TA-4. 13 SH-3D. 14 Super Lynx. 5 AS 532. 16 Bell 206B. 20 HB 350B/AS 355F-2 Esquilo.

**Army Aviation**
4 S-70. 19 AS 550. 36 HB 350-1 Esquilo*. 36 AS 565.

## BRUNEI
**Air Force**
4 PC-7 Mk II. 2 SF.260W. 3 CB-235MPA*. 1 CN-235M. 3 Gulfstream V. 10 Bell 212. 4 UH-60L*. 2 S-70C. 1 Bell 214ST. 6 BO 105CB/CBS. 2 Bell 206B.

## BULGARIA
**Air Force**
21 MiG-29A/UB. 15 MiG-23BN/MF/UM. 70 MiG-21bis. 9 MiG-21RF. 19 MiG-21U/UM. 21 Su-22M/U. 39 Su-25K/U. 35 L-39. 28 L-29. 5 An-26. 1 An-30. 8 L 410UVP-E. 2 Tu-134. 1 Yak-40. 43 Mi-24. 29 Mi-8/17. 14 Mi-2. 6 Bell 206. 1 Bell 430.

**Naval Aviation**
10 Mi-14PL.

## BURKINA FASO
**Air Force**
2 HS.748. 1 King Air 200. 2 N 262. 1 Cessna 337. 1 Cessna 172. 3 Mi-8/17. 2 SA 365N. 1 AS 350.

## BURUNDI
**Army Aviation**
5 SF.260W. 1 Falcon 50. 3 Cessna 150. 2 SA 342L. 3 SA 316B.

## CAMBODIA
**Air Force**
19 MiG-21bis/UM. 5 L-39. 1 F28-1000. 1 Falcon 20. 3 BN-2. 1 King Air 200. 2 Y-12. 2 An-24RV. 1 Cessna 421. 6 P92. 3 Mi-24. 6 Mi-8. 7 Mi-17. 2 Mi-26. 1 AS 365. 1 AS 350B.

## CAMEROON
**Air Force**
5 Alpha Jet. 6 CM 170. 2 Atlas Impala I. 4 Impala II. 1 727-200. 1 Gulfstream III. 2 C-130H. 4 DHC-5D. 1 IAI-201. 2 Dornier 128D-6. 2 PA-23. 1 AS 332L. 2 SA 330C. 1 SA 365N. 3 SA 319B. 1 SA 318C. 3 Bell 206L-3. 4 SA 342L.

## CANADA
**Air Command**
80 CF-18A/B Hornet. 18 CP-140 Aurora. 3 CP-140A Arcturus. 23 CT-114 Tutor. 29 CT-133. 5 CC-150 (A310). 25 CC-130E/H. 2 C-130H-30. 5 KCC-130H. 6 CC-115 Buffalo. 4 CC/CT-142 Dash 8. 4 CC-138 Twin Otter. 6 CE/CC-144 Challenger. 2 CT-145 (King Air). 15 CH-149 Cormorant (EH 101)*. 12 CH-113A Labrador (CH-46). 29 CH-124A/B Sea King. 99 CH-146 Griffon (Bell 412). 13+ CH-139 JetRanger.

**NATO Flying Training in Canada**
18 CT-115 Hawk*. 24 T-6 Harvard II*.

## CAPE VERDE
**Air Force**
3 An-26.

**Coast Guard**
1 Dornier 228. 1 EMB-110.

## CENTRAL AFRICAN REPUBLIC
**Air Force**
1 Rallye 235. 1 AS 350.

## CHAD
**Air Force**
2 PC-7. 4 SF.260W. 2 C-130H/H-30. 1 An-26. 1 PC-6B. 1 Reims-Cessna FTB-337. 2 SA 316.

## CHILE
**Air Force**
15 Pantera (Mirage 50). 25 Elkan (Mirage 5). 16 F-5E/F. 24 A-37B. 1 IAI Phalcon. 21 C-101CC. 13 C-101BB. 20 T-37B/C. 20 T-35A/B Pillan. 14 PA-28. 2 707-320. 1 737-500. 3 C-130B. 2 C-130H. 2 Y-7H-500. 2 Learjet 35. 1 Gulfstream IV. 4 C-212. 14 DHC-6. 9 Beech 99A. 1 King Air 100. 1 King Air 200CT. 6 Extra 300. 3 O-1. 1 S-70A. 8 Bell 412. 1 AS 332. 7 UH-1H. 5 SA 315B. 6 BO 105. 1 BK 117. 4 Bell 206.

**Naval Aviation**
4 P-3A. 2 UP-3A. 6 EMB-111. 2 Falcon 20. 10 PC-7. 10 O-2A. 3 EMB-110CN. 3 C-212. 2 Citation. 7 BO 105. 6 Bell 206. 6 AS 532C.

**Army Aviation**
3 CN-235M. 6 C-212A. 8 Cessna Caravan. 1 King Air 90. 1 Beech Baron. 16 Cessna R172K. 1 PA-31. 3 Cessna 337G. 2 Citation. 2 Falcon 20. 3 AS 332. 11 SA 330F/L. 2 Bell 206B. 12 SA 315B. 15 Enstrom 280FX. 5 MD 530F.

## CHINA
**Air Force**
38 Su-30MKK. 120 H-6 (Tu-16). 250 H-5 (Il-28). 500 Q-5. 250 J-11/Su-27SK*. 400* J-8/J-8II. 600+ J-7 (MiG-21). 2500 J-6 (MiG-19). 500 J-5 (MiG-17). 100 JZ-6. 6 K-8. 50 JJ-7. 500 JJ-5. 150 JJ-6. 1500 CJ-6. CL-601. 30 Y-7/An-24. 12 Y-14/An-26. 8 An-30. 10 Il-18. 25 Y-8 (An-12). 17 Harbin Y-11/Y-12. 300 Y-5.

**Naval Aviation**
30 H-6. 150+ H-5 (Il-28). 20 JH-7. 4 SH-5. 300+ J-6/JJ-6. 100+ J-5. 100 Q-5. 10 Y-7. 40 Y-5. 6+ Z-5. 25 Z-9/SA 365. 20 Ka-28. 20 Z-8/SA 321.

**Army Aviation**
28 S-70C-II. 35 Mi-8. 60 Mi-17. 300 Z-5 (Mi-4). 8 SA 342L-1. 25 Z-9/SA 365. 6 AS 332. 4 Z-11/Fennec.

## COLOMBIA
**Air Force**
13 Kfir C7/TC7. 13 Mirage 5. 21 A-37B. 12 OA-37B. 3 IA-58A. 5 AC-47/-47T. 15 OV-10A. 12 T-37C. 14 EMB-312. 10 T-34A/B. 12 T-41D. 7 C-130B. 2 C-130H-30. 1 707-320C. 3 CN-235M. 3 C-47. 1 C-117. 1 IAI-201. 2 C-212. 2 EMB-110P. 2 C-26. 1 F28-1000. 1 Citation II. 2 DHC-2A. 1 King Air C90. 1 King Air 200. 1 SA2-37A. 3 PA-31. Gallivan 12. 2 PA-34. 1 PA-23. 1 Beech Baron. 1 Queen Air B80. 1 Cessna 206. 2 Cessna 402/441. 2 Cessna 310. 1 Cessna 210. 3 Commander. 2 Bell 412. 14 Bell 212. 26 UH-60A. 7 UH-60L. 23

*ENAER upgraded Chile's Mirage 50s to Pantera standard, with assistance from Israel's IAI – hence the Kfir resemblance. (Alvaro Romero)*

UH-1B/H. 6 Bell 205A. 2 Bell 206L. 13 Hughes 500. 4 MD 530F. 12 Enstrom F28F.
**Naval Aviation**
5 PA-31. 1 King Air. 3 Commander 500. 4 PA-28. 2 AS 555SN. 4 BO 105CB.
**Army Aviation**
28 UH-60L*. 33 UH-1N*. 15 Mi-17. 1 Convair 580. 3 Commander. 1 King Air 90. 1 King Air 200. 2 PA-31. 4 PA-34. 4 PA-28. 2 Cessna U206. 5 UTVA-75.

## COMOROS ISLANDS
**Military Aviation**
1 AS 350B.

## CONGO
**Air Force**
12? MiG-21MF/U. 8 MiG-17F. 1 MiG-15UTI. 3 An-24/An-26. 1 727. 3 Mi-8. 1 SA 365. 2 SA 316. Operational status of these aircraft unknown.

## CONGO (FORMERLY ZAIRE)
**Air Force**
6 Mirage 5. 6 MB-326K. 9 MB-326GB. 5 SF.260MZ. 1 707. 1 727-100. 2 C-130H. 3 DHC-5D. 8 C-47. 1 BN-2A. 2 MU-2J. 12 Reims-Cessna 150. 1 AS 332. 9 SA 330. 7 SA 316. Operational status of some of these aircraft unknown.

## COSTA RICA
**Civil Guard**
2 DHC-4. 1 Cessna O-2. 4 Cessna U206G. 1 PA-23. 1 PA-34. 1 PA-31. 1 PA-32-200. 1 Mi-17. 2 MD 500E.

## COTE D'IVOIRE
**Air Force**
5 Alpha Jet. 4 Beech F33C. 1 Fokker 100. 1 Gulfstream IV. 1 Gulfstream III. 1 King Air. 1 Cessna 421. 1 Cessna 401. 1 SA 330H. 1 SA 365C.

## CROATIA
**Air Force**
36 MiG-21bis/MF/RF/U. ? J-1. ? G-2. ? J-20. 20 PC-9. 3 An-32. 5 CN-235M*. 3 CL-215/-415. 13 An-2. 2 CL-601. 1 Sabreliner 75A. 1 Do 28. 3 PA-28. 2 PA-36. 10 UTVA-75. 1 Cessna T210. 1 Cessna 172. 15 Mi-24V. 25 Mi-8. 10 Bell 206. 4 MD 500. 1 Mi-2.

## CUBA
**Air Force**
18 MiG-29. 2 MiG-29UB. 20 MiG-23M. 45 MiG-23BN. 4 MiG-23U. 85 MiG-21F/MF/PFMA. 80 MiG-21bis. 18 MiG-21U. 18 MiG-17F. 25 L-39C. 20 Zlin Z 326. 4 An-24. 20 An-26. 2 An-32. 1 An-30. 2 Yak-40. 20 An-2. 10 Zlin 142. 12 Mi-24D. 14 Mi-14. 36 Mi-8. 14 Mi-17. 6 Mi-2.

## CYPRUS
**Air Force**
2 PC-9. 1 BN-2B. 4 SA 342L-1. 2 Hughes 500. 3 Bell 206L-3. 2 Kania.

## CZECH REPUBLIC
**Air Force**
24 Gripen. 36 MiG-21MF. 20 MiG-21UM. 22 Su-22M-4/UM. 72 L-159*. 37 L-39. 23 L-29. 12 Zlin Z 142/3. 2 An-24. 4 An-26. 1 An-30. 18 L-410M/T/UVP. 1 L-610. 3 Tu-154. 1 Yak-40. 1 Challenger. 36 Mi-24. 40 Mi-8/17. 33 Mi-2. 11 W-3.

## DENMARK
**Air Force**
69 F-16A/B. 3 C-130J*. 3 C-130H. 1 Gulfstream III. 3 Challenger 604. 14 EH 101*. 8 Sikorsky S-61A. 28 T-17 Supporter.
**Naval Aviation**
8 Lynx.
**Army Aviation**
12 Hughes 500M. 12 AS 550.

## DJIBOUTI
**Air Force**
1 An-28. 1 Falcon 50. 1 Cessna 402. 1 Cessna 206. 5 Mi-8. 2 Mi-2. 2 AS 355F.

## DOMINICAN REPUBLIC
**Air Force**
6 A-37B. 2 O-2A. 10 EMB-312H*. 8 T-35. 5 T-34B. 3 C-212-400. 3 C-47. 2 Aero Commander 680. 1 King Air 90. 2 Queen Air 80. 1 PA-31. 1 Cessna 210. 1 Cessna 207. 3 T-41D. 9 Bell 205A/UH-1H. 10 AS 350B*. 2 SA 316. 1 Alouette II. 1 SA 365C.

## ECUADOR
**Air Force**
14 Mirage F1JE/JB. 17 Kfir C2/TC2. 8 Jaguar International S/B. 9 Strikemaster Mk 89. 23 A-37B. 22 AT-33. 19 T-34C. 2 T-41D. 4 Cessna 150. 4 C-130B. 1 C-130H. 1 L-100-30. 1 DHC-5D. 1 HS.748. 3 DHC-6-300. 4 Sabreliner. 24 UH-1H. 2 UH-1B. 1 Bell 212. 9 Bell 206. 5 SA 316.
**Naval Aviation**
3 T-34C. 2 CN-235M. 1 Citation I. 2 King Air 200/300. 1 Cessna 320. 4 Bell 206B. 2 Bell 222.
**Army Aviation**
1 DHC-5D. 1 CN-235M. 6 IAI-101. 3 PC-6B. 1 Citation II. 1 Sabreliner 40. 1 Learjet 24D. 2 King Air 100/200. 3 Cessna 172. 1 Cessna 185. 13 SA 342K/L. 4 AS 332B. 2 SA 330L. 1 Bell 214B. 1 UH-1. 4 AS 350B. 4 SA 315B.

## EGYPT
**Air Force**
30 F-4E. 36 F-16A/B. 178 F-16C/D*. 17 Mirage 2000C/B. 90 Mirage 5DE/E2. 11 Mirage 5SDR/SDD. 60 F-7. 60 MiG-21. 45 F-6/FT-6. 38 Alpha Jet. 46 L-59E. 80 K-8*. 6 E-2C. 6 Beech 1900C. 3 707. 26 C-130H/H-30. 9 DHC-5D. 1 A340. 7 Gulfstream III/IV. 1 King Air. 3 Falcon 20. 40 L-29. 46 L-59E. 46 EMB-312. 74 Grob G 115*. 35 AH-64A. 79 SA 342K/L/M. 19 CH-47D. 28 Commando. 40 Mi-8. 20 Mi-17. 4 UH-60*. 17 Hiller UH-12E. 2 AS-61.
**Naval Aviation**
10 SH-2G(E). 5 Sea King 47. 12 SA 342L.

## EL SALVADOR
**Air Force**
8 A-37B. 13 O-2A. 4 AC-47. 7 T-41C/D. 1 IAI-201. 1 DC-6. 4 C-47/Turbo-67. 8 T-35B. 4 T-34B. 1 T-41D. 1 Merlin IIIB. 5 Rallye 235GS. 7 MD 500ME. 27 UH-1H/N.

## EQUATORIAL GUINEA
1 An-32. 1 Falcon 900.

## ERITREA
**Air Force**
5 MiG-29. 5 MB-339FD. 4 Y-12. 7 Redigo. 1 Mi-35. 4 Mi-17. 2 Mi-8. 1 Dornier 228.

## ESTONIA
**Air Force**
2 An-2.

## ETHIOPIA
**Air Force**
10 Su-27A/U. 22 MiG-23BN/UB. 35 MiG-21MF/U. 15 MiG-17. 15 L-39ZO. 12 SF.260TP. 11 An-12. 1 An-32. 4 C-130B. 1 Yak-40. 11 Mi-24. 21

*Egyptian F-16s overfly the pyramids. Egypt is building up a fleet of over 200 F-16s. (Lockheed Martin)*

*Finnish air force F/A-18Cs. (Lassi Tolvanen)*

Mi-8/-17. 20 SA 316.2 Mi-14.
### Army Aviation
2 DHC-6. 1 Cessna 401.

## FINLAND
### Air Force
64 F/A-18C/D. 52 Hawk 51/51A. 28 L-70. 9 L-90. 3 F27. 3 Learjet 35. 6 PA-31-350. 7 PA-28.
### Army Aviation
20 NH 90*. 7 Mi-8. 2 Hughes 500D.

## FRANCE
### Air Force
5 Mirage IV-P. 60 Mirage 2000N. 60 Mirage 2000D. 234 Rafale C/D (requirement)*. 35 Mirage F1C/C-200. 40 Mirage F1CR-200. 40 Mirage F1CT. 10 Mirage F1B. 125 Mirage 2000C/B/-5F. 60 Jaguar A/E. 5 E-3F. 99 Alpha Jet E. 92 Epsilon. 48 EMB-312. 9 CAP 10/20/231. 14 C-135FR. 2 A310-300. 3 DC-8-72. 66 C-160/C-160NG. 6 C-160H (command post/ECM). 14 C-130H/H-30. 14 CN-235M. 19 Nord 262. 6 DHC-6. 14 Falcon 20. 4 Falcon 50. 2 Falcon 900. 2 A319CJ*. 17 TBM 700. 32 EMB-121. 10 Jodel D 140E. 7 AS 332C/L. 7 AS 532. 4 AS 532 Mk2*. 29 SA 330B/H. 47 AS 355F-1/N. 3 Alouette III.
### Naval Aviation
60 Rafale M (requirement)*. 52 Super Etendard. 28 Atlantic I. 28 Atlantique ATL2. 4 E-2C*. 5 Falcon 50*. 5 Falcon 20H Gardian. 16 Nord 262. 10 CAP 10B. 15 Rallye 100S/100ST. 6 Falcon 10/10MER. 12 EMB-121. 16 SA 321. 37 Lynx HAS.2(FN)/HAS.4 (FN). 9 SA 365F. 24 AS 565MA*. 30 Alouette III.
### Army Aviation
80 Tiger*. 68 NH 90*. 124 SA 330B/H. 22 AS 332M. 64 AS 532M. 114 SA 341M/F. 30 SA 342L1. 155 SA 342M. 4 AS 532UL Horizon. 18 AS 555. 2 Cessna F406. 8 TBM 700. 5 PC-6.

## GABON
### Air Force
9 Mirage 5G. 1 C-130H. 2 L-100-20/-30. 1 CN-235. 1 ATR 42F. 2 EMB-110P. 1 Falcon 900EX. 1 Gulfstream IV. 1 DC-8. 1 Nord 262. 1 Bell 412SP. 1 AS 350.

### Presidential Guard
3 CM 170. 4 T-34C-1. 1 EMB-110P. 1 AS 355.
### Army Aviation
3 SA 341. 2 SA 330.

## GEORGIA
7 Su-25. 4 L-29. 4 Yak-52. 1 Tu-134. 6 An-2. 4 Mi-24. 4 Mi-8. 1 Mi-2.

## GERMANY
### Air Force
145 F-4F. 180 Eurofighter (requirement)*. 193 Tornado IDS. 35 Tornado ECR. 23 MiG-29A/UB. 83 C-160. 7 A310. 2 707-320. 1 Tu-154M. 7 CL-601. 2 L 410UVP. 30 NH 90*. 82 UH-1D. 3 AS 332U2. US based training units operate 10 F-4F, 10 T-38 and 35 T-37B.
### Naval Aviation
49 Tornado IDS. 18 Atlantic 1. 4 Dornier 228. 38 NH 90*. 21 Sea King 41. 15 Sea Lynx 88. 7 Lynx 88A*.
### Army Aviation
80 Tiger UHT. 96 CH-53G. 120 UH-1D. 204 BO 105P. 96 BO 105M. 15 EC 635. 30 Alouette II.

## GHANA
### Air Force
5 MB-326K. 4 MB-339A. 1 MB-326E. 12 L-29A. 10 Bulldog 122/122A. 3 F27. 1 F28-3000. 4 Skyvan 3M. 4 BN-2T. 2 AB 412. 2 SA 319. 2 A 109.

## GREECE
### Air Force
62 F-4E/RF-4E. 49 Mirage 2000EG/BG*. 134 F-16C/D*. 87 A-7E/H/TA-7H. 24 Mirage F1CG. 4 EMB-145 SA*. 2 Argus. 6 P-3B. 5 C-130B. 10 C-130H. 2 YS-11A. 1 C-47. 15 CL-215. 10 CL-415*. 8 Do 28. 45 T-6A*. 16 T-33A. 20 T-41D. 34 T-37B/C. 35 T-2E. 12 G-164 Ag-cat. 21 PZL Dromader. 6 AS 532C. 4 AB 212. 10 AB 205A. 1 AB 206A. 7 Bell 47G.
### Naval Aviation
10* S-70B. 10 AB 212ASW. 3 Alouette III.
### Army Aviation
24 AH-64A. 12 UH-60. 16 CH-47D*. 29 UH-1H. 80 AB-205A. 1 AB 212. 1 26 NH 300C. 5 OH-13. 3 King Air 200. 3 Commander. 20 Cessna 185.

## GUATEMALA
### Air Force
8 A-37B. 7 PC-7. 7 IAI-201. 4 Basler Turbo C-47. 3 F27. 1 PA-21. 4 T-35B. 6 T-41D. 2 Cessna 206. 2 Cessna T210. 4 King Air. 6 Bell 412. 6 Bell 212. 4 UH-1H. 4 Bell 206B. 3 Bell 206L. 3 S-76.

## GUINEA REPUBLIC
### Air Force
5 MiG-21? 4 MiG-17F? 2 MiG-15UTI? 1 An-24. 4 An-14. 1 SA 342K. 2 SA 316B. 1 AS 350.

## GUINEA-BISSAU
### Air Force
3 MiG-17F. 1 MiG-15UTI. 1 An-24. 1 Falcon 20. 1 SA 318. 2 SA 319.

## GUYANA
### Air Corps
1 BN-2A. 2 Skyvan 3M. 1 Y-12*. 2 Mi-8. 1 Bell 412. 1 Bell 206B.

## HAITI
### Air Corps
6 O-2/337. 5 SF.260TP. 1 F33. 4 172/150. 3 C-47. 1 DHC-6-200. 1 BN-2A. 1 Beech Baron. 1 Cessna 402. Operational status of some of these aircraft unknown.

## HONDURAS
### Air Force
11 F-5E/F. 13 A-37B. 4 C-101B. 10 EMB-312. 6 T-41D. 2 C-130A. 1 C-130D. 6 C-47. 1 IAI-201. 1 L-188A. 1 Westwind. 1 PA-42. 2 PA-31. 1 Cessna 401. 1 Commander 1000. 1 Cessna 310. 2 Cessna 182. 6 Cessna 185. 4

*A CFM56 powered French air force Stratotanker, wearing a unique paint scheme complete with engine cutaways on the nacelles, commemorating 15 years of cooperation with engine manufacturer CFM. (Paul Merritt)*

UH-1H. 9 Bell 412EP. 2 MD 500D. 3 TH-55. 1 A 109.

## HUNGARY
### Air Force
14 Gripen*. 27 MiG-29A/UB. 19 L-39ZO. 9 An-26. 4 Zlin 43. 30 Mi-24D/V. 5 Mi-17. 20 Mi-8.

## ICELAND
### Coast Guard
1 F27-200. 1 AS 332L1. 1 AS 365N. 1 AS 350B.

## INDIA
### Air Force
50 Su-30MKI*. 140 HAL SU-30MKI*. 50 Mirage 2000H/TH*. 75 MiG-29. 135 Jaguar*. 133 MiG-27M. 5 MiG-25R/U. 78 MiG-23BN/UM. 30 MiG-23MF. 213 MiG-21bis. 15 MiG-21M. 40 MiG-21FL. 38 MiG-21U. 10 Canberra B(I).58/T.54. 169 Kiran 1/2. 50 TS-11. 1250 HPT-32. 24 CFM Shadow. 4 Il-76MD. 6 Il-78. 2 707-320C. 4 737-200. 110 An-32. 45 HS.748. 3 Gulfstream III. 2 Learjet 29. 15 Dornier 228. 117 Mi-8. 40 Mi-17*. 50 Mi-24/Mi-35. 15 Mi-26. 39 Chetak. 12 Cheetah. 6 SA 365.
### Naval Aviation
4 Tu-22M-3*. 46 MiG-29K*. 15 Sea Harrier FRS.51. 3 Harrier T.60. 2 Harrier T.2. 12 Kiran 1/2. 8 HPT-32. 13 BN-2A. 8 Tu-142M. 5 Il-38. 24 Dornier 228. 11 Sea King 42/42A. 20 Sea King 42B/C. 7 Ka-31*. 12 Ka-28 Helix. 5 Ka-25. 26 Chetak.
### Coast Guard
1 F27. 36 Dornier 228*. 6 Chetak.
### Army Aviation Corps
116 Chetak. 40 Cheetah.

## INDONESIA
### Air Force
10 F-16A/B. 10 F-5E/F. 15 A-4E/TA-4H. 2 TA-4J. 30 Hawk 200. 5 OV-10F. 8 Hawk 53. 7 Hawk 100. 19 T-34C. 19 SF.260*. 7 KT-1*. 3 737-2X9 Surveiller. 3 CN-235MPA. 2 KC-130B. 17 C-130B/H/H-30. 5 L-100-30. 7 F27-400M. 3 F28. 1 Skyvan 3M. 11 NC 212. 5 PC-6B. 1 707-320C. 17 CN-235. 7 401/402. 23 T-34C. 6 T-41D. 6 MD3-160. 39 AS 202. 18 NAS 332. 10 NAS 330J. 12 EC 120*. 10 Bell 47G. 1 Bell 412. 7 NBO 105C/CB. 10 S-58T. 12 Hughes 500C.
### Naval Aviation
35 Nomad. 2 DHC-5D. 6 CN-235. 7 NC-212. 6 PA-38. 4 Commander 100. 4 PA-34. 2 Beech F33A. 1 Socata TB 9. 16 NAS 332L. 13 NBO 105C. 4 NB-412. 2 Mi-17*. 8 Mi-2*. 2 SA 313. 9 Wasp HAS.1. 3 EC 120*.
### Army Aviation
3 DHC-5D. 4 NC-212. 1 BN-2A. 2 Cessna 310. 2 Commander 680. 18 PZL Wilga 32. 28 NB-412SP. 30 Bell 205A-1. 17 NBO 105. 15 Hughes 300C. 1 Alouette III.

## IRAN
### Air Force
40 F-4D/E. 6 RF-4E. 20 F-14A. 40 MiG-29. 30 Su-24MK. 44 Su-20/22. 45 F-5E/F. 18 F-7. 18 F-6. 19 Mirage F1. 3 P-3F. 10 EMB-312. 45 PC-7. 26 Beech F33A/C. 25 Mushshak. 11 747. 14 707-320. 13 Il-76. 10 An-74. 23 C-130E/H.

Two Luftwaffe F-4Fs taxi behind a MiG-29 at Rheine Hopsten. The colourful schemes commemorate JG 72 wing's 40th anniversary. The wing is due to disband in 2002 and the base will close in 2006. (Harold van Eupen)

2 RC-130H. 14 Y-7*. 10 F27. 5 Dornier 228. 1 Jetstar. 2 Falcon 20. 3 Falcon 50. 9 Y-12. 3 Aero Commander 690. 10 PC-6B. 5 CH-47C. 25 Bell 214A. 5 AB 212.
### Revolutionary Guard
? Su-25. 20 PC-7. 6 An-74. 20 Mi-8*.
### Naval Aviation
4 Falcon 20E. 7 Commander 690. 1 Commander 500. 2 RH-53D. 10 SH-3D. 6 AB 212AS. 5 AB 205. 10 AB 206.
### Army Aviation
70 AH-1J. 2 Falcon 20E. 6 Commander 500/690. 1 Commander 500. 15 Cessna 185. 20 CH-47C. 100 AB 214A. 20 AB 212. 10 AB 205A-1. 40 AB 206A/B. Operational status of some of these aircraft unknown.

## IRAQ
### Air Force
60 Mirage F1EQ/BQ. 10 MiG-25. 60 MiG-23MF/ML. 40 F-7. 35 MiG-21PFM/MF. 30 Su-7/20/22. 13 Su-25. 50 L-39. 10 PC-9. 40 EMB-312. 20 PC-7. 18 AS 202. 3 An-12. 9 An-24. 2 An-26. 10 SA 321. 20 SA 330. 20 SA 342L. 20 Alouette III. 10 Bell 214ST. 3 AS-61TS. 10 BK 117A/B. 40 BO 105C. 20 Mi-24/Mi-25. 80 Mi-8/Mi-17. 2 Mi-6. 15 MD 500D/530F. 1 Adnan AEW. Operational status of some of these aircraft unknown.

## IRELAND
### Air Corps
7 SF.260. 6 FR172. 2 CN-235MP. 1 BN-2T 4000.1 King Air 200. 1 Gulfstream IV. 4 AS 365N. 7 SA 316B. 2 SA 342L. 1 AS 355N.

## ISRAEL
### Air Force
40 F-4E. 53 F-4E 2000. 12 RF-4E. (many F-4s in storage). 25 F-15I*. 44 F-15A/B. 27 F-15C/D. 102 F-16I*. 104 F-16A/B. 125 F-16C/D. 50 Kfir C7/TC7 (some in storage). 105 A-4N (some in storage). 4 E-2C. 40 CM 170. 35 PA-18. 9 747-200. 16 707-320. 19 IAI-201. 4 KC-130H. 10 C-130H. 6 C-130E. 2 EC-130. 11 C-47/RC-47. 4 King Air 200. 13 RU-21A/RC-12D King Air. 16 Queen Air B80. 12 Do 28. 3 Seascan. 21 Cessna U206C. 49 AH-64A/D*. 25 UH-60A. 59 UH-60L*. 40 AH-1G/1S. 33 500MG. 43 CH-53. 60 Bell 212. 44 206/206L. 9 HH-65A Dauphin.

## ITALY
### Air Force
121 Eurofighter (requirement)*. 30 F-16A/B*. 24 Tornado ADV. 89 Tornado IDS. 15 Tornado ECR. 85 F-104ASA. 20 TF-104. 102 AMX. 24 AMX-T. 90 MB-339A. 14 MB-339CD. 38 SF.260AM. 18 Atlantic. 4 707-320. 12 C-130J*.

Italy operates 89 Tornado IDS strike fighters. (Joris van Boven/Sentry Aviation News)

*Kuwait operates 16 Shorts built Tucanos. (Dave Fraser)*

10 C-130J-30*. 12 C-27J*. 33 G222. 5 G222VS/RM. 2 A319CJ. 2 Falcon 900EX. 1 Gulfstream III. 4 Falcon 50. 16 P.180. 6 PD-808RM/ECM. 1 P-166M. 6 P-166DL-3. 40 S.208M. 33 AS-61R (HH-3F). 10 NH 90*. 2 SH-3D-TS. 35 AB 212. 49 NH-500E.

**Naval Aviation**
16 AV-8B Plus. 2 TAV-8B. 20 EH 101*. 46 NH 90*. 31 ASH-3D/3H. 49 AB 212ASW. 1 A 109.

**Air Calvary**
60 A 129*. 60 NH 90*. 38 CH-47C. 25 AB 412. 14 AB 212. 80 AB 205. 28 A 109. 115 AB 206A. 3 P.180. 3 Dornier 228-200. 50 SM 1019.

**JAMAICA**
**Defence Force Air Wing**
1 BN-2A. 1 King Air 100. 1 Cessna 210M. 3 Bell 412EP. 4 AS355N.

**JAPAN**
**Air Self Defence Force**
110 F-4EJ. 25 RF-4E/EJ. 190 F-15J/DJ. 130 F-2*. 61 F-1. 4 E-767. 13 E-2C. 55 T-2. 168 T-4*. 11 T-33. 54 Fuji T-1A/B. 50 Fuji T-3. 21 Fuji T-7*. 27 C-1. 16 C-130H. 8 YS-11. 2 747-400. 30 U-125*. 4 Gulfstream IV. 11 T-400. 5 Queen Air A65. 18 MU-2J/S. 29 CH-47J*. 18 KV-107. 22 UH-60J.

**Maritime Self Defence Force**
95 P-3C. 4 EP-3C/NP-3C. 3 UP-3D. 10 US-1/1A. 10 YS-11T/M. 35 King Air TC-90/LC-90/UC-90. 35 Fuji T-5 (KM-2D). 5 Learjet 36A. 10 MH-53J*. 9 S-61A. 39 SH-3A/B. 60 SH-60J*. 13 UH-60J. 15 OH-6D.

**Ground Self Defence Force**
85 AH-1F. 16 OH-1*. 16 MU-2. 4 King Air 350*. 48 CH-47J*. 5 KV-107-II. 3 AS 332L. 170 UH-1H/J*. 185 OH-6D/J.

**JORDAN**
**Air Force**
16 F-16A/B. 29 Mirage F1B/C/E. 42 F-5E/F. 18 C-101CC. 17 Bulldog 125/125A. 5 Extra 300. 4 C-130H. 2 C-130B. 5 C-130H. 2 C-212. 2 CN-235. 1 TriStar 500. 1 Gulfstream. 2 Challenger 604. 20 AH-1F. 3 S-70A. 36 UH-1H. 18 UH-1L. 10 AS 332M-1. 3 BO 105CBS. 6 Hughes 500D. 1 SA 316C. 1 Socata TB 20.

**KAZAKHSTAN**
**Air Force**
20 Su-27. 40 MiG-29. 40 MiG-31. 100? MiG-23M/U. 15 MiG-25PD/U. 25 Su-24. 15 Su-25. 5 An-12. 1 An-24. 14 An-26. 8 An-30. 1 757-200. 1 Falcon 900. 2 Tu-154. 2 Tu-134. 40 Mi-24. 60 Mi-8. 6 Mi-6. 24 Mi-26.

**KENYA**
**Air Force**
7 F-5E/F. 8 Hawk 52. 11 Shorts Tucano 51. 7 Bulldog 103/127. 1 Fokker 70. 8 DHC-5D. 3 Dash 8-100. 12 Y-12. 6 Do 28. 1 PA-31-350. 12 SA 330/IAR-330. 32 Hughes 500. 1 BO 105S.

**KUWAIT**
**Air Force**
40 F/A-18C/D. 12 Hawk 64. 16 Shorts Tucano. 1 DC-9. 1 MD-83. 3 L-100-30. 3 AS 532AF. 8 SA 330H. 16 SA 342K.

**LAOS**
**Air Force**
3 An-24. 5 Y-7. 7 Y-12. 2 Yak-40. 10 An-2. 1 Mi-6. 6 Ka-32T. 12 Mi-17. 9 Mi-8.

**LATVIA**
**Air Force**
2 An-2. 3 Mi-2. 1 L 410.

**LEBANON**
**Air Force**
6 Hunter F.70/T.66C. 5 CM 170. 5 Bulldog 126. 1 Falcon 20. 9 SA 330L. 24 UH-1H. 3 SA 342L. 7 AB 212. 2 Alouette II. 6 Alouette III.

**LESOTHO**
**Air Squadron**
2 C-212-300. 1 Cessna 182Q. 3 Bell 412. 2 BO 105CBS. 1 Bell 47G.

**LIBERIA**
**Army Aviation**
2 DHC-4. 2 IAI-101B. 1 Cessna Caravan 1. 1 Cessna 185. 2 Cessna 172. Operational status of these aircraft unclear.

**LIBYA**
**Air Force**
12 Su-24MK. 8 Tu-22A/U. 49 MiG-25. 35 Mirage F1AD/BD/ED. 130 MiG-23/BN/U. 49 Mirage 5. 50 MiG-21MF. 80 Su-20/-22. 80 G-2A Galeb. 24 J-1E. 135 L-39. 12 CM-170. 190 SF.260W. 8 Rallye 235GT. 1 Falcon 50. 25 Il-76. 1 707. 10 C-130H/L-100-30/L-100-20. 2 KC-130H. 10 An-26. 16 G222. 15 L 410UVP. 21 Mi-24. 20 Mi-2. 7 Mi-8. 2 AB 212. 4 CH-47. 4 SA 321.

**Army Aviation**
10 O-1E. 10 CH-47C. 5 AB 205. 5 AB 206A. 40 SA 342L.

**Naval Aviation**
7 SA 321. 12 Mi-14PL.

**LITHUANIA**
**Air Force**
8 L-39. 2 L 410. 6 An-2. 3 An-26. 17 Mi-8. 4 Mi-2.

**National Guard**
10 An-2. 4 Wilga.

**MACEDONIA**
**Army Air Force**
4 Su-25. 1 King Air. 2 An-2. 3 Zlin 242. 8 Mi-24. 7 Mi-8/-17. 2 UH-1H.

**MADAGASCAR**
**Air Force**
10 MiG-21FL/U. 4 MiG-17F. 5 An-26. 1 C-47. 1 HS.748. 2 Yak-40. 1 PA-23. 1 Cessna F337. 4 Cessna 172.

**MALAWI**
**Army Air Force**
2 Basler Turbo C-47. 4 Dornier 228. 1 125-800. 2 AS 332. 3 SA 330F. 1 AS 565N. 5 AS 350.

**MALAYSIA**
**Air Force**
18 MiG-29SE/U. 8 F/A-18D. 16 F-5E/F. 2 RF-5E. 17 Hawk 200. 7 Hawk 100. 10 MB-339A. 9 PC-7 MkII. 38 PC-7. 12 MD3-160. 3 C-130H-MP. 2 C-130H-30. 9 C-130H. 6 CN-235. 11 DHC-4A. 4 King Air 200. 1 Global Express. 1 F28-1000. 1 Falcon 900. 9 Cessna 402B. 28 S-61A Nuri/AS-61N. 2 S-70A. 2 Mi-17. 1 A 109C. 13 Alouette III.

**Naval Aviation**
6 Super Lynx*. 6 AS 555N*. 6 Wasp HAS.1.

**Army Aviation**
10 Alouette III.

**MALI**
**Air Force**
11 MiG-21. 6 L-29. 2 Yak-18. 4 Yak-11. 1 An-26. 1 An-24. 2 An-2. 1 Mi-8. 2 AS 365. 1 AS 350B.

**MALTA**
**Armed Forces**
2 BN-2B. 5 Bulldog T.1. 2 Bell 47G. 2 NH-500M. 5 Alouette III.

**MAURITANIA**
**Air Force**
1 DHC-5D. 1 Y-7. 1 Basler Turbo DC-3. 2 Y-12. 7 BN-2A. 4 Cessna 337. 2 PA-31T. 5 SF.260E. 4 Hughes 500M.

**MAURITIUS**
**Coast Guard**
1 Dornier 228-101. 1 BN-2T. 1 AS 350.

## MEXICO
### Air Force
10 F-5E/F. 29 AT-33A. 75 PC-7. 35 F33C/F-33F. 10 Maule MXT-7-180. 69 Cessna 182S*. 9 C-130A. 4 An-32. 12 C-47. 5 IAI-201. 1 Skyvan. 1 EMB-145 SA*. 2 EMB-145MP*. 1 Schweizer SA 2-37A. 3 727-100. 3 737-200. 1 757-200. 2 Gulfstream III. 1 JetStar. 9 Sabreliner. 7 King Air. 4 C-26. 2 Merlin IV. 12 Commander 500. 4 Turbo Commander. 1 Convair 580. 4 PC-6. 2 Mi-26. 4 Mi-17. 2 S-70A. 9 UH-60L. 15 Bell 212. 60 UH-1H. 17 MD 530F. 18 Bell 206. 5 Bell 206L. 3 AS 332L. 2 SA 330F. 2 AS 355. 4 Mi-2.
### Naval Aviation
5 An-32. 1 DHC-5D. 1 Dash 8 Q200. 8 C-212-200. 10 TP-90. 10 F-33C Bonanza. 3 Maule MXT-7-180. 9 Lancair. 3 Tonatiuh. 1 DHC-5D. 1 FH-227. 1 Learjet 24D. 1 King Air 90. 1 Mu-2. 3 Commander. 4 Cessna 402/404/421. 1 PA-31. 3 B55 Baron. 2 PA-23. 1 Cessna 337G. 1 Cessna 210. 1 Cessna 206. 1 Cessna 182. 6 Cessna 152. 19 Mi-17. 5 Mi-2. 2 UH-1H. 8 MD Explorer (MH-90)*. 11 BO 105C/CB. 3 Alouette III. 4 MD 500E. 1 AS 365. 2 AS 550. 2 R22. 1 R44.

## MOLDOLVA
### Air Force
3 An-72. 1 Tu-134. 1 An-24. 1 Il-18. 10 An-2. 8 Mi-8.

## MONGOLIA
### Air Force
3 An-26. 4 An-24. 10 An-2. 4 Y-11. 11 Mi-24. 12 Mi-8.

## MOROCCO
### Air Force
34 Mirage F1CH/EH. 26 F-5E/F. 11 F-5A/B. 2 RF-5A. 6 OV-10A. ? K-8*. 20 Alpha Jet. 14 T-37C. 20 CM 170. 10 T-34C. 10 AS 202A. 9 CAP 10/231. 15 C-130H. 2 KC-130. 7 CN-235M. 3 Do 28D. 1 707. 2 Falcon 20. 1 Falcon 50. 2 Gulf-stream II/III. 2 Citation V. 11 King Air 100/200/300. 9 CH-47C. 30 SA 330C. 38 AB 205A. 5 AB 212. 20 AB 206A/B. 23 SA 342.
### Gendarmerie
2 S-70A. 7 SA 330C. 5 SA 342K. 2 AS 365N. 2 SA 315B.

## MOZAMBIQUE
### Air Force
8 An-26. 2 C-212. 1 Cessna 172. 2 Cessna 152. 4 PA-32. 7 Zlin 326. 4 Mi-24. 5 Mi-8.

## MYANMAR
### Armed Forces
12 MiG-29. 34 F-7M/FT-7. 22 A-5M. 12 K-8. 9 PC-9. 15 PC-7. 6 F27/FH-227. 4 Y-8D. 2 C-212. 5 PC-6B. 1 Citation II. 6 Cessna 180. 11 Mi-17. 2 Bell 205A-1. 10 W-3. 6 Bell 206. 15 Mi-2.

## NAMIBIA
### Defence Force
4 K-8. 6 O-2A. 1 F406. 1 Falcon 900. 1 Lear 31. ? Y-12. 2 SA 316B.

## NATO
### E-3 Component
17 E-3A. 4 707-320.

## NEPAL
### Air Force
1 HS.748. 2 Skyvan 3M. 2 AS 332L. 2 SA 330C/G. 2 SA 316B. 2 Bell 206L.

## NETHERLANDS
### Air Force
128 F-16AM/BM. 13 PC-7. 2 KDC-10. 2 C-130H-30. 4 Fokker 60. 2 Fokker 50. 2 F27 Maritime. 1 Gulfstream IV. 13 PC-7. 30 NAH-64D*. 27 BO 105C. 9 Alouette III. 3 AB 412SP. 13 CH-47D. 13 CH-47D. 17 AS 532U2 Cougar Mk2.
### Naval Aviation
13 P-3C. 1 King Air 200. 20 NH 90*. 21 SH-14D Lynx.

## NEW ZEALAND
### Air Force
6 P-3K. 13 CT-4E Airtrainer. 5 C-130H. 2 727-100C. 3 King Air 200. 14 UH-1H. 5 Bell 47GB-2.
### Navy
5 SH-2G(NZ)*.

## NICARAGUA
### Air Force
4 An-26. 2 An-2.1 Cessna 404. 1 Cessna 180. 2 Cessna U-17. 5 Cessna 172. 10 PA-18. 15 Mi-17.

## NIGER
### Defence Force
1 C-130H. 1 An-26. 1 737-200. 1 Do 28D. 1 Dornier 228.

## NIGERIA
### Air Force
15 Jaguar SN/BN. 16 MiG-21MF/U. 18 Alpha Jet. 18 L-39MS. 12 MB-339AN. 58 Air Beetle. 8 C-130H/H-30. 20 CN-235*. 5 G222. 1 727-200. 2 Falcon 900. 2 Gulfstream II/IV. 1 Hawker 1000. 1 Citation II. 6 Dornier 228. 18 Dornier 128-6. 15 Do 28D. 7 Mi-35. 3 SA 330. 2 AS 332. 18 BO 105D. 14 Hughes 300C. 3 Mi-34.
### Naval Aviation
2 Lynx Mk 89. 2 A 109.

## NORTH KOREA
### Air Force
50 H-5 (Il-28). 40 MiG-29. 56 MiG-23ML/U. 40 F-7. 160 MiG-21PF/PFM/U. 30 F-7. 110 F-5. 25 FT-5. 40 A-5. 100 F-6. 30 Su-7BMK. 40 Su-25. 30 FT-2. 12 L-39. 170 CJ-6. 10 CJ-5. 280 Y-5/An-2. 3 Il-76. 12 An-24. 5 Il-14. 2 Il-18D. 3 Tu-154B. 4 Il-62M. 4 Tu-134. 20 Mi-24. 10 Mi-14PL. 86 Hughes 500. 16 Mi-8/-17. 48 Mi-4. 140 Mi-2. 48 Z-5.

## NORWAY
### Air Force
57 F-16AM/BM. 6 P-3C/N. 6 C-130H. 3 Falcon 20. 3 DHC-6 100/200. 16 MFI-15. 14 NH 90*. 12 Sea King Mk 43. 18 Bell 412SP. 6 Lynx 86.

## OMAN
### Air Force
12 F-16C/D*. 22 Jaguar S/B. 11 Hawk 200. 4 Hawk 100. 12 PC-9M. 2 747SP. 2 Gulfstream IV. 6 BN-2A. 3 C-130H. 10 Skyvan 3M. 3 BAC One-Eleven 475. 4 AS 202. 3 Mushshak. 2 Super Falke. 3 AS 332. 3 SA 330J. 4 AS 202. 5 Bell 214B. 3 Bell 206B. 20 AB 205A. 3 AB 212. 20 Super Lynx 300*.

## PAKISTAN
### Air Force
32 F-16A/B. 40 F-7MG*. 143 F-7M/P. 13 FT-7. 43 A-5. 50 F-6/FT-6. 36 Mirage IIIEP/B. 15 Mirage IIIRP/DP. 43 Mirage IIIO. 6 Mirage IIIB. 52 Mirage 5. 30 FT-5. 6 FT-2. 10 T-33A/RT-33A. 41 T-37B. 30 Mushshak. 8 K-8. 2 707-320C. 1 737-300. 13 C-130B/E/L-100-20. 4 CN-235*. 2 F27. 3 Falcon 20E. 2 Y-12. 1 Citation V. 1 King Air. 1 Baron. 1 PA-34. 4 Cessna 172N. 15 Alouette III.
### Naval Aviation
2 P-3C. 3 Atlantic 1. 5 F27. 3 Lynx HAS.3. 6 Sea King 45. 3 Lynx. 2 Maritime Defender. 8 Alouette III.
### Army Aviation Corps
19 AH-1F. 115 Mushshak. 30 O-1E. 2 Commander 840/SMA. 1 Cessna 421. 2 Y-12. 25 SA 330J. 33 Mi-17*. 10 Mi-8. 10 Bell 205/UH-1H. 28 Bell 206B. 20 Alouette III. 15 SA 315B. 10 Schweizer 300. 12 Bell 47G.

*Once were warriors. New Zealand has disbanded its Air Combat Force, retiring its only front line fighters, A-4 Skyhawks, without replacement. (RNZAF)*

## PANAMA
### National Air Service
6 T-35D Pillan. 1 727. 5 C-212. 1 CN-235M. 1 Gulfstream II. 1 BN-2A. 1 PA-31T. 1 PA-34. 13 UH-1H. 2 Bell 205. 4 Bell 212. 1 S-76.

## PAPUA NEW GUINEA
### Defence Force
2 CN-235. 4 N22 Nomad. 3 IAI-101. 4 UH-1H. 1 NBO 105.

## PARAGUAY
### Air Force
12 F-5E/F. 5 EMB-326. 4 EMB-312. 2 AT-6. 12 T-35A/D Pillan. 3 T-23 Uirapuru. 1 707-320. 1 Citation II. 4 C-212. 1 Convair C-131D. 3 C-47. 1 King Air 200. 1 DHC-6. 2 Cessna 402. 1 Beech Baron. 2 Cessna 210. 6 Cessna 206. 1 Cessna 185. 1 PA-23. 1 PA-32. 1 DHC-3. 2 PZL-104. 1 A 109. 2 UH-1H. 9 UH-1B. 2 HB 350B. 1 Hughes 300
### Naval Aviation
1 Cessna 401. 2 Cessna 310. 1 Cessna 210. 2 Cessna 150. 2 HS 350B. 1 UH-12E. 1 OH-13H.

## PERU
### Air Force
12 Mirage 2000P/DP. 20 MiG-29. 39 Su-20/22M/U. 15 Mirage 5. 18 Su-25. 15 Canberra. 22 A-37B. 13 MB-339AP. 27 EMB-312. 15 T-41D. 2 Cessna 150. 6 Il-103. 18 Zlin 242L. 3 707-320C. 1 737-500. 8 L-100-20/C-130A. 3 An-74. 18 An-32. 13 DHC-5A. 6 DHC-6. 2 DC-8-62CF. 1 FH-227. 8 Y-12. 1 F28-1000. 1 Falcon 20F. 2 Learjet 36A. 6 DHC-6. 1 King Air. 5 Y-12. 4 Metro III. 1 King Air. 1 PA-31T. 1 Cessna 421. 2 PC-6B. 1 PA-34. 3 Cessna 185. 10 Mi-24/-35. 5 Mi-6. 3 Mi-8. 35 Mi-17. 2 Bell 412HP. 10 Bell 212. 5 Bell 214ST. 10 UH-1H. 5 BO 105. 3 AS 350B.
### Naval Air Service
3 F27-200. 3 EMB-111. 2 An-32. 1 EMB-110. 5 T-34C. 2 An-32. 4 C-47. 5 King Air 200T. 1 DHC-6. 1 Cessna 206. 6 AS-61D. 5 AB 212ASW. 4 Mi-8. 4 Bell 206.
### Army Aviation
4 An-32. 1 Queen Air. 1 Cessna 337. 2 Cessna T303. 7 Cessna 206. 1 Cessna 152. 1 Cessna 172. 25 Mi-8. 13 Mi-17. 3 Mi-26. 2 Mi-6. 2 Bell 412. 10 A 109. 6 Alouette III. 5 SA 315B. 8 Enstrom F28F.

## PHILIPPINES
### Air Force
10 F-5A/B. 20 OV-10C. 18 S.211. 33 SF.260M/W. 15 T-41D. 1 F27 Maritime. 8 C-130B. 2 C-130H. 2 L-100-20. 6 F27. 1 F28. 12 N22 Nomad. 1 Cessna 210. 1 S-70A. 5 AUH-76. 1 SA 330L. 6 Bell 412. 59 UH-1H/205. 5 Bell 205A-1. 33 MD 520MD.
### Naval Aviation
8 BN-2A. 8 BO 105C. 1 Cessna 177. 1 Cessna 152.

## POLAND
### Air Force
22 MiG-29/UB. 80 MiG-21bis. 32 MiG-21UM/US. 97 Su-22. 135 TS-11. 29 PZL-130*. 8 C-295*. 10 An-26. 4 An-28*. 25 An-2. 2 Tu-154M. 9 Yak-40. 8 Mi-8. 65 Mi-2. 18 W-3. 1 Bell 412HP.
### Naval Aviation
27 MiG-21bis/UM. 18 TS-11. 13 An-28*. 5 An-2. 13 Mi-14PL/PS. 1 Mi-17. 6 Mi-2. 6 W-3.
### Army Aviation
30 Mi-24. 35 Mi-8. 3 Mi-17. 73 Mi-2. 32 W-3W*.

## PORTUGAL
### Air Force
40 F-16A/B. 45 Alpha Jet. 16 Epsilon. 5 P-3B. 12 Cessna FTB337G. 7 DHC-1. 24 C-212. 3 C-130H-30. 3 C-130H. 1 Falcon 20. 3 Falcon 50. 20 Alouette III. 10 SA 330C. 12 EH 101*.
### Army Aviation
10 NH 90*. 9 EC 635*.
### Naval Aviation
5 Lynx Mk 95.

## QATAR
### Air Force
12 Mirage 2000-5EDA/DDA. 6 Alpha Jet. 1 747SP. 1 A340-200. 1 707-320. 1 727-200. 1 Falcon 900. 6 AS 332F. 11 Commando 2A/2C/3. 10 SA 342L/G.

## ROMANIA
### Air Force
18 MiG-29/UB. 4 MiG-23MF/UM. 182 MiG-21. 33 MiG-21U. 60 IAR-93A/B. 4 H-5R (Il-28). 21 L-39. 45 L-29. 39 IAR-99*. 20 Yak-52. 36 IAR-823. 5 An-24/-26. 3 An-30. 1 Tu-154. 2 707-320. 4 C-130B. 3 BN-2A. 17 An-2. 79 IAR-330. 2 Mi-17. 24 Mi-8. 2 Mi-17. 99 IAR 316. 12 IAR 317. 3 SA 365N.
### Naval Aviation
6 IAR 330. 5 IAR 316.

## RUSSIA
### Air Force
15 Tu-160. 68 Tu-22M. 50 Tu-95. 450 Su-27. 300 MiG-31. 600 MiG-29. 40 MiG-25R. 25? Su-30. 350 Su-24. 5 Su-27IB. 195 Su-25/-39. 15 A-50. 950 L-39. 200 Il-76. 18 Il-78M. 60 An-12. 100 An-26. 25 An-24. 30 An-30. 50 An-32. 20 An-72/74. 28 An-124. 150 L-410. 130 An-2. 20 Il-18/22. 6 Tu-134UBL. 12 Il-62M. 25 Yak-40. 95 Mi-8. 110 Mi-2.
### Naval Aviation
65 Tu-22M/MR. 45 Tu-142. 51 Su-27. 45 Su-24/MR. 5 Su-25. 35 Il-38. 2 Il-20. 12 Be-12. 25 An-12. 20 An-26. 10 An-24. 18 An-2. 2 Tu-154. 3 Tu-134. 12 Yak-40. 35 Mi-8. 60 Mi-14. 4 Ka-31. 25 Ka-29. 65 Ka-25. 85 Ka-27.
### Army Aviation
12 Ka-50/52. 1000+ Mi-8. 700+ Mi-24. 100 Mi-6. 35 Mi-26. 99 Mi-2. 25 An-2.
### Border Guards
Approx 200 Mi-8, Mi-24, Mi-26 and Ka-27 helicopters. 6 An-72P. 15 SM-92 Finist. Approx 70 An-24, An-26, An-72, Il-76, Tu-134, & Yak-40 transports.
### Space and Rocket Forces
Operates transport & support aircraft.

## RWANDA
### Air Force
2 Mi-24. 3 Mi-8. 1 AS 365CS. 1 AS 355F.

## SAUDI ARABIA
### Air Force
72 F-15S. 109 F-15C/D. 24 Tornado ADV. 90 Tornado IDS. 67 F-5E/F. 10 RF-5E. 15 F-5B. 5 E-3A. 8 KE-3A. 45 Hawk 65. 45 PC-9. 13 Cessna 172. 1 Jetstream 31. 7 KC-130H. 36 C-130E/H. 2 C-130H-30. 6 VC-130H. 3 L-100. 4 CN-235. 1 747SP. 1 747-300. 2 MD-11. 2 707-320. 1 707-120. 1 757-200. 1 737-200. 2 TriStar. 1 A340. 2 Gulfstream III. 4 125-800. 2 JetStar 8. 2 Learjet 25/35A. 1 Cessna 310. 12 AS 532A2. 2 AS 61A. 16 AB 412*. 24 AB 212. 13 AB 206A.
### Army Aviation
12 AH-64A. 12 S-70A. 13 Bell 406CS.
### Naval Aviation
24 AS 565. 12 AS 532AL.

## SENEGAL
### Air Force
4 CM 170. 3 Rallye 235. 6 F27-400M. 1 727-200. 1 BN-2T. 2 SA 318C. 1 SA 341.

## SEYCHELLES
### Coast Guard – Air Wing
1 BN-2A. 1 Cessna 152.

## SINGAPORE
### Air Force
62 F-16C/D*. 7 F-16A/B. 38 F-5E/F. 14 RF-5E. 50 A-4SU. 18 TA-4S-1 27 S.211. 20 SF.260M/W. 4 E-2C. 5 Fokker 50 Enforcer 2. 4 KC-135R. 4 Fokker 50 Utility. 4 C-130H. 2 C-130H-30. 4 KC-130B. 8 CH-47SD*. 8 AH-64D*. 6 CH-47D. 34 AS 332M/UL. 16 UH-1H. 11 UH-1B. 8 Bell 205A. 20 AS 550C-2/U-2.

## SLOVAKIA
### Air Force
24 MiG-29/UB. 16 MiG-21MF/US/UM. 12 Su-25K/UBK. 8 Su-22M-4/U. 6 L 410M/T/UVP. 18 L-39. 11 L-29. 2 An-24. 2 An-26. 19 Mi-24. 20 Mi-8/17. 6 Mi-2.

*A line-up of Singaporean air force upgraded A-4SU Skyhawks on exercise in Australia. (Lenn Bayliss)*

*Spanish AV-8B Harrier II Pluses operating off the carrier* Principe de Asturias. *(Andrew Siddons/Rolls-Royce)*

## SLOVENIA
### Air Force
9 PC-9 Mk II. 3 PC-9. 2 PC-6. 8 Zlin 242L. 2 Zlin 143. 1 UTVA 75. 1 Let L 410VP-E. 8 Bell 412. 3 Bell 206B.

## SOUTH AFRICA
### Air Force
9 Gripen*. 37 Cheetah C. 14 Cheetah D. 34 Atlas Impala II. 35 Impala I. 59 PC-7 Mk II. 5 707-320. 9 C-130B. 3 C-130E*. 1 CN-235. 12 C-47/C-47TP. 4 C-212. 1 PC-12. 1 737BBJ. 1 Falcon 900. 2 Falcon 50. 5 HS.125-400B. 2 Citation II. 4 King Air 200. 14 Cessna 185. 11 Cessna 208. 16 AH-2*. 51 Oryx. 30 A 109*. 9 BK 117A-1/3. 56 Alouette III.

## SOUTH KOREA
### Air Force
60 F-4D. 69 F-4E. 18 RF-4C. 180 F-16C/D*. 39 F-16A/B. 179 F-5E/F. 55 F-5A/B. 5 RF-5A. 95 T-50*. 27 A-37B. 7 OV-10D. 16 Hawk 60. 30 T-38. 35 T-33A. 25 T-37C. 15 T-41B. 25 KT-1*. 10 O-2A. 12 CN-235-100. 20 CN-235-200. 4 C-130H-30. 8 C-130H. 2 HS.748. 8 Hawker 800*. 1 737-300. 3 Commander 520/560F. 5 DHC-2 Beaver. 20 O-1A/E. 6 CH-47D. 3 AS 332L. 3 Bell 412. 4 Bell 212. 5 UH-1D/H.
### Army Aviation
60 AH-1J/S/F. 17 CH-47D. 138 UH-60P*. 3 AS 332L. 20 UH-1H. 175 MD 500. 12 BO 105*.
### Naval Aviation
8 P-3C. 3 F406 Caravan II. 24 Lynx 99. 25 MD 500M/ASW. 2 Bell 206B.

## SPAIN
### Air Force
14 RF-4C. 87 Eurofighter (requirement)*. 105 EF-18A/B. 66 Mirage F1C/E/B/D. 24 F-5A/B. 76 C-101B. 37 T-35C. 23 Beech Bonanza. 7 P-3A/B. 3 F27 Maritime. 2 A310. 4 707-320. 5 KC-130H. 6 C-130H. 1 C-130H-30. 9 C-295*.

20 CN-235. 78 C-212. 15 CL-215T. 2 Citation V. 5 Falcon 20. 1 Falcon 50. 2 Falcon 900. 5 Beech Baron. 21 Do 27. 15 EC 120*. 13 Hughes 269C/TH-55. 8 S-76. 19 SA 330. 19 AS 332.
### Naval Aviation
8 EAV-8B Plus. 9 EAV-8B. 3 Citation II. 13 SH-3H. 12 SH-60B. 10 AB 212ASW. 10 Hughes 300.
### Army Aviation
48 UH-1H. 79 BO 105. 6 AB 212. 15 AS 532UL*. 16 AS 332UC. 17 CH-47D. 11 OH-58D.

## SRI LANKA
### Air Force
10 Kfir C2. 1 Kfir TC2. 6 MiG-27. 4 F-7. 1 FT-7. 2 FT-5. 3 K-8. 10 CJ-6. 2 IA-58. 6 SF.260TP. 10 SF.260W. 3 C-130B. 4 An-32. 5 Y-12. 1 Y-8. 1 Cessna 421. 5 Cessna 150. 5 King Air 200. 1 HS.748. 10 Mi-24/-35. 11 Bell 212. 6 Bell 412. 3 Bell 206B. 8 Mi-17. 1 Chetak.

## SUDAN
### Air Force
6 MiG-23FL. 20 F-7. 8 F-6/FT-6. 5 F-5/FT-5. 3 Jet Provost 55. 3 Strikemaster. 2 C-130H. 4 Y-8. 3 DHC-5D. 1 F27-200. 1 DHC-6-300. 1 Falcon 20. 1 Falcon 50. 8 IAR 330 Puma. 4 AB 212. 8 Mi-24. 6 Mi-8. 5 BO 105.

## SURINAM
### Air Force
2 C-212-400. 1 Cessna 310. 1 Cessna 172.

## SWAZILAND
2 IAI-201. 1 PA-28. 3 Alouette III.

## SWEDEN
### Air Force
204 JAS 39*. 134 JA 37 (65 JA 37D*). 47 AJSF/AJSH 37. 15 Sk 37. 2 Sk 35C. 6 S 100B. 106 Sk 60. 60 Sk 61 (Bulldog). 8 C-130E/H. 2 Tp 86 Sabreliner. 1 Tp 100 (Saab 340). 3

Tp 101 (King Air). 10 AS 332M-1. 4 Gulf-stream IV. 1 Citation II.
### Helicopter Wing
1 C-212. 18 NH 90*. 14 BV 107/KV-107. 11 AS 332M. 5 AB 412. 8 AB 204A/B. 20 A 109. 20 BO 105CB. 29 AB 206A/B. 15 Hughes 300C.

## SWITZERLAND
### Air Force
33 F/A-18C/D. 102 F-5E/F. 16 Mirage IIIRS. 2 Mirage IIID. 19 Hawk 60. 38 PC-7. 16 PC-9. 1 Falcon 50. 1 Learjet 36. 18 PC-6B. 12 AS 332UL*. 15 AS 332M-1. 66 Alouette III.

## SYRIA
### Air Force
14 Su-27. 60 MiG-29/UB. 40 MiG-25PD/RB/PU. 80 MiG-23MF/ML/MS. 66 MiG-23BN/UM. 220 MiG-21. 30 MiG-17F. 20 Su-24MK. 96 Su-20/22BKL. 70 L-39. 40 L-29. 15 MiG-15UTI. 48 Flamingo. 6 Mushshak 4 Il-76. 4 An-26. 2 An-24. 2 PA-31. 2 Yak-40. 2 Tu-134. 2 Falcon 20F. 2 PA-31. 35 Mi-24. 100 Mi-8/17. 10 Mi-6. 20 Mi-2. 55 SA 342L.
### Naval Aviation
20 Mi-14. 5 Ka-25.

## TAIWAN
### Air Force
130 Ching-Kuo. 145 F-16A/B*. 57 Mirage 2000-5. 97 F-5E/F. 8 RF-5E. 40 T-38A. 53 AT-3/3B. 36 T-34C. 15 T-CH-1B. 6 E-2C*. 4 E-2T*. 19 C-130H. 3 Fokker 50. 5 C-47. 11 Beech 1900C-1. 1 737-800. 2 727-100. 17 S-70C.
### Army Aviation
62 AH-1W. 12 Chinook*. 90 UH-1H. 30 TH-67. 15 TH-55.
### Naval Aviation
26 S-2T. 20 S-70B. 12 MD 500MD/ASW.

## TAJIKISTAN
1 Tu-134. 5 Mi-24. 10 Mi-8.

*Britain is to upgrade its Harrier GR.7s to GR.9 standard with a liquid crystal display, new INS/GPS, and improved avionics. (Paul Merritt)*

## TANZANIA
### Defence Force
11 F-7. 10 F-6. 8 F-5. 2 MiG-15UTI. 4 DHC-5D. 2 F28-1000. 2 Y-12. 2 Cessna 404. 1 Cessna 402. 1 King Air A100. 2 Bell 206B. 4 Alouette III.

## THAILAND
### Air Force
49 F-16A/B*. 41 F-5E/F. 1 RF-5A/B. 7 F-5A/B. 19 OV-10C. 22 AU-23. 20 Alpha Jet*. 35 L-39ZA. 4 T-33A. 3 RT-33A. 30 Fantrainer 400/600. 23 PC-9. 12 SF.260MT. 23 CT-4A. 24 CT-4E*. 7 C-130H. 5 C-130H-30. 6 G222. 2 CN-235. 6 HS.748. 6 C-47TP. 3 C-212. 19 N22B. 3 IAI-201. 1 A310-300. 1 737-400. 1 737-200. 3 Learjet 35A. 3 Merlin IVA. 22 AU-23. 6 T-41D. 28 O-1. 4 Cessna 150H. 12 H-36 Dimona. 2 AS 332L2. 5 S-58T. 19 UH-1H. 9 Bell 412. 2 UH-1N. 3 AS 332L2. 6 Bell 206.
### Naval Aviation
18 A-7E/TA-7. 7 AV-8S. 2 TAV-8S. 2 P-3T. 1 UP-3T. 6 S-2F. 3 F27 Maritime. 2 CL-215. 2 F27-400M. 6 Dornier 228. 11 Summit Sentry 0-2-337. 5 N24A Searchmaster. 4 U-17B. 4 O-1A/E. 6 S-70B-7. 5 S-76N. 2 Super Lynx 300*. 5 Bell 214ST. 6 Bell 212ASW. 4 UH-1H.
### Army Aviation
2 C-212-300. 2 Jetstream 41. 2 Shorts 330UTT. 2 Beech 1900C. 2 King Air 200. 7 T-41D. 10 O-1A/E. 18 Maule. 10 Cessna U-17. 5 Cessna U-27A. 3 AH-1F. 6 CH-47C/D. 2 UH-60L*. 38 Bell 212. 98 UH-1H*. 40 TH-300. 10 Bell 206A.

## TOGO
### Air Force
4 Alpha Jet. 4 EMB-326G. 3 Epsilon. 1 DHC-5D. 1 707-320B. 1 F28-3000. 2 Beech 58 Baron. 2 King Air. 2 Reims-Cessna F337. 1 AS 332L. 3 SA 318B. 1 SA 319.

## TONGA
### Air Wing
1 Beech G18S. 1 Citabria.

## TRINIDAD & TOBAGO
### Air Wing
1 Cessna 402. 1 Cessna 310. 1 Cessna 172.

## TUNISIA
### Air Force
15 F-5E/F. 8 MB-326K 12 L-59T. 8 MB-326B/L.

18 SF.260C/W. 2 C-130H. 5 C-130B. 5 G222. 3 L 410UVP. 2 SIAI Marchetti S.208A. 4 HH-3E. 12 AB-205A. 17 UH-1H/N. 5 SA 341. 6 Alouette II. 6 AS 350B. 1 AS 365. 3 SA 316. 6 AS 350B.

## TURKEY
### Air Force
163 F-4E. 44 RF-4E. 194 F-16C/D*. 139 F-5A/B. 11 RF-5A. 69 T-38A. 66 T-37B/C. 40 SF.260D. 29 T-41D. 9 KC-135R. 7 C-130B. 7 C-130E. 20 C-160. 49 CN-235M. 3 Gulfstream IV. 2 Citation VII. 4 Citation II. 1 King Air 200. 2 BN-2A. 39 UH-1H. 20 AS 532AL*. 5 AB 412*.
### Army Air Arm
9 AH-1W. 36 AH-1P. 95 S-70A*. 30 AS 532UL*. 35 UH-1H. 30 Citabria 150S. 5 King Air 200. 2 Dornier 28D. 4 Cessna 421. 30 Cessna U-17. 24 T-41D. 5 T-42A. 120 AB 205. 2 AB 212. 12 AB 204B. 30 AB 206B. 25 Hughes 25.
### Naval Aviation
9 CN-235MPA*. 8 TB 20. 16 S-70B*. 4 MH-60S. 13 AB 212ASW/EW. 3 AB 204AS.

## TURKMENISTAN
### Air Force
24 MiG-29. 50 MiG-23. 24 MiG-25. 3 MiG-21. 65 Su-17. 45 Su-25. 2 L-39. 3 An-12. 1 An-24. 10 Mi-24. 10 Mi-8. Many aircraft in storage

## UGANDA
### Defence Force
7 MiG-21. 3 L-39. 4 SF.260. 1 AS 202. 1 Gulfstream IV. 3 Mi-24. 7 Mi-17. 5 AB 412. 4 Bell 212/412. 3 AB 206.

## UKRAINE
### Air Force
50 Tu-22M. 26 Tu-22R. 70 Su-27. 225 MiG-29. 230 Su-24. 65 Su-25. 55 Su-17. 14 Be-12. 1 Il-22. 450 L-39. 230 Yak-52. 30 Il-78M. 70 Il-76. 26 An-72. 2 An-32. 28 An-26. 13 An-24. 21 An-12. 1 Il-22. 2 An-30. 2 Tu-134. 6 Yak-40. 50 An-2. 110 Mi-8. 20 Mi-6. Many aircraft likely in storage.
### Naval Air Arm
12 Ka-27. 4 Ka-29. 18 Ka-25. 5 Mi-14PL. 1 An-12. 1 An-26. 8 Mi-8.
### Ground Forces
250 Mi-24. 240 Mi-8. 40 Mi-6. 25 Mi-26. 50 Mi-2.

## UNITED ARAB EMIRATES
### Abu Dhabi
80 F-16C/D Block 60*. 30 Mirage 2000-9*. 33 Mirage 2000E/D. 32 Mirage VAD/RAD/DAD. 18 Hawk 100. 20 Hawk 63. 24 PC-7. 12 Grob G 115 Acro. 4 C-130H. 7 CN-235M. 4 CN-235MPA*. 4 C-212-200. 1 BN-2A. 10 AS 532UC/SC. 28 SA 330. 16 AS 565SA. 14 AS 350. 30 AH-64. 12 SA 342L. 4 BO 105CBS. 7 Alouette III. 1 AB 206B. Royal Flt – 1 747SP. 2 A300-600. 1 146-100. 3 Falcon 900. 2 King Air 350. 2 AS 332L.
### Dubai
3 MB-326KD. 8 Hawk 61. 4 MB-339. 2 MB-326LD. 5 SF.260TP. 2 C-130H-30/ L-100-30. 1 Shorts 330UUT. 1 Skyvan. 1 BN-2T. 10 IAR-330. 6 AB 412. 2 Bell 212. 4 Bell 214B. 6 AB 205A. 5 206B/AB-206A. 1 Bell 206L. 3 BO 105CBS. 1 Bell 407. Royal Flt – 1 747SP. 2 GulfstreamII/IV. 1 S-76A. 1 AS 365N.

## UNITED KINGDOM
### Air Force
232 Eurofighter (requirement)*. 130 Tornado GR.1/GR.1A/GR.1B/GR.4/GR.4A. 94 Tornado F.3. 52 Jaguar GR.1/GR.3/T.2/T.4. 62 Harrier GR.7/T.10. 97 Hawk T.1/T.1A. 73 Tucano T.1. 25 Nimrod MR.2 (21 MRA.4*). 3 Nimrod MR.1P. 7 Sentry AEW.1. 7 Canberra PR.9/T.4. 5 Global Express ASTOR*. 4 C-17. 9 TriStar K.1/KC.1/K.2. 4 VC10 K.3. 5 VC10 K.4. 11 VC10 C.1K. 10 Hercules C.4. 15 Hercules C.5. 30 Hercules C.1/C.2/C.3. 3 BAe 146 CC.2. 6 HS.125 CC.3. 10 Dominie T.1. 11 Jetstream T.1. 2 Islander CC.2. 14 Chinook HC.3*. 35 Chinook HC.1/2. 22 Merlin HC.3*. 40 Puma HC.1. 25 Sea King HAR.3/3A. 14 Wessex HC.2. 9 Griffin HT.1. 38 Squirrel HT.1/HT.2. 2 Twin Squirrel HCC.1. 35 Gazelle HT.3/HCC 4.
### Navy Fleet Air Arm
28 Sea Harrier F/A.2. 7 Harrier T.8. 12 Hawk T.1. 12 Jetstream T.2/3. Grob Heron 5. 43 Merlin HAS.1/2*. 60 Sea King HAS.5/6. 9 Sea King AEW.2A. 33 Sea King HC.4. 59 Lynx HAS.3/HMA.8. 6 Lynx AH.7. 9 Gazelle AH.1.
### Army Air Corps
67 WAH-64D*. 105 Lynx AH.7. 24 Lynx AH.9. 118 Gazelle AH.1. 5 Islander AL.1. 3 Bell 212. 4 A 109A.

## USA
### Air Force
21 B-2A. 72 B-1B. 85 B-52H. 295 F-22 (requirement)*. 613 F-15A/B/C/D/E. 782 F-16A/B/C/D. 52 F-117. 215 A-10/OA-10. 21 AC-130. 35 U-2S/TU-2S. 19 RC-135. 81 C-5A/B. 2 VC-25. 120 C-17*. 59 KC-10. 139 C-141. 4 C-137. 4 C-32A. 6 C-135. 255 KC-135. 2 C-18. 23 C-9. 191 C-130E/H. 10 C-27. 5 C-37*. 76 C-21. 13 C-20. 3 C-23. 34 C-12. 4 E-4. 32 E-3. 20 E-8*. 1 EC-137. 2 WC-135. 22 EC-130. 2 E-9. 53 MC-130. 9 HC-130. 4 NC-130. 2 OC-135. 2 NKC-135. 413 T-38. 93 AT-38. 372 T-6*. 417 T-37. 180 T-1A. 3 T-41. 3 NT-39. 11 T-43/CT-43. 3 UV-18. 4 RQ-1. 63 HH-1/UH-1. 40 MH-53. 47 HH-60. 9 MH-60.
### Air Force Reserve
9 B-52H. 71 F-16A/B/C/D. 52 A/OA-10. 32 C-5A. 48 C-141B. 72 KC-135E/R. 110 C-130E/H. 7 HC-130. 13 MC-130. 10 WC-130. 23 HH-60G.

*F-15Es are workhorses of the USAF fleet, and have seen active service over Iraq, Kosovo/Yugoslavia and Afghanistan. (USAF)*

## Air National Guard

20 B-1B. 116 F-15. 607 F-16. 101 A/OA-10. 13 C-5. 3 C-22. 18 C-141. 1 C-135. 225 C-130. 13 HC-130. 8 EC-130. 3 C-40*. 4 C-21. 16 C-26. 2 C-38. 223 KC-135. 16 HH-60G.

## Navy & Marines

220 F-14A/B/D. 545 F/A-18E/F*. 287 F/A-18A. 33 F/A-18B. 343 F/A-18C. 138 F/A-18D. 200 AV-8B. 18 TAV-8B. 38 F-5E/F. 124 EA-6B. 293 P-3. 17 S-3A. 119 S-3B. 17 C-130F/T. 77 KC-130. 11 KC-130J*. 7 LC-130F/R. 5 VP-3A. 6 C-40*. 7 C-20D/G. 8 CT-39E/G. 2 C-28A. 38 C-2A. 29 C-9. 2 C-26. 94 E-2C. 16 E-6B. 1 EC-24A. 10 EP-3E/J. 16 ES-3A. 3 DC-130A. 9 UP-3A/B. 5 US-3A. 6 UC-35. 85 U-21A. 2 U-6A. 85 UC-12B/F/M. 4 RC-12F/M. 1 RP-3A. 5 VP-3A. 169 T-45A*. 13 T-2C. 339 T-6*. 317 T-34C. 11 TP-3A. 2 TC-130G/Q. 17 T-39N. 57 T-44A. 4 TC-4C. 2 TC-18F. 155 AH-1W. 141 CH-53E. 75 CH-53D. 27 CH-46D. 241 CH-46E. 42 HH-46D. 24 HH-60H. 45 MH-53E. 425 MV-22*. 19 RH-53D. 50 SH-3H. 160 SH-60B. 76 SH-60F. 94 TH-57B/C. 150 UH/HH-1N. 47 UH-3A/H. 13 UH-46D. 8 VH-60N. 15 VH-3A/D.

## Army

557 AH-64A/D. 334 OH-58D. 253 OH-58A/C. 20 AH-6J. 19 MH-6J. 418 CH-47D. 921 UH-60A/L. 59 EH-60A. 60 MH-60K/L*. 11 MH-47D. 25 MH-47E. 286 UH-1H/V. 137 TH-67A. 2 C-31 (F27-400). 3 UC-35. 13 RC-7. 7 C-23. 47 C-12. 5 UC-35. 46 RC-12D/H/K. 4 U-21. 11 C-26. 6 UV-18. 2 UV-20.

## National Guard & Army Reserve

184 AH-64A. 291 AH-1E/F/G/P/S. 15 OH-58D. 292 OH-58A/C. 183 CH-47. 441 UH-60A/L. 5 EH-60A. 838 UH-1H/V. 67 C-12. 2 C-20. 1 C-21. 31 C-23. 3 RC-12. 4 UC-35.

## URAGUAY
### Air Force

11 A-37B. 5 IA-58B. 6 PC-7U. 13 SF.260. 3 C-130B. 3 EMB-110. 3 C-212. 1 F27-100. 2 Beech Baron. 2 Queen Air. 5 U-17. 5 T-41D. 1 Commander. 4 Cessna U-17. 1 Cessna 210. 10 Cessna 206. 1 Cessna 182. 1 PA-18. 6 Wessex HC.2 2 Bell 212. 6 UH-1H. 2 AS 365.

### Naval Aviation

4 S-2A/G. 1 King Air 200T. 2 Jetstream T.2. 2 T-34B. 2 T-34C. 2 PA-34. 2 Wessex 60. 4 Wessex HC.2.

## UZBEKISTAN
### Air Force

31 Su-27. 38 MiG-29. 32 Su-24. 30 Su-17. 20 Su-25. 10 Il-76. 20 An-12. 15 An-26. 1 An-24. 1 Tu-134. 45 Mi-24. 50 Mi-8. 30 Mi-6. 1 Mi-26.

## VENEZUELA
### Air Force

21 F-16A/B. 16 Mirage 50EV/DV. 16 F-5A/B. 8 AMX-T*. 22 OV-10E. 18 T-2D. 30 EMB-312. 12 SF.260E*. 2 707-320C. 1 737-200. 6 C-130H. 8 G222. 2 Gulfstream II/III. 3 Falcon 20D. 1 Learjet 24D. 2 Citation I/II. 5 King Air 200. 4

Pitts S-2. 6 AS 532AC. 8 AS 332. 4 Bell 412SP. 4 Bell 214ST. 1 212. 18 Mi-17. 4 UH-1H. 1 UH-1B. 10 UH-1N. 10 Alouette III.

### Naval Aviation

1 Dash 7. 9 C-212. 1 King Air 90. 1 King Air 200. 1 Cessna 402C. 2 Cessna 310R. 1 Commander 695. 4 Heli-Dyne Bell 412*. 12 AB 212ASW.

### Army Aviation

4 IAI-201. 12 M-28 Skytruck. 1 King Air 200. 1 King Air 90. 1 Queen Air. 1 BN-2A. 3 Cessna 206/207. 3 172/182. 4 AS-61A. 4 UH-1H. 3 Bell 205A. 2 206B/L. 6 A 109A.

### National Guard

12 M-28 Skytruck. 3 IAI-201. 1 King Air 200. 1 King Air 90. 2 Queen Air. 1 BN-2. 1 Cessna 206. 10 AS 355. 1 Bell 214ST. 5 Bell 206. 1 Bell 206L. 8 A 109.

## VIETNAM
### Army Air Force

11 Su-27P/UB. 145 MiG-21bis/UM. 50 Su-22BKL. 25 L-39. 20 Yak-18/CJ-6. 30 An-26. 9 An-24. 2 An-30. 5 Yak-40. 30 Mi-24. 5 Ka-25. 14 Ka-28/-32. 60 Mi-8. 10 Mi-6.

## YEMEN
### Air Force

34 MiG-29*. 25 MiG-23BN/UM. 70 MiG-21. 13 F-5E/B. 35 Su-22BKL/M-2/U. 12 L-39C. 4 MiG-15UTI. 18 Yak-11. 3 C-130H. 3 An-12B. 1 An-24. 6 An-26. 1 Il-76. 2 Skyvan. 15 Mi-24. 49 Mi-8. 6 AB 212. 2 AB 204B. 6 AB 206B.

## YUGOSLAVIA
### Air Force

? MiG-29A/B. ? MiG-21. ? J-1. ? G-4M. ? J-22. 14 UTVA-66. 30 UTVA-75. 25 An-26. 6 An-2. 6 Yak-40. 2 Falcon 50. 6 Yak-40. 4 Learjet 25. 14 PC-6. 35 UTVA-75. ? Mi-8/-17. ? SA 342.

## ZAMBIA
### Air Force

16 MiG-21MF/U. 8 F-6. 2 FT-5. 8 Z-8. 2 J-1E. 10 CJ-6. 8 SF.260MZ. 15 MFI-17. 4 An-26. 4 DHC-5D. 7 Do 28. 1 HS.748. 1 Yak-40. 5 Y-12. 1 King Air 90. 7 Do 28. 7 Mi-8. 10 AB 205A. 5 AB 212. 12 AB 47G. Operational status of some of these aircraft unknown.

## ZIMBABWE
### Air Force

10 F-7. 2 FT-7. 10 Hunter FGA.9. 1 Hunter T.81. 10 Hawk 60/60A. 15 Reims-Cessna C337G. 2 O-2. 23 SF.260M/F. 6 SF.260TP. 9 C-212. 5 BN-2A. 5 Mi-35. 2 AS 532UL. 7 AB 412.

# GLOSSARY OF TERMS AND ACRONYMS

**AAA** – Anti aircraft artillery.

**AAC** – Army Air Corps (UK).

**AAM** – Air-to-air missile.

**ABM** – Anti ballistic missile. A missile capable of destroying hostile ballistic missiles or their payloads before they impact on their target.

**ACC** – Air Combat Command (USAF).

**ACM** – Air combat manoeuvring.

**ACMI** – Air combat manoeuvring instrumentation.

**ACMR** – Air combat manoeuvring range.

**ADF** – Australian Defence Force.

**ADIZ** – Air defence identification zone.

**AEW** – Airborne early warning.

**AEW&C** – Airborne early warning and control.

**AF** – Air force.

**AFB** – Air force base (US).

**AFMC** – Air Force Materiel Command (USAF).

**ALBM** – Air launched ballistic missile.

**ALCM** – Air launched cruise missile.

**AMC** – Air Mobility Command (USAF).

**Amraam** – Advanced medium range air-to-air missile, the Raytheon AIM-120.

**ANG** – Air National Guard (USA).

**APU** – Auxiliary power unit.

**ARM** – Anti radiation missile.

**ASM** – Air-to-surface missile.

**ASPJ** – Airborne self protection jammer.

**Asraam** – Advanced short range air-to-air missile. An advanced IR guided AAM missile developed by Matra BAe.

**AST** – Air staff target.

**ASTOVL** – Advanced short takeoff and vertical landing

**ASV** – Anti surface vessel.

**ASW** – Anti submarine warfare.

**ASuW** – Anti surface warfare.

**ATBM** – Anti tactical ballistic missile.

**AUW** – All up weight.

**AWACS** – Airborne Warning and Control System. In particular refers to Boeing E-3 Sentry.

**BAe** – British Aerospace, now BAE Systems.

**BVR** – Beyond visual range.

**C2** – Command and control.

**C3** – Command, control and communications.

**C3I** – Command, control, communications and intelligence.

**CAF** – Canadian Armed Forces, now Canadian Forces.

**CAP** – Combat air patrol.

**CAS** – Close air support.

**CDU** – Control display unit.

**CEA** – Circular error average.

**CEP** – Circular Error Probable. A measure of the accuracy of missiles or bombs, the CEP is the radius of a circle in which half the shots are statistically likely to fall.

**CF** – Canadian Forces.

**CFE** – Conventional Forces Europe.

**CIWS** – Close-In Weapon System (US).

**COIN** – Counter insurgency.

**CRT** – Cathode ray tube.

**CV** – Attack aircraft carrier, conventionally powered (US).

**CVN** – Attack aircraft carrier, nuclear powered (US).

**DEW** – Distant early warning (US).

**DFC** – Distinguished Flying Cross: air force decoration.

**DGPS** – Differential GPS.

**DoD** – Department of Defence/Defense.

**DVI** – Direct Voice Input.

**ECCM** – Electronic counter countermeasures.

**ECM** – Electronic countermeasures.

**ECR** – Electronic combat reconnaissance, SEAD Panavia Tornado variant.

**EFIS** – Electronic flight instrument system.

**ELINT** – Electronic intelligence. Intelligence derived from enemy electronic transmissions other than telecommunications (ie radar).

**Endurance** – The length of time an aircraft's fuel load will permit it to remain airborne.

**ESM** – Electronic support measures.

**EW** – Electronic warfare • Early warning.

**FA** – Frontal Aviation, Russian AF command in charge of tactical fighters.

**FAA** – Fleet Air Arm (UK, Aus) • Fuerza Aerea Argentina, Argentine AF.

**FAB** – Forca Aerea Brasileira, Brazilian AF.

**FAC** – Forward air control/forward air controller • Fuerza Aerea de Chile, Chilean AF • Fuerza Aerea Colombiana, Colombian AF.

**FAE** – Fuel air explosives • Fuerza Aerea Ecuatoriana, Ecuadorian AF.

**FBW** – Fly-by-wire (electronic signalling of flight controls).

**fire and forget missile** – AAM or ASM with self guiding capability.

**FLIR** – Forward looking infrared.

**fly-by-wire** – Flight-control system with electric signalling.

**FMS** – Foreign military sale (US).

**g** – Force of gravity.

**GAM** – GPS-Aided Munition. Mk 82 bombs with a GPS guidance tail kit, developed for the B-2.

**GCA** – Ground controlled approach. An instrument approach procedure provided by a ground controller on the basis of radar displays. The aircraft is 'talked down' to within sight of the runway when weather conditions would otherwise preclude a safe landing. Predates ILS.

**GCI** – Ground-controlled intercept.

**GE** – General Electric.

**GPS** – Global positioning system. A worldwide system by which the user can derive his position by receiving signals from navigation satellites.

**HF** – High frequency: 3 to 30 MHz.

**HOTAS** – Hands on throttle and stick.

**HOTCC** – Hands on throttle, collective and cyclic.

**hp** – Horsepower

**hr** – Hour/s

**HUD** – Head-up display.

**HUDWAC** – HUD weapon aiming computer.

**HUDWASS** – HUD weapon aiming subsystem.

**IADS** – Integrated air defence system.

**IAS** – Indicated airspeed shown on the airspeed indicator, when corrected for instrument error.

**ICBM** – Intercontinental ballistic missile. Land based missile with range in excess of 5600km (3000nm).

**IFF** – Identification friend or foe.

**IGE** – In ground effect.

**ILS** – Instrument landing system.

**Imp** – Imperial (UK).

**INS** – Inertial navigation system. A navigation system in which displacement from the point of departure is determined by measuring the acceleration exerted upon a gyroscopically stabilised platform by vehicle movement.

**IOC** – Initial operational capability. Date when a weapon system can be considered capable of being used by personnel even though not fully developed and personnel not fully trained (US).

**IR** – Infrared.

**IRAN** – Inspect and Repair As Necessary.

**IRBM** – Intermediate range ballistic missile. Land based missile with range of 2780km (1500nm) to 5600km (3000nm).

**IRCM** – Infrared countermeasure.

**ISA** – International Standard Atmosphere.

**IRS** – Inertial reference system.

**IRST** – Infrared search and track.

**JASDF** – Japan Air Self Defence Force.

**JAST** – Joint Advanced Strike Technology.

**JDAM** – Joint Direct Attack Munition. INS and GPS guidance kits for conventional bombs. Mk 84 with JDAM is GBU-31.

**JGSDF** – Japan Ground Self Defence Force.

**JMSDF** – Japan Maritime Self Defence Force.

**Joint-STAR** – Joint Surveillance Target Attack Radar System, as in Northrop Grumman E-8.

**JSOW** – Joint Stand-Off Weapon. Currently being developed in GPS/INS guided AGM-154 form.

**JSF** – Joint Strike Fighter (USA), replaced JAST. Program to field a multirole fighter for the USAF, USN, USMC, RAF and RN. Lockheed Martin F-35 selected.

**JTIDS** – Joint Tactical Information Distribution System.

**KCAS** – Calibrated airspeed in knots.

**kg** – Kilogram/s.

**KIAS** – Knots indicated airspeed.

**km** – Kilometre.

**km/h** – Kilometres per hour.

**kN** – KiloNewton (1000 Newtons, 1 Newton = 0.2248lb of force).

**Knot** – Aviation and maritime unit of velocity. 1 knot = 1 nautical mile per hour.

**KT** – Kiloton. Explosive yield equivalent in effect to 1000 tons of TNT.

**Kt/kt** – Knot/s

**KTAS** – True airspeed in knots.

**kW** – KiloWatt. SI measure of power.

**LAMPS** – Light airborne multi purpose system (US).

**LANTIRN** – Low altitude targeting infrared for night.

**LABS** – Low Altitude Bombing System.

**LAPES** – Low Altitude Parachute Extraction System.

**lb** – Pounds, either of mass or thrust.

**LCD** – Liquid crystal display.

**LF** – Low frequency: 30 to 300 kHz.

**LGB** – Laser guided bomb.

**LO** – Low observables, ie stealth.

**LRMP** – Long range maritime patrol aircraft.

**LZ** – Landing zone.

**Mach number, M** – Ratio of true airspeed to speed of sound in surrounding air (which varies as square root of absolute temperature). In standard conditions, the speed of sound (Mach 1) is 1223km/h (661kt) at sea level and 1063km/h (575kt) at 36,000ft.

**MAC** – Military Airlift Command, now AMC (USAF).

**MAD** – Magnetic Anomaly Detector. ASW equipment designed to detect disturbances in the Earth's magnetic field.

**MAP** – Military Assistance Program (USA).

**MAW** – Marine Air Wing (USMC).

**MCM** – Mine countermeasures.

**MFD** – Multi Function Display.

**min** – Minute/s.

**MLU** – Mid life update.

**MoD** – Ministry of Defence.

**MPA** – Maritime patrol aircraft.

**MR** – Maritime reconnaissance.

**MRBM** – Medium range ballistic missile. Land based missile with range of 1100km (600nm) to 2780km (1500nm).

**MSIP** – Multi Stage Improvement Program (US).

**MTOW** – Maximum takeoff weight.

**NAS** – Naval air station.

**NASA** – National Aeronautics & Space Administration (US).

**NATO** – North Atlantic Treaty Organisation. Current members are Belgium, Canada, Czech Republic, Denmark, France, Germany, Greece, Hungary, Iceland, Luxembourg, Netherlands, Norway, Poland, Portugal, Spain, Turkey, UK, USA.

**Nautical mile** – Unit of measurement of distance. 1nm is one minute of great circle of the earth, standardised at 6080ft (1853m) but actually varying with latitude from 6046ft to 6108ft (1842 to 1861m).

**nav/attack system** – One offering either pilot guidance or direct command of aircraft to ensure accurate navigation and weapon delivery against surface target.

**nm** – Nautical mile.

**OCU** – Operational Conversion Unit.

**OGE** – Out of ground effect; supported by lifting rotor(s) in free air with no land surface in proximity.

**OTH-B** – Over-the-Horizon Backscatter Radar. Transmits signals that extend beyond the line-of-sight along the ground. Range is of the order of 2900km (1570nm).

**OTHR** – Over-the-horizon radar.

**OTHT** – Over the horizon targeting.

**PACAF** – Pacific Air Force (USAF).

**Passive** – Not itself emitting. Usually used when describing detection devices which do not use electro-magnetic emissions to operate. They cannot be detected in the way that 'active' devices can.

**Payload** – Weapon and/or cargo capacity of an aircraft or missile.

**PGM** – Precision guided munition.

**PID** – Passive identification device.

**PNGDF** – Papua New Guinea Defence Force.

**R&D** – Research and development.

**RAAF** – Royal Australian Air Force.

**RAAWS** – Radar altimeter and altitude warning system.

**RAF** – Royal Air Force (UK).

**RAM** – Radar absorbing material.

**RAN** – Royal Australian Navy.

**RAST** – Recovery assist, secure and (deck) traverse system.

**RATO** – Rocket assisted takeoff.

**RCS** – Radar cross section.

**Recce** – Reconnaissance.

**RMAF** – Royal Malaysian Air Force.

**RN** – Royal Navy (UK).

**RNeAF** – Royal Netherlands Air Force.

**RNZAF** – Royal New Zealand Air Force.

**ROE** – Rules of Engagement.

**RoKAF** – Republic of Korea Air Force (Sth Korea).

**RPV** – Remotely piloted vehicle.

**RR** – Rolls-Royce.

**RSAF** – Republic of Singapore Air Force • Royal Saudi AF.

**RWR** – Radar warning receiver.

**SAAF** – South African Air Force.

**SAC** – Strategic Air Command (USAF, merged into ACC).

**SAM** – Surface-to-air missile.

**SAR** – Search and rescue.

**SEAD** – Suppression of enemy air defences.

**SENSO** – Sensor operator.

**SLAR** – Side looking airborne radar.

**Sigint** – Signals intelligence.

**Smart** – Device possessing precision guidance. Normally used to describe ASMs and bombs with terminal guidance to differentiate them from iron or gravity bombs.

**Sonobuoy** – A small sonar device dropped by aircraft into the sea. The device floats for several hours and transmits information to the aircraft above. It then sinks automatically to prevent retrieval by a hostile agency.

**SSM** – Surface-to-surface missile.

**SRAM & SRAM II** – Cancelled Short Range Attack Missiles (nuclear) for the B-2 Spirit.

**Stealth** – Stealth (or low observables) technology is used to render aircraft or satellites invisible or near invisible to visual, radar or infrared detection. The Northrop Grumman B-2 Spirit and the Lockheed F-117 Nighthawk are stealth aircraft.

**STO** – Short takeoff

**STOL** – Short takeoff and landing.

**STOVL** – Short Takeoff Vertical Landing.

**TAC** – Tactical Air Command (USAF, now merged into ACC).

**TACAMO** – Take Charge And Move Out.

**TACAN** – Tactical Aid to Navigation. Military UHF navaid.

**TACCO** – Tactical coordinator.

**TANS** – Tactical Air Navigation System.

**TBO** – Time Between Overhauls.

**TFR** – Terrain following radar.

**TIALD** – Target Identification Airborne Laser Designation.

**TNI-AU** – Tentara Nasional Indonesia-Angkatan Udara, Indonesian AF.

**TOW** – Tube launched, Optically tracked, Wire guided. Anti armour missile.

**TSSAM** – Tri Service Stand-Off Attack Missile. Cancelled stealthy stand-off weapon.

**UAV** – Unmanned aerial vehicle.

**UHF** – Ultra-high frequency: 300MHz to 3GHz.

**UN** – United Nations.

**USAF** – United States Air Force.

**USAFE** – US Air Forces in Europe.

**USMC** – United States Marine Corps.

**USN** – United States Navy.

**VHF** – Very high frequency: 3 to 300MHz.

**V/STOL** – Vertical or short takeoff and landing.

**VTAS** – Voice, throttle and stick.

**VTOL** – Vertical takeoff and landing.

**WSO** – Weapon system operator (occasionally weapon systems officer).

**zero-zero seat** – Ejection seat qualified for operation at zero height, zero airspeed; ie pilot can safely eject from parked aircraft.

# INDEX

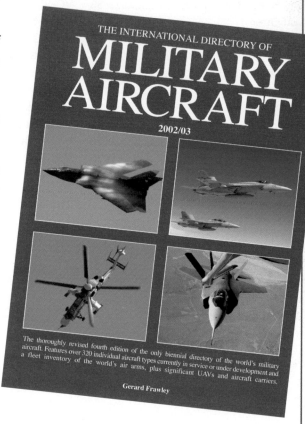
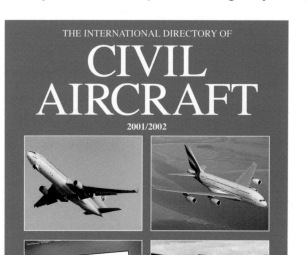